GW00836558

reference
section
WEST
SUSSEX
COUNTY COUNCIL
LIBRARY SERVICE
LIB. 154 D.9342

200459181

THE WORLD'S MAJOR AIRLINES

THE WORLD'S MAJOR AIRLINES

2ND EDITION

DAVID WRAGG

SUTTON PUBLISHING

First published in the United Kingdom in 1998 by Patrick Stephens Limited

This revised and updated edition first published in 2007 by
Sutton Publishing, an imprint of NPI Media Group Limited
Cirencester Road · Chalford · Stroud · Gloucestershire · GL6 8PE

British Library Cataloguing in Publication Data
A catalogue record for this book is available from the British Library.

ISBN 978-0-7509-4481-6

Typeset in Times.
Typesetting and origination by
NPI Media Group Limited.
Printed and bound in England.

Contents

INTRODUCTION

Some maintain that the glamorous days of air travel have gone, but for many of us, the fascination is still there. Nor have the pioneering days gone for good. New routes are still created, but today greater emphasis is being placed on how air transport can develop. There is a world of variety in the activities of the airlines in this book. Bangkok Air, for example, has gone back to basics in actually building airports itself at tourist destinations, while Jet2's predecessor, Channel Express, developed its market in flying flowers from the Channel Islands to the British mainland by using plant to cool the flowers before loading onto the aircraft, preserving their freshness. At the other end of the scale is the movement of exceptionally heavy loads by air, with airlines such as Volga-Dnepr and now the Antonov Design Bureau itself – the railways played a part in developing air transport in a number of countries, but now even railway locomotives can be carried by air.

Traditionally, air travel has been expensive, but over the years, moves have been made to reduce costs. In Europe, inclusive tour, or package holiday, charter airlines have reduced the cost of air travel. Their role is often overlooked in comparisons of air fares between North America and Europe, but they account for more than 40 per cent of all air travel in Europe, as opposed to some 10 per cent in the United States, and once they are taken into account the difference in the average price of a ticket in the United States and Europe is not as vast as a glance at the tariffs of the scheduled airlines might appear.

Now, too, there are many 'low fare, no frills' scheduled airlines. These are also playing a part in cutting the cost of air travel. Not that the established airlines have had everything their own way. Deregulation on both sides of the Atlantic has seen many famous names disappear, notably Braniff, Pan Am and TWA in the United States. The drop in air travel that followed the terrorist acts of 11 September 2001 also created financial pressures that many other airlines couldn't face, so even Swissair, the airline of the land of financial acumen, failed, and took Belgium's Sabena with it.

In Europe, the European Commission has also been forced by the single market rules to look closely at the subsidies given to many bloated and inefficient state-owned airlines. One means of reducing costs on both sides of the Atlantic has been for the major airlines to move away from attempting to operate every kind of route, saving themselves for the domestic trunk routes and the busier international services, but retaining a strong presence by franchising smaller airlines, with lower costs and aircraft well-suited for the less busy and shorter routes.

SMOKE AND MIRRORS?

The big difficulty in compiling a book such as this today is working out exactly which airline flies where, and that's even before one looks at the schedule. Code-sharing has blurred the edges, making it difficult to be sure exactly which airline one has booked with. Look at the airport departure and arrivals boards and one will see a host of exotic flight designators for even a flight between, say, London and Edinburgh. These either clutter up the board reducing the number of flights than can be displayed, or a single departure or arrival is shown, which confuses the passenger by showing an exotic flight designator when it should be showing the airline actually operating the route.

That is bad enough. Returning from holiday recently, a fellow passenger declared that he was flying with airline 'A' as he didn't like airline 'B'. He was wrong. Thanks to a code-share, he was indeed flying with airline 'B'. Personally, I was much happier to be flying with 'B', but that is hardly the point. In an age of increasing consumer choice and consumer power, the airlines are going against the trend and being deliberately misleading and, dare one say it, dishonest.

Global alliances are another aspect of the same problem. In fact, it is also odd to see the British and American regulatory authorities worrying over collusion on fuel surcharges when major airlines are already colluding on frequent flyer programmes. In reality, similar or identical fuel surcharges are inevitable given that on any route, airlines have a choice of two aircraft types, and on the North

Atlantic, the extra fuel cost of one airline flying a Boeing 747-400 between London and New York should be the same as that of a competitor flying the same type of aircraft on the same route. Some believe that one day there will be significantly fewer airlines, with a small number of global airlines, and perhaps the major alliances are going to be the basis for such a move. That's a thought, but do we really want just three major airlines? Where would the regulatory authority for such airlines rest?

Just a step away from the code-share is the franchise arrangement. Some years ago when British Airways first embarked on franchising, one prominent business journalist thought the idea could be taken to its ultimate conclusion, and that the airline could franchise all of its routes and be spared the trouble of flying aircraft. It was seen as a sure way of guaranteeing profits. Life could not be that simple. In fact, the idea of a franchise had just one simple value. It meant that a big international airline could operate feeder services with its own name economically, as it is impossible for an airline with the structure to operate large aircraft over inter-continental distances also to be able to operate short routes with small aircraft. This was the rationale that created airlines such as Delta Connection in the United States. Indeed, the idea is hardly new, as in both the UK and France, separate short- and long-haul airlines were operated for many years, until growth meant that overlap occurred, and Air Inter merged into Air France, and BEA and BOAC merged to become British Airways.

On the other hand, the weakness of a franchise has to be that it is often a costly means of operating the quiet, infrequent, lifeline routes to remote communities. The franchisor probably sees this as a way of ensuring that such passengers interline with the airline's own services rather than those of a competitor, but what if the vast majority of passengers are not interlining, but simply turning up to visit the bank or the hospital? What if costs are inflated, and the air services are subsidised by the taxpayer?

Of course, the economics of air transport operation are complicated and the capacity to make a large loss is always there. This brings us to another example of smoke and mirrors. When is an airline not bankrupt? When it can seek Chapter 11 Bankruptcy Protection. Chapter 11 protects an airline from its creditors, who are deprived of the funds due to them, and even though the airlines concerned got themselves into such a position by being uneconomic, they are allowed to continue trading, making life difficult for their otherwise viable competitors. Chapter 11 also removes much of the discipline from running an airline, since it is easier to seek protection than to make hard decisions such as cutting staff, or aircraft, or routes, or non-essential activities, or in reality, some of all of these.

Sir Rod Eddington, the Australian who took over as chief executive of British Airways, after running Qantas for many years, and stepped down in 2005, maintains that Chapter 11 distorts competition. 'America, the land of the free, is turning itself into the land of the free ride,' he continued. American airlines were swallowing public funds and could still not make a profit. 'America would do itself a favour by going back to the long lost principles of real and honest competition.'

Chapter 11 is in fact nothing more than simple protectionism, which is what anything that allows economic reality to be distorted is all about. In fact, simple bankruptcy would probably do the world air transport market a power of good. It would sort out the wheat from the chaff, the strong from the weak, and the well-managed from the poor, or, frankly, mismanaged. As the Swiss and Belgian experiences have shown, there is still aviation after bankruptcy, but it means that a different organisation continues to provide the service. The collapse of an airline forces those with an interest in the continuance of air transport to recreate an airline, but it is a different airline. Gone are the routes that were added because everyone else was doing it, gone are the pilots bickering over seniority or whether the aircrew at a lower cost subsidiary can operate larger aircraft. There is a fresh sheet of paper and a fresh start.

One just has to compare the Sabena network of a decade ago with that of SN Brussels today, or the Swiss International network with that of Swissair. Swissair had another problem, with French-speaking Geneva wanting parallel rights with German-speaking Zurich, but this, too, disappeared overnight. Despite Switzerland's much lower population, Swiss has a better route network than SN Brussels, but in both cases it is a slimmed-down and more viable network. The Swiss have also swallowed national pride and allowed Lufthansa to buy their airline.

LOW FARES, HIGH RETURNS

> Anyone can make a small fortune from air transport; all that is needed is a large one to start with!
>
> *Anon*

Once upon a time, there were two types of airline. The big, established carriers, usually referred to as flag carriers, were not always, but often, owned by the state, but certainly protected by it. Then, on the fringes of air transport were the smaller airlines. In the United States, these were regional carriers, and sometimes supplemental carriers, that is, to Europeans, charter airlines. In Europe, the fringes were occupied by the charter airlines, and sometimes by airlines offering a particular service, such as flying motorists and their cars across the English Channel or the Mediterranean. The big difference was that the major airlines were protected, and in many countries, if there was a problem, the taxpayer always had deep pockets. The carriers on the fringes struggled to survive, but some did, and often, as they did so, they became valuable prey for the hungry major airlines, anxious to gobble up carriers who had proved that they had a viable route network.

The pattern of air transport also varied between different parts of the world. European restrictions on competition, again to protect the national carriers who operated as a series of cartels, meant that cheap flights were only available as part of a package holiday. This boosted the inclusive tour charter airlines, many of which became substantial and reliable, even buying new aircraft rather than using the hand-me-downs from the larger airlines. It meant that air charter traffic counted for around 40–50 per cent of all air travel in the United Kingdom, for example, as against just 10 per cent in the United States.

Everything changed when the low-cost airlines came into being on the back of deregulation, first in the United States, then between the UK and the Netherlands, and then within the European Union, and finally, on other international routes, so that operations into Brazil, Canada, Dubai and Singapore are encouraged rather than reserved for a select duo of airlines. Southwest Airlines in the United States led the way, and indeed, became the only airline formed in the wake of deregulation of air transport in the United States to survive the first ten years, but the irony was that this observation was made from the safe haven of Chapter 11 Bankruptcy Protection! In Europe, Ryanair also found that low cost could mean high risk, but then everything changed.

Today, it is the low-cost airlines that are making the profits, including those operating in the once-difficult market. It is also the low-cost airlines that are showing themselves to be safer than many of the established carriers, after the low-cost sector gave everyone an unwelcome shock with a completely unnecessary accident at Valujet in the United States, due to the loading of unsuitable cargo.

There are three types of low-cost airlines. There are those like Southwest Airlines in the United States, Ryanair and EasyJet in Europe, and Virgin Blue in Australia, who have been created from the start as low-fare airlines. Then there are those created by the inclusive tour charter airlines, often on the back of their 'seat-only' business, which in truth really does fudge the difference between inclusive tour charters and low-cost scheduled services. Good examples in Europe have been the efforts by Condor in Germany, and by Thomsonfly, the old Britannia Airways, and Monarch in the UK. The experience of these has been indifferent, with many of the low-cost subsidiaries reabsorbed into the operations of their parent airlines after a brief period. Indeed, the separation between a one-class and often fairly cramped charter flight and a similar low-cost flight is so small that to differentiate the airlines seems unnecessary. The only difference is that most tour operators specify some kind of meal service, while the low-cost carriers usually charge for everything.

The third route has been for low-cost airlines to be created as offshoots of the major airlines, and this seems to have become the current vogue, even though British Airways soon sold its low-cost operation, Go!, to EasyJet. It remains to be seen whether the major airlines can be as successful in creating low-cost operations as the standalone airlines driven by entrepreneurs who write their own marketing and pricing rules. For the standalone, low-cost airlines, the suspicion is always that the low-cost subsidiaries of the major airlines enjoy a cross-subsidy, although mechanisms exist for them to challenge this. For the major airlines, the problem with a low-cost subsidiary must lie in exactly when it becomes a competitor, eating away at the bottom end of their market.

Already, the introduction of true low-cost competition on the longer routes has been hampered by the uneconomic fares offered by the major airlines for passengers sitting in the economy section of the aircraft. These fares are possible because, once the first and business classes are full, the aircraft is already making a profit, and the economy class seats need to be filled to stabilise the aircraft. At least one airline has recognised the poor conditions of the economy class and protected its market with a 'full fare economy' class offering extra legroom and other extras as well. If 'full fare economy' was to be the basic fare, then true low-cost, long-haul carriers would emerge.

That would be an interesting prospect for the future.

HOW TO USE THIS BOOK

In preparing any work of reference, there has to be a compromise between coverage and convenience. There is no point in covering every airline if the resulting tome is so heavy that it is difficult to use and has to be left at home or in the office. There is another point as well. The failure rate of new businesses, or 'start ups' to use the modern management jargon, is high in any sector, but in transport it is higher than most. Airlines with one or two aircraft are vulnerable, not least because if, for any reason, one aircraft is grounded, the impact on their income is crippling. For this reason, the airlines covered in this book have been restricted to those with five or more aircraft with more than eighteen passenger seats, or the freight equivalent. Helicopter charter operators have also been excluded. However, recognising that limiting the scope of the book could be frustrating for readers who will, in the main, be living in North America or the British Isles, a few exceptions to this rule have been made.

In this book, airlines are grouped together by nationality. The 'fleet' or 'brand' name is given prominence, with the full title, if different, following. In giving the rankings for the fifty largest airlines in the world, revenue is taken as the determining factor since this includes other activities such as air freight, and the provision of ground handling or engineering services to other airlines. When appropriate, passenger figures are also used, but these can be misleading since an airline carrying many passengers on short flights, with aircraft making eight or more flights per day, can be seen to be more important than long-haul airlines with aircraft barely making one flight daily.

The contents are presented alphabetically, by country and then within each country by airline. The registration prefixes have been given for most countries, and for the airlines, two- and three-letter flight designators have been given whenever possible, along with the airline radio callsigns. Each entry includes some background to the airline, which in the case of many of the major airlines, and some of the smaller airlines, amounts to a sometimes substantial history. Details of airline route structures have also been given when available. In addition, for the countries with a long air transport history, the national entry includes a brief overview.

Whenever possible, statistical information has been given, covering traffic figures and revenue, in which case both the US dollar and the pound sterling have been used, at an exchange rate of US $1.50 to the pound. Comparisons can never be exact. The practice of some airlines to devolve most, if not all, of their maintenance and engineering activities into a separate subsidiary can often mean that some airlines look decidedly short of engineering staff. The ratio of flight-deck crew – mainly pilots but in some instances also engineers – to cabin crew will often depend on the type of aircraft which predominate in a fleet. If larger aircraft are operated, there will be many more cabin crew than pilots, but the reverse happens on smaller aircraft, with two pilots and one cabin attendant.

Obviously, air freight operators don't have cabin crew as such, although they may have a loadmaster. It is also important to remember that charter operators will have far fewer ground staff than scheduled airlines, not needing to sell their own tickets but leaving that to the tour operators who have block-booked space. Another factor in airline staffing levels depends on whether they leave ground-handling and passenger-processing arrangements to other airlines or specialised contractors, such as Servisair in the UK, or do this themselves.

ACKNOWLEDGEMENTS

Researching and obtaining material for a book such as this is a demanding task, and I am especially grateful to those who have made it much easier. In each case, the captions note the source of the photographs, aircraft manufacturer or airline.

David Wragg

ALLIANCES

A number of global alliances have emerged in recent years, with airlines cooperating on matters such as frequent flyer programmes, scheduling and code-sharing, and marketing. Some of these have the potential to extend into areas such as maintenance and procurement. The main alliances are:

OneWorld: This alliance includes airlines from across the world such as American Airlines, British Airways, Cathay Pacific, Finnair, Iberia Airlines, Japan Air Lines International, LANChile, Qantas Airways and Royal Jordanian.

Sky Team: Claimed to be a global airline, Skyteam was formed in 2000 by Aeromexico, Air France, Delta Airlines and Korean Air, and now also includes Alitalia, CSA Czech Airlines, KLM Royal Dutch Airlines and Northwest Airlines.

Star Alliance: Brings together frequent-flyer programmes and other services for Adria Airways, Air Canada, Air New Zealand, All Nippon Airways, Asiana, Austrian Airlines, Blue1, bmi, Croatia Airlines, Lauda Air, LOT Polish Airlines, Lufthansa, SAS, Singapore Airlines, TAP Portugal, Thai International, United Airlines and US Airways.

THE WORLD'S MAJOR AIRLINES

AFGHANISTAN – YA

Afghanistan's low population density and poor surface communications should have ensured that it would be a natural growth area for air transport, but the area's poverty and political unrest have combined to ensure that air transport has had an uncertain and relatively brief history. Indeed, air transport was introduced to Afghanistan by an Indian company, Indamer, which had flown pilgrim charters from Kabul to Jeddah, and when it turned to air transport within Afghanistan, it marked the beginning for today's Ariana.

ARIANA

Ariana Afghan Airlines Co. Ltd
Incorporated: 1955

During the early 1950s, Indamer, at the time the largest Indian charter airline, enjoyed a successful business carrying pilgrims on special charters from Kabul to Jeddah. Aware of the commercial opportunities the as then untapped Afghan market offered, Indamer approached the Afghan government with a proposal to establish a national airline, and as a direct result, Ariana was established that year, with Indamer having a 49 per cent interest in the new airline, and the Afghan government holding the rest. Indamer had to supply the equipment. Operations began the following year, initially using a single Douglas DC-3 on internal routes within Afghanistan, but later that year, services to India and some of the Gulf States followed.

Indamer's interest was bought out in 1957 by Pan American World Airways, and Douglas DC-4s were introduced, and the DC-3s refurbished. Using the DC-4s, services reached Beirut in 1958, and this service was extended to Frankfurt in 1959, using a Douglas DC-6B, but cut back again to Beirut in 1961. It was not until 1967 that Frankfurt was again served, and the service extended to London. Later, Boeing 727s joined the fleet.

The emphasis moved away from American equipment after the Soviet invasion in 1979, with Antonov An-24 and An-26, and Yakovlev Yak-40 and Tupolev Tu-154 aircraft joining the fleet, while the emphasis of the route network shifted as well, away from London and Frankfurt and to Prague, Tashkent and Moscow instead. Services to the Indian subcontinent and to Dubai in the Gulf continued.

The collapse of the Soviet Union led to a return to western equipment, although some old Soviet aircraft remain in the fleet. When the Communist regime collapsed in 1992, the resultant civil war within Afghanistan, and the poor shape of the economy, limited operations and made re-equipment almost impossible, while maintenance facilities had to be moved to Pakistan. In 1999, UN sanctions against the Afghan regime limited the airline to domestic operations, and in 2001 the airline was effectively grounded between November and December, but in 2002 operations began once again. With the return of democracy to Afghanistan, the airline is re-equipping and now has a limited international scheduled network. Nevertheless, the internal situation remains difficult and this may hinder development in the near future.

HQ airport & main base: Kabul
Radio callsign: ARIANA
Designator: FG/AFG
Route points: Amritsar, Baku, Delhi, Dubai, Dushanbe, Islamabad, Istanbul, Jeddah, Kabul, Kuwait, Moscow, Sharjah, Tehran, Urumqi
Fleet: 3 Airbus A300B4-200; 2 Boeing 727-200; 4 Boeing 737-700; 1 Antonov An-26; 5 Antonov An-24RV; 1 Antonov An-12; 1 Yakovlev Yak-40; 1 De Havilland Canada Twin Otter Srs 300

ALBANIA – LV

Europe's poorest country, Albania broke away from the Soviet Bloc during the Communist period in power and instead attached itself to China as an ally, so failed to have an Aeroflot-sponsored airline as did the Warsaw Pact countries, and it was left to private enterprise to establish an airline after the fall of the Communist regime in the early 1990s.

ALBANIAN AIRLINES

Incorporated: 1992

The only Albanian airline, founded after the collapse of Communism, Albanian Airlines was founded in 1992, but operations did not commence until 1995. It is privately owned by the Kharafi Group and operates a small, international, scheduled network, mainly with BAe 146 airliners.

HQ airport & main base: Tirana Nene Teresa
Designator: LV/LBC
Route points: Athens, Bologna, Frankfurt, Istanbul, Milan, Pristina, Rome, Tirana, Turin, Zurich
Fleet: 1 BAe 146-300; 1 BAe 146-200; 1 BAe 146-100

ALGERIA – 7T

Algeria's first experience of air transport came when the country was linked to France by the flying boat services operated by French airlines across the Mediterranean. The outbreak of the Second World War and unrest within the country between pro-independence factions and those committed to continued close associations with France, all hindered the development of air transport, although Air Algerie dates from 1953, when it was created by the merger of two airlines, and before independence from France.

Unlike many other countries, and especially those anxious to increase tourist traffic, Air Algerie operates as a monopoly with little private sector competition. Indeed, the scope of its activities, including air taxi work, puts it on a par with the Soviet-era Aeroflot.

AIR ALGERIE

Societe Nationale des Transports Aeriens
Incorporated: 1953

Air Algerie's history pre-dates Algerian independence, to the time when the country was still a French colony. Two airlines had been formed, one of which was called Air Algerie and dated from 1949, while the other was the Compagnie Generale de Transports Aeriens. The two airlines were merged to form Air Algerie in 1953, a mixed state- and private-enterprise undertaking, with Air France at one stage having a 28 per cent interest. From 1963, the airline was recognised as the national airline of Algeria. The airline became completely state owned in 1972, some years after independence from France.

Today, Air Algerie operates both scheduled and charter air services within Algeria and to destinations in Africa and Europe, although services to France were suspended for a period in 1997. Unusually for a modern airline, air taxi work and agricultural aviation are both features of the airline's operations, although the aircraft used on these activities have been dropped from the fleet list below.

HQ airport & main base: Algiers Houari Boumediene
Radio callsign: AIR ALGERIE
Designator: AH/DAH
Employees: 8,800
Route points: Abidjan, Adrar, Algiers, Alicante, Amman, Amsterdam, Annaba, Athens, Bamako, Barcelona, Batna, Bechar, Beirut, Bejaia, Biskra, Bord Badj Mokhtar, Bordeaux, Brussels, Cairo, Casablanca, Constantine, Dakar, Damascus, Djanet, El Golea, El Oued, Frankfurt, Geneva, Ghardaia, Hassi Messaoud, Illizi, In Amenas, In Salah, Istanbul, Jijel, Lille, London, Lyons, Madrid, Marseilles, Metz, Moscow, Niamey, Nice, Nouakchott, Oran, Ouargla, Paris, Rome, Setif, Tamenghest, Tebessa, Tiemcen, Timimoun, Touggourt, Toulouse, Tripoli, Tunis
Links with other airlines: Tunisair (qv)
Fleet: 5 Airbus A330-200; 3 Boeing 767-300; 3 Boeing 727-200; 10 Boeing 737-800; 1 Boeing 737-400; 3 Boeing 737-300; 5 Boeing 737-600; 1 Boeing 737-200C; 1 Fokker F27-400M; 2 Raytheon Beech King Air 100; 7 Cessna Caravan 675

ANGOLA – D2

Although Portugal was by far the poorest of the European colonial powers, air transport was introduced to Angola before the outbreak of the Second World War, although the lack of a Portuguese aircraft industry meant that neutrality was no guarantee of operations continuing unaffected by the conflict. Nevertheless, postwar, the predecessor of the national airline, TAAG, established a domestic network while international flights were operated by TAP.

AIR GEMINI
Incorporated: 1999

Originally a freight charter airline, passenger charters started in 2002. Much of the company's business is for humanitarian relief organisations and for the mining industry.

HQ airport & main base: Luanda International
Designator: GLL
Fleet: 1 Boeing 727-100; 4 Boeing 727-100C; 2 McDonnell Douglas DC-9-30

AAC ANGOLA AIR CHARTER
Angola Air Charter, SARL
Incorporated: 1987

A wholly owned subsidiary of TAAG, Angola Air Charter handles international and domestic, cargo and passenger charters from its main base at Luanda.

Radio callsign: ANGOLA CHARTER
Designator: C3/AGO
Links with other airlines: The charter subsidiary of TAAG (qv)
Fleet: 2 Lockheed L-100-30 Hercules; 2 Boeing 727-100C; 1 Boeing 737-200

SONAIR
Incorporated: 1979

Formed in 1979 as Sonangol, Sonair provides passenger and cargo charters, including air taxi services, in support of the oil industry, as well as a regular service between Angola and Houston.

HQ airport & main base: Luanda 4 de Fevereiro
Radio callsign: SONAIR
Designator: SOR
Route points: Houston, Luanda, Malabo
Fleet: 1 Boeing 727-100F; 3 Boeing 727-100C; 2 Boeing 737-700; 2 Fokker 50; 1 Fokker F27 Friendship Mk500; 1 Shorts SC-7 Skyvan; 9 de Havilland Canada Twin Otter Srs 300; 5 Raytheon Beech 1900D; 1 Raytheon Beech King Air B200; 2 Beechcraft King Air 350; 2 Cessna Caravan 675

TAAG-ANGOLA AIRLINES
TAAG-Angola Airlines (Linhas Aereas de Angola)
Incorporated: 1938

Originally founded in 1938 as Direccuo de Exploracao do Transportes Aereos, operations began in 1940 but the development of services was inhibited at first by shortages of fuel and equipment during the Second World War, despite Angola being a colony of neutral Portugal. Postwar, a network of internal services was developed and cargo and passenger charters operated as well, while most international services remained with the Portuguese national carrier, TAP. On independence in 1973, the current title was adopted and a network of international services has been steadily developed.

The company is entirely state owned, and the international route network reflects Angola's post-independence alliances, while there are still some Russian aircraft, Ilyushin Il-62Ms, in the fleet, although these may be replaced by the new Boeing 777-200ER. The new Boeing 737-700s may replace the older 737-200, although this remains to be seen. A subsidiary is Angola Air Charter.

HQ airport & main base: Luanda 4 de Fevereiro
Radio callsign: DTA
Designator: DT/DTA
Employees: 5,770
Route points: Accra, Brazzaville, Cabinda, Catumbela, Dundo, Huambo, Johannesburg, Kinshasa, Lisbon, Luanda, Lubango, Lusaka, Malange, Menongue, Namibe, Ongiva, Paris, Pointe Noire, Rio de Janeiro, Sal, Sao Tome, Soyo, Windhoek
Fleet: 1 Boeing 747-300 Combi; 2 Boeing 777-200ER; 2 Ilyushin Il-62M; 4 Boeing 737-700; 3 Boeing 737-200; 1 Boeing 737-200C; 1 Fokker F27 Friendship Mk600

TRANSAFRIK
HQ now in Guernsey, Channel Islands, UK associated territory.

ANTIGUA – V2

The former British colonies in the West Indies were served for many years by British West Indies Airways, BWIA, a subsidiary of BOAC, which had created satellite airlines in the Caribbean, East and West Africa, effectively to provide short-haul feeder services for its long-haul operation. In the case of Antigua, there was eventually a local subsidiary of BWIA, Leeward Islands Air Transport, LIAT, which developed inter-island flights.

CARIBBEAN STAR AIRLINES
Incorporated: 2000

A regional scheduled airline for the Caribbean, based in Antigua, Caribbean Star Airlines was founded by a Texas businessmen through Caribbean Star Holdings in 2000. It operates a Bombardier Dash 8 fleet on inter-island flights.

HQ airport & main base: Antigua V.C. Bird International
Designator: 8B/GFI
Route points: Anguilla, Antigua, Beef Island, Bridgetown, Dominica, Georgetown, Grenada, Port of Spain, St Eustatius, St Kitts, St Lucia, St Maarten, St Vincent, San Juan, Santiago, Tobago
Fleet: 11 Bombardier Dash 8 Q300; 1 Bombardier Dash 3 Q100

LIAT
Liat (1974)
Incorporated: 1956

The present Liat was formed in 1974 as the successor to LIAT, Leeward Islands Air Transport, which dated from 1956, when it was established as a subsidiary of British West Indian Airways, itself in turn controlled by the former BOAC, British Overseas Airways Corporation. From its formation, the main purpose of the airline was to establish and operate scheduled air services within the Caribbean. In 1971, the airline was sold to a UK-based inclusive tour charter operator, Court Line, and when this airline and its parent group collapsed in 1974, Liat was rescued and re-established with ownership in the hands of eleven Caribbean governments, including Antigua, Barbuda, Barbados, Dominica, Grenada, Guyana, Jamaica, St Kitts/Nevis, St Lucia, St Vincent and the Grenadines, Montserrat and Trinidad and Tobago, who purchased the airline from the liquidators. When the airline was privatised in 1995, the Caribbean governments retained a substantial minority interest of 30.8 per cent, and BWIA also had a 29.2 per cent stake. Since then, the BWIA stake has fallen to 11.3 per cent, while that of the governments has risen to 73.4 per cent.

The fleet has changed in recent years, with the disappearance of the Hawker Siddeley 748s, which at one time were the backbone of the fleet, followed by the emergence of a completely de Havilland fleet, with Dash 8s augmented by Twin Otters. Over the past decade, the fleet has changed again to the 'Q' series of quiet turboprops, which now have adopted the Bombardier name.

HQ airport & main base: V.C. Bird International, Antigua
Radio callsign: LIAT
Designator: LI/LIA
Employees: 673
Route points: Anguilla, Antiqua, Barbados, Barbuda, Beef Island, Bridgetown, Dominica, Fort de France, Georgetown, Grenada, Nevis, Pointe a Pitre, Port of Spain, St Croix, St Kitts, St Lucia, St Maarten, St Thomas, St Vincent, San Juan, Santo Domingo, Tobago
Links with other airlines: BWIA (qv) has an 11.3 per cent interest
Fleet: 8 Bombardier Dash 8 Q300; 3 Bombardier Dash 8 Q100

ARGENTINA – LV

Although Aerolineas Argentinas, the national flag carrier, only dates from 1949, Argentina's history of air transport goes back at least to 1927 and the formation of Aeroposta Argentina by the French airline, Cie General Aeropostale. There were also operations across the River Plate linking Argentina and Uruguay using flying-boats. The pioneering work of the United States airlines was also vital in opening up air links throughout South America, a continent of mountains, dense rain forest and extensive waterways. Prominent among these was the New York, Rio and Buenos Aires Airline, NYBRA, nicknamed 'near beer', which used a combination of landplanes and flying boats for its lengthy route down the coast of South America, with passengers changing aircraft according to that judged most suitable for each stage of their journey. A competitor to NYBRA was PANAGRA, Pan American Grace Airways, a joint venture between the still relatively new Pan American Airways and the US shipping line, W.R. Grace & Company, which traded extensively with the countries of Latin America and was able to use its local knowedge. Grace had been planning to enter the airline business on its own, but was persuaded to combine its market knowledge with the aviation experience of Pan American.

AEROLINEAS ARGENTINAS
Aerolineas Argentinas, Empresa del Estado
Incorporated: 1949

The main Argentine airline, Aerolineas Argentinas, was formed in 1949 on the nationalisation of all Argentine airlines other than the Air Force-operated LADE. Operations began in 1950.

Of the four airlines brought together to form Aerolineas Argentinas, the most significant was Aeroposta Argentina, which had commenced operations in 1927 using French Latecoere 25s. A subsidiary of the French Cie Generale Aeropostale, Aeroposta's first route had been to Asuncion in Paraguay, but on nationalisation, several other nearby capitals were being served and a network of domestic services within Argentina had been created. Another airline was ALFA, Aviacion del Litoral Fleuva Argentina, which operated Short Sandringham flying boats on services along the Parana River, a tributary of the River Plate. The third airline was ZONDA, Zonas Oeste y Norte de Aerolineas Argentinas, which had only taken over the internal operations of PANAGRA in 1947, using a fleet of Douglas DC-3s. Prior to nationalisation, the Argentine government already had a 20 per cent stake in both ALFA and ZONDA, as well as a one-third interest in the fourth airline, FAMA, Flota Aero Mercante Argentina, which had been formed in 1946 to operate international services.

Bringing together four such disparate airlines in this way meant that Aerolineas Argentinas started life with a very mixed fleet, including Douglas DC-3s, DC-4s and DC-6s, Convair 240s, Vickers Vikings, Avro Yorks and three old Junkers Ju.52/3M trimotors, as well as a small Avro Anson and larger, but entirely unsuitable, Avro Lancastrians, converted from wartime Lancaster bombers. Inevitably, this resulted in many operational difficulties during the early years. Nevertheless, a major step forward came in 1959, when Argentina became just the fourth nation in the world to operate jet airliners, introducing six de Havilland Comet 4 aircraft, and followed these in 1962 with three Sud Aviation Caravelle 6Rs for shorter routes. The first of what was to become a fleet of twelve Hawker Siddeley HS 748 turboprop airliners followed, replacing the last of the DC-3s and Convair 240s, although the DC-4s soldiered on for some time afterwards.

No doubt much of the pressure for modernisation came from the fact that, from 1955 onwards, privately owned airlines were once again permitted in Argentina, and by the mid-1960s, almost all of the domestic network enjoyed competition.

Boeing 707-320s were placed in service in 1966, and the following year a non-stop Buenos Aires–Madrid service was inaugurated using these aircraft, giving the airline what was then the longest non-stop scheduled air service in the world, covering a distance of 6,275 miles.

Denationalisation of Aerolineas Argentinas saw the state's shareholding fall first to 7 per cent, then more recently to 5 per cent, while that for employees was initially 10 per cent but has since dropped to 3 per cent. From 1998, American Airlines had an 8.5 per cent stake, but this has now been sold. The Spanish airline, Iberia had an 85 per cent stake in 1990, but this had dropped to 20 per cent by 2000. In June 2001, the airline went into administration and flights to a number of international destinations were suspended, but a 92 per cent interest was sold to the Marsans Group in November of that year on condition that US $50 million of fresh capital was injected into the airline, and the airline left administration the following year. Some of the suspended routes have been reinstated, including that to Madrid, but others, including Los Angeles and Johannesburg, have not been restarted. Aerolineas Argentinas now has marketing alliances with another Argentine airline, Austral, which operates domestic scheduled services and is now a subsidiary of Aerolineas, and with Aerosur.

HQ airport & main base: Buenos Aires Jorge Newbery
Radio callsign: ARGENTINA
Designator: AR/ARG
Route points: Asuncion, Auckland, Bahia Blanca, Barcelona, Bogotá, Buenos Aires, Caracas, Catamarca, Comodoro Rivadavia, Cordoba (Arg), Corrientes, El Calafate, Esquel, Florianopolis, Formosa (Arg), Iguazu, Jujuy, La Rioja, Lima, London, Madrid, Mar del Plata, Mendoza, Mexico City, Miami, Montevideo, Munich, Newquen, New York, Paris, Porto Alegre, Posados, Punta del Este, Resistencia, Rio de Janeiro, Rio Gallegos, Rio Grande, Rome, Rosario, Salta, San Carlos de Bariloche, Santa Cruz, San Juan (Arg), San Luis, San Martin de los Andes, San Rafael, Santa Rosa, Sante Fe (Arg), Santiago, Santiago del Estero, Sao Paulo, Trelew, Tucaman, Ushuaia, Viedma, Zurich
Links with other airlines: Austral is a subsidiary, and there is a marketing alliance with Austral and Aerosur (both qv)
Annual turnover: US $947 million (£573.9 million)
Fleet: 2 Boeing 747-400; 1 Boeing 747-200B; 6 Airbus A340-600; 4 Airbus A340-200; 3 Airbus A310-324; 15 Boeing 737-200Adv; 1 McDonnell Douglas MD-88

AUSTRAL
Austral Lineas Aereas
Incorporated: 1971

Austral was formed in 1971 on the merger of Austral Compania Argentina de Transportes Aeros and ALA, Aerotransportes Litoral Argentino, although both airlines had effectively been operating an integrated route network for five years prior to this, after Austral CATA had taken a 30 per cent shareholding in ALA in 1966. ALA had been formed as an air taxi company in 1957, and had moved into scheduled domestic services in 1958.

In 1990, the newly privatised Aerolineas Argentinas took a shareholding in Austral, later acquiring the airline outright. When Aerolineas was privatised in 1990, Cielos del Sur and Iberia both invested in the airline, but these shareholdings have now been sold and the airline is owned by Interinvest with a 90 per cent stake, although close operational and marketing links remain with Aerolineas.

At one time the fleet had as many as eight BAC One-Eleven aircraft, but after 1991, these were gradually replaced by McDonnell Douglas MD series aircraft, and more recently Boeing 737s have been added to the fleet.

HQ airport & main base: Buenos Aires Aeroparque Jorge Newbery
Radio callsign: AUSTRAL
Designator: AU/AUT
Route points: More than thirty domestic destinations
Links with other airlines: A marketing alliance with Aerolineas Argentinas (qv)
Fleet: 7 Boeing 737-200; 11 Boeing 737-500; 2 McDonnell Douglas MD-88; 9 McDonnell Douglas MD-83; 2 McDonnell Douglas MD-81

LADE
Lineas Aereas del Estado
Incorporated: 1940

The airline was founded in 1940 by the Argentine Air Force as Lineas Aereas Suroeste to provide a domestic airline network. In 1945, it merged with Lineas Aereas Noreste, also operated by the Air Force, and the combined airline adopted the current title. In addition to scheduled services, it also offers business jet services.

HQ airport & main base: Buenos Aires Aeroparque Jorge Newbery
Designator: SU/LDE
Route points: Alyto Rio Senguer, Bahia Blanca, Buenos Aires, Comodoro Rivadavia, El Bolson, El Calafate, El Maiten, El Palomar, Esquel, General Roca, Gobemador Gregores, Jose San de Martin, Necochea, Par del Plata, Parana, Puerto Deseado, Puerto Madryn, Rio Gallegos, Rio Grande, Rio Mayo, San Antonio Oeste, San Carlos de Bariloche, San Julianj, San Martin de los Andes, Santa Cruz, Trelew, Ushuaia, Viedma
Fleet: 1 Boeing 757-200; 2 Boeing 707-320C; 5 Lockheed Martin C-130A/H Hercules; 4 Fokker F28 Fellowship Mk1000; 4 Fokker F27 Friendship Mk400/600; 9 de Havilland Canada Twin Otter Srs 200; 2 Fairchild Merlin 23; 1 Bombardier Learjet 60; 3 Bombardier Learjet 35A

LAN ARGENTINA
Incorporated: 2005

Created as an Argentine satellite of the Chilean-owned LAN group, LAN Argentina is primarily a domestic airline but has an international route from Buenos Aires to Miami.

HQ airport & main base: Buenos Aires
Designator: 4M
Route points: Buenos Aires, Cordoba, Mendoza, Miami
Links with other airlines: Owned by the LAN group
Fleet: 3 Boeing 767-300GR; 4 Airbus A320-200

ARMENIA – EK

For many years part of the Soviet Union, Armenia is one of the poorer states and after independence, the national airline, Armenian International Airlines, struggled with the country's poor economic prospects, worsened by a civil war, before collapsing in 2001. The airline had been originally founded as a former division of Aeroflot.

AIR ARMENIA
Incorporated: 2003

A passenger charter airline using Soviet-era equipment.

HQ airport & main base: Yerevan
Designator: QN/ARR
Fleet: 3 Antonov An-72; 1 Tupolev Tu-134; 3 Antonov An-12

ARMAVIA
Incorporated: 1996

Founded in 1996, in 2002 Sibir Airlines acquired a 70 per cent stake, with private investors holding the rest, to enable the airline to take over many routes operated by the former Armenian International Airlines, which collapsed in the wake of the civil war. Armavia uses a mixture of Russian and Airbus equipment on international scheduled flights.

HQ airport & main base: Yerevan
Radio callsign: ARMAVIA

Designator: U8/RNV
Route points: Adler/Scohi, Aleppo, Amsterdam, Ashgabat, Athens, Beirut, Dubai, Ekaterinburg, Frankfurt, Istanbul, Kiev, Krasnodar, Mineralnye Vody, Moscow, Nizhniy Novgorod, Novosibirsk, Odessa, Paris, Rostov, St Petersburg, Samara, Simferopol, Stavropol, Tehran, Tel Aviv, Volgograd
Fleet: 2 Ilyushin Il-86; 1 Airbus A320-200; 2 Airbus A319-100; 1 Tupolev Tu-134A

ARMENIAN INTERNATIONAL AIRWAYS
Incorporated: 2002

Founded to acquire many of the routes operated by Armenian International Airlines, which had been founded as Armenian Airlines and was one of the many airlines which were suddenly cast into existence by the break up of the Soviet Union and of the then Soviet airline, Aeroflot. While Armenian was completely state owned, it ran into severe difficulties in the aftermath of the war between Armenia and Azerbaijan, as well as a difficult economic climate. The new airline is privately owned.

HQ airport & main base: Yerevan
Radio callsign: ARMENIAN
Designator: MVRML
Fleet: 1 Airbus A320-200

AUSTRALIA – VH

As a prosperous and well-developed country, with vast distances separating the main centres of population, and also remote from the rest of the world, Australia was almost made for air transport, especially since the railways had developed piecemeal with different track gauges in many of the states. Postwar, Australia was also noted for a two-airline policy on domestic routes that allowed a state-owned airline, Trans Australia Airways and a private enterprise competitor, ANA Australian National Airways, to compete, while the other major Australian airline, Qantas, was confined to international routes.

Although the first Australian airline was West Australian Airways, which commenced operations on 4 December 1921, the history of air transport in Australia is bound up with the history of the Queensland and Northern Territory Aerial Service, QANTAS, founded in 1920, with operations also commencing the following year, flying charters throughout Queensland with an Avro 504K and a Royal Aircraft Factory BE.2. Later, government subsidy enabled scheduled services to start, but it was the links with Imperial Airways and the start of the Empire Air Mail Scheme for the countries of the British Empire during the late 1930s that saw strong international services begin to develop to and from Australia.

Qantas was also present at the formation of an important Australian institution, the Australian, later Royal Australian, Flying Doctor Service, which commenced operations on 15 May 1928, as a joint venture between the Australian Inland Mission, a religious movement, and Qantas, which provided a de Havilland DH50 that had been modified to take two stretchers.

Meanwhile, another major Australian airline was in the making, Ansett, which at one stage was one of the world's major airlines, until it collapsed following the financial difficulties suffered by one of its major shareholders, Air New Zealand, in the aftershocks that hit the world airline industry following the terrorist attacks on New York and Washington on 11 September 2001.

It was named after its founder, Reginald Ansett, whose first venture in transport was simply a taxi service in 1931, but who learned to fly in 1932. In 1936, with his brother Jack and a radial-engined Porterfield aircraft, Ansett won an air race from Brisbane to Adelaide, for which the prize was £500 (US $2,000 at the then rate of exchange). With the money, a six-passenger Fokker Universal was acquired, and an airline, Ansett Airways Pty Ltd, was established, making its first flight between Hamilton and Melbourne, both in Victoria, on 17 February 1936. The following year, the new airline became a publicly quoted company, and the base moved to Melbourne.

Early expansion was rapid, with the vast distances and low population density of much of Australia lending themselves to air transport. Three Lockheed L10B Electras were obtained in 1937, and services introduced from Melbourne to Adelaide, Broken Hill and Sydney. A serious fire at the airline's hangar destroyed four aircraft, and the advent of the Second World War brought an end to most commercial air services. Ansett moved into servicing Allied military aircraft, while its aircraft were used to carry Allied service personnel around Australia, and to evacuate civilians from Darwin and Broome after Japanese air raids on these towns.

Postwar, airline services resumed, with Reginald Ansett obtaining three ex-USAAF Douglas C-47 Dakotas, which were converted to 28-seat airliners. In 1946, the name was changed to Ansett Transport Industries Ltd, or ATI, reflecting the growing diversification of the business, which by this time included coaches and hotels.

When the Australian government decided on a 'two airline' policy, which effectively reserved the trunk routes for the state-owned Trans Australia Airways and its private enterprise competitor, ANA Australian National Airways, Ansett was left to make the best of the non-trunk routes. This situation did not last for long, and when ANA ran into severe financial difficulties in 1957, ATI purchased the company, creating a new airline, Ansett-ANA.

Ansett-ANA began to expand. In 1958, the airline bought New South Wales-based Butler Air Transport and Queensland Airlines. Expansion and acquisition meant that a varied fleet was created, with six Douglas DC-6s and DC-6Bs, two DC-4s, twenty DC-3s, two Vickers Viscount 700s, eight Convair Metropolitans, a Bristol 170 Freighter and two Short Sandringham flying boats, as well as two helicopters. Yet, despite the sense of competition inherent in the two airlines legislation, there were limits, with a balance on the capacity and frequencies offered by the two main airlines on the trunk routes, so that many innovations had to synchronised, as with the first jet aircraft for the two airlines, Boeing 727s in 1964, and the introduction of Douglas DC-9s three years later.

A further name change followed in 1969, with Ansett-ANA becoming Ansett Airlines of Australia. That year, one of the oldest Australian airlines, McRobertson Miller Aviation, dating from 1927, was purchased, making Ansett Australia's largest domestic airline. Ansett's diversifications were to be the airline's undoing, however, and after the collapse of a finance company in which Ansett had invested, the airline was taken over by another transport operator, TNT (originally founded as Thomas Nationwide Transport), working in partnership with the newspaper publisher, News Corporation.

The first steps in expansion outside Australia came in 1987, with the formation of Ansett New Zealand. Back home, Ansett Australia had gained permission to introduce international services, starting with operations to Denpasar Bali from Perth, Darwin, Sydney and Melbourne in September 1993. Boeing 747s were acquired, and services to Osaka, Hong Kong, Kuala Lumpur, Taipei, Jakarta, Auckland and Seoul followed.

In 1996, Air New Zealand acquired TNT's half share in Ansett Australia, while to prevent a monopoly arising on New Zealand's domestic services, News became the sole owner of Ansett New Zealand. Ansett was then restructured so that 51 per cent of the group belonged to Australian institutional investors, with the balance split equally between Air New Zealand and News. Ansett went into voluntary liquidation in 2001, but by this time Qantas was once again flying domestic services and the appearance of new airlines has filled the gap, although like Ansett before it, Qantas has developed many regional and specialised subsidiaries.

ALLIANCE AIRLINES
Incorporated: 2002

Founded in 2002 by Queensland Airline Holdings to operate passenger and cargo contract charters on behalf of the resources industry within Australia and throughout the western Pacific and South-East Asia, as well as wet-leasing aircraft to major airlines.

HQ airport & main base: Brisbane International
Radio callsign: ALLIANCE
Designator: QQ/UTY
Employees: 152
Fleet: 7 Fokker 100

AUSTRALIAN AIR EXPRESS
Incorporated: 1992

Formed and owned by Qantas and the Australian Postal Corporation, the company provides scheduled and charter all-cargo services within Australia, using aircraft operated by National Jet Systems. The Boeing 727s recently in the fleet have been replaced by Boeing 737-300s.

HQ airport & main base: Melbourne Tullamarine International, with a further major base at Sydney Kingsford Smith International
Designator: XM/XME
Employees: 1,300
Route points: Adelaide, Albury, Alice Springs, Amidale, Ayers Rock, Ballina, Brisbane, Broome, Cairns, Canberra, Coffs Harbour, Darwin, Dubbo, Gold Coast, Gove, Grafton, Groote Eylandt, Hamilton Island, Hobart, Kalgoorlie, Karratha, Launceston, Lord Howe Island, Mackay, Melbourne, Mildura, Moree, Mount Isa, Narrabi, Newcastle, Newman, Paraburdon, Perth, Port Hedland, Port Macquarie, Proserpine, Rockhampton, Sunshine Coast, Sydney, Tamworth, Taree, Townsville, Wagga Wagga
Links with other airlines: Qantas (qv) has a 50 per cent interest
Fleet: 5 Boeing 737-300

EASTERN AUSTRALIA
Eastern Australia Airlines Ltd
Incorporated: 1987

Formed during the late 1980s with the support of Australian Regional Airlines, a subsidiary of the then Australian Airlines, which held a 42 per cent stake in the new airline, Eastern Australia started to establish a network of regional air services within New South Wales. The airline can trace its origins back to the start of the Tamworth Air Taxi Service in 1949, with just one aircraft and one pilot. Today, the airline is a wholly owned subsidiary of Qantas.

HQ airport & main base: Sydney Kingsford-Smith International
Designator: QF/ECO
Employees: 684
Route points: Armidale, Coffs Harbour, Dubbo, Grafton, Kempsey, Lord Howe Island, Moree, Narrabri, Port Macquarie, Sydney, Tamworth, Taree
Links with other airlines: A subsidiary of Qantas (qv)
Fleet: 10 Bombardier Dash 8 Q300; 3 Bombardier Dash 8 Q200; 9 Bombardier Dash 8 Q100

JETSTAR
Incorporated: 2003

Jetstar was formed in 2003 as a low-cost subsidiary for Qantas, and began operation in May 2004. The airline was based on another airline, Impulse Airlines, which Qantas purchased. Initial plans include trans-Tasman operations linking Australia and New Zealand.

HQ airport & main base: Melbourne Tullamarine International
Radio callsign: JETSTAR
Designator: JQ/JST
Employees: 1,000
Route points: Adelaide, Ballina, Brisbane, Cairns, Christchurch, Coolangatta, Hamilton Island, Hervey Bay, Hobart, Launceston, Mackay, Melbourne, Newcastle, Proserpine, Rockhampton, Sunshine Coast, Sydney, Townsville
Links with other airlines: A subsidiary of Qantas (qv)
Fleet: 3 Airbus A330-200; 23 Airbus A320-200

MACAIR
Macair Airlines
Incorporated: 1992

Macair was founded as McKinlay Air Charters in 1992, and started scheduled services in 1998. The original owners sold the airline to Transjet in 2000, which merged it into its own airline subsidiary, Transtates Airlines, and adopted the current title. Horizon Airlines was acquired in 2003 and its operations absorbed into Macair.

HQ airport & main base: Townsville
Radio callsign: MACAIR
Designator: CC/MCK
Route points: Bedourie, Birdsville, Boulia, Brisbane, Burketown, Cairns, Charleville, Cloncurry, Cunnamulia, Doomadgee, Edward River, Hughenden, Julia Creek, Kowanyama, Longreach, Moranbah, Mornington, Mount Isa, Normanton, Oakey, Quilpie, Richmond, St George, Thargomindah, Townsville, Windorah, Winton
Fleet: 6 Saab 340B; 1 Shorts SC-7 Skyvan; 5 Fairchild Metro 23

NATIONAL JET SYSTEMS
National Jet Systems Pty Ltd
Incorporated: 1989

National Jet Systems was established in 1989, and commenced operations the following year, initially offering charter flights. The airline soon took on the Australian Airlink network for Australian Airlines, initially providing the major carrier with a regional feeder service in eastern Australia, which was later extended to cover much of the country. The connection survived Australian's absorption into Qantas, so that today National Jet operates services for Qantas. Charter services are still operated, while an important operation is that of Australian Air Express, an all-cargo company owned jointly by Qantas and the Australian Postal Corporation, whose Boeing 727s are flown by National Jet Systems.

National Jet Systems is owned by FR Aviation.

HQ airport & main base: Adelaide
Designator: NC/NJS
Employees: 800
Route Points: (Excluding those operated for Qantas, Australian Air Express or the Australian Postal Corporation) Adelaide, Brisbane, Cairns, Christmas Island, Cocos Islands, Darwin, Launceston, Perth, Ravensthorpe
Links with other airlines: Operates scheduled services on behalf of Qantas (qv)
Fleet: 5 Boeing 727-200F; 8 Boeing 717-200; 2 BAe 146-300QT; 2 BAe 146-300; 4 BAe 146-200;

5 BAe 146-100; 1 BAe Avro RJ70ER; 1 Bombardier Dash 8 Q300; 1 Bombardier Dash 8 Q200; 1 Bombardier Dash 8 Q100

QANTAS
Qantas Airways Ltd
Incorporated: 1920s

By far the largest airline in the southern hemisphere, Qantas is the twelfth largest worldwide by turnover and thirteenth by passenger numbers.

It was as the Queensland and Northern Territory Aerial Service, QANTAS, that Qantas started in 1920, after a period of deliberation over a title since other names had been tried, such as 'The Western Queensland Auto Aerial Service' and then the 'Australian Transcontinental Aerial Services Co.', and rejected. None of these titles would have done justice to the resultant airline.

Operations began in 1921, flying charters throughout Queensland with an Avro 504K and a Royal Aircraft Factory BE.2, while the directors pressed the Australian government to grant a subsidy for scheduled services. Eventually, the government agreed, although the airline still had to compete, producing the best tender to operate the services. The first service was between Charleville and Cloncurry, and began in November 1922.

The early days of the airline saw struggles with the limitations of the aircraft then available, and it was not unknown for aircraft to be cancelled when it became apparent that they could not meet the severe operating conditions of the Queensland summer. Nevertheless, the airline survived, and even held a licence to manufacture aircraft such as the de Havilland DH.50, which proved to be a considerable improvement over earlier types. With commercial aviation still in its infancy, the opportunity to diversify and innovate existed, and in 1926, two flying schools were established, while in 1928, a significant advance in the use of aviation came with the creation of a flying doctor service using a DH.50 modified as an ambulance, although a Queensland doctor had chartered Qantas aircraft before this time for what were literally flying visits to his patients. Qantas held the contract for the flying doctor service for four years, laying the foundations for the Royal Australian Flying Doctor Service.

Meanwhile, the route network had expanded, with the airline moving to a new head office in Brisbane, and its horizons were widening. In 1934, the airline became Qantas Empire Airways Ltd, and the following year its aircraft, four-engined de Havilland DH.86s, took over the Darwin–Singapore section of the Imperial Airways' route to London, which had been extended to Australia the previous year. Over the next five years, several new types of aircraft were introduced, of which the most famous was probably the Short Empire 'C' class flying boat, six of which entered service in 1938, and enabled Qantas to operate the Sydney–Karachi section of the Empire Airmail service to London, although the aircraft landed at Southampton – in practice, aircraft operated the entire route with their passengers and mail, with Qantas crews operating the southern section and those of Imperial Airways operated from the UK to Karachi. This was the same year that Qantas moved its headquarters from Brisbane to Sydney.

The Empire flying boats were later to form the nucleus of a Royal Australian Air Force flying-boat squadron on the outbreak of the Second World War.

While the outbreak of war, initially in Europe in 1939 and then in the Pacific in 1941, meant that further expansion was limited, during the war years Qantas and the newly created British Overseas Airways Corporation – one of the predecessors of British Airways – operated a joint, non-stop Perth–Colombo service after the fall of Singapore. The airline also helped evacuate casualties from New Guinea and maintained some essential Australian domestic air services.

Postwar, ownership of Qantas passed to the Australian government. Qantas embarked on a programme of expansion. Initially, some of the aircraft pressed into service were converted wartime types, including modified Consolidated Liberator and Avro Lancaster (known as the Lancastrian) bombers and Catalina flying boats, but there were also Short Sandringham flying boats, the Douglas DC-3 for services to New Guinea and within both New Guinea and Queensland, as well as new Douglas DC-4s and Lockheed Constellations. Lockheed Super Constellations were introduced in 1954, and four years later, one of these aircraft inaugurated the airline's round-the-world service. The following year, the Lockheed Electra turboprop was introduced and Qantas became the first non-American airline to introduce Boeing 707s, initially using a longer-range variant unique to the airline, the 707-138B, which used the fuselage of the Boeing 720, before these were eventually replaced by Boeing 707-338Cs.

Meanwhile, postwar Australian civil aviation policy had not only seen Qantas become a state-owned airline, it had also dictated that the airline concentrated exclusively on international services, with domestic operations being given to another state enterprise, Trans Australia Airlines, or TAA, which started operations in 1946 with a fleet of Douglas DC-3s. TAA also took over the Flying Doctor service in 1949, and internal services in New Guinea in 1960. A nationwide network of services was developed, with many routes operating in competition with private enterprise airlines, of which the largest was Ansett Australia. Equipment operated included Vickers Viscounts and, later, Boeing 737s and Fokker F27s. In 1986, Trans Australia was renamed Australian Airlines.

It was eventually decided that the state-owned airlines would be privatised, but before this happened, Qantas purchased Australian Airlines in 1992, creating a new large airline carrying the Qantas name. By this time, Australian Airlines had thirty-six aircraft in its own fleet, including Airbus A300s, and another thirty-seven in subsidiary airlines operating regional services.

Today, Qantas has grown from its small beginnings, but the old link with Imperial Airways was resurrected in 1993 when British Airways successfully bid for a 25 per cent shareholding on privatisation of Qantas, but the shareholding was run down to 18.25 per cent and then sold completely in 2004, although cooperation between the two airlines continue. Qantas has become a member of the Oneworld alliance and links exist with a substantial number of major airlines. Qantas is also the parent for a large number of subsidiaries, and has investments in many more, including a number in support services or travel and tourism, but which also include a subsidiary, Qantas Ltd, which was originally Australia-Asia Airlines, formed to inaugurate services to Taipei in 1990. Qantas has six subsidiary airlines, Airlink; Eastern Australia Airlines; JetConnect; Jetstar; Southern Australia Airlines; and Sunstate Airlines; three of which maintain the Qantaslink feeder operation, as well as substantial stakes in Air Pacific, JetStar Asia and Thai Air Cargo.

HQ airport & main base: Sydney Kingsford Smith International, but there are also major hub operations at Adelaide, Brisbane, Melbourne, Perth
Radio callsign: QANTAS
Designator: QF/QFA
Employees: 35,520
Route points: Adelaide, Albury, Alice Springs, Armidale, Auckland, Ayers Rock, Bahrain, Bangkok, Barcaldine, Beijing, Blackall, Blackwater, Brisbane, Broken Hill, Broome, Bundaberg, Burnie, Cairns, Canberra, Charleville, Christchurch, Coffs Harbour, Coolangatta, Darwin, Denpaser Bali, Devonport, Dubbo, Emerald, Frankfurt, Gladstone, Gove, Hamilton Island, Ho Chi Minh City, Hobart, Hong Kong, Honolulu, Horn Island, Jakarta, Johannesburg, Kalgoorlie, Karratha, Kingscote, Kuala Lumpur, Kununmurra, Launceston, London, Longreach, Lord Howe Island, Los Angeles, Mackay, Manila, Melbourne, Mildura, Moree, Mumbai, Mount Isa, Nadi, Narrabri, New York, Newcastle (NSW), Newman, Norfolk Island, Noumea, Osaka, Papeete, Paraburdoo, Perth, Port Hedland, Port Lincoln, Port Macquarie, Port Moresby, Port Vila, Queenstown, Rockhampton, Rome, Rotorua, Santiago de Chile, Seoul, Shanghai, Singapore, Suva, Sydney, Taipei, Tamworth, Tokyo, Townsville, Wagga Wagga, Weipa, Wellington, Wollongong, Zurich.
Links with other airlines: Qantas owns Airlink*; Eastern Australia Airlines* (qv); JetConnect; JetStar(qv), Southern Australia Airlines; and Sunstate Airlines* (qv) (*Qantaslink operators). Qantas has a 49 per cent stake in both JetStar Asia and Thai Air Cargo, with 46.3 per cent in Air Pacific (qv). Member of the Oneworld alliance. Alliances with Air Caledonie International, Air France (qv), Air Malta (qv), Air Nuigini (qv), Air Pacific (qv), Air Tahiti Nui (qv), Air Vanuatu, Alaska Airlines (qv), America West Airlines (qv), Asiana Airlines (qv), Brindabella Airlines, China Eastern Airlines (qv), EVA Air (qv), Gulf Air (qv), Japan Airlines International (qv), Jet Star (qv), Polynesian Airlines, South African Airways (qv), Sunstate Airlines (qv), Swiss (qv), Vietnam Airlines (qv)
Passengers carried: 31.5 million
Annual turnover: US $8,083 million (£5,600 million)
Fleet: 6 Boeing 747-400ER; 24 Boeing 747-400; 3 Boeing 737-300; 2 Boeing 767-300ER; 10 Airbus A330-300; 4 Airbus A330-200; 38 Boeing 737-800; 18 Boeing 737-400; these exclude aircraft operated by the subsidiary airlines (On order: 20 Airbus A380-800; 21 Boeing 787-8/9)

QANTASLINK

Three of the Qantas regional airlines, Airlink, Eastern Australian Airlines and Sunstate Airlines maintain this feeder service for Qantas trunk domestic and international flights.

REGIONAL EXPRESS
Incorporated: 2002

Regional Express was formed when two major Australian regional operators, Hazelton Airlines and Kendell Airlines, who had both interlined with

Ansett, were seriously affected by the latter's collapse in September 2001. A consortium of Australian businessmen and Singaporean investors bought both regional airlines from the administrators, forming the Rex Group as a holding company.

Formed in 1953 by Max Hazelton as an air taxi operator, Hazelton expanded into air charter and agricultural operations before starting its first scheduled air service in 1975, with a service from Orange to Canberra, the federal capital. The airline operations continued to expand, mainly in New South Wales, in family ownership under the name of Hazelton Air Services Pty Ltd, until it was acquired in October 1993 by a newly formed company, Hazelton Airlines, which became listed on the Australian Stock Exchange in December of that year. At the time of Ansett's collapse, Hazelton was operating a network of services out of Sydney.

Unlike Hazelton, Kendell was actually a subsidiary of Ansett, and had originally been founded in 1967 as Premiair Aviation. For the first four years the airline concentrated on charter services, and moved into regional scheduled services in 1971. The Kendell title was adopted in 1982. Although based at Wagga Wagga, an extensive network of scheduled services has been built up operating out of two hubs, Adelaide and Melbourne, with services reaching as far afield as Canberra in 1996, and then into airports in New South Wales.

Once established, Regional rebuilt the networks of its predecessors and rationalised the fleets, so that now an all-Saab turboprop fleet is operated.

HQ airport & main base: Sydney Kingsford Smith International
Designator: ZL/HZL
Employees: 624
Route points: Adelaide, Albury, Armidale, Ballina, Bathurst, Broken Hill, Burnie, Ceduna, Coober Pedy, Cooma, Dubbo, Griffith, King Island, Kingscote, Lismore, Melbourne, Meimbula, Mildura, Moruya, Mount Gambier, Narrandera, Olympic Dam, Orange, Parkes, Port Lincoln, Portland, Sydney, Wagga Wagga, West Wyalong, Whyalla
Fleet: 7 Saab 340A; 23 Saab 340B

SKYWEST
Skywest Airlines
Incorporated: 1963

Skywest Airlines is the largest regional operator within Western Australia, and since its formation in 1963, as Carnarvon Air Taxis, has developed a network of scheduled passenger and freight services out of Perth. In 2004, the airline expanded beyond its regional limits and started international operations to Denpasar Bali.

HQ airport & main base: Perth Domestic Airport
Designator: XR/SLL
Route points: Albany (Aus), Argyle, Broome, Carnarvon, Darwin, Denpasar Bali, Esperance, Geraldton, Kalbarrie, Kalgoorlie, Karratha, Kununurra, Learmonth, Monkey Mia, Perth, Port Hedland, Wiluna
Fleet: 2 Fokker 100; 5 Fokker 50

SUNSTATE AIRLINES
Sunstate Airlines Ltd
Incorporated: 1982

Established as a regional operator within Queensland, Sunstate Airlines was formed in 1982, and the following year merged with Noosa Air. The airline had early support from Australian Regional Airlines, a subsidiary of Australian Airlines, which held a 33 per cent interest before finally buying the airline outright in 1990. In the beginning, Sunstate was a de Havilland Twin Otter operator, expanding to larger aircraft as demand grew, so that it now operates Bombardier Dash 8s. It is now a wholly owned subsidiary of Qantas.

HQ airport & main base: Brisbane International
Designator: QF/SSQ
Employees: 302
Route points: Barnega, Blackwater, Brampton Island, Brisbane, Bundaberg, Cairns, Dunk Island, Emerald, Gladstone, Great Keppel Island, Hervey Bay, Lizard Island, Lord Howe Island, Mackay, Marochydore, Maryborough, Rockhampton, Thursday Island, Townsville
Links with other airlines: A wholly owned subsidiary of Qantas (qv)
Fleet: 7 Bombardier Dash 8 Q400; 6 Bombardier Dash 8 Q300; 2 Bombardier Dash 8 Q200; 1 Bombardier Dash 8 Q100

VIRGIN BLUE
Incorporated: 1999

Virgin Blue was founded in 1999 and commenced operations as a low-cost carrier the following year, initially operating two Boeing 737-700s between Sydney and Brisbane, the first of many domestic routes within Australia, before introducing international services to New Zealand and the Pacific islands. As the name implies, Virgin Atlantic has an interest, but this is currently just 25.26 per cent. In turn, Virgin Blue owns New Zealand-based Pacific Blue 100 per cent and has a 49 per cent stake in Polynesian Blue, a joint venture with the government of Samoa.

HQ airport & main base: Brisbane International, with a further base at Melbourne Tullamarine International
Designator: DJ/VOZ
Employees: 3,818
Route points: Adelaide, Apia, Auckland, Ballina, Brisbane, Broome, Cairns, Canberra, Coffs Harbour, Coolangatta, Christchurch, Darwin, Hamilton Island, Harvey Bay, Hobart, Launceston, Mackay, Melbourne, Nadi, Newcastle, Nuka'alofa, Perth, Port Villa, Proserpine, Raratonga, Rockhampton, Sunshine Coast, Sydney, Townsville, Wellington
Links with other airlines: Virgin Group has a 25.26 per cent stake. Owns Pacific Blue 100 per cent, and has a 49 per cent stake in Polynesian Blue (all qv). Alliances with United Airlines, Virgin Atlantic Airways (all qv)
Fleet: 36 Boeing 737-800; 22 Boeing 737-700; 11 Embraer 190; 3 Embraer 170

AUSTRIA – OE

AIR ALPS
Air Alps Aviation
Incorporated: 1998

Air Alps commenced operations early in 1999, with the main shareholder being Air Engiadina's president, Dietmar Leitgeb, with 51 per cent, while Air Engiadina owned the rest. Today, the Alpen-Air Consortium, based in South Tyrol, owns 88.82 per cent of the shares. The airline operates scheduled and charter feeder flights from Innsbruck.

HQ airport & main base: Innsbruck, but with a secondary hub at Milan Malpensa
Designator: A6/LPV
Links with other airlines: Alitalia (qv)
Fleet: 8 Dornier 328-110

AMERER AIR
Incorporated: 1995

Bearing the name of its founders and joint owners, Heinz Amerer and Susanne Amerer, Amerer Air operates scheduled and charter cargo services.

HQ airport & main base: Linz Horsching
Designator: AMK
Employees: 48
Route points: Liège, Linz, Vienna
Fleet: 2 Lockheed L-188 Electra; 1 Fokker F27 Mk5000

AUSTRIAN AIRLINES
Österreichische Luftverkehrs AG
Incorporated: 1957

Austrian Airlines was formed in 1957, and operations began the following year, twenty years after Olag Osterreichische Luftverkehrs had ceased operations on Germany's occupation of Austria in 1938. Olag Osterreichische Luftverkehrs had dated from 1923, and by 1938 had a network of services from Vienna to many of the major cities of central Europe. Many of OOL's routes and aircraft were taken over by the German airline Lufthansa.

The first service of the new Austrian Airlines was between Vienna and London Heathrow, using one of four chartered Vickers Viscount 700 aircraft, which were later replaced by four of the later Viscount 800s. Domestic services did not restart until 1963, initially using a Douglas DC-3, by which time the international services had seen the Viscounts joined by Sud Aviation Caravelle 6Rs. Two Hawker Siddeley HS 748s were also operated at this time.

Transatlantic services were introduced in 1969, initially using a Boeing 707 chartered from Sabena, and flying from Vienna to New York via Brussels. This service was withdrawn after two years. Development of European services continued, nevertheless, with nine Douglas DC-9-32 aircraft joining the fleet in 1971, and in 1980, these were followed by the first MD-80s. The decision to concentrate on European services must have been correct, since the airline declared its first profit in 1972. Throughout this period, the airline remained in state ownership, but in 1988, 24.2 per cent of the airline's shares were offered to the public, and Swissair took a 3 per cent interest, which was later raised to 8 per cent, while All Nippon Airways acquired 3.5 per cent. Closer collaboration with other European airlines was considered in 1993, with KLM, SAS and Swissair considering whether a form of strategic cooperation, code-named Alcazar, would be beneficial, but in the end the four participants decided not to proceed, as the concept of what would now be described as airline alliances was still some years away.

In 1994, Austrian acquired 42.85 per cent of the shares of Tyrolean Airways, a regional operator.

That same year, a marketing alliance and code-share was instigated with Delta Air Lines on the Vienna–New York route. The arrangement with Delta later led to a Vienna–Atlanta service. Austrian acquired a 36 per cent interest in Lauda Air in 1997. The investments in Tyrolean and Lauda reflected Austrian's policy of creating a single Austrian airline grouping. In 1997 Austrian doubled its stake in Tyrolean to 85.7 per cent, before later absorbing the airline, while Lauda Air is owned completely by Austrian, as is another airline, Austrian Arrows. Austrian has 62 per cent of Slovak Airlines and a 22.5 per cent interest in Ukraine International Airlines. Today a member of the Star Alliance, Austrian is privatised, with a broad base of shareholders, while Air France has a 1.5 per cent stake. An earlier generation of McDonnell Douglas MD-80 series aircraft has been replaced by new Airbus A320/321 aircraft, although the upper end of the fleet is mixed between aircraft of Airbus and Boeing manufacture. Despite being a relatively late arrival among national flag carriers, the airline has grown steadily in recent years, partly through acquisitions of other airlines, both in Austria and outside the country, so that now as an airline group, Austrian is the thirtieth largest in the world by turnover, and forty-ninth in terms of passengers carried.

HQ airport & main base: Vienna
Radio callsign: AUSTRIAN
Designator: OS/AUA
Employees: 7,662
Route points: Aleppo, Altenrhein, Amman, Amsterdam, Ankara, Athens, Baku, Bangkok, Barcelona, Bari, Basle, Beijing, Beirut, Belgrade, Berlin, Bologna, Bratislava, Brussels, Bucharest, Budapest, Cairo, Cancun, Chisinau, Cluj, Cologne, Colombo, Copenhagen, Damascus, Delhi, Dnepropetrovsk, Dresden, Dubai, Düsseldorf, Frankfurt, Fuerteventura, Funchal, Geneva, Gothenburg, Graz, Hamburg, Hanover, Helsinki, Holquin, Hurghada, Innsbruck, Istanbul, Kathmandu, Kharkov, Kiev, Klagenfurt, Kosice, Krasnodar, Larnaca, Las Palmas, Leipzig, Linz, Ljubljana, London, Luxembourg, Luxor, Lvov, Lyons, Madrid, Malaga, Male, Mauritius, Melbourne, Milan, Minsk, Montego Bay, Moscow, Mumbai, Munich, New York, Nice, Nuremberg, Odessa, Ohrid, Osaka, Oslo, Ostrava, Paris, Phuket, Podgorica, Prague, Pristina, Puerto Plata, Punta Cana, Riga, Rome, Rostov, St Petersburg, Sarajevo, Shanghai, Sibiu, Singapore, Skopje, Sofia, Stockholm, Strasbourg, Stuttgart, Sydney, Tbilisi, Tehran, Tel Aviv, Tenerife, Thessaloniki, Timisoara, Tirana, Tobago, Tokyo, Venice, Vienna, Vilnius, Warsaw, Washington, Yerevan, Zagreb, Zurich
Links with other airlines: Air France has 1.5 per cent. Austrian has 100 per cent of Lauda Air and Austrian Arrows, as well as 62 per cent of Slovak Airlines and 22.5 per cent of Ukraine International Airlines (alll qv). Member of the Star Alliance. Marketing alliances with Aeroflot (qv), Aeroflot-Don (qv), Air Burkina, Air China (qv), Air Dolomiti (qv), Air France (qv), Air India (qv), Air Mauritius (qv), Air Moldova (qv), AirBaltic, Azerbaijan Airways, Belavia Belarussian Airlines (qv), El Al (qv), Georgian Airways (qv), IBEX Airlines, Jat Airways, Job Air, Luxair (qv), Macedonian Airlines, Malaysia Airlines (qv), Montenegro Airlines (qv), Pulkovo Aviation Enterprise, Royal Jordanian Airlines (qv), South African Airways (qv), Styrian Spirit, Syrianair (qv), Tarom (qv), Ukraine International Airlines (qv)
Passengers carried: 9.4 million
Annual turnover: US $2,940 million (£1,960 million)
Fleet: 3 Airbus A340-300; 2 Airbus A340-200; 4 Airbus A330-200; 4 Boeing 777-200ER; 4 Boeing 767-300ER; 3 Airbus A321-200; 3 Airbus A321-100; 6 Airbus A320-200; 6 Airbus A319-100; 3 Fokker 70

AUSTRIAN ARROWS
Incorporated: 1978

Originally founded in 1978, on commencing operations in 1980 the airline used the title of Tyrolean Airways, which itself had started life in 1958 as Aircraft Innsbruck. The first scheduled services were domestic, but international services from Innsbruck followed, initially to destinations in Switzerland and what was then West Germany, and then more recently to destinations as far afield as Amsterdam.

Because of the often steep approaches and departure routes from many of the airports served within Austria, the airline uses aircraft with good, short take-off characteristics, and was one of the operators of the then de Havilland Canada Dash 7, a four-turboprop STOL airliner.

Austrian Airlines acquired an interest in the airline, originally 42.85 per cent, which was doubled to 85.7 per cent in 1997, while another major shareholder was Leipnik-Lundenburger Industrie, with 14.3 per cent. In 1998, Austrian bought the airline outright, and turned it into a feeder operation under the name of Austrian Arrows in 2003.

HQ airport & main base: Innsbruck, with an additional hub at Vienna
Radio callsign: TYROLEAN
Designator: VO/TYR
Employees: 1,631
Route points: Within the Austrian network
Links with other airlines: A wholly owned subsidiary of Austrian Airlines (qv) and a member of the Star Alliance. Marketing alliance with Malev (qv)
Fleet: 12 Fokker 100; 6 Fokker 70; 10 Bombardier Dash 8 Q400; 12 Bombardier Dash 8 Q300; 13 Bombardier CRJ200LR; 1 Bombardier CRJ100LR

LAUDA AIR
Lauda Air Luftfahrt
Incorporated: 1979

Founded in 1979 by former racing driver Niki Lauda, the eponymous Lauda Air did not begin operations until 1985, when it used two Fokker F27 Friendships and BAe One-Elevens, leased from Tarom, on charter flights, including inclusive tour operations to Mediterranean destinations using the One-Elevens. Licences for domestic scheduled services were granted in 1987, and in 1990 approval was given for international scheduled services, which had previously been the sole monopoly of Austrian Airlines. The airline established a small fleet of Boeing 767s for long-haul charters, including services to the Far East. An early supporter of the airline was Lufthansa, which took an initial 26.4 per cent interest, which was increased to 39.7 per cent in 1994, although three years later Lufthansa agreed to sell part of its holding to Austrian Airlines, which built up a 36 per cent share. Since then, the airline has been acquired outright by Austrian Airlines.

Lauda Air was the first European operator of the Canadair Regional Jet, which appeared on services operated under the Lufthansa Express banner, but today the airline's business is primarily inclusive tour charters with some scheduled services to holiday destinations. An Italian subsidiary was Lauda Air SpA, later renamed Lauda Air Italia, but this was acquired by Gruppo Ventaglio (which had been a minority shareholder alongside the Lauda family's Volante group) through its subsidiary, Livingston Aviation Group, and is being absorbed into Livingston.
HQ airport & main base: Vienna International
Radio callsign: LAUDA AIR
Designator: NG /LDA
Route points: Bangkok, Budapest, Hong Kong, London, Los Angeles, Manchester, Melbourne, Miami, Phuket, Sydney
Links with other airlines: Owned 100 per cent by Austrian Airlines (qv). Member of the Star Alliance
Fleet: 2 Boeing 767-300ER; 7 Boeing 737-800; 2 Airbus A320-200; 2 Boeing 737-700; 2 Boeing 737-600

NIKI
Incorporated: 2003

In 2003, former Austrian motor racing champion Niki Lauda took a second foray into air transport, having sold his original airline to Austrian Airlines, acquiring Aero Lloyd Austria with the assistance of Air Berlin, and renaming the company Niki, as the title Lauda Air was retained for his original airline after its sale.

Low-cost services to holiday destinations are operated, many of them on behalf of the Neckermann Reisen tour chain, using a fleet that consists entirely of Airbus narrow-bodied aircraft.

HQ airport & main base: Vienna International
Radio callsign: NIKI
Designator: HG/NLY
Route points: Alicante, Düsseldorf, Fuerteventura, Funchal, Jerez de la Frontera, Lanzarote, Las Palmas, Lisbon, London, Luxor, Malaga, Menorca, Munich, Nuremberg, Palma de Mallorca, Paris, Rome, Sharm el Sheikh, Tenerife, Vienna, Zurich
Links with other airlines: Air Berlin (qv) has a 24 per cent stake
Fleet: 1 Airbus A321-200; 8 Airbus A320-200; 2 Airbus A319-100

AZERBAIJAN – 4K

AZAL AVIA CARGO
Incorporated: 1996

Predominantly a cargo charter airline, operating from Baku throughout the CIS.

HQ airport & main base: Baku Heydar Aliev International
Designator: AHC
Fleet: 4 Ilyushin Il-76TD; 1 Antonov An-26B; 2 Antonov An-12

AZERBAIJAN AIRLINES
Azerbaijan Hava Yollari
Incorporated: 1992

Split off from Aeroflot on the break up of the former Soviet Union, Azerbaijan Airlines is suffering from the severe economic climate, as well as the aftermath of the war with Armenia, but it is slowly re-equipping with western aircraft. In 1997, the airline acquired the sole remaining Canadair CL-44 Conroy for air cargo charters involving outsize loads, but has since reverted to a mix of Airbus, Russian and Ukrainian aircraft. It is completely state owned.

HQ airport & main base: Baku
Radio callsign: AZAL
Designator: J2/AHY
Route points: Aktau, Aleppo, Ankara, Bishkek, Chelyabinsk, Delhi, Dubai, Ekaterinburg, Frankfurt, Gaziantep, Gomel, Istanbul, Kabul, Karachi, Kazan, Kharkov, Kiev, Krasnodar, Milan, Mineralnye Vody, Moscow, Nizhniy Novgorod, Orenburg, Paris, Perm, Samara, Tbilsi, Tehran, Tel Aviv, Trabzon, Ufa, Urumqi, Volgograd, Zaporozhye
Fleet: 5 Tupolev Tu-154B; 2 Tupolev Tu-154M; 4 Boeing 757-200; 1 Airbus A320-200; 3 Airbus A319-100; 8 Tupolev Tu-134; 1 Ilyushin Il-76; 1 Antonov An-140-100; 1 Antonov An-26B; 5 Yakovlev Yak-40

BAHAMAS – VP-B

BAHAMASAIR

Bahamasair Ltd
Incorporated: 1973

The operational subsidiary of the Bahamas government-owned Bahamasair Holdings, Bahamasair was founded in 1973 to improve communications between the many small islands in the Bahamas chain. Operations soon reached some twenty islands both in the Bahamas and in neighbouring groups, while international services are operated to New York, Miami and Orlando in the United States.

HQ airport & main base: Nassau International
Radio callsign: BAHAMAS
Designator: UP/BHS
Employees: 725
Route points: Andros Town, Arthur's Town, Crooked Island, Deadmans Cay, Fort Lauderdale, Freeport, George Town, Governor's Harbour, Havana, Inagua, Mangrove Cay, Marsh Harbour, Mayaguana, Miami, Nassau, North Eleuthera, Orlando, Providenciales, Rock Sound, San Andros, San Salvador, Santo Domingo, South Andros, Spring Point, Stella Maris, The Bight, Treasure Cay, West Palm Beach
Links with other airlines: Alliance with US Airways (qv)
Fleet: 4 Boeing 737-200; 8 Bombardier Dash 8 Q300

BAHRAIN – A40

GULF AIR

Incorporated: 1950

Although based in Bahrain, Gulf Air is the airline for four small states in the Gulf: Abu Dhabi, Bahrain, Oman and Qatar. Interest in establishing an airline for these territories came about after an Englishman, Freddie Bosworth, started operating a war-surplus Avro Anson in 1949, offering sightseeing trips and air charters. The following year, Bosworth and several local businessmen founded the Gulf Aviation Company, obtaining a de Havilland Dove and a small Auster. The early operations were largely charter work on behalf of the major oil companies.

In 1951, BOAC became a major shareholder, and in addition to providing operating capital, also provided technical assistance, adding Gulf Air to the network of locally based airlines throughout the world whose operations fed into those of the British airline. New aircraft, de Havilland Herons, were added to the fleet, and services operated from Bahrain to Abu Dhabi, Al Ain, Kuwait, Muscat and Sharjah. Later, Douglas DC-3s were added to the fleet, followed by Fokker F27s and then a BAC One-Eleven jet. A Vickers VC-10 wet-leased from BOAC saw services to London started in 1970.

In 1973, the airline was effectively nationalised, with the four governments buying out the BOAC shareholding, and a treaty the following year officially changed Gulf Aviation into Gulf Air, formally recognising the airline as the flag carrier for the four states. Investment in the airline saw Lockheed L-1011 TriStars and Boeing 737s join the fleet, displacing the older types and providing the equipment suitable for expansion, with a network which stretched from London and Amsterdam in Europe to Hong Kong. Later, in 1992, Gulf Air became the first Arab airline to operate to Melbourne and to Johannesburg.

The airline is now owned by the governments of Bahrain and Oman equally, with Qatar having withdrawn, then followed by Abu Dhabi in 2006, with Abu Dhabi and Muscat no longer operated as hubs. Over the past decade, Airbus aircraft have come to predominate in the fleet. A subsidiary, formed in 2003, is Gulf Traveller, a low-cost airline.

HQ airport & main base: Bahrain International
Radio callsign: GULF AIR
Designator: GF/GFA
Employees: 5,900
Route points: Abu Dhabi, Amman, Amsterdam, Athens, Bahrain, Bangalore, Bangkok, Beirut, Cairo, Chennai, Chang Mai, Damascus, Damman, Delhi, Dhaka, Doha, Dubai, Dublin, Frankfurt, Hong Kong, Islamabad, Istanbul, Jakarta, Jeddah, Johannesburg, Karachi, Khartoum, Kuala Lumpur, Kuwait, Lahore, Larnaca, London, Manila, Mashhad, Mumbai, Muscat, Nairobi, Paris, Peshawar, Phuket, Riyadh, Rome, Sana'a, Sharjah, Shiraz, Singapore, Sydney, Tehran, Triruvananthapuram
Links with other airlines: Owns Gulf Traveller (qv). Alliances with American Airlines, bmi, Cyprus Airways, Egyptair, Garuda Indonesia, Indian Airlines, KLM, Middle East Airlines, Olympic Airlines, Oman Air, Qantas Airways, Royal Jordanian Airlines, Saudi Arabian Airlines, Thai Airways (all qv)
Fleet: 9 Airbus A340-300; 6 Airbus A330-200; 4 Boeing 767-300ER; 10 Airbus A320-200

GULF TRAVELLER

Incorporated: 2003

Founded by Gulf Air in 2003 using five of that airline's Boeing 767s, the airline operates low-cost all-economy flights from Gulf Air's two bases to points on the parent airline's route network, primarily within the Middle East and to the Indian sub-continent.

HQ airport & main base: Abu Dhabi International
Designator: GF/GFA
Links with other airlines: Owned 100 per cent by Gulf Air (qv)
Fleet: 5 Boeing 767-300ER

BANGLADESH – S2

Inevitably, the history of air transport in Bangladesh is bound up with that of Pakistan, of which Bangladesh was a part, known as East Pakistan, until it became independent in 1971. Before an even earlier partition, the division of Pakistan from India in 1947, services to and from the country would have been largely in the hands of Imperial Airways and the predecessors of Air India. Commercial air transport would have been stopped during the Second World War, with Japanese forces in neighbouring Burma. While Bangladesh was part of Pakistan, the Pakistan Air Force played a major role in air transport, operating a service using Bristol Freighters between East and West Pakistan.

BIMAN BANGLADESH AIRLINES

Bangladesh Airlines Corporation
Incorporated: 1972

Biman dates from 1972, when it was formed by the Bangladesh government shortly after secession from Pakistan late the previous year. Prior to this, services to and from what had been East Pakistan had been operated by PIA. Scheduled operations began in February 1972, a month after the airline was founded. The initial services were domestic, with routes into India, while London became an early long-haul destination using Boeing 707s. The 707s were later replaced by DC-10s and Airbus A310s.

In the near future, the Bangladesh government is prepared to offer up to 40 per cent of the airline's shares to a foreign airline on condition that it assumes management control, while a further 9 per cent of the shares will be available to employees.

HQ airport & main base: Dhaka
Radio callsign: BANGLADESH
Designator: BG/BBC
Employees: 5,351
Route points: Abu Dhabi, Bahrain, Bangkok, Barisal, Brussels, Chittagong, Cox's Bazaar, Damman, Delhi, Dhaka, Doha, Dubai, Frankfurt, Hong Kong, Jeddah, Jessore, Karachi, Kathmandu, Kolkata, Kuala Lumpur, Kuwait, London, Mumbai, Muscat, New York, Paris, Rajshahi, Riyadh, Saidpur, Singapore, Sylhet, Tokyo, Yangon
Fleet: 5 McDonnell Douglas DC-10-30; 4 Airbus A310-300; 4 Fokker F28 Mk4000 Fellowship

BELARUS – EW

BELAVIA

Belavia-Belarussian Airlines
Incorporated: 1993

One of the many airlines created out of the breakup of Aeroflot, Belavia is essentially the former Aeroflot Division within what was the Soviet Republic of Belarus and is owned completely by the Belarus government.

HQ airport & main base: Minsk International
Radio callsign: BELARUS AVIA
Designator: B2/BRU
Route points: Anapa, Berlin, Frankfurt, Istanbul, Kaliningrad, Kiev, Larnaca, London, Minsk,

Moscow, Paris, Rome, St Petersburg, Stockholm, Tblisi, Tel Aviv, Vienna, Warsaw, Yerevan
Fleet: 17 Tupolev Tu-154M; 11 Tupolev Tu-134; 2 Boeing 737-500; 1 Boeing Business Jet; 5 Antonov An-24; 4 Yakovlev Yak-40

TRANSAVIAEXPORT AIRLINE
Incorporated: 1993

Founded in 1993, Transaviaexport Airline operates cargo charters throughout the Commonwealth of Independent States and into the Middle East.

HQ airport & main base: Minsk International
Designator: AL/TXC
Fleet: 13 Ilyushin Il-76MD/TD

BELGIUM – OO

The history of air transport in Belgium is mainly the history of one airline, the national carrier, Sabena. In common with France and the United Kingdom, as much emphasis was placed on links with the colonies as with services between European capitals. The growth of Sabena was less dramtic than of its British and French rivals, due in part to the small size of the country and the fact that the only colony of any importance was the Belgian Congo, in contrast to the extensive British and French overseas possessions. Because of the small size of the country, for many years little importance was attached to either internal air services or operations from provincial centres. The idea of Brussels being a pivotal point in European air transport had still to take hold, given that European unification, a single market, was a concept whose time did not come until after the Second World War. It was also not until after the war that a real independent airline sector began to emerge in Belgium.

Sabena, an acronym for the Société Anonyme Belge d'Exploitation de la Navigation Aerienne, was founded in May 1923 as the successor to SNETA, Société Nationale pour l'Etude de Transports Aeriens, which itself dated from 1919, when it had been founded to operate services from Brussels to Amsterdam, London and Paris, using ex-First World War aircraft. Sabena's first service was far less ambitious, flying newspapers from Brussels to Lympne, on the south coast of England, via Ostend. It was in 1924 that a passenger service first started, from Brussels to Basle via Strasbourg with a three-engined Handley Page W.8. Nevertheless, the airline, in common with many other European carriers of the day, had its ambitions set on flights to colonial destinations, and in 1925 a Handley Page W.8 flew to the Belgian Congo, the seventy-five hour journey being spread over fifty-one days. The following year, this was reduced to three days using an Italian Savoia-Marchetti S-73, and in 1938 was further reduced to twenty-four hours with a Savoia-Marchetti S-83, reputed to be the fastest aircraft in commercial service at the time.

Given the capabilities of the aircraft of the day, the priority had to be the creation of a European network, and by 1938, Sabena had a network which extended to Stockholm in the north, and as far south as Vienna, which was reached that year. Services to the Belgian Congo were inaugurated in 1935, initially using a Fokker F.VII landplane, which took five-and-a-half days. This marked another difference between British, French, and for that matter, US experience, in that landplanes figured in the development of Sabena's services rather than the flying boats favoured, and often necessary, for Imperial Airways, Air France and Pan American. It was also the case that, lacking a home aircraft industry, Sabena could be much freer in its procurement decisions, taking the best that was available.

In 1939, on the eve of war in Europe, Sabena took delivery of its first Douglas DC-3, but the invasion and occupation of Belgium in 1940 meant that all air services were suspended, and aircraft which could be evacuated were placed at the disposal of the Allied powers for the duration of the war.

When commercial services were eventually resumed in 1946, the first aircraft were Douglas DC-3s and DC-4s, with the larger aircraft being used to start services to the United States and reintroduce services to the Belgian Congo. In 1947, Sabena became the first European airline to operate the pressurised Douglas DC-6. Yet another European 'first' for Sabena followed in 1949, when helicopter services were introduced. Sabena went on to introduce the world's first international helicopter services in 1953, initially using Sikorsky S-55s and then later with Sikorsky S-58s, until the services were abandoned in 1966 with the realisation that these could never be made to meet their costs.

These innovations apart, there was steady progress elsewhere, with Convair 440 Metropolitans introduced into European services in 1956, and the following year Douglas DC-7Cs were placed on the intercontinental services. The first jet aircraft for the airline were Boeing 707s in 1960, while in 1961,

Sabena introduced Sud Aviation Caravelles to its European routes. Later, the Caravelles were supplemented by Boeing 727s.

Collaboration with Austrian Airlines on transatlantic services from Vienna via Brussels during the late 1960s proved unsuccesful.

In the 1990s, Sabena pressed for its main base at Brussels Zaventem airport to become a major European hub, but, in common with many of the older European airlines, had to struggle to reduce costs. A regional airline, DTA, Delta Air Transport, was acquired in 1986, and this airline's aircraft were used in Sabena colours to operate new routes at a lower cost than the parent airline could manage. Sabena also had a charter subsidiary, Sobelair, in which the airline had a 72 per cent controlling interest. State ownership of the airline was reduced, with Swissair acquiring 49.5 per cent, leaving the Belgian government with 33.8 per cent and private investors with the remainder.

The charter airline Sobelair had been established in 1946 to operate passenger and freight charters, mainly to the former Belgian Congo (now Zaire), but this business was much reduced after independence for the Congo in 1961. The airline then became a subsidiary of Sabena, and the emphasis on operations switched to inclusive tour charters, mainly within Europe, but with a growing business in services across the Atlantic and to the Far East.

Earlier plans for alliances between Sabena and other European airlines did not come to fruition, but the Swissair connection provided what many, ironically, considered to be a strong strategic alliance, given the quality of the Swiss airline which also needed a foothold inside the European Union. The Swissair link was not the only alliance, and in common with most major airlines, Sabena had alliances with Austrian Airlines Maintenance, Delta Air Lines and TAP Air Portugal. In a further attempt to control costs, a number of services, including Rome, London Gatwick, and even most London Heathrow flights, were operated by Virgin Express, while DTA, Delta Air Transport, operated many other, less-heavily used short-haul routes, such as that between Brussels and Edinburgh, using aircraft in Sabena colours. Meanwhile, the short-haul fleet of Boeing 737-200s was being replaced by Airbus narrow bodies, as well as a handful of turboprops, including a couple of ATR-72s and five Bombardier Dash 8s. In 2001, the airline was operating three Airbus A340s, ten A330s, of two different types in each case, as well as three A321s, three A320s and fourteen A319s, while another three A320s and fourteen A319s were on order to replace the fifteen Boeing 737-300s, 400s and 500s, and there were four A340s, which could have replaced the two McDonnell Douglas MD-11s.

In the terrible aftershock that followed the events of 11 September 2001, Sabena collapsed, taking Sobelair with it. In fact it was the Swissair connection, that had seemed so promising at first, that proved fatal for the airline. Swissair failed first, taking Sabena with it. Two European countries were suddenly left without a national flag carrier, the one a major centre of finance and diplomacy, the other supposedly at the heart of the European Union and home to the core of its vast bureaucracy.

In both countries, frantic efforts were made to resurrect a national airline. Wisely, rather than rebuilding Sabena, with its high costs and difficult unions, the decision was taken to start again, using Delta Air Transport as the basis for a new airline, SN Brussels Airlines. The choice of name seems peculiar, since most airlines carrying the name of a city rather than a nation tend to come from the east, reflecting the quasi-military structure of old Communist-era airlines such as Aeroflot or China's CAAC. Perhaps the thinking was that Brussels was far more important in attracting passengers than the name Belgium.

The German tour operator TUI, with ownership of many airlines throughout Western Europe, established its own airline, TUI Airlines Belgium, to fill the gap left in the inclusive tour charter market by the demise of Sobelair.

Meanwhile, a small, independent airline sector had emerged in Belgium,with airlines such as NLM operating from Antwerp, and European Air Transport establishing a strong freight airline, in effect achieving for freight what would have been Sabena's ambition for passengers. NLM in effect also had the merit of serving Flanders, the Flemish-speaking northern area of the country.

ABELAG AVIATION
Incorporated: 1980

Although founded in 1980, Abelag did not commence operations until 1983, operating international cargo and passenger flights, including air ambulance operations, while at one time helicopter executive charters were provided.

HQ airport & main base: Wevelgem
Designator: W9/SKS
Fleet: 1 Bombardier Learjet 45; 1 Cessna Citation Ultra; 1 Dassault Falcon 2000; 3 Raytheon Beech King Air 200

BRUSSELS AIRLINES
Incorporated: 1966
Founded as SN Brussels Airlines and beginning operations in 2002, the airline had existed since 1966, when it was founded in Antwerp as Delta Air Transport, at the time an independent airline operating Fokker F27 Friendship turboprops. Legally known as DAT Walloonies, but to the flying public as DAT Delta Air Transport, DAT had extended its operations beyond what its local market could offer by basing most of its operations on Brussels, and undertaking flying for KLM and Swissair's subsidiary Crossair, as well as for Sabena, which eventually bought the airline outright. Eventually, most of the fleet of thirty-two BAe 146 and Avro RJ airliners, which had replaced the earlier Fokker F28 Fellowship airliners, carried Sabena colours and most flights used the Sabena designator.

In 2002, DAT was renamed SN Brussels Airlines and started to restructure itself as an international and intercontinental airline to replace Sabena. In March 2007 the airline merged with Virgin Express and became simply Brussels Airlines. The BAe aircraft still remain with the company, but a small number of Airbus aircraft enable it to undertake the longer routes to the United States and Africa. Personnel numbers are little more than a fifth of those employed by Sabena in its final years. Unusually, the former DAT designator is still used for flights.

HQ airport & main base: Brussels National
Radio callsign: BRUSSELS
Designator: SN/DAT
Employees: 2,000
Route points: Abidjan, Abu Dhabi, Banjul, Barcelona, Basle/Mulhouse, Berlin, Bilbao, Billunad, Birmingham, Bologna, Bristol, Bucharest, Budapest, Casablanca, Chicago, Conakry, Copenhagen, Dakar, Douala, Entebbe/Kampala, Frankfurt, Freetown, Geneva, Gothenburg, Hamburg, Helsinki, Istanbul, Kiev, Kigali, Kinshasa, Larnaca, Lisbon, London, Luanda, Lyons, Madrid, Malta, Manchester, Marseilles, Milan, Monrovia, Moscow, Munich, Nairobi, New York, Newcastle, Oporto, Oslo, Palermo, Paris, Prague, Seville, Sofia, Stockholm, Strasbourg, Tel Aviv, Toronto, Toulouse, Turin, Venice, Vienna, Vilnius, Warsaw, Yaounde, Zagreb, Zurich
Links with other airlines: Alliances with Air Malta (qv), Air Senegal International, Alitalia (qv), American Airlines (qv), British Airways (qv), Bulgaria Air (qv), Croatia Airlines (qv), CSA Czech Airlines (qv), Cyprus Airways (qv), El Al (qv), Etihad Airways (qv), Finnair (qv), FlyLal (qv), Iberia Airlines (qv), LOT Polish Airlines (qv), Malev (qv), Malmö Aviation (qv), Pulkovo Aviation Enterprise, Royal Air Maroc (qv), Sun-Air of Scandinavia, Swiss (qv), TAP Portugal (qv), Tarom (qv), Ukraine International Airlines (qv)
Fleet: 3 Airbus A330-300; 1 Boeing 767-300ER; 3 Airbus A319-100; 12 BAe Avro RJ100ER; 14 BAe Avro RJ85ER; 5 BAe 146-200

DELTA AIR TRANSPORT
Now renamed as SN Brussels Airlines (qv), the successor to Sabena.

EAT EUROPEAN AIR TRANSPORT
European Air Transport NV/SA
Incorporated: 1971

Originally starting operations with a Beech Queen Air for light charters and air taxi work, EAT European Air Transport soon progressed to a Rockwell 685. In 1975, additional aircraft were purchased to meet growing demand for an air taxi service. EAT was awarded a contract to operate feeder services to Brussels from Cologne, Düsseldorf, Eindhoven and Luxembourg for Sabena in 1976, for which it became the first European operator of the Swearingen Metro. In 1981, the company was acquired by DHL Worldwide Express, whose colours its aircraft now carry. Passenger operations were dropped shortly after the takeover and today the main business is regular scheduled air cargo operations as part of the DHL network, but ad hoc charters, including those for livestock, are also available. Over the past ten years, the fleet has become standardised on high-capacity Airbus and Boeing aircraft.

HQ airport & main base: Brussels National
Radio callsign: EUROTRANS
Designator: QY/BCS
Employees: 600
Route points: Athens, Barcelona, Basle, Budapest, Cologne, Copenhagen, Dublin, East Midlands, Frankfurt, Geneva, Gothenburg, Hamburg, Helsinki, Istanbul, Lisbon, London Heathrow, Lyons, Madrid, Marseilles, Milan, Nuremberg, Oslo, Paris, Rome, Stockholm, Tampere, Toulouse, Valencia, Vienna, Warsaw
Links with other airlines: A subsidiary of DHL Worldwide Express
Fleet: 14 Airbus A300B4-200F; 12 Boeing 757-200SF; 1 Boeing 727-100F

THOMAS COOK AIRLINES
Thomas Cook Airlines Belgium SA
Incorporated: 2001
The Belgian associate of the UK's Thomas Cook Airlines was launched by the tour operator in December 2001 and commenced operations the following March. Initially, inclusive tour operations were flown to the main European holiday resorts, but a seat-only service was offered from 2004.

HQ airport & main base: Brussels National
Designator: FQ/TCW
Employees: 202
Links with other airlines: Owned 100 per cent by Thomas Cook
Fleet: 6 Airbus A320-200

TNT AIRWAYS
Incorporated: 1999

Founded in 1999, TNT Airways began operations early in 2000 on behalf of TNT Express Delivery Services, operating to almost seventy airports within Europe. It absorbed the operations of the UK airline which had dated from 1987, and which transferred to Liège in 1998.

The parent company, TNT, has developed a worldwide network of of overnight scheduled freight services, using locally based airlines to operate its aircraft, usually carrying the TNT livery. Participating airlines are allowed market the aircraft for cargo or, in the case of the quick-change variants, passenger operations during the day and at weekends, provided that the aircraft are always available for their night duties. The initial services were introduced to Europe, with a major hub at Cologne in Germany, while a similar operation has been established in Asia based on Manila in the Philippines. In 1997, the Cologne hub was moved to Liège in Belgium. Airlines participating in this operation include Air Foyle, Hunting Cargo and Pacific East Asia. One of the aircraft operated is BAe 146 QT (for 'quiet trader') because of its low noise levels.

HQ airport & main base: Liège Bierset
Radio callsign: NITRO
Designator: 3V/TAY
Employees: 357
Route points: Arlanda, Barcelona, Belfast, Billund, Birmingham, Budapest, Cologne, Copenhagen, Dublin, Edinburgh, Glasgow, Gothenburg, Helsinki, Liege, Linz, Liverpool, Luton, Lyons, Madrid, Manchester, New York, Nuremberg, Paris, Valencia, Vienna, Zaragoza
Links with other airlines: Aircraft operated by Air Foyle (qv), Eurowings (qv), Hunting Cargo, Malev (qv), Pacific East Asia Cargo, and Sterling Europe
Fleet: 2 Boeing 747-400ERF; 4 Airbus A300B4-200F; 5 Boeing 737-300SF; 1 Boeing 737-300QC; 8 BAe 146-300QT; 2 BAe 146-200QC; 3 BAe 146-200QT

TUI AIRLINES BELGIUM
Incorporated: 2003

TUI Airlines Belgium was established in 2003 by the German tour operator TUI, owner of Condor and several other airlines, in the wake of the collapse of the Belgian charter operator, Sobelair, in which Sabena was the major shareholder. Inclusive tour charters are also flown for other tour operators.

HQ airport & main base: Brussels National
Designator: TB/TUB
Links with other airlines: Owned by TUI (qv), which has extensive airline interests
Fleet: 1 Boeing 767-300ER; 2 Boeing 737-800; 3 Boeing 737-400; 1 Fokker 100

VIRGIN EXPRESS
Incorporated: 1991

Originally founded in 1991 as a 'low-cost, no frills' scheduled airline under the name of EuroBelgium Airlines, backed by the City Hotels Group, the airline was acquired by the Virgin Group in 1996 and the name changed to Virgin Express. The airline has remained at Brussels since the acquisition, although the high social costs of employing staff in Belgium have prompted speculation that the main base might be moved, and meanwhile a further hub is being developed at Paris Charles de Gaulle, where it has a subsidiary, Air Provence Charter. In addition to flying its own services, Virgin Express at one time operated a number of services on behalf of Sabena, before that airline's demise. In 2005, SN Brussels Airlines' holding company, SN Air Holding, acquired Virgin Express outright, and in March 2007 the airlines merged to become Brussels Airlines.

VLM
Vlaamse Luchttransportmaatschappij
Incorporated: 1992

Founded in 1992, VLM commenced operations between Antwerp and London City Airport the following year using a Fokker 50 airliner. A service from London City to Liverpool followed, before the

airline started to concentrate on services to and from London City and European destinations. Charter flights are also operated.
HQ airport & main base: Antwerp International, with a hub at London City Airport
Radio callsign: RUBENS
Designator: VG/VLM
Employees: 367
Route points: Amsterdam, Antwerp, Hamburg, Isle of Man, Jersey, Liverpool, London, Luxembourg, Manchester, Rotterdam
Fleet: 13 Fokker 50; 1 BAe 146-300

BOLIVIA – CP

As with many South American countries, air transport has an important part to play in Bolivia because of the difficult terrain, and despite the relative poverty of many of these nations, the history of air transport is lengthy. In many cases, after the First World War, expatriate Germans fostered the development of air transport in such countries, and Bolivia was no exception, with the Germans enjoying the support of the Bolivian authorities. Frustrated by being unable to establish airlines in their own country due to the conditions of the Treaty of Versailles, the Germans established the first Bolivian airline in 1925. Once these restrictions were eased, the South American airlines provided useful feeder and distributor services from those combined air and sea services operated by Condor, later Deutsche Luft Hansa, across the Atlantic. In Bolivia, international services did not become significant until after the Second World War, and later air transport was nationalised, before eventually being deregulated.

AEROSUR

AeroSur Compania Boliviano de Aereo Privado
Incorporated: 1992

AeroSur was formed by the merger of several air charter companies in 1992, on deregulation of domestic air transport in Bolivia, to compete with the then state-owned LAB. It now competes with LAB on the main routes within Bolivia, usually operating on a hub-and-spoke basis. Innovations for South America have been the introduction of first and business class on internal services, and prepaid ticketing issued with a boarding pass.

The airline claims to have 54 per cent of the domestic air travel market, while since 2000, it has introduced a small number of international destinations within South America. Marketing alliances are in place with a substantial number of international carriers.

HQ airport & main base: Santa Cruz de la Sierra Viru Viru International, with additional hubs at Viru Viru and Trinidad (Bolivia)
Designator: 5L/RSU
Employees: 460
Route points: Buenos Aires, Cobija, Cochabamba, Guayaramerin, La Paz, Puerto Suarez, Santa Cruz, Sao Paulo, Sucre, Tarija
Links with other airlines: Marketing alliances with Aerolineas Argentinas (qv), American Airlines (qv), Iberia (qv), LAN Chile (qv), Lufthansa (qv), Taca Peru, Varig (qv)
Fleet: 1 Boeing 747-100; 1 Boeing 757-200; 5 Boeing 727-200; 2 Boeing 727-100; 4 Boeing 737-200; 3 LET L-410UVE

LAB – LLOYD AERO BOLIVIA

Incorporated: 1925

Lloyd Aero Bolivia was founded in 1925, during a period which saw many South American airlines begin operations. The airline was formed by Germans living in Bolivia, but with the support of the Bolivian government. Initially, operations were within Bolivia, but international operations followed, although these were not a significant part of the airline's operations until well after the Second World War. In 1941, the Bolivian government eventually took control of the airline, but in 1995, the major Brazilian carrier VASP acquired a 49 per cent stake, and there were also some small private interests, leaving just 48.27 per cent in state hands. In recent years, the current executive president of the airline, Ernesto Ausbin, acquired the VASP stake and built up a 50 per cent shareholding, but in August 2006 UK-based Transatlantic Aviation took a 50.1 per cent shareholding.

LAB has a 50.1 per cent stake in Ecuatoriana.

HQ airport & main base: HQ at Cochabama Aeropuerto Jorge Wilstermann, with operations based on La Paz
Radio callsign: LLOYDAERO
Designator: LB/LAB
Route points: Asuncion, Bogotá, Buenos Aires, Cancun, Caracas, Cochabamba, Cordoba, Cuzco, Guayaquil, Havana, Lima, Madrid, Manaus, Mexico City, Miami, Montevideo, Panama City, Rio de Janeiro, Salta, San Joaquin, Santa Ana, Santa Cruz, Santiago de Chile, Sao Paulo, Sucre, Tarija, Trinidad (Bolivia), Washington

Links with other airlines: Holds 50.1 per cent stake in Ecuatoriana. Alliances with Taca Peru, TAME Linea Aerea del Ecuador (qv)
Fleet: 2 Boeing 757-200; 8 Boeing 727-200; 1 Boeing 727-100; 1 Boeing 737-300

BHUTAN – KB

DRUK AIR
Incorporated: 1983

The scheduled airline for the Himalayan kingdom of Bhutan, established by a Royal Proclamation in 1983. Initially, two Dornier 228s were operated, but in 1986, BAe 146s were introduced. It is state owned.

HQ airport & main base: Paro
Radio callsign: DRUK
Designator: KB/DRK
Route points: Bangkok, Delhi, Gaya, Kathmandu, Kolkata, Paro
Fleet: 2 Airbus A319-100; 2 BAe 146-100

BOTSWANA – A2

AIR BOTSWANA
Incorporated: 1972

Air Botswana was formed in 1972 to take over the operations of Botswana Airways, and was nationalised in 1988. The airline operates domestic and regional air services. There are plans to privatise it in the near future.

HQ airport & main base: Gabarone Sir Seretse Khama International
Designator: BP/BOT
Route points: Francistown, Cape Town, Gabarone, Harare, Johannesburg, Kasane, Lanseria, Maun, Victoria Falls, Windhoek
Links with other airlines: Alliance with Air Zimbabwe (qv)
Fleet: 2 BAe 146-100; 3 ATR-42-500; 1 Cessna Caravan 675

BOSNIA-HERZEGOVINA – T9

The fragmentation of the former Yugoslavia has created many small countries, each struggling to develop its own air transport. The extent to which they are successful will depend hugely on whether the tourist traffic lost during the Balkan conflicts can be regained, although there is the very real danger that the tourist markets may have changed, with holidaymakers moving on to more exotic destinations. Paradoxically, those that survive may well have the most modest ambitions, serving domestic destinations and those in neighbouring states.

BH AIRLINES
Incorporated: 1994

A passenger scheduled and charter airline based in the newly independent state of Bosnia-Herzegovina, part of the former Yugoslavia, and owned 51 per cent by the state and 49 per cent by Energoinvest. It was originally called Air Bosnia, but operations were suspended in 2003, and the present name was adopted when it was restarted in 2005.

HQ airport & main base: Sarajevo
Designator: JA/BON
Route points: Banjar Luka, Cologne/Bonn, Istanbul, Mostar, Sarajevo, Stuttgart, Zagreb, Zurich
Fleet: 2 Airbus A319-100; 2 ATR-72-210

BRAZIL – PP

As the largest, most prosperous and most technically advanced nation in South America, Brazil has a substantial air transport sector as well as being one of the leading manufacturers of regional jet aircraft. Air transport has been deregulated in Brazil, and this may have contributed to the difficulties of some of the nation's airlines, including the national carrier, Varig, while the main domestic airline, VASP, which was also the country's second largest airline, has also collapsed. Such upheavals are certainly not unique to Brazil, with the history of air transport in such mature aviation nations as the United States, United Kingdom and Canada littered with failed airlines, while more recently, even such well-established operators as Swissair and Sabena have disappeared.

Originally founded by the state government of Sao Paulo in Brazil in 1933, VASP grew to become Brazil's second largest airline, with an extensive domestic network serving all of the major airports in Brazil as well as regional routes within Sao Paulo, and with a growing international network. In 1991, the airline was privatised, when a majority stake was acquired by the VOE/Canhedo Group. At its peak, VASP had extensive stakes in three other airlines, Ecuatoriana (50.1 per cent), LAB – Lloyd Aero Boliviano (51 per cent) and TAN in Argentina (82 per cent). The most important of the airlines in which VASP had an investment was TAM, a major Brazilian regional carrier which moved out of air taxi operations and into airline work in 1976 with the support of VASP, which held almost a quarter of the shares initially, although this was reduced later. In conjunction with Varig and Transbrasil, VASP was a participant in the Air Bridge Shuttle between Rio de Janeiro and Sao Paulo.

Other airlines which have disappeared in recent years include TABA, founded in 1976 following deregulation, and, much older, Transbrasil, dating from 1955.

BETA CARGO
Brazilian Express Transportes Aereos SA
Incorporated: 1990

Founded in 1990 as Brasair Transportes Aereos, BETA operates domestic and international scheduled and charter air cargo flights.It is owned by Grupo Brazilian Express.

HQ airport & main base: Sao Paulo Guarulhas
Designator: BET
Route points: Manaus, Porto Alegre, Recife, Salvador, Sao Paulo
Fleet: 2 McDonnell Douglas DC-8 Srs 73F; 2 Boeing 707-320C

BRA TRANSPORTES AEREOS
Incorporated: 1999

Originally founded as a passenger charter airline, BRA Transportes Aereos restructured itself as a low-cost scheduled airline during 2006, and now plans long-haul services.

HQ airport & main base: Sao Paulo Guarulhos
Designator: BRB
Fleet: 1 Boeing 767-300ER; 1 Boeing 767-200; 3 Boeing 737-400; 6 Boeing 737-300

GOL
SA Gol Linhas Aereas Inteligentes
Incorporated: 2000

Originally founded in 2000 by Grupo Aurea, owners of Brazil's main long-distance coach operator, the airline commenced operations in 2001 as Gol Transportes Aereos, GTA. It has developed as a low-cost operator and has seen rapid growth, possibly helped by the troubles of the country's major airline, Varig. Grupo Aurea is no longer directly involved since the airline was floated on the Sao Paulo and New York stock exchanges in June 2004. In March 2007 the airline's shareholders agreed to acquire Varig (qv).

HQ airport & main base: Sao Paulo Congonhas International
Radio callsign: GOL
Designator: G3/GLO
Employees: 3,303
Route points: Aracaju, Asuncion, Belem, Belo Horizonte, Boa Vista, Brasilia, Buenos Aires, Campina Grande, Campinas, Campo Grande, Caxias do Sul, Cordoba, Cuiba, Florianopolis, Fortaleza, Goiania, Igassu Falls, Joao Pessoa, Joinville, Londrina, Macapa, Maceio, Manaus, Maringa, Montevideo, Natal, Navegantes, Palmas, Petrolina, Porto Alegre, Porto Seguro, Porto Velho, Recife, Ribeiro Preto, Rio Branco, Rio de Janeiro, Rosario, Salvador, Santa Cruz, Sao Jose do Rio Preto, Sao Luiz, Sao Paulo, Teresina, Uberlandia, Vitoria
Links with other airlines: Alliances with Copa Airlines, Cruiser Linhas Aereas
Fleet: 101 Boeing 737-800; 30 Boeing 737-700

NORDESTE
SA Nordeste Linhas Aereas Regionais
Incorporated: 1976

Founded in 1976, Nordeste is the main regional passenger and cargo airline in north-east Brazil, and was a subsidiary of Rio-Sul, itself in turn a subsidiary of Varig. Over the past decade, it has converted to an all-jet fleet. In March 2007 Nordeste re-established itself as an independent airline.

HQ airport & main base: Salvador, with an additional hub at Belo-Horizonte
Radio callsign: NORDESTE
Designator: JH/NES
Employees: 666
Links with other airlines: Varig (qv) has a 99 per cent stake
Fleet: 5 Boeing 737-300, 4 Boeing 737-500

PANTANAL LINHAS AEREAS
Incorporated: 1993

Founded in the wake of deregualtion of Brazilian air transport in 1992, Pantanal started operations the following year, operating domestic scheduled services in the south of the country. It was the first Brazilian operator of the ATR-42. In addition to its schedules, it also undertakes charters, mainly in connection with the energy industry.

HQ airport & main base: Sao Paulo Congonhas International
Radio callsign: PANTANAL
Designator: P8/PTN
Route points: Aracatuba, Araraquara, Bauru, Juiz de Fora, Marilia, Presidente Prudente, Sao Paulo, Uberaba
Links with other airlines: Alliance with TAM Linhas Aereas (qv)
Fleet: 6 ATR-42-300/320

RICO LINEAS AEREAS

Incorporated: 1979

Rico Lineas Aereas was founded in 1979, and its operational area is largely confined to serving small communities in the Amazon Basin.

HQ airport & main base: Manaus Eduardo Gomes International
Designator: C7/RLE
Route points: Not available
Fleet: 3 Boeing 737-200; 1 Boeing 737-200QC; 1 Embraer EMB-110C Bandeirante; 2 Embraer EMB-120 Brasilia

RIO-SUL

SA Rio-Sul Servicos Aereos Regionais
Incorporated: 1976

Rio-Sul was founded in 1976 as a regional airline operating in the south of Brazil, taking over the feeder services which had been operated by Cruzeiro do Sol after ownership of that airline passed to Varig. In addition, another driving force behind the airline's creation was a government-inspired initiative to rationalise and invigorate Brazil's regional air services, known as SITAR, or the Integrated System of Regional Air Transport. Under SITAR, Rio-Sul was allocated the southern region of the country, which had been divided into five regions for air transport purposes. Rio-Sol was founded by a combination of financial institutions and Varig. In 1995, government policies were reversed, ending geographical divisions and enabling airlines to expand, prompting Rio-Sol to acquire another Brazilian airline, Nordeste Linhas Aereas that year. Varig has 97 per cent of Rio-Sul's shares, effectively making it a subsidiary of the airline. Uncertainty over the future of Varig also means uncertainty for Rio-Sul.

HQ airport & main base: Rio de Janeiro Santos Dumont
Radio callsign: RIOSSUL
Designator: SL/RSL
Employees: 840
Route points: More than fifty domestic destinations, including Belem, Belo Horizonte, Brasilia, Recife, Rio de Janeiro, Rio Grande and Sao Paolo
Links with other airlines: Varig (qv) has a 97 per cent stake. Rio-Sul owns Nordeste (qv)
Fleet: Included in the Varig entry

SKYMASTER AIRLINES

Incorporated: 1995

Formed in 1995, Skymaster Airlines did not commence operations until 1997, and now operates cargo charters throughout the Americas with a mixed fleet of Boeing 707s and McDonnell Douglas DC-8s.

HQ airport & main base: Manaus Eduardo Gomes International
Designator: SKC
Fleet: 2 McDonnell Douglas DC-8-63F; 1 McDonnell Douglas DC-8-62; 4 Boeing 707-320C

TAF LINHAS AEREAS

Incorporated: 1971

Originally founded in 1971 as an air taxi operator, Taxi Aereo Fortaleza, TAF, the current title was adopted after the company moved into charter and then scheduled airline operations. The scheduled services are mainly domestic flights in northern Brazil, but there is also an international service to Cayenne in French Guiana.

HQ airport & main base: Fortaleza Pinot Martins International
Designator: TSD
Route points: Belem, Cayenna, Fortaleza, Macapa, Manaus, Sao Luz
Fleet: 1 Boeing 727-200F; 3 Boeing 737-200; 4 Embraer EMB-110 Bandeirante; 3 Cessna 208 Caravan; 1 Cessna Caravan 675

TAM

TAM Linhas Aereas SA
Incorporated: 1976

TAM Linhas Aereas is the result of a merger in 2000 between TAM – Transportes Aereas Regionais and TAM – Transportes Aereos Meridonais. TAM Transportes Aereos Regionais was founded in 1976 with the support of VASP, which took just under a quarter of the airline's shares, and a holding company, TAM – Taxi Aero Marilia – taking over the services and many of the assets of an earlier airline, VOTEC. The driving force behind the move into airline operations by what was essentially an air taxi operator was a government-inspired initiative to rationalise and invigorate Brazil's regional air services, known as SITAR, or the Integrated System of Regional Air Transport. Under SITAR, the airline TAM was allocated the mid-west region of the country, which had been divided into five regions for air transport purposes.

TAM moved quickly to establish itself as a significant scheduled carrier within its allocated area, using a variety of aircraft including Fokker F27 Friendships and Embraer EMB-110 Bandeirantes, while Fokker 100 jets were introduced in 1992. The VASP stake in the airline was reduced, initially to 3.35 per cent, and has now been sold to other investors following that airline's suspension. Meanwhile, TAM has developed its scheduled network considerably, with routes to North America and France, with a consequent enlargement and strengthening of its fleet with the additional of long-haul aircraft, while employee numbers have trebled in recent years. In addition to its own operations, TAM owns Aerolineas Paraguayas – ARPA – completely and has an 80 per cent stake in Transportes Aereos del Mercosul.

HQ airport & main base: Sao Paulo Guarulhos
Radio callsign: TAM
Designator: JJ/TAM
Employees: 7,374
Route points: Aracaju, Belem, Belo Horizonte, Bordeaux, Brasilia, Buenos Aires, Campo Grande, Caxias do Sul, Corumba, Cuiaba, Curitiba, Dallas, Florianopolis, Fortaleza, Goiania, Igassi Falls, Ilheus, Imperatriz, Ji-Parana, Joao Pessoa, Joinville, Lima, Londrina, Lyons, Macapa, Maceio, Manaus, Maraba, Maringa, Marseilles, Miami, Montepllier, Nantes, Natal (Brazil), Navegantes, New York, Nice, Palmas, Paris, Porto Alegre, Porto Seguro, Porto Velho, Recife, Ribeirao Preto, Rio de Janeiro, Salvador, Santarem, Santiago de Chile, Sao Jose do Rio Preto, Sao Luiz, Sao Paulo, Strasbourg, Teresina, Toulouse, Uberlandia, Una, Vitoria
Links with other airlines: Owns Aerolineas Paraguayas – ARPA. Has an 80 per cent stake in Transportes Aereos del Mercosul. Alliances with Air France (qv), American Airlines (qv), KLM (qv), Panatanal Linhas Aereas (qv), Taca Peru, Transportes Aereas del Mercosul, TRIP Linhas Aereas, UAir, Varig (qv)
Fleet: 16 Airbus A330-200; 4 Airbus A321-200; 92 Airbus A320-200; 18 Airbus A319-100; 19 Fokker 100; 19 Cessna Caravan 675; 4 Cessna 208 Caravan (On order: 10 Airbus A350-900)

TAVAJ LINHAS AEREAS
Incorporated: 1972

Originally founded in 1972 as an air taxi operator in Cruzeiro do Sul, in the north of the country, TAVAJ moved into airline operations and in 1994 was certified as a regional operator. It now operates to destinations throughout northern Brazil.

HQ airport & main base: Rio Branco Presidente Medici
Designator: TVJ
Route points: Belem, Cayenna, Fortaleza, Macapa, Manaus, Rio Branco, Sao Luz, plus many minor airports
Fleet: 2 Fokker F27 Friendship Mk600; 7 Embraer EMB-110P Bandeirante

TOTAL LINHAS AEREAS
Incorporated: 1988

Originally founded in 1988 as Total Taxi Aero, Total operated air taxi and business charters, before moving into airline operations, initially as a charter carrier before taking advantage of the liberalisation of Brazilian air transport to operate scheduled services.

HQ airport & main base: Belo Horizonte Pampulha
Radio callsign: TOTAL
Designator: TTL
Route points: Altamira, Araguaina, Araxa, Belem, Belo Horizonte, Brasilia, Carajas, Diamantina, Governador Valadares, Ipatinga, Itaituba, Manaus, Montes Claros, Parintins, Patos de Minas, Porto Trombetas, Riberao Preto, Santarem, Tucurui, Uberabia, Uberlandia, Vitoria
Fleet: 2 Boeing 727-200F; 2 ATR-72-210; 2 ATR-42-500; 7 ATR-42-300; 1 Embraer EMB-110 Bandeirante

TRIP LINHAS AEREAS
Incorporated: 1998

Founded in 1998, Trip has developed a regional scheduled network in the south of the country. It is owned by the Caprioli Group.

HQ airport & main base: Sao Paulo, with Natal as the main base

Designator: 8R/TIB
Employees: 223
Route points: Alta Floresta, Barbelos, Campo Grande, Carauari, Cascavel, Coari, Cuiba, Curitiba, Dourados, Eirunepe, Fernando de Noronha, Ji-Parana, Labrea, Londrina, Manaus, Maringa, Natal, Port Velho, Recife, Rondonopolis, Santa Isabel de Morro, Sao Gabriel, Sao Paulo, Sinop, Tabatinga, Tefe, Vilhena
Links with other airlines: Alliance with TAM Linhas Aereas (qv)
Fleet: 1 ATR-72-200; 5 ATR 42 300; 1 Embraer EMB-120 Brasilia

VARIG
SA Empresa de Vicao Aerea Rio Grandense
See VRG Linhas

VARIG LOG
Incorporated: 2000

Originally founded as the cargo subsidiary of Varig, Varig Log was sold in March 2006 to Volo, the Brazilian subsidiary of a US investment fund. Scheduled and charter cargo flights are flown, mainly throughout Brazil but also to other destinations in the Americas.

HQ airport & main base: Rio de Janeiro Galeao International
Designator: LC/VLO
Route points (domestic): Belem, Brasilia, Cruzeiro do Sul, Cuiaba, Fortaleza, Manaus, Porto Alegre, Porto Velho, Recife, Rio Branco, Salvador, Sao Paulo
Fleet: 2 McDonnell Douglas MD-11F; 2 McDonnell Douglas DC-10-30F; 1 Boeing 757-200; 4 Boeing 757-200F; 1 Boeing 757-100C

VRG LINHAS
Incorporated: 2006

VRG Linhas was established in 2006 as the successor to Varig, at one time the largest airline in South America and second largest in the southern hemisphere, but which ran into financial difficulties during the early years of the new century.

In 2006, Varig was the thirty-seventh largest airline in the world by revenue, down from thirty-second, and thirty-eighth by passenger numbers. The slide down the league tables was been caused by the withdrawal of a number of services to save money and also because of a shortage of aircraft.

Originally, Varig was founded by a German immigrant, Otto Ernst Meyer, and started operations in 1927 with technical assistance from the German Condor syndicate, which had itself been formed by the then Deutsches Luft Hansa to operate the South American section of the German airline's trans-South Atlantic air-sea mail service. Varig's role was to operate the Brazilian routes, which it did using a Dornier Wal flying-boat, ideal for operations from the many rivers that provided the best landing places in dense jungle.

Although Varig expanded its operations throughout the 1930s and 1940s, despite the shortages of equipment and spares from North America and Europe during the Second World War, it remained a domestic carrier. In 1951, the airline's operations, which had been concentrated on the southern part of Brazil, were expanded by the acquisition of Aero Geral. Two years later, in 1953, the first international service came, with a route to the United States. More significant international expansion did not follow until 1961, when Varig acquired the REAL consortium, including Aerovias Brasilia, Nacionale and Aeronorte, which at a stroke quadrupled Varig's international network, and even doubled the domestic network as well. Transatlantic services eventually came in 1965, when Panair do Brasil collapsed, forcing the Brazilian government to offer the route rights to Varig, which also took over the defunct airline's equipment, including the lease on a Douglas DC-8 used by Panair.

Another major addition to Varig's operations were the routes and equipment of another airline with a mixture of domestic and some international routes within South America, Cruzeiro do Sol, which also dated from 1926, but which had been nationalised in 1943. Varig's owners, the Ruben Berta Foundation, acquired Cruzeiro do Sol in 1975 and integrated its operations with those of Varig to prevent duplication, especially on the international routes. Many of Cruzeiro do Sol's regional services passed to a new airline, Rio-Sul, with a major route network throughout southern Brazil; founded in 1976, Rio-Sul was a subsidiary of Varig, which owned 95 per cent of its shares. A wholly owned subsidiary of Rio-Sul was Nordeste Linhas Aereas Regionais, while a cargo subsidiary was Varig Log, but this was sold to Volo, a US-owned investment group, to help support the parent company.

VRG can be expected to inherit Varig's position as Brazil's leading airline, but no longer can boast a worldwide route network, although, in contrast to many airlines in the region, Varig maintained an outstanding safety record. In recent years, Varig has encountered financial difficulties, including having leased aircraft repossessed. Employee numbers fell by a third over the past decade.

In 1997, Varig joined the 'Star Alliance', which brought together frequent flyer programmes and other services for Air Canada, Lufthansa, SAS, Thai International and United Airlines as well as Varig. It remains to be seen whether VRG Linhas becomes a member of the Star Alliance, which otherwise would be without a South American member. Varig is now being acquired by the owner of low-fare airline GOL (qv).

HQ airport & main base: Rio de Janeiro Galwao International
Radio callsign: VARIG
Designator: RG/VRG
Employees: 11,727
Route Points: Aracaju, Aruba, Asuncion, Belem, Belo Horizonte, Boa Vista, Bogota, Boston, Brasilia, Buenos Aires, Caracas, Caxias do Sul, Chapeco, Chicago, Ciudad del Este, Copenhagen, Curitiba, Fernando de Noronha, Florianopolis, Fortaleza, Frankfurt, Goiania, Igassu Falls, Joao Pessoa, Johannesburg, Joinville, Lima, Lisbon, London, Londrina, Los Angeles, Macapa, Maceio, Madrid, Manaus, Maringa, Mexico City, Miami, Milan, Montevideo, Munich, Natal, Navegantes, New York, Oporto, Paris, Passo Fundo, Petrolina, Porto Alegre, Porto Seguro, Porto Velho, Punta del Este, Recife, Rio Branco, Rio de Janeiro, Rome, Salvador, Santa Cruz, Santiago de Chile, Sao Luiz, Sao Paulo, Teresina, Toronto, Vitoria, Washington
Links with other airlines: Interests in Nordeste Linhas Aereas Regionais, 99 per cent, Rio-Sul Servicos Aereas Regionais, 97 per cent, and Pluna Lineas Aereas Uruguayas, 49 per cent (all qv). Alliances with Aerosur, Alitalia, Aserca, euro-Atlantic Airways, Mexicana, Pluna Lineas Aereas Uruguayas, Rio-Sul Servicos Regionais, South African Airways, TAM Linhas Aereas (all qv)
Annual turnover: US $2,963 million (£1,795.8 million)
Fleet: 1 Boeing 777-200ER; 2 McDonnell Douglas MD-11ER; 2 Boeing 767-300ER; 4 Boeing 757-200; 2 Boeing 737-800; 2 Boeing 737-400; 11 Boeing 737-300

VASP
SA Viacao Aerea de Sao Paulo
Incorporated: 1933

Operations suspended in 2005.

BRUNEI – V8

ROYAL BRUNEI
Royal Brunei Airlines Sendirian Berhad
Incorporated: 1974

Owned by the government of Negara Brunei Darussalam, Royal Brunei Airlines was founded in 1974, initially having a fleet of two Boeing 737s, one of which operated the first scheduled flight from Banar Seri Begawan to Singapore on 14 May. Before the year was out, services had also been introduced to Hong Kong, Kota Kinabalu and Kuching. Further routes were added in the succeeding years and an additional 737 was acquired in 1980. Longer range aircraft followed in 1986 with three Boeing 757-200s, which enabled new services to Taipei, Dubai and Frankfurt to be introduced, with London Gatwick following after the delivery of Boeing 767s in 1990. The following year, services to London switched from Gatwick to Heathrow.

While international air services were being established, the potential for domestic air services was not neglected, with the delivery of Fokker 50 turboprops in 1994, although later these were replaced by Fokker 100s. A joint marketing agreement and code sharing was introduced with United Airlines, although this has since been dropped, but a code-sharing agreement with British Midland, now bmi, has lasted for more than a decade. The airline sold its Boeing 757s in favour of additional 767s, with Airbus A319s and A320s for the regional routes, while the domestic network is no longer operated. Ownership remains with the Brunei government.

HQ airport & main base: Brunei International
Radio callsign: BRUNEI
Designator: BI/RBA
Employees: 1,924
Route points: Auckland, Bangkok, Brisbane, Brunei, Darwin, Denpasar Bali, Dubai, Frankfurt, Hong Kong, Jakarta, Jeddah, Kota Kinabalu, Kuala Lumpur, London, Manila, Perth, Sharjah, Singapore, Surabaya, Sydney
Links with other airlines: Alliances with bmi, Dragonair, Malaysia Airlines, Philippine Airlines, Singapore Airlines (all qv)
Fleet: 6 Boeing 767-300ER; 2 Airbus A320-200; 2 Airbus A319-100

BULGARIA – LZ

If the Bulgarian experience is anything to go by, the transition from a supply-led communist economy to a market-led capitalist one is extremely difficult. While new airlines have emerged, mainly serving the country's growing tourist trade, Balkan Bulgarian Airlines, the national carrier, collapsed in 2002.

AIR VIA BULGARIAN AIRWAYS
Incorporated: 1990

Formed in 1990 to provide inclusive tour charter flights to Bulgaria for major West European tour operators.

HQ airport & main base: Sofia International
Designator: VL/VIM
Fleet: 2 Tupolev Tu-154M; 3 Airbus A320-200

BH AIR
Incorporated: 2001

BH Air was founded at the end of 2001 and began operations the following January, providing inclusive tour passenger flights, mainly for its owners, Balkan Holidays International, bringing visitors from throughout Europe to Bulgaria.

HQ airport & main base: Sofia International
Designator: BGH
Employees: 211
Fleet: 3 Tupolov Tu-154M; 2 Airbus A320-200

BULGARIA AIR
Incorporated: 2002

Formed in 2002 by the Bulgarian government to take over the services abandoned on the collapse of the Balkan Bulgarian Airlines, the country's national airline. Balkan had itself been founded by the Bulgarian government in 1947 as BVS, and operations on domestic routes started the following year. The new airline had but a short existence, however, for in 1949 its services were taken over by TABSO, owned jointly by the Bulgarian government and the Soviet Union. The emphasis remained on domestic operations until 1954, when control of TABSO finally passed to the Bulgarian government, and a start was made on developing an international network. The first services were to Warsaw, Copenhagen, Frankfurt, Paris, Athens, Moscow and Beirut, using Lisunov Li-2s (Russian-built DC-3s) and Ilyushin Il-14s. Turbine equipment did not appear until 1962, when Ilyushin Il-18 turboprops were introduced, and new services were started to Tunisia and Algeria. The potential of the Black Sea resorts for holidaymakers began to be appreciated at this time, and charter flights were operated from the rest of Europe from 1963 onwards.

Other aircraft followed the Il-18s, including Antonov An-12s and An-24s, and the first jets, Tupolev Tu-134s, were introduced in 1968. Later, the larger Tupolev Tu-154 was to enter service with TABSO.

Throughout most of the airline's existence, TABSO was more than simply an airline, but also responsible for many other aspects of civil aviation. This changed in 1986, when the non-airline functions were removed and airline was renamed Balkan Bulgarian Airlines. The breaking up of the old Soviet empire also paved the way for Balkan to obtain modern western equipment, more economical and efficient than the aircraft available from the former Soviet Union. Initially, the fleet became mixed and included both Russian and American aircraft, while considerable route expansion took place across the Atlantic and into Africa and the Middle East. Such rapid expansion may well have contributed to the eventual collapse of the airline in 2002.

The creation of Bulgaria Air enabled services to restart on the most promising of the former Balkan routes, concentrating on the European network with a fleet of Boeing 737 airliners. It is expected that the airline will be privatised in the near future.

HQ airport & main base: Sofia International
Radio callsign: BULGARIA
Designator: FB/LZB
Route points: Amsterdam, Barcelona, Berlin, Brussels, Budapest, Copenhagen, Frankfurt, Lisbon, London, Madrid, Malaga, Manchester, Milan, Moscow, Palma de Mallorca, Paris, Prague, Rome, Sofia, Tel Aviv, Varna, Vienna, Warsaw, Zurich
Links with other airlines: Alliances with Aeroflot Russian Airlines, Air France, CSA Czech Airlines, El Al, LOT Polish Airlines, SN Brussels Airlines (all qv)
Fleet: 7 Boeing 737-300; 4 Boeing 737-500

BULGARIA AIR CHARTER
Incorporated: 2000

Formed as an inclusive tour charter airline to serve the growing volume of travel between the rest of Europe and the Bulgarian Black Sea resorts.

HQ airport & main base: Sofia
Designator: BUC
Employees: 240

Fleet: 2 Tupolev Tu-154M; 4 McDonnell Douglas MD-83; 7 McDonnell Douglas MD-82; 1 McDonnell Douglas MD-81

HEMUS AIR

Incorporated: 1986

Hemus was originally part of Balkan Bulgarian Airlines, but separated from it in 1986 to conduct air work, including ambulance flights, aerial photography and radar calibration. It became a completely independent identity in 1991 and was renamed Hemus Air. It is owned by the Hemus Air Group, and has now moved into scheduled and charter, passenger and cargo operations.

HQ airport & main base: Sofia International
Designator: DU/HMS
Employees: 308
Route points: Athens, Beirut, Bourgas, Bucharest, Cairo, Cologne, Dubai, Hanover, Larnaca, Sofia, Stuttgart, Tirana, Varna, Vienna
Links with other airlines: Alliance with Syrianair (qv)
Fleet: 1 Tupolev Tu-154M; 1 Boeing 737-400; 1 Boeing 737-300; 4 Tupolev Tu-134A/B; 4 BAe 146-300; 3 BAe 146-200; 7 Yakovlev Yak-40

SCORPION AIR

Incorporated: 1990

Primarily a general aviation contractor, which has expanded into passenger and cargo air charter, Scorpion was founded in 1990. Helicopters are also operated.

HQ airport & main base: Sofia International
Radio callsign: SCORPION
Designator: SPN
Fleet: 6 Antonov An-26; 4 Antonov An-12; 1 Let L-410UVP

VEGA AIRLINES

Incorporated: 1997

Founded in 1997 by Aviobroker and Ikar Air Cargo, both air cargo brokers, Vega commenced operations in 1998. In addition to providing cargo charters with its own Antonov An-12s, it is also the agent in Bulgaria for the Antonov Airline's heavy-lift air cargo charters.

HQ airport & main base: Sofia International
Radio callsign: VEGA
Designator: VEA
Employees: 120
Links with other airlines: Agent for Antonov Airlines
Fleet: 6 Antonov An-12

CAMEROON – TJ

CAMEROON AIRLINES

Incorporated: 1971

Cameroon Airlines was formed in 1971 after the Cameroon government decided to cease support of the Air Afrique consortium, and initially the airline was owned 75 per cent by the government and 25 per cent by Air France, although this is now reduced to a nominal shareholding, with the government holding more than 96 per cent of the stock. The airline was in administration briefly during 2005, but this was lifted, although the route network and the fleet have both been reduced.

HQ airport & main base: Douala
Radio callsign: CAM-AIR
Designator: UY/UYC
Route points: Douala, Paris, Yaounde
Links with other airlines: Air France (qv) has a 3.6 per cent interest
Fleet: 1 Boeing 767-300ER; 1 Boeing 757-200

CANADA – C

Vast distances and isolated pockets of population have made Canada the ideal territory for air transport, but so too have the major cities and the dense commuter traffic between them. For many years, Canada enjoyed two major nationwide airlines, both of which were brought into existence by railway companies, with Air Canada tracing its routes back to the formation of Trans Canada Airlines in 1937 by the Canadian National Railway, while Canadian Airlines International was a merger of Canadian Pacific and Pacific Western, of which the former could trace its origins to the formation of Canadian Pacific Airways by the Canadian Pacific Railway, which was also a major shipowner.

The Canadian Pacific Railway had held authority to operate air services as early as 1919. Nevertheless, the early days of Canadian aviation were those of small, pioneering and under-funded bush operations, while travel between the large cities tended to be by railway. The Canadian government had hoped that the Canadian National Railway, which, as its name implies, was state owned, and Canadian Pacific would cooperate in creating a strong national airline, but Canadian Pacific wished to retain its independence, and so Trans Canada emerged in 1937 as a purely state-owned airline with ownership through the railway. Canadian Pacific was established in 1939 and brought together many small airlines.

For many years, Air Canada was the international airline, but Canadian Pacific Airlines, later Canadian Airlines, eventually was allowed to establish an international network. Both airlines had interests in other airline and inter-lining arrangements. The acquisition of Canadian Airlines brought about a considerable reorganisation and rationalisation of Canada's air transport industry. Several famous names found themselves swept into Air Canada or Air Canada Jazz, including Air Alliance, Air Atlantic and Air BC, as well as Canadian Regional and Inter-Canadien.

Of these, Air BC was formed in 1980, again on the merger of several small airlines in the west of Canada. From 1983 to 1986, the airline operated as Canadian Pacific Commuter, but this alliance with the predecessor of Canada's other major airline, Canadian International, ended when Air Canada acquired an 85 per cent shareholding in November 1986, later increasing this to 100 per cent. The fleet included Jetstream 31 and Twin Otter aircraft, but when absorbed it had standardised on BAe 146s and de Havilland Dash 8s.

The biggest single contributor to Air Canada Jazz, however, was Canadian Regional, a wholly owned subsidiary of Canadian Airlines International and the sister company of Canadian Airlines. The airline was established in 1991, three years after the merger which created Canadian Airlines, to take over the shareholdings in smaller regional airlines inherited mainly from PWA, Pacific Western Airlines. The merged operations of two 100 per cent-owned subsidiaries, Time Air and Ontario Express, provided the basis for the fleet and network of Canadian Regional Airlines, but it also was given responsibility for the investments in other airlines, including Inter-Canadien (70 per cent) and Calm Air (45 per cent).

Time Air operated both scheduled and charter flights in the west of Canada, as well as the Yukon and North West Territories, and across the border into the United States. Formed in 1966, at the time of its merger into Canadian Regional, it was operating a fleet consisting mainly of de Havilland Dash 8s, of which there were eighteen, including both 8-10 and 8-300 versions, as well as three older Convair 580s, three Short 360s and its first jet equipment, six Fokker F28 Fellowships. Pacific Western's involvement dated from 1984, when it had acquired a 40 per cent shareholding, and the airline was bought out in 1991.

Ontario Express dated from 1987, and operated in Ontario and Quebec. PWA had a 49 per cent shareholding in the airline, and again this was increased to 100 per cent in 1991. At the time of the merger, Ontario Express was operating fourteen BAe Jetstream 31, nine EMB-120 Brasilia and six ATR42-300.

Canadian Regional Airlines undertook a programme of consolidation and rationalisation and had a route network based on central and western Canada, with no involvement in the east, which remained the preserve of other Canadian Partners.

Inter-Canadien the airline dated from 1991, but could trace its history back to the founding of Air Rimouski in 1946. The name changed to Quebecair in 1952. In 1983, the Quebec Provincial government acquired the airline, but in 1986 announced that Quebecair was to be returned to the private sector. The year 1987 was a remarkable one for this small airline. Not only did it return to the private sector with the support of a 35 per cent shareholding by CP Air, but operations and equipment were merged with two other airlines, Nordair Metro and Quebec Aviation, and the name was changed to Inter-Canadien. The merged airline operated initially as a Canadian Pacific Commuter operator, but in 1989, after the creation of Canadian Airlines, the main body of shareholders, based in Quebec, terminated their agreement with Canadian Airlines, and changed the company name to Intair. During its short life, Intair operated seven Fokker 100 jet airliners and seven ATR-42s.

Intair was in need of restructuring and refinancing by 1991, and at one time operations ceased. Canadian Regional Airlines took a 70 per cent majority shareholding to restart the airline as a regional turboprop operation, and revived the Inter-Canadien title that had been dropped so abruptly some two years earlier. From the start, the revived airline operated as a Canadian Partner. In 1994, the remaining shares were also purchased by Canadian Regional.

AIR CANADA
ACE Holdings/Air Canada
Incorporated: 1937

Sixteenth largest by annual turnover and fifteenth by passenger numbers, Air Canada is now the sole large domestic and international airline in the country, having taken over Canadian Airlines in 2000 and absorbed its operations.

Air Canada itself dates from the formation of Trans Canada Air Lines in 1937, brought into being by the Trans-Canada Air Lines Act of that year. The new airline was owned 100 per cent by Canadian National Railways, a Crown corporation, which meant that from the outset it was nationalised. An earlier plan for a mixed state- and private-enterprise operation with Canadian Pacific Railways as the other partner failed to materialise.

The new airline started operations by purchasing the Canadian Airways Company and its equipment, giving it an initial fleet of two twin-engined Lockheed 10A Electras and a single-engined Stearman biplane. With this equipment, a Vancouver–Seattle service was inaugurated. In 1938, additional services were introduced, with TCA flying from Winnipeg to Vancouver, Montreal and Toronto, and to Edmonton and Lethbridge, so that by the end of the year the fleet had grown to five Lockheed 10A Electras and nine of the larger Lockheed 14Hs. Expansion continued eastwards, even after the outbreak of war in Europe, so that by 1940, operations had reached the Maritime Provinces, and Canada had its first transcontinental air services.

Development of domestic and cross-border services continued until 1943, when the airline obtained what was later to be an invaluable experience of transatlantic operation when it started the Canadian government Trans-Atlantic Air Service, using Avro Lancastrians (converted Lancaster bombers) between Montreal and Prestwick in Scotland. The service carried important passengers and Canadian forces' mail between Canada and Europe.

The return of peace in 1945 saw TCA introduce a fleet of thirty Douglas DC-3s, and further expansion of both its domestic and cross-border services. In 1947, the Canadair DC-4M North Star (a licence-built Douglas DC-4 with Rolls-Royce Merlin engines) was placed in service, and TCA returned to the transatlantic services, this time operating them in its own right. The DC-4 also operated a service to Mexico City. This expansion continued throughout the decade that followed, including, in 1957, a non-stop Toronto–London service operated by Lockheed Super Constellations, which had first been introduced in 1954. In 1955, TCA became the first North American operator of the Vickers Viscount turboprop airliner.

Not all of the expansion was straightforward. In 1955, TCA traded its service to Mexico City in exchange for Canadian Pacific's network of services within Ontario and Quebec.

TCA's first jet airliners were Douglas DC-8-40s, introduced to the transatlantic services in 1960, while on domestic routes another turboprop, the Vickers Vanguard, entered service in 1961. Trans-Canada was one of just two airlines (the other was BEA) to operate this aircraft, which was too slow and too late for passengers enchanted with the idea of jet air travel.

In 1964, the name was changed to Air Canada, finally reflecting the fact that the airline was no longer primarily a domestic operator, and that year the first short-haul jets, Douglas DC-9s, were ordered to begin Viscount replacement.

The airline was privatised in 1989, and the greater flexibility this offered was exercised in 1992, when Air Canada decided to collaborate with Texas-based Air Partners and jointly invest $450 million in the restructuring programme for Continental Airlines, enabling the American airline to emerge from Chapter 11 Protection in 1993. For many years, Air Canada held a 19.6 per stake in Continental.

The irony of Air Canada's acquisition of Canadian Airlines was that the latter company had originally set out to be completely independent. At the time of the acquisition, Canadian was the main operating subsidiary of Canadian Airlines International and the result of a merger between four airlines which took effect in 1988. The two largest of these airlines were Canadian Pacific, which had been Canada's second largest airline for many years, and Pacific Western Airlines, which was one of Canada's largest regional carriers at the time. The other two airlines were Eastern Provincial Airways and Nordair, which had already been acquired by CP Air in 1984 and 1985 respectively, along with Eastern Provincial's subsidiary, Air Maritime.

Canadian Pacific Airlines, more usually known in its latter days as CP Air, was the airline subsidiary of a highly diversified major group, Canadian Pacific, which had been formed in the nineteenth century to build and operate a transcontinental railway, and whose operations had spread to include, at one time, transatlantic ocean liner operation. By the 1960s, the group was involved in container shipping and ferries; hotels; road transport; oil, gas and timber production; mining and property development; in addition to the airline.

Canadian Pacific had rejected Canadian government proposals for a joint venture airline during the late 1930s, leaving the government to form Trans Canada Airlines, the predecessor of Air Canada. Instead, in 1942, Canadian Pacific Airlines was eventually formed on the merger of ten small airlines, most of which were bush operators. The largest of these airlines was Canadian Airways, a Winnipeg-based operator in which the Canadian Pacific Railway had held the controlling interest since 1930. The others included Ginger Coote Airways of Vancouver; Yukon Southern Air Transport of Vancouver and Edmonton; Wings of Winnipeg; Prairie Airways of Moose Jaw; Mackenzie Air Services of Edmonton; Arrow Airways of Manitoba; Starratt Airways of Hudson; Quebec Airways; and Montreal and Dominion Skyways. The CPR had in fact held a permit to operate aircraft commercially since 1919 The decision to press ahead with the formation of Canadian Pacific Airlines had been taken in 1939, realising that many of the small airlines were in poor financial shape and operating aircraft ill suited to their services. Before the new airline was born, the CPR had already been involved directly in aviation, helping to establish the North Atlantic Ferry Service for the delivery of bombers to the Royal Air Force in 1940, and during the war years was to operate six flying schools.

CPA's initial priorities were to continue and consolidate the bush services of its predecessor companies, doing this in the midst of wartime demands which made re-equipment difficult. Postwar, the airline had its strategy firmly set on transpacific operations, and in 1949, services to Sydney and Hong Kong were inaugurated. The Korean War also saw the airline undertake some 700 military charter flights between Vancouver and Tokyo. The airline was one of the select band of airlines to operate the unfortunate de Havilland Comet 1 jet airliner before this was withdrawn during the early 1950s. In exchange for its services in Ontario and Quebec, in 1955 CPA obtained Air Canada's Mexico City route, which it was able to extend to Buenos Aires. That same year, a polar route between Vancouver and Amsterdam was established, using Douglas DC-6Bs. The transformation from bush airline to long-haul operator was completed in 1959, when CPA introduced its first transcontinental service, using Bristol Britannias. The Canadian government then granted the airline authority to expand its transcontinental operations so that by 1970 it could operate 25 per cent of the long-haul domestic market. Jet equipment followed, with Douglas DC-8s for the longer routes, and, later, Boeing 737-100s for the shorter domestic and cross-border services.

Pacific Western dated from 1946, when it was founded as Central British Columbia Airlines, but adopted the title Pacific Western in 1953. In 1955, PWA acquired Queen Charlotte Airlines and Associated Airways. The third-level operations were sold in 1966 to Northward Aviation. During this period a very mixed fleet was operated, including a Douglas DC-3, two DC-4s, two DC-6Bs and two DC-7Cs, four Convair 640s, a Lockheed Hercules and a Boeing 707-138B, although then disposal of the third-level operations at least meant that an Otter and two Beavers left the fleet, along with three Grumman Goose amphibians! PWA took over BC Airlines in 1970, and a further acquisition occurred in 1979 with the merging of PWA and Winnipeg-based Transair, in which PWA had acquired a 72 per cent stake in 1977.

On its formation, Canadian Airlines, found itself with a mixed fleet of Airbus, Boeing and McDonnell Douglas manufacture, but it also had a route network which was well spread across Canada, rather than as previously, heavily slanted towards the western provinces. It also had interests in other airlines, while it also inherited the 'Canadian Pacific Commuter' network of feeder services. Some standardisation of the fleet occurred, so that it no longer operated both Airbus A310s and Boeing 767s, for example. Between 1991 and 1934, the organisation itself was streamlined, and AMR Corporation, the parent company for American Airlines, took a 31 per cent share in Canadian Airlines International, the parent for both Canadian and Canadian Regional Airlines, with the remainder being held by a holding company, Canadian Airlines Corporation.

By the time it was absorbed into Air Canada, Canadian operated transatlantic and transpacific flights, services to Mexico, Brazil and Argentina, and a major transcontinental and trunk route network within Canada itself, augmented by the feeder operations of its Canadian Partner network, which included airlines owned by Canadian's sister company, Canadian Regional Airlines. Shuttle services were run under the 'Canadian Shuttle' branding, linking Toronto and Montreal, Ottawa and Toronto, in the east, and in the west, Calgary and Vancouver, Edmonton and Vancouver, and Calgary and Edmonton. In addition to close cooperation with American Airlines, marketing alliances exist with many other major international airlines.

In common with many larger airlines, Air Canada had created a network of feeder services through the Air Canada Connector operation. The first Air Canada Connector was Air Nova in 1986, followed soon afterwards by Air BC. In Air Canada's case, the feeder airlines were all subsidiaries, and included Air Alliance, Air Ontario and NWT Air as well as Air Nova and Air BC. Meanwhile, Air Canada introduced high frequency 'Rapidair' services between Montreal, Toronto and Ottawa, with flights at half-hourly intervals at peak periods, and every quarter hour on Montreal–Toronto in the early morning peak! A slightly less frequent 'Rapidair' network operated between Calgary and Edmonton International, and Calgary and Vancouver.

The feeder services have now been reorganised and the regional services of Air BC, Air Nova and Air Ontario now operate in a new airline, Air Canada Jazz, while charter flights are provided by Air Canada Jetz.

Despite amalgamating the Canadian routes, or perhaps because of the restructuring costs involved, in April 2003, Air Canada was forced to file for bankruptcy protection, but was able to leave this in October 2004.

The parent organisation for Air Canada is ACE Aviation Holdings. The the airline is a founder-member of the Star Alliance, which brings together frequent-flyer programmes and other services for Lufthansa, SAS, Thai International and, in 1997, United Airlines and Varig as well as Air Canada.

Including the Air Canada Jazz destinations, today Air Canada serves more than 150 destinations worldwide.

HQ airport & main base: Montreal Trudeau, with further hubs at Toronto and Vancouver
Radio callsign: AIR CANADA
Designator: AC/ACA
Employees: 32,000
Route points: (Including those served by Air Canada Jazz) Abbostford, Albany, Allentown, Antigua, Aruba, Atlanta, Bagotville, Baie Comeau, Baltimore, Bathurst, Beijing, Bermuda, Bogotá, Boston, Bridgetown, Buenos Aires, Calgary, Cancun, Caracas, Castlegar, Cayo Coco, Cayo Largo del Sur, Charlotte, Charlottetown, Chibougemau, Chicago, Cleveland, Columbus, Cranbrook, Dallas, Deer Lake, Delhi, Denver, Detroit, Edmonton, Fort Lauderdale, Fort McMurray, Fort Myers, Fort St John, Frankfurt, Fredericton, Gander, Gaspe, Goose Bay, Grand Cayman Island, Grande Prairie, Grenada, Halifax, Harrisburg, Hartford, Havana, Holguin, Hong Kong, Honolulu, Houston, Indianapolis, Iles de la Madeleine, Ixtapa/ Zihuatanejo, Kahului, Kamloops, Kansas City, Kelowna, Kingston (Canada), Klagenfurt, Kona, Las Vegas, Lethbridge, Lima, London (Canada), London, Los Angeles, Manchester, Medicine Hat, Mexico City, Miami, Milwaukee, Minneapolis, Moncton, Montego Bay, Mont Joli, Montreal, Munich, Nanaimo, Nashville, Nassau, New York, Newark, North Bay, Orlando, Osaka, Ottawa, Paris, Penticton, Philadelphia, Phoenix, Pittsburgh, Pointe-à-Pitre, Port au Prince, Port of Spain, Portland, Prince George, Prince Rupert, Providence, Providenciales, Puerto Plata, Puerto Vallarta, Punta Cana, Quebec, Raleigh/Durham, Regina, Roberval, Rochester, Rome, Rouyn, St John, St John's, St Louis, St Lucia, St Maarten, Salzburg, San Diego, San Francisco, San Jose, San Jose Cabo, San Juan, Sandspit, Santiago de Chile, Santo Domingo, Sao Paulo, Sarnia, Saskatoon, Sault Ste Marie, Seattle, Seoul, Sept-Iles, Shanghai, Smithers, Sudbury, Sydney, Taipei, Tampa, Tel Aviv, Terrace, Thunder Bay, Timmins, Tokyo, Toronto, Val d'Or, Vancouver, Varadero, Victoria, Vienna, Wabush, Warsaw, Washington, West Palm Beach, Westchester County, Whitehorse, Windsor (Canada), Winnipeg, Zurich
Links with other airlines: Owns Air Canada Jazz, Air Canada Jetz (both qv). Member of Star Alliance. Alliances exist with Air Jamaica (qv), Air Labrador (qv), Air One (qv), Air Wisconsin (qv), Avianca (qv), Canadian North, EVA Air (qv), Mexicana (qv), Royal Jordanian Airlines (qv), SkyWest Airlines (qv), Swiss Airlines. Star Alliance member with Lufthansa, SAS, Thai International, United Airlines and Varig (all qv). Code-sharing with Continental, Korean Air, Royal Jordanian (all qv)
Passengers carried: (Includes Air Canada Jazz and Air Canada Jetz) 27.6 million
Annual turnover: (Includes Air Canada Jazz and Air Canada Jetz) US $6,858 million (£4,600 million)
Fleet: 3 Airbus A340-600; 2 Airbus A340-500; 10 Airbus A340-300; 8 Airbus A330-300; 2 Boeing 777F; 6 Boeing 777-300ER; 12 Boeing 777-200LR; 33 Boeing 767-300ER; 13 Boeing 767-200; 10 Airbus A321-200; 47 Airbus A320-200; 48 Airbus A319-100; 12 Bombardier CRJ100ER; 54 Embraer 190; 15 Embraer 175 (On order: 14 Boeing 787-8)

AIR CANADA JAZZ
Incorporated: 2001

Air Canada Jazz was established to replace the Air Canada Connector airlines, Air BC, Air Nova and Air Ontario, following the parent airline's acquisition and integration of Canadian Airlines in 2000. It is owned 100 per cent by Air Canada parent, ACE Aviation Holdings.

HQ airport & main base: Halifax International, with further bases/hubs at Calgary International, Montreal Mirabel, Toronto Pearson and Vancouver International

Designator: QK/ARN
Employees: 3,366
Route points: See Air Canada above
Links with other airlines: Air Canada feeder network
Fleet: 15 Bombardier CRJ700-701LR; 36 Bombardicr CRJ200ER; 23 Bombardier CRJ100ER; 26 Bombardier Dash 8 Q300; 36 Bombardier Dash 8 Q100

AIR CANADA JETZ
Incorporated: 2001

Essentially the charter division of Air Canada, the airline has developed to provide a business-class service for professional sports teams and corporate clients.

HQ airport & main base: Montreal Mirabel
Designator: AC/ACA
Links with other airlines: Subsidiary of Air Canada (qv)
Fleet: 4 Airbus A320-200

AIR CREEBEC
Air Creebec, Inc.
Incorporated: 1982

The unusual name reflects ownership of Air Creebec by the Cree Indians' Creeco Corporation. The airline was founded in 1982 to operate regional scheduled and charter services from Val d'Or in Quebec, and in 1989 it acquired the northern routes of Air Ontario.

HQ airport & main base: Val d'Or, Quebec
Radio callsign: CREE
Designator: YN/CRQ
Route points: Attawapiskat, Chibougamau, Chisasibi, East Main, Fort Albany, Kaschechewan, Kuujjuarapik, La Grande, Montreal, Moosonee, Nemiscau, Peawanuk, Roberval, Timmins, Val d'Or, Waskaganish, Wemindji
Fleet: 3 BAe 748 Srs 2A; 1 Bombardier Dash 8 Q300; 6 Bombardier Dash 8 Q100; 1 Raytheon Beech 1900D; 3 Embraer EMB-110P1 Bandeirante; 1 Raytheon Beech King Air 100

AIR GEORGIAN
Incorporated: 1994

Primarily a passenger and freight charter airline, it also operates a number of domestic scheduled services for Air Canada Jazz, for which it uses that company's call sign and designators.

HQ airport & main base: Toronto Pearson International
Designator: ZX/GGN
Fleet: 19 Raytheon Beech 1900D; 2 Raytheon Beech 1900C; 1 Cessna Citation Bravo

AIR INUIT
Air Inuit, Inc.
Incorporated: 1977

Taking its name from its owners who are of Inuit, or Eskimo, origin, Air Inuit was founded in 1977 as a regional scheduled and charter airline, operating mainly in northern Qebec. The airline also operates as Air Alliance, using a code-share with Air Canada Jazz.

HQ airport & main base: Montreal Dorval
Radio callsign: AIR INUIT
Designator: 3H/AIE
Route points: Akulivik, Aupaluk, Inukjuak, Ivujivik, Kangigsualujjuag, Kangirsuk, Kuujjuaq, Kuujjuarapik, La Grande, Montreal, Povungnituk, Quaqtaq, Quebec, Salluit, Saniiluaq, Schefferville, Sept-Iles, Tasiujuaq, Umiujag, Wabush
Links with other airlines: Marketing alliances with First Air (qv)
Fleet: 4 BAe 748; 6 Bombardier Dash 8 Q100; 7 de Havilland Canada Twin Otter Srs 300; 2 Raytheon Beech King Air 100

AIR LABRADOR
Labrador Airways Ltd
Incorporated: 1948

Founded in 1948 as Newfoundland Airways, using floatplanes based on Gander and handling charter flights. The main base later moved to Goose Bay, and then to St John's. In 1983, Provincial Investments, owned by Roger Pike, acquired the airline and an associate company, Labrador Aviation Services. Scheduled services are now operated throughout Labrador, Newfoundland and Quebec.

HQ airport & main base: St John's International, with further bases at Goose Bay and Montreal Trudeau
Radio callsign: LAB AIR
Designator: WJ/LAL
Route points: Black Tickle, Blanc Sablon, Cartwright, Charlottetown, Chevery, Deer Lake, Fox Harbor, Gethsemani, Goose Bay, Havre St Pierre, Hopedale, Iles de la Madeleine, Kegaska, La Tabatiere, Makkovik, Mary's Harbour, Moncton,

Montreal, Nain, Natashquan, Natuashish, Pakuashipi, Port Hope Simpson, Postville, Quebec, Rigolet, St Anthony, St John's, Sept-Iles, Tête-à-La Baleine, Wabush, Williams Harbour
Fleet: 2 Bombardier Dash 8 Q100; 3 de Havilland Canada Twin Otter Srs 300; 1 de Havilland Canada Twin Otter Srs 100; 2 Raytheon Beech 1900D; 1 Cessna 208 Caravan

AIR NORTH
Incorporated: 1977

Founded in 1977 as Air North Charter and Training, today Air North operates scheduled and charter services in the Yukon, North West Territories and across the border into neighbouring Alaska.

HQ airport & main base: Whitehorse
Designator: 4N/ANT
Employees: 150
Route points: Calgary, Dawson City, Edmonton, Fairbanks, Inuvik, Old Crow, Vancouver, Whitehorse
Fleet: 2 Boeing 737-200; 2 BAe 748 Srs 2A

AIR TRANSAT
Air Transat Ltd
Incorporated: 1986

Primarily a passenger charter carrier, Air Transat was founded in 1986, and has created a fleet of Lockheed L-1011 TriStars, to which it added Boeing 757-200ERs during the late 1990s. More recently, it has started to offer scheduled services to destinations as far afield as Paris and London, while building up a fleet comprised entirely of wide-bodied Airbuses.

HQ airport & main base: Montreal Trudeau
Radio callsign: TRANSAT
Designator: TS/TSC
Employees: 2,616
Route points: Fort Lauderdale, Glasgow, London, Manchester, Montreal, Orlando, Paris, Quebec, Tampa, Toronto
Fleet: 1 Airbus A300-300; 3 Airbus A300-200; 12 Airbus A310-300

BUFFALO AIRWAYS
Incorporated: 1970

A passenger and cargo airline formed in 1970, which also undertakes fire-fighting and fuel-supply operations. One of the few operators of the Curtiss Commando and Douglas DC-4 today.

HQ airport & main base: Hay River, Yellowknife
Designator: J4/BVA
Fleet: 8 Douglas DC-4; 2 Curtiss C-46 Commando; 10 Douglas DC-3

CALM AIR
Calm Air Ltd
Incorporated: 1962

Founded by Arnold Morberg and his wife in 1962, Calm Air initially operated charters in northern Saskatchewan. Expansion was boosted by the airline's 1976 acquisition of services operated by Transair in the Northwest Territories, while in 1987, Pacific Western acquired a 45 per cent shareholding, which later passed to Canadian Regional Airlines with Calm Air operating as a Canadian Partner, feeding into the Canadian network at Thompson and Winnipeg. Since the collapse of Canadian, Calm Air has once again reverted to being a completely independent airline with all of its shares privately held.

HQ airport & main base: Thompson, Manitoba
Radio callsign: CALM AIR
Designator: MO/CAV
Route points: Arviat, Baker Lake, Chesterfield Inlet, Churchill, Coral Harbour, Flin Flon, Gillam, Lynn Lake, Rankin Inlet, Repulse Bay, Shamattawa, South Indian Lake, The Pass, Thompson, Whale Cove, Winnipeg
Fleet: 5 BAe 748; 7 Saab 340B; 2 Cessna Caravan 675

CANADIAN NORTH
Incorporated: 1998

A regional scheduled passenger airline created when it was bought from Canadian Airlines in 1998, to establish a locally owned airline specialising in operations in the Northern Territories. It is owned by Norterra, a locally based investment group.

HQ airport & main base: Yellowknife
Designator: 5T/ANX
Route points: Broughton Island, Calgary, Cambridge Bay, Cape Dorset, Colville Lake, Deline, Edmonton, Fort Good Hope, Gjoa Haven, Hay River, Igloolik, Inuvik, Iqaluit, Kimmirut, Norman Wells, Ottawa, Pangnirtung, Pelly Bay, Pond Inlet, Rankin Inlet, Resolute, Taloyoak, Tulita, Yellowknife
Fleet: 6 Boeing 737-200; 1 Fokker F28 Mk1000

CANADA 3000
Canada 3000 Airlines, Ltd
See CanJet

CANJET
Canjet Airlines Ltd
Incorporated: 1999

Originally founded in 1999 as a low-fare airline by the IMP Group, which owned it outright, it was merged with Canada 3000 in May 2001, but when that airline closed later that year, IMP relaunched Canjet in mid-2002. Canjet withdrew from scheduled services in September 2006.

HQ airport & main base: Halifax International
Radio callsign: CANJET
Designator: C6/CJA
Employees: 572
Fleet: 1 Boeing 737-300; 5 Boeing 737-500

CARGOJET AIRWAYS
Incorporated: 2002

An air cargo charter and scheduled airline formed out of the former Canada 3000 Cargo when Ajay Virmani acquired a 50 per cent stake in Canada 3000 Cargo in 2001, and bought the remaining 50 per cent early in 2002 – at which time the current title was adopted. Later that year Winnport Logistics, a forwarding agent, was acquired. The airline also underatkes contract work for other airlines.

HQ airport & main base: Toronto Pearson International
Radio callsign: CARGOJET
Designator: W8/CJT
Route points: Calgary, Edmonton, Halifax, Moncton, Montreal, Ottawa, Regina, Saskatoon, Toronto, Vancouver, Winnipeg
Links with other airlines: Alliance with Korean Air (qv)
Fleet: 13 Boeing 727-200F

FIRST AIR
First Air Ltd
Incorporated: 1946

Dating from 1946, when it was formed as Bradley Flying School, and later moving into scheduled and charter air services as Bradley Air Services, First Air operates throughout Canada, but is best known as a specialist in Arctic air services. In 1971, the company opened what was then the world's most northerly air service, to Eureka on Ellesmere Island, although this is no longer operated. A wholly owned subsidiary of Makivik, a sister company is Air Inuit, and a subsidiary is Ptarmigan Airways.

HQ airport & main base: Ottawa International
Designator: 7F/FAB
Employees: 700
Route points: Broughton Island, Cambridge Bay, Cape Dorset, Clyde River, Edmonton, Fort Simpson, Gjoa Haven, Hall Beach, Hay River, Holman, Igloolik, Inuvik, Iqaluit, Kimmirut, Kugluktuk, Kuujjuaq, Montreal, Nanisivik, Ottawa, Pangnirtung, Pelly Bay, Pond Inlet, Rankin Inlet, Resolute, Taloyoak, Whitehorse, Winnipeg, Yellowknife
Links with other airlines: Owns Ptarmigan Airways
Fleet: 3 Boeing 727-200F; 2 Lockheed L-100-30 Hercules; 3 Boeing 737-200C; 2 Boeing 737-300; 6 ATR-42-300; 3 BAe 748-2A; 1 de Havilland Canada DHC-6 Twin Otter; 2 de Havilland DHC-2 Beaver

HARMONY AIRWAYS
Incorporated: 2002

Formed in 2002 as HMY Airways, an inclusive tour charter airline, the current title was adopted in 2004. The airline is owned by its chairman. In addition to its charter flights to the UK and Mexico, a small scheduled network is also operated.

HQ airport & main base: Vancouver
Radio callsign: HARMONY
Designator: HQ/HMY
Route points: Calgary, Honolulu, Kahului, Kelowna, Las Vegas, Palm Springs, Toronto, Vancouver, Victoria
Fleet: 4 Boeing 757-200

HAWKAIR AVIATION SERVICES
Incorporated: 1994

A scheduled and charter airline operating a small passenger network in the west of Canada.

HQ airport & main base: Terrace, British Columbia
Radio callsign: HAWKAIR
Designator: 8H
Employees: 130
Route points: Dawson Creek, Fort St John, Prince Rupert, Terrace, Vancouver
Fleet: 3 Bombardier Dash 8 Q100

KELOWNA FLIGHTCRAFT AIR CHARTER
Incorporated: 1974

Kelowna Flightcraft was formed in 1970 as an aircraft engineering organisation, specialising in the conversion of Convair 240/340/440 Metropolitan airliners. Its air charter subsidiary dates from 1974 and undertakes cargo charters, usually on a long-term contract basis for couriers such as Purlator and FedEx, and for the Canadian Post Office. Passenger operations take anglers to fishing lodges in British Columbia. An early attempt at low-fare scheduled services with Greyhound Air, which used seven Boeing 727s, was abandoned in September 1997.

The company continues its engineering work, having acquired the rights to the Convair 580 which it remanufactures as the 5800.

HQ airport & main base: Kelowna International, British Columbia
Radio callsign: FLIGHTCRAFT
Designator: KFA
Fleet: 11 Boeing 727-200F; 2 Boeing 727-200; 1 Boeing 727-100F; 6 Convair 580

MORNINGSTAR AIR EXPRESS
Incorporated: 1970

Founded in 1970 as Brooker-Wheaton Aviation, named after the founders, Morningstar Air Express is an all-cargo charter airline, operating between Montreal and Winnipeg for FedEx, as well as undertaking contracts for other freight specialists and providing ad hoc charters.

HQ airport & main base: Edmonton City Cntre
Radio callsign: MORNINGSTAR
Designator: MAL
Links with other airlines: Operates for FedEx (qv)
Fleet: 4 Boeing 727-200F; 6 Cessna Caravan 675

NOLINOR AVIATION
Incorporated: 1992

After being incorporated in 1992, Nolinor did not begin operations until 1997, initially providing air support for hunting and fishing parties, but since developing as a passenger and cargo charter airline.

HQ airport & main base: Montreal Mirabel International
Designator: NRL
Employees: 60
Fleet: 7 Convair 580

NORTH CARIBOU AIR
Incorporated: 1957

North Caribou Air was founded as North Caribou Flying Services in 1957, and provides passenger and cargo charters as well as scenic flights for tourists.

HQ airport & main base: Fort St John
Radio callsign: CARIBOU
Designator: NCB
Fleet: 4 Bombardier Dash 8 Q100; 3 de Havilland Canada Twin Otter Srs 300; 4 Raytheon Beech 1900C/D; 1 IAI Astra; 3 Raytheon Beech King Air 200; 5 Raytheon Beech King Air 100; 1 Raytheon Beech King Air 350; 1 Raytheon Beech King Air B200; 1 Raytheon Beech King Air C90

PACIFIC COASTAL AIRLINES
Incorporated: 1975

Pacific Coastal was formed in 1975 on the merger of Powell Air with the former Port Hardy operations of Air BC, to operate scheduled passenger and cargo service to small communities in British Columbia, as well as charters. The route network expanded with the acquisition of Wilderness Airlines in 1998.

HQ airport & main base: Vancouver International
Designator: 8P/PCO
Employees: 300
Route points: Anahim Lake, Bella Bella, Bella Coola, Campbell River, Comox, Cranbrook, Kiemtu, Masset, Port Hardy, Powell River, Vancouver, Victoria, Williams Lake
Fleet: 5 Saab 340A; 2 Shorts 360; 3 Raytheon Beech 1900C; 1 Raytheon Beech King Air 200

PROVINCIAL AIRLINES
Incorporated: 1972

Provincial was formed in 1972 as an air-work company, providing flight training and aerial survelliance and photography, and did not become a scheduled service airline until 1980. The network of services was enlarged in 1988 with the acquisition of Eastern Flying Service, with its air courier network throughout the Maritime Provinces. Today, Provincial provides not only passenger and cargo, charter and scheduled services, it continues to offer other services, including maritime surveillance under contract to the Canadian authorities.

HQ airport & main base: St John's
Radio callsign: PROVINCIAL
Designator: PB

Route points: Blanc Sablon, Churchill Falls, Davis Inlet, Deer Lake, Goose Bay, Halifax, Hopedale, Makkovik, Nain, Postville, St Anthony, St John's, Sept-Iles, Stephenville, Wabush
Fleet: 3 Bombardier Dash 8 Q100; 2 Saab 340A; 3 de Havilland Canada Twin Otter Srs 300; 1 Fairchild Metro III; 7 Raytheon Beech King Air 200; 1 Raytheon Beech King Air B200

SKYSERVICE AIRLINES
Incorporated: 1994

A Canadian inclusive tour charter operator, Skyservice was founded in 1994 and operates throughout the Americas and across the Atlantic. A mixed Airbus and Boeing fleet is operated.

HQ airport & main base: Toronto Pearson International with a further base at Montreal
Designator: 5G/SSV
Fleet: 1 Boeing 767-300ER; 10 Boeing 757-200; 11 Airbus A320-200; 2 Airbus A319-100

SUNWING AIRLINES
Incorporated: 2006

Sunwing Airlines is a new Canadian airline formed by the parent company, Sunwing Vacations, and using Boeing 737-800s on low-cost but full service flights across Canada and to resorts in Florida, the Caribbean and Central America.

HQ airport & main base: Toronto Pearson International
Route points: Gander, Halifax, London (Ontario), Montreal, Ottawa, Saguenay, St John's, Thunder Bay, Toronto, Vancouver, plus destinations in Florida, the Caribbean and Central America
Fleet: 6 Boeing 737-800

TRANS CAPITAL AIR
Incorporated: 1994

A passenger and cargo charter airline, Trans Capital Air is one of the few still operating the de Havilland Dash 7 short take-off and landing four-engined aircraft.

HQ airport & main base: Toronto Pearson International
Designator:
Fleet: 4 de Havilland Dash 7-100

TRANSWEST AIR
Incorporated: 2000

Transwest Air was formed in 2000 on the merger of Athabaska Airways, which dated from 1955, with Air Sask, which dated from 1960, creating a new regional airline with the largest network in Saskatchewan.

HQ airport & main base: Prince Albert Municipal
Radio callsign: TRANSWEST
Designator: 9T/ABS
Route points: Fond du Lac, La Ronge, Points North Landing, Prince Albert, Regina, Saskatoon, Stony Rapids, Wollaston Lake
Fleet: 2 Saab 340A; 2 BAe Jetstream 31; 4 de Havilland Canada Twin Otter Srs100/200; 2 Raytheon Beech King Air 100

VOYAGEUR AIRWAYS
Incorporated: 1968

Voyageur Airways has been operating charter and scheduled flights for passengers and cargo since 1968, including air ambulance flights, and also offers dry- and wet-leasing services to other airlines. The sole international scheduled service, to New York, started in 2005.

HQ airport & main base: North Bay
Radio callsign: VOYAGEUR
Designator: VAL
Route points: Mont Tremblant, New York, North Bay, Toronto
Fleet: 2 Bombardier CRJ100LR; 4 de Havilland Dash 7-100; 5 Bombardier Dash 8 Q300; 4 Raytheon Beech King Air 200; 7 Raytheon Beech King Air 100

WASAYA AIRWAYS
Incorporated: 1986

Founded in 1986 as Kelner Airways, for many years the airline operated passenger and cargo charters before starting its first scheduled services in 1997. Operations are mainly concentrated on Manitoba, the North West Territories and northern Ontario, serving many small and remote communities.

HQ airport & main base: Thunder Bay International
Designator: WG/WSG
Employees: 180
Route points: Angling Lake, Bearskin Lake, Big Trout Lake, Cat Lake, Deer Lake, Fort Hope, Fort Severn, Kasabonika Lake, Keewaywin, Kingfisher Lake, Landsdown House, Muskratdam, North Spirit Lake, Pickle Lake, Pikangikum, Poplar Hill, Red

Lake, Round Lake, Sachigo Lake, Sandy Lake, Summer Beaver, Thunder Bay, Webequie, Wunnumin Lake
Fleet: 4 BAe 748 Srs2/2A; 3 Raytheon Beech 1900D; 3 Cessna Caravan 675; 7 Pilatus PC-12

WEST WIND AVIATION
Incorporated: 1983

West Wind Aviation was formed in 1983, and operates passenger charter flights and air taxi operations from Saskatoon. Ownership is divided between an Indian tribal council, West Wind Ventures and a small number of individuals.

HQ airport & main base: Saskatoon John G. Diefenbaker International
Designator: WEW
Employees: 116
Fleet: 1 BAe 748 Srs 2A; 2 ATR-42-300; 2 BAe Jetstream 31; 1 Raytheon Beech King Air B200; 2 Raytheon Beech King Air 200; 2 Raytheon Beech King Air 100; 1 Cessna Citation Ultra

WESTJET
Westjet Airlines Ltd
Incorporated: 1996

A low-fare, no-frills carrier, Westjet was formed in 1996 to pioneer this type of operation in the deregulated Canadian market, initially concentrating on the main centres in the western provinces. Expansion accelerated after the airline became publicly quoted on the Toronto Stock Exchange in 1999, and in 2000 the airline began to serve destinations in eastern Canada, with a route to Hamilton, followed by services into the United States in 2004.

HQ airport & main base: Calgary International
Designator: WS/WJA
Employees: 4,800
Route points: Abbotsford, Calgary, Charlottetown, Comox, Edmonton, Fort Lauderdale, Fort McMurray, Fort Myers, Grande Prairie, Halifax, Honolulu, Kahului, Kelowna, Las Vegas, London (Ont), Los Angeles, Moncton, Montreal, Orlando, Ottawa, Palm Springs, Phoenix, Prince George, Regina, St John's, Saskatoon, Tampa, Thunder Bay, Toronto, Vancouver, Victoria, Winnipeg
Fleet: 10 Boeing 737-800; 48 Boeing 737-700; 13 Boeing 737-600

ZOOM AIRLINES
Incorporated: 2002

Founded in 2002, Zoom Airlines commenced inclusive tour charter flights for its parent company, Go Travel Direct, in 2003, initially using an Airbus A320 leased from Monarch Airlines. It is now developing a low-cost network of scheduled services, mainly to Europe and to the Caribbean, with a highly standardised fleet of Boeing 767s. A UK subsidiary was formed in 2006.

HQ airport & main base: Ottawa International
Radio callsign: ZOOM
Designator: Z4/OOM
Route points: Calgary, Camaguey, Cardiff, Cartagena, Cayo Coco, Glasgow, Halifax, La Romana, London, Manchester, Montreal, Orlando, Ottawa, Paris, Port of Spain, Puerto Plata, Puerto Vallarta, Quebec, St Maarten, Toronto, Vancouver, Varadero
Fleet: 4 Boeing 767-300ER

CAPE VERDE – D4

TACV – CABO VERDE AIRLINES
Transportes Aereos de Cabo Verde
Incorporated: 1958

Formed in 1958 to fly scheduled and charter flights within the Cape Verde Islands, this airline suspended operations in 1967 pending a reorganisation. After independence in 1975, the airline became the national carrier, and was nationalised in 1983. For a period, long-haul operations to Amsterdam, Lisbon and Paris were attempted, using a McDonnell Douglas DC-10-30 of Linhas Aereas de Mocambique, but these were abandoned, leaving the airline at the turn of the century operating services within the islands, with regional services to the African mainland. Nevertheless, over the past decade, with Boeing 757-200s in the fleet, a transatlantic service has been introduced to Boston and a number of European destinations.

HQ airport & main base: Santiago Praia
Radio callsign: TRANSVERDE
Designator: VR/TCV
Employees: 795
Route points: Boa Vista, Boston, Fortaleza, Lisbon, Maio, Milan, Munich, Oporto, Paris, Praia, Rome, Sal, Sao Philipe, Sao Vicente
Fleet: 2 Boeing 757-200; 3 ATR-42-300; 1 de Havilland DHC-6 Twin Otter

CAYMAN ISLANDS – VP-C

CAYMAN AIRWAYS
Incorporated: 1968

The Cayman Islands airline providing scheduled passenger and cargo flights within the islands and to destinations in the Caribbean and the United States, Cayman Airways took over the routes of another airline, Cayman Brac Airways, in 1968. It was taken over by the Cayman Islands government in 1977.

HQ airport & main base: Grand Cayman Owen Roberts International
Radio callsign: CAYMAN
Designator: KX/CAY
Route points: Boston, Cayman Brac Island, Chicago, Fort Lauderdale, Grand Cayman, Havana, Houston, Kingston, Little Cayman, Miami, Montego Bay, Tampa
Fleet: 2 Boeing 737-300; 3 Boeing 737-200; 2 de Havilland Canada Twin Otter Srs300

CHILE – CC

As with many countries, the history of air transport in Chile is largely that of the national airline, LAN. Political change in recent years has also discouraged the formation of competing airlines until recently with the formation of Sky Airline, but the new left-leaning government may well inhibit further enterprise. Despite this, LAN has been active in establishing airlines in other Latin American countries, expanding outside its home market.

LAN AIRLINES

Linea Aerea Nacional de Chile
Incorporated: 1929

The story of LANChile dates from 1929 when the Chilean government formed an airline, Linea Aerospostale Santiago-Arica, which was managed by the air force. A fleet of eight de Havilland Gipsy Moths operated the service. Growth was rapid, and during its first three years, the airline acquired a varied fleet, including Ford Trimotors, Curtiss Condors and Potez 56s. The airline passed into civilian control in 1932, and the present title dates from that time.

The first international service was not started until 1946, when a service to Buenos Aires was introduced, using Douglas DC-3s to fly over the Andes. Martin 202s soon augmented the DC-3 fleet and the airline did not acquire its first four-engined equipment until 1955, pressurised Douglas DC-6Bs. The new aircraft were used to establish new services, first to Lima and Guayaquil, and then in 1958, to Panama City. The first jet aircraft were Caravelles, introduced in 1962.

A change of government in 1964 led to a serious attempt to stem the airline's losses and cut the government subsidy, which was reduced substantially over the next two years. In 1966, a modernisation programme started, with Hawker Siddeley (later BAe) 748 turboprops introduced to repace the DC-3s. Long-haul jet equipment followed, although the first Boeing 707-330 was obtained secondhand from Lufthansa, and services were introduced to Miami and New York. In 1974, the airline was the first to link Australia with South America via the South Pole. Another innovation some years later, in 1986, was the use of a Boeing 767 for the first twin-jet scheduled service across the Atlantic, operating from Santiago de Chile to Madrid via Rio de Janeiro. Three years later, the airline was privatised, and control today is in the hands of three major shareholders.

In 1995, LAN acquired Chile's second largest airline, Ladeco, and followed this in 1998 by merging Ladeco with FastAir. The airline was known until 2004 as LAN Chile, but by that time had subsidiaries, LAN Dominica, LAN Ecuador and LAN Peru, which all became part of Lan Airlines to unify the corporate image of the four airlines. Over the past decade, the number of employees in the pan-Latin America LAN group has grown fivefold, while further satellite airlines have been created in neighbouring Argentina.

LAN is the forty-third largest airline in the world by revenue and is a member of the Oneworld alliance.

HQ airport & main base: Santiago International
Radio callsign: LAN
Designator: LA/LAN
Employees: 13,414
Route points: Acapulco, Amsterdam, Antofagasta, Arica, Asuncion, Auckland, Balmaceda, Barcelona, Bilbao, Bogotá, Brussels, Buenos Aires, Calama, Calgary, Cancun, Caracas, Comodoro Rivadavia, Concepcion, Copiapo, Cordoba, Dallas, Easter Island, El Salvador (Chile), Frankfurt, Guadalajara, Guatemala City, Guayaquil, Havana, Iguaazu, Iquique, La Paz, La Serena, Lima, London, Los Angeles, Madrid, Mendoza, Mérida, Mexico City, Miami, Milan, Monterrey, Montevideo, Montreal, Mount Pleasant, New York, Osorno, Papeete, Paris, Puerto Montt, Puerto Vallarta, Punta Arenas, Punta Cana, Quito, Rio de Janeiro, Rio Gallegos, Rome, Rosario, San Carlos de Bariloche, San Jose Cabo, Santiago de Chile, Sao Paulo, Sydney, Temuco, Toronto, Valdivia, Vancouver, Veracruz, Villahermosa, Zurich

Links with other airlines: Has 100 per cent stake in LAN Argentina (qv), and also controls LAN Express (qv), 99.4 per cent, LAN Chile Cargo, 99.4 per cent, with interests in LAN Dominica (qv) and LAN Peru (qv), both 49 per cent, and LAN Ecuador (qv), 45 per cent, ABSA-Aerolineas Brasileiros, 73.3 per cent, MASAir, 39.5 per cent, and Florida West International Airways, 25 per cent. Member of the Oneworld alliance. Alliances with Aeromexico (qv), Aerosur (qv), Alaska Airlines (qv), Florida West International Airways, Korean Air (qv), LAN Express, LAN Peru, TAM Mercosul
Fleet: 6 Airbus A340-300; 1 Boeing 767 Freighter; 24 Boeing 767-300ER; 10 Airbus A320-200; 13 Airbus A319-100; 20 Airbus A318-100; 12 Boeing 737-200

LAN CARGO
Incorporated: 2004

Owned 99.4 per cent by LAN Airlines, LAN Cargo is part of the group's air cargo interests, and was created out of the cargo operations of the LAN airlines, and operates in cooperation with ABSA, Florida West and MAS Air.

HQ airport & main base: Santiago Arturo Merino Benitez International
Designator: LCO
Route points: On the LAN network
Links with other airlines: Owned 99.4 per cent by the LAN Airlines.
Cooperates with ABSA, Florida West and MAS Air, also part of LAN Airlines.
Alliance with Mexicana (qv)
Fleet: 4 Boeing 767 Freighter; 1 Boeing 737-200

LAN EXPRESS
Incorporated: 1958
LAN Express is based on the former Ladeco, Chile's second largest airline. It was acquired by the then LANChile in 1995 and in 1998 merged with another group company, FastAir. Originally founded as a domestic airline, Ladeco expanded into international services, with an alliance with PanAm, at the time one of the leading US airlines, operating Boeing 707s on the international routes and BAe One-Elevens on the domestic routes. At the time of the acquisition, all of the main cities in Chile were on the route network. Under its new ownership, LAN Express is fundamentally a Chilean domestic airline with a few cross-border routes into Argentina.

HQ airport & main base: Santiago de Chile
Radio callsign: LAN EXPRESS
Designator: LU/LCO
Route points: Antofagasta, Arica, Balmaceda, Calama, Concepcion, Iquique, La Serena, Mendoza, Neuquin, New York, Puerto Montt, Punta Arenas, San Jose, San Juan, Santiago, Temuco, Ushaja, Valdivia, Vina del Mar
Links with other airlines: Part of the LAN Airlines group which has a 94.4 per cent stake
Fleet: 4 Airbus A320-200; 6 Boeing 737-200; 2 Airbus A319-100

SKY AIRLINE
Incorporated: 2001

Owned by the two directors, Sky Airline was formed in late 2001 and has developed a network of scheduled domestic services within Chile, running north and south from the capital, Santiago. Passenger charter flights are also operated. It operates an all-Boeing 737 fleet.

HQ airport & main base: Santiago Arturo Merino Benitez
Designator: H2/SKU
Route points: Antofagasta, Arica, Balmaceda, Calama, Concepcion, Iquique, Puerto Montt, Punta Arenas, Santiago de Chile, Temuco
Fleet: 1 Airbus A320-200; 8 Boeing 737-200

CHINA (PEOPLE'S REPUBLIC OF) – B

For many years the development of commercial aviation in China was inhibited by the internal divisions and unrest within the country, aggravated by Japanese intervention during the 1930s, even before the outbreak of the Second World War. Postwar, and post-Communist takeover, a new airline was established in cooperation with the Soviet Union, as well as another airline completely under Chinese control. Growing tension between China and the USSR resulted in the loss of the Soviet link, and the merging of the Soviet-backed Skoga and the Chinese Civil Aviation Corporation in 1964 to create a new airline, Civil Aviation Administration of China, CAAC, which was a typical bureaucratic, all-embracing, air transport organisation. The break-up of CAAC in 1988 led to the creation of first Air China, and then a large number of other airlines, some of which have survived and others of which have fallen by the wayside.

Even before the creation of Air China, CAAC had purchased Western aircraft, no doubt due largely to the lack of supplies from the USSR and also the absence of suitable Chinese-produced types. Initially, the United States was reluctant to trade with China, but this obstacle was overcome, possibly since the country was seen as an ally against the USSR during the Cold War. Despite the familiarity with Western equipment, in the period immediately after the break-up of the CAAC, air safety became a concern along with a shortage of experienced air and ground crew, as the new airlines expanded rapidly, and at one stage the authorities banned further orders for new aircraft until the existing types had been fully absorbed.

The integration of the former British colony of Hong Kong and the former Portuguese colony of Macau into China, albeit with special administrative dispensations, has meant that the Chinese civil aviation scene now embraces airlines with a Western background, most notably in the case of Cathay Pacific. Both Hong Kong and Macau are still taken separately at the end of the section on China.

Despite the short period since the end of the CAAC, the Chinese air transport industry has matured quickly. The major airlines have feeder and regional subsidiaries or associates, and specialised cargo operations are also present. Nevertheless, despite the prosperity of such places as Hong Kong and, within mainland China, Shanghai, and the regions bordering them, much of the country is still poor. Poverty and strict political control, despite burgeoning private enterprise, mean that many of the other aspects of civil aviation well established in the West, such as inclusive tour charter airlines, are unlikely to emerge in the foreseeable future. There has also been some rationalisation, with the disappearance, for example, of Air Great Wall into China Eastern Airlines, and the demise of the large China Northern Airlines, while the links between Air China, China Eastern and China Southern are set to strengthen.

Meanwhile, airlines have appeared, such as Hainan and Shanghai, that have no connection with the old CAAC and are completely independent.

AIR CHINA
Incorporated: 1988

Air China dates from 1988, when the Chinese government decided to reorganise and break up the former CAAC, Civil Aviation Administration of China, which had run the Chinese national airline of that name and almost everything else connected with civil aviation. Today, CAAC is purely an administrative body with responsibility for controlling Chinese civil aviation.

CAAC itself had dated from 1964, when it took over the merged operations of Skoga, a joint Soviet Union–Communist Chinese airline dating from 1950, and the China Civil Aviation Corporation, a wholly Chinese-owned domestic airline. The Soviet interest in Skoga was lost in the takeover, which had followed years of increasing tension between the two countries, and which also meant that the new CAAC was soon operating not only a very mixed fleet, but also a very elderly one. While utility aircraft were built in China to Soviet designs, China looked to the West for new equipment, buying Hawker Siddeley Tridents and Boeing 707-320s, which augmented an earlier purchase of Vickers Viscounts.

After 1988, Air China became the main domestic trunk and international carrier, while other parts of the former CAAC were spun off into regional carriers, many of which soon began to operate international services and even to appear on certain domestic trunk routes. The need to modernise soon saw more American and European aircraft appear in service, not simply because of tensions with the former Soviet Union and its successors, but because of the superior operating economics of these aircraft. Route expansion also followed, so that today Air China serves thirty cities in twenty-three countries. Reflecting a more liberal economic outlook, the airline received a stock exchange listing in both London and Hong Kong during 2000, but the majority shareholding is still that of the Chinese government through China National Aviation Holding, with 69 per cent, while Cathay Pacific has 10 per cent. Air China has in turn investments in other airlines, including Air China Cargo, 51 per cent, Shenzen Airlines, 25 per cent, and Shandong Airlines, 22.8 per cent. Today, it is the twenty-third largest airline in the world by annual turnover, and nineteenth by passenger figures, making it China's largest airline by sales, but lagging behind China Southern Airlines in passenger numbers.

HQ airport & main base: Beijing Capital International
Radio callsign: AIR CHINA
Designator: CA/CCA
Employees: 29,000
Route points: Amsterdam, Bangda, Bangkok, Baotou, Beihai, Beijing, Belgrade, Berlin, Changchun, Changsha, Changzhou, Chengdu, Chicago, Chongqing, Copenhagen, Daegu, Dalian, Datong, Daxian, Dayong, Doha, Dubai, Frankfurt, Fukuoka, Fuzhou, Golmud, Guangzhou, Guilin, Guiyang, Haikou, Hailar, Hangzhou, Harbin, Hefei,

Helsinki, Hiroshima, Hohhot, Hong Kong, Istanbul, Jakarta, Ji An, Jinan, Jinghong, Karachi, Kuala Lumpur, Kunming, Kuwait, Lanzhou, Lhasa, Lijang, Linyi, London, Los Angeles, Luxi, Luzhou, Macao, Melbourne, Mian Yang, Milan, Moscow, Mudanjiang, Munich, Nagoya, Nanchang, Nanking, Nanning, Nantong, New York-JFK, Ningbo, Nuremberg, Osaka, Pan Zhi Hua, Paris-CDG, Qingdao, Rome, San Francisco, Sanya, Sendai, Seoul, Shanghai, Shantou, Shenyang, Shenzen, Singapore, Song Pan, Stockholm, Sydney, Taiyuan, Tianjing, Tel Aviv, Tokyo, Tongliao, Ulan Bator, Urumqi, Vancouver, Vienna, Wanxian, Washington, Wenzhou, Wuhan, Xiamen, Xian, Xiangfan, Xichang, Xilinhot, Xingyi, Xining, Yangi, Yantai, Yibin, Yinchun, Yun Cheng, Zhengzhou
Links with other airlines: Alliances with Air Macau, All Nippon Airways, Asiana Airlines, Austrian, Cathay Pacific, Dragonair, Finnair, Korean Air, Lufthansa, Qatar Airways, Scandinavian Airlines, Shanghai Airlines, THY Turkish Airlines, United Airlines (all qv)
Annual turnover: US $4,050 million (£2,700 million)
Fleet: 4 Boeing 747-400; 8 Boeing 747-400 Combi; 6 Airbus A340-300; 10 Boeing 777-200; 20 Airbus A330-200; 4 Boeing 767-300; 5 Boeing 767-300ER; 5 Boeing 767-200ER; 13 Boeing 757-200; 24 Airbus A321-200; 6 Airbus A320-200; 26 Airbus A319-100; 34 Boeing 737-800; 6 Boeing 737-400; 15 Boeing 737-700; 30 Boeing 737-300; 5 Antonov An-24 (On order: 15 Boeing 787-8)

AIR CHINA CARGO
Incorporated: 2003

Originating in 1994 as the cargo department of Air China, Air China Cargo was founded in 2003, probably a reflection of the increasing success of Chinese manufacturing industry.

HQ airport & main base: Beijing Capital International, with base also at Shanghai Pudong International
Radio callsign: AIR CHINA
Designator: CA/CAO
Employees: 1,800
Route points: Beijing, Chengdu, Chongqing, Frankfurt, Guiyang, Hangzhou, Hong Kong, Hot Springs, Los Angeles, New York, San Francisco, Shanghai, Tianjin-Zhang, Tokyo
Links with other airlines: Ownership is divided between Air China (qv) with 51 per cent, Citic Pacific with 25 per cent and Beijing Capital International with 24 per cent. Air China has a controlling interest
Fleet: 5 Boeing 747-400F; 4 Boeing 747-200F

CHANGAN AIRLINES
Incorporated: 1992

Changan Airlines was registered in 1992 as Air Changan, and commenced regional scheduled passenger services the following year. It is effectively a subsidiary of Hainan Airlines, which has 73.5 per cent of its shares, and in turn owns Shanxi Airlines.

HQ airport & main base: Xian Xianyang International
Designator: CGN
Route points: Xian and Yinchuan Donghe, with destinations in Shanxi and adjoining provinces
Links with other airlines: Hainan (qv) has 73.5 per cent of the shares. Owns Shanxi Airlines (qv)
Fleet: 4 Boeing 737-800; 2 Boeing 737-700; 3 Airbus A319-100

CHINA CARGO AIRLINES
Incorporated: 1998

China Cargo Airlines was founded in 1998, mainly by China Eastern Airlines, which has 70 per cent of the shares, with the China Ocean Shipping Company having the remainder. It is mainland China's first all-cargo airline and its basic route structure initially was that of its main shareholder. At first, it used aircraft from China Eastern, but is now assembling a fleet of its own.

HQ airport & main base: Shanghai Hongqiao International
Designator: CK/CKK
Route points: Anchorage, Beijing, Chicago, Dallas, Los Angeles, Luxembourg, New York, Paris, San Francisco, Seattle, Shanghai
Links with other airlines: China Eastern (qv) has a 70 per cent shareholding
Fleet: 2 Boeing 747-400ERF; 6 McDonnell Douglas MD-11F

CHINA EASTERN
China Eastern Airlines
Incorporated: 1988

One of the remnants of the former CAAC, China Eastern was formed in 1988, and at first ownership remained with the Chinese government. Shanghai-based, the airline has undergone considerable expansion, especially on international services, reflecting a more relaxed economic regime in Shanghai and the surrounding area, where foreign investment in industry has been encouraged. In 1997, the airline floated on both the New York and Hong Kong stock exchanges, the first mainland Chinese airline to do so, selling 32 per cent of its stock to private investors and making the raising of funds for future expansion easier. In 1998, it formed mainland China's first all-cargo airline, China Cargo Airlines.

In recent years, China Eastern has become the thirty-eighth largest airline in the world by revenue, and twenty-fifth by passenger numbers, helped by the acquisition of Air Great Wall in 2001. Air Great Wall had been formed in 1992 by the Civil Aviation Flying Institute of China, and operated regional services mainly in Sichuan province, with its base at Chongqing. In addition, China Eastern has a large number of subsidiaries.

HQ airport & main base: Shanghai Hongqiao International Airport
Radio callsign: CHINA EASTERN
Designator: MU/CES
Employees: 20,817
Route points: Bangkok, Baoshan, Baotou, Beijing, Belhai, Busan, Changdun, Changde, Changsha, Chengdu, Cheongiu, Chongqing, Daegu, Dali City, Dalian, Dayong, Delhi, Dhaka, Diqing, Fukuoka, Fukushima, Guangzhou, Guilin, Guiyang, Gwangui, Haikou, Hangzhou, Harbin, Hefei, Hiroshima, Ho Chi Minh City, Hohhot, Hong Kong, Huangyan, Jeju, Jinan, Jinghong, Jinjang, Kagoshima, Komatsu, Kuala Lumpur, Kunming, Lanzhou, Lhasa, Lianyungang, Lijang, Lincang, Liuzhou, London, Los Angeles, Luoyang, Luxi, Luzhou, Madrid, Mandalay, Matsuyama, Melbourne, Moscow, Nagasaki, Nagoya, Nanchang, Nanjing, Nanning, Niigata, Ningbo, Okayama, Okinawa, Osaka, Pan Zhi Hua, Paris, Phuket, Qindao, Saipan, Sanya, Sapporo, Seoul, Shanghai, Shantou, Shenyang, Shijiazhuang, Siem Reap, Simao, Singapore, Sydney, Taiyan, Tianjin, Tokyo, Tunxi, Urumqi, Vancouver, Vientiane, Wenzhou, Wuhan, Wuxi, Xiamen, Xian, Xining, Xuzhou, Yancheng, Yantai, Yibin, Yinchuan, Zhaotong, Zhengzhou, Zhoushan
Links with other airlines: Has 100 per cent stake in China Eastern Xi Bei, 96 per cent in China Eastern Wuhan, 70 per cent in China Cargo Airlines and 63 per cent in China Eastern Airlines Jiangsu (all qv). Alliances with Air Europa, Air France, American Airlines, Asiana Airlines, China Eastern Yunnan Airlines, Japan Airlines, Korean Air, Qantas Airways, Thai Airways (all qv)
Fleet: 5 Airbus A340-600; 5 Airbus A340-300; 15 Airbus A330-300; 5 Airbus A330-200; 9 Airbus A300-600R; 3 Airbus A310-200; 3 Boeing 767-300ER; 15 Airbus A321-200; 8 Boeing 737-800; 43 Boeing 737-700; 25 Boeing 737-300; 87 Airbus A320-200; 25 Airbus A319-100; 9 McDonnell Douglas MD-90-30; 3 McDonnell Douglas MD-82; 4 BAe 146-300; 2 BAe 146-100; 7 Antonov An-24; 2 Bombardier CRJ200LR; 10 Embraer ERJ-145 (On order: 15 Boeing 787-8)

CHINA EASTERN AIRLINES JIANGSU

Incorporated: 1993

Owned 63 per cent by China Eastern Airlines, China Eastern Airlines Jiangsu is a regional feeder airline using aircraft from the fleet of China Eastern and founded in 1993. Services are provided from its hub and main base at Nanjing, mainly throughout Jiangsu province, whose government owns 24 per cent of the shares.

HQ airport & main base: Nanjing International
Designator: CJI
Route points: Included in China Eastern Airlines network
Links with other airlines: China Eastern Airlines (qv) has a 63 per cent stake
Fleet: Uses aircraft from the China Eastern Airlines fleet – usually BAe, Embraer and Bombardier types

CHINA EASTERN AIRLINES WUHAN

Incorporated: 1986

A subsidiary of China Eastern Airlines, which owns 96 per cent of the shares, China Eastern Airlines Wuhan was founded and commenced operations in 1986 as Air Wuhan. In 1997, it became a member of the Chinese regional airline Xinxing, New Star, alliance. It was not taken over by China Eastern until 2002, at which time it was operating a mixed Boeing and Chinese fleet. It now uses aircraft from the China Eastern fleet, operating a network of regional services from Wuhan in Hubei province, as well as an international route to Thailand.

HQ airport & main base: Wuhan Nanhu
Designator: WU/CWU
Route points: Included in China Eastern network
Links with other airlines: China Eastern (qv) owns 96 per cent of the shares
Fleet: Uses aircraft from the China Eastern fleet

CHINA EASTERN AIRLINES XI BEI
Incorporated: 1989

Originally formed from CAAC as China Northwest Airlines in 1989, it acquired an 80 per cent interest in Nanjing Airlines in 1996, before being taken over by China Eastern Airlines in 2002. By the time of the takeover, the airline was substantially operating from Xian, with more than seventy routes, including international services to Macau, Nagoya and Singapore, and services to Hong Kong, now an autonomous region within China. Before the takeover, China Northwest is believed to have applied for authority to operate to Bangkok. While the fleet already included European aircraft, a number of Russian and Chinese types were also operated. Since the takeover, aircraft are operated from the China Eastern fleet, and the route network is included in that of the parent airline.

HQ airport & main base: Xain, Shanxi Province
Radio callsign: CHINA NORTHWEST
Designator: WH /CNW
Route points: In China Eastern network
Links with other airlines: 100 per cent owned by China Eastern (qv). Has an 80 per cent stake in Nanjing Airlines
Fleet: Uses China Eastern fleet

CHINA EASTERN AIRLINES YUNNAN
Incorporated: 1992

Another airline created out of the break-up of the former Civil Aviation Administration of China and owned by China Eastern Airlines since 2002, China Eastern Airlines Yunnan operates regional and feeder services, primarily in Yunnan province.

HQ airport & main base: Kunming Wujiaba
Designator: 3Q/CYH
Route points: In China Eastern network
Links with other airlines: China Eastern Airlines (qv) owns the airline
Fleet: Uses aircraft from the China Eastern fleet

CHINA FLYING DRAGON
Feilong Airlines
Incorporated: 1981

One of the few airlines to precede the break-up of CAAC, China Flying Dragon, or Feilong Airlines, was established in 1981 by the Harbin Aircraft Manufacturing Corporation and the Ministry of Geological Mineral Resources, to operate short-haul passenger and cargo flights. Initially operations were linked into the founders' business activities, but the airline now operates on a more commercial basis. Maritime surveillance, forestry protection and aerial photographic duties are also undertaken. It has recently disposed of its Twin Otter fleet.

HQ airport & main base: Harbin
Radio callsign: FEILONG
Designator: CFA
Employees: 600
Route points: Primarily local operations
Fleet: 14 HAMC Y-11; 8 HAMC Y-12; 3 HAMC Z-9; 8 Eurocopter Ecureil

CHINA GENERAL AVIATION
China General Aviation Corporation
Incorporated: 1989

Another operator which has emerged from the former CAAC, China General Aviation Corporation is sometimes described as the only substantial general aviation concern in China, reflecting the broad diversity of CAAC's operations. While the company reflects Western ideas of 'general aviation' in some respects, with a fleet which includes Bell 212 and Eurocopter Bo-105 helicopters, as well as Beech Super King Airs, some aircraft in the fleet are larger, including the Antonov An-30s and Yakovlev Yak-42Ds. Again in contrast to Western ideas of general aviation, there is a scheduled network.

HQ airport & main base: Wu-SU Airport, Taiyuan, Shanxi
Radio callsign: TONGHANG
Designator: GP/CTH
Employees: 3,800
Route points: Domestic charter plus a scheduled network covering some 30 destinations
Fleet: 3 Antonov An-30; 7 Yakovlev Yak-42D; 5 HAMC Y-12; 8 SAP Y-5; 3 Xian Y-7-100; 10 Mil Mi-8; 5 de Havilland DHC-6 Twin Otter; 9 Bell 212; 2 Beech Super King Air 200; 2 Eurocopter Bo-105

CHINA POSTAL AIRLINES
Incorporated: 1997

Established in 1997 as a joint venture between the Chinese Postal Bureau and China Southern Airlines, the airline, as its title indicates, is engaged on scheduled mail and parcels operations. Given the size of the country and the small size of the airline, substantial expansion can be expected.

HQ airport & main base: Beijing
Designator: 8Y/CYZ
Route points: Beijing, Chengdu, Guangzhou, Shanghai, Shenyang, Shenzhen, Wuhan, Xiamen
Links with other airlines: China Southern Airlines (qv) has a 49 per cent stake
Fleet: 4 Boeing 737-300

CHINA SOUTHERN

China Southern Airlines
Incorporated: 1989

One of the largest Chinese airlines, but with its origins in the old CAAC, China Southern has an extensive route network which includes many international destinations, while the fleet shows Boeing and Airbus aircraft to be heavily represented. China Southern has a 60 per cent stake in Xiamen Airlines and 49 per cent of China Postal Airlines, which it helped to found. In addition to China Postal, stakes are also held in Guangxi Airlines, Guizhou Airlines, Shantou Airlines, Sichuan Airlines, Xiamen Airlines and Zuahai Airlines.

Today, China Southern is the thirty-first largest airline in the world by turnover, and fourteenth by passenger numbers. The number of employees has more than doubled over the past ten years.

HQ airport & main base: Guangzhou Baiyan
Radio callsign: CHINA SOUTHERN
Designator: CZ/CSN
Employees: 18, 221
Route points: Aksu, Almaty, Amsterdam, An Shun, Baku, Bangkok, Baoshan, Barcelona, Beihai, Beijing, Berlin, Bishkek, Busan, Changchun, Changsha, Changzhou, Chengdhu, Cheongiu, Chongqing, Copenhagen, Daegu, Dali City, Dalian, Dandong, Dayong, Diqing, Dubai, Dushanbe, Enshi, Frankfurt, Fukuoka, Fuzhou, Ganzhou, Guangzhou, Guilin, Guiyang, Haikou, Hangzhou, Hanoi, Hanover, Harbin, Hefei, Hiroshima, Ho Chi Minh City, Hong Kong, Hotan, Islamabad, Jakarta, Jeju, Jiamusi, Jinan, Jinghong, Jinjang, Johannesburg, Juzhou, Kashi, Korla, Kuala Lumpur, Kunming, Lanzhou, Laoag, Lhasa, Lianyungang, Lijang, Ling Ling, Lisbon, Liuzhou, London, Los Angeles, Madrid, Manila, Mei Xian, Melbourne, Milan, Mudanjiang, Munich, Nagoya, Nanchang, Nanchong, Nanking, Nanning, Nantong, Nigata, Ningbo, Novosibirsk, Osaka, Paris, Penang, Phnom Penh, Qiemo, Qingdao, Quilin, Rome, Saipan, Sanya, Sapporo, Sendai, Seoul, Shanghai, Shantou, Shashi, Shenyang, Shenzhen, Shijiazhuang, Singapore, Stockholm, Surabaya, Sydney, Taiyuan, Tashkent, Tianjin, Tokyo, Tongren, Toyama, Tunxi, Urumqi, Vientiane, Wenzhou, Wuhan, Wulumqi, Wuxi, Xiamen, Xain, Xiangfan, Xingyi, Xining, Xuzhou, Yanchen, Yanji, Yantai, Yichang, Yinchaun, Yining, Yiwu, Zhanjiang, Zhengzhou, Zhi Jiang, Zhuhai
Links with other airlines: Holds a 60 per cent stake in Xiamen Airlines (qv)
Fleet: 2 Boeing 747-400F; 6 Boeing 777-200ER; 4 Boeing 777-200; 8 Airbus A330-300; 6 Airbus A330-200; 6 Airbus A300-600R; 20 Boeing 757-200; 45 Airbus A321-200; 49 Boeing 737-800; 64 Airbus A320-200; 28 Boeing 737-700; 26 Boeing 737-300; 2 Boeing 737-300QC; 2 Boeing 737-500; 42 Airbus A319-100; 13 McDonnell Douglas MD-90-30; 15 McDonnell Douglas MD-82; 11 Antonov An-24; 5 ATR-72-500; 1 Cessna Caravan 675 (On order: 5 Airbus A380-800; 10 Boeing 787-8)

CHINA SOUTHWEST

China Southwest Airlines
Incorporated: 1989

By Chinese standards, a medium-sized airline, and another offshoot of CAAC, China Southwest is based at Chengdu in Sichuan. Scheduled and charter operations are undertaken, usually internally, but also to Lhasa in Tibet, an autonomous region, and Kathmandu in Nepal.

HQ airport & main base: Shuangliu Airport, Chengdu, Sichuan Province
Radio callsign: CHINA SOUTHWEST
Designator: SZ/CXN
Employees: 4,000
Main destinations served: More than 70 domestic routes from Chengdu, as well as Lhasa and Kathmandu
Fleet: 1 Boeing 707-320; 5 Tupolev Tu-154M; 13 Boeing 757-200; 20 Boeing 737-300; 4 HAMC Y-12; 3 XAC Y-7

CHINA UNITED

China United Airlines
Incorporated: 1986

Unusually, China United was not one of the airlines resulting from the break-up of CAAC, but instead was established as a unit of the Chinese Air Force, or Air Force of the People's Liberation Army, operating commercial air services in cooperation with local enterprises. Initially, most of the aircraft were of Soviet origin, but US and Canadian aircraft have taken over. Operations were suspended in

2003, but the airline was re-established in 2005 after being taken over by Shanghai Airlines and the China Import & Export Corporation.

HQ airport & main base: Beijing
Radio callsign: LIANHANG
Designator: HR/CUA
Route points: Few details other than entirely domestic, to around 50 destinations
Links with other airlines: Owned 50 per cent by Shanghai Airlines (qv)
Fleet: 2 Tupolev Tu-154M; 14 Ilyushin Il-76MD; 4 Boeing 737-700; 6 Boeing 737-300; 4 Antonov An-26; 1 Antonov An-24RV; 5 Bombardier CRJ700-701ER; 5 Bombardier CRJ100

CHINA XINGHUA AIRLINES
Incorporated: 1992

China Xinghua Airlines was founded in 1992 and began operations the following year. While the main business was scheduled and charter, passenger and cargo operations within China, in 1997 the airline was one of the founders of the Oriental Falcon Jet Service, to provide Dassault Falcon 50 business jet charters throughout China. The main shareholder is Hainan Airlines,with 60 per cent of the issued shares.

HQ airport & main base: Beijing Capital International, with a further base at Tianjun Zhang Guizhuang
Designator: XW/CXH
Route points: Domestic trunk scheduled services and charter flights from Beijing and Tianjun
Links with other airlines: Hainan Airlines (qv) owns 60 per cent
Fleet: 5 Boeing 737-800; 3 Boeing 737-400; 6 Boeing 737-300

HAINAN AIRLINES
Incorporated: 1989

One of the few truly private-enterprise airlines in China, with some ten shareholders including American investors, Hainan Airlines was formed in 1989, but operations did not start until 1993. While scheduled services are operated, the airline also undertakes charters, including executive jet charters. The airline was the first domestic Chinese airline to seek a stock market listing, in this case on the Shanghai Stock Exchange. It later became the first Chinese airline to buy shares in an airport, with a 25 per cent stake in Haikou Meilan International. It also has extensive investments in other Chinese airlines, as detailed below, while it has grown substantially over the past decade.

HQ airport & main base: HQ at Haikou, with bases at Ningbo and Xian
Radio callsign: HAINAN
Designator: H4/CHH
Employees: 8,800
Route points: Bangkok, Baotou, Beijing, Budapest, Changchun, Changdu, Changsha, Changzhi, Chengdu, Chifeng, Chongqing, Dalian, Datong, Dongying, Dunhuang, Enshi, Fuzhou, Guangzhou, Guillin, Guiyang, Haikou, Hailar, Hangzou, Hanzhong, Harbin, Hefei, Hohhot, Hong Kong, Jaimusi, Jinan, Jingdezhen, Kashi, Kuala Lumpur, Kunming, Lanzhou, Manzhouli, Nanchang, Nanjing, Nanning, Ningbo, Osaka, Qingyang, Qintao, Qiqhar, Sanya, Seoul, Shanghai, Shantou, Shenyang, Shenzhen, Shijiazhuang, Taiyuan, Tianjin, Tokyo, Tongliao, Ulanhot, Urumqi, Weifang, Weihei, Wenzhou, Wu Hai, Wuhan, Xiamen, Xian, Xilinhot, Xining, Xuzhou, Yan'an, Yancheng, Yichang, Yinchuan, Yulin, Zhanjiang, Zhengzhou
Links with other airlines: Has shareholdings in Shanxi Airlines, 92.5 per cent; Changan Airlines, 73.5 per cent; China Xinhua Airlines, 60 per cent; Yangtze River Express, 51 per cent (all qv); Shilin Airlines, 48.9 per cent, as well as smaller investments in Dee Jet and Lucky Air. Alliances with Japan Airlines, Malev (both qv)
Fleet: 7 Airbus A330-200; 5 Boeing 767-300ER; 46 Boeing 737-800; 26 Airbus A319-100; 28 Dornier 328Jet (On order: 8 Boeing 787-8; 50 Embraer 190LR/AR; 50 Harbin Embraer GRJ-145)

JADE CARGO INTERNATIONAL
Incorporated: 2006

Jade Cargo International is a joint venture between Shenzhen Airlines,with 51 per cent, Lufthansa Cargo with 25 per cent, and other investors, to provide air cargo charters and, eventually, scheduled services linking into the route networks of the two shareholding airlines.

HQ airport & main base: Shenzhen Baoan International
Designator: J1/JAE:
Employees: 75
Links with other airlines: Shenzhen Airlines (qv) has a 51 per cent stake. Lufthansa Cargo (qv) has a 25 per cent stake
Fleet: 6 Boeing 747-400ERF

SHANDONG AIRLINES
Incorporated: 1994

Shandong Airlines was founded in 1994 in China's Shan Song Province, primarily as a regional carrier and feeder into the services of the main Chinese airlines. A small international network has since been established. Air China has a 22.8 per cent stake, while Shandong in turn has a 10 per cent stake in Sichuan Airlines. The airline was one of six Chinese regional airlines to form the Xinxing Aviation Alliance in 1997.

HQ airport & main base: Jinan Yaoqiang
Radio callsign: SHANDONG
Designator: SC/CDG
Employees: 1,400
Route points: Beijing, Changchun, Changsha, Chengdu, Chongqing, Dalian, Fuzhou, Guangzhou, Guilin, Guiyang, Haikou, Hangzhou, Harbin, Hefei, Heihe, Hohhot, Hong Kong, Jiamusi, Jinan, Kunming, Lanzhou, Linyi, Manzhouli, Mudanjiang, Nanking, Nanning, Ningbo, Qingdao, Seoul, Shanghai, Shenyang, Shenzhen, Simao, Singapore, Taiyan, Tianjing, Urumqi, Weihai, Wenzhou, Wuhan, Xiamen, Xian, Yantai, Yinchuan
Links with other airlines: Air China (qv) owns 22.8 per cent of the shares. Shandong has a 10 per cent stake in Sichuan (qv). Part of the Xinxing Aviation Alliance
Fleet: 18 Boeing 737-800; 3 Boeing 737-700; 14 Boeing 737-300; 2 Bombardier CRJ700-701ER; 8 Bombardier CRJ200LR

SHANGHAI AIRLINES
Incorporated: 1985

Claiming to be the first airline in China independent of any CAAC origins, Shanghai Airlines is a mixed venture airline, and was originally owned 75 per cent by the provincial government of Shanghai and 25 per cent by private interests. In 2002, the airline was floated on the Shanghai Stock Exchange so that today, 44.7 per cent of the shares are held by the public, another 41 per cent by the Alliance Investment group, and the remainder by the state-owned Bank of China. Services are mainly domestic, although international flights have been operated since 1997, and are almost all scheduled. The airline was involved in the rescue and recovery of China United Airlines.

HQ airport & main base: Shanghai Pudong International
Radio callsign: SHANGHAI AIR
Designator: SF /CSH
Route points: Baotou, Beijing, Changchu, Changsha, Chengdu, Chongqing, Dalian, Dayong, Diqing, Fuzhou, Guangzhou, Guilin, Guiyang, Haikou, Hangzhou, Harbin, Hefei, Hohhot, Jinan, Jinghong, Jinzhou, Kunming, Lanzhou, Lijang, Nanchang, Nanking, Nanning, Ningbo, Qingdao, Sanya, Shanghai, Shantou, Shenyang, Shenzhen, Shijiazhunag, Taiyan, Tianjin, Tunix, Urumqi, Wanxian, Weihei, Wenzhou, Wuhan, Wuxi, Xiamen, Xian, Xianfan, Xining, Xuzhou, Yanji, Yantai, Yichang, Yinchang, Yinchuan, Yun Cheng, Zhengzhou, Zhubai
Links with other airlines: Owns 50 per cent of Shanghai Airlines Cargo. Owns 10 per cent of Sichuan Airlines (qv). Alliances with Air China, All Nippon Airways, Lufthansa (all qv)
Fleet: 1 McDonnell Douglas MD-11F; 7 Boeing 767-300ER; 13 Boeing 757-200; 34 Boeing 737-800; 5 Airbus A321-200; 6 Boeing 737-700; 5 Bombardier CRJ200LR (On order: 9 Boeing 787-8)

SHANXI AIRLINES
Incorporated: 2001

Formed in 2001 as a charter airline, which has since been taken over by Jainan Airlines in a state-sponsored rationalisation of the smaller Chinese airlines. A subsidiary is Lucky Air.

HQ airport & main base: Taiyan Wusu
Radio callsign: SHANXI
Designator: 8C/CXI
Links with other airlines: Hainan Airlines (qv) has a 92.5 per cent interest
Fleet: 1 Boeing 737-800; 3 Boeing 737-700; 1 Dornier 328 Jet

SHENZHEN AIRLINES
Incorporated: 1993

Shenzhen Airlines was formed in 1993 by CAAC and the provincial government as a regional carrier, but now operates to many of the more important destinations and has a couple of international services. It is now owned by a number of investment and transport undertakings, including Air China, which has a 25 per cent stake, and has expanded considerably over the past decade from a fleet of just five Boeing 737s.

HQ airport & main base: Shenzhen Huangtian
Radio callsign: SHENZHEN AIR

Designator: ZH/CSZ
Route points: Beihei, Beijing, Changchun, Changde, Changsha, Changzhou, Chengdu, Chongqing, Dalian, Fuzhou, Guangzhou, Guilin, Guiyang, Haikou, Hangzhou, Harbin, Hefei, Hohhot, Huangyan, Jinan, Jingdezhen, Kuala Lumpur, Kunming, Lanzhou, Lijang, Nanchang, Nanking, Nanning, Qingdao, Sanya, Seoul, Shanghai, Shenyang, Shijiazhuang, Taiyuan, Tianjin, Tunxi, Urumqi, Wenzhou, Wuhan, Wuiyshan, Wuxi, Xiamen, Xian, Xiangfan, Yichang, Yinchuan, Yun Cheng, Zhanjiang, Zhengzhou
Fleet: 5 Boeing 737-900; 20 Boeing 737-800; 10 Boeing 737-700; 9 Boeing 737-300; 19 Airbus A320-200; 5 Airbus A319-100

SICHUAN AIRLINES
Incorporated: 1986

Founded in 1986, with operations starting in 1988, Sichuan Airlines is based at Chengdu in Sichuan Province. Following a restructuring in 2002, ownership is divided between the Sichuan Airlines Group, owned entirely by the provincial government, with 40 per cent, China Southern Airlines with 39 per cent, and with both Shandong Airlines and Shanghai Airlines each having 10 per cent.

HQ airport & main base: Chengdu Shuangliu
Radio callsign: CHUANHANG
Designator: 3U/CSC
Employees: 1,844
Route points: Beijing, Chengdu, Chongqing, Dali City, Dalian, Dayong, Guangzhou, Guiyang, Haikou, Hangzhou, Harbin, Hohhot, Hong Kong, Jinan, Jinghong, Kunming, Lanzhou, Lhasa, Lijang, Nanchang, Nanking, Nanning, Ningbo, Pan Zhi Hua, Sanya, Shanghai, Shenzhen, Shijiazhunag, Son Pan, Tianjin, Tongren, Wanxian, Wenzhou, Xiamen, Xian, Xichang, Xining, Xuzhou, Yichang, Yinchang, Yinchuan
Links with other airlines: China Southern Airlines has a 39 per cent stake. Shanghai Airlines and Shandong Airlines each has 10 per cent (all qv)
Fleet: 6 Airbus A321-200; 4 Airbus A321-100; 18 Airbus A320-200; 6 Airbus A319-100; 5 Embraer ERJ-145LR

XIAMEN AIRLINES
Incorporated: 1992

Founded in 1992 and operating scheduled and charter flights from Xiamen in Fuijan Province, Xiamen Airlines has China Southern Airlines as its main shareholder, with 60 per cent of the airline's shares. The airline has grown considerably in recent years, with employee numbers more than doubling and the fleet size trebling.

HQ airport & main base: Xiamen Gaoqi International Airport, Fuijan
Radio callsign: XIAMEN AIR
Designator: MF/CXA
Employees: 4,550
Route points: Beijing, Changchun, Changsha, Changzhou, Chengdu, Chongqing, Dalian, Fuzhou, Guangzhou, Guilin, Guiyang, Haikou, Hangzhou, Harbin, Hefei, Jinan, Jinjang, Kunming, Lanzhou, Nanchang, Nanking, Nanning, Ningbo, Qindao, Sanya, Shanghai, Shenyang, Shenzhen, Shijiazhuang, Taiyuan, Tianjin, Urumqi, Wenzhou, Wuhan, Wuyishan, Xiamen, Xian, Zhengzhou, Zhoushan, Zhuhai
Links with other airlines: China Southern (qv) has a 60 per cent shareholding
Fleet: 41 Boeing 737-800; 15 Boeing 737-700; 4 Boeing 737-300; 9 Boeing 737-200; 6 Boeing 737-500 (On order: 3 Boeing 787-8)

YANGTZE RIVER EXPRESS
Incorporated: 2003

Sounding more like a high-speed ferry service, Yangtze River Express is a cargo airline flying ad hoc and contract charters, including a Chinese internal network for UPS. Hainan Airlines has a 51 per cent stake, while China Airlines acquired a 25 per cent interest in 2005. The other shareholders are shipping companies.

HQ airport & main base: Shanghai
Designator: Y8/YZR
Links with other airlines: Hainan Airlines has a 51 per cent stake, while China Airlines has 25 per cent. Operates under contract to UPS (all qv)
Fleet: 6 Boeing 737-300QC

CHINA (HONG KONG SPECIAL ADMINISTRATIVE REGION) – VR-H

AIR HONG KONG
Air Hong Kong Ltd
Incorporated: 1988

Originally formed as a cargo charter operator, Air Hong Kong started scheduled cargo operations in 1989, initially operating to Manchester and Nagoya.

Cathay Pacific took a 75 per cent interest in the airline and had a management contract, as well as providing three leased Boeing 747-200 freighters, but when Cathay entered a business partnership with DHL in 2002, the shareholding was reduced to 60 per cent with DHL holding the remainder. Air Hong Kong operates certain services for Cathay and DHL, with the intention of collaborating in developing the Asian air freight market. Air Hong Kong was the launch customer for the Airbus A300-600F freighter.

HQ airport & main base: Hong Kong – Chek Lap Kok
Designator: LD/AHK
Route points: Bangkok, Hong Kong, Osaka, Penang, Seoul, Singapore, Taipei, Tokyo
Links with other airlines: Cathay Pacific has a 60 per cent shareholding. DHL has a 40 per cent shareholding (both qv)
Fleet: 9 Airbus A300-600F

CATHAY PACIFIC
Cathay Pacific Airways Ltd
Incorporated: 1947

Although incorporated in 1947, Cathay Pacific's history started two years earlier, in October 1945, when an American, Roy Farrell, who had flown supplies during the Second World War over the 'hump' between India and China, bought a war-surplus Douglas C-47, which he had converted to DC-3 airliner standard. After arriving in Shanghai with the aircraft's first cargo from the United States, Farrell met a former wartime China National Aviation Company colleague, an Australian, Sydney de Krantzow, and the two formed a partnership, flying woollen goods from Australia to China. The business was sufficiently successful for a second DC-3 to be obtained in 1946. Nevertheless, local rivalry led the partners to move to Hong Kong, where Cathay Pacific was founded in 1947.

Initially, the airline operated charter passenger and freight flights from its new base, mainly to Manila, Macau, Bangkok and Singapore, although on occasion the aircraft ranged as far afield as Australia and even the United Kingdom. Five more DC-3s were pressed into service before the year was out, along with two Consolidated Catalina flying boats, although flying-boat operations were abandoned after an aircraft was hijacked, and in the accident which followed all but one of the occupants and the aircraft were lost.

By 1948, the airline was facing competition from Hong Kong Airways, formed by the local trading house of Jardine Matheson and BOAC, British Overseas Airways Corporation, with both airlines fighting to obtain licences for scheduled services. Another of Hong Kong's trading companies came to the rescue, investing in Cathay Pacific, with the support of Australian National Airways. The new Cathay Pacific was owned 45 per cent by Butterfield and Swire, predecessors of today's Swire Group, 35 per cent by ANA, one of the predecessors of Ansett, and with the founders having 10 per cent each. The battle for route licences was resolved by the Hong Kong government's proposal that the available licences be divided among the two companies, with Hong Kong Airways taking those to China and Japan, and Cathay Pacific taking Bangkok, Manila and Singapore. Given the political upheavals taking place in mainland China, the choice was fortunate for Cathay.

With the security of strong backing and lucrative routes, Cathay started a programme of steady expansion. In 1949, Douglas DC-4s were introduced, and in 1950, a maintenance subsidiary, Hong Kong Aircraft Engineering Company or HAECO, was established. P&O, the major British shipping group, bought a shareholding in 1954. Four years later, the airline bought its first new aircraft, Douglas DC-6Bs, introducing pressurised comfort and the safety of radar to its services. By this time, the route network had reached Calcutta in India. In 1959, Cathay purchased its rival, Hong Kong Airways, and introduced its first turboprop aircraft, two Lockheed L-188A Electras.

Faced with strong competition from jet aircraft, including Qantas Boeing 707-120s which forced Cathay off the Sydney service in 1961, Convair 880 Coronado jet airliners were introduced. Nevertheless, having faced competition from a major state-owned airline, for the next decade Cathay became predominantly a regional carrier, ranging as far afield as Calcutta, Kuala Lumpur and Singapore to the west, Seoul and Tokyo to the east, and Manila to the south. Between 1962 and 1967, the airline enjoyed growth of 20 per cent per year, operating a fleet which consisted of just five Convair 880s, although three more were soon added.

Cathay started to break out of the region in 1970, when Perth was added to the route network. Boeing 707-320s were introduced to complement and then replace the Convairs, and later flights to Sydney were resumed. Ten 707s were eventually operated, before being replaced by Lockheed L-1011 TriStars, and then later, in 1979, the airline obtained its first Boeing 747, a 747-200. The next few years saw Cathay move into intercontinental services, with services to London introduced in 1980, Brisbane in 1982, Frankfurt and Vancouver in 1984, Amsterdam, Rome and San Francisco in 1986, Paris in 1987, Zurich in 1988, and Manchester in 1989. Frequencies to its traditional Asian destinations also increased sharply.

More recently, Cathay has become a major operator of Airbus A330 and A340s and the Boeing 777 and Boeing 747-400, and during 1997–8 equipped its fleet with the Future Air Navigation Systems, FANS. The P&O and ANA involvement with the airline are both long past, but the Swire Group remains the largest single shareholder at 45 per cent, with the Chinese government-backed CITIC having a 25 per cent stake. Cathay has interests in other airlines, Air Hong Kong, in which Cathay has a 60 per cent stake, and Dragonair, in which 18 per cent is held by Cathay, but in which the China National Aviation Corporation has taken a 35.9 per cent interest, while there is also a 10 per cent stake in Air China, the main Chinese carrier. Cathay is a member of the Oneworld alliance.

The transfer of Hong Kong's sovereignty to China in 1997 introduced a degree of uncertainty for the future, which was reflected in the traffic figures for the late 1990s. Despite assurances that the existing political and economic structures will remain in place for fifty years, the initial result post-transfer was a 40 per cent drop in air traffic to and from Hong Kong. Cathay itself reported a fall in traffic of around 12–13 per cent. Since then, traffic growth has recovered, and Cathay is now the twenty-second largest airline in the world by annual turnover, and thirty-second by passenger numbers, reflecting its role as a long-haul airline, but passenger numbers have risen by more than 30 per cent annually in recent years.

HQ airport & main base: Hong Kong Chek Lap Kok
Radio callsign: CATHAY
Designator: CX/CPA
Employees: 15,040
Route points: Adelaide, Amsterdam, Auckland, Bahrain, Bangkok, Barcelona, Beijing, Brisbane, Cairns, Cebu, Colombo, Delhi, Denpasar Bali, Dubai, Frankfurt, Fukuoka, Hanoi, Ho Chi Minh City, Hong Kong, Jakarta, Johannesburg, Karachi, Kuala Lumpur, London, Los Angeles, Madrid, Manchester, Manila, Melbourne, Moscow, Mumbai, Nagoya, New York, Osaka, Paris, Penang, Perth, Riyadh, Rome, San Francisco, Santiago, Sapporo, Seoul, Singapore, Surabaya, Sydney, Taipei, Tokyo, Toronto, Vancouver, Xiamen, Zurich
Links with other airlines: Member of the Oneworld alliance. Cathay has a 60 per cent interest in Air Hong Kong, and 18 per cent in Dragonair, as well as 10 per cent in Air China (all qv). 25 per cent interst in HAECO, Hong Kong Aircraft Engineering Company Ltd, as well as a 10 per cent stake in TAECO Engineering with Singapore Airlines and Japan Airlines. Alliances with Aeroflot Russian Airlines, Air China, Japan Airlines, Malaysian Airlines, Philippine Airlines, South African Airways, Vietnam Airlines (all qv)
Passengers carried: 13.7 million
Annual turnover: US $5,016 million (£3,380 million)
Fleet: 21 Boeing 747-400; 4 Boeing 747-400BCF; 7 Boeing 747-400F; 5 Boeing 777-200; 12 Boeing 777-300; 16 Boeing 777-300ER; 15 Airbus A340-300; 29 Airbus A330-300; 3 Airbus A340-600 (On order: 6 Boeing 747-400BRF; 18 Boeing 777-300GR)

CR AIRWAYS

Incorporated: 2003

The first and only new airline to be formed since Hong Kong passed into Chinese control, CR Airways was established as a charter airline but now also operates a limited number of scheduled services. It is owned 40 per cent by China Rich Holdings and 60 per cent by Robert Yip Kwong.

HQ airport & main base: Hong Kong Chep Lap Kok
Designator: N8/CRK
Route points: Guilin, Haikou, Hong Kong, Jinan, Kunming, Laoag, Luzon, Nanning, Sanya, Subic Bay
Fleet: 1 Boeing 737-800; 1 Bombardier CRJ700-701ER; 2 Bombardier CRJ200LR

DRAGONAIR

Hong Kong Dragon Airlines Ltd
Incorporated: 1985

Originally founded in 1985 as a regional carrier, initially concentrating on services between Hong Kong and China, a number of changes in the shareholders eventually led to Cathay Pacific and Swire Pacific taking a 30 per cent holding, while major shareholdings were also taken by China International Trust and Investment of China (CITIC) and the China National Aviation Corporation. Cathay now has just 18 per cent of Dragonair, with CNAC having more than 43 per cent.

In addition to services to China, the airline also operates a number of services to destinations in South-East Asia for Cathay Pacific, and has a growing international cargo network.The number of employees has more than doubled over the past decade, as has the number of aircraft.

HQ airport & main base: Hong Kong Chek Lap Kok
Radio callsign: DRAGONAIR
Designator: KA/HDA
Employees: 2,745
Route points: Bandar Seri Begawan, Bangkok, Beijing, Changsha, Chengdu, Chongqing, Dalian, Dhaka, Fuzhou, Guangzhou, Guilin, Haikou, Hangzhou, Hiroshima, Hong Kong, Kaohsiung, Kota Kinbalu, Kuching, Kunming, Nanjing, Ningbo, Phnom Penh, Phuket, Qingdao, Sanya, Sendai, Shanghai, Taipei, Tianjin, Tokyo, Wuhan, Xiamen, Xian
Links with other airlines: Cathay Pacific (qv) has an 18 per cent interest and provides commercial support. Alliances with Air China, China Southern Airlines, Malaysia Airlines, Royal Brunei Airlines (all qv)
Fleet: 1 Boeing 747-400BCF; 1 Boeing 747-400F; 3 Boeing 747-300SF; 1 Boeing 747-200F; 17 Airbus A330-300; 6 Airbus A321-200; 10 Airbus A320-200

OASIS HONG KONG
Oasis Hong Kong Airlines
Incorporated: 2005

Founded as a long-haul, low-cost airline, OASiS Hong Kong commenced operations between Hong Kong and London Gatwick in late 2006, and plans to introduce five more routes within the next year or two, most probably to Frankfurt in Germany, either Milan or Rome in Italy, and to the United States. A joint booking system with easyJet that would enable passengers to book connecting flights has been suggested, and if this goes ahead it will be a 'first' for low-fare operators.

HQ airport & main base: Hong Kong Chep Lap Kok
Radio callsign: OASIS
Designator: O8/OHK
Route points: Hong Kong, London Gatwick
Fleet: 2 Boeing 747-400

CHINA (MACAU SPECIAL ADMINISTRATIVE REGION) – B-M

AIR MACAU
Incorporated: 1994

Formed in 1994, Air Macau started operations in 1995, with the support of the Portuguese colonial authorities, who have declared that the airline will be the sole designated carrier for the colony for the next twenty-five years. Macau has followed Hong Kong in passing into Chinese authority in the future, but even before the transfer the China National Aviation Corporation had become the single largest shareholder, with 51 per cent, against just 5 per cent for the local administration, while that for TAP Portugal has fallen from 25 per cent to 20 per cent. A new route was opened from Macau to Beijing and Shanghai in November 2005. Since the turn of the century, the number of employees has almost doubled, while the fleet has also grown considerably, with a number of freighters and aircraft of mainly Airbus manufacture.

The airline plans to develop Macau as a hub for Asian air services using a new airport, perhaps taking traffic unable to use congested Hong Kong. It is also establishing a low-cost airline, Macau Asia Express, in which it has a 51 per cent interest.

HQ airport & main base: Macau International
Radio callsign: AIR MACAU
Designator: NX/AMU
Employees: 963
Route points: Bangkok, Beijing, Chengdu, Guilin, Haikou, Kaoshsiung, Kunming, Macao, Manila, Nanking, Qingdao, Sanya, Seoul, Shanghai, Shenzhen, Tapei, Wuhan, Xiamen
Links with other airlines: TAP Portugal has a 20 per cent shareholding. Alliances with Air China, Philippine Airlines (all qv)
Fleet: 1 Airbus A300-600R; 4 Airbus A300B4-200F; 3 Airbus A321-200; 4 Airbus A321-100; 1 Airbus A320-200; 5 Airbus A319-100; 1 Boeing 727-200F

COLOMBIA – HK

No Latin American country can claim as long a history of air transport as Colombia, with the national flag carrier, Avianca, tracing its origins back to 1919, as one of the oldest airlines in the world. As in many other South American countries, difficult surface conditions contributed to the appeal of air transport, despite Bogotá, the capital, being 9,000ft above sea level, and German interests were active in the country's air transport development during the early years.

AEROREPUBLICA
AeroRepublica SA
Incorporated: 1992

Founded in late 1992, AeroRepublica commenced operations the following year, operating internal scheduled and charter, passenger and cargo flights. Despite plans to operate scheduled services to the United States, the only international scheduled service at present is to Panama City. For many years, the airline had a mixed fleet of Boeing 727s and McDonnell Douglas DC-9s, but now has mainly aircraft in the McDonnell Douglas MD series. The Venezuelan airline, Aeropostal has a 33 per cent stake, while Copa Airlines is also a shareholder.

HQ airport & main base: Bogotá, with a second hub at Cali
Radio callsign: AEROREPUBLICA
Designator: 5P/RPB
Route points: Barranquilla, Bogotá, Bucaramanga, Cali, Cartagena, Cucuta, Leticia, Medellin, Monteria, Panama City, Pereira, San Andres Island, Santa Marta
Links with other airlines: Aeropostal has a 33 per cent stake, while Copa also has an interest (both qv)
Fleet: 3 McDonnell Douglas MD-83; 2 McDonnell Douglas MD-82; 5 McDonnell Douglas MD-81; 2 McDonnell Douglas DC-9-30; 8 Embraer E-190LR/AR

AEROSUCRE
Aerosucre SA
Incorporated: 1969

Originally founded in 1969 and starting operations the following year as a small, third-level operator on regional feeder services in the north of the country, Aerosucre moved into scheduled and charter cargo services, initially with two Handley Page Heralds, which were later joined by two Sud Caravelle jets. After the Heralds were retired, two Boeing 727-100Fs were introduced. Operations extend throughout the Americas. Today, the fleet is standardised on aircraft of Boeing manufacture.

HQ airport & main base: Barranquilla (airport), Bogotá Eldorado International (main base)
Radio callsign: AEROSUCRE
Designator: 6N/KRE
Fleet: 1 Boeing 727-200F; 2 Boeing 727-100F; 3 Boeing 737-200

AIRES COLOMBIA
Aerovias de Integracion Regional SA
Incorporated: 1980

Founded in late 1980, Aires Colombia started operations the following February, and has since developed a network of regional passenger services from its base at Bogotá.

HQ airport & main base: El Dorado International Bogotá
Radio callsign: AIRES
Designator: 4C/ARE
Employees: 538
Route points: Apartado, Aruba, Barranquilla, Bogotá, Cali, Cartagena, Cucuta, Curacao, El Yopal, Florencia, Ibaque, Ipiales, Manizales, Maracaibo, Medellin, Montaria, Neiva, Panama City, Pasto, Pereira, Popayan, Puerto Assis, Quibdo, Valledupar, Villavicencio
Fleet: 4 Bombardier Dash 8 Q300; 4 Bombardier Dash 8 Q100; 6 Bombardier Dash 8 Q200

AVIANCA
Aerovias Nacionales de Colombia SA
Incorporated: 1940

Avianca can trace its history back to 1919, when SCADTA, the first airline in the Americas and the second in the world, started operations using a Junkers seaplane to provide a service between Barranquilla and Giradot. SCADTA's founders were three Germans and five Colombians. The many natural difficulties in surface travel in Colombia enabled the new airline to expand rapidly.

SCADTA also managed a number of 'firsts' during its operations over two decades. One of the airline's Fokker aircraft won a prize offered by a newspaper for the first aircraft to land at Colombia's capital, Bogotá, which is nearly 9,000ft (2,700m) up in the Andes. This was followed in 1925 by the first air service between North and South America when a SCADTA flying boat flew from Barranquilla to Florida. In 1931, Pan American, still in its own infancy, acquired an 80 per cent interest in SCADTA.

Avianca was formed in 1940 when SCADTA merged with another Colombian airline, Servicio Aereo Colombiano. During its first few years, attention was paid to consolidation and new equipment was almost impossible to obtain because of the demands of the Second World War on the aircraft manufacturing industries of the world. Nevertheless, once the war ended, Avianca was the first South American airline to fly into Miami in 1947, and the first to reach New York, in 1948. Avianca took over another Colombian airline, SAETA, in 1954. In 1960, the airline introduced the first non-stop jet airliner service between Miami and

Bogotá, and in 1964 the first between New York and Bogotá.

The Pan American interest was gradually reduced over the years, first to 38 per cent and then to 13 per cent, at which stage, in 1978, Avianca finally bought out the Pan Am shareholding. This was clearly a wise move as it pre-empted any difficulties which might have arisen if Pan Am had still been heavily involved with Avianca at the time of the American airline's final collapse. Before this, Avianca acquired SAM Sociedad Aeronautica de Medellin Consolidada.

Although services to the United States have developed over the years, the airline has been a comparatively recent arrival in Europe, with London being served from 1997, following Madrid and Paris which joined Avianca's network earlier. In March 2002, Avianca absorbed its domestic subsidiary, SAM Colombia and merged with ACES Colombia to create a new organisation, the Summa Alliance, with operations beginning in May.

ACES Colombia dated from August 1971, and began operations in February 1972 with de Havilland Twin Otter aircraft playing a prominent role during the early days. The airline's first jet aircraft, Boeing 727s, were introduced in 1981, and then followed by Fairchild FH-227s in 1986, later replaced by ATR-42s. At first the airline concentrated on developing internal scheduled services, often to smaller communities, but international charter flights were introduced in 1986, and more recently international scheduled operations have been operated to Panama. Before the merger, Airbus A320 aircraft were introduced, starting to replace Boeing 727s.

Actually older than ACES, SAM was founded in 1945 and charter operations started a year later, with the first scheduled operations following in 1947. The airline was initially known as Sociedad Aeronautica de Medellin, but the name changed to SAM Colombia in 1962. The airline became a subsidiary of Avianca and developed a largely domestic route network, but with international flights to Havana and Panama City. BAe RJ100s replaced a fleet which at one stage was comprised entirely of Boeing 727s.

The new venture was short-lived, however, and dismantled after Avianca filed for Chapter 11 bankruptcy protection in March 2003. A number of destinations were dropped while the airline was restructured. SAM Colombia remained a separate airline afterwards, although with Avianca holding 94 per cent of its shares.

Throughout its history, Avianca has been a private-enterprise operation.

HQ airport & main base: Bogotá
Radio callsign: AVIANCA
Designator: AV/AVA
Employees: 5,100
Route points: Alicante, Armenia, Aruba, Atlanta, Barcelona, Barrancabermeja, Bogotá, Bucaramanga, Buenos Aires, Cali, Caracas, Cartagena, Cucuta, Curacao, Fort Lauderdale, Guatemala City, Guayaquil, Lima, Madrid, Manizales, Mexico City, Miami, Monteria, New York, Panama City, Paris, Pasto, Pereira, Quito, Rio de Janeiro, San Jose, San Salvador, Santa Maria, Santiago de Chile, Sao Paulo, Valencia, Valledupar
Links with other airlines: Has a 94 per cent stake in SAM Colombia. Alliances with Air Canada, Delta Airlines, Iberia, LACSA-Lineas Aereas Costarricenses, Mexicana, SAM Colombia, TACA International Airlines (all qv)
Fleet: 2 Boeing 767-300ER; 4 Boeing 767-200ER; 6 Boeing 757-200; 15 McDonnell Douglas MD-83; 4 Fokker 50

LINEAS AEREAS SURAMERICANAS

Lineas Aereas Suramericanas Colombia SA
Incorporated: 1972

A cargo charter operator, handling domestic and international flights from Bogotá, Lineas Aereas Suramericanas began operations in 1972 as Aeronorte, but adopted the current title in 1986. International operations to Panama began in 1987, and today the airline operates extensively into the United States, with connections to Luxembourg from Miami.

HQ airport & main base: Bogotá El Dorado International
Radio callsign: SURAMERICANO
Designator: LAU
Fleet: 4 Boeing 727-200F; 2 Boeing 727-100C; 2 Boeing 727-100F; 1 McDonnell Douglas DC-9-10

SAM COLOMBIA

Sociedad Aeronautica de Medellin Consolidada
Incorporated: 1945

SAM was founded in 1945 and charter operations started a year later, with the first scheduled operations following in 1947. The airline was initially known as Sociedad Aeronautica de Medellin, and the present title was adopted in 1962. The airline became a subsidiary of Avianca, which now owns 94 per cent of its shares, and today operates a largely domestic route network, but with international flights to Havana and Panama City. In March 2002, two other Colombian airlines, ACES and Avianca, joined SAM to establish the Alianza Summa, but despite this, the three airlines continued to operate separately, and when ACES was grounded in August 2003, the Alianza Summa was disbanded. Nevertheless, one development has been that SAM is now an entirely domestic operation with its international services transferred to Avianca, and the airline is considerably smaller as a result.

At one stage the fleet was comprised entirely of Boeing 727s, but the airline now operates McDonnell Douglas MD-83s and Fokker 50s.

HQ airport & main base: Bogotá
Radio callsign: SAM
Designator: MM/SAM
Employees: 240
Route points: Aruba, Barranquilla, Bogotá, Bucuramanga, Cali, Cartagena, Cucuta, Medellin, Monteria, Pasto, Pereira, Riohacha, San Andres, Santa Marta, Tumaco, Valledupar
Links with other airlines: A subsidiary of Avianca (qv) which has a 94 per cent stake
Fleet: 3 McDonnell Douglas MD-83; 4 Fokker 100; 4 Fokker 50

SATENA
Servicio de Aereonavegacion a Territorios Nacionales
Incorporated: 1962

The only Colombian state-owned airline, Satena was established to aid development of the Amazon and Orinoco regions of the country, and is operated as a special unit of the Colombian air force. Satena originally provided charter and scheduled operations for passengers and cargo within the two regions, as well as services for mail, but in recent years the network has expanded to include both the Caribbean and Pacific coast of the country. In addition, over the past decade, the fleet has become more standardised with the retirement of the BAe 748s and the CASA 212s.

HQ airport & main base: Bogotá, with a further base at Medellin
Radio callsign: SATENA
Designator: ZT/NSE
Employees: 300
Route points: Apartado, Araracuara, Arauca, Bahia Solano, Bogotá, Bucaramanga, Buenaventura, Cali, Corazal, Cucuta, Florencia, Guapi, Ipiales, La Chorrera, La Pedrera, Larnacarena, Leticia, Medellin, Mitu, Neiva, Nuqui, Pasto, Pereira, Popayan, Providencia, Puerto Asis, Puerto Carreno, Puerto Inirida, Puerto Leguizamo, Quibdo, San Andres Island, San Jose del Gua, San Vicente, Saravena, Tame, Tarapaca, Tumaco, Villagarzon, Villavicencio
Fleet: 1 Embraer 170; 5 Embraer ERJ-145LR; 6 Dornier 328-110

SEARCA COLOMBIA
Incorporated: 1992

Few detailsof the scheduled services offered by this airline are available, other than that operations are from Medellin. Unusually for an airline in the western world, it operates a fleet that is predominantly Russian in origin.

HQ airport & main base: Medellin Enrique Olaya Herrera
Designator: SRC
Fleet: 6 Let L-410UVP; 6 Raytheon Beech 1900C

TAMPA CARGO
Transportes Aereos Mercantiles Panamericanos
Incorporated: 1973

Tampa Airlines dates from 1973 and operates international scheduled cargo services as well as cargo charters from its base at Medellin and from Bogotá. Marketing alliances were established with Martinair and Millon Air, although only the latter remains, while Martinair acquired a 58 per cent stake in the airline in 1996. Medellin is now the main base.

HQ airport & main base: Medellin Jose Maria Cordova International
Radio callsign: TAMPA
Designator: QT/TPA
Employees: 875
Route points: Barranquilla, Bogotá, Cali, Caracas, Guadalajara, Lima, Medellin, Mexico City, Miami, Panama City, Paramaribo, Philadelphia, Quito, San Juan, Santiago de Chila, Sao Paulo, Valencia
Links with other airlines: Martinair (qv) has a 58 per cent stake
Fleet: 4 Boeing 767-200F; 2 McDonnell Douglas DC-8-71F

CONGO, REPUBLIC OF – TN

AERO-SERVICE
Incorporated: 1967

Originally founded as the air transport department of a company producing frozen food, Aero-Service became an independent airline later, and now provides charter operations, mainly for freight.

HQ airport & main base: Pointe-Noire
Designator: BF/RSR
Fleet: 1 Antonov An-24RV; 1 Yakovlev Yak-42; 3 CASA C-212 Aviocar; 2 Britten-Norman BN2A Islander

TAC
Trans Air Congo
Incorporated: 1994

Formed in 1994, Trans Air Congo provides charter and scheduled services for passengers and cargo in the former French Congo, and to neighbouring states, using a fleet largely consisting of Russian and Ukrainian aircraft.

HQ airport & main base: Pointe Noire Agotino Neto
Designator: Q8/TSG
Route points: Brazzaville, Cotonou, Douala, Pointe Noire
Fleet: 1 Boeing 727-200; 3 Boeing 737-200; 2 Antonov An-24B/RV; 1 Antonov An-12; 2 Let L-410

CONGO, DEMOCRATIC REPUBLIC OF (FORMERLY ZAIRE) – 9Q

BRAVO AIR
Incorporated: 2006

Owned by the Spanish Grupo Bravia Airlines, Bravo Air is currently operating a domestic network within the Congo and services to other countries in Africa as well as services to western Europe.

HQ airport & main base: Kinshasa N'Djili
Radio callsign: Bravo
Designator: K6
Route points: Brazzaville, Brussels, Johannesburg, Kinshasa, Madrid, Nairobi, Paris
Links with other airlines: Part of the Spanish Bravia Airlines Group
Fleet: 1 Boeing 767-200ER; 4 McDonnell Douglas DC-9-30

CAA
Compagnie Africaine d'Aviation
Incorporated: 1992

A charter and scheduled airline, although operations have been affected by the unstable internal situation.

HQ airport & main base: Kinshasa N'Dolo
Fleet: 3 Antonov An-26; 1 Boeing 727-200F; 2 McDonnell Douglas MD-81

HEWA BORA AIRWAYS
Incorporated: 1994

Hewa Bora Airways was originally founded as Zaire Express, a subsidiary of Express Cargo, in 1994. When Zaire changed its name to the Democratic Republic of Congo, the airline became Congo Airlines, and more recently has adopted the Hewa Bora title. It operates scheduled passenger services in addition to scheduled and ad hoc charter cargo services. A marketing alliance existed with Air Zaire before that airline suspended operations following the civil war.

HQ airport & main base: Kinshasa
Designator: EO/EZR
Employees: 1,100
Route points: Brazzaville, Brussels, Douala, Gemena, Goma, Johannesburg, Kananga, Kinshasa, Kisangani, Kolwezi, Lagos, Lubumbashi, Mbandaka, Mbuji, Mayi, Warri
Fleet: 1 Lockheed L-1011-500 TriStar; 1 Boeing 767-200ER; 3 McDonnell Douglas DC-8-55; 4 Boeing 707-320C; 5 Boeing 727-200; 4 Boeing 727-100; 1 Boeing 727-100F; 1 McDonnell Douglas DC-9-50

KINSHASA AIRWAYS
Incorporated: 2002

A cargo charter airline operating throughout Africa and the Middle East.

HQ airport & main base: Kinshasa N'Djili
Designator:
Fleet: 1 McDonnell Douglas DC-8-55; 2 Boeing 707-320; 1 Tupolev Tu-154B; 1 Boeing 727-200

COSTA RICA – TI

LACSA
Lineas Aereas Costarricenses SA
Incorporated: 1946

Originally formed in 1946 as a joint venture between the Costa Rican government, Pan American World Airways and private interests based in Costa Rica, in

1952 the company acquired Taca de Costa Rica, which dated from 1939. An extensive Caribbean network has been created, with services further afield to New York and Rio de Janeiro. A subsidiary is SANSA, Servicios Aereos Nacionales, which operates a small domestic network with a fleet of four Cessna Caravans. International services are now operated as TACA Costa Rica.

The government shareholding today is small, and share ownership is highly fragmented.

HQ airport & main base: San Jose, Costa Rica
Radio callsign: LACSA
Designator: LR/LRC
Employees: 1,150
Route points: Barranquilla, Cancun, Caracas, El Salvador, Guatemala, Guayaquil, Havana, Lima, Los Angeles, Managua, Mexico City, Miami, New Orleans, New York, Orlando, Panama City, Quito, Rio de Janeiro, San Jose, San Juan, San Pedro Suala, Santiago, Tegucigalpa
Links with other airlines: TACA International Airlines has a 10 per cent stake. Alliance with Avianca (both qv)
Fleet: Uses aircraft from the TACA fleet, based in El Salvador

NATUREAIR
Incorporated: 1991

Founded in 1991 as Travelair, Natureair has a small, scheduled domestic network and one international route. Charter flights are also operated.

HQ airport & main base: San Jose Tobias Bolanos International
Designator: 5C
Route points: Barra Colorado, Bocas del Toro, Golfito, Liberia, Nosara Beach, Palmar, Puerto Jiminez, Punta Islita, Quepos, San Jose, Tamarindo, Tambor, Tortuquero
Fleet: 2 Let L-410UVP; 4 de Havilland Canada Twin Otter Srs 300; 3 Britten-Norman BN2A Islander

CROATIA – 9A

AIR ADRIATIC
Incorporated: 2001

Air Adriatic was founded in late 2001 and commenced operations in spring 2002, providing international and domestic charter flights for passengers and cargo. The first flights were inclusive tour passenger flights between Ireland and Croatia, while the airline has also handled relief flights under contract for United Nations operations in the Balkans.

HQ airport & main base: Dubrovnik
Designator: AHR
Employees: 76
Fleet: 4 McDonnell Douglas MD-82; 2 McDonnell Douglas MD-83

CROATIA AIRLINES
Incorporated: 1989

Originally formed in 1989 as Zagal, the current title had been adopted by the time operations of Croatia started in 1991, as the national airline of the newly independent Croatian Republic after the break-up of the former Yugoslavia. Being some distance away from the conflict in Bosnia, the new airline was able to develop an international route network, although tourist traffic is still far below pre-independence levels. The airline's shares were originally split among six shareholders, including Zagreb Airport, but the state is now the majority shareholder, with 94.8 per cent of the shares. The airline is a member of the Star Alliance.

HQ airport & main base: Zagreb
Radio callsign: CROATIA
Designator: OU/CTN
Employees: 1,037
Route points: Amsterdam, Brussels, Dubrovnik, Frankfurt, Istanbul, London, Milan, Mostar, Munich, Paris, Prague, Pula, Rome, Sarajevo, Skopje, Split, Vienna, Warsaw, Zadar, Zagreb, Zurich
Links with other airlines: Alliances with Air France, Alitalia, CSA Czech Airlines, Lufthansa, SN Brussels Airlines. THY Turkish Airlines (all qv)
Fleet: 4 Airbus A320-200; 4 Airbus A319-100; 3 ATR-42-300

DUBROVNIK AIRLINE
Incorporated: 2005

An inclusive tour charter airline flying passengers into Croatia from originating points thoughout Europe, including France, Ireland, Sweden and Switzerland. Despite its passenger emphasis, the airline was started by and is owned by a freight forwarder, Atlanska Plovidba.

HQ airport & main base: Dubrovnik
Radio callsign: DUBROVNIK
Designator: DBK

Employees: 117
Fleet: 2 McDonnell Douglas MD-83; 3 McDonnell Douglas MD-82

CUBA – CV

One of the few old-style Communist states outside of the Chinese Peoples' Republic, Cuba has nevertheless several airlines, albeit all government-owned, rather than a single monolithic structure such as the former Soviet Aeroflot or the CAAC in China. While the national airline, Cubana, can trace its origins back to 1929, before that time, air links between the United States – under whose influence Cuba remained for many years – and the island were largely in the hands of American-owned companies, notably Pan American Airways.

The growth in tourism to Cuba in recent years, with the island seen as a low-cost Caribbean destination, and the end of Soviet patronage, has seen the introduction of some Western types to airline service, but only from European and Brazilian sources, due to continued restrictions on the supply of US equipment to Cuba.

AEROCARIBBEAN
Incorporated: 1982

Originally founded as the Cuban charter operator, handling passengers and cargo internationally and also operating a domestic scheduled network, it has since introduced international destinations within the Caribbean and Central America. It is state-owned by Cubana de Aviacion. Originally an operator of Antonov and Ilyushin types, it now also includes Western equipment.

HQ airport & main base: Havana Jose Marti International
Designator: 7L/CRN
Route points: Cayo Coco, Grand Cayman, Havana, Holguin, Managua, Port au Prince, San Pedro Sula, Santiago, Santo Domingo
Fleet: 3 Antonov An-26; 1 Antonov An-24RV; 4 ATR-72-210; 2 ATR-42-300; 6 Yakovlev Yak-40; 3 Embraer EMB-110P Bandeirante

AEROGAVIOTA
Incorporated: 1994

Aerogaviota was founded in 1994 by the Cuban government, which remains its sole shareholder, to operate passenger and cargo charter flights, mainly for tourists.

HQ airport & main base: Havana Jose Marti International
Designator: KG/GTV
Fleet: 18 Antonov An-26; 3 ATR-42-500; 1 Yakovlev Yak-40

CUBANA
Empresa Consolidada Cubana de Aviacion
Incorporated: 1929

Originally formed in 1929 as the Compania Cubana de Aviacion Curtiss, with operations beginning the following year, Cubana initially operated internal services from its base in Havana. In 1932, the airline was acquired by Pan American Airways, and the name changed to Compania Nacional Cubana de Aviacion, which was shortened in 1944 to Compania Cubana de Aviacion. In 1945, a majority stake in the company was sold to Cuban investors, with Pan American retaining a substantial minority shareholding of 42 per cent. International services started in 1946 with a scheduled service from Havana to Miami, and in 1948, Cubana's first transatlantic service followed, with a service between Havana and Madrid.

The airline was nationalised and the current title adopted in 1959 after the Cuban revolution saw Fidel Castro sweep into power. At the time, Cubana was operating a fleet of Douglas DC-3s and modern Bristol Britannia airliners to destinations throughout the Caribbean. The Britannias remained in service for more than fifteen years after the revolution, but increasingly equipment procurement switched to aircraft of Soviet manufacture, including Antonov An-24s and Ilyushin Il-14s and Il-18s. For many years, the only Western aircraft in the fleet were Fokker F27 Friendships, but these have now gone.

Since the collapse of the Soviet Union, the scope of the international network has increased, largely in an attempt to boost tourist revenues, although American sanctions and the lack of Soviet sponsorship have effectively cut the country off from what were historically its main trading partners. New aircraft continue to come from the countries of the former Soviet Union, but there are a couple of Western aircraft also in service.

HQ airport & main base: Havana
Radio callsign: CUBANA
Designator: CU/CUB
Route points: Bogotá, Buenos Aires, Camaguey, Cancun, Caracas, Cayo Coco, Cayo Largo del Sur, Cienfugos, Fort de France, Frankfurt, Guatemala City, Havana, Holguin, London, Madrid, Mexico

City, Montreal, Nassau, Paris, Pointe-à-Pitre, Rome, Santiago (Cuba), San Jose, Santo Domingo, Toronto
Fleet: 5 Ilyushin Il-96-300; 6 Ilyushin Il-62M; 2 Tupolev Tu-204-100; 3 Tupolev Tu-154B-2; 1 Boeing 737-300; 4 Antonov An-26; 14 Antonov An-24B/RV; 1 ATR-42-500; 7 Yakovlev Yak-42

CYPRUS – 5B

As with many former British colonies, Cyprus initially depended on British airlines for its air transport services, with many services routed via Athens because of the strong links between the island's majority Greek community and Greece. Even Cyprus Airways was initially a joint venture with the British airline British European Airways, BEA, one of the two main predecessors of British Airways.

Paradoxically, it was after the division of the island into Greek and Turkish zones that the tourist industry really became important, with restrictions on hotel construction lifted, and this was accompanied by strong growth in the local air transport industry, which now also includes an independent airline as well as a charter subsidiary of Cyprus Airways.

CYPRUS AIRWAYS

Cyprus Airways Ltd
Incorporated: 1947

Cyprus Airways celebrates its sixtieth anniversary in 2007. Originally the airline had been formed as a joint venture between British European Airways, predecessor of today's British Airways and the Cyprus government, both of which held 40 per cent of the shares, leaving 20 per cent for private interests. In the beginning, the airline operated services from Nicosia to Athens and destinations in the Middle East, using aircraft leased from BEA, but in 1948, it acquired three Douglas DC-3s. Additional DC-3s followed in 1950, when Rome and destinations in Arabia were added to the route network. Increases in the airline's capital to cater for this expansion meant that, by 1950, the shareholdings were BEA, 23 per cent, BOAC, British Overseas Airways Corporation, 23 per cent, the Cyprus government, 31 per cent, and private interests, 23 per cent.

The rapid expansion of the airline went into a sharp reverse during 1955 and 1956, when terrorist action on Cyprus led to a sharp drop in traffic and heavy losses. This came at a time when the airline had been planning to replace its DC-3s with its own fleet of Vickers Viscounts, but in order that the airline itself should survive, the route network was pruned dramatically, the DC-3s were sold, and instead of buying Viscounts, the airline opted to lease two aircraft from BEA.

The revival of the old relationship with BEA was to last more than twenty years, taking Cyprus Airways into the jet age with five Hawker Siddeley Tridents leased from BEA, while the Cypriot government acquired BOAC's interest. A further setback occurred when Cyprus was invaded by Turkey in 1973, resulting in partitioning of the island and the eventual closure of Nicosia Airport.

Over the last thirty years, Cyprus Airways has recovered strongly, buying its own aircraft and building up a fleet of Airbus airliners, some of which replaced an interim fleet of BAe One-Elevens, which had augmented the Tridents. A charter subsidiary, Eurocypria, has been established, recognising the potential to carry more of the many visitors to Cyprus, many of whom arrive on inclusive tour charter flights, on the airline's own aircraft. Cyprus Airways also owns Greek-based Hellas Jet. The airline now flies from the airports at Larnaca and Paphos. Today, Cyprus Airways is owned 70 per cent by the government of Cyprus and 30 per cent by private shareholders.

HQ airport & main base: HQ is at Nicosia, but the main base/hub is Larnaca International, with operations also from Paphos
Radio callsign: CYPRUS
Designator: CY/CYP
Employees: 1,696
Route points: Amman, Amsterdam, Athens, Bahrain, Beirut, Birmingham (UK), Brussels, Cairo, Damascus, Dubai, Frankfurt, Heraklion, Jeddah, Kiev, Larnaca, London, Manchester, Milan, Moscow, Odessa, Paris, Riyadh, Rome, Strasbourg, Tel Aviv, Thessaloniki, Vienna, Warsaw, Zurich
Links with other airlines: Owns Eurocypria and Hellas Jet. Marketing alliances with Aeroflot Russian Airlines, AeroSvit Airlines, Alitalia, El Al, Gulf Airways, KLM, LOT Polish Airlines, Olympic Airlines, Royal Jordanian Airlines, SN Brussels Airlines, Syrianair (all qv)
Fleet: 2 Airbus A330-200; 7 Airbus A320-200; 2 Airbus A319-100

EUROCYPRIA

Eurocypria Airlines Ltd
Incorporated: 1991

Eurocypria was founded in 1991 by Cyprus Airways as its charter subsidiary, and began operations in 1992.

HQ airport & main base: Larnaca International
Radio callsign: EUROCYPRIA
Designator: UI/ECA
Links with other airlines: A subsidiary of Cyprus Airways (qv)
Fleet: 4 Boeing 737-800

CYPRUS (NORTHERN) – TC

KIBRIS TURK HAVA YOLLARI (CYPRUS TURKISH AIRLINES)

Kibris Turk Hava Yolari
Incorporated: 1974

The airline of Turkish Northern Cyprus, Kibris was founded in December 1974 after the Turkish invasion of Cyprus led to partition of the island. The first services were operated early the following year, using aircraft and crews loaned by THY Turkish Airlines. An airfield was put into service at Ercan, some eight miles east of Nicosia, and the first services were from the airport to Ankara in Turkey. Ownership of the airline was divided between THY and the Turkish Cypriot government, but both have now sold their interests to private investors.

Despite Northern Cyprus only being officially recongnised by Turkey, the airline has developed a small international network in recent years.

HQ airport & main base: Ercan, near Nicosia
Radio callsign: AIRKIBRIS
Designator: YK/KYV
Employees: 726
Route points: Adana, Ankara, Anatalya, Dalaman, Ercan, Istanbul, Izmir
Links with other airlines: Closely allied with THY (qv), which has a 50 per cent stake
Fleet: 3 Boeing 737-800; 3 Airbus A320-200

CZECH REPUBLIC – OK

Czechoslovakia became an independent state after the collapse of the Austro-Hungarian Empire at the end of the First World War. The national airline, CSA, traces its history back to 1923, when Czechoslovak State Airlines, Cesholsovenske Stani Aerolinie, was formed using aircraft belonging to the army. The first flight used a Czech-designed and built Aero A-14, which inaugurated a service linking Prague, Brno and Bratislava on 1 March 1923. Air services to neighbouring countries were established in the years before the German invasion in 1938, but were suspended on the outbreak of the Second World War, and the airline was among the first European operators of the Douglas DC-2. Postwar, the airline was re-established in 1946, using salvaged Luftwaffe transports, but became another Aeroflot satellite following the Soviet takeover in 1948.

The collapse of the Soviet Union and the Warsaw Pact was followed by a division of the country into the Czech Republic and Slovakia, and the national airline, Ceskoslovenske Aerolinie, also had its assets divided pro-rata between the two countries. In the Czech Republic, the airline became CSA Czech Airlines. An independent sector has emerged, of a kind, in the form of a low-cost carrier, Smart Wings, but this is owned by Travel Service Airlines, itself owned by the state travel and tourism service!

CSA

CSA Czech Airlines
Incorporated: 1923

Originally Ceskoslovenske Aerolinie, the present title was adopted in 1995 after the division of Czechoslovakia into the Czech Republic and Slovakia.

The history of CSA dates from 1923, when a state air transport group was formed, carrying the title Czechoslovak State Airlines, which used military Brandenburg A-14s and military personnel. The new airline conducted trial flights on a route between Prague and Bratislava, now in the Slovak Republic, and scheduled services along this route followed in 1924. That same year, the first Czech-built and designed aircraft, the Aero 10, entered service between Prague and Kosice. The Aero aircraft factory also operated a route between Prague and Marianske Lazne between 1925 and 1927, when the state-owned airline took over the service.

During the next few years, the state airline expanded rapidly, and civil airports were opened at Brno, Marianske Lazne and Bratislava, reducing the dependence on military aerodromes, while a succession of ever more modern aircraft brought advances in comfort, reliability and speed. These aircraft included the de Havilland 50, the Farman Goliath (eventually manufactured under licence in Czechoslovakia) and the country's own Aero 23s and 38s. While CSA concentrated on internal services, international routes were being developed by CLS, Ceskoslovenska Letecka Spolecnost, a privately owned airline which was founed in 1927, and commenced services to Berlin, Rotterdam and Vienna in 1928. In 1930, CLS inaugurated services from Prague to Balse, Munich and Zurich. It was not until 1930 that CSA started international services, to Zagreb.

It was CSA which had the distinction of becoming the first Western airline to offer an air service to the Soviet Union, using Airspeed Envoys in 1936. The aircraft became known as the 'Russian Express', but it still took ten hours, although this was highly competitive when compared with the forty-five hours taken by a fast train! Another innovation for CSA in 1936 was the airline's first stewardesses, introduced on Douglas DC-2s first delivered that year. The DC-2s were soon followed by their larger development, the famous DC-3.

Both CSA and CLS had extensive networks by 1938, when operations abruptly ceased on the German occupation of Czechoslovakia.

A new airline was established after the end of the Second World War. Ceskoslovenske Aerolinie started operations in 1945, initially using three salvaged ex-Luftwaffe Junkers Ju.52/3ms and some lighter aircraft. Ex-military Douglas C-47s, the military variant of the DC-3, were soon purchased and modified for airline operations, so that services from Prague to Bratislava and Brno could begin early in 1946. The old routes were re-established rapidly, urged on by the war-battered state of the European railway network, so that by the end of 1946, many of the pre-war European destinations were being served once more. Meanwhile, Czechoslovakia was being dragged into the postwar Soviet Bloc, and in 1948, the airline was nationalised.

Equipment purchases soon began to reflect the new regime, with Ilyushin Il-12s being the next new aircraft, followed by Il-14s. The route network also began to become more concerned with links to East European capitals than those in the West. The first jet equipment, Tupolev Tu-104s, was introduced in 1957, and remained prominent in the fleet for more than a decade. Ilyushin Il-18 turboprop airliners were also acquired. Tupolev Tu-134s and the long-range Ilyushin Il-62 appeared during the 1960s. For a short period during the late 1960s, a turboprop Bristol Britannia 318 was leased. In common with many Soviet Bloc airlines, CSA's operations were all-embracing, including air taxi services and aerial crop-spraying.

The break-up of the Soviet Union and the dismantling of the Warsaw Pact, which was an economic as well as a military entity, saw Western equipment placed in service, so that today the last Tupolev aircraft have departed, leaving the fleet dominated by Western types. The route network also extends now to every European capital with the exception of Oslo. On the debit side, the division of Czechoslovakia has meant that the airline has lost its secondary hub at Bratislava, although for a time Slovak Air Services was a subsidiary. Over the past decade, CSA has transformed its fleet, which is now entirely made up of Western aircraft, while the number of employees has grown by a third. The airline is still basically state controlled.

Marketing alliances exist with several European airlines, and the airline is a member of the Sky Team alliance.

HQ airport & main base: Prague Ruzyne
Radio callsign: CSA LINES
Designator: OK/CSA
Employees: 4,860
Route points: Amsterdam, Athens, Barcelona, Basle/Mulhouse, Beirut, Belgrade, Berlin, Birmingham, Bologna, Bratislava, Brno, Brussels, Bucharest, Budapest, Cairo, Dubai, Dublin, Düsseldorf, Edinburgh, Ekaterinburg, Frankfurt, Hamburg, Hanover, Harrisburg, Helsinki, Istanbul, Karlovy Vary, Kiev, Kosice, Krakow, Larnaca, Las Vegas, Ljubljana, London, Luxembourg, Madrid, Manchester, Marseilles, Milan, Munich, New York, Oslo, Ostrava, Paris, Prague, Riga, Rome, St Louis, St Petersburg, Samara, Sarajaevo, Skopje, Sliac, Sofia, Split, Stockholm, Stuttgart, Tallion, Tel Aviv, Thessaloniki, Toronto, Venice, Vienna, Vilnius, Warsaw, Yerevan, Zagreb, Zilina, Zurich
Links with other airlines: Alliances with Aeroflot Russian Airlines (qv), Aerosvit Airlines (qv), Air Malta (qv), Atlantis European Airways, Azerbaijan Airlines (qv), Belavia Belarussian Airlines (qv), Bulgaria Air (qv), Comair (qv), Croatia Airlines (qv), Finnair (qv), Iberia Airlines (qv), Jat Airways (qv), Malev (qv), Olympic Airlines (qv), SkyEurope Airlines (qv), SN Brussels Airlines (qv), Swiss (qv), Tarom (qv), THY Turkish Airlines (qv), Ural Airlines (qv)
Fleet : 4 Airbus A310-300; 2 Airbus A321-200; 8 Airbus A320-200; 6 Airbus A319-100; 14 Boeing 737-400;15 Boeing 737-500; 4 ATR-72-200; 5 ATR-42-500; 2 ATR-42-400

SMART WINGS
Incorporated: 2004

A new Czech low-cost airline planning an international network from its base at Prague, founded in 2004 by parent company Travel Service Airlines.

HQ airport & main base: Prague Ruzyne
Designator: QS/TVS

Links with other airlines: Alliance with Air Europa (qv)
Fleet: 2 Boeing 737-500

TRAVEL SERVICE AIRLINES
Incorporated: 1997

Founded by the Czech government's flying service, Travel Service Airlines is primarily an inclusive tour charter airline and is now owned by Lerox and the Unimex Group. A small, international scheduled network has been established, while the airline owns Smart Wings, the Czech low-cost carrier. It has an associated company in Hungary.

HQ airport & main base: Prague Ruzyne
Designator: QS/TVS
Employees: 550
Route points: Las Palmas, Madrid, Milan, Paris, Prague, Rome
Links with other airlines: Owns Smart Wings. Associated with Travel Service Hungary
Fleet: 2 Boeing 737-900; 4 Boeing 737-800

DENMARK – OY

(*See also* SCANDINAVIA)

The unique international collaboration that resulted in the creation of Scandinavian Airlines System, SAS, means that the history of air transport in the three participating countries is shared. Nevertheless, of the three airlines that combined to form SAS, the Danish airline, DDL, was the oldest, dating from 1919. Air transport also played an important part in linking isolated communities in Greenland, still officially part of Denmark, and in linking the Faroes with Denmark.

Despite the small population of Denmark, the country has been home to one of Europe's leading inclusive tour charter airlines, Sterling, which has now absorbed Maersk, for many years an operator of domestic air services within Denmark and which had a British subsidiary. Sterling itself is now Norwegian owned, although still Danish based, while Premiair, the other Danish charter airline, has become part of the British-owned My Travel group. SAS has a small Danish operation which is covered in the SAS entry under Scandinavia.

AIR GREENLAND
Incorporated: 1960

Originally founded by SAS and a mining company in 1960 as Greenlandair, or Gronlandsfly, in 1962 the Danish government and the Greenland Home Rule government took an interest and now own equal one-third shares with SAS. The airline was formed to provide air transport to the many small and remote settlements in Greenland, where air transport is the only option due to sparse population and rugged terrain, and this has led to a varied fleet, including small helicopters, and operations which include air taxi, special lift, offshore supply and ice reconnaissance in addition to internal passenger and freight, scheduled and charter operations. Many smaller communities receive air transport on what amounts to a scheduled air taxi basis, often on a concessionary fare basis, and a number of destinations can only be reached by helicopter. The first jet airliner, a Boeing 757-200 was introduced in 1998, allowing the airline to operate its own longer-haul operations, while the current title was adopted in 2002. Services to Canada, Denmark and Iceland are operated through arrangements with SAS, First Air and Icelandair.

HQ airport & main base: Nuuk
Radio callsign: GREENLANDAIR
Designator: GL/GRL
Employees: 548
Route points: Aasiaat, Alluitsup Paa, Copenhagen, Ilulissat, Iqaluit, Kangerlussuaq, Kulusuk, Maniitsoq, Nanortalik, Narsaq, Narsarsuaq, Nuuk, Paamiut, Qaanaaq, Qaqortoq, Qasigiannguit, Qeqertarsuaq, Sisimuit, Tasiilaq, Upernavik, Uummannaq
Links with other airlines: SAS has a 33.3 per cent shareholding. Alliances with SAS, First Air and Icelandair (all qv)
Fleet: 1 Airbus A330-200; 1 Boeing 757-200; 6 Bombardier Dash 7-100; 2 de Havilland Canada Twin Otter Srs 300; 1 Raytheon Beech King Air 200; plus several small helicopters, including MDH-500s

ATLANTIC AIRWAYS (FAROE ISLANDS)
Atlantic Airways (Faroe Islands) A/S
Incorporated: 1987

Owned by the government of the Faroe Islands, Atlantic Airways was formed in 1987 and began operations the following year, initially with CimberAirways as a partner and shareholder, but full control passed to the Faroese authorities in 1989. It also includes a helicopter-operating element, originally known as SL Helicopters but part of the airline since 1994.

HQ airport & main base: Vagar
Designator: RC/FLI
Employees: 110
Route points: Billund, Copenhagen, Reykjavik, Stavanger
Links with other airlines: Alliance with Air Iceland (qv)
Fleet: 4 BAe 146-200; 2 BAe RJ100ER

CIMBER
Cimber Air A/S
Incorporated: 1950

Cimber Air was formed in 1950 by Captain Ingolf Lorenz Nielsen, who took over Sonderjyllands Flyveselskab. Initially the airline operated charter flights, and the early fleet included a de Havilland Heron as well as Piper Apache and Beech King Air C90 aircraft. In 1964, the airline was granted a licence for a scheduled service between its base at Sonderborg and Copenhagen, operating a feeder into the international services of SAS. The route was later, in 1967, to see the introduction of the Nord 262 turboprop feeder-liner. In November 1971, Cimber's scheduled services were merged into those of Danair, a consortium between SAS, Maersk and Cimber, in which the latter held a 5 per cent stake.

The airline received its first jet equipment in 1975, as launch customer for the German VFW 614 airliner, although these were replaced three years later by two Fokker F28 Fellowships. Given the small size of the Danish market, Cimber had to look for other business opportunities, and in 1980, the airline's aircraft started to operate feeder services in Saudi Arabia for Saudi Arabian Airlines. While services from Sonderborg grew, and the airline started operations from Aarhus, in 1987 a further development was the provision of feeder services from Kiel in Germany, on sub-charter to DLT (now Lufthansa CityLine), for which a German subsidiary, Cimber Air GmbH, had to be established. By this time, Cimber had introduced three ATR-42 regional airliners.

Services to Montpellier in southern France were introduced in 1989. The following year, Cimber negotiated an alliance with Lufthansa for operation of further feeder services in Germany, for which an additional three ATR-42s were acquired, with a seventh joining the fleet in 1992, the same year that the two F-28s were sold. Eventually the ATR-42 fleet peaked at twelve aircraft.

Danair ceased operations in 1995, largely replaced by SAS Commuter. In 1998, SAS purchased a 26 per cent interest, but this was sold back to the Nielsen family in 2003, so that today, Cimber Air remains in the hands of the Nielsen family, with a third generation running the business. It has a fleet of eight ATR-42 and 72s, but all recent deliveries have been Bombardier CRJ200LR regional jets. While Sonderborg remains the airline's home base, it continues to develop services elsewhere, including Copenhagen and Billund, but no longer operates within Germany even though the alliance with Lufthansa continues.

HQ airport & main base: Sonderborg, with additional bases at Copenhagen Kastrup and Billund
Radio callsign: CIMBER
Designator: QI/CIM
Employees: 368
Route points: Aalborg, Basle/Mulhouse, Billund, Bornholm, Bucharest, Copenhagen, Karup, Munich, Oslo, Sonderborg, Stockholm, Warsaw
Links with other airlines: Alliance with Lufthansa (qv)
Fleet: 7 Bombardier CRJ200LR; 2 Bombardier CRJ100LR; 1 ATR-72-500; 5 ATR-72-200; 1 ATR-42-500; 1 ATR-42-300

DANISH AIR TRANSPORT
Incorporated: 1989

Originally founded as a cargo charter airline, whose business soon developed to transporting horses, Danish Air Transport moved into passenger charters in 1994, and in 1996 the first scheduled services were added. The Rungholm family owns 60 per cent of the shares, with the remainder held by private individuals, while Danish owns Danu Oro Transportas, a small airline operating a single ATR-42-300, out of Vilnius in Lithuania.

HQ airport & main base: Esbjerg
Designator: DX/DTR
Route points: Bergen, Billund, Bornholm, Copenhagen, Ebsjerg, Floro, Oslo, Palanga, Skien, Stavanger
Links with other airlines: Owns Danu Oro Transportas. An alliance with Aria (qv)
Fleet: 5 ATR-72-200; 2 ATR-42-300; 1 ATR-42-320; 1 Saab 340A; 1 Raytheon Beech 1900D

JET TIME
Jet Time A/S
Incorporated: 2006

Founded by a group of investors, Jet Time is a new passenger charter airline that also provides aircraft and crews on a wet-lease basis to other operators.

HQ airport & main base: Copenhagen Kastrup
Fleet: 1 Boeing 737-300; 1 Boeing 737-500

MYTRAVEL
MyTravel Airways a/s
Incorporated: 1994

Until 2002, MyTravel's Danish operation was known as Premiair. The airline was formed in 1994 following the merger of two airlines, Scanair of Sweden and Conair of Denmark. Scanair had been originally founded as a Danish charter carrier in 1961, specialising in the inclusive tour market, but in 1965 had been reorganised by the three parent airlines of SAS as a Scandinavian charter airline, and operated as an independent charter airline within the SAS group, with the main base moving to Stockholm. Conair, or Consolidated Aircraft Corporation, was also an inclusive tour charter operator, founded in 1964 and beginning operations in 1965.
From the outset, the airline was owned by the Simon Spies travel organisation, and operated exclusively for them. The merged airline, Premiair, was itself owned by Simon Spies, until that company in turn was acquired by Airtours, the British tour operator and travel agency group in 1996, as a result of which Premiair came to be controlled by the holiday charter airline, Airtours.

In 2002, the parent company changed its name to MyTravel, and this name was adopted by both Airtours and Premiair. The two airlines cooperate on procurement, so that there is considerable similarity in the equipment used, with McDonnell Douglas aircraft having been replaced in recent years by those of Airbus manufacture.

HQ airport & main base: Copenhagen, with additional bases at Stockholm and Oslo
Radio callsign: VIKING
Designator: DK/VKG
Employees: 465
Links with other airlines: A subsidiary of MyTravel of the UK
Fleet: 2 Airbus A330-300; 2 Airbus 767-300ER; 2 Airbus A330-200; 3 Airbus A321-200; 5 Airbus A320-200

STAR AIR
Star Air A/S
Incorporated: 1987

A subsidiary of the A.P. Moller shipping group, one-time owners of Maersk Air, Star Air was formed in 1987, taking its name from the parent company's trade mark. The airline operates charter and contract freight services, including several scheduled routes on behalf of UPS, which requires all eight of the airline's Boeing 767s, which replaced the original 727s.

HQ airport & main base: Copenhagen, with a further base at Cologne/Bonn Konrad Adenauer
Radio callsign: WHITESTAR
Designator: DQ/SRR
Links with other airlines: Operates UPS scheduled freight services from Copenhagen
Fleet: 11 Boeing 767-200F

STERLING
Sterling Airlines A/S
Incorporated: 1993

Sterling was founded as Sterling European Airways at the end of 1993, just a few months after the bankruptcy of Sterling Airways in September of that year. The original airline had been founded in 1962 by the Tjaereborg Rejser travel group to operate inclusive tour charters from points throughout Scandinavia, initially using Douglas DC-6s, which were later joined by Sud Caravelle jets. At the time of the airline's collapse, a fleet of Caravelles and Boeing 727-200s was being operated. Initially the Sterling European fleet consisted of Boeing 727s, but these were replaced by new generation Boeing 737-700 and 737-800s, as well as by the smaller 737-500. The new airline's shareholders initially included the management team plus two companies, Ganger Rolf and Bonheur, in which the Norwegian Fred Olsen Group had an interest, and in 1999, Sterling became a completely Norwegian-owned company.

While the 'new' Sterling continued the inclusive tour charter operations of the original company, in 2000 it restructured and became a low-cost airline operating scheduled services. In 2005, it merged with the Danish Maersk Air, and dropped the 'European' from its name to become simply Sterling Airlines.

Maersk Air had started operations in 1970, initially operating charter flights but rapidly developing a network of scheduled flights within Denmark. During the early 1990s, a network of international scheduled services was started, initially with a route from Billund to Southend, on the Thames Estuary, but this has since developed to serve a number of major destinations within Europe, operating from both Billund and Copenhagen. Maersk had a 38 per cent stake in Danair, as one of the three partners, and had aircraft and routes operating under the Danair brand until operations ceased in 1995.

Expanding outside Denmark, Maersk was a shareholder in the Plimsoll Line, which at one time was the holding company for both Brymon Airways and Birmingham European Airways, which later became Maersk Air UK. Maersk Air UK was eventually purchased by its management, which renamed the airline Duo, and re-formed it as a low-cost airline operating from bases in Birmingham and Edinburgh, before it collapsed. Meanwhile, Maersk acquired a 49 per cent stake in Estonian Air when that airline was privatised by the Estonian government. Throughout its existence, Maersk was a subsidiary of the A.P. Moller shipping group.

HQ airport & main base: Copenhagen Kastrup, with additional bases at Billund, Oslo and Stockholm
Radio callsign: STERLING
Designator: NB/SNB
Employees: 1,630
Route points: Alicante, Amsterdam, Barcelona, Bergen, Berlin, Billund, Bologna, Budapest, Copenhagen, Edinburgh, Faro, Gothenburg, Lanzarote, Las Palmas, Malaga, Montpellier, Murcia, Nice, Oslo, Palma de Mallorca, Paris, Prague, Rome, Stavanger, Stockholm, Tenerife
Links with other airlines: Flynordic, Norwegian, SkyEurope Airlines (all qv)
Fleet: 10 Boeing 737-800; 9 Boeing 737-700; 4 Boeing 737-500; 1 Bombardier Challenger 604

SUN-AIR
Sun-Air Of Scandinavia A/S
Incorporated: 1978

Originally founded in 1978 as an air taxi and business charter service, Sun-Air began to develop as a regional scheduled airline in 1987, and in 1998 it became a British Airways franchisee, with its aircraft wearing BA colours. It is owned by its chief executive, Niels Sundberg.

HQ airport & main base: Billund
Designator: EZ/SUS
Employees: 220
Route points: Feeder services from Aalborg, Aarhus, Billund and Copenhagen
Links with other airlines: BA franchisee; alliances with Finnair, SN Brussels Airlines (all qv)
Fleet: 2 Dornier 328Jet; 5 Dornier 328-110; 3 BAe Jetstream 31

DJIBOUTI – J2

DAALLO AIRLINES
Airline of Horn of Africa
Incorporated: 1992

Founded in 1992 as a privately owned charter cargo and passenger operator with a fleet of Cessna Caravans, Daallo has since acquired a fleet of aircraft of Eastern European origin. Scheduled and charter flights are operated to a number of destinations in East Africa and the Middle East.

HQ airport & main base: Aeroport International de Djibouti
Radio callsign: DAALLO AIRLINES
Designator: D3/DAO
Route points: Addis Ababa, Bossasso, Burao, Djibouti, Galcaio, Hargeisa, Jeddah, London, Mogadishu, Nairobi, Paris
Links with other airlines: Alliances with Djibouti Airlines, Yemania (qv)
Fleet: 2 Antonov An-24B/RV; 1 Antonov An-12; 2 Let L-410UVP-E

DOMINICAN REPUBLIC – HH

With the end of operations by state-owned Dominicana, air services are largely provided by LAN Dominicana, which uses aircraft from other companies in the Chilean-controlled LAN group, and by the privately owned Servicios Aereos Professionales.

LAN DOMINICANA
Incorporated: 2003

Part of the Chilean-based LAN Airlines group, LAN Dominicana uses aircraft from other companies within the group to maintain a scheduled service between Santo Domingo and Miami. The company is owned 49 per cent by LAN Airlines.

HQ airport & main base: Santo Domingo
Designator: 4M/LNC
Route points: Miami, Santo Domingo
Links with other airlines: Owned 49 per cent by LAN Airlines.

SERVICIOS AEREOS PROFESSIONALES
Incorporated: 1981

Servicios Aereos Professionales originated as a charter airline and business aircraft operator, but now operates a number of scheduled services from Santo Domingo.

HQ airport & main base: Santo Domingo Las Americas
Designator: SS/PSV
Route points: Aruba, Caracas, Curacao, Miami, Port-au-Prince, San Juan, Santo Domingo and a number of domestic destinations
Fleet: 3 Let L-410; 3 Raytheon Beech 1900C/D; 1 Grumman G1; 2 de Havilland Canada Twin Otter Srs 100; 1 BAe Jetstream 326P; 1 Embraer EMB-120 Brasilia; 1 Cessna Caravan 675

ECUADOR – HC

AEROGAL
Incorporated: 1986

Based at Quito, Aerogal is mainly involved in operating scheduled and charter flights between destinations in mainland Ecuador and the Galapagos Islands.

HQ airport & main base: Quito Mariscal Sucre
Designator: 2K/GLG
Route points: Cuenca, Guayaquil, Quito
Fleet: 1 Boeing 727-200; 8 Boeing 737-200

ICARO
Icaro Air
Incorporated: 1971

A domestic scheduled passenger airline, Icaro Air has a small route network based on Quito. A subsidiary is Icaro Express.

HQ airport & main base: Quito Mariscal Sucre
Radio callsign: ICARO
Designator: XB
Route points: Coca, Cuenca, Esmeraldas, Guayaquil, Manta, Quito, San Cristobal
Fleet: 2 Boeing 737-200; 3 Fokker F28 Fellowship Mk4000; 1 Bombardier Dash 8 Q200

LAN ECUADOR
Incorporated: 2002

First founded in 2002, LAN Ecuador is part of the Chilean-based LAN Airlines group. LAN Airlines owns 45 per cent of the shares, while Translloyd owns 55 per cent. Operations commenced in 2003, using aircraft from other airlines within the group as needed.

HQ airport & main base: Quito Mariscal Sucre
Designator: XL/LNE
Route points: Bogotá, Buenos Aires, Lima, Madrid, New York, Quito, Santiago de Chile
Links with other airlines: Ownership is divided between Translloyd, 55 per cent, and LAN Airlines, 45 per cent, with operations integrated with the latter

TAME
TAME Linea Aerea del Ecuador
Incorporated: 1962

Ecuador's largest airline, TAME was founded in 1962 as a domestic carrier and is owned by the Fuerza Aerea Ecuatoriana, or air force. Originally, the airline was called Transportes Aereos Militares Ecuadorianos, which was later amended to Transportes Aereas Mercantiles Ecuadorianos.

It was not until 1990 that it was separated operationally from the air force, although the FAE retains ownership and senior officers occupy a number of important positions in the otherwise mainly civilian management structure. Despite considerable fleet expansion in recent years, strangely, the airline has few international routes.

HQ airport & main base: Quito Mariscal Sucre
Radio callsign: TAME
Designator: EQ/TAE
Route points: Bahia, Cali, Coca, Cuenca, Esmeraldas, Galapagos Islands, Guayaquil, Lago Agrio, Loja, Macas, Manta, Quito, Salinas, San Cristobal, Santiago de Chile, Tulcan
Links with other airlines: Alliance with Lloyd Aero Boliviano
Fleet: 4 Boeing 727-200; 1 Boeing 727-100; 2 Airbus A320-200; 1 Embraer 190; 2 Embraer 170; 2 Fokker F28 Fellowship Mk4000; 3 BAe 748 Srs 2; 2 de Havilland Canada Twin Otter Srs 300

EGYPT – SU

Egypt has one of the longest histories of air transport in Africa, largely because it was not officially a European colony after the fall of the Ottoman Empire, even though Britain and France wielded considerable influence. It was a British-backed company, Misr Airwork, established in 1932, that was the predecessor of the present-day Egyptair, and which was responsible for developing a domestic route network, initially using de Havilland Dragon biplanes.

In recent years, the growth in tourism to Egypt has seen a number of new airlines established, including the small charter operator, Flash, but Egyptair remains state owned and has interests in some of the new companies.

AIR CAIRO
Incorporated: 1997

Founded in 1997 to operate inclusive tour chartered flights between Europe and Egypt, initially using Tupolev aircraft, Egyptair has a 40 per cent stake.

HQ airport & main base: Cairo International
Designator: CCE
Links with other airlines: Egyptair is a major shareholder
Fleet: 1 Airbus A321-200; 5 Airbus A320-200

AIR MEMPHIS
Incorporated: 1995

Air Memphis was founded in 1995 and began passenger and cargo charter operations the following year. While its main base is at Cairo, a considerable volume of business is conducted at Aswan.

HQ airport & main base: Cairo International
Designator: MHS
Fleet: 2 Boeing 707-320C; 2 Airbus A320-200; 1 McDonnell Douglas DC-9-30

EGYPTAIR
Incorporated: 1932

By African standards, Egyptair has a long history, dating from 1932 and the formation of Misr Airwork with a single de Havilland DH60 trainer. The new operator was being supported by a British company, Airwork, a predecessor of British United Airways and, eventually, British Airways. The first scheduled service appeared the following year, linking Cairo, Alexandria and Mersa Matruh using de Havilland Dragon Rapide aircraft. By 1936, the fleet consisted of nine aircraft, all of de Havilland manufacture, including two Dragon Rapides, five Rapides and two Dragon Expresses. Progress with these aircraft continued, so that by 1939, in addition to destinations within Egypt, the airline also served many important points in the Middle East.

While the Second World War saw many restrictions placed on airline operations, with such activity as existed confined to the movement of Allied officers, postwar the airline was able to introduce Vickers Vikings. In 1949 the name was changed to Misrair, and during the period under this title the airline introduced Vickers Viscount turboprop airliners and then became the first Middle East airline to operate jet aircraft when it introduced de Havilland Comet 4Cs in 1960.

At this time, Egypt and Syria declared that they were to become a United Arab Republic, and although this concept had practical limitations, Egypt immediately declared itself as the 'United Arab Republic', and in 1960 the state-owned Misrair became United Arab Airlines, incorporating the privately owned Syrian Airways, while the Misrair title was retained for a new domestic airline. Even after Syria decided to operate its own airline in 1961, the United Arab Airlines title was retained by the Egyptian airline until October 1971, when the present title was chosen.

While the Comet fleet eventually reached seven aircraft, in 1968 the airline introduced three Boeing 707-366 aircraft, while Egypt's alignment with the Soviet Union at the time also meant that Antonov An-24s entered the fleet on loan from both the air force and Misrair.

The airline has now absorbed its domestic subsidiary and operates a strong fleet of Airbus and Boeing origin. Ownership remains with the Egyptian government. It owns a small airline, Air Sinai, and has a 40 per cent stake in the charter airline, Air Cairo.

HQ airport & main base: Cairo International
Radio callsign: EGYPTAIR
Designator: MS/MSR
Employees: 18,000
Route points: Abu Dhabi, Abu Simbel, Accra, Addis Ababa, Aden, Al Ain, Aleppo, Alexandria, Algiers, Amman, Amsterdam, Asmara, Assiut, Aswan, Athens, Bahrain, Bangkok, Barcelona, Beijing, Beirut, Benghazi, Berlin, Brussels, Budapest, Cairo, Casablanca, Copenhagen, Damascus, Damman, Dar-es-Salaam, Dharan, Doha, Dubai, Düsseldorf, Entebbe, Frankfurt, Geneva, Hurghada, Istanbul, Jeddah, Johannesburg, Kano, Khartoum, Kuwait, Lagos, Larnaca, London, Luxor, Madrid, Milan, Moscow, Mumbai, Munich, Muscat, Nairobi, New York, Osaka, Paris, Riyadh, Rome, Sana'a, Sharjah, Sharm el Sheikh, Stockholm, Tokyo, Tripoli, Tunis, Vienna, Zurich
Links with other airlines: Alliances with Austrian Airlines, Gulf Air, Malaysian Airlines, Olympic Airlines, Royal Air Maroc, Swiss, Thai Airways (all qv)
Fleet: 3 Airbus A340-200; 5 Boeing 777-200ER; 6 Airbus A330-200; 1 Airbus A300-600F; 2 Airbus A300B4-200F; 1 Airbus A300-600R; 3 Airbus A321-200; 12 Boeing 737-800; 12 Airbus A320-200; 4 Boeing 737-500

PETROLEUM AIR SERVICES
Incorporated: 1982

An operator of charter services mainly for passengers, Petroleum Air Services had de Havilland Dash 7 aircraft in the Western Desert and the Gulf of Suez for some years, and has recently added Dash 8s. At one time, light helicopters were also operated. Ownership rests with the state-owned Egyptian General Petroleum Corporation (75 per cent) and Air Logistics International (25 per cent).

HQ airport & main base: Cairo (HQ), Al-Arish (main base)
Designator: PAS
Employees: 500
Fleet: 5 Bombardier Dash 8 Q300; 5 de Havilland Dash 7-100

EL SALVADOR – YS

TACA
TACA International Airlines
Incorporated: 1931

Unusual in that it is the flag carrier for two countries, Honduras and neighbouring El Salvador, TACA was originally formed in Honduras by Lowell Yerex in 1931, but in 1939, the airline's main emphasis moved to El Salvador as TACA El Salvador, although it did not become El Salvadorean owned until 1960. The airline developed a scheduled service network initially in Central America, but in 1990 the network reached New York and Washington. The airline acquired a 30 per cent stake in Aviateca of Guatemala in 1989 when that airline was privatised, and also has a 49 per cent stake in TACA-Peru, a 20 per cent stake in Islena Airlines and 10 per cent interest in LACSA of Costa Rica. Over the past decade, the fleet has changed from all-Boeing to all-Airbus, and has enjoyed considerable expansion, including absorbing Aviateca outright, although the aircraft for TACA-Peru are included in the TACA International Airlines fleet.

HQ airport & main base: El Salvador International
Radio callsign: TACA
Designator: TA/TAI
Route points: Belize, Bogotá, Boston, Buenos Aires, Cancun, Caracas, Chicago, Cuzoo, Dallas/Fort Worth, Flores, Guatemala City, Houston, La Ceiba, La Paz, Lima, Los Angeles, Managua, Mexico City, Miami, New York, Panama City, Quito, San Francisco, San Jose, San Pedro Sula, Santa Cruz, Santiago de Chile, Sao Paulo, Tegucigalpa, Washington
Links with other airlines: Owns Aviateca of Guatemala. Has interests in TACA-Peru, 49 per cent; Islena Airlines (qv), 20 per cent, and 10 per cent interest in LACSA (qv) of Costa Rica
Fleet: 5 Airbus A321-200; 31 Airbus A320-200; 12 Airbus A319-100

ERITREA – E3

ERITREAN AIRLINES
Incorporated: 2003

Originally a ground handling company dating from 1991, Eritrean Airlines moved into scheduled operations in 2003. It is wholly owned by the government of Eritrea.

HQ airport & main base: Asmara International
Radio callsign: ERITREAN
Designator: B8/ERT
Route points: Amsterdam, Asmara, Frankfurt, Jeddah, Milan, Nairobi, Rome
Fleet: 1 Boeing 767-200ER; 1 Airbus A320-200

ESTONIA – ES

One of the Baltic States annexed by the Soviet Union early in the Second World War, postwar aviation in Estonia was provided by Aeroflot. Since the break-up of the Soviet Union, the country has had a number of airlines established, often with outside assistance. The national airline, Estonian Air, originally a division of Aeroflot, has had investment first from Denmark's Maersk Air and more recently from SAS.

AERO AIRLINES
Incorporated: 2002

Founded by Finnair, which retains complete ownership, to provide regional passenger and cargo air services between the Baltic countries, including Finland, Aero Airlines operates an all-turboprop fleet. The attraction of this venture is that the company would have substantially lower costs than Finnair itself.

HQ airport & main base: Tallin, with a second base at Tampere
Radio callsign: AERO
Designator: EE/EAY
Employees: 120

Route points: Helsinki, Joensuu, Jyvaskyla, Kajaani, Kokkola, Kuopio, Mariehamn, Tallin, Tampere, Turku, Vaasa, Vilnius
Fleet: 7 ATR-72-200

ENIMEX
Incorporated: 1994

A charter airline specialising in cargo, but with some passenger operations, and wet-lease activities.

HQ airport & main base: Tallinn Ulemiste
Designator: ENI
Fleet: 1 Antonov An-72; 1 BAe ATP

ESTONIAN AIR
Incorporated: 1991

Originally the local division of Aeroflot, Estonian Air assumed its independence in 1991 as a state-owned concern. In 1995, the Estonian government offered 66 per cent of the shares for sale, and Maersk Air obtained a 49 per cent stake in the airline, with an Estonian investment group, the Baltic Cresco Investment Group, obtaining the remaining 17 per cent. The Maersk stake has now passed to SAS.

The fleet has seen the rapid disappearance of Tu-134 and Yak-40 equipment of Aeroflot origin as Maersk provided more up-to-date Western equipment, and today the airline has standardised on the Boeing 737-500.

HQ airport & main base: Tallinn
Radio callsign: ESTONIAN
Designator: OV/ELL
Employees: 347
Route points: Amsterdam, Berlin, Brussels, Copenhagen, Dublin, Frankfurt, Hamburg, Helsinki, Kiev, London, Manchester, Milan, Moscow, Oslo, Riga, Stockholm, Tallinn, Vilnius
Links with other airlines: SAS has a 49 per cent interest. Alliances with Aeroflot Russian Airlines, AeroSvit Airlines, Air Baltic, SAS (all qv)
Fleet: 3 Boeing 737-500; 3 Boeing 737-300

ETHIOPIA – ET

ETHIOPEAN AIRLINES
Incorporated: 1945

Founded in 1945, Ethiopean Airlines commenced scheduled services the following year, receiving technical and operational assistance from TWA. The airline now operates both internal and international services. It is wholly owned by the Ethiopean government.

HQ airport & main base: Addis Ababa Bole International
Radio callsign: ETHIOPEAN
Designator: ET/ETH
Employees: 4,520
Route points: More than 20 domestic destinations served from Addis Ababa, plus Abidjan, Accra, Addis Ababa, Amsterdam, Asmara, Athens, Bamako, Bangkok, Beijing, Beirut, Brazzaville, Bujumbura, Cairo, Dakar, Dar-es-Salaam, Delhi, Djibouti, Douala, Dubai, Entebbe, Frankfurt, Guangzhou, Harare, Hargeisa, Hong Kong, Jeddah, Johannesburg, Khartoum, Kigali, Kilimanjaro, Kinshasa, Lagos, Lilongwe, Lome, London, Luanda, Lusaka, Mumbai, Nairobi, Ndjamena, Paris, Rome, Stockholm, Tel Aviv, Washington
Links with other airlines: Alliances with South African Airways (qv)
Fleet: 2 McDonnell Douglas DC-10-30F; 6 Boeing 767-300ER; 1 Boeing 767-200ER; 1 Boeing 757; 6 Boeing 757-200; 2 Lockheed L-100-30 Hercules; 6 Boeing 737-700; 1 Boeing 737-200; 5 Fokker 50; 1 Antonov An-12; 3 de Havilland Canada Twin Otter Srs 300 (On order: 8 Boeing 787-8; 2 Boeing 787-9)

FIJI – DO

AIR PACIFIC
Air Pacific Ltd
Incorporated: 1947

Formed in 1947 by an Australian, Harold Gatty, Air Pacific was initially known as Katafaga Estates, but the name of Fiji Airways was adopted in 1951 when the airline started regular air services to the islands within the Fiji group. The early aircraft were of de Havilland manufacture, with first Dragon Rapides, then Herons and the relatively rare tri-motor Drovers manufactured in Australia. Later, these were replaced by de Havilland Canada Turbo Beavers and Douglas DC-3s, as well as Hawker Siddeley 748s.

The current title was adopted in 1972, reflecting the airline's move into longer-haul services, and that same year the first jet aircraft were acquired, three BAe One-Elevens. Today the route network extends as far as Japan, the west coast of the United States, Australia and New Zealand, while domestic services are operated by smaller feeder airlines. The airline is controlled by the Fiji government with 51 per cent of the shares, while Qantas holds 46 per cent, Air New

Zealand 1.9 per cent, and a number of small island administrations hold the remaining shares.

HQ airport & main base: Nadi
Radio callsign: PACIFIC NADI
Designator: FJ/FJI
Route points: Apia, Auckland, Brisbane, Christmas Island, Honiara, Honolulu, Los Angles, Melbourne, Nadi, Nuku'alofa, Port Vila, Suva, Sydney, Tokyo, Vancouver
Links with other airlines: Qantas owns 46 per cent of Air Pacific shares, while Air New Zealand (qv) has 1.9 per cent. Alliances with Air Vanuatu, American Airlines (qv), Polynesian Airlines, Qantas (qv)
Fleet: 2 Boeing 747-400; 1 Boeing 767-300ER (leased); 2 Boeing 737-800; 2 Boeing 737-400; 1 Boeing 737-700 (On order: 5 Boeing 787-9)

FINLAND – OH

Seizing independence during the Russian Civil War, civil aviation in Finland began in 1923 with the formation of an airline called Aero, operating Junkers seaplanes. While for many years Finnish air transport was dominated by Finnair, there was also a small domestic scheduled and international charter airline, Kar-Air, which dated from 1950. While Kar-Air no longer exists, a number of airlines have been established in recent years following the liberalisation of air transport after Finland became a member of the European Union, with the emphasis on low-cost flights, while SAS has also bought Blue1 as a Finnish feeder, and Finnair now has its own independently owned feeder, Finncomm.

AIR FINLAND
Incorporated: 2002

Air Finland was founded in 2002 and commenced operations the following year with a single Boeing 757-200, initially on charter flights but later introducing low-cost scheduled flights.

HQ airport & main base: Helsinki Vantaa
Designator: OF/FIF
Employees: 150
Route points: Alicante, Faro, Helsinki, Malaga
Fleet: 3 Boeing 757-200

BLUE1
Incorporated: 1987

Originally formed as Air Botnia in 1987, the airline began operations in the following year. It was taken over by Scandinavian Airlines in 1998 and repositioned as a feeder airline supporting SAS operations out of Stockholm and Copenhagen. The current name was adopted in 2004, and the airline became the first regional member of the Star Alliance.

HQ airport & main base: Helsinki Vantaa
Designator: KF/BLF
Employees: 506
Route points: Amsterdam, Berlin, Copenhagen, Gothenburg, Hamburg, Helsinki, Kittila, Kuopio, Oslo, Oulu, Rovaniemi, Stockholm, Tampere, Turku, Vaasa
Links with other airlines: A susbidiary of SAS (qv)
Fleet: 3 McDonnell Douglas MD-90-30; 2 BAe Avro RJ100ER; 7 BAe Avro RJ85ER; 5 Saab 2000

FINNAIR
Finnair O/Y
Incorporated: 1923

Finnair was founded in 1923 under the title of 'Aero' by Bruno Lucander, who commenced operations the following March using a single Junkers F.13 monoplane seaplane. During the summer months this aircraft served Tallinn and Stockholm from Helsinki, and during the winter months services were operated within Finland. For the summer of 1925, the Helsinki–Tallinn service was extended to Berlin. During the severe winter which followed, when the ferry services between Helsinki and Tallinn were cancelled and those between Helsinki and Stockholm were severely curtailed, the Finnish Parliament became convinced of the potential offered by air transport. This led to the Finnish government providing the new airline with a loan to purchase a Junkers G.24, and a subsidy for the Stockholm route, as well as a contract to provide airmail services.

By 1928, the fleet consisted of five aircraft, four Junkers F.13s and a single G.24. That year, an ambitious new route was introduced: the 'Scandinavian Air Express' was inaugurated linking Tallinn and Helsinki to London and Paris via Stockholm, Malmö, Copenhagen and Amsterdam, taking twenty-four hours end to end. Several new routes were added to the airline's network over the next few years, and Finnair played a significant role in the development of overnight airmail services, which were helped significantly during the early 1930s by the introduction of a Junkers Ju.52/3m, which was able to establish its position using signals from a ground-based radio station. Yet another advance was the opening of airports at both Turku and Helsinki in 1935 and 1936 respectively, enabling the airline to convert to an all-landplane fleet. In the years immediately before the outbreak of the Second World War, a domestic route network was built up, using two de Havilland Dragon Rapide biplanes.

Although not initially involved with the war in Europe, Finland was dragged in after being attacked by the Soviet Union, which wished to annex the country. Most civil operations had to stop during the war, although until the winter of 1944–5, the service from Helsinki to Stockholm was maintained. The position of Finland during the closing months of the war was made more difficult after Finland had allied herself with Germany, facing a common enemy in the Soviet Union. Nevertheless, an early resumption of domestic services was possible once the war ended, using Douglas DC-3s, although international services did not resume until 1947 when the Helsinki–Stockholm service was reintroduced.

The expansion of both domestic and international services continued throughout the 1950s, and in 1956, the airline became the first Western airline to be allowed to operate services to Moscow, although this concession was probably allowed because postwar Finland had neutrality forced upon her. While the DC-3s remained in service throughout this period, they were increasingly confined to domestic services, while international routes were taken over by the Convair 340 and 440 Metropolitan.

Finnair entered the 1960s with the introduction of the airline's first jet airliners, Sud Aviation Caravelles, which by the mid-1960s were used on all of the airline's main international routes. In 1969, the airline introduced two Douglas DC-8-62s for its first transatlantic services. By this time, another change had occurred. After using the name 'Finnair' for some years, but officially remaining Aero O/Y, the legal title was also changed to Finnair.

Finnair's broader horizons did not mean that domestic services were neglected, and relative to the population, one of the most intensive domestic networks anywhere was developed.

In 1996, a major reorganisation of Finnish civil aviation led to Finnair absorbing the operations of two other airlines, Finnaviation and Karair.

Karair had dated from 1950, when it had been formed as Karhumaki Airways, the operating offshoot of the Karhumaki Group, which dated from the 1920s and had itself been founded by three brothers with an interest in aircraft manufacturing and operations. At first, the new airline had operated de Havilland Dragon Rapides on a service between Helsinki and Joensuu, but these were soon joined by two Lockheed Lodestars, and the route was extended to Sundsvall in Sweden via two other domestic route points, although the Swedish section soon had to be dropped. A service to Tampere was later introduced, and Douglas DC-3s added to the fleet.

The name was changed to Karair in 1957, the same year as a Convair 440 Metropolitan was introduced to the fleet, and soon followed by a second aircraft. In addition to a small network of domestic services, Karair was by this time expanding into the air charter business, and Douglas DC-6B Cloudmasters soon joined the fleet, including a swing-tail variant for cargo. Finnair acquired a 29.8 per cent stake in Karair in 1963, and an operating agreement between the two airlines effectively left Karair to operate charters, apart from two scheduled domestic routes, and Finnair scheduled services. This arrangement continued for some time, although eventually Karair became a domestic scheduled airline operating ATR-72s and a Twin Otter, serving sixteen destinations as well as undertaking some international operations on behalf of Finnair, and charter operations became much less significant. The airline also became a subsidiary of Finnair.

Finnaviation also dated from 1950, when it had been formed as Lentohuolto, later changing to Wihuri Finnwings and finally to Finnaviation in 1979, when Oy Nordair, which dated from 1970, was acquired. Finnair eventually acquired a 90 per cent shareholding in the airline. The airline operated a domestic network, night mail and air taxi operations, as well as undertaking a number of services on behalf of Finnair. By the 1990s, the fleet included six Saab 340s, one of which was configured for executive use and flown on charters for business and government customers.

Finnair today is still owned 57.04 per cent by the state, down by around three per cent over the past decade, with the remaining shares belonging to banks and insurance companies, nominees and individuals. Finnair serves more than twenty domestic destinations in addition to a comprehensive European network and transatlantic and Asian services. Expansion outside the limited confines of the Finnish market has seen Finnair start a subsidiary, Aero Airlines in Estonia in 2005, while the following year it bought the low-cost Swedish operator Flynordic. Finnair is a member of the Oneworld alliance, which it joined in 1999, having earlier, in 1997, signed a marketing alliance with Lufthansa.

For most of its history, Finnair has been a staunch supporter of Douglas and then McDonnell Douglas aircraft, but after Boeing acquired McDonnell Douglas, the emphasis seems to have switched to Airbus aircraft, although four Boeing 757s were introduced to the fleet for charter traffic, and a further three were added later.

While Finland has a small population, the airline is the forty-second largest in the world by revenue, but is outside the 'Top 50' by passenger numbers.

HQ airport & main base: Helsinki Vantaa
Radio callsign: FINNAIR
Designator: AY/FIN
Employees: 9,447
Route points: Amsterdam, Athens, Bangkok, Barcelona, Beijing, Berlin, Billund, Brussels, Budapest, Copenhagen, Dubai, Düsseldorf, Frankfurt, Fuerteventura, Geneva, Gothenburg, Guangzhou, Hamburg, Helsinki, Hong Kong, Ivalo, Joensuu, Jyvaskla, Kajaani, Kemi/Tornio, Kiev, Kittila, Kokkola/Pietarsaari, Kuopio, Kuusamo, Lanzarote, Larnaca, Las Palmas, Lisbon, London, Madeira, Madrid, Malaga, Manchester, Mariehamn, Miami, Milan, Moscow, Munich, Murcia, New York, Osaka, Oslo, Ostersund, Oulu, Paphos, Paris, Ponta Delgado, Prague, Riga, Rome, Rovaniemi, St Petersburg, San Francisco, Shanghai, Singapore, Stockholm, Stuttgart, Tallinn, Tampere, Tenerife, Tokyo, Turku, Vaasa, Vienna, Vilnius, Warsaw, Zurich
Links with other airlines: Owns 100 per cent of Aero Airlines of Estonia and Flynordic of Sweden (both qv). Alliances Aeroflot Russian Airlines, Air China, Air France, American Eagle Airlines, City Airline, CSA Czech Airlines, Emirates Sky Cargo, Finncomm Airlines, FlyLal, Japan Airlines, SN Brussels Airlines, Sun-Air of Scandinavia, Swiss, Ukraine International Airlines (all qv)
Annual turnover: US $2,148 million (£1,432 million)
Fleet: 3 Airbus A340-300; 1 McDonnell Douglas MD-11ER; 6 McDonnell Douglas MD-11; 7 Boeing 757-200; 6 Airbus A321-200; 12 Airbus A320-200; 11 Airbus A319-100; 10 Embraer 190; 10 Embraer 170 (On order: 9 Airbus A350-900)

FINNCOMM AIRLINES
Incorporated: 1993

A regional feeder airline in independent ownership, Finncomm Airlines was established in 1993 and commenced operations in 1997, providing feeder services for both Finnair and Golden Air. Unusually for a feeder, it also operates to some international destinations.

HQ airport & main base: Seinajoki, with a hub at Helsinki Vantaa
Radio callsign: FINNCOMM
Designator: FC/WBA
Employees: 145
Route points: Düsseldorf, Enontekio, Helsinki, Joensuu, Jyvaskyla, Kemi/Tornio, Kokkola/Pietersaari, Lappeenranta, Oslo, Pori, Savonlinna, Seinajoki, Stuttgart, Tampere, Vaasa, Varkaus
Links with other airlines: Alliances with Finnair and Golden Air, for whom feeder flights are flown (both qv)
Fleet: 7 ATR 72-500; 4 ATR-42-500; 2 Embraer ERJ-145LR

FRANCE – F

France could claim to have the longest history of air transport as, during the siege of Paris by Prussian forces in 1870, letters were sent from the city using unmanned balloons. Perhaps more to the point, the aircraft manufacturer Farman started an air service between Paris and London on 8 February 1919, using converted wartime Farman Goliath bombers.

The use of converted bombers was a feature of the early air services in many countries, including the United Kingdom and the United States as well as France. While the early flights linked Paris and London, the next priority became regular flying boat services across the Mediterranean, linking metropolitan France with her North African territories. During the 1920s and into the early1930s, even travellers between the United Kingdom and her colonial possessions would make the journey across France by railway rather than by air. Air France then embarked on the task of linking France with her further-flung colonial possessions, initially in sub-Saharan Africa and then in French Indo-China (now Vietnam, Laos and Kampuchea).

After the disruption of the Second World War, most French aviation was dominated by the state airline, Air France, with Air Inter as a domestic airline and, from 1991, Aeropostale as a night airmail operator, but also offering day cargo flights. There was also an inclusive tour charter airline, known somewhat unimaginatively as Air Charter, and which managed to achieve a lower load factor at times than some scheduled airlines! Air Inter has been absorbed into Air France, initially as Air France Europe, but it is now completely integrated. A fourth French airline was Union de Transportes Aeriens, UTA, which was initially established as a 'second force' airline, although overlap and competition with Air France was virtually nonexistent. UTA mainly operated to Africa and the French Pacific territories, and was instrumental in establishing Air Afrique, the multinational airline for former French African colonies away from the stronger economies of North Africa. As with its UK counterpart, British United Airways (later British Caledonian), UTA was eventually absorbed by the national flag carrier, as indeed have been both Aeropostale and Air Charter.

While Air France had a number of 'firsts' to its credit, being the first Western airline to operate a short-haul jet airliner, the Sud Caravelle, and shared with British Airways the distinction of operating supersonic services with the Concorde airliner, it has also shown a number of weaknesses. It was one of the three Allied airlines allowed to operate German domestic services out of Berlin during the period of German partition, but proved uncompetitive against British European Airways and Pan American, and so operated only a Berlin–Paris service.

In recent years, liberalisation of air transport has seen many new French airlines develop. British Airways even became involved in the French market, acquiring a substantial minority stake in the French airline Touraine Air Transport, TAT, although later relinquishing this as the policy of investing in airlines outside the UK was abandoned amidst mounting losses. Since that time, there has been some consolidation of the French air transport industry, with the disappearance of Air Liberté, Air Littoral and TAT, and AOM Airlines.

In some ways, AOM was a successor to UTA. The airline dates from 1992, when it was formed from the merger of two older airlines, Air Outre Mer and Minerve. Air Outre Mer had been formed almost five years earlier, and had been operating scheduled services with three McDonnell Douglas DC-10s between Paris and Reunion in the Indian Ocean. Minerve, Compagnie Française de Transports Aeriens, had been founded in 1975 by René Meyer, and had been operating charter and scheduled services, with the former including ad hoc worldwide cargo operations as well as incluisve tour passenger charters. The Minerve fleet included a Boeing 747 and a McDonnell Douglas DC-10, as well as several DC-8s and MD-83s.

AOM operated McDonnell Douglas DC-10s and MD-83s on inclusive tour charters worldwide, with scheduled services within France and to destinations in the Indian and Pacific Oceans.

AIGLE AZUR
Aigle Azur Transports Aeriens
Incorporated: 1970

Originally formed in 1970 as Lucas Aviation, and then as Lucas Aigle, operating scheduled domestic services. Today, the airline operates passenger and cargo charters, provides wet-leased aircraft and also operates domestic scheduled passenger services within France and Algeria.

HQ airport & main base: Aeroport de Paris-Pontoise
Designator: Z1/AAF
Route points: Algiers, Annaba, Batna, Bejaia, Constantine, Djanet, Hassi Messaoud, Lille, Lyons, Marrakesh, Marseilles, Mulhouse/Basle, Oran, Oujda, Paris, Tamenghest, Tlemcen, Toulouse
Fleet: 3 Airbus A321-200; 4 Airbus A320-200; 2 Airbus A319-100

AIR FRANCE
Compagnie Nationale Air France/Air France-KLM Group
Incorporated: 1933

Following the merger with KLM, the combined airline is now the world's largest in terms of annual turnover, although ranking fifth in terms of passenger numbers. Although Air France itself dates from 1933, it was formed upon the merger of five airlines, the oldest of which, Farman Airlines, dated from 1919. The other four airlines were CIDNA, Cie International de Navigation Aerienne, Air Union, Air Orient and Aeropostale.

Farman Airlines, owned by the aircraft manufacturer of that name, had been among the first generation of airlines when it was formed in 1919, and among the first to operate on the Paris–London service, soon followed by a service from Paris to Brussels. On both these services, the airline used Farman Goliath 13-seat converted bombers. Steady expansion ensured that the airline was serving most western European capitals by 1930.

Air Union concentrated on services to the Mediterranean area of France, while Air Orient, as the name implied, operated from France to the Far East. The airline operated its first service in 1931, from Marseilles in the south of France to Saigon in what was then French Indo-China, flying via Damascus. The jounrey took ten days, and two aircraft, with a Loire-et-Olivier 242 on the Mediterranean section, and a Brequet 280 for the remainder.

Aeropostale was already owned by the French government, which had rescued the airline after it became bankrupt, restarting its postal operations. The airline had been started in the early 1920s, and had also played a part in the development of an ancestor airline to Aerolineas Argentinas.

The French government had a 25 per cent interest in Air France. The new airline expanded rapidly after its formation, so that by 1939 it had a fleet of ninety aircraft, of which fifteen were seaplanes. On the outbreak of the Second World War, the airline's operations were diverted entirely to the war effort, with the needs of the diplomats and the military being met by an hourly frequency on the Paris to London route in 1939. The fall of France in 1940 led to operations being abandoned until 1942, when the airline was reassembled in North Africa, where it operated a small network of services based on Algiers and Dakar, with Damascus being added later after the Allies had occupied Vichy French territory in North Africa. When the war ended, the airline was nationalised, although provision was later made for 30 per cent of the shares to be held by private individuals or organisations.

Normal services were not resumed until 1946, when the airline restarted services to the French colonies and inaugurated its first transatlantic services, using a fleet of Douglas DC-4s, with DC-3s for the shorter routes. More modern aircraft were to follow, including Lockheed Super Constellations for intercontinental services, and, for routes in Europe and to North Africa, Vickers Viscounts. The airline was the first in the West to introduce jet aircraft to short-haul services, as the launch airline for the Sud Aviation Caravelle in May 1959, and this subsequently went on to become the first, and only, French airliner to enjoy commercial success. In January 1976, Air France became one of just two Western airlines to operate supersonic air services when the airline and British Airways launched the first such services simultaneously.

Throughout this period, Air France also became heavily involved in the formation of airlines in French colonies as these approached independence. Among these were Air Vietnam, in which Air France had a 25 per cent interest; Royal Air Cambodge (30 per cent); Tunis Air, 49 per cent; Air Algerie, per cent; Air Madagascar, 30 per cent; Royal Air Maroc, 21 per cent; and Middle East Airlines, 30 per cent. Air France also took an interest in Air Afrique, the airline created to provide services to the former colonies. When a French domestic airline, Air Inter (now Air France Europe) was established, Air France took a 25 per cent shareholding. A charter subsidiary, Société Aerienne Français d'Affrètement, was formed in 1966, later becoming Air Charter in which Air France had an 80 per cent interest and its sister company, Air France Europe, 20 per cent.

In 1991, Air France acquired a majority 84.95 per cent stake in UTA, Union de Transportes Aeriens, which had been formed in 1963 following a merger between UAT, Union Aeromaritime de Transport, and TAI, Transport Aeriens Intercontinentaux, which both dated from the early postwar period and both had strong shipping connections. UAT had been one of the few airlines to operate the ill-starred de Havilland Comet 1 airliner and had concentrated on services to Africa, while TAI had operated as a charter airline until starting services to the Pacific, including Tahiti, in 1956. At the time of the acquisition by Air France, UTA was operating a fleet of three Boeing 747-300s and six McDonnell Douglas DC-10-30s. The acquisition meant that Air France gained a well-established route network in Africa and the Pacific which complemented its own.

In 1994, a major restructuring of French air transport took place to cut costs and state support, made necessary both by pressure from the European Union to end massive state subsidies to state-controlled airlines, and by growing competition both on domestic routes by the independent French airlines, and on international routes by strong competition encouraged by the free market. A new holding company, Groupe Air France SA, was established to take over both Air France and Air Inter, which became Air France Europe and now operates a number of international services. As a transitional stage, Air France Europe operated as Air Inter Europe, but in 1997, Air France Europe was fully absorbed into Air France.

Air Inter had been formed in 1954 as a domestic airline for France. The founders were Air France, SNCF (the French railways), and the Compagnie de Transports Aeriens, with banks, regional groups and some private companies also providing some capital, the latter including the airline TAI. Services were started in 1958 using chartered aircraft, but suspended after a few months, so that it was not until June, 1960, that a more determined effort was made, this time successfully. The first route was Paris to Toulouse, and before the end of the first year, Paris–Pau and Lille–Lyon–Nice were also introduced, with services to Dinard, Quimper, La Baule, Tarbes and Biarritz following shortly afterwards. The early routes were coordinated with the services of both Air France and SNCF, with some of the routes intended to fill in gaps in existing air and railway services, or to bypass Paris, as in the case of Lille–Lyon–Nice.

Once the operation was established, ex-Air France Vickers Viscount 700 series aircraft were acquired, with the first five introduced in 1962, when the airline also established its maintenance base at Paris-Orly, to this day the main hub for French domestic air services. In 1963, TAI became part of UTA, the leading French independent airline, and UTA became a shareholder in Air Inter, so that Air France and SNCF each held a 25 per cent stake in the airline, with UTA having a further 15 per cent. The Viscount fleet continued to grow during the early 1960s, while in 1964, Air Inter also received four small 26-seat Nord 262 airliners for the quieter routes.

Air Inter's first jet aircraft were Sud Aviation Caravelle III jet airliners, with the first two leased from Air France. These were later augmented and then replaced during the early 1970s by eleven Dassault Mercure jet airliners, of which the airline was the sole operator in a market dominated by the similarly sized Boeing 737. Meanwhile, Fokker F27 Friendships were introduced to fill the size gap between the Nord 262s and the Caravelles.

The airline was forbidden by law for its first three decades to operate scheduled services outside France, but it developed charter services. In 1977, Air Inter agreed with Air France to cease competing in the charter market, and in return received 20 per cent of Air Charter. Slightly more than a decade later, and Air Inter was able to operate scheduled services to Ibiza and Madrid, using an Air France designator, while in return, Air France was able to operate from Paris Charles de Gaulle to Marseilles. In 1987, a night cargo airline, Intercargo Service, was established in conjunction with Europe Air Service and Banque Paribas. By this time, Air Inter was owned 37 per cent by Air France and 35.8 per cent by UTA, and Air France's acquisition of almost 90 per cent of UTA's shares in 1991 effectively made Air Inter a subsidiary of Air France.

Since its merger in 2004 with KLM, Air France-KLM has become the world's largest airline. Air France itself operates an extensive route network and with the other group companies has more than 250 aircraft. The company's own network extends to more than 234 destinations in 119 countries. Air France was partially privatised on the Paris Stock Exchange in 1999, and the following year became a founder member of the Sky Team alliance. In 2004, the French government sold further shares and its stake in Air France is now reduced to slightly less than 20 per cent. Since the merger with KLM, both airlines have retained their own branding, but schedules have been coordinated throughout their entire route networks, although the benefits naturally enough lie in the international networks. Cooperation agreements exist with some thirty airlines.

Air France has extensive investments in other airlines. It owns Brit Air, CityJet and Regional outright, with a substantial stake in Air Ivoire, while it has 11.95 per cent in CCM Airlines, 7.5 per cent in Air Tahiti, 5.58 per cent in Tunisair, 3.75 per cent in Cameroon Airlines, 3.17 per cent in Air Madagascar, 2.86 per cent in Royal Air Maroc, 2.78 per cent in Air Mauritius, 2.09 per cent in Air Caledonie, all of which are either French regional operations or reflect the company's own involvement in the country's colonial past, but it also has 2 per cent in the Italian airline, Alitalia, and 1.5 per cent in Austrian Airlines.

HQ airport & main bases: Paris-Orly and Paris-CDG
Radio callsign: AIRFRANS
Designator: AF/AFR
Route points: Aberdeen, Abidjan, Acapulco, Ajaccio, Algiers, Alicante, Amman, Amsterdam, Annecy, Antananarivo, Athens, Atlanta, Avignon, Bangalore, Bangkok, Bangui, Barcelona, Basle/Mulhouse, Bastia, Beijing, Beirut, Belgrade, Berlin, Biarritz, Bilbao, Billund, Birmingham, Bogotá, Bologna, Bordeaux, Boston, Brazzaville, Bremen, Brest, Brussels, Bucharest, Budapest, Buenos Aires, Caen, Cairo, Calvi, Caracas, Casablanca, Cayenne, Chennai, Chicago, Cincinnati, Clermont-Ferrand, Cologne, Conakry, Copenhagen, Cotonou, Dakar, Damascus, Delhi, Detroit, Djibouti, Douala, Dubai, Dublin, Düsseldorf, Edinburgh, Eindhoven, Figari, Fort de France, Frankfurt, Geneva, Genoa, Gothenburg, Guadalajara, Guangzhou, Hamburg, Hanoi, Hanover, Helsinki, Ho Chi Minh City, Hong Kong, Houston, Ibiza, Istanbul, Jakarta, Jeddah, Johannesburg, Kiev, Kinshasa, Kuala Lumpur, Kuwait, Lagos, Lannion, Le Havre, Libreville, Lille, Limoges, Lisbon, Ljubljana, Lome, London, Lorient, Los Angeles, Lourdes, Luanda, Luxembourg, Lyons, Madrid, Mahe Island, Malabo, Malaga, Manchester, Marrakesh, Marseilles, Mauritius, Mérida, Metz/Nancy, Mexico City, Miami, Milan, Monterrey, Montpellier, Montreal, Moscow, Mumbai, Munich, Nagoya, Nantes, Naples, Ndjamena, New York, Newark, Newcastle, Niamey, Nice, Nouakchott, Nuremberg, Osaka, Oslo, Ougadougou, Palma de Mallorca, Papeete, Paris, Pau, Perpignan, Philadelphia, Pisa, Pointe Noire, Pointe-à-Pitre, Port-au-Prince, Port Harcourt, Porto, Prague, Puerto Vallarta, Punta Cana, Quimper, Rabat, Rennes, Rio de Janeiro, Riyadh, Rodez, Rome, Rouen, St Denis de la Reunion, Dominique, St Maarten, St Petersburg, Salzburg, San Francisco, Santiago, Santo

Domingo, Sao Paulo, Seoul, Seville, Shanghai, Singapore, Sofia, Southampton, Stockholm, Strasbourg, Stuttgart, Tehran, Tel Aviv, Tokyo, Toronto, Toulon, Toulouse, Trieste, Tunis, Turin, Valencia, Valladolid, Venice, Verona, Vienna, Vigo, Warsaw, Washington, Yaounde, Zagreb, Zurich
Links with other airlines: Member of Sky Team alliance. Alliances with Aeroflot (qv), Air Caledonie (qv), Air Europa (qv), Air Mauritius (qv), Air Seychelles, Air Tahiti (qv), Air India (qv), Austrian Airlines (qv), bmi (qv), Brit Air (qv), Bulgaria Air (qv), CCM Airlines (qv), China Eastern Airlines (qv), China Southern Airlines (qv), CityJet (qv), Comair (qv), Croatia Airlines (qv), Finnair (qv), Japan Airlines (qv), JAT (qv), Luxair (qv), Malev (qv), Middle East Airlines (qv), PGA Portugalia Airlines (qv), Qantas Airways (qv), Regional (qv), Royal Air Maroc (qv), TACA (qv), TAM (qv), Tarom (qv), Tunisair (qv), Ukraine International (qv), Vietnam Airlines (qv)
Passengers carried: (inc. KLM) 64.1 million
Annual turnover: (inc. KLM) US $24,054 million (£16,018 million)
Fleet: 10 Boeing 747-400; 6 Boeing 747-400 Combi; 5 Boeing 747-400ERF; 1 Boeing 747-300 Combi; 7 Boeing 747-300F; 20 Airbus A340-300; 29 Boeing 777-300ER; 25 Boeing 777-200ER; 5 Boeing 777F; 16 Airbus A330-200; 10 Airbus A321-200; 5 Airbus A321-100; 54 Airbus A320-200; 13 Airbus A320-100; 46 Airbus A319-100; 18 Airbus A318-100 (On order: 10 Airbus A380-800)

AIR MEDITERRANEE
Incorporated: 1997

Founded in 1997, passenger and cargo charter operations began that same year, including flights to the Roman Catholic shrine at Lourdes, where the airline has located its operational base.

HQ airport & main base: Lourdes Tarbes International
Designator: BIE
Fleet: 1 Boeing 757-200; 3 Airbus A321-200; 3 Airbus A321-100; 1 Airbus A320-200

AIRLINAIR
Incorporated: 1998

Airlinair was formed in 1998 and commenced operations in 1999. It provides regional aircraft on wet-lease for a number of airlines, including Air France, while Brit Air has a 19.5 per cent stake in the airline.

HQ airport & main bases: Paris Orly and Charles de Gaulle
Designator: A5/RLA, or more usually that of airline for whom services are operated
Links with other airlines: BritAir (qv) has a 19.5 per cent interest
Fleet: 2 ATR-72-500; 4 ATR-72-200/210; 10 ATR-42-500; 5 ATR-42-300

AXIS AIRWAYS
Incorporated: 1999

Founded in 1999 in Grenoble as Sinair, the original owners, Pan European Air Services, sold the airline to Axis Partners in 2000 and the current title was adopted the following year. Passenger and cargo charter flights are operated from Marseilles and Toulouse.

HQ airport & main base: Marseilles Provence
Designator: 6V/AXY
Fleet: 2 Boeing 757-200; 1 Boeing 737-400; 3 Boeing 737-300QC

BLUE LINE
Incorporated: 2002

A passenger charter airline operating inclusive tour holiday flights and some VIP operations.

HQ airport & main base: Paris Charles de Gaulle
Designator: BLE
Employees: 160
Fleet: 2 Fokker 100; 2 McDonnell Douglas MD-83

BRIT AIR
Brit Air SA
Incorporated: 1973

Founded in 1973, Brit Air commenced operations in 1975 to provide direct air services from western France to the rest of the country and to other European destinations. A service to London Gatwick was introduced in 1979. The fleet at one time included six Saab 340s, but these have been replaced by Bombardier Regional Jets and Fokker 100s. The airline was the launch customer for the stretched Bombardier CRJ-700 regional jet. In 1995, the airline became an Air France franchisee, and in 1997 reached an agreement with Air France that all services would be flown as franchises, with Air France transfering twelve routes to Brit Air, while in 2000, the airline became a wholly owned subsidiary of Air France. In turn, Brit Air owns 19.5 per cent of the shares of Airlinair. HQ is at Morlaix, but services operate from Brest, Caen, Deauville, Le Havre, Nantes, Rennes, Toulouse

Radio callsign: BRITTANY
Designator: DB/BZH (or Air France AF)
Employees: 1,260
Route points: Include Brest, Caen, Deauville, Le Havre, Limoges, London, Lyons, Marseilles, Montpellier, Nice, Paris, Quimper, Rennes, Southampton, Toulouse
Links with other airlines: Owned by Air France (qv)
Fleet: 13 Fokker 100; 15 Bombardier CRJ700-701LR; 19 Bombardier CRJ100ER

CCM AIRLINES
Compagnie Corse Méditerranée
Incorporated: 1990

Founded in 1990 as Corse Méditerranée, the airline adopted its current title in 2000. CCM is a regional airline operating passenger scheduled and charter services from its base at Ajaccio in Corsica. It specialises in providing direct services from the island to important destinations in southern Europe, but in 1997 two Boeing 747-300s were acquired from Singapore Airlines for long distance charters, but these have been dropped following an agreement with Air France, which has a 12 per cent stake in the airline, although there has been expansion elsewhere. Maintenance is carried out by a subsidiary, Compagnie Aerienne Corse Méditerranée.

HQ airport & main base: Ajaccio Campo dell'Oro, with operations also from Bastia and Calvi
Radio callsign: CORSICA
Designator: XK/CCM
Employees: 653
Route points: Ajaccio, Bastia, Calvi, Figari, Geneva, Lyons, Marseilles, Milan, Nice, Paris, Rome, Zurich
Fleet: 2 Airbus A320-200; 2 Airbus A319-100; 2 ATR-72-200; 6 ATR-72-500

CORSAIRFLY
Corse Air International SA
Incorporated: 1981

Corse Air International was founded in 1981 as a charter airline specialising in services to destinations in the Mediterranean, maintaining bases at Paris Orly and Ajaccio. Operations soon expanded to include North America, while the tour operator Nouvelles Frontiers acquired a 30 per cent interest in the airline in 1990, and the airline obtained worldwide traffic rights in 1991. In 2000, the TUI travel group bought the airline. Over the past decade, the airline has more than doubled the number of its employees, while much of its operation now consists of long-distance services, especially to the Caribbean and East Africa, with both scheduled services and charters flown. The present title was adopted in 2005.

HQ airport & main base: Paris Orly
Radio callsign: CORSAIR
Designator: SS/CRL
Employees: 1,723
Route points: Antananarivo, Brest, Fez, Fort de France, Marrakesh, Marseilles, Mombasa, Nairobi, Nates, Paris, Pointe-à-Pitre, Rome, St Denis de la Reunion, St Maarten, Toulouse, Venice
Fleet: 4 Boeing 747-400; 2 Boeing 747-300; 2 Airbus A330-200

EAGLE AVIATION FRANCE
Incorporated: 2002

Provides aircraft and crew on a wet-lease basis to other airlines. Although operations started in 2002, the airline was formed in 1999. The principal shareholder, with 70 per cent, is the chairman.

HQ airport & main base: St Nazaire; main base is Paris Charles de Gaulle
Designator: EGN
Employees: 135
Fleet: 2 Airbus A310-200

EUROPE AIRPOST
Incorporated: 1991

Originally formed as Intercargo Service, Europe Airpost is a subsidiary of Groupe La Poste and operates overnight mail flights for the French Post Office, with charter passenger and cargo flights during the day, including wet-lease scheduled operations for other airlines.

HQ airport & main base: Paris Charles de Gaulle
Radio callsign: AIRPOST
Designator: 5O/FPO
Fleet: 13 Boeing 737-300QC; 1 Boeing 737-300; 1 ATR-72-200

REGIONAL
Regional Compagnie Aerienne Européen SA
Incorporated: 2001

Regional Airlines was founded in 1992 on the acquisition of Airlec and Air Vendée, two regional airlines. Air Vendée, by far the larger of the two, dated from 1975, and operated from Nantes, Rouen and Rennes to a dozen destinations within France and neigbouring countries with a fleet which included Dornier Do.228s, Fairchild Metros and a Beech King Air 200. In 2001, it was acquired by Air France, which already had merged two airlines, its subsidiary Proteus and Flandre Air (not to be confused with a former Belgian airline) in 1999. Flandre Air had been founded in 1976 and began air taxi and executive air charter operations the following year, not moving into scheduled services until 1985. By the time of the acquisition by Proteus, a number of domestic scheduled routes were operated, mainly from the airline's base at Lille, sometimes on behalf of other airlines. Proteus had been operating since 1986. At the time of the creation of Regional, Proteus was operating a mix of Embraer ERJ-135 and 145, Fokker 100 and Raytheon Beech 1900 regional aircraft, while Flandre was also a Beech 1900 and Embraer regional jet operator, as well as having a number of Embraer Brasilia turboprops, with the substantial level of commonality between the three fleets helping the merger when it finally took place in 2001.

The new airline has been created with the aim of providing a feeder service for the parent company, Air France, and has five main hubs.

HQ airport & main base: Nantes Atlantique, with hubs at Bordeaux, Clermont Ferrand, Lyons and Paris Charles de Gaulle
Radio callsign: REGIONAL
Designator: YS/RAE
Employees: 1,700
Route points: Included in the Air France list of destinations
Links with other airlines: Owned by Air France (qv)
Fleet: 9 Fokker 100; 6 Embraer 190; 5 Fokker 70; 28 Embraer ERJ-145EU/MP; 9 Embraer ERJ-135ER; 6 Saab 2000; 9 Embraer EMB-120 Brasilia

TWIN JET
Incorporated: 2001

A French airline founded in 2001 and operating a mainly domestic route network, but with services to Switzerland and to Jersey.

HQ airport & main base: Marseilles Provence
Designator: T7/TJT
Employees: 85
Route points: Angoulême, Basle/Mulhouse, Cherbourg, Epinal, Geneva, Jersey, Lyons, Marseilles, Metz/Nancy, Paris, St Etienne, Toulouse
Links with other airlines: Alliance with CCM Airlines (qv)
Fleet: 8 Raytheon Beech 1900C/D

XL AIRWAYS FRANCE
Incorporated: 1995

This French inclusive tour charter airline was formed as Star Europe in 1995. The airline was bought by a tour operator, Look Voyages, in late 1996 and became Star Airlines the following year. Look Voyages sold the airline in 2003 and it became completely independent until purchased by the Iceland-based Avion Group in 2006. The present title was adopted in December 2006. While operations include flights to Mediterranean resorts, North Africa and the Near East, it also undertakes long-haul flights, to destinations in the Far East and the Americas.

HQ airport & main base: Paris Charles de Gaulle
Designator: SE/SEU
Employees: 480
Links with other airlines: Sister companies in France and Germany (both qv). Owned by Avion Group (Air Atlanta Iceland)
Fleet: 2 Airbus A330-200; 1 Airbus A310-300; 4 Airbus A320-200

FRENCH GUIANA – F

AIR GUYANE EXPRESS
Incorporated: *c.* 2003

A scheduled airline owned by Guyana Aero Invest, providing domestic services and international services to neighbouring countries.

HQ airport & main base: Cayenne Rochambeau
Designator: 3S/GUY
Route points: Cayenne, Maripasoula, St Georges, Saul
Fleet: 1 ATR-42-500; 1 ATR-42-300; 3 de Havilland Canada Twin Otter Srs 300

FRENCH POLYNESIA – F

AIR TAHITI
Incorporated: 1953

Air Tahiti dates from the formation of Reseau Aerien Interinsulaire in 1953, when the French colonial authorities in French Oceania nationalised the operations of the original Air Tahiti, which had been founded in 1950. The airline's operations consisted entirely of inter-island services, and in 1958 the airline was acquired by TAI, Transportes Aeriens Intercontinentaux, the predecessor of UTA, Union Transportes Aeriens, which has since been acquired by Air France.

The title Air Polynésie was taken in 1970, and the present title was adopted in 1987. The French Polynesian government owns 13.7 per cent of Air Tahiti, down from 19 per cent over the past decade, with Air France being another significant shareholder with 7.5 per cent. The company has grown substantially over the past decade, with employee numbers almost doubling, while its fleet has been largely updated with later versions of the ATR-72 series. The company owns 8.4 per cent of Air Tahiti Nui, which is effectively its international tourist counterpart.

HQ airport & main base: Papeete International de Tahiti Faa'a
Radio callsign: AIR TAHITI
Designator: VT/VTA
Employees: 1,017
Route points: Ahe, Anaa, Apataki, Aluona, Bora Bora, Fakarava, Gambier, Hao, Huahine, Makemo, Manihi, Mataiva, Maupiti, Moorea, Nuku Hiva, Papeete, Raiatea, Rairua, Rangiroa, Rurutu, Takapoto, Takora, Tikehau, Tubuai, Ua Huka, Ua Pou, Marquesas
Links with other airlines: Marketing alliance with Air France (qv), which has a 7.5 per cent stake in the airline
Fleet: 10 ATR-72-500; 4 ATR-42-500; 2 Fairchild Dornier 228-212

AIR TAHITI NUI
Incorporated: 1996

Although founded in 1996, Air Tahiti Nui did not begin operations until 1998, and is effectively Tahiti's international airline providing long-haul scheduled and charter operations between the islands and its main tourist markets in the Pacific area and North America. The main shareholder is the government of French Polynesia with 58.37 per cent, while the internal airline, Air Tahiti, has 8.4 per cent.

HQ airport & main base: Papeete International de Tahiti Faa'a
Designator: TN/THT
Employees: *c.* 771
Route points: Auckland, Los Angeles, New York, Osaka, Papeete, Paris, Sydney, Tokyo
Links with other airlines: Marketing alliances with Air France, Japan Airlines, Qantas (all qv)
Fleet: 5 Airbus A340-300

GABON – TR

AIR GABON INTERNATIONAL
Incorporated: 2005

A joint venture between the government of Gabon and Royal Air Maroc, Air Gabon International was expected to commence services in 2006 using a Boeing 757-200 and a 737-200 wet-leased from the Moroccan airline.

Main base: Libreville Leon M'Ba International
Links with other airlines: Royal Air Maroc (qv) has a 51 per cent interest

GAMBIA – C5

SLOK AIR GAMBIA
Incorporated: 2004

Slok Air Gambia has its origins in an earlier airline, Slok Nigeria, which had its operating certificate suspended by the authorities in 2004, and subsequently moved to the Gambia. It intends to develop a scheduled network.

HQ airport & main base: Bathurst
Designator: SO
Fleet: 7 Boeing 737-200

GEORGIA – 4L

GEORGIAN AIRWAYS
Incorporated: 1994

An independently owned passenger airline operating passenger charters, the airline was founded in 1994 as Airzena. International scheduled flights were introduced in 1997. In 1999, the airline merged with Air Georgia to form Airzena Georgian Airlines, but the current title was adopted in 2004.

HQ airport & main base: Tblisi International Lochini
Designator: A9/TGZ
Route points: Amsterdam, Athens, Dubai, Moscow, Paris, Prague, Tel Aviv, Vienna

Links with other airlines: An alliance with Austrian Airlines (qv)
Fleet: 1 Boeing 737-400; 1 Boeing 737-300; 1 Boeing 737-500; 2 Yakovlev Yak-42D; 2 Yakovlev Yak-40

GERMANY – D

After the First World War, German ambitions in air transport were seriously inhibited by the conditions of the Versailles Treaty, which banned the country from aviation. German aircraft designers worked abroad, but so too did those interested in developing commercial air transport, South America proving to be the main beneficiary of their work.

The situation changed in 1926 with the creation of Deutsche Luft Hansa by a merger of two new airlines, Deutsche Aero-Lloyd, ownership of which was divided between the Deutsche Bank and the Hamburg-Amerika Line and North German Lloyd shipping companies, with Junkers Luftverkehr, the operating subsidiary of the famous aircraft manufacturer, which had been formed from the rationalisation of several smaller companies which had been engaged in unprofitable competition.

Deutsche Luft Hansa was owned by the founding airlines, with 27.5 per cent, the central German government, 26 per cent, the German state, or länder, governments, with 19 per cent, and various private interests with 25 per cent. Immediately, the new airline was one of the largest in the world at the time, with a combined fleet of 120 aircraft, although some 80 of these were small, single-engined types.

The history of the airline is covered more fully in the Lufthansa entry below, but it included ambitious plans and in Germany, beacons were established along its routes for night flying, building on earlier experience in developing night flying by Junkers, and creating a chain of seventy-three radio stations along its routes as additional navigation aids.

On the Atlantic, an associate, the Condor syndicate, had been paving the way for South American services with Dornier Wal flying boats, and a number of today's airlines in South America owe their origins to these German pioneers, having been formed to provide connecting services. Occasionally Zeppelin airships were operated.

By the outbreak of the Second World War in Europe, Lufthansa had a route network which extended to Santiago de Chile in the west, and to Bangkok in the east. With the exception of routes to neutral countries such as Sweden and Switzerland, and even these were confined to important official business, operations ceased during the war years. Postwar, Lufthansa was liquidated, starting in 1951. An associate company, Eurasia, in which Lufthansa held a one-third interest and the Chinese Transport Ministry the remainder, became China Air Transport, predecessor of CAAC's airline operations after the Chinese Communists swept to power.

In 1952, the Allied Powers agreed to the formation of a new German airline by the German government. Known initially as Luftag, the old title of Lufthansa was adopted in 1954, and operations began the following year with eight Lockheed Super Constellations, four Convair 340 Metropolitans and three Douglas DC-3s. Such an impressive start was made possible by support of airlines from the Western countries, with TWA, Trans World Airlines and Eastern Airlines providing captains for the Super Constellations, while BEA did the same for the other aircraft. The more important European destinations saw services introduced during 1955, as did New York. By 1958, the South American route once again reached Santiago de Chile, and in 1964, a polar route was opened to Tokyo.

Meanwhile, with the postwar partition of Germany, only the airlines of the wartime allies were allowed to operate into Berlin, and those of France, the United Kingdom and the United States, were confined to three strictly regulated air corridors linking West Berlin with the then West Germany. At one stage, the Soviet Union blockaded West Berlin, forcing the allies to mount a tremendous airlift, initially with military aircraft, but many commercial aircraft were also chartered in and this marked an early boost to many of the fledgling independent airlines. Later, operations between West Berlin and West Germany became the preserve of British European Airways and Pan American, later British Airways and Pan Am, and although in theory Air France could have done the same, it failed to make an impact on the market and was limited to operations to Paris. One of the British independent airlines that had participated in the Berlin airlift, Dan Air, later returned to operate inclusive tour charters out of the city, mainly to Mediterranean holiday resorts.

At the same time, a new airline, Interflug – Gessellschaft fur Internationalen Flugverkehr – was also being developed in East Germany, with the support of Aeroflot. Originally formed in 1954, initially it bore the title of Deutsche Lufthansa. Charter operations started in September 1955, initially on domestic routes. International services did not begin until February 1956, with a service from East Berlin to Warsaw, with domestic services following in June 1957. The Interflug title was not adopted until September 1963. In the years that followed, a network of services throughout Eastern Europe, to the Middle East and West Africa was developed, and at the time of German reunification the airline was operating a fleet that included Ilyushin Il-18s and Il-62s, Antonov An-24s and Tupolev Tu-134s and Tu-154s. It also followed Aeroflot practice to the end by including all aspects of aviation, including general aviation and air work activities. When Germany was reunified, Interflug was allowed to wither, as there was no question of its being absorbed into Lufthansa in the way that the Luftwaffe absorbed elements of Luftstreitkrafte und Luftverteidigung, the East German air force.

A small number of Vickers Viscount turboprop airliners entered service in 1958, followed by Boeing 707 jet airliners in 1960, marking the start of a programme to virtually standardise on Boeing aircraft, with the exception of a fleet of McDonnell Douglas DC-10s for which there was no Boeing equivalent, which lasted until the introduction of the Airbus range some fifteen years later. Lufthansa was the first airline to operate the Boeing 737-100, which it dubbed the 'City Jet'. Lufthansa later became a major customer for Airbus, not surprisingly since the narrow-bodied A320 family are assembled in Hamburg.

Meanwhile, other airlines were emerging, and while the German air transport industry did not become as varied as that of the UK, it not only saw regional feeder and inclusive tour charter airlines emerge, it also attracted attention from outside. With the ending of what had effectively been a British Airways–Pan Am duopoly on the West Berlin–West Germany routes, BA decided to set up its own German domestic and charter airline, Deutsche BA, but while this expanded quickly and took a substantial share of the market, it failed to produce a satisfactory financial return and eventually BA sold the airline, which is now DBA. This was not the only act of retrenchment from its external interests by BA, but Lufthansa had also developed a portfolio of external interests of its own, notably Lauda Air in Austria, but this was sold to Austrian Airlines, while in 2005, Lufthansa acquired the new Swiss International, which had been created from Crossair, a former subsidiary of the failed Swissair.

AIR BERLIN
Air Berlin GmbH
Incorporated: 1992

Originally founded as a charter operator based in Oregon, from 1992 the airline has been based in Berlin. Air Berlin initially offered executive charters as well as inclusive tour charters to the Mediterranean and the Canary Islands, but now operates an extensive domestic and international low-fare scheduled network. The company has risen quickly to become the fiftieth largest airline in the world by revenue, and fortieth by passenger numbers, while its employee numbers have grown ninefold over the past eight years.

It is currently introducing fifty-nine Airbus A320s but continues to operate its Boeing 737 fleet.

HQ airport & main base: Berlin-Tegel, with a hub at Nuremberg
Radio callsign: AIR BERLIN
Designator: AB/BER
Employees: 2,700
Route points: Agadir, Alicante, Almeria, Amsterdam, Antalya, Barcelona, Basle/Mulhouse, Berlin, Bilbao, Bournemouth, Bremen, Budapest, Catania, Cologne, Dortmund, Dresden, Düsseldorf, Erfut, Faro, Frankfurt, Fuerteventura, Funchal, Glasgow, Hamburg, Hurghada, Ibiza, Jerez, Karlsruhe/Baden Baden, Lanzarote, Las Palmas, Leipzig/Halle, Lisbon, London, Luxor, Madrid, Malaga, Manchester, Milan, Monastir, Munich, Münster, Murcia, Nuremberg, Paderborn, Palma de Mallorca, Paris, Porto, Rome, Rostok, Santa Cruz de la Palma, Santiago de la Compostela, Seville, Sharm-el-Sheikh, Stuttgart, Tenerife, Thessaloniki, Turin, Valencia, Vienna, Zurich
Fleet: 59 Airbus A320-200; 19 Airbus A319-100; 95 Boeing 737-800; 35 Boeing 737-700; 3 Fokker 100

AUGSBURG AIRWAYS
Augsburg Airways GmbH
Incorporated: 1980

Originally founded as an air charter operator under the name of Interot Airways, scheduled services began in 1986 with a Beech King Air 200 operating between Augsburg and Düsseldorf. A year later, the original aircraft was replaced by a Beech 1900 on this route, offering more than twice as many seats! The airline then started to expand the route network, first to Hamburg, then to Berlin-Tempelhof, and Colgne/Bonn, while from 1992 onwards, expansion took place to destinations in what had been East Germany. This expansion was helped by the introduction of larger aircraft, starting with the delivery of the airline's first de Havilland Dash 8 in late 1993.

The first international service was introduced in 1994, to Florence, and was followed by a service to

Birmingham in 1995, and then from Cologne/Bonn to London-City Airport later that year (although this service is no longer operated). The following year, the airline adopted its present title.

Augsburg Airways was a subsidiary of a freight forwarding agency, Interot Speditions, but ownership has now passed to Gerd Brandecker. Many of its services were operated under the Lufthansa designator as 'Team Lufthansa', and in 2002, after operations were restructured, this became the case for all flights, with 'Team Lufthansa' changing its name to Lufthansa Regional in 2003, with Augsburg as one of the founding partner airlines.

HQ airport & main base: Augsburg, with a main hub at Munich
Radio callsign: AUGSBURG AIR
Designator: LH
Employees: 334
Route points: On the Lufthansa network
Links with other airlines: Part of Lufthansa Regional (qv)
Fleet: 5 Bombardier Dash 8 Q400; 5 Bombardier Dash 8 Q300

AVANTI AIR
Incorporated: 1994

Founded by its directors as an aircraft management company, Avanti Air started operations on its own account in 1996 with two Beech 1900s, and today provides ad hoc charters and undertakes corporate contract operations.

HQ airport & main base: Airport Siegerland
Designator: ATV
Employees: 45
Fleet: 1 ATR-72-200; 4 ATR-42-300; 3 Raytheon Beech 1900D

CIRRUS AIRLINES
Incorporated: 1995

Originally founded as an executive aircraft charter company in 1995, in 1998 Cirrus moved into scheduled operations. It now operates scheduled and charter airline operations, with many of the former on behalf of Lufthansa.

HQ airport & main base: Saarbrücken Ensheim
Radio callsign: CIRRUS
Designator: C9/RUS
Employees: 650
Route points: Berlin, Billund, Brno, Cologne, Dresden, Erfurt, Frankfurt, Hamburg, Herinsdorf, Leipzig/Halle, London, Mannheim, Munich, Saarbrücken, Skopje, Westerland, Zurich
Links with other airlines: Operates scheduled feeder services for Lufthansa. Alliances with Lufthansa and Swiss (both qv)
Fleet: 1 Boeing 737-500; 1 Embraer 170; 2 Bombardier Dash 8 Q300; 4 Bombardier Dash 8 Q100; 1 Embraer ERJ-145MP; 2 Dornier 328Jet; 6 Dornier 328-110

CONDOR
Condor Flugdienst GmbH
Incorporated: 1961

Condor takes its name from one of the great pioneering airlines, the Condor Syndicate, which helped to develop air transport in South America, and particularly in Brazil, to support the transatlantic ambitions of Lufthansa during the interwar years. The present airline was formed in 1961 on the acquisition of Condor Luftreederei by Deutsche Flugdienst, a subsidiary of Lufthansa. Condor Luftreederei had been formed by the Hamburg-based Oetker Group and dated from 1957, when it began operations with two Convair 440 Metropolitans. Deutsche Flugdienst dated from 1955, and had been acquired by Lufthansa in 1959.

The new airline commenced operations with the Metropolitans and two Vickers Vikings, although the latter were relegated to cargo charters when Vickers Viscounts 800s joined the airline in its first year, with these aircraft also gradually displacing the Metropolitans as a fleet of four was eventually created. Inclusive tour holiday charters were seen as Condor's main business, and in 1965, the airline introduced its first Boeing 727, by which time it was carrying 40 per cent of German package holidaymakers. Long-haul flights to destinations as far afield as Bangkok and Kenya were introduced in 1966, although the first long-haul jet, a Boeing 707, was not introduced until 1967. By 1969, the fleet included six Boeing 727s, three Boeing 737s and a Boeing 707, although a Douglas DC-8 was also operated on a short lease. Transatlantic charters to the United States did not begin until 1972, by which time the airline had become the first package holiday charter airline to operate the Boeing 747.

In 1979, the Boeing 747s in the fleet were replaced by the McDonnell Douglas DC-10, which although smaller were more flexible, since the need for this had been shown by recession in Germany, and by crisis in the oil industry. The airline has always attempted to maintain a modern fleet, being one of the first in its category to operate the Airbus A310. During the 1990s, a fleet of Boeing 757s and 767s was introduced, as well as later marks of the Boeing 737.

After an attempt in 1964 to operate scheduled services from Düsseldorf to Bremen, Hanover and Münster had been abandoned in 1966, Condor returned to scheduled services in 1991, with flights to the Seychelles and Mauritius. Other changes included the transfer of operations to a subsidiary, Condor Südflug, which provided flights for the parent company under contract, although this arrangement was terminated in 1992, and the transfer of operations at Berlin to Schonefeld. By this time Condor was not just chartering flights to tour operators, but also selling seat-only tickets through more than 2,000 travel agents. More recently, Condor took over Lufthansa's 40 per cent stake in the Turkish airline Sun Express. In 1998, a Berlin-based subsidiary, Condor Berlin, was established. The airline was the launch customer for the stretched Boeing 757-300.

After many years as a Lufthansa subsidiary, control of the airline passed to C&N Touristic, which had acquired the British travel agency and tour operator, Thomas Cook, and in 2003, the airline was renamed Thomas Cook – Powered by Condor, but the decision was reversed the following year. Today, Thomas Cook owns 90 per cent of the shares, leaving Lufthansa with 10 per cent.

HQ airport & main base: Frankfurt Main, with a further hub at Munich International
Radio callsign: CONDOR
Designator: DE/CFG
Route points: Agadir, Alicante, Almeria, Antigua, Arrecife, Athens, Bahamas, Bangkok, Barbados, Cancun, Cayo Coco, Colombo, Corfu, Crete, Dakar, Dubai, Faro, Fort Lauderdale, Fort Myers, Fuerteventura, Goa, Grenada, Havana, Holquin, Hurghada, Ibiza, Jamaica, Jerez de la Frontera, Kilimanjaro, Kos, La Romana, Lanzarote, Larnaca, Las Palmas, Las Vegas, Madeira, Mahe, Malaga, Malta, Marsa Alam, Mauritius, Menorca, Mombasa, Monastir, Naples, Orlando, Palermo, Palma de Mallorca, Paphos, Porlamar, Puerto Plata, Puerto Vallarta, Punta Cana, Rhodes, Rimini, Sal, Samos, St Lucia, San Jose, San Juan, Santa Cruz de la Palma, Santo Domingo, Seychelles, Shannon, Sharjah, Sharm-el-Sheikh, Tampa/St Petersburg, Tenerife, Tobago, Varadero
Links with other airlines: Thomas Cook owns 90 per cent. Lufthansa (qv) owns 10 per cent. Alliance with Air Seychelles
Fleet: 9 Boeing 767-300; 13 Boeing 757-300

CONDOR BERLIN
Incorporated: 1998

Founded as the Berlin-based subsidiary of Condor Flugdienst in 1998, to operate inclusive tour charters, the company was merged into Thomas Cook Airlines (Germany) in 2002, but the decision was reversed the following year. Following Thomas Cook's purchase of a majority stake in Condor Flugdienst, Thomas Cook became the sole owner of Condor Berlin.

HQ airport & main base: Berlin Schonefeld
Designator: CIB
Links with other airlines: Subsidiary of Thomas Cook
Fleet: 12 Airbus A320-200

CONTACT AIR
Contact Air Flugdienst GmbH
Incorporated: 1974

Formed in 1974, Contact Air started operations as a charter carrier based at Stuttgart. Scheduled domestic services were introduced operating for DLT, the predecessor of Lufthansa CityLine, and when this airline decided to maintain an all-jet fleet, its Fokker 50s were transferred to Contact Air, also replacing a small fleet of de Havilland Dash 8s operated by the airline. In turn, these have now been replaced by ATR-42s and 72s.

Contact Air is owned by its president, Gunther Eheim. It is now part of the Lufthansa Regional network, the successor to Lufthansa CityLine.

HQ airport & main base: Stuttgart
Radio callsign: CONTACTAIR
Designator: 3T/KIS (or Lufthansa LH)
Employees: 253
Route points: Charters, plus scheduled services under the Lufthansa CityLine banner
Links with other airlines: Operates on behalf of Lufthansa CityLine (qv)
Fleet: 8 ATR-42-500; 6 ATR-72-500

DAUAIR
Incorporated: 2005

Founded in 2005 as a low-cost regional airline by Hans-Jorg Dau, the airline serves a small network from Dortmund.

HQ airport & main base: Dortmund
Designator: D5/DAU

Route points: Berlin, Dortmund, Hanover, Paderborn, Poznan, Stuttgart, Warsaw, Zurich
Fleet: 3 Saab 340B

DBA
DBA Luftfahrtgesellschaft GmbH
Incorporated: 1992

Originally the German subsidiary of British Airways, known as Deutsche BA, the airline was founded in 1978 by an industrialist, Alfred Scholpp, as Delta Air Regionalflugverkehr, and based at Friedrichshafen on Lake Constance. The airline had been formed to fill a gap in the air transport network, and operations to begin with were from Friedrichshafen to Stuttgart and Zurich using de Havilland Twin Otters. In 1982, the Swiss regional airline, Crossair, acquired a 25 per cent stake, and the industrialist Justus Dornier also acquired an interest. A Metroliner was put into service that year, and a service opened between Zurich and Bremen.

In 1986, Saab 340As were introduced. Cooperation with Lufthansa started in 1988, with Delta operating a Friedrichshafen–Frankfurt service for the national airline. Crossair increased its stake in Delta to 40 per cent. Additional Saabs were acquired, and the airline also took over more Lufthansa services during the late 1980s and early 1990s.

In March, 1992, British Airways and three German banks acquired the airline, with BA taking 49 per cent, the maximum permitted to a non-German airline at that time. The title Deutsche BA was adopted in May 1992, and the fleet was repainted into British Airways livery. At the time of the involvement of BA, the airline was operating six Saab 340s and a single Dornier Do228. Under BA, the airline moved rapidly to an all-jet fleet, with Boeing 737s and Fokker 100s, and repositioned to provide scheduled services for business travellers on weekdays, with scheduled and charter flights for holidaymakers at weekends, the airline ceasing to be a regional feeder and becoming a domestic trunk airline with international services. Although supposedly a low-cost airline, inflight service was provided and seats were upholstered in leather. As part of the changes, the main base was moved from Friedrichshafen to Munich, with Berlin as another major base.

BA's involvement had been driven to some extent by its long association with the German internal airline market, having provided flights from West Berlin to West German destinations at a time when only airlines of the occupying powers could gain access through the air corridors over East Germany to West Berlin. This business ended with German reunification, enabling German airlines the usual access to what once again became the federal capital.

When the European air transport market was finally liberalised in 1997, BA acquired the remaining shares in Deutsche BA, but the airline never made a profit under BA ownership and in 2003, British Airways sold the airline for a single euro to a consultancy, Verwaltungsgesellschaft, which today owns 60 per cent, with the remaining shares owned by Aton, owned by an entrepreneur, Lutz Helmig, with 25 per cent, and two of the directors. The new owners rebranded the airline as DBA, but continued with low-fare operations both within Germany and throughout Europe, but added charter flights to the existing schedules. In March 2005, Germania Express was acquired.

HQ airport & main base: Munich International
Radio callsign: SPEEDWAY
Designator: DI/BAG
Employees: 700
Route points: Berlin, Bremen, Cologne/Bonn, Dresden, Düsseldorf, Frankfurt, Hamburg, Hanover, Karlsruhe/Baden Baden, London, Munich, Münster, Nice, Nuremberg, Paris, Rome, Stuttgart
Fleet: 10 Boeing 737-700; 14 Boeing 737-300; 1 Boeing 737-500; 14 Fokker 100

EUROPEAN AIR EXPRESS
Incorporated: 1999

Based in Düsseldorf, European Air Express operates scheduled passenger services both domestically and internationally to neighbouring countries, as well as charter flights.

HQ airport & main base: Düsseldorf Express Münchengladbach
Designator: EA/EAL
Employees: 80
Route points: Amsterdam, Berlin, Cologne, Düsseldorf, Geneva, Münster, Nuremberg, Osnabrück, Stuttgart, Zurich
Fleet: 5 ATR-42-300; 1 Fairchild Metro IIIh

EUROWINGS
Eurowings Luftverkehrs AG
Incorporated: 1994

Eurowings was formed by the merger of NFD Luftverkehrs and RFG Regionalflug on 1 January 1994. NFD, based at Nuremberg, dated from 1974, and had developed an extensive domestic and international passenger operation, including flights undertaken for Lufthansa, as well as inclusive tour and cargo charters, including operation of a BAe 146-200QT for TNT. RFG operated feeder services from Dortmund to destinations in Germany and to London Gatwick, as well as a Stuttgart–Lyon service. While both fleets had a variety of aircraft, they also included ATR-42s, and this provides the backbone of the merged airline.

Unusually, in 1995, the new airline was able to swap its NS IATA designator with the EW code previously used by East-West Airlines of Australia. At one time, Eurowings claimed to be Europe's largest independently owned regional carrier, but Lufthansa has since acquired a 49 per cent interest and the airline's scheduled flights are now part of the Lufthansa Regional network. The main base has also moved from Nuremberg to Dortmund.

HQ airport & main base: Dortmund, with hubs at Frankfurt and Munich
Radio callsign: EUROWINGS
Designator: EW/EWG
Employees: 1,700
Route points: On the Lufthansa Regional network
Links with other airlines: Lufthansa has a 49 per cent interest. Part of the Lufthansa Regional network (both qv)
Fleet: 10 BAe 146-300; 4 BAe 146-200; 5 Bombardier CRJ200LR; 12 Bombardier CRJ200LR

GERMANIA EXPRESS
Incorporated: 2003

Formed by the parent company Germania Fluggesellschaft in 2003 as a low-cost scheduled subsidiary, the airline's European services were absorbed by DBA in 2005, and the airline's aircraft are wet-leased to DBA.

HQ airport & main base: Berlin Tegel
Designator: Now DI/BAG
Links with other airlines: Owned 100 per cent by Germania Fluggesellschaft (qv)
Fleet: 4 Fokker 100

GERMANIA FLUGGESELLSCHAFT
Incorporated: 1978

Germania was founded in 1978 as the inclusive tour charter airline, SAT, and renamed Germania in 1986. After the reunifiaction of Germany, the base was moved to Berlin from Cologne/Bonn.

HQ airport & main base: Berlin Tegel, with most operations from Cologne/Bonn
Radio callsign: GERMANIA
Designator: ST/GMI
Fleet: 8 Boeing 737-700

GERMANWINGS
Incorporated: 2002

Formed as a low-fare domestic and international scheduled airline in 2002 by parent company Eurowings, Germanwings has seen rapid growth in its first few years.

HQ airport & main base: Cologne/Bonn Konrad Adenauer
Designator: 4U/GWI
Employees: 704
Route points: Athens, Barcelona, Berlin, Birmingham, Bologna, Budapest, Cologne/Bonn, Dresden, Dublin, Düsseldorf, Edinburgh, Hamburg, Helsinki, Istanbul, Krakow, Leipzig, Lisbon, London, Madrid, Milan, Moscow, Munich, Nice, Oslo, Paris, Prague, Rome, Split, Stockholm, Stuttgart, Thessaloniki, Toulouse, Verona, Vienna, Warsaw, Zagreb, Zurich
Links with other airlines: Owned by Eurowings (qv). Alliance with Centralwings (qv)
Fleet: 3 Airbus A320-200; 38 Airbus A319-100

HAMBURG INTERNATIONAL
Incorporated: 1998

Not to be confused with the regional airline, Hamburg Airways, which interlined with Lufthansa, Hamburg International was formed in 1998 and started passenger charter flights the following year, initially using Boeing 737-700s. It is owned by its management and local interests, and in addition to inclusive tour charters, it also undertakes ad hoc charters and wet-leases to other airlines. Rapid expansion is envisaged, with fourteen Airbus A319s on order.

HQ airport & main base: Hamburg
Designator: 4R/HH
Employees: 215
Fleet: 6 Boeing 737-700 (On order: 14 Airbus A319-100)

INTERSKY
Incorporated: 2001

Founded in 2001, Intersky began operating low-cost scheduled services out of Friedrichshafen in 2002.

Inclusive tour charter flights are flown to Mediterranean destinations during summer, and from the UK to the Swiss ski resorts during the winter months.

HQ airport & main base: Friedrichshafen
Designator: 3L/ ISK
Employees: 70
Route points: Berlin, Cologne, Friedrichshafen, Graz, Hamburg, Prague, Vienna
Fleet: 2 Bombardier Dash 8 Q300

LTU
LTU International Airways/Lufttransport-Unternehmen GmbH & Co
Incorporated: 1955

Originally founded as Lufttransport Union, the airline was established to operate inclusive tour and freight charters. The present title was adopted in 1958. Feeder services were operated from Düsseldorf to a number of destinations on behalf of Lufthansa, usually using Fokker F27 Friendships and Nord 262s, while Caravelles were used for the IT charter work. The airline has acquired tour operating subsidiaries of its own, and owns a Munich-based operation, LTU Süd International Airways, as well as helping to found the Spanish charter carrier, LTE International Airways, in which LTU had a 25 per cent stake before acquiring outright ownership between 1993 and 2001. LTE operated three Boeing 757-200s from its base at Palma de Mallorca. LTU is expanding its international scheduled network, concentrating on tourist destinations. It is owned by Verwaltungsgesellschaft with 60 per cent, Rewe Touristik holding the remainder. Over the past decade, it has moved from being a Boeing 757 and 767 operator to an all-Airbus fleet.

HQ airport & main base: Düsseldorf International, with a further base at Munich
Radio callsign: LTU
Designator: LT/LTU
Employees: 2,610
Route points: Agadir, Alicante, Almeria, Antalya, Athens, Bangkok, Beirut, Cancun, Cape Town, Catania, Colombo, Djerba, Faro, Fort Myers, Fuerteventura, Havana, Holquin, Hurghada, Ibiza, Kavala, La Romana, Lanzarote, Las Palmas, Lisbon, Luxor, Madeira, Madrid, Malaga, Male, Marsa Alam, Mauritius, Miami, Mombasa, Monastir, Montego Bay, New York, Orlando, Palma de Mallorca, Phuket, Puerto Plata, Punta Cana, Rome, Santa Cruz de la Palma, Sharm-el-Sheikh, Tenerife, Thessaloniki, Valencia, Varadero, Vienna, Windhoek
Links with other airlines: An alliance with Air Mauritius (qv)
Fleet: 4 Airbus A330-300; 9 Airbus A330-200; 4 Airbus A321-200; 9 Airbus A320-200

LUFTHANSA
Deutsche Lufthansa AG
Incorporated: 1926

The Lufthansa Group is the world's second largest airline by annual turnover, and the largest 'one nation' operation, although ranking eighth in passenger numbers.

Although the present airline was established in 1955, after a prolonged period during which commercial aviation was banned in Germany following the Second World War, the history of Lufthansa goes back much further to the formation of an airline of the same name in 1926. The original Lufthansa was formed by a merger of Deutsche Aero-Lloyd, ownership of which was divided between the Deutsche Bank and the Hamburg-Amerika Line and North German Lloyd shipping companies, with Junkers Luftverkehr, the operating subsidiary of the famous aircraft manufacturer.

The new airline's capital was held by the founding airlines, with 27.5 per cent, the central German government, 26 per cent, the German state, or länder, governments with 19 per cent, and various private interests with 25 per cent. In addition to an extensive domestic route network, the new airline inherited international services which stretched as far as London in the west and Stockholm in the north.

Immediately, the new airline set about expanding its network further, both in Germany and elsewhere, with ambitious plans for services across the Atlantic and to the Far East. In Germany itself, beacons were established along its routes for night flying, building on earlier experience in developing night flying by Junkers, and creating a chain of seventy-three radio stations along its routes as additional navigation aids.

On the Atlantic, an associate, the Condor syndicate, had been paving the way for South American services with Dornier Wal flying boats, and a number of today's airlines in South America owe their origins to these German pioneers, having been formed to provide connecting services. The aircraft of the day lacked the range and reliability for true transoceanic flight, but it was possible to accelerate the mail service through catapulting a small seaplane from a liner as the ship approached the coast. On the South Atlantic, a further acceleration of the mail was also possible on the South American service by flying mail to Las Palmas in the Canary Islands. The huge Dornier X twelve-engined flying-boat made a flight to South America in 1932, and occasionally Zeppelin airships could be used instead of a steamer.

By 1934 on the South Atlantic route and 1936 on the North Atlantic, flying boats could be used for the crossing, using three ships converted as floating bases. The aircraft would land close to one of the ships, would be hoisted aboard for servicing and refuelling, and then be launched again to continue the flight. Even so, the service was confined to mail, and the North Atlantic service had to be routed southwards via the Azores and the Bahamas rather than by the more direct northerly route because of the shorter over-water stages and better sea conditions. The aircraft used included the Wal and a larger development, the 'Ten Ton Wal', which were followed later by the diesel-engined Dornier Do.18 and Blohm und Voss Ha.139 flying boats. Overland sections of route in Europe were often flown by the Junkers Ju.52/3m trimotor, of which Lufthansa eventually operated seventy-nine, and in South America, the Dornier Wal proved ideal for operating up-country from the many waterways.

By the outbreak of the Second World War in Europe, Lufthansa had a route network which extended to Santiago de Chile in the west, and to Bangkok in the east. The start of hostilities saw most services suspended, except for a few operated to neutral countries such as Sweden and Switzerland, and even these were restricted to those on urgent government business, especially as shortages of fuel and aircrew began to take effect. All services were officially suspended in 1945, and eventually Lufthansa was liquidated starting in 1951. An associate company, Eurasia, in which Lufthansa held a one-third interest and the Chinese Transport Ministry the remainder, became China Air Transport, predecessor of CAAC's airline operations after the Chinese Communists swept to power.

In 1952, the Allied Powers agreed to the formation of a new German airline by the German goverment. Known initially as Luftag, the airline adopted the old title of Lufthansa in 1954, and operations began the following year with eight Lockheed Super Constellations, four Convair 340 Metropolitans and three Douglas DC-3s. Such an impressive start was made possible by support of airlines from the western countries, with Trans World Airlines, TWA, and Eastern Airlines providing captains for the Super Constellations, while BEA did the same for the other aircraft. The more important European destinations saw services introduced during 1955, as did New York. By 1958, the South American route once again reached Santiago de Chile, and in 1964 a polar route was opened to Tokyo.

A small number of Vickers Viscount turboprop airliners entered service in 1958, followed by Boeing 707 jet airliners in 1960, marking the start of a programme virtually to standardise on Boeing aircraft, with the exception of a fleet of McDonnell Douglas DC-10s for which there was no Boeing equivalent, which lasted until the introduction of the Airbus range some fifteen years later. Lufthansa was the first airline to operate the Boeing 737-100, which it dubbed the 'City Jet', as well as operating a large fleet of Boeing 727s and, of course, the Boeing 747 from 1970 onwards.

One of the world's largest airlines, Lufthansa has reorganised in recent years. It had for many years operated its charter subsidiary, Condor, as a separate entity, but more recently sold off 90 per cent of the airline to Thomas Cook, now German-owned. The growth of air cargo, and especially whole-aircraft scheduled cargo services, led Lufthansa to establish its cargo operation, Lufthansa Cargo, as a separate entity while retaining ownership. A feeder operation created around the network of another subsidiary, DLT, later became Lufthansa Cityline. Establishing a strong base for itself in Europe's strongest economy and largest country also led Lufthansa to take an interest in other airlines, buying a 20 per cent stake in Austria's Lauda Air, which also operated services on its behalf, until this airline was acquired by Austrian Airlines, while interests have been held in Luxair, Sun Express and DHL International, the parcels and courier service. Over the past decade, these interests have changed, so while Lufthansa Cargo and Lufthansa CityLine remain wholly owned subsidiaries and have been joined by Air Dolomiti of Italy, Lufthansa has a 50 per cent stake in Thomas Cook and 30 per cent in the British airline bmi, as well as 49 per cent in both Air Trust and Eurowings. There is still a 13 per cent stake in Luxair and 10 per cent in Condor.

The postwar development of Germany, and the division of the country for four decades, meant that operations have been from many more German cities than might otherwise have occurred. Services to the former East Germany started in 1989. In contrast to the Luftwaffe, there was no attempt to absorb the aircraft of the former East German airline.

For many years, the German, or at the time, West German, government held 65 per cent of Lufthansa's shares, but this holding was dramatically reduced after a 1994 share issue in which the German government did not participate, leaving control of the airline with private investors, so that the state involvement fell initially to 36 per cent of the airline's shares, and in late 1997, Lufthansa became a completely privatised airline. Lufthansa has code-sharing and marketing alliances with a number of airlines, but the most significant of these is the Star Alliance, announced in May, 1997, and which includes Lufthansa, Air Canada, SAS, Thai Airways and United Airlines.

Despite German reunification causing the capital to move from Bonn to Berlin, the airline continues to be based at Cologne, but the most important hub for the airline and its main operational base remains at Frankfurt. A major acquisition in 2005 was that of Swiss International Air Lines, the successor to Swissair, which collapsed in 2002.

HQ airport & main base: Cologne/Bonn, with a main base at Frankfurt Main, and additional bases/hubs at Berlin, Bremen, Düsseldorf, Hamburg, Hanover, Munich, Stuttgart
Radio callsign: LUFTHANSA
Designator: LH/DLH
Employees: 32,144
Route points: (including those of Lufthansa Cityline) Aberdeen, Abu Dhabi, Abuja, Accra, Addis Ababa, Alexandria, Algiers, Almaty, Amman, Amsterdam, Ancona, Ankara, Ashgabat, Asmara, Athens, Atlanta, Bahrain, Baku, Bangkok, Barcelona, Bari, Basle/Mulhouse, Beijing, Beirut, Belfast, Belgrade, Bergen, Berlin, Berne, Bilbao, Billund, Birmingham, Bologna, Bordeaux, Boston, Bratislava, Bremen, Brno, Brussels, Bucharest, Budapest, Buenos Aires, Cairo, Calgary, Cape Town, Caracas, Casablanca, Catania, Charlotte, Chennai, Chicago, Cologne/Bonn, Copenhagen, Dalian, Dallas/Fort Worth, Damman, Delhi, Denpasar Bali, Denver, Detroit, Dnepropetrovsk, Doha, Donetsk, Dortmund, Dresden, Dubai, Dublin, Dubrovnik, Durham, Düsseldorf, Edinburgh, Ekaterinburg, Erfurt, Faro, Frankfurt, Freidrichshafen, Gdansk, Geneva, Genoa, Glasgow, Gothenburg, Graz, Guangzhou, Hamburg, Hanover, Helsinki, Ho Chi Minh City, Hof, Hong Kong, Houston, Hyderabad, Innsbruck, Inverness, Istanbul, Izmir, Jakarta, Jeddah, Johannesburg, Karachi, Karlstad, Katowice, Kazan, Khartoum, Kiel, Kiev, Klagenfurt, Krakow, Kuala Lumpur, Kuwait, Lagos, Lamezia, Larnaca, Leeds, Leipzig/Halle, Linz, Lisbon, Ljubljana, London, Los Angeles, Luxembourg, Lyons, Madeira, Madras, Madrid, Malaga, Malmö, Malta, Manchester, Mannheim, Manila, Marseilles, Mexico City, Miami, Milan, Minsk, Montreal, Moscow, Mumbai, Munich, Münster/Osnabrück, Muscat, Nagoya, Naples, New York, Newark, Newcastle, Nice, Nizhniy Novgorod, Nuremberg, Oporto, Osaka, Oslo, Palermo, Palma de Mallorca, Paderborn, Paris, Perm, Pescara, Philadelphia, Pisa, Port Harcourt, Portland, Poznan, Prague, Reggio Calabria, Riga, Rio de Janeiro, Riyadh, Rome, Rostov, Saarbrücken, St Peterburg, Salzburg, Samara, San Francisco, Sana'a, Santiago de Chile, Sao Paulo, Sarajevo, Seoul, Shanghai, Singapore, Skopje, Sofia, Split, Stavanger, Stockholm, Strasbourg, Stuttgart, Tallinn, Tbilisi, Tehran, Tel Aviv, Thessaloniki, Timisoara, Tokyo, Toronto, Toulouse, Trieste, Tripoli, Tunis, Turin, Ufa, Valencia, Vancouver, Venice, Verona, Vienna, Vilnius, Warsaw, Washington, Westerland, Wroclaw, Yerevan, Zagreb, Zurich
Links with other airlines: Member of the Star Alliance. Owns Swiss International Air Lines, Lufthansa Cargo, Lufthansa CityLine, Air Dolomiti (all qv). Stakes in Thomas Cook (qv), 50 per cent, Air Trust, 49 per cent, Eurowings (qv), 49 per cent, bmi (qv), 30 per cent, Luxair (qv), 13 per cent, Condor (qv), 10 per cent. Alliances with Aegean Airlines, Aerosur, Air China, Air Dolomiti, Air India, Air One, Augsburg Airways, bmi, Carpatair, Cimber Air, Cirrus Airlines, Contact Air Flugdienst, Jat Airways, Luxair, Mexicana, Privatair, QatarAirways, Shanghai Airlines, Swiss (all qv)
Passengers carried: 50.9 million
Annual turnover: US $21,101 million (£14,068 million)
Fleet: 7 Boeing 747-400 Combi; 23 Boeing 747-400; 23 Airbus A340-600; 29 Airbus A340-300; 15 Airbus A330-300; 2 Airbus A330-200; 2 Airbus A300-600R; 11 Airbus A300-600; 21 Airbus A321-200; 20 Airbus A321-100; 46 Airbus A320-200; 33 Boeing 737-300; 23 Airbus A319-100; 29 Boeing 737-500; 12 Bombardier CRJ900 (On order: 15 Airbus A380-800; 20 Boeing 747-8)

LUFTHANSA CARGO
Lufthansa Cargo AG
Incorporated: 1996

On 1 January 1996, Lufthansa separated its cargo operations from the mainstream airline to operate as an autonomous business; the first airline to do so. In addition to maintaining its separate cargo network and selling cargo space on Lufthansa flights,

Lufthansa Cargo also operates freight charters. At one time, the airline had a 40 per cent shareholding in an Indian joint venture airline, Hindja Cargo Services, which used a fleet of Boeing 727 freighters to feed freight into a hub-and-spoke operation at Sharjah, in the Persian Gulf. Lufthansa Cargo has pioneered the use of rail freight to feed cargo into its Frankfurt hub. Today, the sole overseas investment is in Jade Cargo, the Chinese joint venture with Shenzhen Airlines. Over the past decade, the fleet has standardised on the McDonnell Douglas MD-11F freighter.

HQ airport & main base: Frankfurt Main
Radio callsign: LUFTHANSA CARGO
Designator: GEC
Employees: 5,042
Route points: Included in the Lufthansa detsinations
Links with other airlines: A subsidiary of Lufthansa (qv). Has a 25 per cent shaerholding in Jade Cargo International (qv)
Fleet: 19 McDonnell Douglas MD-11F

LUFTHANSA CITYLINE
Lufthansa CityLine GmbH
Incorporated: 1958

Lufthansa CityLine's history dates back to 1958 when Jan Janssen and Martin Decker established Ostfriesische Lufttaxi, or OLT (the name stood for East Friesian Air Taxi Service), in Emden, backed by a shipping line, Fisser & van Dornum. In 1970 an industrial group, AGIV, also became a shareholder, before acquiring the company outright in 1973, by which time the fleet included a de Havilland Canada DHC-6 Twin Otter. The following year, a change of name and restructuring occurred, with the adoption of the new title DLT, Deutsche Luftverkehrs-gesellschaft.

The new airline began to develop a network of regional services, acquiring larger aircraft, including a fleet of Short 330s, and started to operate services on behalf of Lufthansa. In 1978, the airline took over a couple of short international services, Bremen–Copenhagen and Hanover–Amsterdam, and operated these under the Lufthansa name. In return, Lufthansa subscribed to new share capital, leaving the national carrier with a 26 per cent shareholding in DLT. By 1984, most of DLT's operations were functioning under the Lufthansa designator. Meanwhile Hawker Siddeley 748 turboprops had been introduced, marking a further increase in the size of aircraft operated by the airline. These were soon joined by Embraer EMB-120 Brasilias, and in 1987 DLT became the first operator of the new Fokker 50.

Lufthansa acquired a controlling interest in 1989, before finally acquiring the airline outright in 1993. Meanwhile, in 1992, the name was changed from DLT to Lufthansa CityLine, and the new Canadair Regional Jet was added to the fleet. Under Lufthansa ownership, planning and marketing tasks were transferred to the parent airline, and the decision was taken to move the fleet away from turboprop operation to jet operation as far as possible, with Avro RJ85s being added to the fleet. The Lufthansa livery was adopted, and onboard facilities were modelled on those offered on Lufthansa's domestic and European services. The airline introduced Canadair Regional Jets during the late 1990s, following which the remaining turboprop operations were transferred to Contact Air, which now operates as a partner to Lufthansa CityLine. Until its acquisition by Austrian Airlines, Lauda Air was a partner of Lufthansa CityLine.

In addition to operating a domestic network, the airline also handles some of the thinner European routes for its parent. A number of training subsidiaries are owned, including simulator operations.

HQ airport & main base: Cologne/Bonn Konrad Adenauer
Radio callsign: HANSALINE
Designator: CLH
Employees: 2,500
Route points: Included in the Lufthansa domestic network
Links with other airlines: A subsidiary of Lufthansa (qv). Partner airlines include Contact Air (qv)
Fleet: 18 BAE Avro RJ85ER; 12 Bombardier CRJ900; 20 Bombardier CRJ700-701ER; 10 Bombardier CRJ200LR; 16 Bombardier CRJ100LR

OLT
Ostfriesische Lufttransport GmbH
Incorporated: 1958

Originally founded as an air taxi operator, OLT did not expand into airline operations until 1991, when it introduced charter flights. It has since developed a network of scheduled services based on Bremen.

HQ airport & main base: Bremen
Designator: OL/OLT
Employees: 120
Route points: Berlin, Borkum, Bremen, Bremerhaven, Bristol, Brussels, Copenhagen,

Emden, Hamburg, Heide-Buesum, Heligoland, London, Nuremberg, Toulouse, Zurich
Fleet: 3 Saab 2000; 2 Saab 340A/B; 3 Fairchild Metro III; 1 Cessna Caravan 675; 3 Britten-Norman BN2B Islander

PRIVATAIR
Privatair GmbH
Incorporated: 2003

The German subsidiary of the Swiss-owned Privatair Group. Business class-only flights are operated using Airbus aircraft, including corporate shuttles for Airbus and transatlantic flights for Lufthansa.

HQ airport & main base: Düsseldorf International
Designator: PTG
Route points: Include Hamburg and Toulouse as well as Lufthansa destinations
Links with other airlines: Subsidiary of Privatair of Geneva (qv). Operates for Lufthansa (qv)
Fleet: 4 Airbus A319-100LR

TUIFLY
Incorporated: 1973

Developed as Hapag-Lloyd and originally a subsidiary of the German shipping line. The airline was founded in 1973 and in 1979 acquired Bavaria Flug – another charter airline, which had been formed in 1957 as an air taxi operator, moving into air charter operations in 1964 with Handley Page Heralds – enabling Hapag-Lloyd to become a major German charter airline. The airline's main area of operations was to resorts in the Mediterranean and North Africa and to the Dominican Republic. In 1987, the airline was acquired by Preussag, and is now owned by TUI, which also owns Hapag-Lloyd Express, a new low-fares German internal and European airline, and Air Berlin. The title was amended to Hapagfly in 2005 to reposition the airline as a low-cost scheduled carrier, building on the seat-only offers on its charter flights, while a low fares subsidiary, Hapag-Lloyd Express, was established in 2002. The fleet has grown considerably over the past decade, and includes a mixture of Airbus and Boeing products.

In January 2007, Hapagfly and Hapag-Lloyd Express were merged by the parent company to form TUIfly.

HQ airport & main base: Hanover Langenhagen
Radio callsign: TUIFLY
Designator: HF/HLF
Employees: 3,500
Route points: Agadir, Alicante, Almeria, Antalya, Barcelona, Bari, Basle/Mulhouse, Berlin, Bilbao, Cairo, Catania, Cologne, Djerba, Dublin, Faro, Fuerteventura, Hamburg, Hanover, Ibiza, Jerez de la Frontera, Klagenfurt, Lanzarote, Laranca, Las Palmas, Lisbon, Madeira, Madrid, Malaga, Malta, Manchester, Marrakesh, Marsa Alam, Marseilles, Milan, Monastir, Munich, Murcia, Naples, Newcastle, Nuremberg, Olbia, Palma de Mallorca, Pathos, Pisa, Porto, Rijeka, Rome, Salzburg, Santa Cruz de la Palma, Santiago de la Compostela, Seville, Stockholm, Stuttgart, Tenerife, Thessaloniki, Valencia, Vienna
Links with other airlines: Alliance with Air Berlin
Fleet: 35 Boeing 737-800; 9 Boeing 737-700; 5 Boeing 737-500

WALTER
Luftfahrtgesellschaft Walter GmbH
Incorporated: 2000

A small regional airline operating internal services from its base at Dortmund, with some services to German islands in the North Sea.

HQ airport & main base: Dortmund
Radio callsign: WALTER
Designator: HE/LGW
Route points: Berlin, Cologne, Dortmund, Dresden, Düsseldorf, Erfurt, Leipzig/Halle, Nuremberg, Stuttgart, Westerland
Fleet: 5 Dornier 228-212; 1 Dornier 228-100

WDL AVIATION
WDL Flugdienst GmbH
Incorporated: 1955

WDL offers passenger and freight charter services, and has in the past also offered aerial survey work and undertaken passenger schedules for DLT, predecessor of Lufthansa CityLine. Originally based at Essen, the airline is now based at Cologne/Bonn.

HQ airport & main base: Cologne/Bonn Konrad Adenauer International
Radio callsign: WDL
Designator: WDL
Fleet: 1 BAe 146-200; 2 BAe 146-100; 4 Fokker F27 Friendship Mk600; 2 Bombardier Dash 8 Q300

XL AIRWAYS GERMANY
Incorporated: 2006

This new German airline mainly operates charter flights, but has plans to move into the German market. Air Atlanta Iceland owns 49 per cent of the shares and aircraft are leased from Air Atlanta or from the French and UK sister companies as required.

HQ airport & main base: Frankfurt
Designator: GXL
Links with other airlines: Air Atlanta Iceland has a 49 per cent stake and there are close links with XL Airways France and XL Airways UK
Fleet: Chartered from other group companies as required.

GHANA – 9G

Air services to and from West Africa were initiated by Imperial Airways in the 1930s, and during the Second World War included a service between West and East Africa operated by the new British Overseas Airways Corporation, BOAC. Postwar, services within the region, and especially between the British colonies, were developed by the West African Airways Corporation, WAAC, which essentially operated as an affiliate of BOAC. When the colony of the Gold Coast became independent and was renamed Ghana, in 1958, a national airline was established, Ghana Airways, to take over the Ghana services of WAAC.

Initially, long-haul services, which meant the route between Accra and London, were operated by BOAC aircraft in Ghana Airways colours, while domestic services were operated by Douglas DC-3s and de Havilland Herons. Initially, BOAC held a 40 per cent stake in the airline, but full control was taken by the Ghana government in 1961. The new airline could be seen as a national status symbol, along with a national flag, and was probably never viable. Despite this, during the 1960s an ambitious but commercially unrealistic expansion programme started. Anxious to increase its influence in West Africa, the Soviet Union supplied aircraft, while the airline itself ordered two Vickers VC-10s. A change of government in 1966 saw the route network cut back drastically, with many services to the Middle East and Eastern Europe dropped, while a VC-10 was sold, leaving the airline with a single VC-10, two VickersViscount turboprop airliners, a Hawker Siddeley 748 turboprop, and a few Douglas DC-3s. Domestic air services were dropped in 1991, and the airline struggled on, operating international services until operations were suspended in 2005.

In an attempt to resume a Ghanaian international operation, a new airline, Ghana International Airlines, has been formed.

GHANA INTERNATIONAL AIRLINES
Incorporated: 2004

The original Ghanaian national airline, Ghana Airways, dating from 1958, was liquidated and the new Ghana International Airlines is a joint venture between the government, with a 70 per cent shareholding, and an American consortium, GIA-USA, set up in 2004. Operations began in 2005 between Accra and London.

HQ airport & main base: Accra Kokoka International
Radio callsign: GHANA
Designator: GO/GHB
Employees: 125
Route points: Accra, Düsseldorf, London, New York
Fleet: 1 Boeing 767-300ER

GREECE – SX

International services to and from Greece were started by several Western European airlines during the 1930s, and Athens was a calling point on the Imperial Airways route from Southampton to India and Australia. Services were suspended during the Second World War, even before the Italian and German invasions. Postwar, three airlines were formed, Aero Metaforai Ellados, Hellos, which developed a route network to Europe and the Middle East, and TAE, mainly operating a domestic route network. Initially, all three were private ventures, but when TAE ran into financial difficulties it was nationalised. In 1951, all three airlines were merged to form TAE National Greek Airlines.

Despite the pivotal position of Greece between Europe and the Middle East and, later, the expansion of tourism, TAE National Greek Airlines did not perform well, and in 1955 the shipping magnate Aristotle Onassis was granted a fifty-year concession to run a Greek national airline, and Olympic Airways was formed to operate as a monopoly domestic and international airline. Jet equipment in the form of de Havilland Comet 4C airliners was introduced and a helicopter operated summer services to Greek islands, many of which were without airports initially, although a massive programme of airfield construction followed, accompanied by turboprop aircraft, with the airline being the only European operator of the Japanese NAMC YS-11 turboprop. Despite expansion and heavy investment in new aircraft, and a monopoly on services to the islands, with foreign airlines banned from the island airports for many years, the airline encountered financial difficulties in 1974. Onassis withdrew from the airline and operations were suspended. The airline was restructured and resumed operations in 1976 as a nationalised concern.

With state support, Olympic has grown steadily in recent years, but real expansion of the Greek air transport market has followed the liberalisation of air transport that followed Greek entry to the European Union. Several new airlines have sprung up, and one of these, Aegean Airlines, is seen as a 'second force' carrier, that is, it is a Greek competitor to the national airline on certain routes. Even so, it is possibly significant that one of Europe's leading low-cost carriers, EasyJet, is owned by the scion of a Greek shipping family, and yet is registered and based in the United Kingdom. History repeats itself, and once again the Greek government is looking to divest itself of Olympic. A Greek-based inclusive tour charter airline, Venus, which started operations in 1993, flying holidaymakers to Greek resorts from Western Europe, ceased operations in the late 1990s, at which time it had a fleet of six aircraft, including Boeing 737s and 757s.

AEGEAN AIRLINES
Incorporated: 1977

Although originally incorporated in 1977, airline operations did not begin until 1992, and in the meantime, as Aegean Aviation, the company operated executive charters and air ambulance operations throughout the Aegean. The airline became the first Greek independent airline in 1992, operating charter flights initially and adopting its present title when scheduled services were introduced in 1999. It merged with Cronus Airlines in 2001 and for a while was known as Aegean Cronus Airlines before finally absorbing the smaller company. It is now effectively the 'second force' in Greek commercial aviation.

HQ airport & main base: Athens International, with a further base at Heraklion and a hub at Thessaloniki
Radio callsign: AEGEAN
Designator: A3/AEE
Employees: 1,500
Route points: Alexandropolis, Athens, Chania, Chios, Düsseldorf, Frankfurt, Heraklion, Ionnina, Kavala, Kerkyra, Kos, Larnaca, Mikonos, Milan, Munich, Mytilene, Rhodes, Rome, Stuttgart, Thessaloniki, Thira
Fleet: 14 Airbus A320-200; 6 BAe Avro RJ100ER; 6 Boeing 737-400; 9 Boeing 737-300

EUROAIR
Incorporated: 1995

This business charter airline for passengers and cargo was formed in 1995, operating from Athens to some of the islands using mainly wet-leased aircraft.

HQ airport & main base: Athens International
Designator: 6M/EUP
Route points: Athens, Mykonos, Syros
Fleet: 1 Let L-410UVP-E

GREECE AIRWAYS
Incorporated: 2003

Greece Airways was founded in 2003 by Dhai Al-ani, and began operations in 2004, flying a Boeing 757-200 on wet-lease to Air Scotland.

HQ airport & main base: Athens, but main base is Glasgow
Designator: GRE
Links with other airlines: Operates for Air Scotland
Fleet: 1 Airbus A320-200

OLYMPIC
Olympic Airlines SA
Incorporated: 1957

Olympic Airlines was known as Olympic Airways until December 2003, and had started operations in 1957 as the successor to TAE National Greek Airlines, which had been formed in 1951 by the merger of Hellos, serving several destinations in Europe and the Middle East; TAE, concentrating mainly on domestic routes; and Aero Metaforai Ellados. All three airlines had been formed shortly after the end of the Second World War, and with the exception of TAE, which had been acquired by the Greek government after experiencing financial difficulties, all were privately owned.

The new airline was owned by the shipping magnate Aristotle Onassis, who had been given a fifty-year concession by the Greek government, and with his backing, Olympic Airways was able to expand quickly. The initial fleet of aircraft included a Fairchild Argus, a Douglas DC-4 and fourteen Douglas DC-3s, all of which had belonged to TAE. Douglas DC-6Bs were acquired urgently, and the new de Havilland Comet 4Bs were ordered. The Comets were introduced in 1960, and immediately produced a London–Athens record of 3 hours 13 minutes. Re-equipped, the airline was able to add new routes, so that it was soon serving the major destinations in Europe and the Middle East, and around the Mediterranean. In 1966, the arrival of Boeing 707s saw the airline inaugurate an Athens–New York service. At this time, the airline also had a single Sud Aviation Super Frelon helicopter for summer services to some of the Greek islands.

The Boeing 707s were soon joined by Boeing 720s and 727s, which replaced the Comets. Construction of airports on the Greek islands led to the development of conventional air services to many of them, and Japanese-built NAMC YS-11 turborprop airliners and small Short Skyvan aircraft were introduced onto these routes. Olympic also conducted trials with two Yakovlev Yak-40 airliners, the first airline outside of what was then the Soviet Bloc to test these aircraft, the forerunners of today's small regional jets. Meanwhile, the route network reached Sydney in 1972, and the following year, Olympic received its first Boeing 747.

This optimistic picture changed during the early 1970s, with continuing heavy losses forcing Onassis to withdraw in 1974, and operations were suspended. After reaching a settlement with Onassis the following year, the airline was nationalised and operations started again in January 1976.

The airline quickly re-established itself, helped by the growing popularity of Greece as a holiday destination. One of the early moves was to acquire Boeing 737s, and in 1979 the first Airbus A300s were introduced.

Today, Olympic remains in state ownership, and continues to operate domestic, international and intercontinental services from its main base at Athens. In 1999, British Airways took over the management of the airline, but this agreement ended, and it is common knowledge that the Greek government would like to offer a majority stake in Olympic Airlines to a buyer. Employee numbers have fallen dramatically over the past decade. At one time a subsidiary was Macedonian Airlines, which operated four aircraft from Skopje in Macedonia, but this is now independently owned, while another subsidiary, Olympic Aviation, has been reintegrated with Olympic, which has retained its ATR-42 and 72 aircraft for use on services to the smaller Greek islands.

HQ airport & main base: Athens International
Radio callsign: OLYMPIC/OLYMPAIR
Designator: OA/OAL
Employees: 1,800
Route points: Alexandria, Alexandropolis, Amsterdam, Astypalaia, Athens, Beirut, Belgrade, Berlin, Brussels, Bucharest, Cairo, Chaia, Chios, Corfu, Dubai, Düsseldorf, Frankfurt, Geneva, Heraklion, Ikaria, Ioannina, Istanbul, Johannesburg, Karpathos, Kasos, Kastelorizo, Kuwait, Larnaca, Leros, Limnos, London, Madrid, Manchester, Mikonos, Milan, Milios, Montreal, Moscow, Munich, Mytilene, Naxos, New York, Paris, Paros, Preveza, Rhodes, Rome, Samos, Sitia, Skiathos, Skiros, Sofia, Stuttgart, Syros, Tel Aviv, Thessaloniki, Thira, Tirana, Toronto, Vienna, Zakynthos
Links with other airlines: Alliances with AeroSvit Airlines (qv), Air Malta (qv), CSA Czech Airlines (qv), Cyprus Airways (qv), Egyptair (qv), Gulf Air (qv), Hellas Jet, Kuwait Airways (qv), TAP Air Portugal (qv)
Fleet: 4 Airbus A340-300; 1 Airbus A300-600R; 1 Airbus A320-200; 14 Boeing 737-400; 3 Boeing 737-300; 3 Boeing 717-200; 7 ATR-72-200; 6 ATR-42-320; 4 Bombardier Dash 8 Q100

OLYMPIC AVIATION

Olympic Aviation SA
Incorporated: 1971

Originally formed as a private airline, Olympic Aviation was taken over by the Greek government in 1974, becoming an operator of feeder services for Olympic Airways, now Olympic Airlines, of which it became a wholly owned subsidiary. The airline also provided charter operations and air taxi services, including the use of small helicopters. It has now been reintegrated with Olympic Airlines, which operates its fleet of ATR-42s and 72s on services to the Greek islands.

GUADELOUPE – FOG

AIR CARAIBES

Incorporated: 1969

Originally founded as Air Guadaloupe by the Guadaloupe government and Air France, services started in 1970. Originally owned 45 per cent by the government and 45 per cent by Air France, it is now owned by the Dubreuil Group, which has an 85 per cent shareholding. A service to Paris was started in 2003, although this is officially operated by a subsidiary, Air Caraibes Atlantique. Most of the airline's services are within the Caribbean.

HQ airport & main base: Point-à-Pitre Raizet, Guadaloupe
Designator: TX/FWI
Employees: 630
Route points: Belem, Bridgetown, Canouan Island, Cayenne, Fort de France, Havana, Marie Galante, Paris, Pointe-à-Pitre, Port-au-Prince, St Barthélemy, St Lucia, St Maarten, St Martin, Santo Domingo, Tierre-de-Haut, Union Island
Links with other airlines: Alliances with LIAT (qv), Winair
Fleet: 2 Airbus A330-300; 3 Airbus A330-200; 3 ATR72-500; 2 ATR42-500; 1 Embraer 195LR; 1 Embraer 175LR; 2 Embraer ERJ-145MP; 3 Dornier 228-200; 5 Cessna Caravan 675

GUATEMALA – TG

The national airline Aviateca was privatised, with TACA of El Salvador acquiring a 30 per cent initial stake, but TACA nows owns the airline outright and in 2004 absorbed its fleet and routes into its structure.

TIKAL JETS

Incorporated: 1992

Tikal Jets was founded in 1992 and has developed into a regional passenger airline with a domestic scheduled service and a small number of International routes. It also undertakes charters and provides sightseeing flights for tourists.

HQ airport & main base: Guatemala City La Aurora
Radio callsign: TIKAL
Designator: WU/TKC
Route points: Cancun, Flores, Guatemala, Havana, Mexico City
Fleet: 2 McDonnell Douglas DC-9-50; 1 McDonnell Douglas DC-9-30; 3 Let L-410UVP

GUINEA – 3X

AIR GUINEE EXPRESS

Compagnie Nationale Air Guinée
Incorporated: 2002

Formed in 2002 to take over the services of Air Guinée, the national airline of the former French African colony of Guinea which was formed after independence in 1960 with assistance from the then Soviet Union and Czechoslovakia. Not surprisingly, initially Antonov aircraft types predominated.

The airline remains state owned and concentrates on domestic and regional services to neighbouring states.

HQ airport & main base: Conakry
Radio callsign: AIR GUINEE EXPRESS
Designator: 2U/GIB
Route points: Abidjan, Bamako, Conakry, Dakar, Freetown, Lagos, Monrovia
Fleet: 4 Antonov An-24B; 1 Bombardier Dash 7; 4 Antonov An-12; 1 Bombardier Dash 7 Srs100

HONDURAS – HR

ATLANTIC AIRLINES DE HONDURAS

Incorporated: 2001

Atlantic Airlines de Honduras operates scheduled regional passenger services throughout Central America, and is associated with a small Nicaraguan airline of the same name which also operates Let L-410s.

HQ airport & main base: La Ceiba
Designator: ZF/HHA
Route points: Belize, Bluefields, Com, Guanaja, La Ceiba, La Palma, Managua, Puerto Cabezas, Roatan, San Pedro Sula, Tegucigalpa, Utila
Links with other airlines: Associated with Atlantic Airlines, Nicaragua
Fleet: 3 Boeing 737-200; 1 BAe 748 Srs 2B; 2 Fokker F27; 10 Let L-410UVP

ISLENA AIRLINES

Incorporated: 1981

Islena Airlines operates a small network of domestic scheduled and international charter services. The scheduled services are essentially feeders for TACA of El Salvador, which has a 20 per cent stake in Islena.

HQ airport & main base: La Ceiba Goloson International
Designator: WC/ISV
Route points: Guanaja, La Ceiba, Roatan, San Pedro Sula, Tegucigalpa
Links with other airlines: TACA has a 20 per cent interest. Alliance with TACA (qv)
Fleet: 3 ATR-42-300; 3 Shorts 360; 2 Let L-410UVP; 1 Embraer EMB-110P2 Bandeirante

SOSA
Aerolineas SOSA
Incorporated: 1984

SOSA operates domstic and regional scheduled and charter services with a small, but varied, fleet.

HQ airport & main base: La Ceiba
Designator: P4/NSO
Route points: Ahuas, Brus Laguna, Cauquira, Guanaja, La Ceiba, Palacios, Puerto Lempira, Roatan, San Pedro Sula, Tegucigalpa, Utila
Fleet: 1 Fokker F27 Friendship; 4 Let L-410UVP; 2 BAe Jetstream 31

HUNGARY – HA

FARNAIR HUNGARY
Farnair Air Transport Hungary Kft
Incorporated: 1990

Originally founded in 1990 as NAWA Air Transport, it was the first privately owned airline in Hungary since the end of the Second World War. It was acquired by the Swiss Farnair Air Transport in 1993, and was renamed Farnair Air Transport Hungary, the name changing again in 1997 to the present Farnair Hungary. Charter passenger and cargo flights are operated, including regular cargo contract flights.

HQ airport & main base: Budapest Ferihegy
Designator: FAH
Links with other airlines: A wholly owned subsidiary of Farnair Switzerland
Fleet: 6 Fokker F27 Mk500; 1 Let L-410UVP-E

MALEV
Malev – Magyar Legikozlekedesi Vallalat
Incorporated: 1946

Hungary's national airline, Malev, was formed in March 1946, as Maszovlet, Magyar-Szovjet Polgari Legiforgalmi Tarsasag, the Hungarian-Soviet Airlines Company, and operations started later that year. At first, the airline was confined to domestic services, operating Ilyushin Il-12 aircraft, but by 1950 international services were being operated to Prague, Bucharest, Belgrade and Warsaw, and there was also a short-lived service to Venice.

The present title was adopted in 1954, when control of the airline passed into Hungarian hands. Expansion gained pace at this time, and services began to be introduced to major centres in western Europe, starting with Vienna. A service to Cairo was started in 1963, followed by Damascus in 1965 and Beirut in 1966. The fleet by this time included Ilyushin Il-18s and Il-14s. Malev had been the first Warsaw Pact country to put the Il-18 into service. The Il-14s were withdrawn, starting in 1968, when the first jets, Tupolev Tu-134s, were introduced.

While expansion of the international network continued, heavy losses on the domestic network meant that the 1960s saw domestic services steadily reduced, and then abandoned altogether. Fares, which were low, could not cover costs, and repairs to the war-damaged infrastructure had also meant that road and rail travel had become feasible once more.

Larger aircraft in the form of the Tupolev Tu-154 were introduced in 1973, and later these aircraft were to introduce first-class service on Malev flights. The airline remained committed to purchasing Soviet aircraft until 1988, when Malev leased the first of three Boeing 737-200s and was also selected to operate BAe 146-200QT aircraft for TNT. The move to more productive, Western equipment marked the beginning of the end for the old Tupolev aircraft, which started to be replaced. Eventually, the airline was operating a dozen Boeing 737s, when, in 1993, Boeing 767-200ER aircraft were introduced on long-haul services. No less significant a sign of changing times in eastern Europe, in 1992 Malev became a public limited company, although it has yet to be completely privatised, with the state holding 97 per cent of the share capital while employees and municipal interests combined hold just over 1 per cent.

After a period during which the Tu-154s were relegated to charter duties, today, Malev operates a modern fleet which is completely of Western manufacture, and its services extend throughout Europe, and to the Middle East, Africa and North America. Alliances exist with a large number of airlines, although Malev has not, as yet, committed to any of the major alliances. A feeder subsidiary, Malev Express, was established in 2002, operating Bombardier CRJ200s, but this was reintegrated into the parent airline in 2005.

HQ airport & main base: Budapest Ferihegy
Radio callsign: MALEV
Designator: MA/MAH
Route points: Amsterdam, Athens, Bangkok, Barcelona, Beijing, Beirut, Berlin, Birmingham, Bologna, Brussels, Bucharest, Budapest, Cairo, Chisinau, Cluj, Cologne, Constanta, Copenhagen, Damascus, Dublin, Düsseldorf, Frankfurt, Geneva, Gothenburg, Guangzhou, Hamburg, Hanover, Helsinki, Istanbul, Kiev, Krakow, Larnaca, Lisbon,

London, Lyons, Madrid, Malaga, Manchester, Milan, Moscow, Munich, New York, Odessa, Palma de Mallorca, Paris, Prague, Pristina, Riga, Rome, Santo Domingo, Sarajevo, Shanghai, Skopje, Sofia, Stockholm, Stuttgart, Tallinn, Tel Aviv, Tenerife, Thessaloniki, Timisoara, Tirana, Tirgu Mares, Toronto, Varna, Venice, Vienna, Vilnius, Warsaw, Zagreb, Zurich
Links with other airlines: Alliances with Aeroflot Russian Airlines, AeroSvit Airlines, Air Europa, Air France, Alitalia, Austrian Arrows, Carpatair, City Airline, CSA Czech Airlines, Hainan Airlines, Japan Airlines International, KLM, LOT Polish Airlines, Moldavian Airlines, Northwest Airlines, SN Brussels Airlines, Swiss, TAP Portugal, Tarom (all qv)
Fleet: 2 Boeing 767-200ER; 5 Boeing 737-800; 7 Boeing 737-700; 6 Boeing 737-600; 5 Fokker 70; 4 Bombardier CRJ200ER

SKYEUROPE HUNGARY
Incorporated: 2003

The Hungarian subsidiary of Slovakia's SkyEurope Airlines, it uses aircraft from the parent company as required.

HQ airport & main base: Budapest Ferihegy
Designator: 5P/HSK
Route points: Under SkyEurope
Links with other airlines: A subsidiary of SkyEurope (qv)
Fleet: Aircraft from the SkyEurope fleet

TRAVEL SERVICE HUNGARY
Incorporated: 2001

Formed by Travel Service Airlines of the Czech Republic, Travel Service Hungary is an inclusive tour charter airline, mainly flying to the Mediterranean and southern Europe.

HQ airport & main base: Budapest Ferihegy
Designator: TVL
Links with other airlines: Associated with Travel Service Airlines of the Czech Republic (qv)
Fleet: 1 Boeing 737-800

WIZZ AIR
Incorporated: 2003

A European low-cost airline originally registered in London in 2003, Wizz Air is based in Hungary and started operations in 2004. It is owned by a private consortium, Indigo Partners.

HQ airport & main base: Budapest Ferihegy
Radio callsign: WIZZ
Designator: W6/WZZ
Route points: Amsterdam, Brussels, Dortmund, Frankfurt, Gdansk, Hamburg, Katowice, Kaunas, Liverpool, Malmö, Milan, Paris, Poznan, Rome, Sofia, Stockholm, Warsaw, Wroclaw
Fleet: 8 Airbus A320-200 plus 32 on order

ICELAND – TF

AIR ATLANTA ICELANDIC
Incorporated: 1986

Originally founded to offer wet-leasing services to international scheduled carriers, Air Atlanta moved into charter operations in 1993, although wet-leasing to airlines such as Iberia remains the major element of the business ,since the airline's capacity is well beyond that of a country with a population of around 250,000. The airline was owned completely by Captain Arngrimur Johannsson, who is its President, and his family. In 2004, the company acquired a 40.5 per cent stake in the British charter airline, Excel Airways, later increasing this to 76.9 per cent, and the following year, Air Atlanta Icelandic merged with Islandflug and ownership was vested in a new holding company, the Avion Group. Meanwhile, in 2002, a British subsidiary, Air Atlanta Europe, was formed at London-Gatwick with a single Boeing 747-300, and undertook wet-lease operations for Excel and Virgin Atlantic as well as a number of other airlines, but this operation has now been absorbed by Excel. The Boeing 777 Freighters are in course of delivery, and may result in some rationalisation of the fleet.

HQ airport & main base: Reykjavik
Designator: CC/ABD (on wet-leasing, the client airline's designator is used)
Fleet: 8 Boeing 777-200WRF; 1 Boeing 747-400F; 5 Boeing 747-300; 5 Boeing 747-200B; 6 Boeing 747-200F; 1 Airbus A300-600F; 1 Airbus A310-300

AIR ICELAND
Incorporated: 1997

The successor to Flugfelag Nordurlands, Air Iceland was founded in 1997. Flugfelag Nordurlands originated in 1975, when it took over the services of Nordurflug. Today, the airline operates scheduled services and charter flights within Iceland and to Greenland and the Faroes. It is owned by the FL Group.

HQ airport & main base: Reykjavik Keflavik International
Designator: NY/FXI
Employees: 225
Route points: Akureyri, Eglisstadir, Faroe Islands, Grimsey, Hornafjordur, Isafjordur, Kulusuk, Neerlerit Inaat, Reykjavik, Thorshofn, Vopnafjordur
Links with other airlines: Atlantic Airways (qv)
Fleet: 6 Fokker 50; 2 de Havilland Canada Twin Otter Srs 300; 1 Bombardier Dash 8 Q100

ICELAND EXPRESS
Incorporated: 2002

Operates international low-cost scheduled flights.

HQ airport & main base: Reykjavik Keflavik International
Designator:
Employees: 73
Route points: Alicante, Berlin, Copenhagen, Friedrichshafen, Hahn, London Stansted, Stockholm
Fleet: 2 McDonnell Douglas MD-82

ICELANDAIR
Flugleidir hf
Incorporated: 1973

Icelandair was formed by the merger of two much older airlines, Icelandair and Loftleidir, in 1973.

The original Icelandair had been founded in 1937 as Flugfelag Akureyrar, or Flugfelag Islands, operating a seaplane service. The first international service came in 1945, when a Consolidated Catalina flying boat was used for a route to Glasgow. A second service, to Copenhagen, soon followed. Landplane services were introduced the following year, using converted Liberator bombers leased from Scottish Aviation for services to Prestwick, near Glasgow, and Copenhagen. Douglas DC-4s were purchased in 1948. The title of Icelandair was introduced in 1950, when the Icelandic government acquired a 13.2 per cent shareholding. In 1957, the airline bought two Vickers Viscounts and these were followed by DC-6s.

A thirteen-point domestic network was established postwar, especially after Loftleidir's decision to concentrate on international services, reflecting the considerable distances and sparse population which make road building uneconomic. Initially DC-3s were used, but they were eventually replaced by Fokker F27 Friendships. Although originally formed as a domestic carrier in 1944, with just one Stinson seaplane, Loftleidir developed postwar into a pioneer of low-cost transatlantic air services, using a loophole because of the need to change planes in Iceland. The domestic operations were withdrawn in 1952, by which time the airline had been operating to Copenhagen since 1947, and New York since 1948 using Douglas DC-4s. In 1960, the airline was given a government-guaranteed loan to buy Douglas DC-6Bs, later augmenting and then replacing these with Canadair CL-44s, stretched Bristol Britannias with Rolls-Royce Tyne engines, so that the airline marketed the aircraft as the Rolls-Royce 400. Eventually, the airline moved into the jet age with the acquisition of Douglas DC-8 airliners.

After the merger in 1973, Icelandair initially acted as a holding company for the two airlines, but operations were merged in 1979. The route network still offers transatlantic opportunities for the traveller. The domestic route network was initially trimmed back to ten points, aided by the emergence of a third-level carrier, Islandsflug, with a fleet of small aircraft well suited to services to the smaller communities, before a domestic subsidiary, Air Iceland, was formed in 1997. In 2005, the holding company, the Flugleidir Group,changed its name to FL Group. The airline is one of the country's largest employers, numbers having almost doubled over the past decade, and now concentrates exclusively on international services, using an exclusively Boeing fleet. A sister company is Icelandair Cargo, which markets cargo capacity for Icelandair, and uses aircraft from Icelandair as necessary for whole-plane loads.

HQ airport & main base: Reykjavik Keflavik International
Radio callsign: ICEAIR
Designator: FI/ICE
Employees: 2,565
Route points: Amsterdam, Baltimore, Boston, Copenhagen, Frankfurt, Glasgow, London, Luxembourg, Minneapolis, New York, Orlando, Oslo, Paris, Reykjavik, Stockholm
Links with other airlines: Through the parent FL Group, is linked to Air Iceland (qv) and Icelandair Cargo. Alliance with SAS (qv)
Fleet: 1 Boeing 757-300; 15 Boeing 757-200; 1 Boeing 757-200PF; 6 Boeing 737-800 (On order: 4 Boeing 787-8)

JET X
Incorporated: 2004

Jet X operates inclusive tour charters between Iceland and Italy, as well as scheduled services from Iceland to Copenhagen and London.

HQ airport & main base: Reykjavik Keflavik International
Designator: JXX
Route points: Copenhagen, London, Reykjavik
Fleet: 1 Boeing 737-800; 1 McDonnell Douglas MD-83; 1 McDonnell Douglas MD-82

LANDSFLUG
Incorporated: 2004

Landsflug was formed in 2004 by City Star Airlines to acquire the operations of Islandsflug, and operates a purely domestic network of scheduled passenger services.

HQ airport & main base: Reykjavik Keflavik International
Designator: X9/ISL
Employees: 80
Route points: Bildudalur, Gjogur, Hofn, Saudarkrokur, Westman Island
Links with other airlines: A subsidiary of City Star Airlines (qv)
Fleet: 1 Dornier 328 Jet; 3 Dornier 228-212

INDIA – VT

Air services linked India with the UK during the early 1930s, and later the country was on the Empire Air Mail route between the UK and Australia. The predecessor of Air India, Tata Airlines, was founded in 1938, but operations had started earlier, in 1932, as Tata & Sons operating charters. Initially, the airline concentrated mainly on airmail services. Operations continued during the Second World War, operating on special services for the government and the armed forces. In 1946, using war surplus aircraft, the airline started to expand rapidly and the name was changed to Air-India, with assistance from the American airline, Trans World Airways, which provided training for the introduction of Douglas C-47s and C-54s converted to airline DC-3 and DC-4 standard.

After India became independent, the airline adopted the title of Air-India International, and the state took a 49 per cent stake, with an option on another 2 per cent. Meanwhile, Indian businessmen were busy establishing an airline in Afghanistan. Nationalisation of Indian air transport came in 1953, with Air-India and six other airlines merged and two airlines were established, Air-India International Corporation for the international routes, and Indian National Airlines Corporation for domestic services. Both airlines developed independently, but eventually became known simply as Air India and Indian Airlines. In 1981, India established a third-level operation, Vayudoot, in which Air India had a 50 per cent stake, but following a number of accidents, Vayudoot's routes and aircraft were integrated into Indian Airlines.

Greater freedom for the private sector was accompanied by permission for Indian Airlines to move into international services, mainly to the Gulf States where many Indian expatriate workers are employed. Several new airlines have been formed over the years, including two ventures with Lufthansa, Hindujah Cargo Services, and Modiluft, as well as NEPC, but the new airlines have often found it difficult to maintain services and the three mentioned no longer exist. Not the least of their problems is that of finding and retaining experienced air crew – a problem not unique to India and which it shares with mainland China, which also has a fast-growing economy.

AIR DECCAN
Incorporated: 2003

Founded by Deccan Aviation, a fixed-base and helicopter charter company, to expand into low-cost domestic scheduled air services in 2003, Air Deccan has a growing route network based on Bangalore. Ambitious plans call for a ninefold increase in its Airbus A320 fleet. It is trying to replicate its success in Sri Lanka, where it has a 48 per cent stake in Deccan Lanka.

HQ airport & main base: Bangalore
Radio callsign: DECCAN
Designator: DN/DKN
Route points: Ahmedabad, Amritsar, Aurangabad, Bagdogra, Bangalore, Belgaum, Bhavnagar, Bhopal, Chandigarth, Chennai, Coimbatore, Dehra Dun, Delhi, Goa, Guwahati, Gwalior, Hubli, Hyderabad, Indore, Jabalpur, Jaipur, Jammu, Jamnagar, Kandla, Kanpur, Kochi, Kolhapur, Kolkata, Kozhikode, Lucknow, Madurai, Mangalore, Mumbai, Nagpur, Pune, Raipur, Rajkot, Srinagar, Thiruvananthapuram, Tiruchirappalli, Tirupati, Vadodara, Vijayawada, Vishakhapatnam
Links with other airlines: Subsidiary of Deccan Aviation. 48 per cent stake in Deccan Lanka
Fleet: 18 Airbus A320-200; 7 ATR-72-500; 9 ATR-42-500; 2 ATR-42-320; 3 ATR-42-300 (On order: 59 Airbus A320-200)

AIR INDIA
Air India Ltd
Incorporated: 1932

Air India's history dates from 1932, when J.R.D. Tata formed an airline which was known initially as Tata & Sons, but which became Tata Airlines in 1938. The airline had been formed to operate airmail services, and for the first few years mail used almost all of the payload of the aircraft, de Havilland Puss Moths carrying mail to and from the Empire Air Mail services of Imperial Airways. It was not until 1938 that passenger services started, with the introduction of de Havilland Rapide biplanes.

The start of the Second World War ended the airmail services, and such flying as was permitted was confined to operations on behalf of the government and armed forces. Progress continued, and during the war Tata Airlines had experience of operating larger and more modern aircraft. Postwar, the airline was able to expand rapidly using war surplus aircraft, becoming a public company and changing the name to Air-India in 1946. TWA provided assistance in training cabin crew for the Douglas C-47s and C-54s converted to airline DC-3 and DC-4 standard, and in return, Air-India became a sales agent in India for the American airline.

In early 1948, a few months after Indian independence, the airline changed its name again, to Air-India International, while the Indian government took a 49 per cent share in the airline, with an option on another 2 per cent. The airline had still to start international operations, and this came later the same year with a service from Bombay to London. The frequency of this service was soon increased, but it was not until 1950 that the next international service could be introduced, from Bombay to Nairobi. This steady progress continued until 1953, when all Indian airlines were nationalised, and the aircraft and routes of Air India and six other airlines were merged into two corporations, Indian National Airlines Corporation for domestic routes, and Air-India International Corporation for international services. The new airline continued to expand its network of services, helped by the introduction of Lockheed Super Constellations in 1954. A further name change occurred in 1962, to Air-India.

Traditionally, the airline's route structure favoured services to the United Kingdom as the former colonial power and because of immigration, while East Africa was also important at first because of the substantial Indian communities there. The growth of the oil economies of the Middle East, often in countries with small populations, also created new traffic patterns as expatriate Indian workers moved to these areas.

The early 1960s saw the airline introduce Boeing 707 jet airliners, developing what was for the day a small, but modern fleet of nine aircraft, with routes from Bombay and Delhi ranging as far afield as New York, Moscow, Tokyo and Sydney. The airline continued this progress, replacing the 707s with Boeing 747s and later augmenting these with Airbus A300 and A310 aircraft. Occasionally, aircraft such as Ilyushin Il-62 and Il-76s were chartered in for a short period, with the latter aircraft used on freight duties.

In 1981, Air India and Indian Airlines, as Indian National Airlines had become, established a third airline in which both had equal shares, Vayudoot, to operate feeder services with aircraft that included Indian-built Hawker Siddeley 748s, Fokker F27 Friendships and Dornier Do.228s.

Today, Air India is still in state control, although privatisation has been considered. It has a number of subsidiaries, mainly involved in hotels, and Air India Charters, established in 1971, which does not have aircraft of its own but instead operates with aircraft provided by the parent airline. Future plans are to introduce what the airline describes as 'medium capacity long range' aircraft for medium-density long-haul routes, offering more non-stop flights. A low-cost subsidiary, Air India Express, was founded in 2004 and began operations in 2005 using three Boeing 737-800s from Mumbai. Many of the 737-800s being introduced may be passed to this subsidiary if demand justifies it.

The airline is forty-eighth largest in the world by revenue. Employee numbers have fallen by around a sixth over the past seven or eight years. It has a 2.56 per cent stake in Air Mauritius. Deliveries of the Boeing 777 fleet may reduce the 747 fleet further.

HQ airport & main base: Mumbai International (Bombay), with Delhi Indira Ghandi International
Radio callsign: AIRINDIA
Designator: AI/AIC
Employees: 15,535
Route points: Abu Dhabi, Ahmedabad, Amritsar, Amsterdam, Bahrain, Bangalore, Bangkok, Birmingham, Chennai, Chicago, Damman, Dar-es-Salaam, Delhi, Dhaka, Doha, Dubai, Frankfurt, Goa, Hong Kong, Hyderabad, Istanbul, Jakarta, Jeddah, Kochi, Kolkata, Kozhikode, Kuala Lumpur, Kuwait, London, Los Angeles, Lucknow, Manchester, Mauritius, Moscow, Mumbai, Munich, Muscat, Nairobi, New York, Newark, Osaka, Paris, Pune, Riyadh, Rome, San Francisco, Seoul, Shanghai, Singapore, Tel Aviv, Thiruvananthapuram, Tokyo, Toronto, Vienna, Zurich
Links with other airlines: Alliances with Aeroflot Russian Airlines, Air France, Air Mauritius, Asiana

Airlines, Austrian Airlines, Emirates, Kuwait Airways, Lufthansa, Malaysian Airlines, Singapore Airlines, Thai Airways, THY Turkish Airlines (all qv). Hub-and-spoke operations at Mumbai (Bombay) and Delhi operated jointly with Indian Airlines (qv), as are operations from Calcutta to the Gulf
Annual turnover: US $1,670 million (£1,060 million)
Fleet: 8 Boeing 747-400; 1 Boeing 747-400 Combi; 2 Boeing 747-300 Combi; 1 Boeing 747-200; 15 Boeing 777-300ER; 3 Boeing 777-200ER; 9 Boeing 777-200LR; 19 Airbus A310-300; 22 Boeing 737-800 (On order: 27 Boeing 787-8)

AIR SAHARA
Sahara India Airlines Ltd
Incorporated: 1991

Founded in 1991 as Sahara Indian Airlines, the operating division of the Sahara Group, the airline did not commence operations until 1993, when two Boeing 737-200s were introduced, which were joined the following year by two 737-400s. The airline developed a network of scheduled passenger and cargo services from Delhi and Mumbai (Bombay), adding ATR-42s for its shorter routes, although these have since been replaced and an all-jet fleet is now operated. The names was changed to Air Sahara in 2000. International routes were started in 2003, flying to Colombo and Kathmandu, to which Singapore has now been added. A merger with Jet Airways is in prospect, with regulatory approval having been gained, which will create a substantial Indian private sector airline.

HQ airport & main base: Delhi Indira Gandhi International, with further hubs at Calcutta International, Chennai International, Hyderabad and Mumbai
Designator: S2/SHD
Route points: Ahmedabad, Allahabad, Bangalore, Bhubaneswar, Calcutta, Chennai, Coimbatore, Colombo, Delhi, Dibrugarh, Goa, Gorakhpur, Hyderabad, Jaipur, Kathmandu, Kochi, Kolkata, Lucknow, Mumbai, Patna, Pune, Ranchi, Singapore, Srinagar, Varanasi, Vishakhapatnam
Fleet: 17 Boeing 737-800; 3 Boeing 737-400; 8 Boeing 737-700; 21 Boeing 737-300; 4 Bombardier CRJ200LR; 3 Bombardier CRJ200ER

ALLIANCE AIR
Alliance Air Ltd
Incorporated: 1996

Alliance Air was formed by Indian Airlines in 1996 as a regional subsidiary operating to destinations in the west, initially operating four of the parent airline's Boeing 737s. The airline has now developed into a low-cost operation, operating to more than forty destinations within India.

HQ airport & main base: Delhi-Safdarjung
Designator: CD/LLR
Route points: Delhi, Goa, Mumbai and another 40 destinations on the Indian Airlines network
Links with other airlines: A subsidiary of Indian Airlines (qv)
Fleet: 11 Boeing 737-200; 4 ATR-42-300

BLUE DART AVIATION
Incorporated: 1994
Founded in 1994, Blue Dart did not commence operations until 1996, operating scheduled overnight cargo services, mainly within India, as well as charter operations.

HQ airport & main base: Meenambakkan Airport, Tamil Nadu
Designator: BZ/BDA
Employees: 625
Route points: Banaglore, Calcutta, Chennai, Delhi, Hyderabad, Kolkata, Mumbai
Fleet: 2 Boeing 757-200SF; 5 Boeing 737-200

INDIAN AIRLINES
Indian Airlines Ltd
Incorporated: 1953

Indian Airlines was formed in 1953 as the Indian National Airlines Corporation on the nationalisation of all Indian airlines, and was allocated the domestic services hitherto operated by the then Air-India International and six other airlines. Initially, the airline's fleet included a large number of Douglas DC-3s, but these were later replaced by Indian-built Hawker Siddeley 748 turborprop airliners. As air travel developed in India, the airline became one of the world's largest domestic carriers, with larger aircraft needed for the trunk routes. This led in 1981 to the formation of a third level airline, Vayudoot, as a 50:50 joint venture with Air India.

Vayudoot had Indian Airlines' fleet of HS 748s transferred to it, and also operated Fokker F27 Friendships and Dornier Do.228s. A third-level carrier, its operations were reabsorbed by Indian Airlines in 1995, after concerns over safety.

In recent years, Indian Airlines has moved beyond purely domestic operations and now operates to neighbouring countries as well as to South-East Asia and to the Gulf, the latter in cooperation with Air India. The growth in flights between the Indian subcontinent and the Gulf States has been aided by the number of expatriate Indian workers in these countries. Changes in the route network have been made possible by the types of aircraft now operated, which have the range and capacity to relieve Air India of some of that airline's shorter routes.

A subsidiary, Alliance Air, was established in 1996 as a regional airline. The Boeing 737 fleet is gradually being transferred to the new airline.

Although Indian Airlines is still nationalised and under the control of the Ministry of Tourism and Civil Aviation, it is no longer operated as a state corporation but as a limited company.

HQ airport & main base: New Delhi (HQ), with main base at Hyderabad and additional hubs and bases at Calcutta, Chenna and Mumbai
Radio callsign: INDAIR
Designator: IC/IAC
Employees: *c.* 25,000
Route points: Argatala, Agatti, Ahmedabad, Aizawl, Al-Fujairah, Amritsar, Aurangabad, Bagdogra, Bahrain, Bangalore, Bangkok, Bhopal, Bhubaneswar, Chandigarth, Chennai, Coimbatore, Colombo, Delhi, Dhaka, Dibrugarth, Dimapur, Doha, Dubai, Gaya, Goa, Guwahati, Hyderabad, Imphal, Indore, Jaipur, Jammu, Jamnagar, Jodphur, Jorhat, Kabul, Karachi, Kathmandu, Khajuraho, Kochi, Kolkata, Kozhikode, Kuala Lumpur, Kuwait, Lahore, Leh, Lilabari, Lucknow, Madurai, Male, Mangalore, Mumbai, Muscat, Nagpur, Patna, Port Blair, Pune, Raipur, Rajkot, Ranchi, Ras-al-Khaimah, Sharjah, Shillong, Silchar, Singapore, Srinagar, Udaipur, Vadodara, Varanasi, Vishakhapatnam, Yangon
Links with other airlines: Owns Alliance Air (qv). Alliances with Gulf Air, Pakistan International Airlines, Sri Lankan Airlines (all qv)
Fleet: 3 Airbus A300B4-200; 20 Airbus A321-200; 51 Airbus A320-200; 24 Airbus A319-100; 2 Dornier 228-212

INDIGO AIRLINES
Incorporated: 2005

Not operational at the time of writing, this is an ambitious plan for an independently owned low-cost Indian airline with 100 Airbus A320-200s on order.

HQ airport & main base: New Delhi Indira Ghandi International
Radio callsign: INDIGO
Designator: TBA
Fleet: Up to 30 Airbus A321-200 and 100 Airbus A320-200

JET
Jet Airways (India) Ltd
Incorporated: 1992

One of the largest independent airlines in India, Jet Airways was founded in April 1992, and commenced operations a little over a year later, in May 1993. Support was provided by Gulf Air and Kuwait Airways, each with a 20 per cent stake in the new airline, although the largest shareholder was Tailwinds, an Indian company owned by Naresh Goyal, the airline's chairman. In 1997, a new Indian government demanded that Gulf Air and Kuwait Airways dispose of their shareholdings and that all airlines must be completely Indian-owned, which resulted in Tailwinds taking an 80 per cent share while other investors took the remaining 20 per cent.

Meanwhile, the airline, which when formed was officially classified as an 'air taxi operator', despite operating four Boeing 737-300s, and had been limited to charter operations, was permitted by a change in the law in India in 1994 to commence scheduled operations. The support of Gulf Air and Kuwait Airways plus a cooperation agreement with KLM, including a common frequent-flyer programme, ensured rapid growth. Jet Airways plans to acquire Sahara Airlines in the near future.

HQ airport & main base: Mumbai International, with additional hubs at Bangalore, Chennai and Delhi
Radio callsign: JET AIRWAYS
Designator: 9W/JAI
Employees: 7,600
Route points: Agartala, Ahmedabad, Aurangabad, Bagdogra, Colombo, Delhi, Diu, Goa, Guwahati, Hyderabad, Imphal, Indore, Jaipur, Jammu, Jodpur, Jorhat, Kathmandu, Khajuraho, Kochi, Kolkaata, Kozhikode, Kuala Lumpur, Leh, London, Lucknow, Madurai, Mangalore, Mumbai, Nagpur, Patna, Portbandar, Pornandar, Port Blair, Pune, Raipur, Rajkot, Singapore, Srinagar, Thiruvananthapuram, Udaipur, Vadodara, Varanasi
Fleet: 3 Airbus A340-300; 10 Boeing 777-300ER; 10 Airbus A330-200; 2 Boeing 737-900; 34 Boeing 737-800; 4 Boeing 737-400; 13 Boeing 737-700; 8 ATR-72-500 (On order: 10 Boeing 787-8)

KINGFISHER AIRLINES
Incorporated: 2004

Founded in 2004 as a low-cost airline, Kingfisher began operations in 2005 and has ambitious plans for a substantial domestic and international route network.

HQ airport & main base: Delhi Indira Gandhi International
Designator: IT
Route points: Agartala, Ahmedabad, Bangalore, Chennai, Delhi, Dibrugarh, Goa, Guwahati, Hyderabad, Kochi, Kolkata, Mumbai, Pune
Fleet: 4 Airbus A321-200; 10 Airbus A320-200; 4 Airbus A319-100 (On order: 5 Airbus A380-800; 5 Airbus A330-200; 5 Airbus A350-800; 35 Airbus A320-200; 35 ATR-72-500)

PARAMOUNT AIRWAYS
Incorporated: 2005

Founded in 2005 by the Paramount textile group, Paramount is a new airline aimed at business travellers to and from Coimbatore.

HQ airport & main base: Coimbatore Pilameedu
Radio callsign: PARAMOUNT
Designator: 17/PMW
Route points: Chennai, Coimbatore, Delhi
Fleet: 3 Embraer 175; 2 Embraer 170

INDONESIA – PK

Indonesia is one of a number of countries in Asia with a dynamic, locally owned air transport industry, with independent airlines blossoming despite the presence of a substantial state-owned airline. The independent airlines have established the Indonesian National Air Carriers' Association, which in addition to representing their interests, also operates an endorsable ticketing system so that passengers can transfer between any of the participating carriers.

Despite the dynamism, there have been a few airlines that have failed, and over the past decade one of these has been Sempati.

ADAMAIR
Incorporated: 2003

Founded in 2003 as an international and domestic scheduled and charter airline handling both passengers and cargo, using two leased Boeing 737s, the airline is a wholly owned subsidiary of PT Adam SkyConnection Airlines. It has an all-Boeing 737 fleet.

HQ airport & main base: Jakarta
Designator: KI/DHI
Employees: 2,300
Route points: Balikpapan, Banda Aceh, Bandar Lampung, Banjarmasin, Batam, Bengkulu, Denpasar Bali, Jakarta, Manado, Medan, Padang, Palembang, Pangkalpinang, Pejkanbaru, Penang, Pontianak, Samarang, Singapore, Surabaya, Ujung Pandang, Yogyakarta
Fleet: 7 Boeing 737-200; 7 Boeing 737-300; 6 Boeing 737-400; 1 Boeing 737-500

AIRFAST
Airfast Indonesia
Incorporated: 1971

Originally founded to provide air services for the oil industry in Indonesia, Airfast has expanded its operations to include contract and ad hoc passenger and freight charters, with a very wide variety of aircraft, ranging from small Piper and Beech air taxis and Bell helicopters to Boeing 737s.

HQ airport & main base: Jakarta Soekarno Hatta International
Radio callsign: AIRFAST
Designator: AFE
Employees: 450
Fleet: 1 Boeing 737-200; 2 McDonnell Douglas MD-82; 4 BAe 748; 1 Embraer GRJ-145; 1 Raytheon Beech 1900D; 3 de Havilland DHC-6 Twin Otter; 1 CASA/IPTN 212-200 Aviocar; 3 Sikorsky S-58ET; 2 Bell 412; 1 Bell 212; 1 Beech Queen Air B80; 2 Bell 204; 2 Bell 206B JetRanger; 1 Piper Apache

BALI AIR
Incorporated: 1973

A wholly owned subsidiary of Bouraq, Bali provides regional air charter services.

HQ airport & main base: Jakarta Soekarno Hatta International
Designator: BLN
Links with other airlines: Owned by Bouraq
Fleet: 1 Boeing 737-200; 3 BAe 748 Srs 2

BATAVIA AIR
Incorporated: 2002

Originally founded as Metro-Batavia using Fokker F27s wet-leased from Sempati, mainly handling cargo charter flights, the airline started scheduled services in 2002 and moved into passenger operations the following year, changing its name. It currently operates a domestic and regional scheduled network, with longer-term plans to operate to Australia. Metro-Batavia remains as the holding company.

HQ airport & main base: Jakarta Soekarno Hatta International
Designator: 7P/BTV
Route points: Balikpapan, Banjarmasin, Batam, Biak, Denpassar Bali, Guangzhou, Jakarta, Jambi, Jayapura, Jogyakarta, Kuching, Kupang, Manado, Manokwari, Medan, Padang, Palangkaraya, Palembang, Pankal Pinang, Pekanbaru, Pontianak, Surabaya, Semarang, Tanjung Pandan, Tarakan, Ujung Pandang
Fleet: 4 Boeing 737-400; 9 Boeing 737-300; 4 Airbus A319-100; 13 Boeing 737-200; 1 Fokker F28 Mk4000

BOURAQ
Bouraq Indonesia Airlines
Incorporated: 1970

Bouraq operates throughout the eastern part of the Indonesian archipelago, including Bali and Java, and to parts of Malaysia. In recent years, its five BAe 748 turboprop aircraft have been replaced by Boeing 737s and an MD-82, but Bouraq's current status is unclear and operations may have ceased in 2005.

HQ airport & main base: Jakarta Soekarno Hatta International
Radio callsign: BOURAQ
Designator: BO/BOU
Employees: 731
Route points: Balikpapan, Banjarmasin, Berau, Datadawai, Jakarta, Ketapang, Kotabaru, Long Agung, Long Bawan, Nunukan, Pangkalanbuun, Pontianak, Putussibau, Salekhard, Samarinda, Sampit, Sintang, Tanjung Selor, Tarakan, Ujung Pandang
Fleet: 2 Boeing 737-200; 1 McDonnell-Douglas MD-82

DERAYA AIR TAXI
Incorporated: 1967

Despite the title, Deraya Air Taxi now operates charter and a number of regional scheduled services within Indonesia for cargo and passengers, as well as maintaining a number of ancillary activities, such as medical evacuation, a flying school and aerial photography. It is a subsidiary of the Boediharjo Group.

HQ airport & main base: Jakarta Halim Perdanakusuma International
Designator: DRY
Route points: Services out of Jakarta and Bandung
Fleet: 3 Shorts 360-300; 2 Shorts 330-100; 3 Indonesian Aerospace 212-100; 1 Shorts SC-7 Skyvan

DIRGANTARA AIR SERVICE
Incorporated: 1971

Originally founded in 1971 as a charter and aerial work company, Dirgantara moved into scheduled flights in 1995, and these continue, mainly within Indonesia. The airline's employees own 30 per cent of the shares.

HQ airport & main base: Banjamasin Syamsudin Noor
Radio callsign: DIRGANTARA
Designator: AW/DIR
Employees: 232
Route points: Balikpapan, Banjarmasin, Berau, Datadawai, Ketapang, Kotabaru, Long Agung, Long Bawan, Nunukan, Pangkalanbuun, Pontianak, Putussibau, Salekhard, Samarinda, Sampit, Sintang, Tanjung Selor, Tarakan, Ujung Pandang
Fleet: 1 ATR-42-300; 6 Indonesian Aerospace 212-200; 2 Indonesian Aerospace 212-100; 7 Britten-Norman BN2A/B Islander

GARUDA
PT Garuda Indonesia Airways
Incorporated: 1949

Air services in Indonesia were originally started by KLM in the 1930s, which operated an Inter Island Division in Indonesia before establishing a subsidiary airline, KNILM, or Royal Dutch East Indies Airlines, before the outbreak of the Second World War. Postwar operations were slow to start as, after the defeat of Japan, Indonesia pressed hard for independence.

Garuda itself was founded by the government of the newly independent Indonesia and KLM in 1949, and commenced operations the following year as Garuda Indonesian Airways. KLM's interest was taken over by the Indonesian government in 1954, and during the next decade the airline acquired many of the smaller airlines operating within Indonesia. While the initial objective was to create a viable air transport operation within Indonesia, a large country with tropical rain forest and mountains, spread over a large number of islands, intercontinental services were also introduced later. Having originally commenced operations with Douglas DC-3s, Convair 340 and 440 Metropolitans were acquired, and then Fokker F27s and Lockheed Electras, some of which were ex-KLM, before a move into the jet age with Comvair 990s and Douglas DC-8s, which were followed by DC-9s.

In 1962, Garuda acquired the domestic services operated by a KLM subsidiary, de Kronduif, but after two years these were passed to the new airline formed by the Indonesian government to operate domestic services, Merpati. In 1978, Garuda acquired Merpati, which by this time operated an intensive network of domestic air services, but now no longer owns the airline although retaining a small 6.8 per cent share. In 2001 Garuda established a low-cost domestic operator, Citilink, which it owns outright and which operates three Boeing 737s.

Today, in terms of annual turnover, Garuda is no longer one of the world's top fifty airlines. Having risen from thirty-fourth in 1996 to thirty-first in 1997, the airline fell out of the list by 2004, although it is still forty-eighth in terms of passenger numbers. The route network extends throughout Asia and the Pacific and to the primarily European destinations, as well as to Los Angeles. A major domestic route network is also operated. Alliances exist with a number of major airlines.

The question of the airline being denationalised, to reduce its dependence on the government, possibly by an offering of shares to raise capital for future expansion, has been raised repeatedly over the past decade. Employee numbers have halved over the same period.

HQ airport & main base: Jakarta Soekarno Hatta International
Radio callsign: INDONESIA
Designator: GA/GIA
Employees: 6,825
Route points: Adelaide, Amsterdam, Auckland, Balikpapan, Banda Aceh, Bangkok, Banjarmasin, Batam, Beijing, Biak, Brisbane, Damman, Darwin, Denpasar Bali, Doha, Frankfurt, Fukuoka, Guangzhou, Ho Chi Minh City, Hong Kong, Jakarta, Jayapura, Jeddah, Kendari, Kuala Lumpur, Kuching, London, Manado, Manchester, Manila, Mataram, Medan, Melbourne, Nagoya, Osaka, Padang, Palembang, Paris, Pekanbaru, Penang, Perth, Pontianak, Riyadh, Semarang, Seoul, Shanghai, Singapore, Solo City, Surabaya, Sydney, Taipei, Tarakan, Tembagapura, Tokyo, Ujung Pandang, Vienna, Yogyakarta, Zurich
Links with other airlines: Owns Citilink 100 per cent. Has a 6.8 per cent stake in Merpati (qv). Alliances with China Airlines, China Southern Airlines, Gulf Air, Korean Air, Malaysia Airlines, Philippine Airlines, Qatar Airways, Silk Air (all qv)
Passengers carried: 9.8 million
Fleet: 5 Boeing 747-400; 3 Boeing 747-300; 6 Boeing 777-200ER; 4 Boeing 767-300GA; 9 Airbus A330-300; 2 Boeing 737-800; 18 Boeing 737-700; 19 Boeing 737-800; 24 Boeing 737-400; 5 Boeing 737-500

JATAYU AIR

Jatayu Airlines
Incorporated: 2000

Jatayu was founded in 2000 and operates passenger charter flights and is developing a scheduled network based on Jakarta.

HQ airport & main base: Jakata Soekarno Hatta International
Radio callsign: JATAYU
Designator: VJ/JTY
Fleet: 6 Boeing 727-200; 3 Boeing 737-200

LION AIRLINES

Incorporated: 1999

Founded in 1999, Lion Airlines commenced operations in 2000, operating scheduled and charter flights handling passengers and cargo. Operations began with a service between Jakarta and Pontianak with a leased Boeing 737-200, but this was replaced by McDonnell Douglas MD series aircraft which were joined by Boeing 737-400s. At present, the airline is in the midst of a re-equipment programme that will see it standardise on Boeing 737-900ERs. A subsidiary is Wings Air, while the airline itself is owned by the president and his family.

HQ airport & main base: Jakarta Soekarno Hatta International
Designator: JT/LNI
Route points: Ambon, Balikpapan, Bandung, Batam, Cialcap, Denpasar Bali, Jakarta, Kuala Lumpur, Manado, Mataram, Medan, Padang, Pekanbaru, Penang, Solo City, Sorong, Surabaya, Ternate, Ujung, Pandang, Yogyakarta
Links with other airlines: Owns Wings Air (qv)
Fleet: 40 Boeing 737-900EX; 7 Boeing 737-400; 2 Boeing 737-300

MANDALA AIRLINES
PT Mandala Airlines
Incorporated: 1969

Among the first privately owned airlines in Indonesia after nationalisation of air transport in the 1950s, Mandala initially operated charters before establishing a network of scheduled services. During the past decade, the fleet has become all-jet and standardised on the Boeing 737, replacing a fleet of five Lockheed Electra turboprops and a couple of Fokker F28 Fellowships.

HQ airport & main base: Jakarta Soekarno Hatta International
Radio callsign: MANDALA
Designator: RI/MDL
Employees: 1,325
Route points: Ambon, Balikpan, Banjarmasin, Batam, Denpasar Bali, Jakarta, Jambi, Makassar, Manado, Medan, Padang, Pekanbaru, Semarang, Surabaya, Tarakan, Yogyakarta
Fleet: 2 Airbus A320-200; 2 Boeing 737-400; 11 Boeing 737-300; 6 Boeing 737-200

MERPATI
Merpati Nusantara Airlines
Incorporated: 1962

Merpati is Indonesia's main domestic airline, operating scheduled passenger and cargo services throughout the Indonesian archipelago, as well as charter flights. The airline was founded by the Indonesian government in 1962, as a domestic partner to Garuda, and although that airline continued to operate an extensive domestic trunk network, the services previously operated by de Kroonduif, a subsidiary of KLM, and which Garuda had been operating, were transferred to Merpati in 1964. The core of Merpati's operations at first were routes which had been flown by the Indonesian Air Force, which had been developing services to isolated communities from 1958 onwards.

In 1978, ownership of Merpati was transferred to Garuda, but the airline maintained its own identity and management team for most of the time afterwards, except between 1989 and 1993, when it was integrated into Garuda. Afterwards, in 1997, a restructuring of shareholdings saw Garuda left with a token 6.8 per cent share while the Indonesian government held the rest. Merpati itself has a subsidiary, Sabang Merauke Raya Air Charter, operating feeder services, air charters and medical flights within Sumatra with a Britten-Norman Islander and Indonesian Aerospace 212s. At one time, in terms of airports used, Merpati had one of the world's largest domestic networks, reaching more than 130 destinations all within Indonesia, but this may have been cut back somewhat as the airline has contracted over the past decade. It also has a limited regional international network.

HQ airport & main base: Jakarta Soekarno Hatta International, with additional hubs at Denpasar (Bali) and Padang
Radio callsign: MERPATI
Designator: MZ/MNA
Employees: 2,150
Main route points: Balikpapan, Bandar Lampung, Bandung, Batam, Bengkulu, Biak, Denpaser Bali, Dili, Jakarta, Jayapura, Kendari, Kuala Lumpur, Kupang, Manado, Manokwari, Mataram, Medan, Merauke, Padang, Palangkaraya, Palembang, Palu, Pekanbaru, Sorong, Surabaya, Tembagapura, Ternate, Ujiung Pandang, Yogyakarta
Links with other airlines: Garuda (qv) has a 6.8 per cent interest. Merpati owns Sabang Merauke Raya Air Charter. Alliances with Airnorth, Kuwait Airways (qv), Silk Air (qv)
Fleet: 2 Boeing 737-300; 9 Boeing 737-200; 1 Fokker 100; 4 Fokker F28-4000 Fellowship; 1 Fokker F27-500 Friendship; 5 Indonesian Aerospace CN-235; 3 Indonesian Aerospace CN-212; 5 de Havilland DHC-6 Twin Otter Srs 300

PELITA
Pelita Air Service
Incorporated: 1963

Pelita was founded in 1963, but operations did not begin until 1970, operating as part of the state oil company, Pertamina. The company was allowed to operate independently of its parent in 1981, providing executive air services, passenger and freight charter and contract operations, and developing a small scheduled network. Today, Pertamina still holds 90 per cent of the shares, while Patra Jara has 10 per cent. The fleet has slimmed down and rationalised considerably in recent years, and no longer operates such heavy freighters as the Lockheed Hercules, of which there were four at one time.

HQ airport & main base: Jakarta Halim Perdanakusuma
Radio callsign: PELITA
Designator: EP/PAS

Route points: Bandung, Denpasar Bali, Gorontalo, Jakarta, Manokwari, Sorong, Surabaya, Tarakan, Ujung Pandang, Yogyakarta
Links with other airlines: Alliances with Bouraq Indonesia Airlines (qv), Indonesian Air Transport
Fleet: 2 Fokker 100; 1 BAe Avro RJ85ER; 2 Fokker F28 Fellowship Mk4000; 5 de Havilland Canada Dash 7-100; 7 Indonesian Aerospace 212-200

SABANG
Sabang Merauke Raya Air Charter
Incorporated: 1969

Originally founded as a joint venture with a Malaysian company and known as Malaysian Air Charter, in 1972, the airline split from the Malaysian interests and adopted the current title. Although the airline's operations are predominantly charter, some scheduled services are now operated in and around Sumatra.

HQ airport & main base: Medan, Sumatra
Radio callsign: SAMER
Designator: SMC
Fleet: 4 CASA/IPTN 212-100; 2 Pilatus Britten-Norman BN-2A Islander

SRIWIJAYA AIRLINES
Incorporated: 2003

Owned by local government and by other interests, Sriwijaya Airlines was established in 2003 and is building a domestic scheduled network based on Jakarta, using a fleet of Boeing 737s.

HQ airport & main base: Jakarta Soekarno Hatta International
Designator: SJ/SJY
Route points: Bandung, Denapsar Bali, Gorontalo, Jakarta, Manokwari, Sorong, Surabaya, Tarakan, Ujung Pandang, Yogyakarta
Fleet: 15 Boeing 737-200

TRANSWISATA PRIMA AVIATION
Incorporated: 2002

Founded in 2002 by a group of local businessmen, Transwisata Prima Aviation is primarily a passenger charter airline, but it is developing a scheduled network.

HQ airport & main base: Jakarta Halim Perdanakusuma International
Fleet: 1 Fokker 100; 2 Fokker F28 Fellowship Mk4000; 4 Fokker 50

TRIGANA AIR SERVICE
Incorporated: 1991

Originally founded in 1991, Trigana Air Service is primarily a charter airline but is developing a scheduled route network.

HQ airport & main base: Jakarta Halim Perdanakusuma
Designator: TGN
Fleet: 1 Boeing 737-200; 1 ATR-72-200; 1 ATR-42-300F; 6 ATR-42-300; 6 Fokker F27 Friendship Mk200/500/600; 3 de Havilland Canada Twin Otter Srs 300

WINGS AIR
Incorporated: 2003

Wings Air was formed in 2003 by the owners, Lion Airlines, and is developing a domestic route network, with plans to introduce services to Malaysia and Singapore later.

HQ airport & main base: Jakarta Soekarno Hatta International
Designator: IW/WON
Route points: Jakarta, Manado, Medan, Merauke, Padang, Palangkaraya, Palembang, Palu, Surabaya, Tembagapura, Ternate, Ujiung Pandang
Fleet: 4 McDonnell Douglas MD-82; 2 Bombardier Dash 8 Q300

IRAN – EP

IRAN AIR
Iran Air/Homa
Incorporated: 1944

The predecessor of Iran Air, Iranian Airways, was founded in 1944 as a private compnay with TWA holding 10 per cent of the shares. Operations did not begin until the following year, when charter flights were operated, with the first scheduled flights starting in 1946, with services from Tehran to Baghdad, Beirut and Cairo. At this time the airline was mainly using Douglas DC-3 aircraft, although these were soon joined by Douglas DC-4s. A domestic route network was developed during this time, while international expansion continued, with services to Athens, Paris and Rome being introduced in 1947.

Convair 240 Metropolitans and Douglas DC-6s, including DC-6Bs, were introduced later, and in 1959 the airline received two Vickers Viscount 700s. Two years later, at the request of the government, the airline absorbed Persian Air Services, which was in serious financial difficulties. Persian Air Services had dated from 1954, and had had the benefit of assistance from both Sabena and KLM. The merger resulted in an extensive reorganisation of Iranian Airways, and it was nationalised in 1962, becoming the Iran National Airlines Corporation, or Iranair. Post-nationalisation, a three-year technical assistance agreement was reached with Pan American in 1964.

The first jet equipment, Boeing 727s, was introduced in 1966, and enabled the airline to inaugurate a service to London. Both Boeing 707s and 737s soon followed.

Revolution in Iran and the creation of an Islamic republic saw a slight change to the name, becoming Iran Air, but now otherwise known as HOMA, based on the acronym of the airline's name in Persian. Operations were disrupted after the revolution and then again during the lengthy war with Iraq. Despite frequent diplomatic difficulties with the West, the airline has built up a substantial fleet of European and American aircraft, although many of these are now elderly, and Iran Air has been planning to modernise its fleet with Airbus A321 and A330 aircraft, although at the time of writing no orders have been announced. Possibly due to the country's political difficulties, the number of employees has dropped by around 40 per cent over the past decade.

A subsidiary is Iran Air Tours, operating a charter fleet of Russian origin, while Iran Air remains completely state owned.

HQ airport & main base: Tehran Mehrabad
Radio callsign: IRANAIR
Designator: IR/IRA
Employees: 7,500
Route points: Abadan, Amsterdam, Ardabil, Ashgabat, Athens, Bahrain, Baku, Bandar Abbas, Bandar Lengeh, Beijing, Beirut, Birjand, Bushehr, Chah-Bahar, Cologne, Copenhagen, Damascus, Dhaka, Doha, Dubai, Frankfurt, Geneva, Gheshm, Gothenburg, Hamburg, Isfahan, Istanbul, Jeddah, Karachi, Kerman, Kermanshah, Kish, Kuala Lumpur, Kuwait, London, Mashhad, Milan, Moscow, Mumbai, Paris, Rasht, Rome, Sary, Seoul, Shahre-Kord, Sharjah, Shiraz, Stockholm, Tabriz, Tashkent, Tehran, Tokyo, Urumieh, Vienna, Yazd, Zahedan
Links with other airlines: Owns Iran Air Tours (qv)
Fleet: 2 Boeing 747-200F; 2 Boeing 747-200; 7 Boeing 747-100F; 1 Boeing 747-100B; 2 Boeing 747SP; 4 Airbus A300-600R; 4 Airbus A300B2; 2 Airbus A310-300; 3 Airbus A310-200; 4 Boeing 727-200; 2 Boeing 727-100; 4 Boeing 737-200; 8 Fokker 100

IRAN AIR TOURS

Incorporated: 1973

Although formed as a subsidiary of Iran Air in 1973, Iran Air Tours did not start operating aircraft until 1990, and while today most of its business is air charter, including pilgrimage flights, it has also developed a network of domestic services and an international route to Dubai. The size of the fleet has reduced substantially in recent years.

HQ airport & main base: Tehran Mehrabad, with a further base at Mashhad
Designator: IRB
Route points: Abadan, Ahwaz, Bandar Abbas, Bushehr, Chah-Bahar, Dubai, Isfahan, Kermanshah, Mashhad, Rasht, Sary, Shahre-Kord, Shiraz, Tabriz, Tehran, Urmieh, Yazd, Zahedan
Links with other airlines: A subsidiary of Iran Air (qv)
Fleet: 10 Tupolev Tu-154M

IRAN ASEMAN

Iran Aseman Airlines
Incorporated: 1980

Iran Aseman Airlines was founded after the Iranian revolution in 1980, on the nationalisation and merger of four operators: Air Taxi, dating from 1958; Air Service, formed in 1962; Paris Air, formed in 1969; and Hoor Asseman. The aircraft included a number of types suitable for air taxi and feeder services.

Today, the airline remains in state ownership but independent of and distinct from Iran Air. A high-frequency domestic network is operated, to which some international destinations have been added in recent years, as well as domestic and international charters.

HQ airport & main base: Tehran Mehrabad
Designator: Y7/IRC
Employees: 1,300
Route points: Abu Dhabi, Abadan, Ahwaz, Ardabil, Asaloyeh, Bahrain, Bam, Bandar Abbas, Birjand, Bohnord, Bushehr, Doha, Dubai, Dushanbe, Gheshm, Gurgan, Ilaam, Kabul, Kermanshah, Khoy, Kuwait, Lamerd, Lar, Mashhad, Now Shahr,

Rafsanjan, Ramsar, Rasht, Sabzevar, Sahand, Sanandaj, Shiraz, Tabriz, Tehran, Yasouj, Yazd
Fleet: 4 Boeing 727-200; 11 Fokker 100; 2 ATR-72-500; 3 ATR-72-210; 5 Fokker F28 Fellowship Mk1000/4000; 5 Dornier 228-212; 6 Dassault Falcon 20

KISH AIR
Kish Airlines
Incorporated: 1991

Kish Airlines was founded in 1991 and started operations the following year, operating from its base on Kish Island, off the coast of Iran. The airline was originally completely owned by the Kish Free Zone organisation, which now owns 79 per cent, with the remaining shares in the hands of other local organisations, while the main base has moved from Kish to Tehran. It operates scheduled services and passenger charters.

HQ airport & main base: Tehran Mehrabad
Radio callsign: KISHAIR
Designator: Y9/IRK
Employees: 303
Route points: Dubai, Isfahan, Kermanshah, Kish, Mashhad, Shiraz, Tabriz, Tehran
Fleet: 2 Tupolev Tu-154M; 1 McDonnell Douglas MD-82; 5 Fokker 50

MAHAN AIR
Incorporated: 1991

Founded in 1991, Mahan Air started operations the following year, and has since built up a domestic and international scheduled network, primarily for passengers, while also operating international charters including pilgrimage flights. Airbus aircraft predominate in the fleet, although a couple of Tupolev aircraft are still operated.

HQ airport & main base: Tehran Mehrabad
Designator: W5/IRM
Employees: 1,400
Route points: Asaloyeh, Bandar Abbas, Bandar Mahshahr, Bangkok, Birmingham (UK), Delhi, Dubai, Düsseldorf, Iran Shahr, Kerman, Mashhad, San Borja, Tehran, Zabol, Zahedan
Fleet: 2 Airbus A300B2; 4 Airbus A300B4; 4 Airbus A310-300; 1 Tupolev Tu-204-120; 1 Tupolev Tu-154M; 3 Airbus A320-200

SAHA AIRLINES
Incorporated: 1990

Owned by the Islamic Republic of Iran Air Force, Saha operates international and domestic passenger and cargo charters as well as providing links between major IRIAF bases.

HQ airport & main base: Tehran Mehrabad
Radio callsign: SAHA
Designator: IRZ
Fleet: 2 Boeing 747-200F; 4 Boeing 707-320C; 2 Fokker F27 Friendship Mk600

IRAQ – YI

IRAQI AIRWAYS
Incorporated: 1945

After almost fifteen years with flights banned after the 1991 Gulf War, Iraqi Airways is gradually resuming operations.

Originally founded in 1945 as a branch of the state-owned railways, Iraqi Airways commenced operations the following year with a service between Baghdad and Basra, using de Havilland Rapide biplanes. Douglas DC-3s followed soon after, and by the end of the first year the airline had services operating from Baghdad to Beirut, Damascus, Lydda and Cairo. Assistance was then received from BOAC, the British Overseas Airways Corporation, and this arrangement lasted until 1960.

Early expansion was steady, with Tehran and Kuwait added to the network in 1947, and in 1948, services were introduced to Athens, Bahrain and Cyprus. The Rapides and DC-3s were replaced by de Havilland Doves and Vickers Vikings, and it was not until 1957 that the airline received its first four-engined aircraft, Vickers Viscount 735s. The Viscounts enabled the airline to start a service from Baghdad to London via Istanbul and Vienna in 1957. In 1965, the first jet equipment, Hawker Siddeley Trident 1Es, joined the fleet.

While Boeing aircraft were acquired in subsequent years, increasingly the fleet marked Iraq's close collaboration with the Soviet Union, so that Antonov and Ilyushin aircraft joined the fleet. Operations were affected by the long war between Iraq and Iran. The Gulf War of 1991 saw a complete ban on fixed-wing flights as part of the ceasefire terms. Nevertheless, the United Nations Security Council eventually agreed to a resumption of civil internal flights, and a service between Baghdad and Basra using Antonov An-24s was restarted in January 1992, but shortly afterwards operations were suspended again. The resumption of flights following the invasion led by US and British forces came in September 2005, with a service between Baghdad and Amman. It will take some time before the full route network is restored and the fleet is rebuilt.

HQ airport & main base: Baghdad International
Radio callsign: IRAQI
Designator: IA/IAW
Fleet: 1 Boeing 767-200; 5 Airbus A310-200; 1 Boeing 727-200; 4 Boeing 737-200

IRELAND – EI

Air transport in Ireland was for several decades the preserve of Aer Lingus, but in recent years the market has opened up and a substantial number of independent airlines have been established. The most successful of these has been Ryanair, which although Irish-registered and -based, has other bases across Europe and has overtaken the national carrier as Ireland's largest airline. Not every new Irish airline has been a success, and in recent years both EUJet and Ireland Airways have disappeared.

While for most of its post-independence history Ireland was a poor nation, this has been transformed in recent years, with the economy growing strongly. Nevertheless, the Irish market is a small one, with the Republic of Ireland having a population of less than four million, while a further difficulty is that air travel between Ireland and the United Kingdom, the biggest single market, is highly seasonal, with a short, sharp peak in the summer and an even shorter one at Christmas and the New Year. The country is also relatively small, and despite low average speeds on the railway network, has not lent itself to viable domestic air services.

AER ARANN/AER ARANN ISLANDS
Incorporated: 1970

Originally formed as a third-level carrier providing services between the Arann Islands off the west coast of Ireland and the mainland, the airline moved its main base to Dublin in 1998, when the airline was effectively divided into Aer Arann and a new entity, Aer Arran Islands. It continued to concentrate on services within Ireland until it opened new routes to the UK and the Isle of Man in 2002, followed by charter flights to France in 2004. Ownership is with Aer Arann Islands, the smaller airline, which continues to operate its vital lifeline services between Connemara Regional Airport and the islands.

HQ airport & main base: Aer Arann: Dublin, with hubs at Cork and Galway; Aer Arran Islands: Connemara Regional Airport
Radio callsign: ARANN
Designator: RE/REA
Employees: 400
Route points: Aer Arann: Belfast, Birmingham, Bristol, Cork, Donegal, Dublin, Edinburgh, Galway, Glasgow, Isle of Man, Kerry, Liverpool, London, Manchester, Sligo, Southampton, Waterford; Aer Arann Islands: Connemarra, Inisheer, Innishmaan, Inishmore
Fleet: Aer Arann: 7 ATR-72-200; 5 ATR-42-200; Aer Arran Islands: 3 Britten-Norman BN2A/B Islander (On order: 10 ATR-72-500)

AER LINGUS
Aer Lingus Ltd
Incorporated: 1936

Aer Lingus operates as a single airline, but is in fact two airlines as a result of a 1993 reorganisation – Aer Lingus, which operates European services, and Aer Lingus Shannon, which operates transatlantic services. (Aer Lingus is Gaelic for 'air fleet'.) Although this is the result of legislation passed in 1993, it also reflects the history of the airline, with Aer Lingus being formed in 1936 and Aerlinte Eireann formed in 1947 to operate a transatlantic service.

Operations began in May 1936, with a flight by a de Havilland Dragon Rapide biplane from Dublin to Bristol, although by the end of the year the service had been extended to London. Steady expansion took place up to the outbreak of the Second World War in 1939 when, despite Irish neutrality, operations were limited to a Dublin–Liverpool service, largely due to concerns over safety when flying in a combat zone, but also because of a severe shortage of fuel in Southern Ireland.

Aerlinte Eireann's first routes linked Dublin and Shannon with New York and Boston, using Lockheed Super Constellation airliners. The Constellations were later replaced by three Boeing 707s, which in turn were replaced by Boeing 747-100s, before these too were replaced by Airbus A330s. The airline's transatlantic operations were restricted for many years by an enforced call at Shannon in the west of Ireland for political reasons, largely to protect the local economy after transatlantic flights began to bypass the airport. Today, a compromise has been reached, with the A330s starting their transatlantic flights by flying eastwards from Shannon to Dublin, before beginning their 'non-stop' transatlantic flights: a measure considered important to tap into the potential market offered from airports in England and Scotland.

Today, Aer Lingus operates transatlantic services and services to most of the major centres in Europe, as well as providing charter flights for package holidays and for pilgrims to Lourdes. From 1984, a wholly owned subsidiary, Aer Lingus Commuter, operated feeder services within Ireland and from Great Britain, initially using Short 360 aircraft but later progressing to Fokker 50 and then BAe 146-300s, but was merged into the parent company in 2001. A number of services to Europe are routed through airports in England, and especially Manchester, because of the limited market offered by Ireland's small population. A major overhaul facility at Shannon, TEAM Aer Lingus, is used by a large number of airlines. The airline was slimmed down considerably in the wake of the September 2001 terrorist attacks in New York, which led to a fall in air travel, especially over the North Atlantic, but another factor affecting the airline has been the emergence of low-cost 'no frills' services between Ireland and Europe, including the important UK routes. The airline has a 20 per cent stake in the Spanish inclusive tour charter operator, Futura International Airways. Although Aer Lingus was a member of the Oneworld alliance, it left in 2006.

HQ airport & main base: Dublin, with transatlantic services located at Shannon, where the main maintenance base is situated
Radio callsign: SHAMROCK
Designator: EI/EIN
Employees: 3,900
Route points: Alicante, Almeria, Amsterdam, Barcelona, Berlin, Birmingham, Boston, Bordeaux, Bristol, Brussels, Budapest, Chicago, Cork, Dublin, Düsseldorf, Edinburgh, Faro, Frankfurt, Fuerteventura, Geneva, Glasgow, Hamburg, Krakow, Lanzarote, Lisbon, Liverpool, London Heathrow, Los Angeles, Madrid, Malaga, Manchester, Milan, Munich, Newcastle, New York-JFK, Nice, Paris, Prague, Riga, Rome, Salzburg, Shannon, Tenerife, Venice, Vienna, Warsaw, Zurich
Links with other airlines: Marketing alliances with JetBlue, British Airways and KLM (all qv)
Fleet: 4 Airbus A330-300; 3 Airbus A330-200; 6 Airbus A321-200; 24 Airbus A320-200

AIR CONTRACTORS
Incorporated: 1972

Founded in the United Kingdom as Air Bridge Carriers, the airline became part of the Hunting Group and adopted the title of Hunting Cargo Airlines in September 1992, operating Vickers Merchantmen (cargo conversions of the Vanguard airliner) on scheduled and charter freight services throughout the British Isles and Europe. In 1998, the airline was acquired by Compagnie Maritime Belge, with a 51 per cent interest, and by Safair, and the current title was adopted with a move to the Irish Republic. Most of the current workload consists of mail and express parcels, with the current fleet consisting of aircraft smaller than the Merchantmen of the past.

HQ airport & main base: Dublin International
Designator: AG/ABR
Route points: Bournemouth, Dublin, Glasgow, London, Paris
Links with other airlines: Safair (qv) has a 49 per cent stake
Fleet: 1 Lockheed C-100-30 Hercules; 3 ATR-72-200F; 4 ATR-72-200; 11 ATR-42-300F; 4 Fokker F27 Mk500; 2 Shorts 360

CITYJET
Incorporated: 1992

Formed in 1992, Cityjet did not begin operations until 1994, initially flying between Dublin and London City Airport as a franchisee of Virgin Atlantic Airways. In 1997, it began to operate under its own name, while also starting to fly between London City and Paris on behalf of Air France. The French airline took a 25 per cent stake in Cityjet in 1999 in partnership with Air Foyle Ireland, but then acquired Cityjet outright in 2000. Since then, the airline has operated many services under the Air France name.

HQ airport & main base: Dublin International with a hub at Paris Charles de Gaulle
Designator: WX/BCY
Employees: 555
Route points: Dublin, London, Paris, as well as points on the Air France network
Links with other airlines: A subsidiary of Air France (qv)
Fleet: 2 BAe 146-300; 19 BAe 146-200; 3 BAe Avro RJ85ER

RYANAIR
Incorporated: 1985

The pioneer in 'low fares, no frills' service within the British Isles, Ryanair was formed in 1985, and initially operated Rombac One-Elevens on services between Ireland and England, with its main UK base at London Luton. Now Europe's largest low-fare airline, Ryanair has since moved its main UK hub to London Stansted, and also introduced a wide range low-fare services within Great Britain and to Europe, using many UK airports, including Glasgow Prestwick. The One-Elevens were replaced by Boeing 737-200s, and these were replaced in turn by 737-800s, as the company's policy is to operate a modern, low-maintenance fleet.

While most of the airline's progress has been through organic growth, in 2003 Ryanair acquired the UK-based, low-fare operator buzz (sic) from KLM, further strengthening its position at Stansted. Ryanair's rapid growth can be seen in its rise between 2003 and 2004 from the fifty-second largest airline in the world to forty-seventh, just behind its main low-cost rival, EasyJet, while Ryanair is ahead of EasyJet at sixteenth largest by passenger numbers. Although Dublin-based, the airline has made a point of establishing bases throughout Europe, but connecting flights are not offered. The airline's growth has been controversial, using many minor and sometimes remote airports to keep costs to the absolute minimum. Over the past decade, the fleet has grown from twelve Boeing 737-200s to well over a hundred 737-800s, which, with orders, could rise to almost 300. The airline is planning 'Open Skies' transatlantic operations, possibly through a subsidiary.

HQ airport & main base: Dublin International, but bases are also at Bergamo Orio Al Serio, Brussels South Charleroi, Franksfurt Hahn, Gerona, Glasgow Prestwick International, London Luton, London Stansted, Rome Ciampino G.B. Pastine, Shannon International, Stockholm Skavsta
Radio callsign: RYANAIR (Ireland) BUDGET JET (UK)
Designator: RYR (Ireland) CYR (UK)
Route points: Aarhus, Aberdeen, Alghero, Almeria, Ancona, Bari, Bergerac, Berlin, Biarritz, Birmingham, Blackpool, Bournemouth, Bratislava, Brest, Brindisi, Bristol, Brno, Brussels, Bydgoszcz, Carcassonne, Cardiff, Cork, Dinard, Doncaster, Dublin, Durham, Düsseldorf, East Midlands, Edinburgh, Eindhoven, Esbjerg, Faro, Forli, Frankfurt, Friedrichshafen, Gdansk, Genoa, Gerona, Glasgow, Gothenburg, Granada, Graz, Hamburg, Haugesund, Jerez de la Frontera, Karlsruhe/Baden Baden, Kerry, Knock, Kuanas, Krakow, La Rochelle, Lamezia-Terme, Leeds/Bradford, Limoges, Linz, Liverpool, Lodz, London, Londonderry, Lyons, Malaga, Malmö, Manchester, Marseilles, Milan, Montpellier, Murcia, Nates, Newcastle, Newquay, Nîmes, Oporto, Oslo, Palermo, Paris, Pau, Perpignan, Pescara, Pisa, Potiers, Poznan, Reus, Riga, Rodez, Rome, Rzeszow, St Etienne, Salzburg, Santander, Santiago de Compestela, Seville, Shannon, Stockholm, Szczecin, Tampere, Toulon, Tours, Trieste, Turin, Valencia, Valladolid, Venice, Verona, Vitoria, Wroclaw, Zaragoza
Fleet: Up to 281 Boeing 737-800

ISRAEL – 4X

ARKIA

Arkia Israeli Airlines Ltd
Incorporated: 1949

Israel's domestic airline, Arkia was formed in 1949 and commenced operations in 1950 as Arkia Inland Airlines, with El Al having half of the airline's shares. In addition to operating domestic services, the airline also moved into the air charter market, initially with equipment leased from El Al, although El Al sold its shares in Arkia in 1980, and now operates inclusive tour charters into Israel from Europe. Present ownership is with the Kanaf-Arkia Airlines Group with 75 per cent, while employees own the remaining 25 per cent.

HQ airport & main base: Tel Aviv Ben Gurion International, with a hub at Tel Aviv Dov Hoz
Radio callsign: ARKIA
Designator: IZ/AIZ
Employees: 718
Route points: Amman, Dead Sea, Eilat, Gush Katif, Haifa, Jerusalem, Lod, Masada, Rosh Pina, Tblisi, Tel Aviv
Links with other airlines: Alliance with Uzbekistan Airways (qv)
Fleet: 2 Boeing 757-300; 1 Boeing 757-200; 4 ATR-72-500; 5 Bombardier Dash 7-100; 1 Bombardier Global 5000; 1 Britten-Norman BN2A Islander (On order: 2 Boeing 787-9)

EL AL

El Al Israel Airlines Ltd
Incorporated: 1948

Israel's national airline, El Al (from the Hebrew, meaning 'to the skies'or 'onward and upward') was founded in November 1948, and commenced operations in July 1949, with services from Tel Aviv to Rome and Paris using Douglas DC-4 Skymasters. Early development of the route network was rapid, with Athens, Vienna, Zurich, London, Nairobi, Johannesburg and New York soon being added, with Lockheed Super Constellations flying the transatlantic services. Before long, El Al was flying to every capital city in western Europe.

Turboprop airliners were introduced in 1957, with Bristol Britannias operating the transatlantic flights via London. Four years later, Boeing 707s were introduced on these services, and within months of their introduction were operating from Tel Aviv to New York nonstop, a record at the time. The airline moved into receivership in 1982 and did not re-emerge until 1995. Fluctuating traffic, often due to the uneasy political situation in the Middle East, and restrictions which prevented the airline from operating on the Sabbath, meant that the airline has encountered financial difficulties in the past, and delayed the privatisation of El Al until 2003. Since privatisation, the parent company of Arkia, Knafaim-Arkia Holdings, has built a 40 per cent stake in El Al, starting in 2004, and has expressed its intent to acquire El Al, leading to the possibility of a merger, but at present El Al operates international services only, with domestic operations handled by Arkia. The irony is that El Al had a 50 per cent interest in Arkia until 1980.

HQ airport & main base: Tel Aviv Ben Gurion International
Radio callsign: ELAL
Designator: LY/ELY
Employees: 3,213
Route points: Amsterdam, Athens, Bangkok, Barcelona, Beijing, Berlin, Brussels, Bucharest, Budapest, Cairo, Chicago, Chisinau, Cologne/Bonn, Dnepropetrovsk, Frankfurt, Geneva, Hong Kong, Istanbul, Johannesburg, Kiev, Krakow, Larnaca, London, Los Angeles, Madrid, Marseilles, Miami, Milan, Minsk, Moscow, Munich, New York, Newark, Odessa, Paris, Prague, Rome, St Petersburg, Simferopol, Sofia, Tel Aviv, Toronto, Vienna, Warsaw, Zurich
Fleet: 5 Boeing 747-400; 3 Boeing 747-200F; 2 Boeing 747-200B/C; 6 Boeing 777-200ER; 3 Boeing 767-300ER; 2 Boeing 767-200ER; 4 Boeing 767-200; 6 Boeing 757-200; 2 Boeing 737-700; 6 Boeing 737-800

ISRAIR
Israir Airlines and Tourism
Incorporated: 1989

A scheduled and charter airline which has its roots in an air taxi and executive charter business. The scheduled services are entirely within Israel, while inclusive tour charters are flown internationally.

HQ airport & main base: Tel Aviv Dov Hoz
Designator: 6H/ISR
Route points: Elat, Haifa, Tel Aviv
Fleet: 1 Boeing 767-300ER; 1 Boeing 757-200; 2 Airbus A320-200; 4 ATR-42-320

ITALY – I

Despite its popularity as a tourist destination, for many years the development of air transport in Italy was stifled by the presence of a single international airline and a single major domestic airline. This has now changed with deregulation and the country is now home to a number of independent airlines. The disposition of the new airlines clearly reflects the fact that the most properous part of the country is in the north, especially around Milan, while the south is much poorer, so that not all of the tourist traffic is inward.

AIR DOLOMITI
Air Dolomiti SpA
Incorporated: 1989

After being founded in 1989, Air Dolomiti started operations in May, 1991 using a single de Havilland Dash 8 on a service between Trieste and Geneva. During the late 1990s, the fleet consisted entirely of aircraft of ATR manufacture, but these have since been joined by BAe 146 jets. Employee numbers have more than doubled over the past eight years.

HQ airport & main base: Verona Villafranca International, with further hubs at Trieste Intrnational and at Munich
Radio callsign: DOLOMITI
Designator: EN/DLA
Employees: 558
Route points: Ancona, Bari, Bergamo, Düsseldorf, Florence, Frankfurt, Genoa, Milan, Munich, Naples, Paris-CDG, Pisa, Stuttgart, Trieste, Turin, Venice, Verona, Vienna
Fleet: 5 BAe 146-300; 8 ATR-72-500; 6 ATR-42-500

AIR EUROPE
Air Europe Italy SpA
Incorporated: 1988

Established in 1988 as part of the Airlines of Europe Group, which collapsed in 1991 with the parent

International Leisure Group, Air Europe Italy has since passed into wholly Italian ownership. Operations originally began in 1989 with a single Boeing 757, but the fleet is now completely standardised on the larger Boeing 767. The airline initially flew long-distance inclusive tour charters.

HQ airport & main base: HQ at Varese, with operations based on Rome Fiumicino Leonardo da Vinci and Milan Malpensa
Radio callsign: AIR EUROPE
Designator: VA/VLE
Employees: 500
Links with other airlines: Alitalia owns 24.6 per cent of the airline's shares
Fleet: 7 Boeing 767-300ER

AIR ITALY
Incorporated: 2005

A new Italian international passenger charter airline, with BV Asset Management and Guiseppe Gentile, the chief executive, each holding 40 per cent of the shares.

HQ airport & main base: Milan Malpaesa
Designator: I9/AJR
Fleet: 1 Boeing 767-300ER; 2 Boeing 757-200

AIR ONE
Air One SpA
Incorporated: 1983

Originally founded in 1983 as Aliadriatica, a flying school, the company was taken over by the Toto Group, a major Italian civil engineering contractor, in 1988. A Boeing 737 was acquired in 1994, initially for charter operations, but in April 1995 the airline started scheduled operations between Milan and Brindisi and Reggio Calabria. That November, a new corporate identity was unveiled to coincide with Air One's move onto the Rome Fiumicino to Milan Linate trunk route, Italy's busiest domestic route and the fifth busiest in Europe, offering competition on this route for the first time with up to thirteen flights in each direction daily.

In 1996, Air One took over the operations on a three-year lease of another Italian airline, Noman, which had originally been called Fortune Aviation before taking its new name in 1994.

Air One has grown rapidly, and now operates as far afield as Athens and London Stansted, flying domestic scheduled services and international charters, although the latter account for around just 5 per cent of traffic. Until the collapse of Swissair, the airline was a member of the Swissair Qualiflyer frequent-flyer programme. It has been replacing its Boeing 737 fleet with Airbus A320s.

HQ airport & main base: Rome Fiumicino Leonardo da Vinci, with further bases at Milan Linate and Turin International
Radio callsign: HERON
Designator: AP/ADH
Employees: 1,381
Route points: Albenga, Alghero, Bari, Bologna, Brindisi, Cagliari, Catania, Crotone, Genoa, Lamezia-Terme, Lampedusa, Milan, Naples, Palermo, Patelleria, Pecara, Pisa, Reggio Calabria, Rome, Trapani, Trieste, Turin, Venice
Links with other airlines: Marketing alliances with Aegean Airlines, Air Canada, Darwin Airline, Lufthansa, TAP Portugal, US Airways (all qv)
Fleet: 35 Airbus A320-200; 22 Boeing 737-400; 6 Boeing 737-300; 10 Bombardier CRJ900

ALITALIA
Linee Aeree Italiane SpA
Incorporated: 1946

Alitalia was formed in September 1946 as one of two airlines supported by the Italian government through the Istituto per la Ricostruzione Industrial, with the technical and operational assistance of BEA, British European Airways. The other airline was Linee Aeree Italiane, which received assistance from TWA, Trans World Airlines. Under its agreement, BEA held a 30 per cent shareholding in Alitalia.

Operations by Alitalia began in May 1947, and for the next ten years both airlines developed separately, and absorbed all other Italian airlines during this time. Both airlines operated on domestic and European routes, while Alitalia also operated to the Middle East, Africa and South America, and LAI operated to Egypt and to North America. In 1957, the two airlines were merged at IRI's behest, largely to eliminate the overlap on many domestic and European routes, but also to provide a single, strong airline rather than dividing the available resources. The fleet name Alitalia was chosen for the merged airline, which immediately started a major rationalisation programme. The combined fleet in 1958 included six Douglas DC-7Cs for the North Atlantic services, eight Douglas DC-6Bs and three DC-6s, twelve DC-3s, six Vickers Viscounts and six Convair 440 Metropolitans. The Viscount fleet was enlarged, so that eventually fifteen aircraft, all series 785s, were operated.

Alitalia's first jet equipment entered service in 1960, with Douglas DC-8s for the longer-haul routes and Sud Aviation Caravelles for the European and Middle Eastern services. The route network continued to grow, and soon reached Australia.

The airline replaced its Viscounts during the late 1960s with a fleet of Douglas DC-9s, while it also took later versions of the DC-8 and its successor, the DC-10. Before this, in 1963, most of the domestic services were hived off into a new airline, ATI, Aero Transporti Italiani, which was a wholly owned subsidiary of Alitalia. ATI also took over services which had been operated by SAM, Societal Aerea Mediterranea, which became Alitalia's charter subsidiary. ATI continued the relationship with Douglas, acquiring a fleet of DC-9s and then adding McDonnell Douglas MD-82s to this, as well as a fleet of ATR-42s. The route network included mainland Italy, Sicily and Sardinia.

The operations of SAM were incorporated into those of ATI in 1985. In 1994, in a complete reversal of the decision taken more than thirty years earlier, ATI was absorbed into Alitalia. Further integration came in 1996, when the operations of Avianova, which operated services from Olbia and had been formed by Alitalia and Alisarda (now Meridiana) in 1986, were also taken over by Alitalia. Alitalia was owned 89.31 per cent by IRI, the state-owned vehicle for investment in industrrial enterprises, but in recent years the state involvment has been reduced to 49.9 per cent, held now by the Italian treasury, while private shareholders, including employees, own 35.7 per cent. Other shareholders include investment organisations, while Air France has 2 per cent. The airline has shareholdings in several other airlines, including Malev (30 per cent), Eurofly (45 per cent) and Air Europe Italy (24.6 per cent), while in 1997 it established a low-cost regional subsidiary and charter airline, Alitalia Express, whose services were initially based on the former Avianova network. Alitalia was a founder-member of the Sky Team alliance. At one time predominantly an operator of McDonnell Douglas aircraft, Alitalia now operates a significant number of Boeing and Airbus aircraft in its fleet.

Currently, Alitalia is twenty-first in the world both by annual turnover and by passengers carried.

HQ airport & main bases: Rome Fiumicino Leonardo da Vinci, and Milan Malpensa
Radio callsign: ALITALIA
Designator: AZ/AZA
Employees: 18,180
Route points: Aberdeen, Accra, Algiers, Amsterdam, Ancona, Athens, Atlanta, Bangkok, Barcelona, Bari, Beijing, Beirut, Belgrade, Bergen, Berlin, Biarritz, Bilbao, Birmingham, Bologna, Bolzano, Bonaire, Bordeaux, Boston, Bremen, Brest, Brindisi, Bristol, Brussels, Bucharest, Budapest, Buenos Aires, Cagliari, Cairo, Cancun, Caracas, Cardiff, Casablanca, Catania, Chicago, Clemont-Ferrand, Cluj, Cologne/Bonn, Copenhagen, Dakar, Damascus, Delhi, Doha, Dubai, Dublin, Durham (UK), Düsseldorf, Edinburgh, Florence, Frankfurt, Fuerteventura, Geneva, Genoa, Glasgow, Gothenburg, Guatemala, Hamburg, Hanover, Helsinki, Humberside, Ibiza, Istanbul, Johannesburg, Kiev, Krakow, Kristiansand, Lagos, Lamezia, Lanzarote, Larnaca, Las Palmas, Leeds/Bradford, Lima, Lisbon, London, Los Angeles, Lyons, Maastricht, Madrid, Malaga, Malta, Manchester, Marseilles, Menorca, Mérida, Mexico City, Miami, Milan, Montpellier, Moscow, Mumbai, Munich, Nantes, Naples, New York, Newark, Newcastle, Nice, Norwich, Osaka, Oslo, Palermo, Palma de Mallorca, Paris, Pau, Porto, Perugia, Pisa, Prague, Punta Cana, Reggio Calabria, Rennes, Riga, Rimini, St Maarten, St Petersburg, San Francisco, Santiago de la Compestela, Santo Domingo, Sao Paulo, Sarajevo, Seoul, Shanghai, Singapore, Skopje, Southampton, Split, Stavanger, Stockholm, Strasbourg, Stuttgart, Taipei, Tallinn, Tehran, Tel Aviv, Tirana, Tokyo, Toronto, Toulouse, Trieste, Tripoli, Trondheim, Tunis, Turin, Valencia, Venice, Verona, Vienna, Vigo, Warsaw, Washington, Zagreb, Zurich
Links with other airlines: Owns Alitalia Express (qv). Alliances with Aeroflot (qv), Air Alps Aviation, Air Europa (qv), China Airlines (qv), City Airline (qv), Croatia Airlines (qv), Cyprus Airways (qv), Japan Airlines (qv), Malev (qv), Palestinian Airlines (qv), Qatar Airways (qv), SN Brussels Airlines (qv), Tarom (qv), Varig (qv)
Passengers carried: 22.3 million
Annual turnover: US $5,068 million (£3,400 million)
Fleet: 1 Boeing 747-200F; 4 McDonnell Douglas MD-11F; 10 Boeing 777-200ER; 13 Boeing 767-300ER; 23 Airbus A321-100; 11 Airbus A320-200; 12 Airbus A319-100; 74 McDonnell Douglas MD-82

ALITALIA EXPRESS
Incorporated: 1997

The feeder and charter operation of Alitalia, which owns the airline outright, based on the operations of an earlier airline, Avianova.

HQ airport & main base: Rome Fiumicino Leonardo da Vinci, with a major hub at Miland Malpensa
Radio callsign: ALITALIA EXPRESS
Designator: XM/SMX
Employees: 720
Route points: Part of the Alitalia network
Links with other airlines: A wholly owned subsidiary of Alitalia (qv)
Fleet: 6 Embraer 170; 6 ATR-72-500; 4 ATR-72-210; 1 ATR-42-300; 14 Embraer ERJ-145LR

ALPI EAGLES
Incorporated: 1979

Owned by banking and travel interests, Alpi Eagles operates scheduled and charter services, mainly within Italy and the Mediterranean area.

HQ airport & main base: Venice Marco Polo
Designator: E8/ELG
Route points: Athens, Barcelona, Bari, Bologna, Brindisi, Bucharest, Cagliari, Catania, Lamezia-Terme, Milan, Naples, Palermo, Reggio Calabria, Rome, Timisoara, Tirana, Venice, Verona
Fleet: 9 Fokker 100

BLUE PANORAMA AIRLINES
Incorporated: 1998

Primarily an inclusive tour charter airline, Blue Panorama also plans scheduled services.

HQ airport & main base: Rome Fiumicino Leonardo da Vinci
Designator: BV/BPA
Links with other airlines: Alliances with Cubana de Aviacion (qv)
Fleet: 4 Boeing 767-300ER; 2 Boeing 757-200; 4 Boeing 737-400 (On order: 4 Boeing 787-8)

EUROFLY
Eurofly SpA
Incorporated: 1989

Eurofly was formed in May 1989, and commenced operations the following February, flying inclusive tour charters within Europe and to North Africa and the Middle East. Transatlantic operations began in 1998. At first, it was owned 45 per cent each by Alitalia and Olivetti, with the remaining 10 per cent held by San Paolo Finance, but in 2000 Alitalia took the airline over until it was privatised in 2003, with 80 per cent of the shares being purchased by Banca Profio Spinnaker. Today, it is owned by the Effe Luxembourg Investment Fund,and a number of scheduled services are also operated. The headquarters has moved from Turin to Milan.

HQ airport & main base: Milan Orio al Serio
Radio callsign: SIRIOFLY
Designator: GJ/EEZ
Route points: Cancun, Colombo, Fuerteventura, Male, Milan, Mombasa, Naples, Punta Cana, Rome
Fleet: 5 Airbus A330-200; 8 Airbus A320-200; 1 Airbus A319CJ (On order: 3 Airbus A350-800)

ITALI AIRLINES
Incorporated: 2003

Itali was formed in 2003 and is developing a regional scheduled network, as well as operating inclusive tour charter services.

HQ airport & main base: Pescara
Designator: 9X/ACL
Fleet: 3 McDonnell Douglas MD-82; 2 Dornier 328Jet; 2 Fairchild Metro III

ITALY FIRST
Incorporated: 1999

Operates charter flights and is developing scheduled flights in the Mediterranean and Adriatic.

HQ airport & main base: Rimini
Designator: 1F/IFS
Fleet: 2 ATR-42-320

LIVINGSTON
Incorporated: 2003

A new airline established by the Viaggi del Ventaglio travel group, it absorbed the Italian operations, Lauda Air Italy, of the Volante Group, controlled by the Austrian Lauda motor racing family. The main emphasis is on charter operations, including long-haul operations to East Africa, the Indian Ocean resorts and the Caribbean and Brazil, but a low-cost scheduled network is also likely to be developed, possibly based on 'seat-only' deals on charter flights.

HQ airport & main base: Milan Malpensa
Radio callsign: LIVINGSTON
Designator: LM/LVG
Employees: 169
Fleet: 3 Airbus A330-200; 1 Boeing 757-200; 3 Airbus A321-200

MERIDIANA
Meridiana SpA
Incorporated: 1963

Meridiana was founded by the Aga Khan in March 1963, as Alisarda, and commenced air taxi and light charter operations the following year. Alisarda started its first scheduled services in 1966, and the airline soon established a network of services, initially from Olbia in northern Sardinia, but later from Cagliari and Catania. Having developed into a substantial carrier, the need arose for a new third-level operator, and in 1986 Alisarda and Alitalia established Avianova as a joint venture, although the operations of this company were absorbed into Alitalia in 1996.

The current title was adopted in 1991 to match a similarly named Spanish operator formed by air taxi and air charter airlines to take advantage of deregulation of air transport in Europe – but the Spanish airline, Meridiani Air, had to suspend operations the following year. Since then, Meridiana has continued to grow. It is one of the few airlines able to operate jet aircraft from Florence (most operators have to use Pisa), and remains completely privately owned, although the Aga Khan's stake is now less than 18 per cent and most of the shares are held by institutions.

HQ airport & main base: Olbia, with further bases at Catania, Florence and Verona
Radio callsign: MERAIR
Designator: IG/ISS
Employees: 500
Route points: Amsterdam, Barcelona, Bologna, Cagliari, Catania, Florence, Lampedusa, London, Madrid, Milan, Naples, Olbia, Palermo, Pantelleria, Paris, Rome, Turin, Verona
Fleet: 4 Airbus A319-100; 8 McDonnell Douglas MD-83; 9 McDonnell Douglas MD-82

MINILINER
Incorporated: 1981

Founded in 1981 to provide a parcels and package service for express parcels operators, Miniliner began operations in 1982, becoming the first Italian overnight small consignment operator. Services have been provided for FedEx, UPS and the Italian postal authorities since 1988. Ad hoc charters are also provided.

HQ airport & main base: Bergamo Orio al Serio
Designator: MNL
Employees: 75
Links with other airlines: Operates for FedEx and UPS (both qv)
Fleet: 6 Fokker F27 Friendship Mk500; 1 Fokker F27 Friendship Mk400

MISTRAL AIR
Incorporated: 1981

Although founded in 1981, Mistral Air did not begin operations until 1984, providing scheduled cargo services with BAe 146 Quiet Traders for its parent company, TNT Post Group.

HQ airport & main base: Rome Ciampino
Radio callsign: MISTRAL
Designator: MSA
Links with other airlines: A wholly owned subsidiary of TNT
Fleet: 1 Boeing 737-300QC; 2 BAE 146-200QT

MYAIR
My Way Airlines SpA
Incorporated: 2004

Founded in 2004 as a low-cost scheduled airline, Myair operates both domestic and international services, mainly from Milan and Venice.

HQ airport & main base: Bergamo Orio al Serio
Radio callsign: MYAIR
Designator: 8I/MYW
Employees: 150
Route points: Barcelona, Bari, Bergamo, Bologna, Brindisi, Bucharest, Catania, Madrid, Milan, Naples, Palermo, Paris, Reggio Calabria, Venice
Fleet: 5 Airbus A320-200; 19 Bombardier CRJ900

NEOS
Incorporated: 2001

Founded by travel group interests in 2001, Neos began operations in 2002, flying mainly inclusive tour charters. Although the German company TUI was one of the founders, since 2004 the airline has been owned 99.99 per cent by the Alpitour Group.

HQ airport & main base: Milan Malpensa
Designator: NO/NOS
Employees: 275
Fleet: 2 Boeing 767-300ER; 4 Boeing 737-800

OCEAN AIRLINES
Incorporated: 2003

Founded in 2003, Ocean Airlines began scheduled cargo operations from Italy to the Middle East and Asia in 2003.

HQ airport & main base: Brescia Montichiari
Radio callsign: OCEAN
Designator: VC/VCX
Route points: Almaty, Brecia, Dubai, Hong Kong, Shanghai, Verona
Fleet: 2 Boeing 747-200F

VOLAREWEB
Volare Airlines
Incorporated: 1997

Volare was founded by businessmen in the north of Italy in 1997 and commenced operations from Milan Linate the following year, during which SAirLines, owners of Swissair and part of the SAirGroup, acquired a 34 per cent stake. A merger with Air Europe was announced in 2000, although both airlines were to retain their individual identities. When Swissair collapsed, Volare was bought by Gino Zoccai, but operations had to be suspended in 2004. A resumption of operations followed in 2005, and the current title has since been adopted.

HQ airport & main base: Milan Linate
Designator: VA/VLE
Route points: Bari, Brindisi, Catania, Milan, Naples, Palermo, Paris
Fleet: 1 Airbus A321-200; 4 Airbus A320-200

WIND JET
Incorporated: 2003

Wind Jet was formed in 2003 to operate scheduled and charter passenger flights from Catania in Italy. As yet, only domestic schedules are operated. It is owned by the Finaria Group.

HQ airport & main base: Catania Fontanarossa
Designator: IV/JET
Route points: Catania, Forli, Milan, Palermo, Rome, Venice
Fleet: 10 Airbus A320-200; 1 Airbus A319-100

IVORY COAST – TU

The Ivory Coast was for many years the home of Air Afrique, Société Aerienne Africaine Multinationale, which was established in 1961 to provide an international airline for a large number of French colonies as they became independent, on the assumption that none of these would be able to support an international airline of its own. The states consisted of Benin, Burkina Faso (originally Upper Volta), Cameroon, Central African Republic, Chad, Congo, Gabon, Ivory Coast, Mauritania, Niger, Senegal and Togo, each of which contributed 7.2 per cent of the share capital, with Sodetraf, Société pour le Développement du Transport Aerien en Afrique, holding the remainder. The airline was at first established in Cameroon.

Initially the airline operated Douglas DC-8s, and there was a marketing and technical alliance with the then independent French airline, UTA. Cameroon left the consortium in 1971, causing the base to move to the Central African Republic, while Chad left in 1972 and Gabon in 1977. Later, an Airbus wide-body fleet of five A310s and six A300s, as well as two A330s, was built up, supported by two Boeing 737-330s and an Antonov An-24.

In its final days, Air Afrique was based in the Ivory Coast and was owned 70.4 per cent by the remaining states, with Air France having 12.6 per cent, and DHL 3.2 per cent. In turn, Air Afrique had a 20 per cent stake in Air Mauritania, 46 per cent in Air Mali and 17 per cent in Air Burkina. The first signs of problems arose in 1998, when four of its Airbus A310s had to be returned to the leasing companies, leading to the suspension of several long-haul services. Other aircraft followed and services were suspended in February 2002, after attempts to restructure the airline failed. Probably part of the problem lay in getting so many different national shareholders to agree to a recovery programme.

JAMAICA – 6Y

AIR JAMAICA
Incorporated: 1968

Air Jamaica was formed in October 1968, and commenced operations the following April, operating from Kingston to both Miami and New York Kennedy. Ownership was initially divided between the Jamaican government and Air Canada, but in 1980 the airline became completely state owned.

Services expanded, with a service to London operated jointly with British Airways, and using one of that airline's aircraft. Most of the emphasis in expansion was placed on the North American market, largely with tourism to Jamaica in mind. In 1994, the airline was partially privatised, with the government share reduced to 25 per cent, and afterwards underwent extensive modernisation with the purchase of many new aircraft, while the route structure expanded considerably. In December 2004, after substantial losses had been incurred, the government renationalised the airline.

Meanwhile, during the period of private ownership, a subsidiary, Air Jamaica Express, originally known as Trans Jamaican Airlines, was established to provide feeder services using a single AI(R) ATR-42 and three Fairchild Dornier Do.228s. Operations ceased early in 2005, on the same day that the old management relinquished control of Air Jamaica, due to high fuel costs.

In 1997, a marketing alliance was agreed with Delta Air Lines, and this remains, along with alliances with other airlines.

HQ airport & main base: Kingston Norman Manley International, with a further base at Montego Bay Sangster International
Radio callsign: JULIET MIKE
Designator: JM/AJM
Employees: 2,848
Route points: Atlanta, Baltimore, Bonaire, Bridgetown, Chicago, Curaçao, Fort Lauderdale, Grand Cayman, Grenada, Havana, Kingston, London, Los Angeles, Miami, Montego Bay, Nassau, New York, Newark, Orlando, Philadelphia, Toronto
Links with other airlines: Marketing alliances with Air Canada, Delta Air Lines, Cubana de Aviacion (all qv)
Fleet: 2 Airbus A340-300; 6 Airbus A321-200; 9 Airbus A320-200

JAPAN – JA

Often regarded as an industrial powerhouse, Japan was slow to embrace deregulation and greater competiveness in air transport, with three large airlines dominating the market. Deregulation of air transport in 1998 has seen four new airlines created between then and 2006.

AIR CENTRAL
Incorporated: 1988

Although founded in 1988, Air Central did not commence operations until 1991, providing scheduled and charter flights as Naka Nihon Airlines, but adopted the Air Central name in 2005. All Nippon Airways had an interest initially, and this was increased to 55 per cent in late 2004, while the other shareholder is the Nagoya Railroad Group with 45 per cent.

HQ airport & main base: Nagoya
Designator: NV/ALS
Employees: 140
Route points: Fukushima, Matsuyama, Nagoya, Niigata, Sendai, Tokyo, Tokushima, Tottori, Yonago
Links with other airlines: Major shareholder is All Nippon (qv), with whom there is an operational alliance
Fleet: 2 Bombardier Dash 8 Q400; 4 Fokker 50

AIR NEXT
Incorporated: 2005

Established as a low-cost subsidiary of All Nippon Airways, Air Next operates from Fukuoka to the main Japanese cities.

HQ airport & main base: Fukuoka International
Designator: 7A/NXA
Route points: Fukuoka, Fukushima, Hiroshima, Nagasaki, Nagoya, Okinawa, Osaka, Toyama, Tsushima
Links with other airlines: Owned by All Nippon Airways
Fleet: 8 Boeing 737-500

AIR NIPPON
Air Nippon Co. Ltd
Incorporated: 1974

Air Nippon was founded in 1974 as Nihon Kinkyori Airways by All Nippon Airways, Toa Domestic (predecssor of Japan Air System) and Japan Airlines, to operate the less heavily used domestic services. The airline has since become Air Nippon, reflecting ANA outright ownership. In turn, Air Nippon owns Air Next, which operates four Boeing 737-500s on scheduled regional services, while it now has its own feeder operation in the Air Nippon Network.

HQ airport & main base: Tokyo Haneda
Radio callsign: ANK AIR
Designator: EL/ANK
Employees: 1,637
Route points: Fukuoka, Nagoya, Osaka, Taipei, Tokyo
Links with other airlines: A subsidiary of Air Nippon (qv). Marketing alliances with ANA and Eva (qv)
Annual turnover: Included in Air Nippon figures
Fleet: 8 Boeing 737-700; 17 Boeing 737-500

AIR NIPPON NETWORK
Incorporated: 2001

Air Nippon Network was founded by All Nippon Airlines in 2001 to provide feeder services for both Air Nippon and All Nippon using turboprop aircraft. Operations began in 2002.

HQ airport & main base: Sapporo City
Designator: EH/AKX
Fleet: 11 Bombardier Dash 8 Q400; 5 Bombardier Dash 8 Q300

ANA ALL NIPPON AIRWAYS
All Nippon Airways Co. Ltd
Incorporated: 1952

The second largest airline both in Japan and in Asia, All Nippon Airways remains ninth largest worldwide both by sales and by passenger numbers. The company dates from 1952, the first year that Japanese ownership and operation of commercial aircraft was permitted postwar, and operations began in December 1953, as Japan Helicopter and Airplane. From the start, the airline operated scheduled services. Growth was aided by a number of mergers and acquisitions, merging with Far Eastern Airlines in 1957, and then acquiring Fujita Airlines in 1963, Nakanihon Air Services in 1965, and Nagasaki Airways in 1967, helping the airline towards becoming the second largest Japanese airline, as well as the ninth largest in the world on the basis of annual turnover. The present title was adopted following the merger with Far East Air Transport.

The early growth of the airline was confined to domestic routes, with Japan Airlines having a monopoly of international services up to its privatisation in 1986. Since that time, ANA has developed an extensive network of international services, beginning with a Tokyo–Guam service in 1986. By 1989, services had been introduced between Tokyo and London Gatwick, and a service to Paris was introduced the following year. A network of international alliances was quickly established to help accelerate the introduction of international services. Domestic operations were not neglected, however, and today ANA has more than a 50 per cent of Japan's domestic air travel market.

In 1974, the airline was one of the founders of Air Nippon, which today is a wholly owned subsidiary, operating domestic services as feeders into the ANA trunk network. Ownership of ANA itself is spread between a large number of Japanese private shareholders, who hold more than 76 per cent of its shares, financial institutions and the Nagoya Railroad. The airline owns outright Air Nippon Network, Air Japan, Air Nippon and Air Next, as well as 80 per cent of Air Hokkaido and 55 per cent of Air Central. Air Japan is a charter operation which leases aircraft from the parent company as required. The airline was a founder member of the Star Alliance. It was the first customer for the high-capacity, short-haul variant of the Boeing 747, while more recently it became the launch customer for the Boeing 787. In recent years, the route network has come to include a growing number of destinations in China.

HQ airport & main base: Tokyo Narita International, with further hubs at Osaka Kansei and Osaka Itami, and Tokyo International
Radio callsign: ALL NIPPON
Designator: NH/ANA
Employees: 12,090
Route points: Akita, Asahikawa, Bangkok, Beijing, Chengdu, Chicago, Chongqing, Dalian, Doha, Frankfurt, Fukue, Fukuoka, Fukushima, Guam, Guangzhou, Hachijo Jima, Hakodate, Hangzhou, Hiroshima, Ho Chi Minh City, Hong Kong, Honolulu, Ishigaki, Iwami, Kagoshima, Kochi, Komatsu, Kuala Lumpur, Kumamoto, Kushiro, London, Los Angeles, Matsuyama, Memanbetsu, Miyake Jima, Miyako, Miyazaki, Monbetsu, Nagasaki, Nagoya, Nakashibetsu, New York, Nigata, Odate Noshiro, Oita, Okayama, Okinawa, Osaka, Oshima, Paris, Qingdao, Rishiri, Saga, San Francisco, Sapporo, Seattle, Sendai, Seoul, Shanghai, Shenyang, Shenzhen, Shonai, Singapore, Sydney, Takamatsu, Tokushima, Tokyo, Toronto, Tottori, Toyama, Tsushima, Ube, Vancouver, Vienna, Wajima, Wakkanai, Washington, Xiamen, Yonago
Links with other airlines: Air Nippon is a subsidiary. 100 per cent ownerships of Air Nippon Network, Air Japan, Air Nippon and Air Next (all qv); 80 per cent of Air Hokkaido and 55 per cent of Air Central (qv). Marketing alliances with Air China, IBEX Airlines, Malaysia Airlines, Mexicana, Qatar Airways, Shanghai Airlines, Skynet Asia Airways, Vietnam Airlines (all qv)
Passengers carried: 48.6 million
Annual turnover: US $12,043 million (£8,030 million)
Fleet: 23 Boeing 747-400; 13 Boeing 777-300ER; 7 Boeing 777-300; 7 Boeing 777-200ER; 16 Boeing 777-200; 24 Boeing 767-300ER; 34 Boeing 767-300; 4 Boeing 767-300F; 7 Airbus A321-100; 33 Airbus A320-200; 37 Boeing 737-700; 3 Bombardier Dash 8 Q400 (On order: 20 Boeing 787-8; 30 Boeing 787-3)

J-AIR
Incorporated: 1991

Although founded in 1991, J-Air did not begin operations until 2001. Originally based at Hiroshima, it was moved to Nagoya in 2005 and it provides feeder services for Japan Airlines, which owns J-Air.

HQ airport & main base: Nagoya
Designator: uses JAL codes
Employees: 200
Route points: In JAL domestic network
Links with other airlines: Japan Airlines (qv) owns J-Air. Provides feeder services for JAL
Fleet: 9 Bombardier CRJ200ER

JAL EXPRESS
Incorporated: 1997

JAL Express was founded in 1997 and began operations the following year with services between Osaka and Kagoshima and Miyazaki. It is a low-cost subsidiary of Japan Airlines.

HQ airport & main base: Osaka Itami
Designator: JC/JEX
Employees: 360
Route points: Kumamoto, Nagasaki, Nagoya, Oita, Osaka, Sapporo, Sendai
Links with other airlines: Japan Airlines (qv) owns 100 per cent
Fleet: 7 Boeing 737-400; 5 McDonnell Douglas MD-81

JALWAYS
Japan Air Charter
Incorporated: 1990

Established in 1990 as the air charter subsidiary of Japan Air Lines and commenced operations as Japan Air Charter the following year. The initial fleet was small, with aircraft wet-leased from other companies in the same group as required, which could mean operations with five or more Boeing 747-200Bs and four or more McDonnell Douglas DC-10-40s at any one time. In 1998, the current title was adopted as the airline had started its own scheduled services, operating low-cost services to holiday destinations in Asia and the Pacific. The JAL interest was increased from 82 per cent to outright ownership in 2001, while the airline has lost its DC-10s in favour of using the equipment of its parent and sister companies.

HQ airport & main base: Tokyo Narita International
Radio callsign: JAPAN CHARTER
Designator: JO/JAZ
Links with other airlines: Japan Airlines (qv) has a 100 per cent interest
Fleet: Uses JAL aircraft as required on a wet-lease basis

JAPAN AIR COMMUTER
Japan Air Commuter Co. Ltd
Incorporated: 1983

The feeder network operator for Japan Airlines, Japan Air Commuter has a fleet of turboprop aircraft and operates from two hubs at Kagoshima and Osaka. It was founded by Japan Air System in 1983, and the JAS 60 per cent interest passed to Japan Airlines when JAS was acquired in 2004. The remaining shares are divided among fourteen municipalities in Kagoshima Prefecture.

HQ airport & main base: Kagoshima, with further hubs at Amani O Shima, Fukuoka and Osaka
Radio callsign: COMMUTER
Designator: 3X/JAC
Route points: Included in Japan Airlines Domestic network
Links with other airlines: Japan Airlines (qv) has a 60 per cent interest. Provides feeder services for JAS
Fleet: 10 Bombardier Dash 8 Q400; 7 NAMC YS-11A-500; 11 Saab 340B

JAL JAPAN AIRLINES DOMESTIC
Japan Airlines Co. Ltd
Incorporated: 1971

Japan Airlines Domestic itself dates from the merger of Japan Air System with Japan Airlines in 2004, and the name is meant to distinguish the essentially domestic scheduled operation (with overseas charters) of the former JAS network from that of Japan Airlines, which in turn has had International added to its title. At the time of the merger, JAS had the largest network of scheduled domestic air services throughout Japan, while it also had scheduled services to China and Korea, which were transferred to JAL.

Japan Air System had come into existence in 1971 as Toa Domestic Airlines, on the merger of Japan Domestic Airlines, which was founded in 1964, with Toa Airways. The predecessors of JDA had included Nito Airlines and Fuji Airlines, both dating from 1952, and North Japan Airlines, which started in 1953, the same year that Toa Airways was founded. In 1988, Toa Domestic Airlines adopted the title of Japan Air System, and a completely new corporate identity. JAS shareholders included a number of industrial groups, including the Kinki Nippon Railway with a 9 per cent stake, as well Japan Airlines, which also held 9 per cent of the shares.

On the merger, the JAS 60 per cent stake in the feeder airline Japan Air Commuter passed to JAL. A new holding company was established to control both domestic and international airlines, the Japan Airlines Corporation. Japan Airlines Domestic in turn has shareholdings in Hokkaido Air System at 51 per cent, and a modest 2 per cent stake in Amakusa Airlines. Japan Airlines Domestic was merged back into Japan Airlines International in October 2006, recreating Japan Airlines.

HQ airport & main base: Tokyo International
Radio callsign: AIR SYSTEM
Designator: JL/JLJ
Employees: 4,257
Route points: Akita, Amami O Shima, Aomori, Asahikawa, Fukuoka, Kukushima, Hakodate, Hanamaki, Hiroshima, Izumo, Kagoshima, Kita Kyushu, Kochi, Komatsu, Kumamoto, Kushiro, Matsumoto, Matsuyama, Memanbetsu, Misawa, Miyazaka, Nagasaki, Nagoya, Niigata, Obihiro, Oita, Okayama, Okinawa, Sapporo, Sendai, Shirahama, Takamatsu, Tokunoshima, Tokushima, Tokyo, Toyama, Ube, Yamagata
Links with other airlines: Part of the Japan Airlines Corporation. Has a 60 per cent stake in Japan Air Commuter (qv), 51 per cent in Hokkaido Airlines and 2 per cent in Amakusa Airlines
Fleet: 2 Boeing 777-300; 8 Boeing 777-200; 22 Airbus A300-600; 3 Boeing 767-300ER; 3 Boeing 767F; 30 Boeing 737-800 (On order: 13 Boeing 787-8)

JAL JAPAN AIRLINES

Incorporated: 1951

Now the world's third largest airline, and sixth largest by passenger numbers, Japan Airlines was formed in 1951, during the Korean War, when permission was granted by the Supreme Commander, Allied Powers, for the operation of domestic air services by a Japanese airline, but only on condition that the aircraft and crews would be supplied by a non-Japanese operator. Five companies bid for the right to start services, and Japan Airlines was selected on condition that it formed a union with its four competitors to strengthen the new airline.

Japan Airlines had a predecessor, Dai-Nippon Airways, which had been formed in 1938 on the amalgamation of the Japan Air Transport Company and several smaller operators. Although the airline was not formally disbanded until the end of the Second World War in 1945, its wartime operations were increasingly limited, and had to be abandoned completely before the end of hostilities because of the acute shortage of fuel.

The first services of JAL were operated by Martin 202s of Northwest Orient Air Lines, now Northwest, with the first services on 25 October 1951, when services started between Tokyo and Osaka, with some flights extended to Fukuoka, and between Tokyo and Sapporo. This arrangement lasted for exactly a year, until the first Japanese-owned and crewed aircraft, Douglas DC-4s, entered service on 25 October 1952. The new airline ordered two de Havilland Comet 2s, but did not take delivery after the failure of the original de Havilland Comet 1 aircraft in a series of accidents. JAL's next aircraft, the first of which were delivered in 1953, were Douglas DC-6B Cloudmasters, and after route proving throughout the rest of the year, in February 1954 a new service was opened between Tokyo and San Francisco, with the aircraft operating via Wake Island and Honolulu. Meanwhile, the Japanese government had taken a 50 per cent share in the airline to increase its capital for expansion, and later this was increased to 58 per cent.

A service from Tokyo to Hong Kong via Okinawa was inaugurated in 1955, and at the end of the year Douglas DC-8 jet airliners were ordered – followed by an order for DC-7C piston-engined airliners in April 1956! The DC-7Cs entered service on the Tokyo–San Francisco route early in 1958, while services by this time had extended as far as Bangkok, reached via Singapore. While consolidation of services in Asia and across the Pacific continued, in 1960 a Tokyo–Paris service was started, flying over the North Pole in a Boeing 707 belonging to Air France. The first Douglas DC-8 jet airliners arrived later in the year, and were used initially on services from Tokyo to the west coast of the United States, although later these were also used on the polar routes to Paris, Amsterdam and London. For less busy services, the smaller Convair 880 entered service in 1961.

During the early 1960s, the airline also developed freight services, initially using converted DC-4s, while later, in 1965, DC-8-55F mixed passenger and cargo aircraft were introduced. JAL participated in the formation of Southwest Airlines, now Japan TransOcean Air, in 1967, when the airline was formed to improve air services between Japan and the Ryukyu Islands, including Okinawa. As the decade progressed, Boeing 727s were introduced, followed by Boeing 747s in 1970, although the airline's first trans-Siberian services, via Moscow to Paris, launched that same year, were operated by Douglas DC-8-62s. One of the innovations made by the airline was the use of the specially developed Boeing 747SR, a high-capacity, short-range variant of the aircraft, which had 498 seats and was used first on the Tokyo–Okinawa service in 1973. Seven years later, an even higher capacity version, with 550 seats, was introduced on the same route. The airline was also among the first to operate Boeing 747 freighters. Today, JAL has the world's largest fleet of Boeing 747s.

Political difficulties between Communist China and Taiwan led to the formation of Japan Asia Airways in 1975, with JAL taking a 91 per cent stake in this airline, formed specifically for services between Japan and Taiwan. A 9 per cent stake was taken in Japan Domestic Airways.

The airline's shares were launched on the Tokyo Stock Market in 1986, as the first stage in privatisation of the airline. That same year, JAL lost its monopoly of international services, and competition from All Nippon Airways started on international services. The government sold its remaining shares the following year. Reacting to changes in travel patterns elsewhere, JAL established a charter subsidiary, Japan Air Charter, in 1990.

The structure of the airline changed with the merger with Japan Air System in 2004, with a holding company, Japan Airlines Corporation, owning the two operational airlines, Japan Airlines Domestic and Japan Airlines International. The latter airline consists primarily of the old JAL international routes and aircraft and the international scheduled services of JAS, while JAL Domestic took the domestic services of JAL. In addition, both JAL Express, J-Air and Japan Air Commuter provide feeder services. The split between domestic and international was reversed in October 2006.

Today, Japan Airlines is owned by a number of Japanese financial institutions, primarily banks and insurance companies. It has interests in a number of major Japanese airlines, and in tour operators and ground handling. Marketing alliances of various kinds exist with a number of the world's major airlines, with JAL one of the latest members of the Oneworld alliance. Over the past decade, the McDonnell Douglas DC-10-40 fleet was first converted to freighters and then replaced by a mix of Boeing 767s and 777s. In turn, Japan Airlines owns J-Air and JALways, as well as having taken over Japan Asia Airways completely and having a 51 per cent stake in Japan TransOceanAir.

HQ airport & main base: Tokyo International, Tokyo Narita International
Radio callsign: JAPANAIR
Designator: JL/JAL
Employees: 15,869
Route points: Amsterdam, Auckland, Bangkok, Beijing, Brisbane, Busan, Cairns, Chicago, Dalian, Dallas/Fort Worth, Delhi, Denpasar Bali, Dubai, Frankfurt, Guangzhou, Haikou, Hangzhou, Hanoi, Ho Chi Minh City, Hong Kong, Istanbul, Jakarta, Kuala Lumpur, Las Vegas, London, Los Angeles, Madrid, Manila, Melbourne, Mexico City, Milan, Moscow, New York, Papeete, Paris, Qindao, Rome, San Francisco, San Jose, Sao Paulo, Seoul, Shanghai, Singapore, Sydney, Tianjin, Vancouver, Xiamen, Xian, Zurich
Links with other airlines: Owns J-Air, JALways, Japan Asia Airways, all 100 per cent, plus a 51 per cent stake in Japan TransOceanAir (all qv). Member of the Oneworld alliance. Alliances with Aeromexico, Air France, Air New Zealand, Air Tahiti Nui, Alitalia, American Airlines, British Airways, Cathay Pacific, China Eastern Airlines, China Southern Airlines, Emirates, Finnair, Hainan Airlines, Iberia Airlines, Korean Air, Malev, Mexican, Qantas Airways, Swiss, Thai Airways, THY Turkish Airlines, Vietnam Airlines, Xiamen Airlines (all qv)
Passengers carried: 59.5 million
Annual turnover: US $19,841 million (£13,228 million)
Fleet: 2 Boeing 747-400F; 41 Boeing 747-400; 10 Boeing 747-300; 9 Boeing 747-200F; 5 Boeing 747-200B; 13 Boeing 777-300ER; 5 Boeing 777-300; 11 Boeing 777-200ER; 7 Boeing 777-200; 1 Boeing 767F; 15 Boeing 767-300ER; 19 Boeing 767-300; 3 Boeing 767-200

JAA

Japan Asia Airways Co. Ltd
Incorporated: 1975

Japan Asia Airways was formed by Japan Airlines in 1975 for operations between Japan and Taiwan, removing any obstacles which might have prevented JAL operating to Beijing, because of Chinese Communist objections to businesses which recognised the regime in Taiwan. Initially, aircraft were wet-leased from the JAL fleet, but later JAA assumed responsibility for purchasing its own aircraft. At first, JAL had a 91 per cent stake in the airline, which also used a variation of the JAL colour scheme on its aircraft, but this has now been increased to 100 per cent. Since its formation, the airline has extended its range of destinations to include other popular centres in Asia.

HQ airport & main base: Tokyo International, plus Nagoya and Osaka
Radio callsign: ASIA
Designator: EG/JAA
Employees: 761
Route points: Denpasar Bali, Hong Kong, Jakarta, Kaohsiung, Nagoya, Okinawa, Osaka, Taipei, Tokyo
Links with other airlines: A subsidiary of Japan Airlines (qv)
Fleet: 2 Boeing 747-300; 2 Boeing 747-200B; 3 Boeing 767-300

JAPAN TRANSOCEAN
Japan TransOcean Air
Incorporated: 1967

Originally founded in 1967 as Southwest Airlines with the backing of Japan Airlines, which took a 51 per cent stake in the new company. The new airline took over the services to Okinawa and the Ryukyu Islands, which had hitherto been operated by Air America. A subsidiary, Ryukyu Air Commuter, operates feeder services into the main hubs from the smaller islands. Over the past decade, the fleet has been rationalised considerably to just one aircraft type, the Boeing 737-400.

HQ airport & main base: Okinawa Naha, with a further hub at Miyako
Radio callsign: JAI OCEAN
Designator: NU/JTA
Employees: 750
Route points: Fukuoka, Fukushima, Ishigaki, Kita Kyushu, Kochi, Komatsu, Kume-jima, Matsuyama, Miyako, Okinawa, Osaka, Tokyo, Yonaguni
Links with other airlines: Japan Airlines (qv) holds a 51 per cent interest. Ryukyu Commuter (qv) is a subsidiary
Fleet: 16 Boeing 737-400

NIPPON CARGO AIRLINES
Incorporated: 1978

The first Japanese scheduled and charter cargo airline, Nippon Cargo Airlines was formed in 1978, but did not commence operations until 1985, largely due to delays in obtaining government approval. The airline's original shareholders included All Nippon Airways and the Mitsui OSK shipping line., but over the past decade these have changed and now include Global Logistics Investments, with more than 55 per cent, and other interests.

HQ airport & main base: Tokyo Narita International
Radio callsign: NIPPON CARGO
Designator: KZ/NCA
Route points: Amsterdam, Anchorage, Bangkok, Beijing, Chicago, Frankfurt, Hong Kong, Kuala Lumpur, London, Los Angeles, Louisville, Manila, Milan, Nagoya, New York, Osaka, San Francisco, Seoul, Shanghai, Singapore, Tokyo
Fleet: 10 Boeing 747-400F; 6 Boeing 747-200F (On order: 8 Boeing 747-8F)

RYUKYU AIR COMMUTER
Incorporated: 1985

As the name suggests, Ryukyu Air Commuter operates passenger scheduled services from Okinawa to the offshore Ryukyu and Amami island groups. It is a subsidiary of Japan TransOcean Air, which has almost 70 per cent of the shares, while the Okinawa Prefecture has just over 5 per cent and the rest are with a variety of shareholders.

HQ airport & main base: Nahu
Radio callsign: RYUKYU
Designator: RAC
Route points: Most of the islands in the Amami and Ryukyu chains
Links with other airlines: Japan TransOcean Air (qv) has a 69.8 per cent stake
Fleet: 1 Bombardier Dash 8 Q300; 4 Bombardier Dash 8 Q100; 3 Britten-Norman BN-2 Islander

SKYMARK AIRLINES
Incorporated: 1996

Skymark Airlines was formed in 1996 and began operations in 1998 following deregulation of the Japanese domestic market, developing a network of regional routes and an international service between Tokyo and Seoul. It also operates international passenger charters.

HQ airport & main base: Tokyo Narita International
Radio callsign: SKYMARK
Designator: BC/SKY

Route points: Fukuoka, Kagoshima, Osaka, Seoul, Tokushima, Tokyo
Links with other airlines: Alliance with Japanese Airlines Domestic (qv)
Fleet: 6 Boeing 767-300ER; 4 Boeing 737-800

SKYNET ASIA AIRWAYS
Incorporated: 2002

Founded in 2002 as Pan Asia Airlines, Skynet Asia Airways is a low-cost carrier based on Fukuoka and controlled by the Industrial Revitalisation Corporation of Japan, with 57 per cent of the stock, and by a number of other interests. As with many low-cost airlines, it has standardised on a single aircraft type, in this case the Boeing 737. Unlike many low-cost airlines, the route network is still small.

HQ airport & main base: Fukuoka
Radio callsign: SKYNET
Designator: 6J/SNJ
Route points: Fukuoka, Kumamoto, Miyazaki, Tokyo
Links with other airlines: Alliance with All Nippon Airways (qv)
Fleet: 8 Boeing 737-400

JORDAN – JY

As with many Middle Eastern countries, air transport in Jordan was once the preserve of a single, state-owned monopoly, but the past decade has seen at least four independent airlines, primarily charter, established.

AIR RUM
Incorporated: 2002

Air Rum was founded as a passenger charter airline by Mohammad Abu Sheikh in 2002.

HQ airport & main base: Amman
Designator: RUM
Fleet: 2 Lockheed L-1011 TriStar 1; 1 Boeing 727-100

AIR UNIVERSAL
Incorporated: 2002

A Jordanian passenger charter airline, operating mainly in the Middle East, Air Universal dates from 2002. A long-haul charter operator, Air Universal (Cyprus) is planned for the future.
HQ airport & main base: Amman Queen Alia International
Designator: UVS
Employees: 225
Fleet: 3 Boeing 747-200B; 1 Lockheed L-1011-250 TriStar

JORDAN AVIATION
Incorporated: 2000

Started as a passenger charter airline, Jordan Aviation is now moving into scheduled operations, concentrating on the Middle East and Africa.

HQ airport & main base: Amman Civil Airport, but most operations from Aqaba
Designator: RS/JAV
Employees: 410
Route points: Amman, Aqaba
Fleet: 1 Airbus A310-300; 1 Airbus A310-200; 2 Boeing 727-200; 2 Boeing 737-300; 1 Boeing 737-200C; 1 Boeing 737-500

ROYAL JORDANIAN
Royal Jordanian Airlines
Incorporated: 1963

Originally known as Alia Royal Jordanian Airlines, the name 'Alia' meaning 'high flying', the airline was founded and commenced operations in 1963 with a fleet of two Handley Page Heralds and a Douglas DC-7. The airline replaced an earlier operation, Air Jordan. The first routes were from Amman to Jerusalem, at that time partly within Jordan, as well as to Beirut, Cairo and Kuwait. Initially, ownership was divided equally between private interests and the state, but today the airline is completely state owned.

The first jet equipment, Sud Aviation Caravelles, entered service in 1965, with operations extended to Rome that year, and to Paris and London the following year.

The current title was adopted in 1986. While the question of privatisation has been raised from time to time, the airline remains in government ownership although it now is a public limited company. The number of employees has fallen by a third over the past decade. The fleet has been restructured in recent years with the retirement of the Lockheed TriStars and Boeing 707s, with Airbus products for the longer and busier routes, and Embraer 195s for the domestic and regional services. The airline has two subsidiaries: the feeder operator Royal Jordanian Express, and Royal Wings Airlines, which operates a business-class network in the Middle East (although marketed by Royal Jordanian) and charter flights;

and a 25 per cent stake in the business and executive charter operator, Arab Wings. Both subsidiaries are small, with Royal Jordanian Express having two Bombardier Dash 8 Q400 turboprops and Royal Wings having a single Dash 8 Q300. Royal Jordanian is expected to become a member of the Oneworld alliance in 2007.

HQ airport & main base: Amman Queen Alia International
Radio callsign: JORDANIAN
Designator: RJ/RJA
Employees: 3,337
Route points: Abu Dhabi, Aden, Al Ain, Al Arish, Aleppo, Alexandria, Amman, Amsterdam, Athens, Aqaba, Baghdad, Bahrain, Bangkok, Barcelona, Basra, Beirut, Cairo, Chicago, Colombo, Damascus, Damman, Delhi, Detroit, Doha, Dubai, Erbil, Frankfurt, Geneva, Istanbul, Jeddah, Khartoum, Kiev, Kolkata, Kuwait, Larnaca, London, Madrid, Milan, Moscow, Mumbai, Munich, Muscat, New York, Paris, Riyadh, Rome, Sana'a, Sharm-el-Sheikh, Tel Aviv, Tripoli, Tunis, Vienna, Zurich
Links with other airlines: Owns both Royal Jordanian and Royal Wings Airlines (both qv), 100 per cent, and has a 25 per cent stake in Arab Wings. Alliances with Aeroflot Russian Airlines, Air Canada, America West Airlines, Austrian Airlines, Cyprus Airways, Gulf Air, Iberia Airlines, Syrianair, Thai Airways (all qv)
Fleet: 4 Airbus A340-200; 2 Airbus A310-300F; 4 Airbus A310-300; 4 Airbus A321-200; 8 Airbus A320-200; 7 Embraer 195LR; 2 Bombardier Challenger 604

SKY GATE INTERNATIONAL
Incorporated: 2004

An inclusive tour charter airline, mainly operating within the Middle East and to Africa, Sky Gate International was formed in 2004 and is owned by its directors. The fleet is standardised on the Lockheed TriStar.

HQ airport & main base: Amman Queen Alia International
Designator: SGD
Employees: 102
Fleet: 4 Lockheed L-1011-250 TriStar

KAMPUCHEA – XU

KAMPUCHEA AIRLINES
Incorporated: 1997

Originally founded in 1997 as SK Air, Kampuchea Airlines is re-establishing air transport links between Kampuchea and its neighbouring states using leased Boeing 757s and McDonnell Douglas MD-82s. The government has a controlling 51 per cent interest, with the remainder held by Orient Thai Airlines, which also provides management and maintenance support.

HQ airport & main base: Pochentong International Airport
Designator: KT/KMP
Links with other airlines: Orient Thai Airlines (qv) has a 49 per cent interest and provides operational support
Fleet: Boeing 757s and McDonnell Douglas MD-82s are leased as required

KAZAKHSTAN – UN

While the immediate aftermath of the break-up of the Soviet Union saw many new countries emerge and establish their own airlines, usually from the local division of Aeroflot, progress was not always smooth. In Kazakhstan, Kazakhstan Airways emerged from the local Aeroflot division in 1993, operating under the name of Kazair, but in 1996 the new airline was declared bankrupt. A new company, Air Kazakhstan, was established from the remnants of the airline with the addition of some regional airlines and state backing, and in 1999 the government decreed that this would be the national airline, but it has now ceased operations. Nevertheless, in the meantime a second airline has also been established with government support, Air Astana, and a number of independent airlines have also emerged, some with the support of the local energy industry.

AIR ASTANA
Incorporated: 2001

Founded as a new national airline for Kazakhstan in 2001, operations commencing the following year. It is a partnership between the national government, with 51 per cent, and BAe Systems.

HQ airport & main base: Almaty International, with a second base at Astana
Radio callsign: ASTANA
Designator: 4L/KZR
Employees: 1,000
Route points: Aktau, Aktyubinsk, Almaty, Amsterdam, Astana, Atyrau, Bangkok, Beijing,

Delhi, Dubai, Dzhambyl, Frankfurt, Hanover, Istanbul, Karaganda, Kostenay, Kzyl-Orda, London, Moscow, Pavlodar, Petropavlovsk, Semipalatinsk, Seoul, Shimkent, Uralsk, Ust-Kamenogorsk, Zhezkazgan
Fleet: 3 Boeing 757-200; 4 Airbus A320-200; 2 Boeing 737-800; 2 Boeing 737-700; 5 Fokker 50

ATYRAU AIRWAYS
Incorporated: 1996

Formed as a regional carrier based on Atyrau Airport in 1996, but in 1999 became part of the Air Kazakhstan Group, before being transferred to the control of the state oil company, Kaztransoil, the following year.

HQ airport & main base: Atyrau
Designator: IP/JOL
Fleet: 2 Tupolev Tu-154; 4 Tupolev Tu-134A

BERKUT AIR
Incorporated: 1997

A charter airline specialising in VIP flights and other specific requirements.

HQ airport & main base: Almaty
Designator: BEK
Fleet: 1 Boeing 757-200; 1 Ilyushin Il-76TD; 1 Antonov An-12; 5 Let L-410UVP; 4 Yakovlev Yak-40

EURO-ASIA AIR
Incorporated: 1997

Euro-Asia commenced operations in 1997, and today operates a network of passenger and cargo services within Kazakhstan and to the neighbouring Asian republics of the former USSR, and to Russia. Ownership is with KazMunayGas.

HQ airport & main base: Atyrau
Designator: 5B/EAK
Employees: 500
Fleet: I Ilyushin Il-76TD; 2 Tupolev Tu-134A; 1 Antonov An-24RV; 2 Yakovlev Yak-40; 1 Let L-410UVP; 1 Gulfstream GIV-SP

KAZAIR WEST
Incorporated: 1996

Not to be confused with an earlier airline, Kazair, which was a forerunner of Air Kazakhstan, Kazair West operates passenger and cargo charter flights from Almaty. It is owned by an American investor, Clintondale Aviation.

HQ airport & main base: Almaty
Fleet: 1 Tupolev Tu-134B; 2 Let L-410UVP-E; 2 Yakovlev Yak-40

KOKSHETAU AIRLINES
Incorporated: 2000

This airline currently operates charter flights and is in the process of developing a scheduled network.

HQ airport & main base: Kokshetau
Designator: OK/KRT
Employees: 240
Fleet: 1 Airbus A310-300; 2 Ilyushin Il-62M; 6 Yakovlev Yak-40

SCAT
Incorporated: 1997

Founded by the two shareholders, Vladimir Denissov and Vladimir Sytnik, in 1997 as a passenger and cargo airline providing charters as well as a scheduled service network.

HQ airport & main base: Shymkent
Radio callsign: SCAT
Designator: DV/DSV
Employees: 321
Route points: Aktua, Aktyubinsk, Almaty, Astana, Astrakhan, Atyrau, Bayankhongor, Kostanay, Kzyl-Orda, Mineralnye Vody, Petropavlovsk, Shimkent, Uraalsk, Ust-Kamenogorsk, Yerevan
Fleet: 20 Antonov An-24B/RV; 2 Yakovlev Yak-40

KENYA – 5Y

In common with many British colonies, after the Second World War air transport in Kenya was provided by an offshoot of the British Overseas Airways Corporation, BOAC, East African Airways Corporation. East African had been formed in 1946 by BOAC and the colonial administrations of Kenya, Uganda, Tanganyika and Zanzibar. At first, the airline provided feeder services within East Africa for BOAC's trunk routes, and operated six de Havilland Dragon Rapide biplanes. These aircraft were soon replaced by new de Havilland Doves, which were followed by Lockheed Lodestars, then by much larger

Douglas DC-3s, all in quick succession until additional DC-3s were purchased in 1952.

EAAC broke out of the regional role in 1957, when international services were started to London, Karachi, Aden and Salisbury (now Harare) using Canadair DC-4M Argonauts (Canadian-built versions of the Douglas DC-4, using Rolls-Royce Merlin engines). A significant improvement in travelling times and passenger comfort followed when a Bristol Britannia 'Whispering Gaint' turboprop airliner was leased to operate these routes before jet airliners, de Havilland Comet 4s, were introduced in 1960. In 1966, when the first of four Vickers VC-10 airliners were introduced, the Comets were downgraded to services within Africa. Meanwhile, many of the DC-3s had been replaced by Fokker F27 Friendship turboprops on the domestic services, augmented by a handful of remaining DC-3s and, for the thinner routes, de Havilland Canada Twin Otters.

Throughout this period, British Overseas Airways Associated Companies remained the main shareholder with a 53 per cent stake. EAAC even had a subsidiary of its own for tourist services, Seychelles-Kilimanjaro Air Transport, operating just one de Havilland Dragon Rapide. While EAAC operated with its aircraft registered with the participating nations in proportion to their shareholdings, after independence the strains of multinational ownership soon showed, even though at one time a fleet of BAC One-Eleven regional airlines was planned to replace the F27s and remaining DC-3s. In 1977, the participating nations opted to disband the airline and establish their own national operations, although only Kenya had the potential to do so.

The growth of tourism in Kenya has also seen the country establish a diverse air transport sector, although, inevitably it seems, this has also meant that a few companies have fallen by the wayside, including AirKenya, which dated from 1985, when it was formed on the merger of Air Kenya and Sunbird Aviation, and operated scheduled and charter services within Kenya, mainly to tourist centres, and a similar airline, dating from 1986, Eagle Aviation.

BLUE BIRD AVIATION
Incorporated: Not known

A Kenyan charter airline mainly serving holidaymakers travelling within the country.

HQ airport & main base: Nairobi
Designator: BBZ
Fleet: 5 Fokker 50; 2 Bombardier Dash 8 Q100; 8 Let L-410; 1 Raytheon Beech 1900D; 3 Raytheon Beech King Air 200

KENYA AIRWAYS
Incorporated: 1977

Kenya Airways came into existence in 1977, founded by the Kenyan government following the collapse of East African Airways, which had operated since 1946 with the assistance of BOAC, British Overseas Airways Corporation, and had been owned by British Overseas Airways Associated Companies and the governments of Kenya, Uganda, and Tanganyika and Zanzibar (later Tanzania).

The new airline's first flight was on 4 February 1977, from London Heathrow to Nairobi, using a Boeing 707, one of three such aircraft in the fleet. While the 707s were used on services to Europe, African and domestic services used a McDonnell Douglas DC-9-30, a Boeing 720 and two Fokker F27 Friendships. The airline's growth was helped by the growing importance of Kenya as a tourist destination.

In 1996 the airline was privatised, and it is now quoted on the Nairobi Stock Exchange. KLM bought 26 per cent of the airline's shares, and a marketing alliance also exists between the two carriers, while the government retains a 22 per cent interest. In 2004, Kenya Airways Cargo was established to market its cargo operations and in due course to operate aircraft in its own right, while a domestic subsidiary, Flamingo Airlines, was terminated and its operations reabsorbed. The fleet, which had included Airbus A310s, is now all Boeing with the exception of two ex-Flamingo Saab 340s.

HQ airport & main base: Nairobi Jomo Kenyatta International Airport
Radio callsign: KENYA
Designator: KQ/KQA
Employees: 2,300
Route points: Abidjan, Accra, Addis Ababa, Amsterdam, Bamako, Bangkok, Bombay, Bujumbura, Cairo, Copenhagen, Dakar, Dar-es-Salaam, Djibouti, Douala, Dubai, Entebbe, Freetown, Guangzhou, Harare, Hong Kong, Istanbul, Jeddah, Johannesburg, Khartoum, Kigali, Kinshasa, Kisumi, Lagos, Lamu, Lilongwe, London, Lusaka, Mahe, Malindi, Maputo, Mombasa, Mumbai, Nairobi, Paris, Rome, Seychelles, Stockholm, Yaounde, Zanzibar
Links with other airlines: KLM owns 26 per cent. Alliances with Air Malawi (qv), East African Airlines, KLM (qv), Rwandair Express

Fleet: 4 Boeing 777-200ER; 6 Boeing 767-300ER; 1 Boeing 767-300; 3 Boeing 737-800; 4 Boeing 737-700; 4 Boeing 737-300; 3 Boeing 737-200; 2 Saab 340B (On order: 9 Boeing 787-8)

KOREA (SOUTH) – HL

ASIANA

Asiana Airlines, Inc.
Incorporated: 1988

Asiana Airlines was formed in 1988, as Seoul Air International, by the present major shareholders, the Kumho Group, with the encouragement of the South Korean government, which wanted the country to have a second major airline, or flag carrier. Initially, the new airline operated scheduled domestic services and international charters, building up a fleet of Boeing 737s, but in 1990 the airline moved into international scheduled services, initially to destinations in Japan and China. The present title was adopted in advance of the start of international services. The airline received its first wide-bodied aircraft, a Boeing 767 and a Boeing 747, in November 1991, and introduced a service from Seoul to Los Angeles.

In a decade, the airline has grown from nothing to be not only South Korea's second largest airline, but also one of the top forty airlines in the world by annual turnover. There are alliances of various kinds with a number of other major international airlines.

In recent years, Asiana has been the thirty-sixth largest airline in the world by revenue, and thirty-ninth in passenger numbers. It is a member of the Star Alliance.

HQ airport & main base: Seoul Incheon International
Radio callsign: ASIANA
Designator: OZ/AAR
Employees: 7,183 (exc. Asiana Airport, Inc.)
Route points: Almaty, Auckland, Bangkok, Beijing, Brussels, Busan, Cairns, Cebu, Changchun, Chengdu, Chiang Mai, Chiang Rai, Chicago, Chongqing, Daegu, Delhi, Detroit, Frankfurt, Fukuoka, Fukashima, Guangzhou, Guilin, Gwangiu, Haikou, Hangzhou, Hanoi, Harbin, Hiroshima, Ho Chi Minh City, Hong Kong, Istanbul, Jeju, Jinju, Khabarovsk, Koror, Kota Kinabalu, Kumamoto, London, Los Angeles, Luzon, Manila, Matsuyama, Miyazaki, Mokpo, Nagoya, Nanking, New York, Okinawa, Osaka, Phuket, Pohang, Pusan, Qintao, Saipan, San Francisco, Seattle, Sendai, Seoul, Shanghai, Shenyang, Shenzhen, Siem Reap, Singapore, Sydney, Taipei, Takamatsu, Tashkent, Tianjin, Tokyo, Toyama, Ulsan, Vancouver, Viennna, Weihai, Xian, Yantai, Yanyi, Yeosu, Yonago, Yuzhno-Sakhalinsk
Links with other airlines: Alliances with Air China, Air India, China Eastern Airlines, China Southern Airlines, Qantas Airways, South African Airways, THY Turkish Airlines (all qv)
Passengers carried: 12.3 million
Annual turnover: US $2,628 million (£1,752 million)
Fleet: 2 Boeing 747-400; 6 Boeing 747-400 Combi; 5 Boeing 747-400F; 10 Boeing 777-200ER; 6 Airbus A330-300; 2 Boeing 767ER; 7 Boeing 767-300; 11 Airbus A321-200; 2 Airbus A321-100; 4 Airbus A320-200; 7 Boeing 737-400; 3 Boeing 737-500

KOREAN AIR

Korean Air Lines
Incorporated: 1962

Eighteenth largest in the world by turnover and twenty-second by passenger numbers, Korean Air was founded in 1962 as the successor to Korean National Airlines, which had dated from 1948. Initially, the new airline was owned by the Korean government, but was acquired by the Hanjin Group in 1969, although today the ownership is much more broadly based, with Hanjin having 7.82 per cent, employees 6.22 per cent and the Yang-Ho Cho family 12.13 per cent. It was until recently one of the three largest in Asia, but the rapid growth of Chinese airlines and the merger between Japan Airlines and Japan Air System have combined to push Korean into fifth place. It operates an extensive domestic network as well as a large international network, which includes a substantial number of scheduled cargo services, reflecting the country's status as one of the 'tiger economies' of Asia. It is a member of the Sky Team alliance. Over the past decade, the airline fleet has standardised on Boeing and Airbus products, with the disappearance of McDonnell Douglas aircraft, but some Cessna and Gulfstream business jets are also operated.

HQ airport & main base: Seoul Gimpo International
Radio callsign: KOREANAIR
Designator: KE/KAL
Employees: 15,000
Route points: Akita, Amsterdam, Aomori, Atlanta, Auckland, Bangkok, Beijing, Brisbane, Busan, Cairo, Cheongui, Chicago, Dallas, Denpasar Bali, Dubai, Frankfurt, Fukuoka, Guam, Gwabgui, Hanoi,

Ho Chi Minh City, Hong Kong, Honolulu, Jakarta, Jeju, Jinan, Jinju, Kagoshima, Kormatsu, Kota Kinabalu, Kuala Lumpur, Kunming, London, Los Angeles, Manila, Moscow, Mumbai, Nadi, Nagasaki, Nagoya, New York, Nigata, Oita, Okayama, Osaka, Paris, Penang, Phuket, Pohang, Prague, Qingdao, Rome, San Francisco, Sanya, Sapporo, Seattle, Seoul, Shanghai, Shenyang, Shenzen, Singapore, Sydney, Taipei, Tianjin, Tokyo, Toronto, Ulan Bator, Ulsan, Vancouver, Vladivostok, Washington, Weihai, Wongju, Wuhan, Xiamen, Xian, Yangyang, Yantai, Yeosu, Zurich
Links with other airlines: Member of the Sky Team alliance. Alliances with Aeroflot Russian Airlines (qv), Air China (qv), Cargojet Airways, China Airlines (qv), China Eastern Airlines (qv), China Southern Airlines (qv), Emirates (qv), Garuda Indonesia (qv), Japan Airlines International (qv), LAN Airlines, Malaysia Airlines (qv), SAS Cargo, Vietnam Airlines (qv)
Passengers carried: 21.3 million
Annual turnover: US $6,332 million (£4,224 million)
Fleet: 8 Boeing 747-ERF; 10 Boeing 747-400F; 1 Boeing 747-400 Combi; 23 Boeing 747-400; 4 Boeing 777-300; 18 Boeing 777-200ER; 5 Boeing 777F; 16 Airbus A330-300; 3 Airbus A330-200; 10 Airbus A300-600R/F; 20 Boeing 737-900; 14 Boeing 737-800; 1 Gulfstream GIV; 4 Cessna Citation Ultra (On order: 5 Airbus A380-800; 5 Boeing 747-8F; 10 Boeing 777-300ER; 10 Boeing 787-8)

KOREA, NORTH – P-

AIR KORYO
Incorporated: 1955

Air Koryo, the airline of the People's Republic of North Korea, was founded in 1955, taking over from SOKAO, a joint Soviet–Korean airline founded in 1950. Initially the airline was called Chosonminhang Korean Airways, but the present title was adopted in 1994. The airline is primarily domestic scheduled, although there is a limited international network, and international freight charters are flown. Given the state of the North Korean economy, it is not clear how many of the airline's aircraft are operational, while the route network seems to concentrate on international services, doubtless for political and diplomatic reasons.

HQ airport & main base: Pyongyang Sunan
Radio callsign: AIR KORYO
Designator: JS/KOR
Employees: 2,500
Route points: Bangkok, Beijing, Khabarovsk, Moscow, Pyongyang, Shenyang
Fleet: 3 Ilyushin Il-76MD; 4 Ilyushin Il-62M; 4 Tupolev Tu-154B; 2 Tupolev Tu-134B; 2 Antonov An-24

KUWAIT – 9K

JAZEERA AIRWAYS
Incorporated: 2004

Jazeera Airways is the first independently owned airline in Kuwait. It was founded in 2004, and started scheduled passenger operations in 2005, with a service from Kuwait to Dubai. Further expansion is planned.

HQ airport & main base: Kuwait
Radio callsign: JAZEERA
Designator: J9
Route points: Amman, Bahrain, Beirut, Damascus, Dubai, Kuwait
Fleet: 10 Airbus A320-200

KUWAIT AIRWAYS
Kuwait Airways Corporation
Incorporated: 1954

It was as the Kuwait National Airways Company that Kuwait Airways commenced operations in 1954 with two Douglas DC-3 aircraft on routes to Iraq, Syria, the Lebanon, Jordan and Iran. The airline was an immediate success, and added two Handley Page Hermes aircraft the following year, and in 1957 these were joined by Douglas DC-4s. The name of the company was changed in 1957 to the Kuwait Airways Company. BOAC, British Overseas Airways Corporation, became responsible for the airline's technical management in 1958, for five years.

Although the airline had been formed as a 50:50 venture between the state and private interests, ownership passed to the state in 1962, and the current title was adopted. That same year, the airline introduced its first jet aircraft, a leased de Havilland Comet 4, and later three of these aircraft were purchased, eventually being joined by Hawker Siddeley Trident 1Es and Boeing 707s.

Despite the considerable wealth of Kuwait and its pivotal position on routes between the East and Europe, the airline has suffered mixed fortunes due to the aggressive posture adopted towards Kuwait by Iraq. Although a threatened invasion during the early

1960s was prevented by prompt action by British forces, the country was overrun by Iraq in August 1990. Many of the airline's aircraft were caught on the ground in Kuwait and seized, while the airline's management set up a temporary head office in Cairo, and the remaining aircraft – four Boeing 747-200 Combis, a Boeing 767 and three Boeing 727s – operated a temporary service from Cairo to Bahrain, Dubai and Jeddah. By 2000, the airline had recovered from the invasion, and rebuilt a modern fleet, although the resumption of transatlantic flights is of more recent origin. To diversify from its small base, a 20 per cent stake was been taken in the Indian operator, Jet Airways, but this has since been sold. The airline remains in state ownership.

HQ airport & main base: Kuwait International
Radio callsign: KUWAITI
Designator: KU/KAC
Employees: 4,050
Route points: Abu Dhabi, Alexandria, Amman, Amsterdam, Assiut, Athens, Bahrain, Bangkok, Beirut, Cairo, Chennai, Colombo, Copenhagen, Damascus, Damman, Delhi, Dhaka, Doha, Dubai, Frankfurt, Islamabad, Jakarta, Jeddah, Kochi, Kuwait, Lahore, Larnaca, London, Luxor, Manila, Mumbai, Muscat, New York, Paris, Riyadh, Rome, Sharm-el-Sheik, Tehran, Trivandrum
Links with other airlines: Alliances with Air India, Merpati Nusantera, Olympic Airlines, THY Turkish Airlines (all qv)
Fleet: 1 Boeing 747-400 Combi; 4 Airbus A340-300; 2 Boeing 777-200ER; 6 Airbus A300-600R; 4 Airbus A310-300; 4 Airbus A320-200; 3 Gulfstream GV

KYRGYZSTAN – EX

KYRGYZSTAN AIRLINES
Kyrgyzstan Aba Yolduru National Airlines
Incorporated: 1992

A former Aeroflot division, Kyrgyzstan Airlines is now the national airline following the break-up of the Soviet Union. Strong links remained with Aeroflot for a number of years, but these seem to have been discontinued. The airline is 81 per cent government owned.

HQ airport & main base: Bishkek
Radio callsign: KYRGHYZ
Designator: R8/KGA
Route points: Bishkek, Delhi, Dushanbe, Frankfurt, Hanover, Jalalabad, Karachi, London, Moscow, Novosibirsk, Omsk, Osh, Sharjah, Tashkent, Urumqi
Fleet: 2 Ilyushin Il-76TD; 9 Tupolev Tu-154B/M; 3 Tupolev Tu-134; 5 Antonov An-28; 1 Antonov An-26; 2 Yakovlev Yak-40

LAOS – XW

LAO AIRLINES
Incorporated: 1991

Formed in 1991 as Lao Aviation and as the national airline, initially ownership was spread among import–export agencies and China Travel Air Service, based in Hong Kong. The name was changed to Lao Airlines in 2003, and the airline has been nationalised. Both domestic and international services are operated.

HQ airport & main base: Vientiane Wattay International
Radio callsign: LAO
Designator: QV/LAO
Route points: Bangkok, Chiang Mai, Hanoi, Ho Chi Minh City, Houeisay, Kunming, Luang Namtha, Luang Prabang, Oudomxay, Oakse, Phnom Penh, Phongsay, Sayaboury, Siem Reap, Vientiane, Xieng Khouang
Fleet: 6 Antonov An-26; 5 Antonov An-24RV; 2 ATR-72-200; 2 Cessna Caravan 675

LATVIA – YL

AIRBALTIC
Incorporated: 1995

One of the newer airlines to emerge from the ruins of the former Soviet empire, AirBaltic is a joint venture between the state, SAS and Transaero. The state decided that AirBaltic would become the national carrier, taking over from Latavio, which had been a former Aeroflot division. Initially, all routes were international, but its first domestic service was started in 2005 between Riga and Liepaja. The airline has concentrated on creating a fleet of European aircraft, standardising on two types after operating a more varied fleet initially, and has seen considerable expansion in recent years, while the SAS shareholding has risen from 29 per cent to more than 47 per cent.

HQ airport & main base: Riga
Radio callsign: AIRBALTIC
Designator: BT/BTI
Employees: 482

Route points: Barcelona, Berlin, Brussels, Copenhagen, Dublin, Frankfurt, Hamburg, Helsinki, Istanbul, Kiev, Liepaja, London, Milan, Minsk, Moscow, Munich, Oslo, Palanga, Paris, Riga, St Petersburg, Stockholm, Tallinn, Vienna, Vilnius, Warsaw
Links with other airlines: SAS has a 47.2 per cent shareholding. Alliances with AeroSvit Airlines (qv), Austrian Airlines (qv), Belavia (qv), Donbassaero (qv), Estonian Air (qv), Pulkovo Aviation Enterprise, SAS (qv), Spanair (qv)
Fleet: 7 Boeing 737-500; 6 Fokker 50

LATCHARTER AIRLINES
Incorporated: 1992

A passenger charter airline operating inclusive tour and ad hoc charters, LATcharter was founded in 1992 and started operations the following year. Its shares are held by a number of private investors.

HQ airport & main base: Riga International
Designator: 6Y/LTC
Fleet: 2 Airbus A320-200; 2 Yakovlev Yak-42D

RAF-AVIA AIRLINES
Incorporated: 1990

Latvia's first independently owned airline, founded in 1990, RAF-Avia commenced operations in 1991 delivering spare parts for the RAF commercial vehicle plant. The original business showed little scope for expansion, and in 1994 RAF-Avia became a cargo charter airline, and in 1996 it became independent of the vehicle manufacturer and fully privately owned. It now undertakes contract flying for DHL, TNT, the United Nations and the military.

HQ airport & main base: Riga International
Designator: MTL
Employees: 80
Links with other airlines: Contract flying for DHL (qv) and TNT
Fleet: 1 Antonov An-74; 5 Antonov An-26/26B; 1 Saab 340A

LEBANON – OD

MEA MIDDLE EAST AIRLINES
Middle East Airlines Airliban SARL
Incorporated: 1945

Middle East Airlines was founded in 1945 and commenced operations in 1946 with a fleet of three de Havilland Rapide biplanes, quickly establishing routes from Beirut to Baghdad, Aleppo, Cairo, Lydda, Haifa, Damascus and Amman by the middle of the year, so that Douglas DC-3s had to be acquired. A political crisis in Palestine in 1948 forced the termination of the Haifa and Lydda ervices, but the impact of this was offset by new services to Ankara and Istanbul. The following year, a third DC-3 was acquired and the Rapides were sold.

In 1949, Pan American World Airways acquired a 36 per cent interest in the airline, providing three more DC-3s. This arrangement lasted until 1955, when BOAC, British Overseas Airways Corporation, took a 48.5 per cent shareholding, and assisted with the purchase of three Vickers Viscounts and a new maintenance base. In 1960, BOAC leased two de Havilland Comet 4s to the airline while it awaited delivery of its own aircraft. Meanwhile, the airline had also expanded into the air freight business, initially with a Bristol Freighter and then with three Avro Yorks. Nevertheless, the agreement with BOAC ended in 1961 once MEA started to experience competition from BOAC's sister airline, BEA, British European Airways.

For two years, MEA operated without foreign shareholdings, and even took a 30 per cent shareholding in Jordan Airways until 1963, when Air France took a 30 per cent stake in MEA and the airline was merged with Air Liban, in which the French airline had a controlling interest. Air Liban had operated Douglas DC-4s on services to Europe and West Africa. Once again, the choice of associate had a bearing on MEA's choice of equipment, with Sud Aviation Caravelles joining the fleet.

The airline's operations have been frequently disrupted by the unstable political and military situation in the Middle East. One of the worst incidents came in 1968, on 28 December, when an Israeli attack on the airport at Beirut resulted in a Viscount, a Boeing 707, three Comets and two Caravelles being destroyed, along with a leased Vickers VC.10. The airline started the long process of reconstruction, acquiring Lebanese International Airways in 1969, and later buying Boeing 747s. Yet worse was to come, for between 1975 and 1990, civil war in the Lebanon saw Beirut International Airport closed for some 800 days.

Nevertheless, in 1992 further reconstruction was assisted by the award of a twenty-year exclusivity right to operate as a commercial airline in the Lebanon, effectively making the airline the official flag carrier. Today, the main shareholder is Banque Central, the Central Bank of Lebanon, indirectly making the airline state owned. Alliances are in place with a number of major airlines.

Operations were again disrupted in July and August 2006, when Israeli forces attacked Lebanon, although at least four aircraft were ferried to safety in Amman during the attack. Over the past decade, the fleet has gone from mixed Boeing and Airbus to being completely Airbus, but the number of aircraft has more than halved and employment has dropped by around a third and the route network has seen the loss of long-haul destinations, doubtless reflecting the impact on tourism and commerce of the Lebanon's problems. MEA is a partner with Syrian Airlines in Phoenician Express, a regional airline planned to act as a short-haul feeder service to the two national airlines.

HQ airport & main base: Beirut International Airport
Radio callsign: CEDAR JET
Designator: ME/MEA
Employees: 2,360
Route points: Abidjan, Abu Dhabi, Accra, Amman, Athens, Beirut, Cairo, Damman, Dhahran, Doha, Dubai, Frankfurt, Geneva, Istanbul, Jeddah, Kano, Kuwait, Lagos, Larnaca, London, Milan, Nice, Paris, Riyadh, Rome
Links with other airlines: Alliances with Air France, Gulf Air, Qatar Airways (all qv). Owns 25 per cent of Phoenician Express
Fleet: 7 Airbus A330-200; 6 Airbus A321-200; 4 Airbus A319-100

LIBYA – 5A

AIR LIBYA TIBESTI
Incorporated: 1996

An airline using mainly Soviet-era equipment for scheduled and charter international and domestic services, including locust control and crop spraying. Five Antonov An-140s have recently been introduced.

HQ airport & main base: Tripoli
Designator: 7Q/TLR
Route points: Benghazi, El Fasher, Gadames, Kufrah, Sabha, Sert, Tripoli
Fleet: 1 Ilyushin Il-76MD; 1 Tupolev Tu-154B; 5 Antonov An-140; 1 Antonov An-26; 1 Antonov An-24; 7 Yakovlev Yak-40

BURAQ AIR
Incorporated: 2000

A charter airline operating domestically and internationally, Buraq Air was formed in 2000 by a group of private investors. It now has a small scheduled network.

HQ airport & main base: Mitiga International
Radio callsign: BURAQ
Designator: BRQ
Route points: Aleppo, Benghazi, Istanbul, Misurata, Mitiga, Tripoli
Fleet: 1 McDonnell Douglas DC-10; 2 Ilyushin Il-76TD; 3 Boeing 727-200; 2 Boeing 737-800; 2 Boeing 737-200; 3 Let L-410UVP-E; 1 BAe Jetstream 32

LIBYAN ARAB AIR CARGO
Incorporated: 1979

Libyan Arab Airlines has followed those airlines with an all-cargo subsidiary with the creation of Libyan Arab Air Cargo in 1979, responsible for marketing cargo capacity on the parent airline's passenger services and also providing scheduled cargo operations where necessary on the LAA network. Charter flights are also provided, many of them in support of the oil and natural gas industries. In contrast to LAA, the fleet consists entirely of Russian and Ukrainian equipment.

HQ airport & main base: Tripoli International
Radio callsign: LIB AIR
Designator: LCR
Links with other airlines: A subsidiary of Libyan Arab Airlines (qv)
Fleet: 2 Antonov An-124-100; 1 Ilyushin Il-78; 18 Ilyushin Il-76M/T/TD;4 Lockheed L-100-30 Hercules; 4 Antonov An-32; 2 Antonov An-26

LIBYAN ARAB AIRLINES
Jamahiriya Libyan Arab Airlines
Incorporated: 1964

Originally founded as Kingdom of Libya Airlines, the airline adopted its present title in 1971 after the monarchy was overthrown in a coup. A ban on all flights to and from Libyan airspace was imposed in 1989 by the United Nations after Libya refused to extradite the two men suspected of involvement in the destruction of a Pan Am Boeing 747 over Lockerbie in Scotland in 1988, and this, together with previous embargoes on equipment, meant that the airline spent a number of years in limbo. Sanctions were lifted in 1999 and the airline has steadily rebuilt its operations. The domestic carrier

Air Jamahiriya was absorbed in 2001. Since the lifting of sanctions, an all-western fleet has been built, but many of the aircraft are elderly.

HQ airport & main base: Tripoli International
Radio callsign: LIBAIR
Designator: LN/LAA
Fleet: 2 Airbus A300-600R; 2 Airbus A310-200; 1 Airbus A320-200; 1 Boeing 707-320C; 9 Boeing 727-200; 2 BAe One-Eleven 400; 2 Fokker F28 Mk4000; 16 de Havilland Canada Twin Otter Srs 300; 1 Gulfstream GII; 1 Dassault Falcon 900EX; 1 Dassault Falcon 20

LITHUANIA – LY

AMBER AIR

Incorporated: 2004

Founded as a business and executive charter company, Amber Air expanded into charter and scheduled passenger services in 2005, initially with a route linking Palanga with Billund and Warsaw.

HQ airport & main base: Palanga International
Designator: OA/GNT
Route points: Billund, Hamburg, Palanga, Warsaw
Fleet: 2 Saab 340B

FLYLAL

Incorporated: 1991

FlyLal is the new name for Lithuanian State Airlines, also known as Air Lithuania, which was founded in 1991. The airline started charter operations the following February, but introduced scheduled services in 1993, with a service between Vilnius and Budapest. Lithuanian was the former Kaunas Joint Air Detachment of Aeroflot, dating from 1938. The airline was organised as a company, but ownership rested with the Lithuanian government until the company was privatised, being acquired by LAL Investments and the Swedish airline, FlyMe, in 2005, when the current title was adopted. LAL has two-thirds of the shares, with FlyMe holding the remainder.

HQ airport & main base: Vilnius
Radio callsign: LITHUANIA AIR
Designator: TE/LIL
Employees: 708
Route points: Amsterdam, Brussels, Dublin, Frankfurt, Helsinki, Kiev, London, Milan, Moscow, Palanga, Paris, Stockholm, Vilnius
Fleet: 5 Boeing 737-500; 1 Antonov An-24RV; 4 Saab 2000

LUXEMBOURG – LX

CARGOLUX

Cargolux Airlines International SA
Incorporated: 1970

Cargolux was founded in 1970 by a consortium consisting of Luxair, Loftleidir Icelandic Airlines, the Salen Shipping Group and a number of other private interests. The first aircraft was a Canadair CL-44, a stretched and licence-built variant of the Bristol Britannia with Rolls-Royce Tyne engines, which incorporated a swingtail for easier loading of large items. Eventually, the airline had five of these aircraft before they were supplemented and then replaced by Douglas DC-8 freighters, which enabled the airline to extend its scheduled operations to the United States.

The first Boeing 747-200F was delivered in 1979, followed by a second aircraft in 1980. The first of a number of strategic alliances was established in 1982 with China Airlines. The airline also moved into passenger charters in 1983, operating two 747s and a DC-8 on Hadj pilgrim flights. Lufthansa acquired a 24.5 per cent shareholding in 1987, while Luxair increased its stake to the same level. In 1997, Lufthansa sold its stake to SAir Logistics. The airline became the first operator of the Boeing 747-400 freighter in 1993, and for many years was the only European operator of this aircraft.

Today, the airline operates an extensive international air cargo network. Luxair now owns 34.9 per cent, while the SAir stake of 33.7 per cent is being sold. For the future, the airline has orders for the freight version of the Boeing 747-8F.

HQ airport & main base: Luxembourg Findel
Radio callsign: CARGOLUX
Designator: CV/CLX
Employees: 1,384
Route points: Abidjan, Abu Dhabi, Amman, Auckland, Baku, Bangkok, Barcelona, Beijing, Beirut, Bogotá, Budapest, Calgary, Chennai, Chicago, Damascus, Dubai, Glasgow, Guadalajara, Helsinki, Hong Kong, Houston, Indianapolis, Johannesburg, Karachi, Komatsu, Kuala Lumpur, Kuwait, Latacunga, Los Angeles, Lusaka, Melbourne, Mexico City, Milan, Nairobi, New York, Panama City, San Francisco, Santiago de Chile, Sao Paulo, Seattle, Seoul, Shanghai, Singapore, Taipei, Xiamen

Links with other airlines: Luxair (qv) owns a 34.9 per cent stake
Fleet: 17 Boeing 747-400F (On order: 10 Boeing 747-8F)

LUXAIR
Société Anonyme Luxembourgeoise de Navigation Aerienne
Incorporated: 1962

Luxair was founded in 1962 as the national airline for the Grand Duchy of Luxembourg, with ownership shared between the government, the steel industry and the banks. A predecessor company, Luxembourg Airlines, had been supported by a British company, Scottish Airways, between 1948 and 1951, and then by Seaboard World Airlines, an American company, until 1960. Initially, the fleet consisted of a Vickers Viscount 810 and three Fokker F27 Friendships, while the route network consisted of the main centres in north-western Europe, including London and Paris.

Today, the airline has a more extensive route network, although given the small size of Luxembourg and its small population, it is not surprising that no wide-bodied aircraft are operated. For a while, a subsidiary, Luxair Commuter, operated the shorter and less busy routes, but these have been reintegrated with the main services, and the airline has become all-jet over the past decade. Luxair has an interest in the Luxembourg-based air cargo airline, Cargolux. Lufthansa has a 13 per cent share in the airline, with other shares held by banking groups, while the state shareholding is 23.1 per cent.

HQ airport & main base: Luxembourg
Radio callsign: LUXAIR
Designator: LG/LUX
Employees: 2,190
Route points: Barcelona, Berlin, Budapest, Copenhagen, Dublin, Frankfurt, Fuerteventura, Geneva, Lanzarote, Las Palmas, Lisbon, London, Luxembourg, Madeira, Madrid, Malaga, Malta, Manchester, Milan, Munich, Nice, Oporto, Palma de Mallorca, Paris, Rome, Saarbrücken, Turin, Vienna
Links with other airlines: Lufthansa (qv) owns 13 per cent. Luxair has a 34.9 per cent stake in Cargolux (qv)
Fleet: 3 Boeing 737-700; 2 Boeing 737-500; 3 Bombardier Dash 8 Q400; 8 Embraer ERJ-145EP/LU; 2 Embraer ERJ-135LR

WEST AIR LUXEMBOURG
Incorporated: 2001

Formed in 2001, West Air Luxembourg began operations in 2003, operating cargo charter and scheduled flights from Luxembourg. It is a subsidiary of West Air Sweden.

HQ airport & main base: Luxembourg
Designator: WLX
Employees: 46
Route points: Amsterdam, Luxembourg, Marseilles, Munich, Paris
Links with other airlines: Owned 100 per cent by West Air Sweden (qv)
Fleet: 5 BAe ATP

MACEDONIA – Z3

MAT
Macedonian Airlines
Incorporated: 1994

Although owned by the founders, Zivko Gruevski and Zlatko Petrovski, MAT Macedonian Airlines is regarded as the newly independent country's national airline, with a small route network which includes a single domestic route and links to the major European centres. It has effectively replaced Avioimpex, which operated scheduled and charter flights.

HQ airport & main base: Skopje
Designator: IN/MAK
Route points: Düsseldorf, Hamburg, Ohrid, Rome, Skopje, Vienna, Zurich
Links with other airlines: Alliances with Austrian Airlines, Swiss (both qv)
Fleet: 1 Boeing 737-300; 1 Bombardier CRJ900

MALAGASY REPUBLIC – 5R

AIR MADAGASCAR
Société Nationale Malgache de Transports Aeriens
Incorporated: 1962

The nationalised carrier of Madagascar, Air Madagascar was founded in 1962 by the newly independent Malagasy Republic with the support of Air France, which still retains a 3.17 per cent shareholding. The airline was formed to replace a local operator, Madair. Severe operating difficulties during 2000–2 led to restructuring with assistance from Lufthansa Consulting.

In addition to operating throughout Madagascar, the airline also operates to countries in Africa and to Europe. At one time it used a Boeing 747, giving it an unusually wide range of capacity, but now these services are covered by 767s. Private investment in the airline is minimal at 4.46 per cent, while the Malagasy government holds 90.6 per cent.

HQ airport & main base: Antananarivo Ivato International
Radio callsign: AIR MADAGASCAR
Designator: MD/MDG
Employees: 1,380
Route points: Ambatomainty, Ankavandra, Antalaha, Antananarivo, Antsalova, Antsiranana, Antsohihy, Bangkok, Belo, Besalampy, Djibouti, Dzaoudzi, Fianarantsoa, Fort Dauphin, Johannesburg, Maintirano, Majunga, Mananara, Mandritsara, Manja, Maraontsetra, Mauritius, Morafenobe, Morombe, Morondava, Nairobi, Mossi-be, Paris, Saint Denis de la Reunion, Saint Pierre de la Reunion, Sainte Marie, Sambava, Soalala, Tamatave, Tambohorano, Tsaratanana, Tsioanomandidy, Tulear
Links with other airlines: Air France (qv) has a 3.5 per cent interest. Alliances with Air Mauritius, Inter Air South Africa, Thai Airways (all qv)
Fleet: 2 Boeing 767-300ER; 2 Boeing 737-300; 3 ATR-72-500; 1 ATR-42-300; 4 de Havilland Canada Twin Otter Srs 300

MALAWI – 7Q

AIR MALAWI
Incorporated: 1967

Prior to independence, the British colonies in Central Africa were served by CAA, Central African Airways Corporation, in which a subsidiary, British Overseas Airways Associated Companies (one of the predecessors of British Airways), British Overseas Airways Corporation, BOAC, was a major shareholder.

Air Malawi was established as a subsidiary of CAA in 1964, but when CAA was disbanded the present Air Malawi was established, owned by the Malawi government, in 1967. Mainly domestic and regional services are operated, but there is a route to Dubai.

HQ airport & main base: Blantyre
Designator: QM/AML
Route points: Blantyre, Club Makokola, Dar-es-Salaam, Dubai, Harare, Johannesburg, Lilongwe, Lusaka, Mzuzu, Nampula
Fleet: 1 Boeing 737-300; 1 Boeing 737-500; 1 ATR-42-320; 1 Let L-410UVP; 1 Cessna Caravan 675

MALAYSIA – 9M

AIRASIA
Incorporated: 1993

AirAsia was founded in 1993, but did not begin operations late 1996, initially as a regional airline but later switching, after a change of ownership in 2001, to providing low-cost scheduled domestic and international passenger flights. Expansion has been rapid, and the company has set up new airlines, Thai AirAsia and Indonesia AirAsia, in two neighbouring countries, and because of restrictions on foreign ownership, owns a maximum 49 per cent in each. Originally an operator of Boeing 737-300s, the airline is replacing these with Airbus A320-200s.

HQ airport & main base: Kuala Lumpur International
Designator: AK/AXM
Route points: Alor Setar, Balikpapan, Bandung, Bangkok, Bintulu, Chiang Mai, Denpasar Bali, Hat Yai, Ipoh, Jakarta, Johor Bharu, Kota Kinabalu, Kuala Lumpur, Kuala Terengganu, Kuching, Labuan, Lankawi, Luzon, Macau, Medan, Miri, Padang, Pekanbaru, Penang, Phnom Penh, Phuket, Sandakan, Sibu, Siem Reap, Solo City, Surabaya, Tawau
Links with other airlines: Owns 49 per cent of Thai AirAsia (qv) and Indonesia AirAsia
Fleet: Up to 150 Airbus A320-200; 17 Boeing 737-300

MALAYSIA AIRLINES
Malaysia Airlines Berhad
Incorporated: 1971

Malaysia Airlines can trace its history back to the formation of Malayan Airways in 1937, as a joint venture between Imperial Airways and Straits Steamship and Ocean Steamship. Operations did not begin until after the end of the Second World War, in 1947, with a service from Singapore to Penang via Kuala Lumpur. When the new state of Malaysia was formed, incorporating Singapore, the airline changed its name in 1963 to Malaysian Airways, but in 1966 the governments of Malaysia and Singapore acquired a joint majority stake in the airline, and had it renamed Malaysia–Singapore Airlines. The airline was restructured and renamed yet again after the ending of the federal agreement between the two governments in 1971, becoming Malaysian Airline System, or MAS. The present title was adopted in 1987.

Ownership of the airline rests with a number of financial institutions and investment agencies, and at one time Royal Brunei Airlines was a shareholder, while at one time, Malaysian had a 40 per cent stake in Air Cambodge. The airline has an extensive domestic and international network. Today, Malaysia Airlines is the twenty-eighth largest by turnover, having risen rapidly from thirty-third, while it is twenty-sixth in terms of passenger numbers, two steps up from Singapore Airlines. It has a subsidiary, MASkargo, although as yet all aircraft remain in the Malaysian fleet.

HQ airport & main base: Kuala Lumpur International
Radio callsign: MALAYSIA
Designator: MH/MAS
Employees: 20,789
Route points: Adelaide, Alor Setar, Ahmedabad, Amman, Amsterdam, Auckland, Bakalalan, Bandar Seri Begawan, Bangalore, Bangkok, Bario, Beijing, Beirut, Bintulu, Brisbane, Buenos Aires, Cairo, Cape Town, Cebu, Chengdu, Chennai, Chiang Mai, Colombo, Copenhagen, Darwin, Delhi, Denpasar Bali, Dhaka, Doha, Dubai, Frankfurt, Fukuoka, Gothenburg, Guangzhou, Hanoi, Helsinki, Ho Chi Minh City, Hong Kong, Hyderabad, Ipoh, Istanbul, Jakarta, Jeddah, Johannesburg, Johor Bharu, Kaohsiung, Karachi, Kolkata, Kota Kinabalu, Kuala Lumpur, Kuala Terengganu, Kuantan, Kuching, Kudat, Kunming, Labuan, Lahad Datu, Langkawi, Lawas, Limbang, Long Akah, Long Banga, Long Lellan, Long Seridan, London, Los Angeles, Madrid, Male, Manchester, Manila, Marudi, Mauritius, Medan, Melbourne, Miri, Mukah, Muli, Mumbai, Munich, Nagoya, New York, Newark, Osaka, Padang, Paris, Penang, Perth, Phnom Penh, Phuket, Pontianak, Rio de Janeiro, Rome, Sandakan, Seoul, Shanghai, Sibu, Siem Reap, Singapore, Surabaya, Sydney, Taipei, Tashkent, Tawau, Tokyo, Tomanggong, Ujang Padang, Vancouver, Vienna, Xiamen, Xian, Yangon, Yogyakarta, Zurich
Links with other airlines: Alliances with Air Mauritius, Air India, All Nippon Airways, Austrian Airlines, bmi, Cathay Pacific, Dragonair, Egyptair, Garuda Indonesia, Iran Air, KLM, Korean Air, Myanmar Airways International, Philippine Airlines, Qatar Airways, Royal Brunei Airlines, Silk Air, Singapore Airlines, Sri Lankan Airlines, Swiss, Thai Airways, Uzbekistan Airways (all qv)
Passengers carried: 17.5 million
Annual turnover: US $3,061 million (£2,040 million)
Fleet: 2 Boeing 747-400F; 17 Boeing 747-400; 2 Boeing 747-200F; 17 Boeing 777-200ER; 11 Airbus A330-300; 3 Airbus A330-200; 2 Boeing 737-800; 39 Boeing 737-400; 10 Fokker 50; 5 de Havilland Canada Twin Otter Srs 300 (On order: 6 Airbus A380-800)

TRANSMILE AIR
Transmile Air Services
Incorporated: 1992

Formed in 1992, Transmile Air commenced operations in 1993, initially on passenger and cargo charter flights, and in 1996 was designated the national cargo carrier for Malaysia, and in 1998 launched its first scheduled service between Kuala Lumpur and China. Other scheduled services have since been introduced within Malaysia and to neighbouring states. The main base has moved from Kuala Lumpur to Subang. The airline is owned by the Transmile Group Berhad.

HQ airport & main base: Subang Sultan Abdul Aziz Shah
Radio callsign: TRANSMILE
Designator: 9P/TSe
Employees: *c.* 1,000
Route points: Anchorage, Bangalore, Bangkok, Chennai, Chongqing, Hong Kong, Kota Kinabalu, Kuala Lumpur, Kuching, Los Angeles, Miri, Nagoya, Penang, Shenzgen
Fleet: 4 McDonnell Douglas MD-11; 8 Boeing 727-200F; 2 Boeing 737-200C; 1 Boeing 737-200; 2 Cessna Caravan 675

MALTA – 9H

AIR MALTA
Air Malta Co. Ltd
Incorporated: 1973

Air Malta was founded in 1973 and commenced operations in April 1974, with the assistance of Pakistan International Airways, which also wet-leased the airline two Boeing 720 airliners. The airline had been founded by the Maltese government as the successor to The Malta Airlines, which meant the Malta Airways Company and an associate, Air Malta (which had been formed after the end of the Second World War in 1946, with BOAC, British Overseas Airways Corporation), holding a 34 per cent interest, which passed to BEA, British European Airways, in 1948. The Malta Airlines did not have a fleet of their own; instead BEA services from the UK to Malta generally passed through Rome and Naples, at which point the flight designators changed to a Malta Airlines flight.

The new Air Malta's scheduled services at the outset included London Heathrow, Birmingham, Manchester, Rome, Frankfurt, Paris and Tripoli. The fleet of wet-leased aircraft grew, but in March 1983, the airline introduced the first of three Boeing 737s purchased new from the manufacturer, which were later joined by another two aircraft of the same type.

Air Malta has obvious limits set on its expansion by the small size of its home market, with a population of less than 400,000 people. It was involved with a British charter airline, Excalibur Airways, founded in 1992 to take over the operations of Trans European Airways, but this airline has since ceased operations. More recently, in 1995, Air Malta helped found an Italian regional airline, AZZURRAair, based at Bergamo, and which operated three BAe Avro RJ85s, although these were replaced by three smaller ex-Air Malta RJ70s.

The fleet has grown steadily since 1983, with eleven aircraft undertaking charters, as well as scheduled services to almost forty destinations in Europe, North Africa and the Middle East. The airline is standardising on Airbus narrow bodies.

In 1995, the airline introduced a direct Malta–New York service, using space on a Balkan Bulgarian service for a period, but this operation has now ended. A subsidiary, Malta Air Charter, operates a helicopter service between Malta and its smaller sister island of Gozo using Mil Mi-8 helicopters.

HQ airport & main base: Malta, Luqa International
Radio callsign: AIR MALTA
Designator: KM/AMC
Employees: 1,758
Route points: Abu Dhabi, Amsterdam, Bahrain, Berlin-Tegel, Birmingham, Brussels, Budapest, Cairo, Casablanca, Catania, Copenhagen, Damascus, Dubai, Dublin, Düsseldorf, Frankfurt, Geneva, Glasgow, Hamburg, Istanbul, Larnaca, Lisbon, London, Lyon, Malta, Manchester, Marseilles, Milan, Monastir, Munich, Oslo, Palermo, Paris, Rome, Stockholm, Tunis, Vienna, Zurich
Links with other airlines: A subsidiary is Malta Air Charter. A 25 per cent stake is held in Medavia (qv). Marketing alliance with Balkan Bulgarian (qv)
Fleet: 5 Airbus A320-200; 2 Boeing 737-300; 4 Airbus A319-100

EUROPEAN 2000 AIRLINES
Incorporated: 2000

Although founded in 2000, European 2000 did not commence operations until 2005, operating flights between Malta and Sicily.

HQ airport & main base: Malta, Luqa International
Designator: EUT
Employees: 15
Route points: Catania, Malta, Trapani
Fleet: 2 Fairchild Metro 23

MEDAVIA
Incorporated: 1979

Although based in Malta, a substantial part of Medavia's operations is in support of the oil and natural gas industries in North Africa. Passenger and cargo charter flights are provided. Air Malta has a 25 per cent stake in the airline, with Libyan interests holding the remainder.

HQ airport & main base: Malta, Luqa International
Radio callsign: MEDAVIA
Designator: MDM
Links with other airlines: Air Malta (qv) has a 25 per cent stake
Fleet: 1 Bombardier Dash 8 Q100; 2 Raytheon Beech 1900D; 3 CASA C-212

MAURITIUS – 3B

AIR MAURITIUS
Incorporated: 1967

Air Mauritius was founded in 1967 as the country's national carrier, with the support of Air France, Air India and British Airways, all of which invested in the airline and initially provided block space on their aircraft. In 1977, the airline assumed responsibility for operating its own services, and has now developed a route network embracing Africa, Australia, Asia and Europe.

Air Mauritius Holdings has a 51 per cent majority stake in the airline, with another 20 per cent publicly held, while some 9 per cent remains in the hands of the original three investing airlines and the government has 4.53 per cent.

HQ airport & main base: Sir Seewoosagur Ramgoolam International Airport, Mauritius
Radio callsign: AIRMAURITIUS
Designator: MK/MAU
Employees: 1,481

Route points: Antananarivo, Cape Town, Chennai, Delhi, Dubai, Durban, Düsseldorf, Frankfurt, Geneva, Hong Kong, Johannesburg, Kuala Lumpur, London, Mahe, Mauritius, Melbourne, Milan, Mumbai, Munich, Nairobi, Paris, Perth, Reunion, Rodrigues, Rome, Saint Denis de la Reunion, Saint Pierre de la Reunion, Singapore, Sydney, Vienna, Zurich
Links with other airlines: Air France has a 2.78 per cent interest, British Airways 3.34 per cent, Air India 2.56 per cent (all qv). Marketing alliances with Air Austral, Air France, Air India, Air Madagascar, Air Seychelles, Austrian Airlines, Emirates, LTU International, Malaysian Airlines (all qv)
Fleet: 8 Airbus A340-300; 2 Airbus A319-100; 1 ATR-72-500; 2 ATR-42

MEXICO – XA

The past twenty-five years have seen a substantial number of new airlines started in Mexico, including the country's first low-cost carrier. More recently, free trade with the United States and Canada has fuelled the expansion of air transport in Mexico, but even so, there have been a number of airlines that have failed, including AeroExo.

AERO CALIFORNIA

Aero California SA de CV
Incorporated: 1982

Originally founded in 1982 as a regional airline, operating from La Paz in Baja California, the initial fleet included Douglas DC-3s, which were later joined by a Convair 340 Metropolitan and small Cessna and Beech twins. Domestic services over a wider area started in 1989, and today the airline is the third largest in Mexico, while the route network has extended, and reaches as far north as Los Angeles in the United States and throughout Mexico.

HQ airport & main base: La Paz, Baja California
Radio callsign: AEROCALIFORNIA
Designator: JR/SER
Employees: 1,800
Route points: Aguascalientes, Chihuahua, Ciudad Juarez, Ciudad Obregon, Ciudad Victoria, Colima, Culiacan, Durango, Guadalajara, Hermosillo, La Paz, Leon/Guanajuato, Loreto, Los Mochis, Manzanillo, Mazatlan, Mérida, Mexico City, Monterrey, Puebla, Puerto Vallarta, San Jose Cabo, Tampico, Tepic, Tijuana, Torreon, Verracruz, Villahermosa
Fleet: 2 McDonnell Douglas DC-9-10; 17 McDonnell Douglas DC-9-30

AEROLITORAL

Servicios Aereos Litoral SA de CV
Incorporated: 1989

Founded in 1989, Aerolitoral became a subsidiary of Aeromexico in 1990, and has operated as the parent airline's feeder operator since, using Aeromexico flight numbers. Over the past decade, the Fairchild Metro fleet has been replaced by Embraer regional jets and Saab 340B turboprops.

HQ airport & main base: Monterrey Gen Mariano Escobedo International, but also has a major base and hub at Mexico City
Radio callsign: COSTERA
Designator: Aeromexico AM/AMX
Route points: Included in the Aeromexico network
Links with other airlines: A subsidiary of Aeromexico (qv), and uses Aeromexico flight numbers
Fleet: 25 Embraer ERJ-145LR; 11 Saab 340B

AEROMAR

Transportes Aeromar SA de CV
Incorporated: 1987

Aeromar was formed in 1987 and has taken over a number of shorter and less busy services previously operated by Aeromexico, mainly domestic but with one US route, while a number of other US destinations are served through a code-sharing arrangement with Aeromexico. It has a marketing alliance with both Aeromexico and Mexicana. Ownership rests with the publicly listed Aeromar Group. The fleet has almost doubled in size since 2000.

HQ airport & main base: Mexico City Lic Benito Juarez International
Radio callsign: TRANS-AEROMAR
Designator: VW/TAO
Employees: 995
Route points: Acapulco, Aquascalientes, Campeche, Cancun, Chihuahua, Corpus Christi, Cuidad del Carmen, Ciudad Juarez, Ciudad Victoria, Colima, Culiacan, Durango, Hermosilo, Jalapa, Lazaro Cardenas, Leon/Guanajuato, Manzanillo, Matamoros, Mérida, Mexico City, Minatitlan, Monterrey, Morelia, Oaxaca, Poza Rica, Puebla, Puerto Vallarta, Queretaro, Reynosa, Salina Cruz, San Jose Cabo, San Luis Potosi, Tampico, Tepic, Uruapan, Veracruz, Villahermosa, Zacatacas
Links with other airlines: Marketing alliances with Aeromexico, Mexicana and United Airlines (all qv)
Fleet: 10 ATR-42-500; 5 ATR-42-320

AEROMEXICO
Aerovias de Mexico SA de CV
Incorporated: 1988

Although Aeromexico only dates from 1988, the airline can trace its origins to as early as 1934, when Aeronaves de Mexico was formed with a small fleet of Beech aircraft. The airline was granted an experimental permit by the Mexican government in September of that year to operate a scheduled service between Mexico City and Acapulco, now Mexico's bustling main tourist resort but at the time just a small fishing village. The licence for this service was later made permanent.

In 1940, Pan American World Airways acquired a 40 per cent interest in Aeronaves, and in 1941 services were inaugurated to Mazatlan and La Paz (Mexico). No less important, in 1940 the airline also made the first of many acquisitions, buying Transportes Aereos de Pacifico, following this in 1943 with the acquisition of Taxi Aereo de Oaxaca, giving Aeronaves a route network to the north, west and south of Mexico City. In 1944, when Lineas Aereas Jesus Sarabia collapsed, Aeronaves acquired that airline's route rights.

A major acquisition came in 1952, when a major domestic operator, LAMSA, Lineas Aereas Mexicanas SA, which also dated from 1934, was acquired when United Air Lines decided to dispose of its interest in the Mexican company. This gave Aeronaves important routes in northern and central Mexico. Further expansion in the north of the country followed in 1954, with the acquisition of Aerovias Reforma taking the route network right to the border with the United States, which proved useful, given the great difficulty encountered in obtaining international route permits. One route taken over with Aerovias Reforma, Mexico City to Tijuana, a town on the border and just thirty miles from San Diego in California, became the airline's most important route at the time, to the extent that two Lockheed Constellations were leased from Pan American to operate the service, while the rest of the fleet consisted of Douglas DC-3s and DC-4s.

The airline finally received permission to operate its first international route in 1957, the same year that Pan American finally disposed of its shareholding to Mexican interests. The first route was from Mexico City to New York, and marked a change of emphasis for the airline, away from domestic and towards international route development. The grant of the international permit had probably been helped by Aeronaves forming Aerolineas Mexicanas, at government request, the previous year, as a carrier intended to operate unprofitable but socially necessary services.

This promising progress was arrested in 1959 by a strike by Mexican airline pilots. The impact on Aeronaves was so devastating that it had to be nationalised to remain operational. A government-appointed administrator ensured that the airline covered its expenses without losses as soon as possible. A reorganisation followed, with greater standardisation of the fleet, with Douglas DC-3s and DC-6s, plus two new Bristol Britannia 302s. Domestic air fares were increased to more economic levels, and a Douglas DC-8 was ordered for the prestigous New York service.

Aeronaves was not the only airline to suffer from the pilots' strike, and in 1960 the airline had to acquire two bankrupt airlines, Aerolineas Mexicanas and Trans Mar de Cortes. The former was the airline established by Aeronaves to operate many unprofitable routes, but at least in the latter, Aeronaves gained a valuable route to Los Angeles. The following year, Aeronaves acquired Aerovias Guest when SAS sold its interest to Aeronaves. This gave Aeronaves not only routes into South America, but a profitable Mexico City–Miami service as well. Nevertheless, a shortage of suitable aircraft meant that some of the Aerovias Guest routes had to be suspended for a while. By the middle 1960s, Aeronaves was operating a fleet in which the Douglas DC-3 still played a prominent part, with a dozen of these aircraft, as well as five Douglas DC-8s and nine DC-9s in service.

The difficulties facing any airline which attempts to do, if not everything, then at least everything ranging from local domestic feeder services through to intercontinental operations, was eventually recognised, and in 1970 a government plan saw domestic airlines rationalised into an integrated air transport system under Aeronaves de Mexico, and organised into eight smaller carriers, many of which today operate under Aeromexico flight numbers.

Two years later, the current title was adopted, and the airline continued to operate until 1988, when it was declared bankrupt by the Mexican government, its only shareholder at the time. A bank was appointed as liquidiator and prepared a six-month recovery programme, although the airline which emerged was much reduced from the pre-bankruptcy Aeromexico. Renamed Aerovias de Mexico, it retained the name Aeromexico for trading purposes. A consortium of business interests took a majority shareholding in the airline.

In 1996 CINTRA, a Mexican trading group, acquired 99.2 per cent of Aeromexico's shares and

99.9 per cent of those of its rival, Mexicana. While the two airlines continue to operate with their separate identities, this effectively puts Mexican commercial aviation into one group, along with AeroPeru.

Other group companies in Mexico include Aerolitoral, Aerocaribe and Aeromexpress, with the latter operating freight terminals. Combined, Aeromexico and Mexicana are the twenty-seventh largest airline group by annual turnover and the largest in Latin America, although Varig of Brazil carries more passengers.

Aeromexico was a founder member of the Sky Team global airline alliance in 2000.

HQ airport & main base: Mexico City Lic Benito Juarez International, with additional bases/hubs at Guadalajara, Monterrey, Tijuana
Radio callsign: AEROMEXICO
Designator: AM/AMX
Employees: 6,773
Route points: Acapulco, Aguascalientes, Atlanta, Barcelona, Boston, Campeche, Cancun, Chihuahua, Chicago, Ciudad del Carmen, Ciudad Juarez, Ciudad Obregon, Ciudad Victoria, Colima, Cozumel, Culiacan, Durango, Guadalajara, Guerrero Negro, Hermosilla, Houston, Hualulco, Ixtapa/Zhuatanejo, Las Vegas, Lima, Loreto, Los Angeles, Los Mochis, Madrid, Manzanillo, Matamoros, Mazatlan, Mérida, Mexicali, Mexico City, Miami, Minatitlan, Monterrey, Morelia, New York-JFK, Oakland, Oaxaca, Ontario, Orlando, Paris-CDG, Phoenix, Piedras Negras, Portland, Poza Rica, Perto Vallarta, Punta Arenas, Queretaro, Reynosa, Sacramento, Salina Cruz, Salt Lake City, San Antonio, San Diego, San Francisco, San Jose, San Jose Cabo, San Luis Potosi, San Salvador, Santiago, Sao Paulo, Tampico, Tapachula, Tepic, Tijuana, Torreon, Uruapan, Tucson, Vancouver, Vera Cruz, Villahermose, Zacatecas
Links with other airlines: Member of Sky Team. Sister company of Mexicana, Aerolitoral, Aeromar and Aeromexpress are subsidiaries (all qv). Code-sharing with Delta Airlines (qv), Air Europa (qv), Japan Airlines (qv), LAN Chile, Mexicana (qv)
Annual turnover: US$3,185 million (£2,125 million) (includes turnover for Aeromexico, Mexicana and subsidiaries)
Fleet: 2 Boeing 777-200ER; 1 Boeing 767-300ER; 3 Boeing 767-200ER; 2 Boeing 757-200; 7 Boeing 737-800; 8 Boeing 737-700; 5 McDonnell Douglas MD-82 (leased); 5 McDonnell Douglas MD-83; 14 McDonnell Douglas MD-87; 10 McDonnell Douglas MD-88 (On order: 5 Boeing 787-8)

AEROMEXICO EXPRESS
Incorporated: 1990

Although founded in 1990, Aeromexico Express did not commence operations until 1994. The main shareholder is the Posado Group with 50.01 per cent, but Cintra, Aeromexico's parent, has 49.99 per cent. It does not actually operate aircraft itself, but manages the cargo operations of Aeromexico.

AEROUNION
Aerotransporte de Carga Union
Incorporated: 1998

An international charter airline, mainly operating domestic flights and between Mexico and the United States.

HQ airport & main base: Mexico City Lic Benito Juarez International
Radio callsign: AEROUNION
Designator: 6R/TNQ
Fleet: 4 Airbus A300B4-200F; 1 NAMC YS-11A-200

AVIACSA
Incorporated: 1990

Aviacsa has developed an extensive domestic scheduled network for passengers and cargo within Mexico and into the United States, serving centres as far north as Chicago.

HQ airport & main base: Mexico City Lic Benito Juarez International
Designator: 6A/CHP
Route points: Acapulco, Cancun, Chetumal, Chicago, Ciudad Juarez, Culiacan, Guadalajara, Hermosillo, Houston, Las Vegas, Leon/Guanajuato, Los Angeles, Mérida, Mexicali, Mexico City, Miami, Monterrey, Morelia, Oaxaca, Puerto Vallarta, Tampico, Tapachula, Tijuana, Tuxtla Gutierrez, Villahermosa
Fleet: 6 Boeing 727-200; 2 Boeing 737-300; 23 Boeing 737-200

AZTEC AIRLINES
Lineas Aereas Azteca
Incorporated: 2000

Lineas Aereas Azteca was founded in 2000 and commenced operations the following year, utilising many of the assets of another airline, TAESA, which had ceased operations, and recruiting many of its personnel. Both charter and scheduled operations are provided, including some international routes into the United States. The airline is owned by its president.

HQ airport & main base: Mexico City Lic Benito Juarez International
Radio callsign: AZTEC
Designator: ZE/LCD
Route points: Acapulco, Cancun, Chihauhau, Ciudad Juarez, Guadalajara, Hermosillo, Laredo, Mexico City, Monterrey, Morelia, Oaxaca, Ontario (US), Puerto Vallarta, Tijuana, Uruapan, Veracruz, Zacatecas
Fleet: 3 Boeing 737-700; 6 Boeing 737-300

CLICK MEXICANA

Originally formed by private investors as Aerocaribe, a regional airline serving Mexican centres in Yucatan, the company was bought by Mexicana in 1990 and became part of the CINTA Group, owners of Mexicana and Aeromexico, in 1996. As part of CINTRA, the airline operated feeder flights for Mexicana as Mexicana Inter and also operated charter flights.

The airline was repositioned as a low-cost carrier and rebranded Click Mexicana in July 2005, but in December of that year it was sold to the hotel chain Grupo Posada. It operates an extensive domestic low-cost network and an international service to Havana.

HQ airport & main base: Mexico City Lic Benito Juarez International
Designator: QA/CBE
Route points: Cancun, Chetumal, Guadalajara, Havana, Huatulco, Mérida, Mexico City, Monterrey, Nuevo Laredo, Oaxaca, Puerto Escondido, Saltilla, San Luis Potosi, Toluca, Tuxtla Gutierrez, Veracruz, Villahermosa, Zihuatanejo
Fleet: 13 Fokker 100; 2 Fairchild FH-227

ESTAFETA

Estafeta Carga Aerea
Incorporated: 2000

A scheduled and charter cargo airline operating within Mexico and to the United States, with onward connections throughout the Americas, to Europe and to Asia.

HQ airport & main base: San Luis Potosi
Radio callsign: ESTAFETA
Designator: E7/ESF
Employees: 174
Route points: Cancun, Chihauhau, Culiacan, Hermosillo, Mérida, Mexico City, Monterrey, San Luis Potosi
Links with other airlines: Interline agreements with a substantial number of other airlines
Fleet: 2 Boeing 737-300QC; 1 Boeing 737-300; 3 Boeing 737-200C

INTERJET

Incorporated: 2005

Formed in 2005, Interjet is a new, low-cost carrier operating domestic services within Mexico.

HQ airport & main base: Mexico City
Designator: TBA
Route points: Acapulco, Cancun, Ciudad del Carmen, Guadalajara, Monterrey, Tampico, Toluca, Veracruz
Fleet: 27 Airbus A320-200

MAGNICHARTERS

Incorporated: 1994

Founded in 1994 and commencing operations the following year, Magnicharters has expanded into scheduled services to the main Mexican tourist destinations as well as continuing to operate passenger charters throughout the Americas.

HQ airport & main base: Monterrey Gen Mariano Escobedo International
Designator:
Route points: Acapulco, Cancun, Huatulca, Ixtapa-Zihautanejo, Mazatlan, Mérida, Monterrey, Puerto Vallarta
Fleet: 2 Boeing 737-300; 7 Boeing 737-200

MEXICANA

Compania Mexicana de Aviacion de CV
Incorporated: 1921

Mexico's oldest airline and today one of the two largest, Mexicana was founded in 1921 as Compania Mexicana de Transportes Aereos, taking its present name in 1924. The airline is the second oldest in the Americas and claims to be the fourth oldest in the world, with seventy-five years of continuous operation. It was the first non-American airline to serve a destination within the United States, other than towns on the borders with Mexico or Canada, in 1936 when a service from Mexico City to Los Angeles was introduced.

By this time, Mexicana had already changed ownership twice, being sold in 1924 to two competitors, and again in 1929 to Pan American. It produced a further innovation on the Los Angeles service in 1960, when one of its five de Havilland Comet 4C airliners introduced the first jet service between Mexico City and LA. Pan American sold the airline to Mexican interests in 1968, and in 1982 the Mexican government acquired a 58 per cent controlling interest. State intervention was short lived, however, as the airline was privatised in 1989. Between 1996 and 2005, the airline was owned by the Cintra Group, owners of Aeromexico, but it was then sold to the hotel chain, Grupo Posada. Although under Cintra ownership both Aeromexico and Mexicana were operated as separate companies, in the late 1990s, combined they were the twenty-seventh largest airline group by annual turnover and the largest in Latin America, although Varig of Brazil carried more passengers.

Although Mexicana joined the Star Alliance in 2000, it left in 2004.

The airline has developed a route network within Mexico and to North America, as well as to destinations in Central America and the Caribbean. In 1990, the airline acquired Aerocaribe. which operates many of the airline's feeder services as Mexicana Inter. A major innovation came in 2005, when Mexicana launched Click Mexicana, Mexico's first low-cost airline, with a fleet of ten Fokker 100s.

HQ airport & main base: Mexico City Lic Benito Juarez International, with an additional bases/hubs at Cancun and Guadalajara
Radio callsign: MEXICANA
Designator: MX/MXA
Employees: 6,690
Route points: Acapulco, Aguascalientes, Baltimore, Barcelona, Bogotá, Buenos Aires, Cancun, Caracas, Chetumal, Chicago, Chihauhau, Ciudad del Carmen, Ciudad Obregon, Ciudad Victoria, Colima, Cozumel, Culiacan, Dallas/Fort Worth, Denver, Durango, Frankfurt, Guadelajara, Guatemala City, Guerrero Negro, Havana, Hermosilla, Huatulco, Ixtapa/Zihuatanejo, Jalapa, La Paz, Las Vegas, Lazaro Cardenas, Leon/Guanajuato, Los Angeles, Madrid, Manzanillo, Matamoros, Mazatlan, Mérida, Mexicali, Mexico City, Miami, Minatitlan, Monterrey, Montreal, Morelia, New York, Nuevo Laredo, Oakland, Oaxaca, Ontario, Panama City, Phoenix, Piedras Negras, Portland, Poza Rica, Puebla, Puerto Escondido, Puerto Vallarta, Queretaro, Reynosa, Sacramento, Salina Cruz, Saltillo, San Antonio, San Francisco, San Jose, San Jose Cabo, San Luis Potosi, San Salvador, Santiago de Chile, Sao Paulo, Seattle, Tampico, Tapachula, Tepic, Tijuana, Toronto, Torreon, Tuxtla Gutierrez, Uruapan, Vancouver, Veracruz, Villahermosa, Zavatecas
Links with other airlines: Owns Aerocaribe (qv), which operates Mexicana Inter, and Click Mexicana (qv). Alliances with Aeromar (qv), Aeromexico (qv), Air Canada (qv), Air New Zealand (qv), All Nippon Airways (qv), American Airlines (qv), Avianca (qv), Copa Airlines (qv), Iberia Airlines (qv), Japan Airlines International (qv), LAN Chile Cargo, Lufthansa (qv), SAS (qv), Varig (qv)
Annual turnover: US$3,185 million (£2,120 million) (includes turnover for Aeromexico, Mexicana and subsidiaries)
Fleet: 1 Boeing 767-300ER; 5 Boeing 757-200; 35 Airbus A320-200; 16 Airbus A319-100; 10 Airbus A318-100

VOLARIS

Incorporated: 2005

Originally founded as Vuela, Volaris commenced operations in 2006, operating low-cost flights, initially within Mexico, but with plans for international services. The initial fleet of four Airbus A319s is set to grow to twenty.

HQ airport & main base: Toluca Lic Adolfo Lopez Mateos
Radio callsign: VOLARIS
Designator: VLO
Route points: Cancun, Guadalajara, Mexico City, Monterrey, Tijuana, Tolucca
Fleet: 20 Airbus A319-100

MOLDOVA – ER

One of the many small republics coping with post-Soviet independence, Moldova has established a substantial, yet fragmented, air transport industry over the past twenty years.

AEROCOM

Aeroportual International Marculesti
Incorporated: 1998

The Moldovan pasenger and cargo charter airline, operating a variety of Antonov aircraft.

HQ airport & main base: Chisinau
Radio callsign: AEROCOM
Designator: MCC

Fleet: 3 Antonov An-26; 3 Antonov An-24RV; 1 Antonov An-12

AIR MOLDOVA
Incorporated: 1992

Created as the state-owned flag carrier of the Republic of Moldova when that state became independent of the former Soviet Union, Air Moldova was based on the former local Aeroflot division. Although charter flights are operated, its main business is the operation of scheduled services to European capitals. The fleet is still predominantly Soviet-era, but Western equipment is gradually being introduced.

HQ airport & main base: Chisinau International
Radio callsign: AIR MOLDOVA
Designator: 9U/MLD
Route points: Amsterdam, Athens, Bucharest, Donetsk, Ekaterinburg, Istanbul, Krasnodar, Larnaca, Lisbon, Mineralnye Vody, Minsk, Moscow, Prague, Rome, Samara, Sochi, Tblisi, Volgograd
Fleet: 2 Airbus A320-200; 1 Tupolev Tu-154B; 5 Tupolev Tu-134; 1 Antonov An-26; 4 Antonov An-24; 2 Embraer EMB-120 Brasilia

MOLDAVIAN AIRLINES
Incorporated: 1994

The first privately owned airline for Moldova when established in 1994, Moldavian Airlines is primarily a passenger and cargo charter operator, but with a small scheduled network.

HQ airport & main base: Chisinau International
Radio callsign: MOLDAVIAN
Designator: 2M/MDV
Route points: Budapest, Chisinau, Timisoara
Links with other airlines: Alliances with Carpatair, Malev (both qv)
Fleet: 1 Tupolev Tu-154B-2; 1 Fokker 100; 1 Antonov An-32; 2 Antonov An-24B; 2 Saab 2000; 1 Saab 340B

PECOTOX AIR
Incorporated: 2000

A passenger and cargo charter airline founded in 2000 at Chisinau, operating a Soviet-era fleet.

HQ airport & main base: Chisinau
Designator: PXA
Fleet: 1 Antonov An-32B; 2 Antonov An-26B; 5 Antonov An-24RV

TEPAVIA TRANS
Incorporated: 1999

A small cargo charter airline that wet-leases its aircraft to other airlines, Tepavia Trans was established in 1999 at Chisinau.

HQ airport & main base: Chisinau International
Radio callsign: TEPAVIA
Designator: TEP
Fleet: 3 Antonov An-28; 2 Antonov An-12

TIRAMAVIA
Incorporated: 1998

Tiramavia is a small cargo charter airline founded in 1998, with operations which are mainly concentrated on the Russian states and neighbouring territories.

HQ airport & main base: Chisinau
Designator:
Fleet: 1 Ilyushin Il-76MD; 2 Antonov An-26; 1 Antonov An-24B; 4 Antonov An-12

MONGOLIA – JU

MIAT MONGOLIAN AIRLINES
Mongolyn Irgeniy Agaaryn Teever
Incorporated: 1956

Mongolian Airlines was formed by the Mongolian government in 1956, with assistance from Aeroflot. Because of the country's considerable poverty, the airline's fleet is mainly old and of Russian and Chinese origin, although one of three Boeing 727-200s was donated by Korean Air in the 1990s, and more recently, more modern Airbus and Boeing aircraft have been added, but in single numbers.

HQ airport & main base: Ulan Bator
Radio callsign: MONGOL AIR
Designator: OM/MGL
Route points: Altai, Arvaikheer, Beijing, Berlin, Dalanzadgad, Irkutsk, Mandalgobi, Moron, Moscow, Seoul, Tokyo, Tosontsengel, Ulan Bator, Ulgit, Uliastai
Fleet: 1 Airbus A310-300; 1 Boeing 737-800; 1 Antonov An-30; 1 Antonov An-26; 1 Antonov An-24RV

MOROCCO – CN

Morocco's history of French and Spanish colonial rule meant that the early air transport links with the country were largely provided by the former colonial powers, and especially the French. Both Air France and Iberia played a part in setting up the national airline, Royal Air Maroc, which superseded two struggling independent airlines. In recent years, a thriving independent sector has emerged.

ATLAS BLUE
Incorporated: 2004

Atlas Blue was founded in 2004 as the low-cost scheduled service and charter subsidiary of Royal Air Maroc, which owns 99.9 per cent of the shares. The airline's foundation can be viewed as a defensive measure against the growth of low-cost carriers in Europe.

HQ airport & main base: Marrakesh Menara
Radio callsign: ATLAS
Designator: 8A/BMM
Employees: 167
Route points: Amsterdam, Bordeaux, Brussels, Geneva, London, Lyons, Marrakesh, Milan, Nice, Toulouse
Links with other airlines: Royal Air Maroc (qv) has 99.9 per cent of the shares
Fleet: 1 Airbus A321-200; 1 Boeing 737-800; 6 Boeing 737-400

RAM ROYAL AIR MAROC
Cie Nationale de Transport Aeriens – Royal Air Maroc
Incorporated: 1953
Morocco's national airline, Royal Air Maroc was founded in 1953 as Compagnie Chrefienne, on the merger of Air Maroc with Air Atlas. Both airlines had been experiencing financial difficulties, and the merger had been instigated by the government to both strengthen the two airlines and eliminate duplication on some routes. Air France and Aviaco, the Spanish domestic carrier, provided assistance and took token shares in the new airline.

Of the two predecessor airlines, Air Atlas was slightly older, having been founded in 1946 under the sponsorship of the French Resident-General as a domestic operator, but with some services to southern France. The initial fleet consisted of ten war surplus Junkers Ju.52/3ms, supplemented by some French Martinets for the shorter routes, and replaced in 1948 by Douglas DC-3s for the busiest routes, from Casablanca to Bordeaux and Marseilles.

Air Maroc had been formed a year later, in 1947, but did not start charter operations until 1948, using Douglas DC-3s. Scheduled services started in 1949, and on the merger with Air Atlas the airline was operating from Casablance to Paris and Geneva.

On its formation, the new airline was owned 34 per cent by the government, with Air France having a similar shareholding. When the airline was recognised officially as the national airline in 1956, on the eve of Moroccan independence, the present title was adopted. The level of state ownership grew steadily, with the share rising to 64 per cent by the early 1960s, and today the airline is owned 95.4 per cent by the Moroccan government, with Air France and Iberia having just under 3 per cent.

The airline operated DC-3s throughout the 1950s, replacing these with Sud Aviation Caravelles and Fokker F27s. The route network has grown steadily, helped by growth in tourism. At one stage, domestic services were hived off to a subsidiary airline, Royal Air Inter, but the airline has been reabsorbed and today RAM operates both domestic and international services, including inclusive tour charters. The current fleet consists mainly of Boeing aircraft, but there are a small number of Airbus A321s, and the ATR-42 turboprops used on the less busy domestic services have been withdrawn. Royal Air Maroc has a subsidiary, Atlas Blue, in which a 99.9 per cent stake is held, as well as 51 per cent stakes in Air Gabon International and Air Senegal International.

HQ airport & main base: Casablanca Mohammed V, with bases at Tangier and Marrakesh
Radio callsign: MOROCAIR
Designator: AT/RAM
Employees: 5,629
Route points: Abidjan, Agadir, Al Hoceima, Algiers, Amsterdam, Bamako, Barcelona, Beirut, Bologna, Bordeaux, Brussels, Cairo, Casablanca, Conakry, Cotonou, Dakar, Dhakia, Douala, Dubai, Düsseldorf, Errachidia, Essaouria, Fez, Frankfurt, Geneva, Istanbul, Jeddah, Laayoune, Las Palmas, Libreville, Lille, Lisbon, Lomé, London, Lyons, Madrid, Malaga, Marrakesh, Marseilles, Milan, Montreal, Munich, Nador, Nantes, New York, Niamey, Nice, Nouakchott, Oran, Ouarzazate, Ouagadougou, Oujda, Paris, Rabat, Riyadh, Rome, Strasbourg, Tangier, Toulouse, Tripoli, Tunis, Valencia, Vienna, Zurich
Links with other airlines: Air France and Iberia each have a 2.86 per cent stake. Royal Air Maroc has a 99.9 per cent stake in Atlas Blue and 51 per cent in both Air Gabon (qv) and Air Senegal International. Alliances with Air France (qv), Air Mauritanie, Air Senegal International, Atlas Blue (qv), Delta Air Lines (qv), Egyptair (qv), Emirates (qv), Iberia Airlines (qv), Regional Air

Lines (qv), SN Brussels Airlines (qv), THY Turkish Airlines (qv)
Fleet: 1 Boeing 747-400; 3 Boeing 767-300ER; 2 Boeing 757-200; 4 Airbus A321-200; 2 Boeing 737-200C; 24 Boeing 737-800; 6 Boeing 737-700; 6 Boeing 737-500 (On order: 4 Boeing 787-8)

REGIONAL
Regional Air Lines
Incorporated: 1996

The first privately owned airline to be established in Morocco, Regional was founded in 1996 and began operations the following year, developing a domestic and international network with a small fleet of regional turboprop aircraft. Charter flights, mainly for tour operators, are also operated.

HQ airport & main base: Casablanca Mohammed V
Designator: FN/RGL
Employees: 160
Route points: Agadir, Casablanca, Laayoune, Las Palmas, Libson, Malaga, Tangier
Links with other airlines: Alliances with PGA – Portugalia Air Lines, Royal Air Maroc (both qv)
Fleet: 4 ATR-42-300; 4 Raytheon Beech 1900D; 1 Raytheon Beech King Air 350

MOZAMBIQUE – C9

LINHAS AEREAS DE MOCAMBIQUE
Linhas Aereas de Mocambique LAM
Incorporated: 1936

Linhas Aereas de Mocambique was founded in 1936 by the Department of Railways and Harbours, and as Direccao dos Transportes Aereos, DETA, began operations in late 1937, flying within the country, which was then a Portugese colony. The airline remained state owned after independence, but in 1980 was partly privatised with the employees gaining a 20 per cent shareholding, and the current title was adopted.

HQ airport & main base: Maputo International
Radio callsign: MOCAMBIQUE
Designator: TM/LAM
Employees: 800
Route points: Beira, Chimoio, Dar-es-Salaam, Durban, Harare, Inhambane, Johannesburg, Lichinga, Lisbon, Maputo, Nairobi, Nampula, Pemba, Quelimane, Tete, Vilanculos
Links with other airlines: Alliances with Hi Fly, South African Airways (qv)
Fleet: 3 Boeing 737-200; 1 Antonov An-26; 2 CASA C-212-200 Aviocar; 1 Embraer EMB-120 Brasilia; 1 Beech King Air 200

MYANMAR (FORMERLY BURMA) – XY

MYANMAR AIRWAYS
Incorporated: 1948

Originally founded in 1948 as Union of Burma Airways, the airline became Burma Airways in 1972 and adopted the present title in 1989, when the country changed its name. For most of its history, the airline has been government owned. In 1993, the airline was divided into domestic and international operators, with the latter becoming Myanmar Airways International, although the two airlines use the same flight designators.

HQ airport & main base: Yangon International (formerly Rangoon)
Radio callsign: UNIONAIR
Designator: 8M/UBA
Route points: Bhamo, Dawe, Heho, Kalemyo, Kawthuang, Keng Tung, Khamtis, Kyaukpyu, Lashio, Loikaw, Magwe, Mandalay, Maulmyine, Mong Hsat, Myeik, Myitkyina, Namsang, Nyaung-u, Putao, Sittwe, Tachilek, Thandwe,Yangon
Fleet: 4 Fokker F28 Fellowship Mk1000/4000; 2 ATR-72-210; 2 Fokker F27 Friendship Mk400/600; 1 ATR-42-320

MYANMAR AIRWAYS INTERNATIONAL
Incorporated: 1993

The international services of Myanmar Airways were separated and put into a new airline, Myanmar Airways International, in 1993. Initially, the new airline was operated as a joint venture with Highsonic Enterprises of Singapore, but the partnership ended in 1998. A further joint venture started in 2001 with another Singapore organisation, Region Air Group, whose Myanmar subsidiary, Regional Air Myanmar, today holds 49 per cent of the shares, with Myanmar Airways holding 40 per cent. Both Myanmar Airways and Myanmar Airways International share the same flight designators.

Development of the airline has been hampered by the isolationist stance taken by the country's government.

HQ airport & main base: Yangon International (formerly Rangoon)

Radio callsign: MYANMAR
Designator: 8M/UBA
Route points: Bangkok, Doka, Kuala Lumpur, Singapore, Yangon
Links with other airlines: Alliances with Jetstar Asia, Malayan Airlines, Qatar Airways (qv), Thai Airways (qv)
Fleet: 2 McDonnell Douglas MD-82

NAMIBIA – V5

AIR NAMIBIA

Incorporated: 1946

Air Namibia predates the country's independence, being formed in South West Africa in 1946, with operations beginning in 1948 under the name South West Air Transport, with its main base at Windhoek. In 1959 the airline changed its name to South West Airways, and when it merged with Namib Air in 1978, adopted that title. In 1987, in the run-up to independence from South Africa, the airline was appointed as the national airline, and on independence in 1991, became Air Namibia. It has been nationalised since independence. International and domestic scheduled services are operated, using an unusually wide range of aircraft, from a Cessna Caravan to an Airbus A340.

HQ airport & main base: Windhoek International
Designator: SW/NMB
Route points: Cape Town, Frankfurt, Johannesburg, London, Luanda, Luderitz, Maun, Mpacha, Ondangwa, Oranjemund, Swakopmund, Victoria Falls, Walvis Bay, Windhoek
Alliances: TAAG Angola Airlines (qv)
Fleet: 2 Airbus A340-300; 3 Boeing 737-200; 4 Raytheon Beech 1900C/D; 1 Cessna Caravan 675

NEPAL – 9N

COSMIC AIR

Incorporated: 1997

Founded in 1997 by the current chairman, Rabindra Pradhan, Cosmic began operations the following year with two Mil Mi-17 helicopters, to which were soon added Dornier 228 turboprop feeder airliners. Most of the airline's operations are connected with the tourist industry and both scheduled and charter flights are operated.

HQ airport & main base: Kathmandu
Designator: F5/COZ
Route points: Bhairahawa, Bharatpur, Biratnahar, Delhi, Dhaka, Jomsom, Kathmandu, Kolkata, Nepalgunj, Pkhara, Simara, Tumling Tar, Varanasi
Fleet: 4 Fokker 100; 2 Dornier 228-100/212

ROYAL NEPAL

Royal Nepal Airlines
Incorporated: 1958

Royal Nepal Airlines was formed by the Nepalese government in 1958 to take over domestic services and also the routes from India to Nepal that had been operated by Indian Airlines. The airline was the first to place the Boeing 757-200 Combi in service. The fleet has contracted in recent years, possibly due to a fall in tourism because of guerilla activity within Nepal.

HQ airport & main base: Kathmandu Tribhuvan
Radio callsign: ROYAL NEPAL
Designator: RA/RNA
Route points: Bangalore, Bangkok, Delhi, Dubai, Hong Kong, Kathmandu, Kuala Lumpur, Mumbai, Osaka, Shanghai, Singapore
Fleet: 2 Boeing 757-200; 4 de Havilland Twin Otter Srs 300

NETHERLANDS – PH

The Netherlands has one of the longest histories of commercial aviation in Europe, with the national flag carrier, KLM, tracing its history back to 1919. While colonial air links were as much a driving force with the Dutch as with the British and French, the Dutch were mainly advocates of landplane operation rather than of the flying boats favoured by Imperial Airways and Air France. Despite the country's neutrality, the Netherlands were invaded by Germany during the Second World War and air transport was grounded. Postwar, the country has had one of the most liberal regimes, allowing airlines to develop – and, of course, some of them collapsed. The national carrier, KLM, was active in investing in airlines outside of its home country, including Air UK, which it later absorbed. The 'open skies' agreement between the UK and the Netherlands was the first of its kind when it was signed in 1986. Although at one time a merger between KLM and British Airways was considered, this may have been ahead of its time, especially since there have been several earlier examples of British–Dutch business cooperation, and the result has been that KLM has effectively merged with Air France, although both airlines have retained their national identities, at least for the foreseeable future.

ARKEFLY
Incorporated: 2003

Formed by the Excel Aviation Group in 2003 and commencing operations early the following year, the airline was initially known as HollandExcel, but after the parent company ran into difficulties its main customer, the TUI Group, acquired the airline and renamed it. It operates international passenger charters for holidaymakers.

HQ airport & main base: Amsterdam
Designator: YZ/HXL
Fleet: 3 Boeing 767-300ER; 1 Boeing 737-800

DENIM AIR
Incorporated: 1996

Denim Air is a wet-lease operator, offering fully crewed aircraft to regional airlines, mainly in Europe. Initially scheduled operations were also flown on the airline's own account, but these have now ceased. The airline was taken over by the Spanish airline, Air Nostrum, in 1999, but a management buyout in 2005 saw Denim regain its independence, only to be taken over by Panta Holdings, the parent company for VLM Airlines of Belgium, at which stage scheduled operations were dropped.

HQ airport & main base: Eindhoven
Radio callsign: DENIM
Designator: 3D/DNM or that of the airline wet-leasing the aircraft
Employees: 275
Links with other airlines: Owned by Panta Holdings, which also owns VLM (qv)
Fleet: 8 Fokker 50; 7 Bombardier Dash 8 Q300

KLM CITYHOPPER
Incorporated: 1991

KLM Cityhopper operates KLM's domestic network and the less heavily used and shorter European services. The airline was formed in 1991 on the merger of KLM's regional subsidiary, NLM, which dated from 1966, and Netherlines, which KLM had acquired in 1988. It is owned 100 per cent by KLM. In a major restructuring of the parent group in 2002, KLM's regional subsidiaries, including companies such as KLMuk, were merged into KLM Cityhopper, with the main emphasis on feeding into the KLM network. KLMuk had previously built up a substantial UK route network, and in addition linked many regional UK centres with Amsterdam.

HQ airport & main base: Amsterdam Schiphol
Radio callsign: CITY
Designator: WA/KLC
Employees: 919
Route points: Domestic services plus many of the shorter flights on the KLM network, including many international flights from Eindhoven and Rotterdam
Links with other airlines: A subsidiary of KLM (qv)
Fleet: 19 Fokker 100; 21 Fokker 70; 14 Fokker 50

KLM ROYAL DUTCH AIRLINES
Koninklijke Luchvaart Maatschappij NV/Air France-KLM Group
Incorporated: 1919

Part of the Air France KLM Group, created through a share exchange between the two airlines in May 2004, which has created the world's largest airline in terms of combined annual turnover, KLM itself dates from 1919, when it was formed at the Hague. KLM operated its first scheduled service between Amsterdam and London the following year, using a single-engined two-passenger biplane, making this the oldest scheduled air service in the world to be operated by the same company. The airline introduced services from Amsterdam to other major European cities before introducing the world's first intercontinental air service in 1929, between Amsterdam and Jakarta in Indonesia, then a Dutch colony, using a Fokker F-VIIB trimotor. KLM was the first European airline to operate the Douglas DC-2 and DC-3 before the outbreak of the Second World War, and postwar, in 1946, the airline introduced its first transatlantic services using Douglas DC-4s from a fleet of eighteen of these aircraft, with thirty DC-3s for European services.

Postwar, the airline expanded its interests in other ways. In 1965, KLM Helikopters (now KLM/ERA Helicopters) was launched, in time for the massive growth in offshore oil and gas exploration in the North Sea. A year later, a domestic subsidiary, NLM, now KLM Cityhopper, was launched, separating international and domestic services, although now this airline also undertakes some of the less busy European scheduled services for its parent. In 1988, NetherLines, a Dutch regional carrier, was acquired. The airline also built up a shareholding in the British regional carrier, Air UK, before acquiring this airline

1. Despite adding Airbus products, the Qantas fleet still includes Boeing 747-400s, such as this one seen over Sydney Harbour. *(Qantas)*

2. Qantas also has a feeder operation, Qantaslink, using aircraft such as this Bombardier Dash 8 Q200 operated by a subsidiary, Sunstate Airlines. *(Bombardier)*

3. The Virgin empire seems set to expand throughout the English-speaking world, with a subsidiary now in Australia, the low-cost airline Virgin Blue, which operates this Boeing 737-800. *(Boeing Airplane)*

4. Austrian Airlines operates Airbus A319s on its European network. *(Austrian Airlines)*

5. Whenever they can afford to do so, the airlines of the states that have emerged from the break-up of the former Soviet Union have invested in more efficient Western equipment, such as this Airbus A319-100 of Azerbaijan Airlines. *(Airbus Industrie)*

6. SN Brussels was the new national airline for Belgium following the demise of Sabena – here is one of its Airbus A319s used on European routes, shortly to be rebranded as Brussels Airlines. *(SN Brussels Airlines)*

7. Above: The other component of the new Brussels Airlines is the low-cost operator Virgin Express. *(Virgin Express)*

8. Below: GOL, the new Brazilian low-cost airline, is unusual in that it is owned by a long-distance bus company. It has standardised on the Boeing 737-800, one of which is seen here climbing away after take-off. *(Boeing Airplane)*

9. Opposite top: Royal Brunei operates six Boeing 767-300ERs on its long-haul routes. This one is seen at Brunei International at dawn. *(Royal Brunei)*

10. Opposite bottom: Air Canada operates Airbus A319s, A320s and A321s, and operates in often extreme winter weather conditions – here is an A320 being de-iced in mid-winter. *(Air Canada)*

AIR CANADA
C-FTJO

11. Above: Air China is one of many airlines that have emerged from the break-up of the old Civil Aviation Administration of China, CAAC, which was once the country's equivalent of the Soviet Aeroflot. This is one of its long-haul Airbus A330-200s. *(Airbus Industrie)*

12. Opposite top: The rapid expansion of air transport in China has included substantial numbers of regional jets, such as this China Yunnan Airlines CRJ200. Poor road and rail surface links will have added to the demand for air travel. *(Bombardier)*

13. Opposite centre: Another Airbus A330, this time operated by China Southern Airlines. *(Airbus Industrie)*

14. Opposite bottom: A Cathay Pacific Airbus A340-600 takes off from Hong Kong's Chek Lap Kok airport. *(Oneworld)*

中國雲南航空
CHINA YUNNAN AIRLINES
B-3013

中国南方航空
SOUTHERN

CATHAY PACIFIC
A9W
09L-27R

15. The Czech Republic's national airline, CSA, is an Airbus A320-200 operator. *(Airbus Industrie)*

16. Egyptair is one of the more recent operators of the Boeing 737-800, which because of the airline's location can reach all of Europe and the Middle East, as well as much of Africa. *(Boeing Airplane)*

17. TACA is the flag carrier for two countries, Honduras and neighbouring El Salvador, as well as having a subsidiary in Peru. The fleet includes Airbus A321-200s, such as this one seen taking off. *(Airbus Industrie)*

18. The Boeing 767-300ER is an ideal aircraft for the longer, thinner routes. One operator is Ethiopean Airlines. *(Boeing Airplane)*

19. In addition to its traditional inclusive tour charters, Sterling has also developed into a low-cost scheduled airline, as the blue plane in the background indicates on its fuselage. *(Sterling Airlines)*

20. Estonian Airlines, part of the SAS empire, operates a small fleet consisting entirely of Boeing 737-500s, one of which is seen here in the hangar. *(SAS)*

21. Blue1 is the Finnish subsidiary of SAS, and this is a close-up of the tailplane of one of its BAe Avro RJ regional jets. *(SAS)*

22. Finnair's small feeder network is operated by Finncom, whose fleet includes ATR-72 turboprops. *(Finnair)*

23. Longer-haul routes are served by Air France Airbus A330s. *(Air France)*

24. In common with many major carriers, Lufthansa has feeder services operated by smaller regional airlines, such as this Augsburg Airways' Bombardier Dash 8 Q400. *(Bombardier)*

25. One of the new generation of European airlines is Germany's Air Berlin, which operates the new generation Boeing 737s. *(Air Berlin)*

26. Originally the charter division of Lufthansa, Condor is now owned by a tour operator and also operates low-fare flights. It is one of the few operators of the stretched Boeing 757-300, seen here in a special anniversary livery. *(Condor)*

27. A line-up of Lufthansa aircraft, with an Airbus A320 in the foreground and an A300 just beyond it. *(Lufthansa)*

28. Hungarian airline Malev moved quickly to adopt Western equipment – here is one of its Boeing 737s at Budapest Ferihegy. *(Malev)*

29. In recent years, the airline has also operated Airbus products, such as this A310-300, especially on routes within Asia. *(Air India)*

30. Liberalisation of the Indian economy has brought growth and increasing prosperity to the country, including the air transport sector with many new airlines, among them Indigo, whose Airbus A320-200 is seen here. *(Airbus Industrie)*

31. Above: Originally founded to maintain links between the Irish mainland and the Arran Islands off the west coast, Aer Arran has expanded and become a successful low-cost domestic airline operating aircraft such as this ATR-72-500. *(Air Arran)*

32. Opposite top: An Aer Lingus Airbus A321-200. At one time the leading Irish airline, Aer Lingus has repositioned itself as a low-fares carrier, doubtless spurred on by competition from operators such as Ryanair, which now has several times the number of aircraft of the older airline. *(Oneworld)*

33. Opposite centre: The Irish low-cost carrier Ryanair has expanded outside of its home country and now has aircraft based throughout Western Europe, and in so doing it has become several times larger than the national airline, Aer Lingus. Just one aircraft type is operated, the Boeing 737-800. *(Boeing Airplane)*

34. Opposite bottom: Air One is a fast-growing Italian independent airline, one of many that have taken advantage of deregulation of air transport in the European Union. This is one of its Airbus A320-200s. *(Airbus Industrie)*

Aer Lingus
A8
09L-27R

RYANAIR

Air One

35. Above: A Japan Airlines Boeing 747-400 in flight. At one time, the Boeing 747 series were unrivalled on long-haul operations, and despite opposition from wide-bodied twins and the Airbus A340, the aircraft still plays an important part on the busiest long-haul routes. In Japan at one time, a special short-haul version was also operated. *(Oneworld)*

36. Opposite top: A Kenya Airways Boeing 767 enters the hangar at Nairobi for maintenance. *(Kenya Airways)*

37. Opposite centre: In recent years, Asiana of South Korea has become a substantial airline in the Far East. This is a Boeing 777-200ER carrying Star Alliance colours – each airline is committed to painting at least one aircraft in Star livery. *(Star Alliance)*

38. Opposite bottom: Jazeera is Kuwait's first independent airline, operating Airbus A320-200s. *(Airbus Industrie)*

Kenya Airways
The Pride of Africa

STAR ALLIANCE
Asiana

jazeera
طيران الجزيرة
9K-CAA

39. Above top: Liberalisation of air transport has come belatedly to Africa, but even in Libya, independent airlines are appearing. This is a Buraq Boeing 737-800. *(Boeing Airplane)*

40. Above: Despite its small size, Luxembourg has a number of airlines, and in addition to the national airline Luxair, it has Cargolux, one of Europe's major all-cargo airlines. Here a Boeing 747-400F is loaded. *(Cargolux)*

41. Opposite top: Malaysian low-cost carrier AirAsia is building its fleet around Airbus A320-200s – carrying the slogan 'Now everyone can fly'. *(Airbus Industrie)*

42. Opposite bottom: Aeromexico is Central America's largest airline. Its fleet includes Boeing 777-200ERs for long-haul routes. *(Boeing Airplane)*

NOW EVERYONE CAN FLY
go
holiday
9M-AFA
MALAYSIA
AIRBUS

AEROMEXICO
aeromexico.com
N745AM
745

43. Above: One of Royal Air Maroc's new Boeing 737-700s takes off. *(Boeing Airplane)*

44. Opposite top: A Pakistan International Airlines, PIA, Boeing 777-200LR takes off. *(Boeing Airplane)*

45. Opposite centre: KLM was a loyal customer of Douglas and then McDonnell Douglas aircraft for several decades, but the MD11, seen here in flight, was the last. *(KLM)*

46. Right: Air New Zealand's feeder operation is branded as 'Air New Zealand Link', and is flown by operators such as Air Nelson, one of whose Bombardier Dash 8 Q300s is shown here. *(Bombardier)*

PIA

KLM
KLM

C-FCPO
link

47. Now known as SAS Braathens, operating domestic services within Norway and Sweden, Braathens has a longer history than its parent airline, and at one time operated to South America and the Far East, hence it was namedBraathens SAFE (South America and Far East). This is a Boeing 737-400. *(SAS)*

48. For longer-haul services, Philippine Airlines has adopted the Airbus A340-300. *(Philippine Airlines)*

49. On its less-busy routes, LOT uses Embraer EMB-170s. *(LOT Polish Airlines)*

50. TAP Portuguese Airlines includes three Airbus A321-200s in its fleet serving European destinations, here showing a new livery with the name TAP in the colours of the national flag. *(TAP Portuguese)*

VA
RA-85689

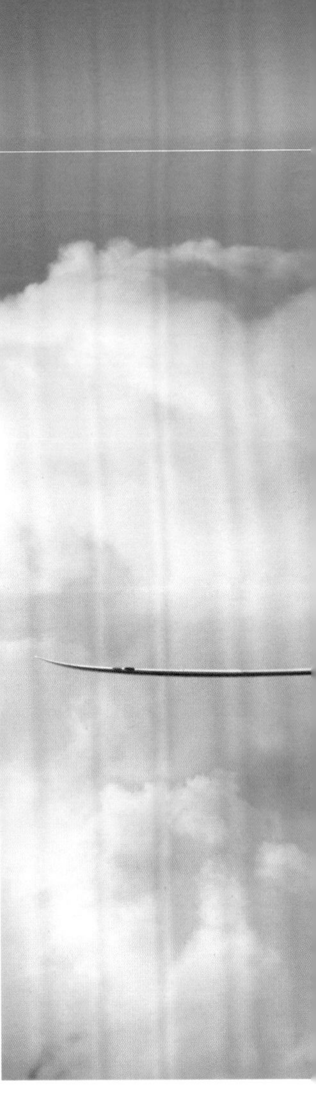

ADRIA
Slovenija

IBERIAregional
AIR NOSTRUM

51. Opposite top: Vladivostok also continues to use the Tupolev Tu-154 trijet on its longer routes. *(Vladivostok Airlines)*

52. Opposite centre: Adria, the main airline for the newly-independent Slovenia, operates two Airbus A320-200s. *(Adria Airways)*

53. Left: Air Nostrum has a substantial fleet of Bombardier CRJ200 regional jets. The CRJ series is claimed to be the world's most popular regional jet. *(Bombardier)*

54. Above: For the future, Singapore Airlines will be operating both the Boeing 787 'Dreamliner', as in this artist's impression, and the large Airbus A380. *(Boeing Airplane)*

SE-RDS
FlyNordic
FlyNordic

THAI

55. Right: Emirates has made the most of its strategically placed main base at Dubai, with a rapidly expanding route network that includes destinations such as Glasgow. Here is an Emirates A330-200 in flight. *(Emirates)*

56. Opposite top: Flynordic of Sweden is a subsidiary of Finnair, operating McDonnell Douglas MD-82s and MD-83s, such as this. *(Flynordic)*

57. Opposite centre: A Thai Airways Airbus A340-600 comes in to land. *(Star Alliance)*

58. Below: Jet2 is a British low-cost and inclusive tour charter carrier, and its origins include Channel Express, an air freight carrier. These are Boeing 737s at Manchester. *(Jet2)*

59. Left: Air Tran and Midwest received the last aircraft off the Boeing 717-200 production line before it closed. *(Boeing Airplane)*

60. Right: Frontier's less-busy routes are served by Bombardier Dash 8 Q400 turboprops operated by associated airlines. *(Bombardier)*

61. Left: One of the world's largest airlines, American Airlines is the only US major not to have sought bankruptcy protection. This is one of its Boeing 767s. *(American Airlines)*

62. Right: Federal Express operates through a fleet of more than 600 aircraft, many of them owned by contractors, while its own aircraft include this Airbus A300. *(Federal Express)*

63. Left: One of the largest airlines in the world, Delta still needs the support of feeder services under the Delta Express brand, here operated by Skywest with a Bombardier CRJ200. *(Bombardier)*

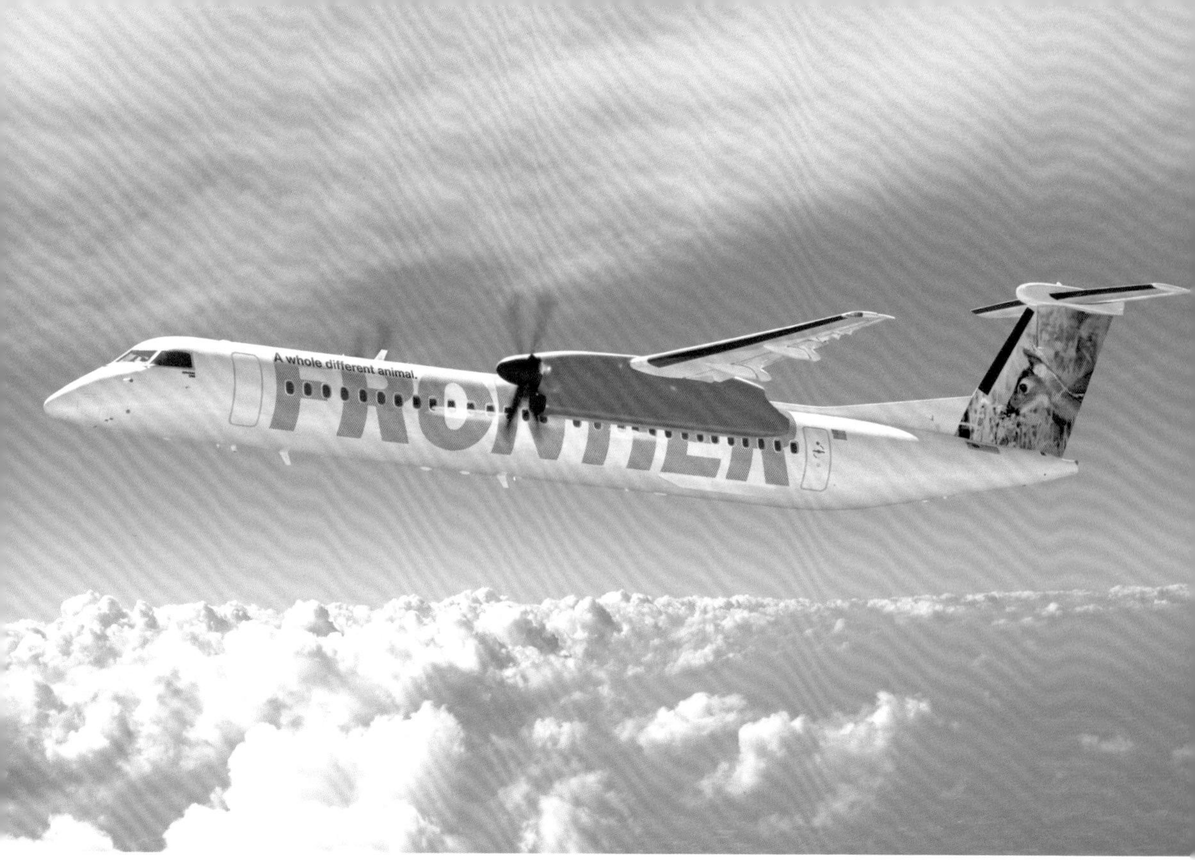

A whole different animal.
FRONTIER

FedEx
FedEx
Express
FedEx

64. A Mesa Airlines Bombardier CRJ700 is pushed back ready for an America West Express feeder service, while behind a Dash 8 Q200 prepares for flight. *(Bombardier)*

65. South West Airlines was the original low-cost carrier. It is set to merge with US Airways, but separate identities will be retained at first. *(South West Airlines)*

66. A United Airlines Boeing 747-400 flying over hostile terrain. *(United Airlines)*

outright in 1997. An 80 per cent stake in Transavia has also been taken, as well as a 50 per cent stake in Martinair and a 26 per cent stake in Kenya Airways. Before this, KLM was among the first to create a transatlantic alliance, taking 19 per cent of the shares in the US airline, Northwest in 1989, and operating a code-share arrangement with this airline. But KLM later agreed to dispose of its shares in Northwest, selling these of in four tranches by 2000.

Even before the merger with Air France, in terms of annual turnover, KLM was the thirteenth largest airline in the world, and fifth largest in Europe, despite the relatively small size of its home market. At its Amsterdam Schiphol hub, the airline introduced a 'wave system' of arrivals and departures, to provide better onward connections between incoming and departing flights, and Air UK and KLM Cityhopper services were included in the system.

For most of its postwar existence, the airline was owned 50.5 per cent by the state, with the remainder in private hands, but the state involvement has been reduced, and a major share offering in 1994 meant that the state shareholding was reduced to just 38.2 per cent. In 1997, KLM took a 30 per cent stake in Braathens SAFE, the Norwegian airline, but later relinquished this. Air UK was bought outright, renamed KLMuk, and then later merged into KLM Cityhopper. Since the merger with Air France, both airlines have been owned 100 per cent by Air France-KLM Group. In return, KLM owns 100 per cent of the shares in KLM Cityhopper and Transavia Airlines, as well as 50 per cent of Martinair and 26 per cent of Kenya Airways. Since the merger with Air France, KLM has also joined the Sky Team alliance. The two airlines have integrated their scheduled and frequent-flyer programmes, but for the foreseeable future are likely to retain their separate national identities.

HQ airport & main base: Amsterdam Schiphol
Radio callsign: KLM
Designator: KL/KLM
Route points: Aberdeen, Abu Dhabi, Abuja, Accra, Addis Ababa, Almaty, Amman, Amsterdam, Aruba, Athens, Atlanta, Bahrain, Bangkok, Barcelona, Beijing, Beirut, Bergen, Berlin, Birmingham, Bologna, Bonaire, Bordeaux, Boston, Bremen, Bristol, Brussels, Bucharest, Budapest, Cairo, Cape Town, Cardiff, Chicago, Clermont-Ferrand, Cologne, Copenhagen, Curaçao, Damascus, Damman, Dar-es-Salaam, Delhi, Denpasar Bali, Detroit, Doha, Dubai, Durham, Düsseldorf, Edinburgh, Eindhoven, Entebbe, Frankfurt, Geneva, Glasgow, Guangzhou, Guayaquil, Hamburg, Hanover, Helsinki, Hong Kong, Houston, Humberside, Hyderabad, Istanbul, Jakarta, Johannesburg, Kano, Khartoum, Kiev, Kilimanjaro, Kristiansand, Kuala Lumpur, Kuwait, Lagos, Larnaca, Leeds/Bradford, Lima, Lisbon, London, Los Angeles, Luxembourg, Lyons, Maastricht, Madrid, Manchester, Manila, Marseilles, Memphis, Mexico City, Milan, Minneapolis/St Paul, Monterrey, Montreal, Moscow, Münster, Mumbai, Munich, Nairobi, New York, Newark, Newcastle, Nice, Norwich, Nuremberg, Osaka, Oslo, Paphos, Paramaribo, Paris, Porto, Prague, Quito, Riga, Rio de Janeiro, Rome, Rotterdam, St Maarten, St Petersburg, San Francisco, Sao Paulo, Seattle, Seoul, Shanghai, Singapore, Stavanger, Stockholm, Strasbourg, Stuttgart, Taipei, Tallinn, Tblisi, Tehran, Tel Aviv, Tokyo, Toronto, Toulouse, Tripoli, Trondheim, Vancouver, Venice, Vienna, Warsaw, Washington, Zurich.
Links with other airlines: Part of Air France-KLM Group. Member of the Sky Team alliance. Has 100 per cent stake in KLM Cityhopper, Transavia; 50 per cent in Martinair, 26 per cent in Kenya Airways (all qv). Alliances with Aer Lingus (qv), Air Alps Aviation (qv), Air Europe (qv), China Southern Airlines (qv), Comair (qv), Cyprus Airways (qv), DAE, FlyLal (qv), Gulf Air (qv), Horizon Air (qv), Kenya Airways (qv), KLM Cityhopper (qv), Malaysia Airlines (qv), Malev (qv), PGA-Portugalia Airlines (qv), Philippine Airlines (qv), Pinnacle Airlines, PrivatAir (qv), Surinam Airways – SLM, TAM Linhas Aereas (qv), Transavia Airlines (qv), Ukraine International Airlines (qv)
Passengers carried: Air France-KLM: 64.1 million
Annual turnover: Air France-KLM: US $24,054 million (£16,018 million)
Fleet: 4 Boeing 747-400ERF; 5 Boeing 747-400; 17 Boeing 747-400 Combi; 4 Boeing 777-300GR; 13 Boeing 777-200ER; 9 Airbus A330-200; 10 McDonnell Douglas MD-11; 9 Boeing 767-300ER; 5 Boeing 737-900; 24 Boeing 737-800; 13 Boeing 737-400; 14 Boeing 737-300; 1 Boeing BBJ (for VIP and Royal use)

MARTINAIR

Martinair Holland NV
Incorporated: 1958

Martinair takes its name from its founder, Martin Schroder, who founded the airline in 1958 as Martin's Air Charter. Before founding the airline, Martin Schroder had operated Piper and Auster aircraft on air taxi work and pleasure flights.

Initially, the airline wet-leased aircraft as required, but in 1961 an ex-BEA Douglas DC-3 Pionair was purchased, and a Douglas DC-4 and a de Havilland Dove soon followed. In addition to air charters and executive flights, the airline soon started to undertake contract flying for KLM.

Eventually KLM acquired an interest in the company, initially at just 28.8 per cent, while a larger shareholder was the Royal Nedlloyd shipping group with 49.2 per cent, which later passed to the Danish Maersk Group when it acquired Nedlloyd. For some years, the airline has had the distinction of operating and maintaining a Fokker 70 used by the Dutch Royal Family and by members of the government, having previously also handled this work on a Fokker F28 Fellowship. The airline also operates under contract to the Dutch government a Dornier 228 on offshore surveillance duties.

In addition to a growing inclusive tour charter business, the airline moved into low-cost scheduled transatlantic flights during the late 1980s, and unusually continued its executive charters as well.

Today, Martinair continues to offer the mix of scheduled (mainly to holiday destinations in the Americas and the Indian Ocean), inclusive tour charter, contract and executive flying, although the latter fleet is not included below, while ownership is now divided equally between KLM and Maersk. A subsidiary is Tampa Cargo, in which Martinair holds a 58 per cent stake.

HQ airport & main base: Amsterdam Schiphol
Radio callsign: MARTINAIR
Designator: MP/MPH
Employees: 3,647
Route points: Amsterdam, Cancun, Colombo, Havana, Holguin, Male, Miami, Mombasa, Montego Bay, Montreal, Orlando, Porlamar, Puerto Plata, Punta Cana, San Jose, Tobago, Toronto, Varadero
Links with other airlines: KLM (qv) owns 50 per cent of the shares. Martinair has a 58 per cent stake in Tampa Cargo
Fleet: 4 Boeing 747-200B/C/F; 7 McDonnell Douglas MD-11F/CF; 6 Boeing 767-300ER; 4 Airbus A320-200; 1 Fokker 70 (owned by the Dutch government); 1 Dornier Do.228-212 (fitted as surveillance aircraft)

SCHREINER AIRWAYS
Incorporated: 1945

Originally founded in 1945, Schreiner has been heavily involved in the operation of flying schools, including one for professional commercial and military pilots opened in 1968. The company's airline operations centre around operating a fleet of aircraft, including helicopters, on behalf of major oil companies and other airlines.

HQ airport & main base: Hoofddorp, with bases at Amsterdam, Brussels, Den Helder, Rotterdam
Radio callsign: SCHREINER
Designator: AW/SCH
Fleet: 2 Bombardier Dash 8 Q300; 4 de Havilland Canada Twin Otter Srs300; plus many smaller aircraft and helicopters

TRANSAVIA
Transavia Airlines NV
Incorporated: 1966

Transavia was established in 1966 as an air charter operator, initially known as Transavia Limburg, operating a fleet of five Douglas DC-6s, to which a Boeing 707-320 was soon added for transatlantic charters. The name was soon changed to Transavia Holland, before the present title was adopted in 1986. The airline took the opportunity of greater freedom in air transport to introduce scheduled services to European destinations during the late 1980s, taking advantage of an earlier open skies agreement – the world's first – between the UK and the Netherlands in 1986 to introduce a service between Amsterdam and London Gatwick. Later, in 1998, the airline became the first non-Greek airline to operate a domestic route within Greece, following liberalisation of the Greek air transport market.

KLM acquired a 40 per cent interest in 1991 from the airline's major shareholder, the Nedlloyd shipping and transport group, which it doubled to 80 per cent in the late 1990s, before acquiring the remaining shares in 2003. The airline continues to operate inclusive tour charters, but has taken advantage of the deregulation of European air services to restructure itself as a low-cost carrier.

HQ airport & main base: Amsterdam Schiphol
Radio callsign: TRANSAVIA
Designator: HV/TRA
Employees: 1,482
Route points: Agadir, Alicante, Antalya, Barcelona, Berlin, Chambery, Copenhagen, Dublin, Faro, Fuerteventura, Genoa, Gerona, Innsbruck, Lanzarote, Las Palmas, London, Madeira, Madrid, Malaga, Marrakesh, Milan, Naples, Nice, Pisa, Rome, Salzburg, Santa Cruz de la Palma, Tenerife, Venice, Verona

Links with other airlines: KLM (qv) has a 100 per cent interest
Fleet: 13 Boeing 737-800; 10 Boeing 737-700

NEW ZEALAND – ZK

The remote position of New Zealand and its long-standing links with the United Kingdom suggest that air transport is important, also helped by a relatively small and scattered population and the division of the country into two islands. Air transport within the country started in 1920 with the formation of New Zealand Aero Transport, which later became Mount Cook Airlines. Because of its small population, New Zealand did not rank as highly as Australia when the Empire Air Mail Scheme was inaugurated in 1937; and when the governments of the two countries and the United Kingdom founded Tasman Empire Airways, TEAL, in 1940, it was largely as a feeder into the Imperial Airways and Qantas joint service linking Sydney and Southampton. For many years TEAL was an operator of flying boats.

The country's geography presented some interesting problems for which air transport provided a solution, including Straits Air Freight Express, SAFE, which operated air cargo services across the Bass Strait, linking the North and South Islands, using Bristol 170 Freighters. Unlike the English Channel services flown by such aircraft, for SAFE the main cargo was sheep.

Being relatively close – some 1,200 miles – to Australia, it was perhaps natural that New Zealand should been seen as a place for expansion by the Ansett Group, which, with the TNT group, took over Newmans Air, which dated from 1985, in 1987 and renamed it Ansett New Zealand.

Long after TEAL became Air New Zealand, ANZ, the airline was privatised in 1989, and again the Australian connection came through with Qantas buying 19.9 per cent. A reverse move in 1996, when ANZ acquired a 50 per cent shareholding in Ansett Australia, which it increased to 100 per cent in 2000, was to prove ANZ's undoing when Ansett Australia was placed in voluntary liquidation in 2001, and ANZ had to have a major capital injection by the New Zealand government early the following year.

AIR CHATHAMS

Incorporated: 1986

Air Chathams was formed in 1986 and operates commuter services from Chatham Island to both North and South Islands in New Zealand, as well as passenger and cargo charters.

HQ airport & main base: Chatham Island
Radio callsign: CHATHAM
Designator: CV/CVA
Route points: Auckland, Chatham Island, Wellington
Fleet: 4 Convair 580; 1 Fairchild Metro 23; 1 Fairchild Metro III

AIR FREIGHT NZ

Incorporated: 1989

A subsidiary of Freightways Express, the airline operates regular scheduled overnight freight services between major centres in New Zealand.

HQ airport & main base: Auckland International
Designator:
Route points: Auckland, Christchurch, Palmerston North
Fleet: 4 Convair 580; 1 Kelowna Flightcraft/Convair CV580

AIR NELSON

Air Nelson Ltd
Incorporated: 1986

Air Nelson evolved from a flying school and air taxi operation, starting scheduled services in 1986. It was later acquired by Air New Zealand, and operates services which are unprofitable for that airline's larger aircraft as Air New Zealand Link.

HQ airport & main base: Nelson
Designator: PG/RLK
Employees: 417
Route points: Auckland, Napier, Nelson, New Plymouth, Tauranga
Links with other airlines: A wholly owned subsidiary of Air New Zealand (qv)
Fleet: 16 Bombardier Dash 8 Q300; 9 Saab 340A

AIR NEW ZEALAND

Air New Zealand Ltd
Incorporated: 1940

Originally founded in 1940 as Tasman Empire Airways Ltd, or TEAL, Air New Zealand was originally owned by the governments of Australia, New Zealand and the United Kingdom, and was intended to operate air services between New Zealand and Australia. Ownership was left with the governments of these two countries in 1954, when the UK withdrew, although cooperation with BOAC continued. During the early years of its existence,

TEAL was a flying boat operator, although these were later replaced by Lockheed Electras. Australia withdrew from the partnership in 1961, and in 1965 the present title was adopted. The airline began to expand at this time, introducing Douglas DC-8s and developing routes to the Far East and the United States in addition to those to Australia. Later, McDonnell Douglas DC-10s supplemented and then replaced the DC-8s.

The airline did not operate domestic services for many years, because a domestic airline, also owned by the government, New Zealand National Airways (trading as National Airways), was formed after the Second World War, while ANZ also bought stakes in Mount Cook Airline and SAFEAIR, with the latter flying Bristol 170 Freighters on vehicle ferry and livestock flights across the Cook Straits between the South and North Islands. National, by this time operating a fleet of Boeing 737s, was merged into Air New Zealand in 1978. A feeder operation, Air New Zealand Link, was started using aircraft operated by Air Nelson, Eagle Airways and Mount Cook Airlines.

Air New Zealand was privatised in 1989, with Brierley Investments taking 35 per cent, Qantas, 19.9 per cent, American Airlines, 7.5 per cent, and Japan Airlines, 7.5 per cent. Brierley later increased their share to 41.8 per cent. In 1996, ANZ acquired a 50 per cent shareholding in Ansett Australia, which forced the Ansett Group to sell its share in Ansett New Zealand to prevent a domestic monopoly emerging, and in 2000 ANZ acquired the remaining shares in Ansett Australia, by which the two airlines were members of the Star Alliance. Brierley Investments sold its stake to Singapore Airlines, and at one time this company owned a 25 per cent stake in ANZ. After Ansett Australia was placed in voluntary liquidation in 2001, ANZ had to have a major capital injection by the New Zealand government early in 2002, reducing the stakes of the remaining shareholders, with Singapore Airlines selling its share, by this time just 6.25 per cent, in 2004.

Today, Air New Zealand has an extensive network, reaching almost thirty domestic points as well as destinations in Australia, South-East Asia, the United States and Europe. Feeder services are operated under the name Air New Zealand Link. Despite the small population of the country, Air New Zealand is the forty-first largest airline in the world by revenue, and forty-fourth by passenger numbers.

HQ airport & main base: Auckland International
Radio callsign: NEW ZEALAND
Designator: NZ/ANZ
Employees: 10,829
Route points: Auckland, Apia, Bangkok, Blenheim, Brisbane, Cairns, Christchurch, Denpasar, Dunedin, Frankfurt, Fukuoka, Gisborne, Hamilton, Hobart, Hoktika, Hong Kong, Honolulu, Invercargill, Kaitaia, Kerikeri, London, Los Angeles, Melbourne, Nadi, Nagoya, Napier, Nelson, New Plymouth, Norfolk Island, Noumea, Osaka, Palmerston North, Papeete, Perth, Queenstown, Rarotonga, Rotorua, Seoul, Singapore, Sydney, Tauranga, Timaru, Tonga, Wanaka, Wanganui, Wellington, Westport, Whakatane, Whangarei
Passengers carried: 11,200,000
Links with other airlines: ANZ owns Air Nelson, Eagle Airways, Freedom Air and Mount Cook Airlines, as well as 1.94 per cent in Air Pacific (all qv). In addition to Star Alliance membership, the airline has alliances with Air Caledonie International, EVA Air, Japan Airlines, Mexicana and South African Airways (all qv)
Annual turnover: US $2,200 million (£1,450 million)
Fleet: 8 Boeing 747-400; 7 Boeing 777-200ER; 6 Boeing 767-300ER; 14 Boeing 737-300 (On order: 4 Boeing 787-8)

EAGLE AIRWAYS
Incorporated: 1969

Originating as a regional airline, Eagle Airways is now a wholly owned subsidiary of Air New Zealand and operates feeder services as a member of Air New Zealand Link.

HQ airport & main base: Hamilton
Designator: WEG
Employees: 196
Route points: Destinations on the Air New Zealand domestic network from hubs at Auckland, Christchurch, Wellington
Links with other airlines: Subsidiary of Air New Zealand (qv). Air New Zealand Link carrier
Fleet: 16 Raytheon Beech 1900D; 1 BAe Jetstream 326P

FREEDOM AIR
Incorporated: 1995

Originally founded in 1995 as South Pacific Air Charters by Mount Cook Airlines, the airline was rebranded as Freedom Air after Mount Cook's acquisition by Air New Zealand. It has also moved into trans-Tasman Sea scheduled services, while continuing to fly charters within New Zealand.

HQ airport & main base: Auckland International
Designator: SJ/FOM
Route points: Auckland, Brisbane, Christchurch, Coolangatta, Dunedin, Hamilton, Melbourne, Nadi, Palmerston North, Sydney, Wellington
Fleet: 12 Airbus A320-200

MOUNT COOK AIRLINES

Mount Cook Airlines Ltd
Incorporated: 1920

Originally founded in 1920 as New Zealand Aero Transport, Mount Cook changed its name several time before adopting the current title with the start of scheduled services in 1961. It has now become a domestic scheduled service operator and is now wholly owned by Air New Zealand, and with its services operated under the Air New Zealand Link banner. Since its acquisition by ANZ, the airline has been steadily replacing its BAe 748s, of which it had eight at one stage. The airline established a charter subsidiary, South Pacific Charters, which has been taken over by Air New Zealand and rebranded as Freedom Air.

HQ airport & main base: Christchurch International
Radio callsign: MOUNTCOOK
Designator: NM/NZM (or Air New Zealand NZ/ANZ)
Employees: 378
Route points: Included in the Air New Zealand domestic network
Links with other airlines: A wholly owned subsidiary of Air New Zealand (qv)
Fleet: 11 ATR-72-500; 1 ATR-72-210; plus Cessna and Piper light aircraft for air taxi/sight-seeing flights

PACIFIC BLUE

Pacific Blue (NZ)
Incorporated: 2003

Founded in 2003, Pacific Blue commenced low-cost operations in 2004 with a route linking Christchurch and Brisbane. The airline is wholly owned by Australian-based Virgin Blue, and its main area of operations is between Australia and New Zealand.

HQ airport & main base: Christchurch International
Designator: DJ/PBI
Employees: 124
Route points: Auckland, Brisbane, Christchurch, Sydney
Links with other airlines: Owned by Virgin Blue (qv)
Fleet: 3 Boeing 737-800

NIGERIA – 5N

While Nigeria was served by Imperial Airways, and then by its successor, the British Overseas Airways Corporation, BOAC, services within the region had been developed by the Royal Air Force during the Second World War. The former RAF services were taken over by the West African Airways Corporation, or WAAC, which had been formed in 1946 by the governments of Nigeria, the Gold Coast (now Ghana), Sierra Leone and Gambia, when these were all British colonies, with investment by British Overseas Airways Associated Companies. In 1958, following independence, WAAC's services were taken over by Nigeria Airways, which also took over the Lagos–Kano service of Nigeria Air Services, and then added extensions from Lagos to Freetown, Bathurst and Dakar.

International services were not new to WAAC. Apart from operating between the then British colonies in West Africa, in 1950 the British Colonial Office called upon the airline to operate a trans-Africa service to Khartoum, and for this and the Dakar service WAAC purchased a number of Bristol Wayfarers, the all-passenger version of the Bristol 170 Freighter. The remaining routes at this time were operated by de Havilland Doves. In 1956, the Wayfarers were replaced by Douglas DC-3s, a much older aircraft, and by de Havilland Herons, which were also replaced shortly afterwards by DC-3s.

The new Nigeria Airways inherited this fleet and continued to operate it until 1963, when the first of the airline's Fokker F27 Friendships arrived, initially working the Lagos–Dakar service, but then gradually taking over the domestic services as well. Even before the airline's foundation, from 1957 a 'pool' service was operated from Lagos to London with BOAC, British Overseas Airways Corporation, using that airline's aircraft. Initially Canadair Argonauts (licence-built DC-4s with Rolls-Royce Merlin engines) were used, followed briefly by Boeing Stratocruisers, then Bristol Britannias, de Havilland Comet 4s and then Vickers VC.10s. This arrangement soon had its counterpart in a service between Lagos and New York, operated with Pan American World Airways using that airline's Douglas DC-8s.

The ownership of Nigeria Airways at the time of its formation in 1958 was with the Nigerian government, 51 per cent, BOAC, 32.6 per cent and

Elder Dempster Lines, 16.4 per cent, but in 1961 the government took complete control of the airline, and this situation remains to this day. Under new ownership, the airline started to acquire its own jet equipment, Boeing 707s and then Boeing 737s, later adding Airbus A310 and McDonnell Douglas DC-10 aircraft to this fleet. This rapid expansion, fuelled by a booming economy with revenue from crude oil production, nevertheless resulted in a period of financial difficulties during the late 1980s, which called for reorganisation and other remedial measures, such as reducing the workforce and suspending unprofitable services.

The problems of the airline nevertheless would not go away, and despite repeated attempts to put the airline on a sound financial footing, in 2003 it suspended operations and was declared bankrupt. Since then, a new airline, Virgin Nigeria, has been formed, operating a domestic feeder service, while Virgin operates some of its flights between the UK and South Africa via Nigeria.

ADC AIRLINES
Incorporated: 1984

Although founded in 1984, ADC did not commence operations until 1991. The company's parent, Aviation Development, became the first publicly quoted airline in Nigeria in 1994. Scheduled and charter flights are operated for passengers and cargo.

HQ airport & main base: Lagos Murtala Muhammed
Designator: Z7/ADK
Route points: Abuja, Calabar, Lagos, Port Harcourt, Sokoto, Yola
Fleet: 1 Boeing 727-200; 4 Boeing 737-200

AEROCONTRACTORS
Incorporated: 1958

Aerocontractors provides a variety of scheduled and charter operations within Nigeria and West Africa, and has a fleet of light aircraft and helicopters for air taxi work. Much of its operation is in support of the oil industry. Ownership is mainly by the Nigerian Mofta West Africa Group, with 60 per cent, but also includes a 40 per cent stake by Canadian Helicopters.

HQ airport & main base: Lagos Murtala Muhammed
Designator: AJ/NIG
Employees: 700
Route points: Abuja, Accra, Benin City, Calabar, Lagos, Malabo, Port Harcourt, Warri
Fleet: (Excluding rotary-wing and light aircraft) 2 Boeing 737-300; 4 Bombardier Dash 8 Q300; 2 de Havilland Canada Twin Otter

ARIK AIR
Incorporated: 2006

Arik Air was founded by the owners, Ojemai Investments, to take over the domestic routes of the former Nigeria Airways, with the first service between Lagos and Abuja on 30 October 2006, using a Bombardier CRJ900ER.

HQ airport & main base: Lagos Murtala Muhammed
Radio callsign: Arik
Designator: W3/ARA
Route points: Abuja, Benin City, Calabar, Enugu, Lagos, Port Harcourt
Fleet: 2 Boeing 737-300; 4 Bombardier CRJ900ER; 1 Bombardier Dash 8 Q300

DANA
Dornier Aviation Nigeria
Incorporated: 1979

Operating scheduled and charter flights in Nigeria, as well as running a fixed-base operation and undertaking air work such as agricultural flying and photography, Dornier Aviation Nigeria was founded in 1979. As the name implies, it uses Dornier aircraft exclusively. Ownership is divided, Nigeria Airways holding 40 per cent of the shares and other interests, mainly foreign, holding the remainder.

HQ airport & main base: Kaduna
Designator: DAV
Employees: 207
Route points: Services operated from Abuja, Lagos and Port Harcourt
Links with other airlines: Nigeria Airways has a 40 per cent share
Fleet: 2 Dornier 328-110; 14 Dornier 228-212

KABO AIR
Incorporated: 1980

A Nigerian domestic airline, Kabo Air was founded in 1980 and commenced operations the following year, developing a network of services from its base at Kano and using two Boeing 727s and a McDonnell Douglas DC-8. The airline also undertook international charters, including pilgrimage flights to Saudi Arabia. It is named after its founder, who was chairman for many years.

HQ airport & main base: Kano Mallam Aminu International
Radio callsign: KABO
Designator: KO/QNK
Main destinations served: Scheduled flights linking domestic destinations, plus international charters
Fleet: 3 Boeing 747-200B; 2 Boeing 747-100; 2 Boeing 727-200; 1 Boeing 727-100

VIRGIN NIGERIA
Incorporated: 2003

Founded in 2003 by Virgin Atlantic Airways, with a 49 per cent stake, and Nigerian institutional investors, Virgin Nigeria began operations in 2004, operating both domestic and international services in place of the bankrupt national carrier, Nigeria Airways. Links with London and Johannesburg use Virgin Atlantic aircraft.

HQ airport & main base: Lagos Murtala Muhammed
Radio callsign: NIGERIA
Designator: VK
Route points: Abuja, Accra, Dakar, Douala, Johannesburg, Lagos, London, Port Harcourt
Links with other airlines: Virgin Atlantic (qv) has a 49 per cent stake
Fleet: 1 Airbus A340-300; 1 Airbus A330-200; 2 Airbus A320-200; 7 Boeing 737-300

NORWAY – LN

(*See also* SCANDINAVIA)

As Norway is one of the countries that comprise the consortium owning Scandinavian Airlines System, SAS, this section should be read in conjunction with that for Scandinavia.

Norway, with its long and heavily indented coastline, is ideal territory for internal air transport, otherwise anyone travelling any distance is either compelled to change between road or rail transport and ferries, or take a slow, coasting steamer. The oldest surviving Norwegian airline is Wideroe, albeit now owned by SAS, founded in 1934.

Nevertheless, while Norway's own airline, NDL, was the country's contribution when SAS was formed, there were other airlines, and of these the most interesting was Braathens South American and Far East Air Transport, Braathens SAFE. Braathens was born out of the need for a shipowner to move his crews around without bringing ships back to home waters – a reflection of the strength of Norwegian shipping, which did more than simply transport goods to and from Norway but was also heavily involved in the 'cross trades', that is, shipping services linking other countries. Later, Braathens' routes were contributed to the SAS network, leaving the airline for many years as Norway's main domestic airline, despite its exotic title.

In recent years, one Norwegian airline that has disappeared, Fred Olsen's Air Transport, also had a shipowning connection, while Braathens is now part of SAS. Nevertheless, new airlines have also appeared, including a low-cost carrier, Norwegian.

KATO AIRLINE
Incorporated: 1995

A small airline owned by the Karlsen family and formed in 1995, Kato operates scheduled passenger and cargo flights from Evenes as well as night mail flights for the Norwegian postal authorities.

HQ airport & main base: Harstad Evenes
Radio callsign: KATO
Designator: 6S/KAT
Route points: Bodo, Evenes, Narvik, Rost
Fleet: 2 Dornier 228-212; 2 Cessna Caravan 675

NORWEGIAN
Incorporated: 2002

Norwegian was formed in 2002 as a low-cost airline, initially operating on domestic routes. A number of international destinations have since been added. The airline can trace its history back to the formation of Busy Bee Air Service in 1967, which became Air Executive Norway in 1972, while a further change of name to Norwegian Air Shuttle followed in 1980. Ownership rests with a number of financial institutions and transport groups.

HQ airport & main base: Oslo Gardemoen
Radio callsign: NORWEGIAN
Designator: DY/NAX
Employees: 500
Route points: Alicante, Alta, Bergen, Berlin, Bodo, Budapest, Copenhagen, Dubrovnik, Faro, Gdansk, Geneva, Hamburg, Harstad/Narvik, Krakow, London, Malaga, Murcia, Nice, Oslo, Paris, Prague, Riga, Rome, Salzburg, Stavanger, Stockholm, Tromso, Trondheim, Turin, Warsaw

Links with other airlines: Alliances with Flynordic, Sterling (both qv)
Fleet: 14 Boeing 737-300

SAS BRAATHENS
Incorporated: 2004

SAS Braathens was founded in 2004, although SAS had acquired Norway's largest airline, Braathens, some years earlier, in 2001. Known for most of its existence as Braathens South American and Far East Air Transport, Braathens SAFE, the airline took its name from its founder, Ludvig Braathen, a Norwegian shipowner. Braathens SAFE was formed in 1946 and three Douglas DC-4 Skymasters were delivered the following year for the airline to commence charter flying. Initially, the movement of ships' crews was a major part of the business, and flights were between Europe and the Middle East, although gradually these were extended to the Far East. In 1949, the airline was awarded a five-year licence to fly from Norway to the Far East, the journey taking four days. Occasional charter flights were operated to Caracas in Venezuela.

Domestic air services started in 1952, using de Havilland Herons, which were soon supplemented, and eventually replaced, by Douglas DC-3s. The services to the Far East were abandoned in 1954 on the expiration of the original licence because of Norway's involvement in the then new internationally owned Scandinavian Airlines System, SAS. Although the Far East scheduled services were lost, the airline continued to operate charter flights, eventually replacing the DC-4s with pressurised DC-6s, while the DC-3s were in turn replaced on the domestic routes by turboprop Fokker F27 Friendships and, later, the jet Fokker F28 Fellowship. Occasionally, Fokker 50 aircraft were chartered from Norwegian Air Shuttle, which operated four of these aircraft and acted as a sub-carrier for several airlines in northern Europe.

In 1996, Braathens bought a 50 per cent share in Transwede, acquiring the rest of the airline later, giving it a strong position in the Swedish domestic market. The following year, marketing links were established with the Dutch airline, KLM, which acquired a 30 per cent stake in Braathens, as the airline had become known, dropping the, by this time, obsolete South American and Far East, as a domestic scheduled airline with a growing European scheduled network and inclusive tour charter flights. In 1998, Braathens developed its Swedish network still further, acquiring the airline Malmö Aviation Schedule.

By the time of the SAS acquisition in 2001, an all-Boeing 737 fleet was operated with no fewer than twenty-seven aircraft on domestic and international scheduled flights, with a substantial inclusive tour charter operation to resorts in the Mediterranean and the Canary Islands, which accounted for a sixth of the airline's annual revenue.

Today, SAS Braathens has been fully integrated into the SAS network, although the fleet has expanded to thirty-six aircraft and remains all-Boeing, in contrast to that of its parent airline. The main base has moved from Fornebu to Gardermoen.

HQ airport & main base: Oslo Gardermoen
Designator: SK/BRA
Employees: 4,300
Route points: In the SAS network
Links with other airlines: A wholly owned subsidiary of SAS (qv)
Fleet: 9 Boeing 737-800; 4 Boeing 737-400; 14 Boeing 737-700; 8 Boeing 737-600; 13 Boeing 737-500; 16 Fokker 50

WIDEROE
Wideroe's Flyveselskap
Incorporated: 1934

Norway's oldest airline, Wideroe was formed in 1934 and operates mainly scheduled domestic services, although there are also services to neighbouring countries and charter operations as well. The airline acquired Norsk Air in 1989. At one time, the airline counted among its shareholders Fred Olsen, Braathens SAFE and SAS, which obtained 29 per cent of the shares in 1997, and later increased this holding to 100 per cent following its purchase of Braathens.

Since the acquisition by SAS, the numbers employed have doubled.

HQ airport & main base: Bodo
Radio callsign: WIDEROE
Designator: WF/WIF
Employees: 1,438
Route points: Aberdeen, Alta, Batsfjord, Bergen, Berlevag, Bodo, Bronnoysund, Copenhagen, Forde, Gothenburg, Hammerfest, Harstad-Narvik, Hasvik, Honningsvag, Kirkenes, Lakselv, Leknes, Mehamn, Mo I Rana, Mosjoen, Namsos, Newcastle, Orsta-Volda, Oslo, Roervik, Roros, Sandane, Sandnessjoen, Songnal, Sorkjosen, Stavanger, Stockholm, Stokmarknes, Svolvaer, Tromso, Trondheim, Vadso, Vardoe
Links with other airlines: A subsidiary of SAS (qv)

Fleet: 3 Bombardier Dash 8 Q400; 9 Bombardier Dash 8 Q300; 16 Bombardier Dash 8 Q100

OMAN – A40

OMAN AIR

Oman Aviation Services
Incorporated: 1981

Originally founded on the merger of what had been Gulf Air's Light Aircraft Division and Oman International Services, for the first ten years or so of its existence, Oman Air operated domestic services within the Sultanate. In recent years, the network has grown to include other Gulf destinations and the Indian subcontinent. The fleet, which included Fokker and Airbus aircraft at one time, now consists of Boeing 737s and ATR-42s. Ownership is varied, with the Sultanate holding 33.8 per cent, and private individuals the remainder.

HQ airport & main base: Muscat Seeb International
Radio callsign: OMAN AIR
Designator: WY/OMA
Employees: 2,630
Route points: Abu Dhabi, Amman, Bahrain, Bangkok, Beirut, Chennai, Colombo, Delhi, Doha, Dubai, Frankfurt, Hyderabad, Jeddah, Kochi, Khasab, Kuala Lumpur, Kuwait, London, Mumbai, Muscat, Riyadh, Salalah, Trivandrum, Zurich
Fleet: 3 Boeing 737-800; 3 Boeing 737-700; 2 ATR-42-500

PAKISTAN – AP

Pakistan emerged as an independent nation with the partition of India in 1947. Initially, the country was divided in two, separated by India, and with the national airline operating out of both West and East Pakistan, with the former being the larger, more populous and prosperous. For many years, the Pakistan Air Force maintained a regular air transport operation between the two halves of the country, using Bristol 170 Freighters, as air transport saved a considerable distance by sea going round the Indian subcontinent. When East Pakistan gained its independence, all operations were concentrated on what had been West Pakistan. Pakistan was the first non-Communist country to be able to operate air services into Communist China.

While air transport was originally in the hands of Pakistan International Airlines, in recent years a healthy private sector has developed.

AERO ASIA INTERNATIONAL

Incorporated: 1993

A private enterprise carrier, Aero Asia International was founded in 1993 using aircraft leased from Tarom to operate scheduled services and charter flights. At first a leased Boeing 707-320 and six Romanian-built Rombac One-Eleven 500s were used, but these have been replaced by Boeing 737s and McDonnell Douglas DC-9s. Operations are mainly within Pakistan and to the Gulf States.

HQ airport & main base: Karachi Quaid-e-Azam International
Radio callsign: AERO ASIA
Designator: E4/RSO
Employees: 500
Route points: Abu Dhabi, Al Ain, Doha, Dubai, Faisalabad, Islamabad, Karachi, Lahore, Multan, Muscat, Peshawar
Fleet: 3 Boeing 737-200; 1 McDonnell Douglas MD-83; 1 McDonnell Douglas MD-82; 3 McDonnell Douglas DC-9-50

AIRBLUE

Incorporated: 2004

Another example of the spread of the low-cost concept, AirBlue operates within Pakistan on the main routes and also to Dubai, which has many Pakistani migrant workers.

HQ airport & main base: Karachi
Designator: ED/ABQ
Route points: Dubai, Islamabad, Karachi, Lahore, Peshawar, Quetta
Fleet: 2 Airbus A321-200; 10 Airbus A320-200

PIA PAKISTAN

Pakistan International Airlines Corporation
Incorporated: 1954

Pakistan International Airlines was established in 1954, commencing operations with a single Lockheed Super Constellation which operated a direct service between West and East Pakistan, now Bangladesh. The following year, the airline merged at the behest of the Pakistani government with Orient Airways, creating the present Pakistan International Airlines Corporation. That same year, the airline introduced its first international service, operating Lockheed Constellations from Karachi to London via Cairo and Rome, while Douglas DC-3s operated domestic services.

Turboprop operations started in 1959 with the arrival of the airline's first Vickers Viscounts, and in 1960 these were joined by Fokker F27 Friendships, which started to replace the DC-3s. Jet operations began in 1960, using a wet-leased Boeing 707 from Pan American, and a service between Karachi and New York was introduced in 1961. PIA's own Boeing 720s were introduced in 1962. The difficult nature of the terrain in East Pakistan meant that fixed-wing operations were difficult, so in 1962 PIA introduced three Sikorsky S-61 helicopters to the network, although by 1966 traffic, and the runways, had improved enough for fixed-wing operations to take over.

In 1963 PIA became the first airline from the non-Communist world to operate to Peking, now Beijing, in China.

During the late 1960s, the fleet was modernised with the delivery of Boeing 707-320s and Hawker Siddeley Trident 1E airliners, although the Tridents were later sold to CAAC, the Communist Chinese airline of the day.

The war of December 1971, between Pakistan and India saw East Pakistan break away and establish itself as an independent nation, thus at a stroke cutting off a significant part of PIA's domestic network and forcing changes to some international services as well. PIA was then, from 1972 onwards, closely involved with the founding and early years of Air Malta, seconding a management team to the airline and wet-leasing two Boeing 720s in 1973, the same year that the first McDonnell Douglas DC-10s were delivered. Two years later, the first Boeing 747s were introduced, initially using leased aircraft.

In addition to its connection with Air Malta, PIA was also involved in establishing Somali Airlines and Yemen Airways, predecessor of today's Yemania.

Today PIA continues to operate an intensive domestic network, having resisted the fashion towards passing the less busy routes to a subsidiary or a franchisee, and a growing international network. The fleet is predominantly Boeing, but Airbus A310s are also operated, while the Fokker F27 Friendships have been replaced by ATR-42s, while deliveries of Boeing 777s may see some of the older 747s or A310s replaced. Unusually, the airline, which was owned 56 per cent by the state, with the remainder of the shares with private institutions, has seen the state share rise to 87 per cent over the past decade.

HQ airport & main base: Islamabad Chaklala, with additional hubs at Karachi, Lahore and Peshawar
Radio callsign: PAKISTAN
Designator: PK/PIA
Employees: 19,615
Route points: Abu Dhabi, Al Ain, Amsterdam, Bahawalpur, Bahrain, Bangkok, Beijing, Birmingham (UK), Chicago, Chitral, Colombo, Copenhagen, Damman, Delhi, Dera Ghazi Khan, Dera Ismail Khan, Dhaka, Doha, Dubai, Faisalabad, Frankfurt, Gilgit, Glasgow, Gwadar, Hong Kong, Islamabad, Jeddah, Kabul, Karachi, Kathmandu, Kuala Lumpur, Kuwait, Lahore, London, Manchester, Mashhad, Milan, Mohenjo Daro, Moscow, Multan, Mumbai, Muscat, Nairobi, New York, Oslo, Panigur, Paris, Pasri, Peshawar, Quetta, Rahim Yar Khan, Riyadh, Rome, Saidu Sharif, Sharjah, Singapore, Skardu, Sukkur, Tokyo, Toronto, Tripoli, Turbat, Urumqi, Zhob
Links with other airlines: Alliances with Indian Airlines, Saudi Arabian Airlines (both qv)
Fleet: 6 Boeing 747-300; 2 Boeing 747-200B; 3 Boeing 777-300ER; 1 Boeing 777-200LR; 4 Boeing 777-200ER; 12 Airbus A310-300; 2 Airbus A321-200; 7 Boeing 737-300; 7 ATR-42-500; 2 de Havilland Canada Twin Otter Srs 300

SHAHEEN AIR INTERNATIONAL
Incorporated: 1993

Founded in 1993 by the Shaheen Foundation, part of the Pakistan Air Force, and the following year officially designated as the second airline of Pakistan. Initially, domestic services were operated, but the first international service was inaugurated in 1995 between Peshawar and Dubai. The Shaheen Foundation remains a shareholder, alongside the directors, but other interests are also included.

HQ airport & main base: Karachi Quaid-e-Azam International
Radio callsign: SHAHEEN
Designator: NL/SAI
Employees: 500
Route points: Abu Dhabi, Al Ain, Doha, Dubai, Islamabad, Karachi, Kuwait, Muscat, Lahore, Peshawar
Fleet: 2 Tupolev Tu-154B-2; 3 Boeing 737-200

PALESTINE

PALESTINIAN AIRLINES
Incorporated: 1995

Founded in 1995, Palestinian Airlines did not begin operations until 1997. It was intended to be based on Gaza rather than in the more substantial Palestinian territory on the West Bank of the River Jordan, but disputes and hostilities with neighbouring Israel have disrupted plans. Initially, the first services, charter flights carrying pilgrims to Jeddah, had to be operated from Port Said on Egypt's Mediterranean coast, but the base was later moved to El Arish, from where scheduled services to Jordan and Saudi Arabia were started. Although services were transferred to the new airport at Gaza when it opened in 1998, the airline was unable to operate from October 2000, following unrest in the region, and returned to El Arish late the following year. It has a substantial workforce for its two aircraft.

HQ airport & main base: Gaza International
Designator: PF/PNW
Employees: 398
Route points: Amman, Cairo, Gaza, Jeddah
Fleet: 2 Fokker 50

PANAMA – HP

AEROPERLAS

Aerolineas Pacifico Atlantico SA
Incorporated: 1969

Grandly named, reflecting the country's strategic position between two continents and between two oceans, AeroPerlas was founded in 1969 as Aerolineas Islas de las Perlas and operations commenced the following year. From 1976, the airline was owned by the Panamanian government, remaining in state hands until 1987, when it was sold to Raul Espinosa, who became its president for a period. International services began in 1996, with a route to Costa Rica. It is now owned by Apair, but American Eagle Airlines has a 20 per cent stake. Operations are primarily domestic scheduled and international charter.

HQ airport & main base: Panama City Tocumen International
Radio callsign: AEROPERLAS
Designator: WL/APP
Route points: Bahai Pinas, Bocas del Toro, Carli, Changuinola, Colon, Contadora, Corazon de Jesus, David, El Porvenir, El Real, Garachine, Jaque, La Palma, Mamitupo, Malatupo, Panama City, Playon Chica, Puerto Obaldia, Rio Sidra, Sambu, Ustopo
Links with other airlines: Marketing alliance with American Airlines (qv). American Eagle (qv) has a 20 per cent interest
Fleet: 3 Convair 580; 8 Short 360-200; 1 Embraer EMB-110 Bandeirante; 3 de Havilland Canada DHC-6 Twin Otter; 5 Cessna Caravan 675; 1 Raytheon Beech King Air 100

COPA AIRLINES

Incorporated: 1944

Although founded in 1944, with the assistance of Pan American, which took a 32 per cent interest, the airline did not begin operations until 1947, operating domestic services with Douglas DC-3s and ex-military C-47s. In 1972, the airline became entirely Panamanian owned, but in 1999 Continental Airlines took a 49 per cent interest. Services are now operated throughout the Americas and the Caribbean, and the airline is Panama's largest, while a subsidiary is AeroRepublica. Over the past decade, the airline has grown considerably, with a route network that stretches from Buenos Aires to New York, and an up-to-date and enlarged fleet, while employment has almost quadrupled.

HQ airport & main base: Panama City Tocumen International
Radio callsign: COPA
Designator: CM/CMP
Employees: 2,400
Route points: Barranquilla, Bogotá, Buenos Aires, Cali, Cancun, Caracas, Cartagena, Guatemala City, Guayaquil, Havana, Houston, Kingston, Lima, Los Angeles, Managua, Medellin, Mexico City, Miami, New York, Newark, Orlando, Port-au-Prince, Quito, San Andres, San Jose, San Juan, San Salvador, Santiago de Chile, Santo Domingo, Sao Paulo, Tegucigalpa
Links with other airlines: Continental (qv) has a 49 per cent shareholding and there is a marketing alliance between the two airlines. Further alliances with Cubana de Aviacion, Gol Transportes Aereos, Gulfstream International Airlines, Mexicana, TACA International Airlines (all qv)
Fleet: 7 Boeing 737-800; 23 Boeing 737-700; 15 Embraer 190

PAPUA NEW GUINEA – P2

AIR NUIGINI

Incorporated: 1973

Air Nuigini was founded in 1973 as a joint venture between the New Guinea government, with 60 per cent of the shares, and the then three main Australian airlines, Qantas, with 12 per cent, Ansett,

16 per cent, and TAA Trans Australia, 12 per cent. The airline eventually became completely government controlled (through a National Airlines Commission) after the Qantas and TAA shares were bought in 1976, followed by those of Ansett in 1980.

There is an extensive domestic network, reflecting the difficult terrain of the island, with regional international services. At one time plans existed to privatise the airline, but these have now been dropped for the foreseeable future.

HQ airport & main base: Port Moresby Jackson
Radio callsign: NUIGINI
Designator: PX/ANG
Route points: Alotau, Brisbane, Buka, Cairns, Goroka, Honiara, Hoskins, Kavieng, Kundiawa, Lae, Lihir, Madang, Manila, Manus, Mendi, Mount Hagenm Popondetta, Port Moresby, Rabaul, Singapore, Sydney, Tari, Tokyo, Vanimo, Wapenamanda, Wewak
Links with other airlines: Marketing alliances with Qantas (qv)
Fleet: 1 Boeing 767-300ER; 2 Fokker 100; 5 Fokker F28 Mk4000 Fellowship; 4 Bombardier Dash 8 Q200

AIRLINES OF PAPUA NEW GUINEA
Incorporated: 1987

Originally founded as Milne Bay Air, the company undertook operations on behalf of the mining and timber industries and did not receive an airline licence until 1997, when it became MBA Airline, before later adopting the current title. It now maintains a domestic scheduled network as well as undertaking charter flights.

HQ airport & main base: Port Moresby Jackson
Designator: CG
Employees: 426
Route points: Aguan, Alotau, Awaba, Baimuru, Balimo, Daru, Goroka, Hivaro, Itokama, Kamusi, Kerema, Kikori, Kiunga, Kokada, Lae, Losuia, Misima, Moro, Mount Hagen, Nomad River, Popondetta, Port Moresby, Rabara, Salamo, Suki, Tabubil, Tufi, Vivigani, Wanigela, Wipim
Fleet: 7 Bombardier Dash 8 Q100; 4 de Havilland Canada Twin Otter Srs 200/300

PERU – OB

The Peruvian air transport sector has seen many airlines come and go, and the departures have not always been the most recent arrivals, but have included one of the oldest airlines in Latin America, Faucett Peru, which dates from 1928. The airline took its name from its founder, the American Elmer J. Faucett. Throughout its existence the airline was primarily a domestic scheduled carrier. At the time of its demise, it was operating a Lockheed TriStar and a Boeing 727-100, as well as seven Boeing 737s. The airline was Peruvian-owned.

AERO CONDOR
Incorporated: 1975

Aero Condor operates a mixed fleet on passenger and cargo charters as well as a domestic scheduled network

HQ airport & main base: Lima Jorge Chavez International and Cuzco
Radio callsign: AERO CONDOR
Designator: Q6/CDP
Route points: Andahuaylas, Arequipa, Ayacucho, Cajamarca, Chiclayo, Cuzco, Iquitos, Lima, Piura, Puerto Maldonado, Tacna, Tumbes
Fleet: 2 Antonov An-24RV; 5 Boeing 737-200; 1 Fokker 50; 2 Fokker F27; 3 Cessna Caravan 675; 1 Raytheon Beech King Air 200

CIELOS DEL PERU
Incorporated: 1997

A scheduled and charter cargo airline founded in 1997 and operational the following year, Cielos del Peru acquired Export Air in 1998. The fleet is standardised on the DC-10.

HQ airport & main base: Lima Jorge Chavez International
Designator: A2/CIU
Route points: Bogotá, Buenos Aires, Caracas, Lima, Medellin, Miami, Panama City, Santiago, Sao Paulo
Fleet: 6 McDonnell Douglas DC-10-10/30F

LAN PERU
Incorporated: 1998

Founded in 1998, LAN Peru began operations the following year, initially operating domestic flights, but an international route to Miami was introduced before the end of the first year. It is part of the Chilean-based LAN Airlines group, which has a 49 per cent interest, the maximum allowed a foreign investor. Aircraft from other group companies augment the airline's own fleet as required.

HQ airport & main base: Lima Jorge Chavez International
Designator: LP/LPE
Employees: 1,500
Route points: Arequipa, Bogotá, Buenos Aires, Caracas, Chiclayo, Cuzco, Guayaquil, Iquitos, Juliaca, Lima, Los Angeles, Mexico City, Miami, Piura, Puerto Maldonado, Quito, Santiago, Sao Paulo, Tacna, Tarapoto, Trujillo
Links with other airlines: LAN Airlines has a 45 per cent stake
Fleet: 2 Airbus A320-200

STAR PERU
Incorporated: 1997

Formed in 1997 by Valentin Kasyanov as Star Up, initially Star Peru was a passenger and cargo charter airline, but the current title was adopted when domestic scheduled services were introduced in 2004.

HQ airport & main base: Lima Jorge Chavez International
Designator: 2I/SRU
Route points: Chiclayo, Cuzco, Iquitos, Lima, Pucallpa, Trujillo, Tatapoto
Fleet: 5 Boeing 737-200; 1 Antonov An-26; 3 Antonov An-24RV

TACA PERU
Incorporated: 1999

TACA Peru was founded in 1999 by TACA International Airlines of El Salvador, which has the maximum 49 per cent stake permitted a foreign airline by the Peruvian government, with the airline's president, Daniel Ratti, holding the remainder. It uses aircraft from the parent company's fleet as required, and for the most part shares many of the destinations of TACA International, but has in addition a domestic route of its own linking Lima with Arequipa.

HQ airport & main base: Lima Jorge Chavez International
Designator: TPU
Links with other airlines: TACA International Airlines (qv) has a 49 per cent stake. Alliances with Aerosur (qv), Alianza Summa, Lloyd Aero Boliviano, TAM Linhas Aereas (qv)

PHILIPPINES – PI

2GO
Incorporated: 1988

Originally founded as Aboitiz Air by Jon Ramon Aboitiz and Carlos Soriano to operate cargo and parcels services within the Philippines. In 1997, it signed a cooperative agreement with Cebu Pacific, under which it leases the cargo holds of that airline's DC-9s. Name changed to 2Go in 2004, but parent company retains the name of Aboitiz One.

HQ airport & main base: Manila
Radio callsign: ABAIR
Designator: BOI
Fleet: 5 NAMC YS-11; 1 Raytheon Beech King Air 200

AIR PHILIPPINES
Air Philippines Corporation
Incorporated: 1995

Air Philippines was founded in 1995, and operations started the following year. Scheduled domestic and international charter flights are operated, while permission was obtained in 1999 to operate scheduled international services to Hong Kong, Japan, South Korea, Taiwan and the United States, but these have still to be introduced. U-Land Airlines acquired a 30 per cent interest in 1998.

HQ airport & main base: Subic Bay International Airport, with a main hub at Manila Ninoy Aquino International
Radio callsign: ORIENT PACIFIC
Designator: 2P/GAP
Route points: Bacolod, Cagayan de Oro, Cebu, Davao, Dumaguete, General Santos, Iloilo, Manila, Puerto Princesa, Subic Bay, Tuguegarao, Zamboanga
Fleet: 9 Boeing 737-200

ASIAN SPIRIT
Incorporated: 1995

Formed in 1995 by former Philippine Airlines' employees, Asian Spirit commenced operations in 1996 as a domestic scheduled and charter operator intended to take advantage of deregulation of air transport in the Philippines. It remains in employee ownership.

HQ airport & main base: Manila Ninoy Aquino International
Designator: 6K/RIT
Employees: 525
Route points: Antique, Baguio, Basco, Busuanga, Cagayan de Oro, Calbayog, Catarman, Caticlan, Cebu, Diosdado, Dipolog, Luzon, Mactan, Manila,

Marinduque, Masbate, Ormoc, Puerto Princessa, San Jose, Sandoval, Surigao, Tandag, Taytay Tugeugarao, Virac
Fleet: 2 BAe 146-200; 2 BAe 146-100; 1 BAe ATP; 4 Bombardier Dash 7-100; 3 Let L-410UVP; 1 Indonesian Aerospace CN-235

CEBU PACIFIC AIR
Incorporated: 1988

Originally founded in 1988, CEBU Pacific did not commence operations until 1996, initially operating DC-9s. It has since developed into a low-cost scheduled airline, mainly operating domestic services, using a fleet in which Airbus aircraft predominate.

HQ airport & main base: Manila Ninoy Aquino International
Designator: 5J/CEB
Employees: 1,361
Route points: Bacolod, Batan, Cagayan de Oro, Cebu, Cotabato, Davao, Dumaguete, Hong Kong, Iloilo, Kalibo, Manila, Puerto Princesa, Roxas City, Seoul, Subic Bay, Tacloban, Tagbilaran, Zamboanga
Links with other airlines: Alliance with Asian Spirit (qv)
Fleet: 2 Boeing 757-200; 4 Airbus A320-200; 10 Airbus A319-100

PAL PHILIPPINE AIRLINES
Philippine Airlines Corporation
Incorporated: 1941

Although Philippine Airlines was founded in February 1941, and commenced operations in March, services soon had to abandoned on the outbreak of the Second World War in the Pacific, with subsequent Japanese occupation of the Philippines. Services restarted in 1946, and the airline was soon operating an extensive domestic network as well as international services. Nevertheless, the international services had to be dropped in 1954, and for the next eight years the airline concentrated on its domestic route network. The return of the international services in 1962 saw routes established initially to other destinations in the Far East, and then to the United States, before spreading to Europe. The airline used a fleet of Douglas DC-8s for its longer-haul routes during the 1960s and 1970s, augmented by BAe One-Elevens and 748s on domestic and regional services.

For many years the airline's main shareholder was PR Holdings, a group of Philippines financial institutions, with 67 per cent of the shares, while the Philippines government held a 33 per cent stake. This has now changed, with the chairman, Lucio Tan, holding a majority 53.73 per cent stake, the government holding just 4.26 per cent, and other institutions the remainder. The current fleet is predominantly of Airbus manufacture with a small Boeing presence. The McDonnell Douglas MD-11 fleet, originally leased from World Airways, was cut from four to two in 1997 when the airline withdrew its services from Manila to Los Angeles and New York-Newark, although services continue to the western United States. The Fokker 50 turboprops have also gone. There has also been some trimming of services to Europe in recent years, but the number of destinations served in China has grown considerably. Over the past decade, PAL has dropped from being the world's fiftieth largest airline on the basis of annual turnover.

HQ airport & main base: Manila Ninoy Aquino International
Radio callsign: PHILIPPINE
Designator: PR/PAL
Route points: Abu Dhabi, Amsterdam, Bandar Seri Begawan, Bangkok, Beijing, Busan, Doha, Dubai, Fukuoka, Guam, Ho Chi Minh City, Hong Kong, Honolulu, Jakarta, Kota Kinabalu, Kuala Lumpur, Las Vegas, Los Angeles, Macau, Manila, Melbourne, Nagoya, Okinawa, Osaka, San Francisco, Seoul, Shanghai, Singapore, Sydney, Taipei, Tokyo, Vancouver, Xiamen
Links with other airlines: Alliances with Air Macau, Air Philippines, Cathay Pacific, Emirates, Garuda Indonesia, KLM, Malaysia Airlines, Qatar Airways, Royal Brunei Airlines, Vietnam Airlines (all qv)
Fleet: 9 Boeing 747-400; 4 Airbus A340-300; 8 Airbus A330-300; 20 Airbus A320-200; 4 Airbus A319-100

SEAIR
Incorporated: 1995

Originally formed in 1995 to provide wet-leasing and charter operations, Seair has developed a small, domestic scheduled network after being authorised in 1995 to serve the Clark Special Economic Zone. The airline specifically serves tourist destinations.

HQ airport & main base: Manila Ninoy Aquino International
Radio callsign: SEAIR
Designator: DG/SRO

Route points: Busuanga, Catician, Cebu, Cotabato, Jolo, Luzon Island, Manila, Puerto Princessa, San Jose, Surigao, Tawitawi, Zamboanga
Fleet: 2 Dornier 328-110; 9 Let L-410UVP-E

POLAND – SP

CENTRALWINGS
Incorporated: 2004

Centralwings was founded at the end of 2004 and commenced low-cost scheduled passenger operations early in 2005. Initially aircraft have been provided by the parent company, LOT Polish Airlines, which plans rapid expansion of its new venture. Both domestic and international services are flown, with the emphasis likely to be increasingly on the latter.

HQ airport & main base: Warsaw Frederic Chopin
Designator: CO/CLW
Route points: Bologna, Cologne, Dublin, Edinburgh, Krakow, Katowice, Lisbon, London, Lyons, Milan, Rome, Shannon, Wroclaw
Links with other airlines: The low-cost subsidiary of LOT (qv)
Fleet: 5 Boeing 737-400; 3 Boeing 737-300

EUROLOT
Incorporated: 1996

Eurolot was formed in 1996 and started operations as a feeder airline for LOT, its parent company, the following year. The airline was established in order to cut LOT's losses on its domestic route network. It also operates charter flights.

HQ airport & main base: Warsaw Frederic Chopin
Radio callsign: EUROLOT
Designator: K2/ELO
Employees: 275
Route points: In the LOT network
Links with other airlines: A subsidiary of LOT (qv)
Fleet: 8 ATR-72-200; 5 ATR-42-500

LOT POLISH AIRLINES
LOT – Polski Linie Lotnicze
Incorporated: 1929

Poland's state-owned flag carrier, LOT, was formed by the Polish government in 1929 to take over two private enterprise airlines, Aerolot and Aero, both of which dated from earlier in the decade. The two airlines had operated domestic services, and LOT continued these before introducing its first international service in 1930, operating to neighbouring states in eastern Europe and, later, to Greece. Steady progress was made during the 1930s, and by the outbreak of war in Europe, LOT's network had reached many European capitals and the airline had a modern fleet of Douglas DC-2s and Lockheed Electras.

Operations were suspended following the German and Soviet invasion of Poland, although many aircraft had been flown to the United Kingdom once the invasion started. LOT was reformed in March 1945, using ex-Polish Air Force Lisunov Li-2s, DC-3s built under licence in the Soviet Union, and operations were supported by Soviet technical assistance. The route network expanded throughout the late 1940s and the 1950s, although as a reflection of the changed political scene, services to Warsaw Pact destinations took precedence. Ilyushin Il-12 and Il-14 airliners were acquired, as were some Convair 240s, but aircraft of Soviet manufacture predominated in the fleet, and Ilyushin Il-18s followed, before the first jets, Tupolev Tu-134s, arrived, followed by the long-range Ilyushin Il-62. By the early 1970s, the route network extended throughout Europe and the Middle East.

After the break-up of the Warsaw Pact, western equipment started to appear in the fleet, including Boeing 767s for transatlantic operations, although foreign exchange problems and the relatively high capital cost of new European and American aircraft meant that Tupolev Tu-154s and Antonov An-24s still figured prominently in the fleet for some years.

Although the state still owned LOT, from 1992 the company had a changed status as a limited company to permit privatisation, while the fleet became formed entirely of modern western aircraft. In July 1997 a low-cost feeder operation, EUROLOT, was established, and LOT's eight ATR-72-200 aircraft were transferred to EUROLOT. Privatisation came eventually in late 1999, with SAirGroup, owners of Swissair, acquiring a 37.6 per cent stake, and this passed to SAirLines Europe after the collapse of Swissair. Today, LOT is owned by the government with 67.97 per cent and SAirLines with 25.1 per cent, while the remainder is held by the airline's employees. LOT in turn owns both Centralwings and EuroLOT. The airline joined the Star Alliance in 2003.

HQ airport & main base: Warsaw Frederic Chopin
Radio callsign: POLLOT
Designator: LO/LOT

Employees: 3,760
Route points: Amsterdam, Athens, Barcelona, Beirut, Berlin, Brussels, Bucharest, Budapest, Bydgoszcz, Bucharest, Brussels, Chicago, Copenhagen, Dubai, Dublin, Düsseldorf, Frankfurt, Gdansk, Geneva, Hamburg, Helsinki, Istanbul, Kaliningrad, Katowice, Kiev, Krakow, Larnaca, Lodz, Ljubljana, London, Lvov, Lyons, Madrid, Manchester, Milan, Minsk, Moscow, Munich, New York, Newark, Nice, Odessa, Oslo, Paris, Prague, Riga, Rome, Rzeszow, St Petersburg, Sofia, Stockholm, Szczecin, Tallinn, Tel Aviv, Toronto, Venice, Vienna, Vilnius, Warsaw, Wroclaw, Zagreb, Zielona Gora, Zurich
Links with other airlines: SAirLines Europe has a 25.1 per cent interest. LOT owns 100 per cent of Centralwings and EuroLOT (both qv). Member of the Star Alliance. Alliances with Aeroflot Russian Airlines (qv), AeroSvit Airlines (qv), Belavia Russian Airlines (qv), Bulgaria Air (qv), Cyprus Airways (qv), El Al (qv), Malev (qv), Pulkovo Aviation Enterprise, Slovak Airlines (qv), SN Brussels Airlines (qv), Tarom (qv), THY Turkish Airlines (qv)
Fleet: 4 Boeing 767-300ER; 2 Boeing 767-200ER; 3 Boeing 737-400; 6 Boeing 737-500; 4 Embraer 175; 10 Embraer 170; 11 Embraer ERJ-145MP (On order: 8 Boeing 787-8)

SKY EXPRESS
Incorporated: 2004

A cargo airline offering charter services on contract and an ad hoc basis, formed in 2004. It is owned by individuals and a financial institution. It has a subsidiary, Direct Fly.

HQ airport & main base: Warsaw Frederic Chopin
Designator:
Links with other airlines: Owns Direct Fly
Fleet: 5 Saab 340A; 3 Let L-410UVP-E

WHITE EAGLE AVIATION
Incorporated: 1993

Named after the old Polish heraldic symbol, White Eagle Aviation was founded initially to provide tourist flights, including aerial sightseeing, but moved into cargo flights later, and in addition to ad hoc cargo charters, provides regular services under contract to UPS.

HQ airport & main base: Warsaw Frederic Chopin
Designator: SA/WEA
Employees: 70
Links with other airlines: Operates under contract to UPS (qv)
Fleet: 2 ATR-42-300; 1 ATR-42-310; 1 Raytheon Beech King Air 350

PORTUGAL – CS

Despite being one of the European colonial powers, the relative poverty of Portugal until recent years meant that air transport did not figure as prominently in communications with the empire as in the case of the United Kingdom and France.

AEROCONDOR
Aerocondor Transportes Aereos
Incorporated: 1951

Although founded in 1951, operations did not begin until 1984. Today the airline operates regional scheduled services within Portugal and to Madeira, as well as a scheduled service in France and cargo charter services internationally.

HQ airport & main base: Cascais
Radio callsign: AEROCONDOR
Designator: 2b/ARD
Employees: 90
Route points: Agen, Braganca, Cascais, Lisbon, Paris, Villa Real
Fleet: 4 Shorts 360; 2 Dornier 228-212

EUROATLANTIC AIRWAYS
Incorporated: 1997

Originally came into existence as Air Madeira, a trading name for Air Zarco, with a single Lockheed TriStar 500 for long-haul inclusive tour charter flights. The present title was adopted in 2000. The airline is owned by a combination of Portuguese and Luxembourg interests.

HQ airport & main base: Lisbon
Designator: MM/MMZ
Employees: 215
Fleet: 1 Lockheed L-1011-500 TriStar; 2 Boeing 767-300ER; 1 Boeing 757-200

HI FLY
Incorporated: 1997

Hi Fly was originally launched as a transatlantic inclusive tour charter airline, with some European flights during the summer, under the name Air

Luxor. Confusion with both the Egyptian airline Luxor Air and Luxair of Luxembourg led to the present name being adopted in 2005, although the flight designator reflects the earlier name. A small, scheduled network has been developed recently.

HQ airport & main base: Lisbon Portela
Designator: LK.LXR
Route points: Lisbon, Paris, Praia
Links with other airlines: Alliances with Air Europa (qv), Linhas Aereas de Mocambique, PGA-Portugalia Airlines (qv)
Fleet: 2 Airbus A330-300; 3 Airbus A320-200

PORTUGALIA
Companhia Portuguesa de Transportes Aereos SA
Incorporated: 1988

A private-enterprise Portuguese airline, Portugalia was founded in 1988 and commenced operations in 1990 following the liberalisation of air transport in Portugal, with domestic scheduled and international charter flights, mainly from Lisbon, but also from Faro and Oporto. International scheduled flights followed later. The airline is controlled by the Grupo Espirito Santo, with an 84 per cent stake.

HQ airport & main base: Lisbon Portela, with further bases at Faro and Oporto
Radio callsign: PORTUGALIA
Designator: NI/PGA
Employees: 750
Route points: Alicante, Amsterdam, Barcelona, Basle/Mulhouse, Bilbao, Bologna, Bordeaux, Brussels, Casablanca, Copenhagen, Faro, Frankfurt, Fuerteventura, La Corunna, Lanzarote, Las Palmas, Lisbon, London, Lyons, Madeira, Madrid, Malaga, Marseilles, Milan, Munich, Nice, Oporto, Palma de Mallorca, Pamplona, Paris, Rome, Tenerife, Toulouse, Valencia, Zurich
Links with other airlines: Alliances with Air Europa (qv), Air France (qv), Hi Fly, KLM (qv), Regional Air Lines (qv), TAP Portugal (qv)
Fleet: 6 Fokker 100; 8 Embraer ERJ-145EP

SATA AIR ACORES
Servicion Acoreano de Transports Aereos SA
Incorporated: 1941

The airline for the Azores, a group of islands in the North Atlantic, originally started in 1941 as a study group, when a group of local people founded the Azorean Society of Aeronautic Study, or Sociedada Acoreana de Estudos Aereos. The first services did not come until 1947, when a Beechcraft AT11 was introduced on an internal service within the islands. The following year, a de Havilland Dove was added to the fleet, and remained there until 1971, by which time a Douglas DC-3 Dakota was also operated, and replaced by a BAe 748 turboprop airliner.

The airline was taken over by the Azores regional government in 1980, when the current title was adopted. While the airline continued to develop, and at one time operated a leased Boeing 737-300 on a number of routes to the mainland and on charter services, as well as a service linking Madeira and Jersey for migrant workers and their families, the international services were hived off in 1998 to a new airline, SATA International, leaving the original airline to confine itself to meeting its original aim of an inter-island service. While privatisation has been discussed, this is unlikely in the near future.

HQ airport & main base: Ponta Delgada
Radio callsign: SATA
Designator: SP/SAT
Employees: 570
Route points: Corvo, Flores, Graciosa, Horta, Pico, Ponta Delgada, Santa Maria, Sao Jorge, Terceira
Links with other airlines: Owns SATA International (qv) 100 per cent
Fleet: 4 BAE ATP; 1 Dornier Do.228-212

SATA INTERNATIONAL
Incorporated: 1998

Although originally founded in 1990 as Ocean Air, a charter airline, SATA Air Acores became a shareholder in 1994, and eventually bought the airline completely after Ocean Air suspended flying. In 1998, the name was changed to SATA International and the operations of SATA Air Acores outside of the Azores were transferred into the airline.

HQ airport & main base: Ponta Delgada
Radio callsign: OCEAN
Designator: S4/RZO
Employees: 413
Route points: Boston, Faro, Funchal, Lisbon, Ponta Delgada, Toronto, Zurich
Links with other airlines: Owned by SATA Air Acores (qv). Alliance with TAP Air Portugal (qv)
Fleet: 3 Airbus A310-300; 3 Airbus A320-200

TAP PORTUGAL
Transportes Aereos Portugueses SA
Incorporated: 1944

Portugal's national carrier, TAP, or Transportes Aereos Portugueses, was founded in 1944 by the Portuguese government, although operations did not begin until two years later, when Douglas DC-3s started flying between Lisbon and Madrid, and, later that same year, to the Portuguese African colonies of Angola and Mozambique. The European network expanded during the late 1940s, reaching London in 1949. Douglas DC-4s were introduced for the longer-haul routes, especially to southern Africa. In 1953, the airline was given private company status, allowing its directors greater commercial freedom.

The important colonial services were much improved in 1955 with the arrival of three Lockheed Super Constellations, which displaced the three DC-4s for other duties, while six DC-3s remained in the fleet. The purchase of modern aircraft proved difficult for what was at the time one of western Europe's poorest nations, so in 1959 a pool arrangement was reached with BEA, British European Airways, on the Lisbon–London route, enabling both airlines to use BEA's Vickers Viscounts. This was followed by a similar arrangement with Air France on the Lisbon–Paris service, using the French airline's Sud Aviation Caravelles. Another pool agreement came the following year, using Douglas DC-7Cs of Panair do Brasil on the Lisbon–Rio de Janeiro route.

TAP eventually introduced its own jet equipment in 1962, when the first of three Caravelles entered service. These were followed by Boeing 707-320s in 1966, and by Boeing 727s in 1968. The airline was nationalised in 1975, following political upheaval in Portugal. The name was changed to TAP Air Portugal in 1978, but changed to TAP Portugal in 2005. In 2005, the airline joined the Star Alliance.

The airline became a public limited company in 1991, but the state remains the majority shareholder. TAP is the forty-ninth largest airline in the world by revenue. Over the past decade, the fleet, at one time all-Boeing, has moved from a mixed Boeing and Airbus operation to one that is completely Airbus. Employee numbers have fallen by around a quarter.

In recent years, TAP has acquired interests in a number of other airlines, including a 75.5 per cent stake in the Portuguese charter carrier White Airways, and 40 per cent each in Air Sao Tome e Principe and Linhas Aereas de Sao Tome e Principe, and 20 per cent in Air Macau.

HQ airport & main base: Lisbon
Radio callsign: AIR PORTUGAL
Designator: TP/TAP
Employees: 5,750
Route points: Amsterdam, Barcelona, Bissau, Brasilia, Brussels, Budapest, Caracas, Copenhagen, Curitiba, Dakar, Faro, Florianopolis, Fortaleza, Frankfurt, Geneva, Igaussu Falls, Johannesburg, Kiev, Lisbon, London, Luanda, Luxembourg, Madeira, Madrid, Maputo, Milan, Münster, Munich, Natal (Brazil), Newark, Oporto, Oslo, Paris, Ponta Delgada, Porto Santo, Prague, Praia, Recife, Rio de Janeiro, Rome, Sal, Salvador de Bada Bahai, Santa Maria, Santo Domingo, Sao Paulo, Sao Tome, Stockholm, Terceira, Venice, Vienna, Vitoria, Zurich
Links with other airlines: Holds 75.5 per cent stake in White Airways (qv); 40 per cent each in Air Sao Tome e Principe and Linhas Aereas de Sao Tome e Principe; 20 per cent in Air Macau. Member of the Star Alliance. Alliances with Air One, Malev, Olympic Airlines, PGA-Portugalia Airlines, SATA International, SN Brussels Airlines, TACV, Ukraine International Airlines (all qv)
Annual turnover: US $1,618 million (£1,080 million)
Fleet: 4 Airbus A340-300; 7 Airbus A330-200; 6 Airbus A310-300; 3 Airbus A321-200; 15 Airbus A320-200; 16 Airbus A319-100 (On order: 4 Airbus A350-900; 6 Airbus A350-800)

WHITE AIRWAYS
Incorporated: 2000

Originally founded in 2000 as Yes Linhas Aereas Charter, with a Lockheed L-100 Tristar 500 for long-haul charters and an Airbus A320 for medium haul charters, the airline adopted its present name in 2005. It now concentrates on long-haul charters, including both inclusive tour and ad hoc charters. TAP Air Portugal has a controlling 75.5 per cent shareholding.

HQ airport & main base: Lisbon Portela
Designator: YSS
Employees: 158
Links with other airlines: TAP Air Portugal (qv) holds 75.5 per cent of the shares
Fleet: 1 Lockheed L-100 TriStar 500; 1 Airbus A310-300

PUERTO RICO – N

ROBLEX AVIATION
Incorporated: 1997

Roblex Aviation dates from 1997 and provides cargo charter flights throughout the Caribbean.

HQ airport & main base: San Juan Isla Grande
Fleet: 7 Shorts 360-300; 1 Britten-Norman BN2A Islander

QATAR – A7

QATAR AIRWAYS
Incorporated: 1993

The national airline of Qatar, Qatar Airways was first owned by members of the Qatar royal family, and dates from 1993, although operations did not begin until January 1994. The airline was relaunched in 1997, and today the shares are divided equally between the government of Qatar and private shareholders.

The airline operates international services as far afield as London and Osaka. Over the past decade, the number of employees has grown tenfold, while the fleet has also shown substantial growth along with the route network. At one time a mixed Boeing and Airbus fleet, it now consists entirely of Airbus aircraft.

HQ airport & main base: Doha International
Radio callsign: QATARI
Designator: Q7/QTR
Employees: 5,300
Route points: Abu Dhabi, Aden, Alexandria, Algiers, Amman, Athens, Bahrain, Bangkok, Beijing, Beirut, Berlin, Cairo, Cape Town, Casablanca, Cebu, Colombia, Damascus, Damman, Delhi, Dhaka, Doha, Dubai, Frankfurt, Hyderabad, Islamabad, Istanbul, Jakarta, Jeddah, Johannesburg, Karachi, Kathmandu, Khartoum, Kochi, Kuala Lumpur, Kuwait, Lahore, London, Luxor, Madrid, Mahe, Male, Manchester, Manila, Milan, Moscow, Mumbai, Munich, Muscat, Nairobi, Osaka, Paris, Peshawar, Riyadh, Rome, Sana'a, Seoul, Shanghai, Singapore, Tehran, Thiruvananthapuram, Tripoli, Tunis, Vienna, Yangon, Zurich
Fleet: 4 Airbus A340-600; 14 Boeing 777-300GR; 6 Boeing 777-200LR; 2 Boeing 777F; 12 Airbus A330-300; 19 Airbus A330-200; 1 Airbus A300-600F; 9 Airbus A300-600R; 7 Airbus A321-200; 11 Airbus A320-200; 2 Airbus A319-100LR (On order: 2 Airbus A380-800)

REUNION ISLAND – F

AIR AUSTRAL
Incorporated: 1974

Air Austral was established in 1974 to operate passenger and freight services within the French overseas territory of Reunion Island in the Indian Ocean, with operations beginning the following year. Initially known as Reunion Air Service, and from 1987 as Air Reunion, the present title was adopted in 1990. A service to Paris was launched in 2003 and the airline also operates charter flights to East Africa and South Africa in addition to its internal scheduled services. Ownership lies with French financial institutions.

HQ airport & main base: St Denis Gillot
Designator: UU/REU
Route points: Paris, Saint Denis de la Reuion, Saint Pierre de la Reunion
Links with other airlines: Air Mauritius, Inter Air South Africa (both qv)
Fleet: 3 Boeing 777-200ER; 1 Boeing 737-300; 1 Boeing 737-500; 1 ATR-72-500

ROMANIA – YR

BLUE AIR
Incorporated: 2004

A Romanion low-cost airline founded in 2004, initially operating to destinations in and around the Mediterranean as well as to Paris and Maastricht.

HQ airport & main base: Bucharest
Designator: OB.JOR
Route points: Barcelona, Bucharest, Cuneo, Istanbul, Lyons, Maastricht, Madrid, Milan, Paris, Rome, Timisoara, Verona
Fleet: 1 Boeing 737-400; 2 Boeing 737-300; 1 Boeing 737-500

CARPATAIR
Incorporated: 1999

A scheduled and charter airline handling both passengers and cargo, Carpatair was originally founded in 1999, as Veg Air using a single leased Yakovlev Yak 40, but the current name was adopted at the end of the year when Swedish and Swiss shareholders acquired 49 per cent of the company, leaving the majority in the hands of private Romanian shareholders. Today the airline has a small domestic network and a much more substantial network of international routes, operated with Saab regional turboprop airliners.

HQ airport & main base: Timisoara
Radio callsign: CARPATAIR
Designator: V3/KRP

Employees: 450
Route points: Ancona, Bologna, Budapest, Chinsinau, Cluj, Düsseldorf, Florence, Lvov, Milan, Munich, Naples, Rome, Timisoara, Turin, Venice, Verona
Links with other airlines: Alliances with Lufthansa, Malev, Moldavian Airlines (all qv)
Fleet: 12 Saab 2000; 3 Saab 340B

ROMAVIA
Romavia Romanian Aviation Company
Incorporated: 1991

Romania's other state-owned airline, Romavia is owned by the Ministry of National Defence and its primary role was originally intended to be the operation of government VIP flights. The natural extension of this service has been the operation of aircraft on behalf of major industrial groups or banks, while the airline has since developed into operating charter flights and has acquired the rights for scheduled services from Bucharest and Constanta to a number of destinations in Europe, North Africa, the Gulf and Pakistan. It remains to be seen whether such a small country facing considerable economic and infrastructural problems can maintain two international airlines.

HQ airport & main base: Bucharest Henri Coanda International
Radio callsign: AEROMAVIA
Designator: WQ/RMV
Route points: Bucharest, Copenhagen, London, St Petersburg, Sofia
Fleet: 1 Boeing 707-320C; 1 Rombac (BAe) One-Eleven 500; 1 BAe 146-200; 1 Antonov An-26

TAROM
Transporturile Aeriene Romane
Incorporated: 1946

In common with many other East European national airlines, Tarom was founded in 1946 with Soviet assistance, with the USSR holding a half share in the airline. The airline replaced a pre-war airline, LARES, which had been formed in 1932 by the Romanian government and which ceased operations in 1939. Full ownership and control of Tarom passed to Romania in 1954, and the period which followed saw steady expansion, with the initial fleet of Lisunov Li-2 (Russian-built Douglas DC-3) aircraft replaced by Ilyushin Il-14 airliners. Later equipment included the airline's first turboprops, Ilyushin Il-18s, introduced in 1962, and Antonov An-24s.

The first jet equipment, BAe One-Elevens, entered service in 1968, and subsequently these aircraft were assembled under licence in Romania as Rombac One-Elevens. The decision may have had much to do with the ending of One-Eleven production in the UK and the desire of the Romanian government to establish an aircraft industry, or it may have been due to the growing rift between Romania and the Warsaw Pact nations, which saw the country increasingly aligned with Communist China.

Tarom has leased and wet-leased Rombac One-Elevens to other airlines, and in the past a major user of these aircraft was Ryanair.

The end of Communist dictatorship in Romania has seen many more Western aircraft types enter service with Tarom, which is developing a comprehensive European network. Over the past decade, transatlantic services have been dropped, as have some other intercontinental operations, but a domestic network has developed from just one route. A subsidiary, Liniile Aeriene Romane, or LAR, was formed in 1975 to provide feeder services, as well as undertaking charter flights, using two Beech 1900Ds, but this airline and its routes have been absorbed into Tarom. Although Tarom may well be privatised in the future, at present ownership rests with the state, mainly the transport ministry but also including Bucharest airport and the civil aviation authority.

HQ airport & main base: Bucharest Henri Coanda International
Radio callsign: TAROM
Designator: RO/ROT
Employees: 2,325
Route points: Aleppo, Amman, Athens, Bacau, Baia Mare, Beirut, Brussels, Bucharest, Budapest, Cairo, Chisinau, Cluj, Constanta, Damascus, Dubai, Frankfurt, Iasi, Istanbul, Larnaca, London, Madrid, Male, Milan, Moscow, Munich, Oradea, Paris, Prague, Rome, Satu Mare, Sibiu, Sofia, Suceava, Tel Aviv, Thessaloniki, Timisoara, Vienna, Warsaw
Fleet: 1 Ilyushin Il-62M; 4 Boeing 737-700; 5 Boeing 737-300; 4 Airbus A318-100; 1 Antonov An-24RV; 7 ATR-42-500

RUSSIAN FEDERATION – RA

One can either be very optimistic or very pessimistic about the state of commercial aviation in the Russian Federation, which, with the Ukraine, really is the rump of the former Soviet Union. The real point is, of course, that so much of aviation in these countries is commercial in name only, with operators having to learn how to operate in a market economy and forget all that they ever learned about the old Soviet-style command economy. For much of its history, Aeroflot was operated on military lines and was almost indistinguishable from the Soviet Air Force's transport elements.

In essence, the history of Aeroflot is the history of Russian civil aviation. The dramatic political, and the accompanying economic, changes which have swept through the old Soviet Union resulted in Aeroflot breaking up into many pieces. The result for what is left today, Aeroflot Russian International Airlines, has been beneficial, with re-equipment and with travellers reporting that, happily, Aeroflot is no longer the airline it used to be. For the rest, the results have varied. Many of the 'new' Russian airlines with a history within the old Aeroflot have failed to survive, and many of those that remain continue to struggle through lean and uncertain times, faced with poor infrastructure, elderly equipment, fuel shortages, poor productivity, and a simple lack of comprehension over what it takes to survive and prosper.

The airlines do not have the market to themselves. In addition to military-operated airlines, perhaps not too dissimilar from those which were once commonplace in Latin America, many research institutes faced with reduced budgetary support from the Russian government have put their aircraft into the charter market. Some industrial concerns have followed suit, although, to be fair, in the case of Antonov, the Ukrainian aircraft manufacturer, this has been an astute move – but Antonov is leading in a niche market.

In an attempt to emulate Western success, and perhaps reconcile socialism with capitalism, many Russian airlines have substantial employee shareholdings. There are also a number of genuinely new airlines, and some of these, most notably Volga-Dnepr, which has shown spectacular growth in a short time and established a reputation to match, and Transaero, show just what can be done. One or two former Aeroflot divisions, such as Aviation Enterprise Pulkovo and Aeroflot-Don Airlines, can also show just what can be achieved in switching from one politico-economic system to another.

For a country such as the Russian Federation, aviation is not a luxury but a necessity, because of the vast distances, the harsh climate and difficult terrain, all of which put aviation at a distinct advantage over other forms of transport. In the far northern wastes, road and railway construction is often simply not an option, with marshland in summer and extreme Arctic temperatures in winter. The failure of the so-called 'Stalin Railway' in northern Siberia proves the point.

In many ways, Russian civil aviation needs consolidation, but consolidating back into the old, over-centralised system will not work in such a large and diverse country. Nevertheless, strong regional groupings need to emerge. At present, so many Russian airlines take the name of their home airport for their own title that there is sometimes difficulty in distinguishing between operators at the same base. This is an unusual feature of the post-Aeroflot era – there are few examples in the West of airlines adopting airport names, with one of the few examples being the former Midway Airlines (not to be confused with the current airline of that name) based at Chicago's second airport.

2ND ARKHANGELSK AVIATION ENTERPRISE
Founded: 1935
Formerly a local division of Aeroflot, today the company operates regional passenger and cargo services, but also contracts for humanitarian and relief work overseas for aid agencies. A mixed fleet of utility aircraft and helicopters is operated.

HQ airport & main base: Archangel
Designator: OAO
Fleet: 6 Antonov An-2; 6 Let L410UVP-E; 4 Mil Mi-8T; 3 Mil Mi-26T

AEROFLOT RUSSIAN AIRLINES
Incorporated: 1932

At one time the world's largest airline, although run more on military than commercial lines, Aeroflot was once one of the top forty airlines in terms of annual turnover, but over the past eight years has dropped out of the top fifty.
Since the break-up of the former Soviet systems, its activities have become more confined, enabling the airline to become both more commercial, and for Aeroflot to divide itself into many regional or state airlines. Gone too are the days when Aeroflot handled everything, from air taxis and crop spraying to long-haul airline operation.

The airline's immediate predecessor was Dobroflot, formed in 1923 at the start of the first five-year plan, on the merger of a several small pioneering airlines. Dobroflot had the then high route mileage of 6,000 miles when, in 1932, Aeroflot was formed, taking over the airline. Expansion was rapid, albeit almost entirely on domestic services, until the German invasion in 1941 halted many services, and subsequent activity was reduced in favour of supporting Russia's war effort.

Extensive military assistance from the United States during the war years saw the Douglas C-47, the military variant of the DC-3, provided for Soviet use, and the aircraft was subsequently produced under licence in the Soviet Union as the Lisunov Li-2. The Li-2 formed the backbone of the airline's fleet after the war ended, with large numbers remaining in service throughout the 1950s, even after Russian aircraft such as the Ilyushin Il-12 and Il-14 entered service. For many years, all Aeroflot aircraft were single or twin-engined types, since travel was restricted to senior government and Communist Party officials, and it was not considered worth spending scant resources on aircraft of Douglas DC-4 or DC-6 type.

Postwar, and the Russian occupation of Eastern Europe, Aeroflot was the chosen instrument for Soviet participation in the national airlines that were established throughout what later became the Warsaw Pact members. Most of these airlines were formed with standard packages of Li-2s.

Aeroflot's first jet was the twin-engined Tupolev Tu-104, introduced in 1956, and first seen in the West during a state visit to the United Kingdom. A shorter-range version of the Tu-104 was the Tu-124, while turboprop aircraft followed soon afterwards, with the Ilyushin Il-18, Antonov An-24 and An-114. These aircraft were followed by the second generation of jet airliners, including the Tupolev Tu-134 and Tu-154, equating to the Douglas DC-9 and Boeing 727 respectively, and by the Ilyushin Il-62, an aircraft of strikingly similar appearance to the Vickers VC-10. The airline operated the unsuccessful Tupolev Tu-144 supersonic jet airliner for a short period, although this never saw service on international routes.

In recent years, the much slimmed-down Aeroflot has become more commercial, with operations confined to what might be regarded as the domestic trunk routes and to international services, developing a more extensive network than hitherto. At one time, the airline rebranded itself as ARIA – Aeroflot Russian International Airlines, but the Aeroflot title has been readopted in recent years. The airline is still controlled by the Russian government but the state shareholding has been reduced to 51 per cent, with the remainder being held by the airline's employees, while in 2000 the present title was adopted. Russian and Ukrainian aircraft types are gradually disappearing from the fleet as increasing numbers of Western aircraft enter service, although whether this continues will depend on the airline's success in earning foreign currency; a compromise might be Russian aircraft with Western engines and avionics.

In 1997 the airline decided to re-establish itself on a broader domestic network, using Moscow Sheremetyevo as a hub. Two Boeing 777-200s were leased for seven years to cover for delays in deliveries of the new Ilyushin Il-86.

Despite having been split into many parts, Aeroflot remains the forty-fifth largest airline in the world by revenue, but because of its predominantely international traffic flying longer distances, it is outside the 'Top 50' by passenger numbers. Over the past few years it has realigned its route network to reflect changing political realities, with fewer flights outside the northern hemisphere, including cutting services to many of the African client states of the former Soviet regime. It has 51 per cent shareholdings in both Aeroflot-Don and Aeroflot-Nord.

HQ airport & main base: Moscow Sheremetyevo, with a further base at St Petersburg
Radio callsign: AEROFLOT
Designator: SU/AFL
Employees: 15,000
Route points: Adler/Sochi, Amman, Amsterdam, Anapa, Anchorage, Ankara, Antalya, Archangel, Astrakhan, Athens, Baku, Bangkok, Barcelona, Barnaul, Beijing, Beirut, Belgorod, Belgrade, Berlin, Bishkek, Bratislava, Brussels, Bucharest, Budapest, Cairo, Chelyabinsk, Copenhagen, Damascus, Delhi, Dnepropetrovosk, Dubai, Düsseldorf, Ekaterinburg, Frankfurt, Geneva, Gothenburg, Hamburg, Havana, Helksinki, Hong Kong, Irkutsk, Istanbul, Kaliningrad, Karlovy Vary, Kemerovo, Khabarovsk, Kiev, Krasnodar, Larnaca, Ljubljana, London, Los Angeles, Luanda, Madrid, Milan, Mineralnye Vody, Moscow, Mumbai, Munich, Murmansk, Naryan-Mar, New York, Nice, Nizhnevartovsk, Novosibirsk, Nurengri, Omsk, Oslo, Paris, Perm, Petropavlovsk-Kamchatsky, Prague, Riga, Rome, Rostov, St Petersburg, Samara, Seoul, Shanghai, Simferopol, Sofia, Stockholm, Tallinn, Tashkent, Tblisi, Tehran, Tokyo, Toronto, Ufa, Ulan Bator, Venice, Vienna, Vilnius, Vladivostok, Volgograd, Warsaw, Washington, Yerevan, Zagreb, Zurich
Links with other airlines: Lufthansa (qv) is assisting with the expansion of Moscow Airport
Fleet: 11 Boeing 767-300ER; 4 McDonnell Douglas DC-10-40; 10 Airbus A321-200; 12 Airbus A320-200; 8 Airbus A319-100; 12 Ilyushin Il-96-300M/T; 7 Ilyushin Il-86; 26 Tupolev Tu-154B/M; 13 Tupolev Tu-134 (On order: 30 Sukhoi Superjet 100)

AEROFLOT-DON
Incorporated: 2000

Based at Rostov-on-Don, Aeroflot-Don was established as Donavia, primarily as a regional carrier, but also operates internationally, mainly to the Middle East, and Aeroflot retains a 51 per cent stake. Donavia was able to trace its origins back to 1925, but was absorbed by Aeroflot until the break-up of the Soviet Union and the fall of Communism, after which it was restructured and relaunched as a private enterprise airline in 1993, owned 51 per cent by its employees and 20 per cent by the state. Aeroflot took its controlling interest in 2000, at which time the current title was adopted.

HQ airport & main base: Rostov-on-Don, with further bases at Moscow Vnukovo and Shermetyevo
Radio callsign: DONAVIA
Designator: D9/DNV
Route points: Adler/Sochi, Dnepropetrovsk, Dubai, Ekaterinburg, Frankfurt, Gyoumri, Istanbul, Moscow, Murmansk, Neryungri, Novosibirsk, Rostov, St Petersburg, Tashkent, Tel Aviv, Yerevan
Fleet: 9 Tupolev Tu-154; 2 Tupolev Tu-134; 2 Boeing 737-500

AEROFLOT-NORD
Incorporated: 2004

Formed in 2004 when Aeroflot acquired a 51 per cent interest in Arkhangelsk Airlines to establish a regional airline, which now has two international services to Scandinavia. It continues to operate a fleet consisting entirely of Russian and Ukrainian aircraft.

HQ airport & main base: Arkhangelsk
Designator: 5N/AUL
Route points: Anapa, Arkhangelsk, Belogrod, Chelyabinsk, Ekaterinburg, Kotlas, Moscow, Murmansk, Naryan-Mar, Omsk, Pechora, St Petersburg, Samara, Simferopol, Solovetsky, Tromso, Volgograd
Links with other airlines: Aeroflot (qv) has a 51 per cent interest
Fleet: 4 Tupolev Tu-154B; 10 Tupolev Tu-134A; 2 Antonov An-26B; 6 Antonov An-24; 4 Boeing 737-500

AIRBRIDGE CARGO
Incorporated: 2003

Formed in 2003 by the parent company Volga-Dnepr Airlines to operate scheduled freight services between Europe and Asia, AirBridge Cargo commenced operations in 2004. It has an all-Boeing 747 fleet.

HQ airport & main base: Moscow
Designator:
Route points: Amsterdam, Beijing, Frankfurt, Krasnoyararsk, Moscow, Nagoya, Shanghai
Links with other airlines: Owned by Volga-Dnepr (qv)
Fleet: 2 Boeing 747-400ERF; 1 Boeing 747-300SF; 2 Boeing 747-200F (On order: 5 Boeing 747-8F)

AIRSTARS
Incorporated: 2000

An all cargo charter airline, formed well after the break-up of the USSR but operating a Soviet-era fleet.

HQ airport & main base: Moscow Domodedovo
Radio callsign: AIRSTARS
Designator: PL/ASE
Fleet: 4 Ilyushin Il-76TD; 1 Ilyushin Il-62M; 2 Antonov An-12

ANGARA AIRLINES
Incorporated: 2000

Founded in 2000, Angara Airlines operates a scheduled passenger service between Irkutsk and Kirensk, as well as charter operations within Russia. It is owned by the Irkutsk Aircraft Repair Factory.

HQ airport & main base: Irkutsk International Airport
Designator: AGU
Route points: Irkutsk, Kirensk
Fleet: 2 Antonov An-26; 3 Antonov An-24RV

ASTRAKHAN AIRLINES
Incorporated: 1994

This airline was created when the former Astrakhan Integrated Airsquad, which was organised on military lines and included both the main airport and air transport operations, was split up, separating the airport and airline. Scheduled flights are operated, alongside charter operations, for both passengers and cargo.

HQ airport & main base: Astrakhan Narimanovo
Designator: OB/ASZ
Fleet: 3 Tupolev Tu-134A; 2 Antonev An-24RV

ATLANT SOYUZ
Atlant Soyuz Airlines
Incorporated: 1993

The City of Moscow is the largest single shareholder in Atlant Soyuz, holding 25 per cent of the stock. The airline provides passenger and cargo scheduled and charter flights from Moscow.

HQ airport & main base: Moscow Sheremetyevo
Designator: 3G/AYZ
Fleet: 5 Tupolev Tu-334-100; 4 Tupolev Tu-154M; 8 Ilyushin Il-76TD; 1 Ilyushin Il-96-300; 4 Ilyushin Il-86; 2 Boeing 737-300; 1 Yakovlev Yak-42

ATRAN
Aviatrans Cargo Airlines
Incorporated: 1942

Formed as an Aeroflot division in 1942. The Russian Federation still holds 25 per cent of the shares, but the employees now own 73 per cent of the shares in this charter and scheduled cargo airline. Over the past ten years there has been some slimming of the fleet and rationalisation in the number of aircraft types operated.

HQ airport & main base: Moscow Domodedovo
Designator: V8/VAS
Fleet: 2 Antonov An-26; 4 Antonov An-12

AVIACON ZITOTRANS
Incorporated: 1995

A charter airline operating both passenger and cargo flights, mainly throughout Eastern Europe and the Near East.

HQ airport & main base: Ekaterinburg
Designator: ZR/AZS
Employees: 190
Fleet: 5 Ilyushin Il-76

AVIAL
Incorporated: 1991

Founded in 1991, Avial commenced operations in late 1992 as the Avial Air Company, operating cargo charter flights with a small fleet of Antonov An-12s. The current name was adopted in 2000.

HQ airport & main base: Moscow
Designator: NV/NVI
Fleet: 6 Antonov An-12

AVIANERGO
Incorporated: 1994

A subsidiary of Russian State Energy, Aviaenergo operates passenger and cargo charter flights primarily in support of the oil industry.

HQ airport & main base: Moscow Sheremetyevo
Designator: 7U/ERG
Fleet: 2 Ilyushin Il-62M; 2 Tupolev Tu-154M; 1 Tupolev Tu-134A

AVIATION ENTERPRISE PULKOVO
Aviation Enterprise Pulkovo
Incorporated: 1932

Originally a part of Aeroflot, since the break-up of that airline's regional network, Pulkovo has remained in state hands. It is one of the more successful of the former Aeroflot divisions, operating to many destinations outside Russia. After autonomy from Aeroflot, it was initially known as the Pulkovo Aviation Concern, but later adopted the above title. In October 2006 the airline was absorbed into Rossiya Airlines, and it will be the Rossiya name that survives.

BAL BASHKIRI AIRLINES
Bashkiri Avialinii
Incorporated: 1992

A scheduled and charter, passenger and cargo airline, based on a former division of Aeroflot, BAL was put into receivership in 2005, but continues to operate while it is being reorganised.

HQ airport & main base: Ufa
Designator: V9/BTC
Route points: Nadym, Nizhnevartovsk, Novyj Urengoj, St Petersburg, Surgut, Ufi
Fleet: 5 Tupolev Tu-154M; 1 Tupolev Tu-134A

BUGULMA AIR ENTERPRISE
Incorporated: 1992

Another airline formed on the demise of the original Aeroflot, Bugulma Air Enterprise operates charter passenger services and also flies schedules on contract to Tatarstan Airlines.

HQ airport & main base: Bugulma
Designator: BGM
Links with other airlines: Operates in connection with Tatarstan Airlines (qv)
Fleet: 11 Yakovlev Yak-40

CHUKOTAVIA
Incorporated: 1996

A charter airline carrying passengers and cargo within Russia, Chukotavia was formed in 1996 by the merger of Anadyr Air Enterprise and Chaunski Air Enterprise, and is today owned by four groups, the Anadyr Air Enterprise, Keperveyen Air Enterprise, Mys Shmidta Air Enterprise and Pevek Air Enterprise.

HQ airport & main base: Anadyr Ugolny
Fleet: 3 Antonov An-26B; 2 Antonov An-24B/RV

DALAVIA
Incorporated: 1953

Originally founded as a division of Aeroflot, the airline changed its name to Khabarovsk Aviation Enterprise on the break-up of Aeroflot and then adopted the current title in 1999.

Scheduled and charter, passenger and cargo flights are operated. Despite the liberalisation of the Russian economy in recent years, the airline is still in public ownership.

HQ airport & main base: Khabarovsk-Novy
Designator: H8/KHB
Route points: Anadyr, Barnaul, Blagoveschensk, Chelyabinsk, Chita, Ekaterinburg, Irkutsk, Khabarovsk, Komsomolsk Na Amure, Krasnodar, Krasnojarsk, Magadan, Moscow, Novosibirsk, Okhotsk, Omsk, Petropavlovsk-Kamchatsky, Rostov, St Petersburg, Samara, Tashkent, Vladivostok, Yuzhno-Sakhalinsk
Fleet: 4 Tupolev Tu-214; 6 Ilyushin Il-62M; 7 Tupolev Tu-154M/B-2; 2 Antonov An-26; 5 Antonov An-24RV

DOMODEDOVO AIRLINES
Incorporated: 1960

Originally formed within Aeroflot, operating from Moscow's Domodedovo Airport, the airline became independent on the break-up of Aeroflot. It continues to operate services from Domodedovo. While the state retains a 50.4 per cent stake in the airline, Kras Air owns the remainder and between them the two airlines have established a joint management company, Air Bridge Management, to coordinate their activities.

The fleet has been slimmed down dramatically over the past ten years, but there are no Western aircraft operated as yet.

HQ airport & main base: Moscow Domodedovo
Radio callsign: DOMODEDOVO
Designator: E3/DMO
Route points: Anadyr, Baku, Blagoveschensk, Khabarovsk, Magadan, Moscow, Noril'sk, Omsk, Petrapavlovsk-Kamchatsky, Samarkand, Tashkent, Vladivostok, Yakutsk, Yuzhno-Sakhalinsk
Links with other airlines: KrasAir (qv) has a 49.6 per cent stake
Fleet: 5 Ilyushin Il-96-300; 5 Ilyushin Il-62M; 3 Tupolev Tu-154M

GAZPROMAVIA
Gazpromavia Aviation
Incorporated: 1995

Essentially a passenger and cargo charter airline supporting the oil and natural gas industries, Gazpromavia was founded in 1995. It also operates a small domestic scheduled network and has a subsidiary, Karat Air, operating scheduled services.

HQ airport & main base: Moscow Vnukovo
Radio callsign: GAZPROM
Designator: 4G/GZP
Route points: Adler/Sochi, Belgorod, Moscow, St Petersburg
Links with other airlines: An alliance with Karat Air (qv)
Fleet: 9 Antonov An-74; 2 Ilyushin Il-76TD; 4 Tupolev Tu-154M; 7 Yakovlev Yak-42D; 6 Yakovlev Yak-40; 5 Dassault Falcon 900

GROMOV AIR
Incorporated: 1995

A charter airline founded by the Gromov Flight Research Institute, operating passenger and cargo flights.

HQ airport & main base: Moscow Zhukovsky
Radio callsign: GROMOV
Designator: GAI
Fleet: 9 Ilyushin Il-76; 4 Tupolev Tu-154; 5 Tupolev Tu-134A; 1 Antonov An-30; 1 Antonov An-26; 4 Antonov An-12; 1 Yakovlev Yak-40

IZHAVIA
Izhevsk Air Enterprise
Incorporated: 1992

Originally Aeroflot's Izhevsk Division, the company has now become the Urmurtia Republic's airline, but unusually only operates charters.

HQ airport & main base: Izhevsk
Designator: IZA
Fleet: 2 Tupolev Tu-134A; 1 Antonov An-26; 3 Antonov An-24RV; 1 Yakovlev Yak-42D

KARAT AIR
Karat Air Company
Incorporated: 1993

Originally founded in 1993 as Rikor, the current title was adopted before a merger with Tulpar Aviation in 2004. The airline operates scheduled and charter flights and is owned by Gazpromavia Aviation.

HQ airport & main base: Moscow Vnukovo
Radio callsign: KARAT
Designator: V2/AKT
Route points: Adler/Sochi, Baku, Chelyabinsk, Dushanbe, Gyoumri, Kazan, Khudzhand, Moscow, Nadym, Novj Urengoj, Rostov, St Petersburg, Yerevan
Links with other airlines: A subsidiary of Gazpromavia (qv)
Fleet: 4 Tupolev Tu-154B; 7 Tupolev Tu-134A; 3 Antonov An-24RV; 5 Yakovlev Yak-42D; 5 Yakovlev Yak-40

KD-AVIA
Kaliningrad Avia
Incorporated: 1945

Originally formed in late 1945 as a local detachment within Aeroflot, operations did not begin until 1948. The airline became independent with the break-up of the old Aeroflot, and in 2004 launched international services. It was grounded for air safety violations in April 2005, but resumed operations in mid-May, and shortly afterwards adopted the title of KD-Avia.

HQ airport & main base: Kaliningrad
Designator: KD/KLN
Route points: Operates throughout the CIS from Kaliningrad
Fleet: 12 Boeing 737-300

KMV
KMV Airlines – Kavminvodyaria
Incorporated: 1961

KMV was founded in 1961 as the Mineralnye Vody Aviation Group, which was later renamed as the Mineralnye Vody Civil Aviation Enterprise in 1988 before being further reorganised as the State United Venture Kavminvodyavia, KMV. During the early years, charter and domestic scheduled flights were operated, mainly within the northern Caucasus, but a number of international services are now operated, many of them, such as those to Malta, on an inclusive tour charter basis.

HQ airport & main base: Mineralnye Vody
Designator: KV/MVD
Route points: Ekaterinburg, Mineralnye Vody, Moscow, Nori'sk, St Petersburg, Stavropol, Yerevan
Fleet: 4 Tupolev Tu-204-100; 7 Tupolev Tu-154B/M; 1 Tupolev Tu-134A

KOLAVIA
Kogalym Avia
Incorporated: 1993

Founded in 1993 at Kogalym, Kolavia serves oil and gas-producing communities in Tyumen, which is part of Western Siberia, with scheduled and charter flights, as well as operating to Moscow and St Petersburg.

HQ airport & main base: Kogalym
Radio callsign: KOLAVIA
Designator: 7K/KGL
Route points: Baku, Kogalym, Krasnodar, Mineralnye Vody Moscow, Rostov, St Petersburg, Samara, Surgut, Tyumen, Volgograd
Fleet: 6 Tupolev Tu-154B/M; 7 Tupolev Tu-134A

KOMINTERAVIA
Incorporated: 1996

Founded in 1996, Kominteravia began operations the following year, operating on a small domestic network, as well as on charter flights, carrying both passengers and cargo.

HQ airport & main base: Syktyvar
Designator: 8J/KMV
Route points: Pechora, Syktyvar, Ukhta, Usinsk, Vorkuta
Fleet: 5 Antonov An-24RV

KRASAIR
Krasnoyarsk Avia
Incorporated: 1982

Originally founded, as were all of the older Russian airlines, as a division of Aeroflot, it was privatised in 1993. In October 2004 a joint management company, Air Bridge, was established with Domodedovo Airlines. The two airlines intended to keep their separate identities, which is probably inevitable given the existence of other shareholders – in the case of Kras Air the Krasnoyarsk municipal authorities – but will integrate their networks, which have little overlap. Meanwhile, Krasair has a 49.6 per cent stake in Domodedovo Airlines and also owns 71 per cent of Omskavia Airlines. Krasair has been more advanced in adopting Western equipment, but as yet the numbers are a token percentage of the total fleet.

HQ airport & main base: Kranoyarsk
Radio callsign: KRASAIR
Designator: 7B/KJC
Route points: Abakan, Adler/Sochi, Almaty, Baku, Barnaul, Blagoveschensk, Chita, Dushanbe, Ekaterinburg, Eniseysk, Hanover, Hatanga, Irkutsk, Kemerovo, Khabarovsk, Khudzand, Komsomolsk Na Amure, Krasnodar, Krasnojarsk, Kyzyl, Lisbon, Tashkent, Mineralnye Vody, Moscow, Noril'sk, Novosibirsk, Omsk, Petropavlovsk-Kamchatsky, Rostov, St Petersburg, Samara, Tomsk, Ulan-Ude, Vladivostok, Yakutsk, Yerevan, Yuzhno-Sakhalinsk
Links with other airlines: Air Bridge Management holds a 49 per cent interest. Krasair has a 71 per cent stake in Omskavia Airlines, and 49.6 per cent in Domodedovo Airlines (both qv). Alliances with AeroSvit Airlines (qv), Avcom, Perm Airlines (qv), Transaero (qv)
Fleet: 3 Boeing 767-200ER; 4 Boeing 757-200; 6 Ilyushin Il-86; 1 Tupolev Tu-214; 4 Tupolev Tu-204-100; 2 Ilyushin Il-76TD; 14 Tupolev Tu-154B/M; 5 Boeing 737-300; 2 Yakovlev Yak-42D

KUBAN AIRLINES
Incorporated: 1932

Kuban Airlines started in 1932 as the Krasnodar division of Aeroflot. Since becoming independent of Aeroflot in 1992, it has developed a largely domestic scheduled network, but with international charters. Ownership is divided between the government with 51 per cent and employees with 49 per cent.

HQ airport & main base: Krasnodar Pashkovsky
Radio callsign: KUBAN
Designator: GW/KIL
Route points: Adler/Sochi, Frankfurt, Kaliningrad, Kazan, Krasnodar, Moscow, Nizhnevartovsk, Novyj Urengoj, St Petersburg, Surgut, Ufa, Yerevan
Fleet: 10 Yakovlev Yak-42

NOVOSIBIRSK AVIA
Incorporated: 1995

Primarily a charter airline for passengers and cargo, unusually, at least by Western standards, the airline also undertakes aerial surveys.

HQ airport & main base: Novosibirsk Tolmachevo
Radio callsign: NOVOSIBIRSK
Designator:
Fleet: 3 Antonov An-30; 6 Antonov An-24RV

OMSKAVIA
Incorporated: 1994

Founded in 1994 when the local state aviation enterprise separated its airport and airline involvement, the airline operates charter and scheduled flights for passengers and cargo. Kras Air has a 71 per cent stake. The Tupolev Tu-154 fleet is being replaced by Tupolev Tu-214s.

HQ airport & main base: Omsk
Radio callsign: OMSK
Designator: N3/OMS
Route points: Moscow, Omsk
Links with other airlines: Kras Air (qv) has a 71 per cent stake
Fleet: 4 Tupolev Tu-214; 2 Tupolev Tu-154M

ORENBURG AIRLINES
Orenburgskoe Gosudarstvennoe
Incorporated: 1992

Originally founded in 1932 as the Orenburg Division of Aeroflot, with the break-up of the Soviet state airline in 1992, Orenburg Airlines established itself as an inclusive tour charter operator with flights to destinations in Western Europe, and created its own small scheduled network. It has the distinction of being the first Russian airline to create a hub-and-spoke operation at Orenburg, and the first to offer through domestic air fares.

HQ airport & main base: Orenburg
Radio callsign: ORENBURG
Designator: R2/ORB
Route points: Dushanbe, Khudzhand, Moscow, Orenburg, Orsk, St Petersburg, Simferopol
Fleet: 4 Tupolev Tu-154B/M; 4 Tupolev Tu-134A; 2 Boeing 737-400; 1 Boeing 737-500

PERM AIRLINES
Perm State Air Enterprise – Permskoe Gosudartsvennoe
Incorporated: 1968

Originally formed as the Aeroflot Perm Division in 1968, Perm was one of the many airlines that became independent with the break-up of the old Aeroflot in the early 1990s. Today, the airline operates domestic and international scheduled services as well as charters. It is owned by the state government.

HQ airport & main base: Perm
Radio callsign: PERM
Designator: 9D/PGP
Route points: Anapa, Baku, Dushanbe, Kazan, Khudzhand, Kurgan, Mineralnye Vody, Moscow, Nakhichevan, Perm, St Petersburg, Samara, Tashkent, Yerevan
Links with other airlines: Alliances with Kras Air (qv), Trans-Aero Samara
Fleet: 5 Tupolev Tu-154B; 3 Tupolev Tu-134A; 2 Antonov An-26

POLAR AIRLINES
Incorporated: 1998

Polar Airlines was formed from four divisions of the former Aeroflot, Batagi, Chokordakh, Kolyma-Indigirka and Tiksi, and provides passenger and cargo services from its base at Yakutsk.

HQ airport & main base: Yakutsk
Route points: Batagi, Chokordakh, Tiksi, Yakutsk
Fleet: 1 Antonov An-74; 6 Antonov An-26; 4 Antonov An-24

POLET AIRLINE
Incorporated: 1988

Claims to offer worldwide charter flights for passengers and cargo as well as internal scheduled flights and flights to a small number of foreign destinations.

Unusually, the airline has expanded into the air ambulance, aerial photography and agricultural markets, while at the other extreme it operates six of the giant Antonov An-124 transports. It is owned by Anatoly Karpov, while in turn Polet has a 24 per cent stake in VoronezAvia.

HQ airport & main base: Voronezh
Radio callsign: POLET
Designator: POT
Route points: Baku, Lipetsk, Moscow, Munich, St Petersburg, Ulyanovsk, Voronezh
Links with other airlines: Owns 24 per cent of VoronehzAvia
Fleet: 6 Antonov An-124; 2 Antonov An-30; 4 Antonov An-24RV; 2 Tupolev Tu-134A; 5 Saab 2000; 2 Yakovlev Yak-40

ROSSIYA AIRLINES
Incorporated: 1992

Another offshoot of Aeroflot, Rossiya nevertheless has the distinction of providing and operating the Russian presidential aircraft and providing VIP flights for members of the Russian government and senior officials. It also provides wet-lease aircraft for Aeroflot. The Russian government ordered Rossiya to absorb Pulkovo Aviation while retaining its own name and this took effect in October 2006.

HQ airport & main base: Moscow Vnukovo
Radio callsign: ROSSIYA
Designator: R4/SDM
Fleet: 2 Ilyushin Il-96-300; 8 Ilyushin Il-86; 3 Tupolev Tu-214; 8 Ilyushin Il-62M; 29 Tupolev Tu-154B/M; 14 Tupolev Tu-134A; 1 Airbus A319-100; 1 Antonov An-74; 5 Boeing 737-500; 6 Yakovlev Yak-40

RUSAIR
Rusair Aviation Company
Incorporated: 1994

Originally formed as CGI Aero, whose callsign it retains, Rusair operates charter and air ambulance flights within Russia and beyond. It is wholly owned by Clintondale Aviation.

HQ airport & main base: Moscow Sheremetyevo
Radio callsign: RUSAIR
Designator: CGI
Fleet: 3 Tupolev Tu-134A; 4 Yakovlev Yak-40

RUSSIAN SKY
Incorporated: 1995

Founded in 1995 and commencing operations in 1996 as East Line Air, the airline became East Line Airlines in 1997, and adopted its current title after a change of ownership in 2005. Originally a passenger and cargo charter airline that developed scheduled flights to Europe and the Middle East, in September 2006 it became an all-cargo airline. Passenger services have been transferred to Vim Avia (qv).

HQ airport & main base: Moscow Domodedovo
Designator: P7/ESL
Fleet: 6 Ilyushin Il-76TD

SAMARA AIRLINES
Aviacompania Samara
Incorporated: 1993

Based on the Kuybyshev Joint Aviation Squadron, which was privatised in 1993, Samara Airlines was established as a joint stock company and began to convert to commercial airline operations. Today, the state still holds 51 per cent of the airline's shares. Scheduled and charter flights are operated, with a small external route network.

HQ airport & main base: Samar International
Radio callsign: SAMARA
Designator: E5/BRZ
Route points: Baku, Dushanbe, Irkutsk, Khudzhand, Krasnodar, Krasnojarsk, Moscow, Nakhichevan, Nizhnevartovsk, Novosibirsk, St Petersburg, Samara, Tainjin, Ufa, Yerevan
Fleet: 2 Antonov An-140; 3 Tupolev Tu-154M; 5 Tupolev Tu-134A; 3 Yakovlev Yak-42

SARAVIA
Incorporated: 1931

Formed in 1931 as the Aeroflot Saratov Division, Saravia became a joint stock company in 1992 on the break-up of the old Aeroflot. A small scheduled network is operated in addition to passenger charter flights. The state retains the controlling 51 per cent shareholding, with the remainder being held by the airline's employees.

HQ airport & main base: Saratov
Radio callsign: SARAVIA
Designator: 6W/SOV
Employees: 1,174
Route points: Moscow, Saratov, Yerevan
Fleet: 5 Yakovlev Yak-42; 1 Yakovlev Yak-40

SAT
SAT Airlines – Sakhalinski Aviatrassy
Incorporated: 1992

One of many airlines spawned from local Aeroflot detachments on the break-up of the old Aeroflot, SAT was the Sakhalin United Air Detachment, a term used to cover an organisation embracing both an airport and the aircraft based there. Although still government owned, the airline was reorganised along joint stock company lines in 2005. Passenger and cargo charters are operated alongside a domestic route network and international services to the Far East.

HQ airport & main base: Yuzhno Sakhalinsk
Radio callsign: SAKHALIN
Designator: HZ/SHU
Employees: 590
Route points: Blagoveschensk, Busan, Hakodate, Khabarovsk, Komsomolsk Na Amure, Sapporo, Seoul, Vladivostok, Yuzhno Sakhalinsk
Fleet: 1 Ilyushin Il-62; 2 Boeing 737-200; 6 Antonov An-24RV; 1 Antonov An-12

SIBAVIATRANS
Sibaviatrans Air Co
Incorporated: 1995

Sibaviatrans was founded in 1995 and has developed as an operator of both scheduled and charter flights for passengers and cargo and, in addition to its aircraft, operates a number of helicopters on charter duties.

HQ airport & main base: Krasnoyarsk
Radio callsign: SIBAVIA
Designator: 5M/SIB
Route points: Abakan, Barnaul, Bratsk, Ekaterinburg, Igarka, Kemerovo, Krasnoyarsk, Nori'sk, Novosibirsk, Ufa, Ulan-Ude
Fleet: 1 Tupolev Tu-154B-2; 5 Tupolev Tu-134A; 1 Antonov An-32; 7 Antonov An-24RV; 1 Yakovlev Yak-40K

SIBIR/SIBERIA AIRLINES
Sibiria Airlines
Incorporated: 1992

Sibir or Siberia Airlines was formed in 1992 by the Tolmachevo States Aviation Enterprise at Ob, using nearby Novosibirsk as a base, and has grown rapidly into a major trunk domestic route and international airline with bases at Novosibirsk and Moscow, with a growing proportion of Western aircraft in its fleet. Initially known as Sibir, it is now promoting itself as Siberia Airlines. Two subsidiaries are Armavia, in which Sibir has a 70 per cent stake, and Vnukovo Airlines, acquired in 2001.

HQ airport & main base: Novosibirsk Toimachevo, with a further major hub and base at Moscow Domodevovo
Radio callsign: SIBIR
Designator: S7/SBI
Employees: 4,000
Route points: Adler/Sochi, Baku, Bangkok, Barnaul, Beijing, Blagoveschensk, Chelyabinsk, Dubai, Dushanbe, Düsseldorf, Ekaterinburg, Frankfurt, Hanover, Hurghada, Irkutsk, Kazan, Kemerovo,

Khabarovsk, Khudzhand, Kiev, Krasnodar, Kutaisi, Magnitogorsk, Makhachkala, Mineralnye Vody, Moscow, Munich, Nizhnevartovsk, Nizhniy Novgorod, Noril'sk, Novokkuznetsk, Novosibirsk, Novj Urengoj, Omsk, Petropavlovsk-Kamchatsky, Rostov, St Petersburg, Samara, Sharm-el-Sheikh, Shenyang, Tashkent, Tbilisi, Tomsk, Ulan-Ude, Urumqi, Ust-Kamenogorsk, Vladikavkaz, Vladivostok, Volgograd, Yakutsk, Yerevan, Yuzhno-Sakhalinsk
Links with other airlines: Owns Vnukovo Airlines. Has a 70 per cent stake in Armavia (qv)
Fleet: 9 Ilyushin Il-86; 6 Tupolev Tu-204-100; 4 Airbus A310-300; 2 Airbus A310-200; 27 Tupolev Tu-154M; 10 Boeing 737-500

TATARSTAN AIR
Incorporated: 1999

Tatarstan Air was formed in 1999 from Tatarstan Airlines and Kazan Air Enterprise, both of which dated from 1992 and had originated in parts of the former Aerovolga Division of the old Soviet-era Aeroflot. The two airlines collaborated from 1997 as Tatarstan/Kazan Air Enterprise, and were formally merged to form Tatarstan Air by the Tatarstan republic, which owns the new airline completely.

HQ airport & main base: Kazan
Radio callsign: TATARSTAN
Designator: U9/TAK
Employees: 1,406
Route points: Baku, Dushanbe, Ekaterinburg, Kazan, Khudzhand, Mineralne Vody, Moscow, Nizhnevartovsk, St Petersburg, Tashkent
Fleet: 3 Ilyushin Il-86; 2 Tupolev Tu-154B/M; 3 Tupolev Tu-134A; 1 Boeing 727-100; 3 Antonov An-24RV; 5 Yakovlev Yak-42; 1 Yakovlev Yak-40

TESIS AIRLINE
Incorporated: 1992

Specialising in cargo charters, mainly to the Middle East and Far East. Unusually for a Russian operator, the Tesis Airline has standardised its fleet, in this case using Ilyushin Il-76 freighters.

HQ airport & main base: Moscow Domodedovo International
Radio callsign: TESIS
Designator: UZ/TIS
Employees: 250
Links with other airlines: Alliance with Aviaprad
Fleet: 7 Ilyushin Il-76MD/TD; 1 Boeing 747-200F

TOMSK AVIA
Incorporated: 1992

Tomsk Avia was founded in 1992, having originated in Aeroflot's Tomsk Division, and continues to operate a small route network and charters, mainly for passengers. In 1999 it absorbed the Kalpashevo Air Enterprise.

HQ airport & main base: Tomsk
Radio callsign: TOMSK
Designator: TSK
Route points: Niznevarartovsk, Novosibirsk, Tomsk
Fleet: 2 Antonov An-26; 5 Antonov An-24RV

TRANSAERO
Transaero Airlines AP
Incorporated: 1990

The first truly private enterprise Russian airline, and the first with non-Aeroflot origins to gain approval for scheduled services, first within Russia and then internationally, Transaero was founded in 1990 and commenced operations in November 1991. The airline's first international service was from Moscow to Tel Aviv, and was inaugurated in November 1993.

Lacking any inherited aircraft, the airline was able to concentrate on creating a fleet which was almost entirely Western in origin, initially using leased older aircraft, but these were updated as new aircraft were delivered. Despite the fact that the Ilyushin and Yakovlev design bureaux were both shareholders, along with the Aerotrans and Ikar joint stock companies, Aeronaviagtion, and the Loriel Partnership, the trend towards buying Western equipment has continued so that today an all-Boeing fleet is operated. The airline also has followed the Western fashion of establishing a commuter or feeder susbidiary, Transaero Express, and has a token 0.2 per cent stake in AirBaltic.

In recent years the main operating base has moved from Moscow's Sheremetyevo Airport to Domodedovo, while the route network has changed, with a greater emphasis on tourist destinations.

HQ airport & main base: Moscow Domodedovo
Radio callsign: TRANSOVIET
Designator: UN/TSO
Employees: 2,400
Route points: Aktau, Almaty, Anadyr, Astana, Bangkok, Berlin, Denpasar Bali, Ekaterinburg, Frankfurt, Irkutsk, Karaganda, Kiev, Kuala Lumpur, London, Male, Montreal, Moscow, Novosibirsk, Odessa, Ovda, Paphos, Petropavlovsk-Kamchatsky,

St Petersburg, Shimkent, Singapore, Tashkent, Tel Aviv, Utapao, Vladivostok, Yuzhno-Sakhalinsk
Links with other airlines: Transaero Express is a subsidiary. 0.2 per cent stake in Air Baltic (qv). Alliances with Air Moldava, Kras Air (both qv)
Fleet: 6 Boeing 747-200B; 4 Boeing 767-300ER; 3 Boeing 767-200ER; 4 Boeing 737-400; 3 Boeing 737-300; 4 Boeing 737-500

URAL AIRLINES
Incorporated: 1993

Although only founded in 1993, Ural Airlines can trace its history back to the creation of Sverdlovsk State Air Enterprises in 1943, which included the airport at Ekaterinburg in a typical Soviet-era structure. The airport and airline were separated in 1993. Ural Airlines has a substantial route network and is owned by Ural Wings, which has a 66 per cent stake, and the Ural Transport Bank, with almost 15 per cent.

HQ airport & main base: Ekaterinburg International
Radio callsign: URAL
Designator: U6/SVR
Employees: 1,320
Route points: Adler/Sochi, Bratsk, Chita, Dubai, Dushanbe, Ekaterinburg, Irkutsk, Istanbul, Khudzhand, Mineralnye Vody, Moscow, Munich, Nadym, Nizhnevartovsk, Novosibirsk, Novyj Urengoj, Paris, Prague, St Petersburg, Salekhard, Samara, Tashkent, Vladivostok, Yerevan
Fleet: 4 Ilyushin Il-86; 16 Tupolev Tu-154B/M; 1 Tupolev Tu-134A; 3 Antonov An-24B/RV; 1 Airbus A320-200

UTAIR AVIATION
Incorporated: 1991

Originally formed within Aeroflot in 1967 as the Tyumen Aeroflot Directorate, the airline was intended to serve energy industry development in Siberia. On the break-up of the old Aeroflot, the airline took its independence as the Tyumenaviatrans Aviation, and then changed to its present title in 2003.

In addition to the aircraft listed, it also maintains a large fleet of Mil helicopters to meet the needs of the energy industry.

HQ airport & main base: Khanty-Mansiysk
Radio callsign: UTAIR
Designator: P2/TMN
Employees: 5,000
Route points: Adler/Sochi, Baku, Belgorod, Bishkek, Cheboksary, Donetsk, Ekaterinburg, Kaliningrad, Khanty-Mansisyk, Kharkov, Khudzhand, Kiev, Kogalym, Krasnodar, Kursk, Magnitogorsk, Makhachkala, Mineralnye Vody, Mimyj, Moscow, Nizhnevartovsk, Nizhniy Novgorod, Nojabrxsk, Novosibirsk, Novyj Urengoj, Omsk, Rostov, St Petersburg, Samara, Surgut, Sykyvkar, Tyumen, Ufa, Ukhta, Uraj
Fleet: 15 Tupolev Tu-154B/M; 38 Tupolev Tu-134A/B; 1 Antonov An-26; 17 Antonov An-24B/RV; 12 Yakovlev Yak-40; 1 ATR-42-320; 1 Gulfstream GIV-SP

VIM AIRLINES
Incorporated: 2003

One of the newest, if not the newest, Russian airlines, VIM is privately owned and operates passenger and cargo charters worldwide, and in September 2006 it acquired the passenger services of Russian Sky (qv).

HQ airport & main base: Moscow Vnukovo
Radio callsign: VIM
Designator: NN/MOV
Employees: 1,000
Fleet: 13 Boeing 757-200

VLADIVOSTOK AIR
Incorporated: 1932

Dating from 1932, when it was formed as the Vladivostok Division of Aeroflot, Vladivostok Air established a separate existence in 1994, and in 2003 acquired Khakasia Airways, a regional operator. The state continues to own 51 per cent of the shares, with the remainder held by employees.

HQ airport & main base: Vladivostok Kievichi
Radio callsign: VLADIVOSTOK
Designator: XF/VLK
Route points: Abakan, Anadyr, Barnaul, Busan, Changchun, Dalian, Ekaterinburg, Harbin, Irkutsk, Kemerovo, Khabarovsk, Krasnodar, Magadan, Moscow, Mudanjiang, Niigata, Novokuznetsk, Novosibirsk, Osaka, Petropavlovsk-Kamchatsky, Seoul, Tomsk, Toyama, Vladivostok, Yakutsk, Yuzhno-Sakhalinsk
Fleet: 1 Airbus A320-200; 12 Tupolev Tu-154B/M; 2 Antonov An-24RV; 6 Yakovlev Yak-40

VOLGA-AVIAEXPRESS AIRLINES
Incorporated: 1992

Based on the Aeroflot Volgograd Division, Volga-AviaExpress Airlines became independent in 1992 and initially operated as Volga Airlines. It is owned by private investors and the airline's employees.

HQ airport & main base: Volgograd Gumrak
Designator: WLG
Route points: Vladivostok, Volgograd
Fleet: 2 Tupolev Tu-134A; 4 Yakovlev Yak-42D

VOLGA-DNEPR
Volga-Dnepr Airlines
Incorporated: 1990

The first airline without its origins in Aeroflot to be able to undertake heavy and outsized cargo charters, Volga-Dnepr was founded in 1990 and commenced operations in 1991. The shareholders include the Ukrainian-based Antonov Design Bureau, builders of the largest aircraft in commercial use, the Antonov An-124 Ruslan, the Aviastar Joint Stock Company and Motor Sich. Volga now also operates scheduled cargo services. The airline has been extremely successful in carving out a specialised niche for itself, and for many years enhanced its marketing efforts through an agreement with the British freight airline, HeavyLift.

A passenger service is operated between Volga's base at Ulyanovsk and Moscow. A wholly owned subsidiary is AirBridgeCargo. The number of employees has increased by half over the past decade.

HQ airport & main base: Ulyanovsk Vostochny International
Radio callsign: VOLGA-DNEPR
Designator: VI/VDA
Employees: 1,392
Route points: Moscow, Nizhniy, Novogorod, Penza, Shenyang, Shenzhen, Tianjin, Ulyanovsk
Links with other airlines: Owns Air BridgeCargo (qv)
Fleet: 10 Antonov An-124-100; 2 Ilyushin Il-76TD; 4 Yakovlev Yak-40

VOSTOK AVIATION
Incorporated: 1945

Originally founded in the Aeroflot era, Vostok is basically an air-work operation, with operations embracing helicopter logging and air ambulance duties as well as charter passenger and cargo operations. It is owned by the Russian Federal Property Fund, which has a 51 per cent stake, and the regional government, which has 38 per cent.

HQ airport & main base: Khabarovsk
Radio callsign: VOSTOK
Designator: VTK
Employees: 679
Fleet: 2 Antonov An-38-100; 5 Antonov An-28

YAKUTIA AIRLINES
Incorporated: 1925

As with so many airlines in the former Soviet Union, Yakutia traces its origins to the formation of an Aeroflot division, in this case the Yakutsk Division. At one stage it was named Yakutaviatrans, and later became Sakhaavia after the break up of the old Aeroflot, operating cargo charters in Europen and to the Middle East and Africa. It entered bankruptcy in 1999, but was saved by the regional government and emerged in 2000, after which it was absorbed by Yakutavia in 2002 and the new airline adopted the current title.

HQ airport & main base: Yakutsk
Designator: K7/SYL
Route points: A number of scheduled services are operated within the CIS
Fleet: 8 Antonov An-140; 7 Tupolev Tu-154M; 2 Antonov An-26; 8 Antonov An-24

YAMAL AIRLINES
Incorporated: 1997

Yamal Airlines operates domestic scheduled services as well as two international routes.

HQ airport & main base: Salekhard
Radio callsign: YAMAL
Designator: YL/LLM
Route points: Baku, Ekaterinburg, Kazan, Khanty-Mansiysk, Moscow, Nadym, Nojabrxsk, Novyj Urengoj, Salekhard, Tyumen, Ufa, Yerevan
Fleet: 3 Tupolev Tu-154B/M; 9 Tupolev Tu-134A; 1 Antonov An-26B; 2 Antonov An-24RV; 6 Yakovlev Yak-40

SAUDI ARABIA – HZ

AL-KHAYALA
Incorporated: 2005

Fundamently an executive and business aircraft charter company, Al-Khayala has developed a premium-class domestic scheduled service between Riyadh and Jeddah, operating Airbus A319s in four-abreast configuration with just forty-four seats. It also provides charters throughout the Gulf area and will undertake longer-distance operations with its Airbus A340-600 airliner. It is owned completely by National Air Services, a private-venture Saudi aviation company.

HQ airport & main base: Jeddah
Designator: 2N
Route points: Jeddah, Riyadh
Fleet: 1 Airbus A340-600; 2 Airbus A320-200; 2 Airbus A319-100; 1 Airbus A319CJ; 2 Boeing Business Jet; plus eight Gulfstream and Dassault Falcon business jets

SAUDI ARABIAN AIRLINES
Saudi Arabia Airlines Corporation
Incorporated: 1945

The largest airline in the Middle East by passenger numbers, but no longer on turnover, Saudi Arabian Airlines was formed in 1945 by the Saudi Arabian government with assistance from TWA, Trans World Airlines, and initially undertook charter flights using Douglas DC-3s, the first of which was a gift from the American president. Scheduled services began in 1947, initially on domestic routes, but these were soon extended to neighbouring states. While Bristol Wayfarers, passenger-carrying versions of the Bristol 170 Freighter, were introduced in 1951, for the first twenty years of the airline's history there was a marked preference for Douglas products. The first jets, Boeing 727s, were introduced in 1962. Services to the United States started in 1979, operated jointly with another American airline, Pan Am.

The airline has enjoyed considerable growth, due not so much to the size of the Saudi population, but to the country's booming oil economy, which has led to substantial numbers of expatriate workers being employed, most of whom are contracted to use the airline's services, on which no alcohol is served. Although the airline does derive some benefit from pilgrims travelling to Mecca, most of this traffic is handled by non-Saudi charter airlines. From 1972 until 1996, the fleet name Saudia was used, but the airline has now reverted to its full title.

The airline remains in state hands. Two unusual aspects of its operations are that a number of aircraft are operated on behalf of the Saudi government, or Royal family, for VIP use, and that, in contrast to many large airlines today, there is no separate feeder or commuter operation. The airline is now the second largest in the Arab world by annual turnover, on which basis it ranks twenty-fifth worldwide, but is twenty-ninth by passenger numbers, although it remains the largest Arab airline on this assessment.

HQ airport & main base: Jeddah King Abdul Aziz, with further bases/hubs at Dhahran and Riyadh
Radio callsign: SAUDI (SAUDI GREEN for VIP flights)
Designator: SV/SVA
Employees: 25,000
Route points: Abha, Abu Dhabi, Addis Ababa, Alahsa, Al-Baha, Alexandria, Algiers, Amman, Arara, Asmara, Bahrain, Beirut, Bisha, Cairo, Casablanca, Chennai, Colombo, Dakar, Damascus, Damman, Delhi, Dhaka, Dharan, Doha, Dubai, Frankfurt, Gassim, Geneva, Gurayat, Hail, Hyderabad, Islamabad, Istanbul, Jakarta, Jazan, Jeddah, Johannesburg, Jouf, Kano, Karachi, Khartoum, King Kalid Military City, Kochi, Kuala Lumpur, Kuwait, Lahore, London, Madinah, Manila, Mashhad, Milan, Mumbai, Muscat, Nairobi, Nejran, New York, Paris, Peshawar, Qaisumah, Rafha, Riyadh, Rome, Sana'a, Sharjah, Sharurah, Singapore, Tabuk, Tehran, Tunis, Turaif, Washington, Wedjh, Yanbu
Links with other airlines: Alliances with Gulf Air (qv), Pakistan International Airlines. Annual passenger numbers: 15.8 million
Annual turnover: US $3,607 million (£2,404 million)
Fleet: 5 Boeing 747-400; 12 Boeing 747-300; 1 Boeing 747-200F; 7 Boeing 747-100B; 1 Boeing 747SP; 23 Boeing 777-200ER; 4 McDonnell Douglas MD-11F; 8 Airbus A300-600; 4 Airbus A320-200; 28 McDonnell Douglas MD-90-30; 15 Embraer 170; 1 de Havilland Canada Twin Otter Srs300; 2 Dassault Falcon 900. There are other aircraft operated on behalf of the government which include: 6 Grumman Gulfstream IV; 5 Gulfstream III; 4 Gulfstream II; 2 Dassault Falcon 900 and a de Havilland Canada DHC-6 Twin Otter. The airline also owns its own training aircraft

SCANDINAVIA

If one excepts the relatively small LIAT, no other set of countries seems to have managed to create an airline in multinational ownership that has stood the test of time and lasted so long and so amicably as Denmark, Norway and Sweden have done with Scandinavian Airlines System, SAS. It is all the more surprising since the three Benelux nations, Belgium, Luxembourg and the Netherlands, managed to cooperate in other fields, while the nations of East Africa and West Africa would have found creating a sustainable intercontinental airline so much easier. Yet, even within one country, there can be tensions, as happened during Swissair days when there was rivalry over long-haul services between French-speaking Geneva and German-speaking Zurich.

On the other hand, had the question of a joint airline arisen much later, after intercontinental air travel had become established, SAS might never have happened. As it was, at the time of its formation, Norway had its own intercontinental airline in Braathens South American and Far East Air Transport. Depending on when the question arose, one could have seen Copenhagen, Oslo and Stockholm competing to be the hub for transpolar air services between Europe and Japan. Norway and Denmark might have hoped that their success in maintaining massive merchant fleets cross trading without visiting home ports could have had its counterpart in air transport, although without an open skies arrangement, all that could have been achieved would have been an international/ intercontinental 'hub and spoke' arrangement.

One only has to look at the fragmentation of air transport in Russia and China to appreciate the SAS achievement.

SAS CARGO
Incorporated: 2001

SAS's version of a cargo entity that markets the cargo capacity of its aircraft and could in the future operate all-cargo aircraft in its own right. The designators of the parent airline are used.

HQ airport & main base: Kasterup
Radio callsign: SCANDINAVIAN
Designator: SK/SAS
Links with other airlines: Wholly owned by SAS (qv). Alliances with Wow, Korean Air (qv)

SAS SCANDINAVIAN AIRLINES SYSTEM
Scandinavian Airlines System
Incorporated: 1946

The world's thirteenth largest airline by annual turnover, but twentieth by passenger numbers, SAS dates from 1946 and the merger of three airlines, the Danish DDL, the Swedish ABA, and the Norwegian DNL. Of these three airlines, the Danish airline, DDL, was the oldest, dating from 1919, although in common with the Norwegian DNL, which dated from 1927, operations had been suspended completely after the German invasion of these two countries during the Second World War. The Swedish airline, ABA, dated from 1924, and had managed to maintain limited operations during wartime because of Swedish neutrality.

From the outset, the new airline was owned in the proportions of 3:2:2 for Sweden, Denmark and Norway respectively, with each national share being divided 50:50 between the state and private investors. More recently, however, the names of the shareholding national airlines have been changed to SAS Sweden AB, SAS Danmark AS and SAS Norge ASA.

Initially, SAS was only concerned with transatlantic operations and was known as OSAS, Overseas Scandinavian Airlines System, but the participating airlines merged their European networks into ESAS, European Scandinavian Airlines System in 1948, and in 1951 ESAS and OSAS were merged to form the current airline. The intercontinental operations of Braathens SAFE were added to those of OSAS before the merger.

SAS soon expanded its route network into Africa and Asia. The new airline also worked hard to make a virtue of its geographical position, which some might have viewed as being isolated on the fringes of northern Europe. In 1954, it made air transport history by inaugurating the first air service over the North Pole, using Douglas DC-6Bs on a service to the west coast of the United States. This was followed by a DC-7C service in 1957, which cut the the journey time between Europe and Japan in half. Ten years later, SAS became the first European airline to operate via Tashkent, in what was then the USSR, now Uzbekistan, cutting 1,350 miles off the journey from Copenhagen to Bangkok and Singapore.

The airline's DC-6s and DC-7s had been complemented by Convair 440 Metropolitans on the European services, but these were later replaced by Sud Aviation Caravelles. SAS for many years proved to be a loyal customer for Douglas, later McDonnell Douglas, also buying Douglas DC-8 long-haul airliners, DC-9s to replace the Caravelles, and then the DC-10, before moving on to the MD series. More recently, however, the airline has concentrated on Boeing 767s for its long-haul operations and introduced Boeing 737-600s for its less busy European routes.

The airline's links with the Far East saw it play a leading role in the establishment of Thai Airways in 1959, and for many years SAS held a substantial stake in that airline, although this was reduced from its initial 30 per cent to 15 per cent, and then in 1977, the Thai government took over the SAS holding.

Originally, it was not intended that SAS should operate domestic services, although it did acquire a 50 per cent holding in the Swedish domestic airline, Linjeflyg, and a 25 per cent interest in Greenlandair was held for many years, although this is now a 37.5 per cent interest in Air Greenland. Nevertheless, the formation of SAS Commuter in 1989 saw expansion into domestic services, while Linjeflyg's operations were absorbed by SAS in 1993, although some of the airline's routes were passed to SAS Commuter. Linjeflyg had been founded in 1957 as a domestic airline to operate passenger and newspaper delivery flights, and quickly established a 38-point domestic network. The airline expanded into operating inclusive tour holiday charter flights, which made a convenient fit with the domestic scheduled services. By the time of its merging into SAS, Linjeflyg was operating eight Boeing 737-500s and sixteen Fokker F28-4000s, as well as four leased Saab 340s, and had another six 737-500s on order.

SAS took a 24.9 per cent shareholding in Airlines of Britain Holdings, owners of British Midland, now bmi, in 1988, and eventually built this up to 40 per cent, before reducing it to the present 20 per cent. bmi has taken over some SAS routes, notably Glasgow to Copenhagen. Spanair was a joint venture between SAS, with 49 per cent, and a Spanish travel group, but SAS now has a controlling 94.9 per cent of the Spanish airline.The airline was a founder-member of the Star Alliance, which brings together frequent-flyer programmes and other services for Air Canada, Lufthansa, Thai International, United Airlines, and, from late 1997, Varig, as well as SAS.

In recent years, the airline has rationalised many of its subsidiaries, including reintegrating the operations and fleet of SAS Commuter into the main airline, and has created SAS Cargo to market the cargo capacity on its aircraft. In 2001, it acquired the long-established Norwegian domestic scheduled and charter airline, Braathens, and in doing so also acquired its Swedish subsidiary, Braathens Sweden, originally known as TransSwede, while Wideroe is another wholly owned subsidiary. It also has a 47.2 per cent stake in AirBaltic, the Latvian airline, and 49 per cent in Estonian Air. Although Sweden is the largest shareholder, the airline has refocused its operations and the main base is now Copenhagen. Each aircraft in the fleet carries the registrations of one of the participating nations, roughly in line with the 2:2:3 split in ownership.

HQ airport & main base: Copenhagen Kastrup, with further bases/hubs at Stockholm Arlanda and Oslo Gardermoen

Radio callsign: SCANDINAVIAN

Designator: SK/SAS

Employees: 19,250

Route points: Aalborg, Aalesund, Aarhus, Aberdeen, Alicante, Alta, Amsterdam, Angelholm/Helsingborg, Arkhangelsk, Arvidsjaur, Athens, Bangkok, Barcelona, Bardufloss, Basle/Mulhouse, Beijing, Bergen, Berlin, Billund, Birmingham, Bodo, Bologna, Borlange, Brussels, Bucharest, Budapest, Cairo, Chicago O'Hare, Cologne/Bonn, Copenhagen, Dublin, Düsseldorf, Edinburgh, Frankfurt, Gdansk, Geneva, Glasgow, Gothenburg, Halmstad, Hamburg, Hanover, Harstad/Narvik, Haugesund, Helsinki, Hemavan, Hong Kong, Istanbul, Jonkoping, Kalmar, Kangerlussaq, Karlstad, Karup, Kiev, Kirkenes, Kiruna, Kramfors, Kristiansand, Kristianstad, Kristiansund, Kuopio, Kuwait, La Corunna, Las Palmas, Linkoping, Lisbon, London, Longyearbyen, Lulea, Luxembourg, Lycksele, Lyons, Madrid, Malaga, Malmö, Manchester, Milan, Molde, Moscow, Munich, Newark, Nice, New York, Newcastle, Nice, Norrkoping, Nuremberg, Orebro, Ornskoldsvik, Osaka, Oslo, Ostersund, Oulu, Palanga, Palma de Mallorca, Paris, Poznan, Prague, Reykjavik, Riga, Rome, Ronneby, Rovaniemi, St John's, St Petersburg, Sao Paulo, Seattle, Shanghai, Singapore, Skelleftea, Stavanger, Stockholm, Stuttgart, Sundsvall, Tallinn, Tampere, Tokyo, Trollhattan, Tromso, Trondheim, Turin, Turku, Umea, Vaasa, Vasteras, Vaxjo, Venice, Vienna, Vilhelmina, Vilnius, Visby, Warsaw, Washington, Zagreb, Zurich

Annual passengers: 23.8 million

Links with other airlines: Owns Blue1 (qv), Scandinavian Airlines Sverige, Scandinavian Airlines Denmark, Braathens Sweden, SAS Braathens, Wideroe's Flyveselskap, SAS Cargo, Snowflake, all 100 per cent. Interests in Spanair, 94.9 per cent, Estonian Air, 49 per cent, AirBaltic, 47.2 per cent, Air Greenland, 37.5 per cent, Aerolineas de Balaires, 25 per cent, and bmi, 20 per cent (all qv). Star Alliance member. Alliances with Air China (qv), AirBaltic (qv), CHC Helikopter Service (qv), Estonian Air (qv), Icelandair (qv), Mexicana (qv), Midwest Connect (qv), Pulkovo Aviation Enterprise, Swiss (qv), Wideroe's Flyveselskap (qv).

Annual turnover: US $7,921 million (£5,280 million)

Fleet: Aircraft have national registrations. 7 Airbus A340-300; 4 Airbus A330-300; 8 Airbus A321-200; 9 Boeing 737-800; 3 Boeing 737-700; 4 Airbus A319-100; 18 Boeing 737-600; 3 McDonnell Douglas MD-90-30; 9 McDonnell Douglas MD-87;

30 McDonnell Douglas MD-82; 4 McDonnell Douglas MD-81; 1 BAe Avro RJ70ER; 24 Bombardier Dash 8 Q400

SERBIA AND MONTENEGRO – YU

AVIOGENEX

Incorporated: 1968

A passenger charter airline founded in 1968 as the aviation division of Generalexport, operations were suspended, due to UN sanctions, between June 1992 and October 1994, and again in 2000 due to the conflict in Kosovo, but resumed by the end of the year. The airline remains a subsidiary of Genex Holdings.

HQ airport & main base: Belgrade
Designator: AGX
Employees: 212
Fleet: 2 Boeing 727-200; 1 Boeing 737-200

JAT AIRWAYS

Jugoslovenski Aerotransport
Incorporated: 1946

Now the airline of newly independent Serbia after the break-up of Yugoslavia and the resultant war, JAT was originally founded in 1946 by the Yugoslav government. A predecessor airline, Aeropout, had ceased operations shortly after the outbreak of the Second World War. JAT commenced operations in 1947, initially operating a small fleet of Douglas DC-3s on domestic routes, but before the year was out, international services to Czechoslovakia, Hungary and Romania were introduced.

The international services were suspended the following year, but restarted in 1949, only to have the routes into eastern Europe suspended yet again in 1950 after Yugoslavia declared itself independent of what had emerged as the Soviet Bloc. The airline's route development then reflected this policy change, with priority given to establishing services to major centres in western Europe. Eventually, services to Prague and East Berlin were reinstated.

The airline also looked to Western suppliers for its equipment, starting with an order for Convair 440 Metropolitans in 1954, and also ordering Douglas DC-6Bs at the same time. Nevertheless, in 1957 a number of Ilyushin Il-14s were introduced. JAT's first jet aircraft were introduced in 1962, with the delivery of its first Sud Aviation Caravelles. These were later augmented and eventually replaced by Douglas DC-9s.

Encouraged by Yugoslavia's growing popularity as a tourist destination, in the years which followed JAT continued to expand, obtaining Boeing 727-20Adv and 737-300s, as well as McDonnell Douglas DC-10s. This steady progress was thrown sharply into reverse during the early 1990s with the start of hostilities between the different communities within Yugoslavia, following the break-up of the state. The new state of Serbia had taken 51 per cent of the airline's shares on the break-up of the country and, following United Nations sanctions against Serbia because of the country's part in the conflict, JAT was reduced to operating just two domestic routes from Belgrade.

The return of peace meant that JAT's international route network has had to be rebuilt, and while this has been substantially achieved, the airline still does not operate transatlantic service, concentrating on Europe and the Middle East. Ownership rests with the government of Serbia and Montenegro.

HQ airport & main base: Belgrade Novi Beograd
Radio callsign: JAT
Designator: JU/JAT
Employees: 3,525
Route points: Amsterdam, Athens, Berlin, Brussels, Copenhagen, Dubai, Düsseldorf, Frankfurt, Gothenburg, Istanbul, Larnaca, Llubljana, London, Malta, Moscow, Munich, Ohrid, Paris, Prague, Rome, Sarajevo, Skopje, Stockholm, Stuttgart, Tel Aviv, Tirana, Trieste, Tripoli, Tunis, Vienna, Zurich
Fleet: 1 Boeing 727-200; 2 Boeing 737-400; 10 Boeing 737-300; 8 Airbus A319-100; 4 ATR-72-200

MONTENEGRO AIRLINES

Incorporated: 1994

Although founded in 1994 as the national airline for Montenegro, Montenegro Airlines did not commence operations until 1997. Officially, the state had a 51 per cent shareholding at the outset, but the remaining shares were held by other state enterprises, including tourism, although some financial institutions were involved, and today the state shareholding is 99 per cent. The European Union imposed a brief ban on flights into member states, but this was lifted in October 1999.

HQ airport & main base: Podgorica
Radio callsign: MONTENEGRO
Designator: YM/MGX
Employees: 228
Route points: Belgrade, Budapest, Frankfurt, Ljubljana, Nis, Paris, Podgorica, Rome, Tivat, Vienna, Zurich

Links with other airlines: Alliances with Adria Airways, Austrian Airlines (both qv)
Fleet: 4 Fokker 100

SINGAPORE – 9V

SILKAIR

Silk Air Ltd
Incorporated: 1989

Originally founded in 1989 as Tradewinds the Airline, using two leased Boeing 737-300s, in 1992 Silk Air became a wholly owned subsidiary of Singapore Airlines and the present title was adopted. Many of its services are operated on behalf of its parent airline, while it has marketing alliances with a number of regional carriers. While it was originally intended to serve tourist destinations, the airline has since developed its route structure to include destinations more likely to appeal to the business traveller.

HQ airport & main base: Singapore Changi
Radio callsign: SILK AIR
Designator: MI/SLK
Employees: 725
Route points: Balikpan, Cebu, Chengdu, Chiang Mai, Chongqing, Christmas Island, Da Nang, Davao, Kochi, Kota Kinabalu, Kuantan, Kuching, Kunming, Langkawi, Manado, Medan, Padang, Palembang, Phnom Penh, Phuket, Shenzhen, Siem Reap, Singapore, Solo City, Surabay, Thiruvananthapuram, Xiamen, Yangon
Links with other airlines: Wholly owned by Singapore Airlines. Alliances with Bouraq Indonesian Airlines, Garuda Indonesian, Malaysian Airlines, Merpati Air, Singapore Airlines (all qv)
Annual turnover: Included in figures for Singapore Airlines
Fleet: 16 Airbus A320-200; 10 Airbus A319-100

SINGAPORE AIRLINES

Singapore Airlines Ltd
Incorporated: 1972

The world's fourteenth largest airline by turnover, up from seventeenth in just one year, Singapore Airlines is twenty-eighth in terms of passengers carried, largely due to many of its passengers travelling on long-haul services and the complete absence of short-haul domestic flights.

For almost the first quarter-century of its operations, the history of Singapore Airlines was inextricably tied up with that of Malaysian Airlines. The present title was not adopted until 1972, after the ending of the agreement the previous year between the governments of Singapore and Malaysia, which had created the relatively short-lived Malaysia–Singapore Airlines.

Initially, Singapore Airlines was a nationalised concern, but the state's holding has been steadily reduced, largely as the airline has sought additional capital from private investors to fund its expansion. Despite the small size of Singapore and the absence of any domestic routes, the airline is the third largest in Asia, a reflection of the rapid economic growth achieved by Singapore, and the pivotal position of the country as a hub.

The airline has made a number of investments elsewhere in the air transport industry, including Singapore Aircraft Leasing Enterprise, which is a joint venture with Boullioun Aviation Services, for which a substantial number of Boeing 777s and Airbus A320s are being delivered. It now owns Silk Air and Singapore Airlines Cargo, as well as having a 49 per cent interest in both Virgin Atlantic Airways and Tiger Airways. Singapore Airlines Cargo was established in 2000 to market the cargo capacity on Singapore Airlines' passenger services as well as on its own fleet of cargo aircraft, of which there are now sixteen. At one time it had minor shareholdings in both Swissair and Delta Air Lines, which had small shareholdings in Singapore Airlines as part of a strategic partnership. The airline has been a member of the Star Alliance since 2001.

HQ airport & main base: Singapore Changi
Radio callsign: SINGAPORE
Designator: SQ/SIA
Employees: 13,572
Route points: Abu Dhabi, Adelaide, Ahmedabad, Amritsar, Amsterdam, Athens, Auckland, Bandar Seri Begawan, Bangalore, Bangkok, Beijing, Brisbane, Cairo, Cape Town, Chennai, Christchurch, Colombo, Copenhagen, Delhi, Denpasar Bali, Dhaka, Dubai, Frankfurt, Fukuoka, Guangzhou, Hanoi, Hiroshima, Ho Chi Minh City, Hong Kong, Hyderabad, Istanbul, Jakarta, Jeddah, Johannesburg, Karachi, Kolkata, Kota Kinabalu, Kuala Lumpur, Kuantan, Kuching, Lahore, London, Los Angeles, Male, Manchester, Manila, Melbourne, Moscow, Mumbai, Nagoya, New York, Newark, Orlando, Osaka, Paris, Penang, Perth, Rome, Rotorua, San Francisco, Seoul, Shanghai, Singapore, Sydney, Taipei, Tokyo, Vancouver, Vienna, Zurich. A number of other destinations are served by Silk Air
Links with other airlines: Owns Silk Air and Singapore Airlines Cargo (qv). Has a 49 per cent stake in Tiger Airways (qv) and in Virgin Atlantic

Airways. A strategic alliance exists with these airlines, with Silk Air also undertaking a number of SIA operations. A member of the Star Alliance. Alliances with Air India, Malaysian Airlines, Royal Brunei Airlines, Silk Air, Vietnam Airlines, Virgin Atlantic Airways (all qv)
Passengers carried: 15.9 million
Annual turnover: US $7,334 million (£4,889 million)
Fleet: 24 Boeing 747-400; 5 Airbus A340-500; 19 Boeing 777-300ER; 12 Boeing 777-300; 46 Boeing 777-200ER; 19 Airbus A330-300 (On order: 10 Airbus A380-800; 20 Boeing 787-9)

SINGAPORE AIRLINES CARGO
Incorporated: 2000

Another example of a major airline with strong cargo traffic establishing a subsidiary to market the cargo capacity on its passenger services and to develop its own fleet of all-cargo aircraft and its own routes within those of the parent company. Singapore Airlines Cargo was established in 2000 and began operations the following year. It now has sixteen Boeing 747 freighters, and a 25 per cent interest in Great Wall Airlines.

HQ airport & main base: Singapore Changi
Radio callsign: SINGAPORE CARGO
Designator: SQ/SQC
Employees: 900
Links with other airlines: A subsidiary of Singapore Airlines (qv). Has a 25 per cent stake in Great Wall Airlines. Alliance with Wow
Fleet: 16 Boeing 747-400F

TIGER AIRWAYS
Incorporated: 2003

Founded in 2003 with the backing of Singapore Airlines as a low-cost venture, Tiger Airways began operations in 2004. It is intended to be a short- and medium-haul scheduled operator.

HQ airport & main base: Singapore Changi International
Radio callsign: TIGER
Designator: TR/TGW
Route points: Bangkok, Chiang Mai, Da Nang, Darwin, Hanoi, Hat Yai, Ho Chi Minh City, Krabi, Luzon, Macau, Padang, Phuket
Links with other airlines: Singapore Airlines (qv) has a 49 per cent stake
Fleet: 20 Airbus A320-200

SLOVAKIA – OM

SKYEUROPE AIRLINES
Incorporated: 2001

Founded in 2001 by its current chairman, Alain Skowronek, and chief executive, Christian Manl, SkyEurope Airlines claims to be the first low-cost airline in central Europe and to be the first airline in the region to have bases in more than one country, in this case in Hungary and Poland as well as Slovakia. Operations began in 2002, initially with Embraer Brasilia turboprops, and growth has been rapid, funded by several financial institutions. The airline is now standardising on Boeing 737s. A subsidiary is SkyEurope Hungary, which uses aircraft from the parent company as required.

HQ airport & main base: Bratislava M.R. Stefanik, with further bases/hubs at Budapest, Krakow and Warsaw
Designator: NE/ESK
Employees: 754
Route points: Amsterdam, Barcelona, Basle/Mulhouse, Bratislava, Bucharest, Budapest, Cologne/Bonn, Copenhagen, Dublin, Innsbruck, Kosice, Krakow, London, Manchester, Milan, Nice, Paris, Poprad, Rome, Salzburg, Sofia, Stuttgart, Warsaw
Links with other airlines: Owns SkyEurope Hungary (qv) 100 per cent
Fleet: 21 Boeing 737-700; 2 Boeing 737-300; 2 Boeing 737-500

SLOVENIA – YU

ADRIA AIRWAYS
Incorporated: 1961

Adria Airways started operations as Adria Aviopromet before the fall of Communism in Yugoslavia, as an inclusive tour charter airline with a substantial employee shareholding. It was unique as being the only charter airline in Eastern Europe. Initially, Douglas DC-6 aircraft were operated, with the first aircraft leased from KLM Royal Ducth Airlines, and the airline grew quickly with the expansion of the country's tourist industry. Between 1968 and 1986, the airline was known as Inex-Adria Airways, when it became connected with Interexport, a Belgrade-based trading organisation. In the mean time, scheduled services were introduced, initially to Larnaca in Cyprus in 1983.

After the break-up of the Yugoslav Federation, Adria became the national airline of the new republic of Slovenia, with a substantial shareholding by state-sponsored institutions, and its base moved from Belgrade to Ljubljana. Today, it operates scheduled and charter flights. Partly privatised in 1996, the airline joined the Star Alliance in 2004.
HQ airport & main base: Ljubljana
Radio callsign: ADRIA
Designator: JP/ADR
Employees: *c.* 900
Route points: Amsterdam, Brussels, Copenhagen, Frankfurt, Istanbul, London, Moscow, Munich, Ohrid, Paris, Podorica, Pristina, Sarajevo, Skopje, Vienna, Warsaw, Zurich
Fleet: 3 Airbus A320-200; 1 Boeing 737-500; 1 Bombardier CRJ100LR; 6 Bombardier CRJ200LR; 1 Fokker F27 Mk500; 2 Let L-410UVP-E; 3 Saab 340A

SOUTH AFRICA – ZS

Given the country's immense size and low population density, combined with wealth and industries such as mining, it is not surprising that South Africa has a varied commercial aviation sector. In addition to the airlines mentioned here, the sector includes often substantial general aviation companies, such as National Airways, with no less than thirty fixed-wing aircraft plus helicopters, with some of the aircraft used (including no fewer than twenty-two Raytheon Beech 1900s in airliner configuration) bordering on the air charter business.

1 TIME AIRLINE
Incorporated: 2003

Operations started in 2004 for this low-cost airline that concentrates on domestic services from its Johannesburg base. Main shareholder is Afrisource Holdings with 50 per cent.

HQ airport & main base: Johannesburg
Designator: RNX
Employees: 300. Flight crew: 60; cabin staff: 36
Route points: Cape Town, Durban, East London, George, Johannesburg, Port Elizabeth
Fleet: 2 McDonnell Douglas MD-82; 1 McDonnell Douglas MD-83; 1 McDonnell Douglas DC-9-10; 4 McDonnell Douglas DC-9-30

AFRICAN INTERNATIONAL AIRWAYS
Incorporated: 1985

An all-cargo airline handling charter flights and subcontracting to major airlines, including Alitalia between 1985 and 1996, as well as on short-term arrangements for other airlines, including South African Airways and British Airways.

HQ airport & main base: Johannesburg International
Designator: AIN
Fleet: 3 McDonnell Douglas DC-8 Srs 62; 2 McDonnell Douglas DC-8 Srs 50

COMAIR
Commercial Airways
Incorporated: 1946

Originally founded as Commercial Air Services in 1946, Comair did not begin operations until 1948, and has since developed a network of domestic services which has recently been extended to neighbouring states.

An important element in the airline's business has been the development of safari tours. At one time the airline operated a service to Gabarone for South African Airways, but the airline is now a British Airways franchisee, with the British airline holding 18 per cent of the shares.

The fleet, which as late as 1991 consisted of a Douglas DC-3 and four Fokker F27 Friendships, now includes Boeing 737s and McDonnell Douglas MD-82s. In 1997, Comair acquired a 25 per cent stake in state-owned SunAir, and also operates low-cost flights using the kulula.com name.

HQ airport & main base: Johannesburg International
Radio callsign: COMMERCIAL
Designator: CAW
Employees: 1, 212
Route points: Cape Town, Durban, Gabarone, George, Harare, Hoodspruit, Johannesburg, Manzini, Port Elizabeth, Richards Bay, Skukuza, Victoria Falls, Windhoek
Links with other airlines: British Airways (qv) has an 18 per cent shareholding. A British Airways franchisee
Fleet: 3 Boeing 737-400; 7 Boeing 737-300; 6 Boeing 737-200; 6 McDonnell Douglas MD-82

EXECUTIVE AEROSPACE
Incorporated: 1984

Executive Aerospace operates passenger charter flights, mainly for inclusive tour operators but also for sports teams and their supporters. Although the headquarters is in Johannesburg, Durban is the main base.

HQ airport & main base: Durban Louis Botha International
Designator: EAS
Fleet: 2 McDonnell Douglas DC-9-30; 4 BAe 748 Srs 2B

INTER AIR SOUTH AFRICA
Incorporated: 1993

Originally formed as a regional domestic scheduled airline in 1993, with operations started the following year, the airline is now concentrating on international services.

HQ airport & main base: Johannesburg International
Designator: D6/ILN
Employees: 243
Route points: Antananarivo, Bamoko, Brazzaville, Cotonou, Libreville, Ndjamena, Ndola, St Denis de la Reunion
Links with other airlines: Alliances with Air Austral (qv), Air Burkina, Air Gabon (qv), Air Madagascar (qv)
Fleet: 2 Boeing 727-200; 2 Boeing 737-200C; 1 Fokker F28 Mk4000

MANGO
Incorporated: 2006

Founded by South African Airways as a low-cost scheduled carrier to increase the number of people using the domestic air network from its present 5 per cent of the population, Mango has an initial fleet of four Boeing 737-800s leased from SAA and with a high-density 186-seat configuration.

HQ airport & main base: Johannesburg International
Route points: Bloemfontein, Cape Town, Durban, Johannesburg
Links with other airlines: Subsidiary of South Africa Airways (qv)
Fleet: 4 Boeing 737-800

NATIONWIDE AIRLINES
Incorporated: 1995

Nationwide was founded in 1995 by the current chief executive, Vernon Bricknell, initially to operate cargo charter flights, including humanitarian relief operations for major aid agencies. Passenger scheduled services started in the first year, and the network has grown rapidly to include most of the major centres within South Africa, as well as international scheduled services to Livingstone and London, the latter introduced in 2003.

The company is structured into four divisions, the airline, Nationwide Air Charter, Nationwide Aircraft Maintenance and Nationwide Aircraft Support. A franchisee, Nationwide Airlines (Zambia), uses the parent company's aircraft as required.

HQ airport & main base: Johannesburg International
Radio callsign: NATIONWIDE
Designator: CE/NTW
Employees: 800
Route points: Cape Town, Durban, George, Johannesburg, Livingstone, London, Nelspruit, Port Elizabeth
Links with other airlines: Alliance with Virgin Atlantic Airways (qv)
Fleet: 1 Boeing 767-300ER; 3 Boeing 727-200; 10 Boeing 737-200; 2 Boeing 737-500

NATURELINK
Incorporated: 1997

Founded as Naturelink Charters in 1997 to serve the tourist industry, the company now also operates contract charters for the energy and construction industries. Helicopters are also operated. Safair has a 60 per cent stake.

HQ airport & main base: Placencia
Designator: NRK
Employees: 160
Links with other airlines: Safair (qv) has a 60 per cent stake
Fleet: 1 Boeing 727-200; 1 Raytheon Beech 1900D; 3 Embraer EMB-110PI Bandeirante; 4 Embraer EMB-120 Brasilia; 5 Cessna Caravan 675; 5 Raytheon Beech King Air B200; 1 Britten-Norman BN2A Islander

SAFAIR
Safair Freighters
Incorporated: 1970

South Africa's main freight airline, Safair was formed in 1970 as a subsidiary of the state-owned shipping line, Safmarine. Initially, the airline concentrated on the domestic and regional cargo market before diversifying into the courier business and aircraft maintenance in 1991. In 1998, Safair acquired a 49 per cent shareholding in the Irish airline, Air Contractors, before being itself acquired by the present owners, Imperial Holdings later that year.

The following year, Safair took control of National Airways Corporation and of the air charter and aircraft sales company, Streamline Aviation. A 60 per cent stake in Naturelink, predominantly a tourist air charter company.

Safair today operates cargo charters nationally and internationally as well as having a domestic scheduled network. The fleet has varied over the years, and has included a Boeing 707 and BAe 146s, and in the 1990s included eight Boeing 727s and nine Lockheed Hercules. Today, the airline has four 727s, two 737s and eight Lockheed Hercules.

HQ airport & main base: Johannesburg International
Radio callsign: CARGO
Designator: FA/SFR
Employees: 509
Route points: Cape Town, Durban, East London, George, Johannesburg, Port Elizabeth, Walvis Bay
Links with other airlines: Owns 60 per cent of Naturelink (qv) and 49 per cent of Air Contractors (qv)
Fleet: 2 Boeing 727-200F; 2 Boeing 727-200; 2 Boeing 737-200; 8 Lockheed C-100-30 Hercules; 2 Raytheon Beech 1900D

SOLENTA AVIATION
Incorporated: 2000

Solenta Aviation provides passenger and cargo charters, including contract flying for DHL and for the oil industry, and wet-leasing of aircraft to other airlines.

HQ airport & main base: Johannesburg International
Radio callsign: SOLENTA
Designator:
Employees: 210
Links with other airlines: Operates cargo services on behalf of DHL (qv)
Fleet: 5 ATR-42-300/320; 7 Raytheon Beech 1900D; 1 Raytheon Beech King Air 220

SOUTH AFRICAN AIRLINK
Incorporated: 1992

South African Airlink was originally known as Airlink Airline when operations began in 1992, taking over the services of the bankrupt Link Airways and initially operating a mixed fleet including four ATR-42s, two Metroliners, a Dornier 228 and two Piper Navajo Chieftains. The airline became SAAirlink in 1995 when it entered into an alliance with South African Airways, operating commuter or feeder services and complementing the operations elsewhere in South Africa of SA Express. That same year it acquired Metavia, another South African airline.

The name has since changed to the more explicit South African Airlink, while South African Airways has now acquired a 10 per cent stake, and South African Airlink in turn has a 49 per cent stake in Zimbabwe Airlink and 40 per cent in Swaziland Airlink. Recently, Embraer regional jets have been added to the fleet, and the Dornier 228s have been replaced.

HQ airport & main base: Johannesburg International
Radio callsign: LINK
Designator: 4Z/LNK
Employees: 500
Route points: Bloemfontein, Durban, Johannesburg, Margate, Mmabatho, Nelspruit, Phalaborwa, Pietersburg, Pietmaritzburg, Plettenberg Bay, Sun City, Umtata
Links with other airlines: South African Airways (qv) has a 10 per cent interest. Owns 49 per cent of Zimbabwe Airlink (qv) and 40 per cent of Swaziland Airlink. Operates in a marketing alliance with South African Airways and SA Express (both qv)
Fleet: 1 Boeing 737-200; 2 Embraer 170; 15 Embraer ERJ-135LR; 12 BAe Jetstream 41

SOUTH AFRICAN
South African Airways
Incorporated: 1934

Africa's largest airline, and the only one in the fifty largest by turnover, was originally founded in 1934 when the South African government acquired Union Airways, a privately owned airline unable to keep pace with the capital demands of rapid growth. South African Airways was soon enlarged by the acquisition of South West African Airways in 1935. South West African had also been privately owned and dated from 1932.

The mainstay of the new airline's fleet was the Junkers F.13, but these were later supplemented by Junkers Ju.52/3m trimotors and then Ju.86s, with a sizeable fleet of Lockheed Lodestars also pressed into service before the outbreak of the Second World War. Wartime demands for aircraft and aircrew, and the difficulty in obtaining spares for the German-built aircraft, meant that all services were suspended in 1940, and the serviceable were aircraft taken over by the South African Air Force. A limited number of services was reinstated in 1944, recognising the significance of air transport in a large country.

After the Second World War, a service to London was started in 1945, with the airline operating the surviving Lockheed Lodestars and Douglas DC-3s on domestic services and Douglas DC-4s and Avro Yorks on the longer-haul routes. Lockheed Constellations were introduced in 1950, until replaced by Douglas DC-7Bs in 1956. Meanwhile, de Havilland Comet 1 jet airliners had been leased from BOAC in 1953, and flown with South African crews until these aircraft were grounded after a spate of serious accidents. Much greater success was experienced with a fleet of Vickers Viscount turboprop airliners, first introduced in 1956 and used on services within South Africa and to neighbouring states.

South African Airways entered the jet age permanently in 1960, with Boeing 707s. Services to New York began in 1969. The extra range of these aircraft soon came to be valued, after a number of newly independent African states banned the use of their airspace by South African aircraft, leading to the European services having to be rerouted via the Cape Verde Islands, at that time a Portuguese colony. The new routes, nevertheless, proved popular with passengers.

Short-haul jet airliners eventually replaced the Vickers Viscounts, with Boeing 727s and then Boeing 737s entering service, while long-haul routes came to be taken over by the Boeing 747. At the other end of the scale, the less heavily used domestic services had most of their DC-3s replaced by Hawker Siddeley, later BAe, HS 748 twin turboprop airliners.

Political change in South Africa has eased the airline's operating conditions considerably, and also led to a massive growth in competition, with more than eighty foreign airlines now operating into the country's airports, as opposed to a handful during the final days of apartheid. The visible change has been the changing of the well-known blue cheat line and orange tail with a springbok symbol to an all-white fuselage and a tailplane design incorporating the colours of the new national flag. Unusually, especially for a large national airline, for many years the fleet included aircraft maintained in active preservation, including DC-3s, DC-4s and a Ju.52/3m, but these have now been separated from the main fleet.

In 1990 ownership of the airline was transferred to Transnet, a state-owned company, ready for privatisation. A degree of privatisation followed in 1999 when the SAirGroup, owners of Swissair, bought a 20 per cent stake in the airline, but when Swissair collapsed in 2002, Transnet bought back the sharehlding to protect South African Airways. After many years when SAA had a 20 per cent stake in SA Express, which operates feeder services, Transnet also bought this company, but SAA has a 10 per cent stake and a marketing alliance with South African Airlink, another feeder operator. SAA has established SAA Cargo to market the cargo capacity on its scheduled services, and this airline could operate aircraft in its own right in the future. Meanwhile, a 49 per cent stake is held in Air Tanzania.

By far the largest airline in Africa, South African Airways recently fell from being the thirty-first largest in the world by revenue to thirty-fourth, and is now outside the 'Top 50' by passenger numbers, although this is largely a reflection of the importance of long-distance passengers to the airline. Overall, the past decade has seen continued growth, including a rise of almost 50 per cent in the number of employees.

HQ airport & main base: Johannesburg International, with additional hubs/bases at Cape Town and Durban
Radio callsign: SPRINGBOK
Designator: SA/SAA
Employees: 14,475
Route points: Abidjan, Accra, Addis Ababa, Amsterdam, Atlanta, Bangkok, Beira, Blantyre, Bloemfontein, Bulawayo, Cape Town, Dakar, Dar-es-Salaam, Dubai, Durban, East London, Entebbe, Frankfurt, Gabarone, George, Harare, Hoedspruit, Hong Kong, Johannesburg, Kigali, Kilimanjaro, Kimberley, Kinshasa, Lagos, Lilongwe, Livingstone, London, Luanda, Lubumbashi, Lusaka, Mala Mala, Manzini, Maputo, Margate, Maseru, Mauritius, Mmabatho, Mumbai, Nairobi, Ndola, Nelspruit, New York, Paris, Perth, Phalaborwa, Pietermaritzburg, Polokwane, Port Elizabeth, Recife, Richards Bay, Rio de Janeiro, Sal, Salvador, Sao Paulo, Sydney, Tel Aviv, Umtata, Upington, Victoria Falls, Walvis Bay, Windhoek, Zanzibar, Zurich
Links with other airlines: Owns SAA Cargo. SAA has a 49 per cent stake in Air Tanzania, and a 10 per cent stake in South African Airlink (qv). Alliances with Air New Zealand (qv), Air Tanzania (qv), Asiana Airlines (qv), Atlantic Southeast Airlines, Austrian Airlines (qv), bmi (qv), Cathay Pacific (qv), Delta Air Lines (qv), El Al (qv), Emirates (qv), Ethiopian Airlines (qv), Linhas Aereas de Mocambique, Lufthansa (qv), Qantas Airways (qv),

TAC Air Services (qv), United Airlines (qv), Varig (qv), Virgin Atlantic Airways (qv), Zimbabwe Airlink (qv)
Annual turnover: US $2,823 million (£1,880 million)
Fleet: 8 Boeing 747-400; 9 Airbus A340-600; 3 Airbus A340-300; 6 Airbus A340-200; 20 Boeing 737-800; 15 Airbus A320-200; 11 Airbus A319-100

SOUTH AFRICAN EXPRESS
South African Express Airways
Incorporated: 1993

South African Express was originally founded in December 1993 as SA Express, and commenced operations the following April, being intended from the start to be a commuter airline to feed into the trunk domestic services of South African Airways, and also take over routes which could not be served economically by jet aircraft, while charter flights were also operated.

Initially, South African Airways acquired a 20 per cent stake in the new airline, while the main shareholder was Thebe Investments with 51 per cent, but Transnet, the state holding company that owns South African Airways, has since acquired the airline outright.

In addition to the SAA connection, the airline also has a marketing alliance with South African Airlink.

HQ airport & main base: Johannesburg
Radio callsign: EXPRESSWAYS
Designator: YB/EXY
Route points: On the domestic services of South African Airways
Links with other airlines: Marketing alliances with SAA (qv) and South African Airlink (qv)
Fleet: 2 Bombardier Dash 8 Q400; 6 Bombardier CRJ200ER; 7 Bombardier Dash 8 Q300

VULKANAIR
Incorporated: 1997

Vulkanair was formed in 1997 and operates a very mixed fleet of aircraft on passenger and cargo charters throughout Africa, the Middle East and Europe.

Although based in South Africa, the airline also has operations elsewhere, including the Congo and Uganda.

HQ airport & main base: Johannesburg International
Employees: 120
Fleet: Aircraft chartered as required

SPAIN – EC

Once one of the most backward nations in western Europe, and the first to have lost its empire, Spain's development of civil air transport was different from that of France and the United Kingdom. It would be wrong to suggest that the Spanish were indifferent to air transport, however, as a fleet of military Junkers Ju.52/3 trimotor transports was used to ferry troops of the Spanish Foreign Legion from Ceuta and Melilla in North Africa to Spain at the outset of the Spanish Civil War.

Much of the history of Spanish commercial aviation has been that of the national airline, Iberia, largely because the Spanish economy was tightly regulated. The airline was originally founded in 1927 as Iberia Air Transport. In 1929 the airline was merged with two other Spanish airlines, CETA and Union Aerea Española, to create a new airline, CLASSA, and a majority shareholding in this airline was taken by the Spanish government. CLASSA was in turn acquired in 1931 by a newly established state-owned carrier, LAPE. These manouevres failed to establish a solid footing for air transport in Spain, largely because of the impact of the Spanish Civil War, which saw many routes suspended and aircraft requisitioned for the war effort by both sides, leaving LAPE in severe financial and operational difficulties by 1938.

The present Iberia was formed in 1938 to acquire the equipment and services of LAPE, and re-establish domestic and international services suspended during the Civil War. The initial fleet consisted almost entirely of ex-military Junkers Ju.52/3M trimotors. Initially the new airline was a mixed enterprise, with the Spanish government holding a 51 per cent majority stake, but the difficulties experienced by the airline during the Second World War, despite Spanish neutrality, resulted in the state acquiring the private shareholdings. Wartime services were limited to links with Portugal, Spanish Morocco and Spain's offshore islands.

Spain's main domestic airline, Aviaco, was formed in 1948 by a group of businessmen in Bilbao, in northern Spain, as an all-cargo charter airline using Bristol 170 Freighters. Scheduled passenger services followed in 1950, initially from Bilbao to Madrid and Barcelona, and before long the airline was etsablishing services from the mainland to the Balearic Islands and to the Canaries. Major expansion of the domestic route network followed, with services based on Madrid, and jet equipment was introduced during the early 1960s, initially using Sud Aviation Caravelles leased from Sabena.

An unusual feature of the airline's operations during the 1960s was the vehicle ferry services from Barcelona to Palma de Mallorca, on the largest of the Balearic Islands, using Aviation Traders Carvairs, converted Douglas DC-4s.

Acquisition of a substantial shareholding in Aviaco by Iberia enabled the airline to take over some of Iberia's domestic services, leaving that airline with a presence on the major trunk routes, such as Madrid to Barcelona. A number of internal services are operated on behalf of Iberia.

In 1999, when Aviaco was operating a fleet of McDonnell Douglas DC-9s and MD-88s, it was absorbed by Iberia.

From the 1950s onwards, Spain increasingly became a major tourist destination. Despite complaints that the foreign visitors were arriving in aircraft owned by foreign airlines, relatively little was done about it until deregulation of air transport in the European Union encouraged many Spainsh airlines to be established. There were a few independent Spanish airlines even before Spain became a member of the European Union, including, for example, Spantax, which dated from 1959, but deregulation proved to be more effective in encouraging the growth of new airlines.

One reason why the tourists used foreign airlines was in fact the impact of strict air transport regulations throughout almost all of the nations of western Europe. High air fares on national flag carriers established to serve the business and diplomatic markets were beyond the reach of would-be private travellers. The solution lay in inclusive tour charter flights on which the seat on an aircraft was part of a packge that included hotel accommodation and food. While a healthy independent sector flourished in many countries, it was confined in what it could achieve.

AEROLINEAS DE BALEARES
Incorporated: 2000

Starting operations in 2000 with the title AB Bluestar, Aerolineas de Baleares operates scheduled domestic and regional services as well as charter flights to mainland Europe. The majority shareholder is Grupo Marsans, the owner of Aerolineas Argentina, with 51 per cent, but another Spanish airline, Spanair has 18 per cent and Aerolineas de Baleares operates franchised services as Spanair Link. The other significant shareholder is SAS.

HQ airport & main base: Palma de Mallorca Son Sant Joan
Radio callsign: BALEARES
Designator: DF/ABH
Links with other airlines: SAS and Spanair (qv) are shareholders. Operates as Spanair Link franchisee
Fleet: 4 Boeing 717-200

AIR EUROPA
Incorporated: 1984

Although founded in 1984, Air Europa did not commence operations until 1994, operating inclusive tour charter flights between Europe and Spanish holiday resorts as part of the Airlines of Europe Group. When Airlines of Europe dissolved, the airline became indpendent, operating for a period from 1998 as an Iberia franchisee. It subsequently moved into, first, domestic scheduled services and then long-haul international scheduled services.

HQ airport & main base: Palma de Mallorca Son San Juan, with a hub at Las Palmas de Gran Canaria
Designator: UX/AEA
Employees: 2,570
Route points: Alicante, Asturas, Barcelona, Beijing, Bilbao, Budapest, Cancun, Caracas, Fuerteventura, Granada, Havana, Ibiza, Madrid, Malaga, Marrakesh, Menorca, Milan, Palma de Mallorca, Paris, Prague, Punta Cana, Rome, Salvador, Santiago de Compostella, Santo Domingo, Seville, Shanghai, Tenerife, Tunis, Valencia, Warsaw, Zaragoza
Links with other airlines: Alliances with Aeromexico (qv), Air France (qv), Air Plus Comet, Alitalia (qv), China Eastern Airlines (qv), Continental Airlines (qv), Cubana de Aviacion (qv), Hi Fly, KLM (qv), Malev (qv), PGA Portugalia Airlines (qv), Smart Wings (qv), Tunisair (qv)
Fleet: 1 Airbus A340-200; 4 Airbus A330-200; 5 Boeing 767-300ER; 67 Boeing 737-800 (in course of delivery) (On order: 10 Airbus A350-800)

AIR NOSTRUM
Air Nostrum SA
Incorporated: 1994

Privately owned Air Nostrum was formed in 1994 to operate scheduled services from Valencia to other major Spanish cities, to the Balearic Islands and to southern France. A Dutch airline, DenimAir, was owned between 1999 and 2002. In 1997, Air Nostrum became an Iberia franchisee, operating as an Iberia Regional partner. Recently, it has replaced its fleet of Bombardier Dash 8 turboprops with Bombardier Regional Jets.

HQ airport & main base: Valencia
Designator: YW/ANS
Employees: 1,767
Route points: Biarritz, Bilbao, Ibiza, Madrid, Menorca, Nice, Palma de Mallorca, Valencia, Vitoria
Fleet: 16 Bombardier CRJ900; 34 Bombardier CRJ200ER; 1 BAe 146-200; 7 ATR-72-500; 11 Bombardier Dash 8 Q300

AIR COMET
Incorporated: 1996

Originally founded as Air Plus Comet in 1996 by Grupo Marsans, this airline commenced operations the following year. It operates both scheduled and charter flights within Spain and Europe, as well as long-haul operations to the Americas and, more recently, China. The present title was adopted in January 2007.

HQ airport & main base: Madrid
Designator: A7/MPD
Route points: Barcelona, Beijing, Bogotá, Lima, Madrid, Milan, New York, Puerto Plata, Rome, Santo Domingo, Shanghai
Links with other airlines: Alliance with Air Europa (qv)
Fleet: 4 Boeing 747-200B; 1 Airbus A340-300; 2 Airbus A310-300; 2 Boeing 737-300; 2 McDonnell Douglas MD-88

AUDELI AIR
Incorporated: 1987

A subsidiary of Cygnus Air, Audeli Air grew out of an executive aircraft charter business and today provides executive and other passenger charter flights.

HQ airport & main base: Madrid Barajas
Designator: ADI
Fleet: 2 Boeing 757-200; 1 Embraer ERJ-135; 3 Dassault Falcon 20

BINTER
Binter Canarias SA
Incorporated: 1988

Established in 1988 as a subsidiary of Iberia, Binter Canarias commenced operations the following year, taking over many of the routes within the Canary Islands hitherto operated by Iberia and Aviaco. Iberia retained a controlling interest in the airline, which extended its operations to Madeira until 1999, when privatisation of the airline saw control pass to Hesperia Inversiones Aereas, a group of Canary Islands-based investors. Since then, the route network has expanded to include additional international destinations.

HQ airport & main base: Gran Canaria Las Palmas, with a further base at Tenerife Norte
Designator: NT/IBB
Employees: 420
Route points: Fuertaventura, Funchal, Laayoune, Lanzarote, Las Palmas, Marrakesh, Milan, Paris, San Sebastian de la Gomera, Santa Cruz de la Palma, Tenerife, Valverde
Fleet: 2 Boeing 737-400; 7 ATR-72-500; 5 ATR-72-210

CLICKAIR
Incorporated: 2006

Iberia has a 20 per cent stake in this low-cost Spanish airline, but 80 per cent control, along with four other equity partners. The airline is planning an all-Airbus A320 fleet and intends to serve thirty European destinations from the main Spanish holiday resorts.

HQ airport & main base: Barcelona
Radio callsign: Clickair
Designator: XG/CLI
Route points: Barcelona, Malaga, Seville, Valencia
Links with other airlines: Iberia has a 20 per cent stake
Fleet: 8 Airbus A320-200 with another 22 on order

CYGNUS AIR
Incorporated: 1994

Founded in 1994, operations began as Regional Lineas Aereas, owned by Regional Airlines of France and Gestair, a Spanish business airline, operating regional Spanish scheduled passenger flights from Madrid. In 1998, the airline was repositioned as a cargo operator and adopted the current name. Gestair has retained a 60 per cent stake, with the remainer held by IMES, and Cygnus has a subsidiary, Audell Air, in which it holds a 90 per cent share.

HQ airport & main base: Madrid Barajas
Designator: RGN
Fleet: 1 McDonnell Douglas DC-8-73AF; 2 McDonnell Douglas DC-8-62

FUTURA
Futura International Airways SA
Incorporated: 1989

Founded in 1989 by Aer Lingus and Spanish tour operating interests, Futura began charter operations in 1990. Initially Aer Lingus held a 25 per cent interest, but this is now 20 per cent, with the remainder held by Futura's management.

HQ airport & main base: Palma de Mallorca
Designator: FH/FUA
Employees: 712
Links with other airlines: Aer Lingus (qv) has a 20 per cent interest
Fleet: 8 Boeing 737-800; 6 Boeing 737-400

GIRJET
Incorporated: 2003

A passenger charter airline specialising in operations in support of conferences, as well as ad hoc charters.

HQ airport & main base: Barcelona
Designator: GJT
Fleet: 1 Boeing 757-200; 4 Fokker 100

HOLA AIRLINES
Incorporated: 2002

Established by a former chief executive of Air Europe Express in 2002, Hola provides ad hoc, VIP, corporate and inclusive tour passenger charters.

HQ airport & main base: Palma de Mallorca
Designator: HOA
Fleet: 2 Boeing 757-200; 1 Boeing 737-300

IBERIA
Iberia Airlines – Lineas Aereas de Espana SA
Incorporated: 1927

Spain's national airline, Iberia, is the nineteenth largest airline in the world by annual turnover, and seventeenth by passenger numbers. The airline was originally founded in 1927 as Iberia Air Transport. In 1929, the airline was merged with two other Spanish airlines, CETA and Union Aerea Española, to create a new airline, CLASSA, and a majority shareholding in this airline was taken by the Spanish government. CLASSA was in turn acquired in 1931 by a newly established state-owned carrier, LAPE. These manouevres failed to establish a solid footing for air transport in Spain, largely because of the impact of the Spanish Civil War, which saw many routes suspended and aircraft requisitioned for the war effort by both sides, leaving LAPE in severe financial and operational difficulties by 1938.

The present Iberia was formed in 1938 to acquire the equipment and services of LAPE, and re-establish domestic and international services suspended during the Civil War. The initial fleet consisted almost entirely of Junkers Ju.52/3M trimotors. Initially, the new airline was a mixed enterprise, with the Spanish government holding a 51 per cent majority stake, but the difficulties experienced by the airline during the Second World War, despite Spanish neutrality, resulted in the state acquiring the private shareholdings. Wartime services were limited to links with Portugal, Spanish Morocco and Spain's offshore islands.

Postwar, Iberia began a programme of expansion, acquiring a new fleet of Douglas DC-3s for internal and European services, and then DC-4s for longer-distance operations, including the airline's first transatlantic services. The DC-4s were augmented and then replaced by Lockheed Super Constellations on the longer-distance routes, while the DC-3s remained on domestic services but were replaced on European routes by Convair 440 Metropolitans. The airline's first jet equipment, Douglas DC-8s for the transatlantic routes, was introduced in 1961, while Sud Aviation Caravelles were introduced on European routes in 1962. A fleet of Fokker F27 Friendship airliners was introduced in 1967 to replace the DC-3s on the domestic routes.

As the jet age progressed, Iberia operated a mix of Boeing and Douglas types, notably the Boeing 727 and 747, and different marks of Douglas DC-9. In more recent years, the airline has also operated aircraft of Airbus manufacture, as well as the Boeing 757.

After Iberia took a shareholding in the Spanish domestic carrier, Aviaco, many of the domestic services were handed over to Aviaco, although Iberia continued to maintain a presence on the trunk routes. Iberia also took a 20 per cent stake in the Argentine airline, Aerolineas Argentinas, when that airline was privatised in 1990. Another South American carrier in which Iberia had a substantial interest for many years was Viasa of Venezuela. There is a token 3 per cent stake in Royal Air Maroc. For many years, Iberia itself was owned by the state holding company, SEPI, itself a major shareholder in Aviaco in addition to Iberia's 32.9 per cent stake.

An abrupt change in policies started in 1999. Aviaco was taken over and its services fully integrated into those of Iberia. In the years that followed, the interests in airlines such as Aerolineas Argentinas and Viasa were sold. Iberia itself became a member of the Oneworld alliance, while closer links were established with British Airways when that airline acquired a 9 per cent shareholding in Iberia after Iberia was privatised, and American Airlines has a 1 per cent stake in Iberia. In an attempt to contain costs, Iberia participated in the creation of low-cost regional carriers, such as Binter Canarias, itself since sold to local interests, and a new airline, Viva Air, operating both scheduled and charter flights for the leisure market. A marketing alliance with American Airlines was agreed in 1997. An indication of the success of cost-cutting measures is that today, despite having absorbed Aviaco, Iberia employs more than a thousand fewer personnel than ten years ago.

Inevitably the composition of the fleet has changed over the past decade, with the last of the McDonnell Douglas types having departed, leaving the airline with an all-Airbus fleet now and for the foreseeable future.

HQ airport & main base: Madrid Barajas, with a further hub/base at Barcelona
Radio callsign: IBERIA
Designator: IB/IBE
Employees: 24,677
Route points: Acapulco, Albacete, Alicante, Almeria, Amman, Amsterdam, Asturias, Asuncion, Athens, Badajoz, Barcelona, Berlin, Bilbao, Birmingham, Bogotá, Bologna, Bordeaux, Brussels, Buenos Aires, Cairo, Cali, Cancun, Caracas, Casablanca, Chicago, Copenhagen, Dakar, Damascus, Delhi, Dublin, Düsseldorf, Edinburgh, Frankfurt, Fuerteventura, Geneva, Granada, Guadalajara, Guatemala, Guayaquil, Havana, Helsinki, Ibiza, Istanbul, Jerez de la Frontera, Johannesburg, Kiev, La Coruna, Lagos, Lanzarote, Las Palmas, Leon, Lima, Lisbon, Logrono, London, Madrid, Malabo, Malaga, Managua, Manchester, Marrakesh, Marseilles, Melilla, Menorca, Mérida, Mexico City, Miami, Milan, Monterrey, Montevideo, Moscow, Munich, Murcia, New York, Nice, Oporto, Oaxaca, Quito, Palma de Mallorca, Pamplona, Panama City, Paris, Prague, Puerto Vallarta, Quito, Rio de Janeiro, Rome, San Jose, San Juan, San Pedro Sula, San Salvador, San Sebastian, Santa Cruz de la Palma, Santa Cruz de Tenerife, Santander, Santiago de Chile, Santiago de Compostella, Santo Domingo, Sao Paulo, Seville, Stockholm, Stuttgart, Tangier, Tel Aviv, Tenerife, Tokyo, Tunis, Turin, Valencia, Vallodolid, Venice, Veracruz, Verona, Vienna, Vigo, Vitoria, Zurich
Passengers carried: 26.7 million
Links with other airlines: British Airways (qv) has a 9 per cent stake. American Airlines (qv) has a 1 per cent stake. Iberia has a 3 per cent stake in Royal Air Maroc (qv)
Annual turnover: US $5,895 million (£3,900 million)
Fleet: 13 Airbus A340-600; 18 Airbus A340-300; 4 Boeing 757-200; 19 Airbus A321-200; 64 Airbus A320-200; 24 Airbus A319-100; 12 McDonnell Douglas MD-88; 18 McDonnell Douglas MD-87

IBERWORLD AIRLINES
Incorporated: 1998

Founded in 1998 as an inclusive tour charter operator by Grupo Iberostar, a tour operator, Iberworld now also has a scheduled service to Havana in addition to flying tourists to destinations in Europe, North Africa and the Caribbean.

HQ airport & main base: Palma de Mallorca
Designator: TY/IWD
Employees: 407
Route points: Havana, Palma de Mallorca
Fleet: 2 Airbus A330-300; 1 Airbus A330-200; 4 Airbus A320-200

ISLAS
Islas Airways
Incorporated: 2002

A small inter-island airline based in the Canaries, Islas Airways was founded in 2002 and began operations the following year. A subsidiary is Santa Barbara Airlines, which operates a scheduled network out of Caracas in Venezuela.

HQ airport & main base: Tenerife Norte Los Rodeos
Designator: 1F/ISW
Route points: Fuertaventura, Las Palmas, Santa Cruz de la Palma, Tenerife
Links with other airlines: Owns 100 per cent of Santa Barbara Airlines (qv)
Fleet: 4 ATR-72-200; 1 ATR-42-300

NAYSA
Navegacion y Servicios Aereos Canaria
Incorporated: 1969

NAYSA commenced operations from Cordoba on mainland Spain in 1969, operating charter and air taxi flights. The company moved to the Canary

Islands in 1973, and in 1977 changed owners. Today, scheduled and charter flights, including air ambulance flights and airline crew transfers, are operated between the Canary Islands for passengers and cargo.

HQ airport & main base: Gran Canaria Las Palmas
Designator: NAY
Route points: Lanzarote, Las Palmas, Tenerife
Fleet: 6 ATR-72-500; 5 Raytheon Beech 1900C/D

ORIONAIR
Incorporated: 2006

A passenger charter airline operating mainly to the Balearic and Canary Islands.

HQ airport & main base: Valencia
Fleet: 2 BAe 146-300

PAN AIR
Incorporated: 1987

Founded in 1987, Pan Air began operations the following year and has developed into a cargo carrier operating on the European Express Network of its owners, TNT Express Spain.

HQ airport & main base: Madrid Barajas
Designator: PV/PNR
Employees: 195
Links with other airlines: Owned 100 per cent by TNT Spain
Fleet: 1 Airbus A300B4-200F; 6 BAE 146-200QT

SPANAIR
Spanair SA
Incorporated: 1986

Spanair was founded in 1986 as a joint venture between the Viajes Marsans travel agency group and SAS, and began charter operations in 1988, using a single McDonnell Douglas MD-83, with most of the flights being inclusive tour charters from mainland European centres to the Balearic Islands. Transatlantic charter flights started in 1991, followed by scheduled services in 1994, the same year that Spanair moved into ground handling, hitherto the preserve of Iberia and Aviaco.

Although the airline's headquarters and main base is at Palma de Mallorca, the main hub for its growing scheduled network is Madrid. Following the creation of the European single market and the lifting of restrictions on airline ownership by foreign companies, the SAS shareholding in Spanair has grown from 49 per cent to 94.9 per cent, with Marsans now holding 5.1 per cent, while Spainair has an 18 per cent stake in Aerolineas de Baleares.

HQ airport & main base: Palma de Mallorca, with bases/hubs at Madrid and Barcelona
Radio callsign: SUNWING
Designator: JK/JKK
Employees: 2,953
Route points: Alicante, Ancona, Asturias, Bangkok, Barcelona, Bilbao, Billund, Bremen, Copenhagen, Düsseldorf, Frankfurt, Fuerteventura, Hamburg, Ibiza, Jerez de la Frontera, La Coruna, Lanzarote, Larnaca, Las Palmas, Linz, Lisbon, London, Madeira, Madrid, Malabo, Malaga, Menorca, Munich, Palma de Mallorca, Philadelphia, Prague, Riga, Rome, Salzburg, Santiago de Compostella, Seville, Stockholm, Stuttgart, Tenerife, Valencia, Vienna, Vigo, Vilnius, Warsaw
Links with other airlines: SAS (qv) has a 94.9 per cent shareholding. Spanair has an 18 per cent stake in Aerolineas de Baleares (qv)
Fleet: 5 Airbus A321-200; 16 Airbus A320-200; 11 McDonnell Douglas MD-87; 19 McDonnell Douglas MD-83; 10 McDonnell Douglas MD-82; 2 McDonnell Douglas MD-81; 2 Fokker 100

SWIFTAIR
Incorporated: 1986

Primarily a passenger and cargo charter airline, Swiftair is developing scheduled services. It was founded in 1986 and is completely independent.

HQ airport & main base: Madrid Barajas
Designator: SWT
Fleet: 1 Airbus A300B4-200F; 1 Boeing 727-200F; 2 Boeing 727-200; 2 ATR-72-200F; 6 ATR-72-200; 1 ATR-42-300F; 1 ATR-42-300F; 4 ATR-42-300; 2 McDonnell Douglas MD-83; 1 McDonnell Douglas MD-82; 9 Embraer EMB-120 Brasilia; 2 Fairchild Metro

VOLAR AIRLINES
LTE Volar Airlines
Incorporated: 1987

LTE Volar Airlines was formed in 1987 by Spanish business interests with the backing of the German airline LTU, as an inclusive tour charter airline mainly flying passengers from western Europe to holiday destinations in mainland Spain, the Balearic Islands and the Canary Islands. Initially LTE had a

25 per cent stake in the airline, but in 1993 the airline became wholly owned by LTU. Control has now passed to the Gaserer group. Originally, the airline had three Boeing 757s, but these have now been replaced by Airbus A320s.

HQ airport & main base: Palma de Mallorca
Designator: XO/LTE
Fleet: 4 Airbus A320-200

VUELING AIRLINES
Incorporated: 2004

Vueling Airlines is a new Spanish low-cost carrier based on Barcelona. Services commenced in 2004 and link many of the busiest tourist destinations in Spain and also extend to several European capitals. Ownership rests with institutional investors, the management team and a number of private investors.

HQ airport & main base: Barcelona, with a hub at Valencia
Designator: VY/VLG
Route points: Amsterdam, Barcelona, Brussels, Bilbao, Lisbon, Madrid, Malaga, Milan, Palma de Mallorca, Paris, Rome, Seville, Valencia
Fleet: 21 Airbus A320-200

SRI LANKA – 4R

As with many countries, the history of air transport in Sri Lanka has been essentially that of one airline, Sri Lankan Airlines (the name adopted for Air Lanka in 1999) and its colonial-era predecessor, Air Ceylon.

The airline has had a difficult history, with Sri Lanka riven by civil war and guerilla activities, although the fleet is stronger today than ever before. At the same time, the airline has been associated with and managed by a succession of airlines from outside the country, of which the current one, Emirates, which also has a 43.6 per cent stake in the airline, seems have had the most impact.

SRI LANKAN AIRLINES
Air Lanka Corporation
Incorporated: 1979

Until 1999, Sri Lankan Airlines was known as Air Lanka, which was formed as the national airline of Sri Lanka in 1979, a wholly government-owned airline to take over the operations of Air Ceylon, which had itself been established by the government in 1947. Air Ceylon had initially operated three Douglas DC-3s on services within Ceylon and to India. Services to London and Sydney followed in 1949 after the airline entered into an operating agreement with Australian National Airways, and two Douglas DC-4s were obtained for these services. Later, in 1951, the airline was restructured, becoming a corporation rather than a department of the Ministry of Communications and Works, and under the new arrangement, the Ceylon government held 51 per cent of the shares and ANA the remainder. ANA's interest was purchased in 1955 by KLM, Royal Dutch Airlines, and from 1956 onwards a service was also operated to Amsterdam.

The agreement with KLM was terminated in 1961, when the airline became wholly government owned and had to suspend operations other than within Ceylon and to India until BOAC, British Overseas Airways Corporation, was able to start a London–Colombo service in association with Air Ceylon, initially using one of BOAC's de Havilland Comet 4s, although later this was replaced by a Vickers VC10.

The airline's own jet equipment arrived soon afterwards, with a Hawker Siddeley Trident 1E for services to India, while turboprop Hawker Siddeley (later BAe) HS 748 and Nord 262s were used on internal services alongside two surviving DC-3s and on services to southern India. After the ending of the agreement with BOAC, the French independent airline, UTA, provided management assistance, and services once again extended to Europe and Australia, using a Douglas DC-8.

The change of name and restructuring in 1979 also reflected the new name adopted for Ceylon. Once again, a foreign airline provided assistance, in this case Singapore Airlines, which remained with Air Lanka for its first two years of existence. The network continued to expand, with the airline's first wide-bodied aircraft, Lockheed TriStars, while a Boeing 737-200 was acquired for the shorter routes.

After Singapore Airlines, in place of the agreements with UTA, BOAC and KLM, Air Lanka had marketing alliances with a number of airlines in the Indian subcontinent, the Gulf and South-East Asia. This eventually led to one of the Gulf airlines, Emirates, purchasing a 43.6 per cent stake in the airline in 1998, and the following year the airline changed its name to Sri Lankan Airlines. While the government continued to hold a controlling 51 per cent stake, the airline's employees received 5.3 per cent.

Despite a difficult history, with civil war and guerilla activity blighting Sri Lanka's (and the airline's) development, including one occasion when many of its aircraft were destroyed on the ground, the past decade has seen steady progress.

HQ airport & main base: Colombo Bandaranaike International
Radio callsign: AIR LANKA
Designator: UL/ALK
Employees: 5,163
Route points: Abu Dhabi, Amsterdam, Bahrain, Bangalore, Bangkok, Beijing, Bentota River, Birmingham (UK), Brisbane, Brussels, Chennai, Colombo, Damman, Delhi, Dickwella, Doha, Dubai, Düsseldorf, Frankfurt, Hong Kong, Hyderabad, Jakarta, Karachi, Koggala, Kuala Lumpur, Kuwait, Larnaca, London, Male, Manchester, Munich, Muscat, New York, Paris, Riyadh, Singapore, Sydney, Thiruvananthapuram, Tiruchirappalli, Tokyo, Vienna, Weerawila, Zurich
Links with other airlines: Emirates has a 43.6 per cent stake in the airline. Alliances with bmi, Emirates, Indian Airlines, Malaysia Airlines, Oman Air (all qv)
Fleet: 5 Airbus A340-300; 4 Airbus A330-200; 4 Airbus A320-200; 2 Antonov An-12

SUDAN – ST

AZZA TRANSPORT
Incorporated: 1993

A cargo charter airline owned by a number of financial institutions, operating within Africa and the Middle East.

HQ airport & main base: Khartoum
Designator: AZZ
Employees: 350
Fleet: 2 Ilyushin Il-76TD; 2 Boeing 707-320C; 1 Antonov An-26B; 1 Antonov An-12

BADR AIRLINES
Incorporated: 1997

Owned by two private shareholders, BADR Airlines is primarily an air cargo charter operator, with much of its work concentrated within Sudan itself, on contract to international relief agencies.

HQ airport & main base: Khartoum and also Sharjah International
Designator: BDR
Fleet: 1 Ilyushin Il-76TD; 3 Antonov An-74; 1 Antonov An-26B

SUDAN AIRWAYS
Sudan Airways Corporation
Incorporated: 1946

Sudan Airways was founded in 1946 by the Sudanese government-owned Sudan Railways System, beginning operations in 1947 with the assistance of a British company, Airwork, at that time also involved in airline operations. Initially, three de Havilland Dove light transports operated on domestic services, linking the more important Sudanese centres. The route network expanded, so that by 1960 Sudan Airways was operating to a number of important points in the Middle East, still with four Doves, augmented by seven Douglas DC-3s and a single Vickers Viscount turboprop airliner.

Three Fokker F27 Friendship airliners were introduced in 1962, and in 1963 the airline received its first jet equipment, the first of two de Havilland Comet 4Cs, which enabled the airline to extend its route network south to Nairobi and north to Frankfurt and London. The Comets were later joined by Boeing 707s in 1974, with the first short-haul jets, Boeing 737s, the following year. In recent years Airbus aircraft and Fokker 50 turboprops have been added, as well as a number of Antonov turboprops, but the number of European destinations has been substantially reduced. The airline remains in government ownership.

HQ airport & main base: Khartoum Civil
Radio callsign: SUDANAIR
Designator: SD/SUD
Employees: 2,400
Route points: Abu Dhabi, Addis Ababa, Al Ain, Bamako, Cairo, Damascus, Damman, Doha, Dubai, Entebbe, Jeddah, Kano, Khartoum, Lagos, Nairobi, Niamey, Riyadh, Tripoli
Fleet: 3 Airbus A300-600; 2 Airbus A310-300; 2 Boeing 707-320C; 1 Boeing 737-200; 3 Antonov An-24; 5 Fokker 50; 1 Yakovlev Yak-42D; 2 de Havilland Canada Twin Otter Srs 300; 1 Raytheon Beech King Air 200; 1 Raytheon Beech King Air C90B

TRANS ATTICO
Incorporated: 1998

A Sudan-based charter cargo airline, Trans Attico's operations largely centre around the Gulf, with an operations base at Sharjah.

HQ airport & main base: Khartoum Civil, with a base at Sharjah International

Designator: ML/ETC
Fleet: 2 Ilyushin Il-76TD; 1 Antonov An-32B; 2 Antonov An-26; 2 Antonov An-12; 2 Let L-410UVP-E

SWEDEN – SE

(*See also* SCANDINAVIA)

The single largest market for Scandinavian Airlines System, SAS, and also the largest shareholding nation, Sweden has also had a number of airlines of its own, usually independent but also including subsidiaries of SAS. The involvement of the tri-national airline in the home market has been a sensitive issue at times, as there is reluctance to see it take a disproportionate share of the Swedish market.

Swedish air transport nevertheless dates back much further, to the formation of AB Svenska Air Transport after the First World War. The airline was the first to operate trimotor transports, with a fleet of four Junkers G.23 all-metal airliners, with which it introduced a service between Malmö, Hamburg and Amsterdam in May 1925. The aircraft was built with Swedish cooperation, as Germany was at the time banned from building aircraft under the terms of the Treaty of Versailles.

Inevitably, just as new airlines appear, others disappear. Missing from the current line-up is Transwede, originally founded in 1985 by NRT Nordisk as an inclusive tour charter airline. Transwede moved into scheduled services with a service from Stockholm to London Gatwick in 1991. At one time operating long-haul charters, this aspect of the business was split off in 1996 to a new airline, Transwede Leisure, leaving Transwede to develop scheduled services within Sweden and to neighbouring countries. Ownership was transferred to Transwede Holdings and Braathens SAFE, with each holding 50 per cent, after which Braathens exercised its option to take full control of Transwede, which was absorbed by the Norwegian airline after its acquisition by SAS.

While many Swedish domestic services are now operated by SAS Braathens, Finnair has also invested in the country, with the acquisition of Flynordic.

AMAPOLA FLYG

Incorporated: 2004

A wholly owned subsidiary of the Salenia Group, Amapola operates on charter to the Swedish Post Office, carrying mail.

HQ airport & main base: Stockholm Arlanda
Designator: APF
Employees: 13
Fleet: 2 Fokker 50

AVITRANS

Incorporated: 2003

Formed as Flygtransporter I Nykoping in 2003, the airline commenced operations in 2005 as Avitrans, primarily as a charter airline but with a single scheduled service at present.

HQ airport & main base: Stockholm Skavsta
Designator: 2Q/ETS
Route points: Ronneby, Stockholm
Fleet: 7 Saab 340A/B; 1 CASA C-212

CITY AIRLINE

Incorporated: 1997

A small, regional scheduled service airline operating from Gothenburg, privately owned but with alliances with several major airlines. City Airline also offers charters and wet-lease operations. From its founding in 1997 to 2001, it provided aircraft on wet-lease to bmi.

HQ airport & main base: Gothenburg Landvetter International
Designator: CF/SDR
Employees: 65
Route points: Birmingham, Gothenburg, Helsinki, Lulea, Lyons, Manchester, Zurich
Links with other airlines: Alliances with Alitalia, bmi Regional, Finnair, Malev (all qv)
Fleet: 3 Embraer ERJ-145EU/MP; 3 Embraer ERJ-135ER; 2 Saab 2000

FLYNORDIC

Incorporated: 2000

A Swedish charter and scheduled passenger airline, Flynordic was founded in 2000 as Nordic Airlink. In 2003, Finnair bought an 85 per cent interest, increasing this to outright ownership in 2004, and shortly afterwards the current title was adopted.

HQ airport & main base: Stockholm Arlanda
Designator: LF/NDC
Employees: 240
Route points: Copenhagen, Gotenburg, Kiruna, Lulea, Lyons, Oslo, Ostersund, Stockholm, Turin, Umea

Links with other airlines: Owned by Finnair (qv)
Fleet: 3 McDonnell Douglas MD-83; 6 McDonnell Douglas MD-82; 1 Saab 340A

GOLDEN AIR
Incorporated: 1993

Founded in 1993, Golden Air operates regional scheduled passenger services within Sweden and to Finland, as well as operating charters. It is owned by the shipping company Erik Thun.

HQ airport & main base: Trollhattan
Designator: DC/GAO
Route points: Angelholm, Helsinki, Stockholm, Trollhattan, Turku, Visby
Links with other airlines: Alliance with Finncomm Airlines (qv)
Fleet: 4 Saab 2000; 13 Saab 340A/B

MALMÖ AVIATION
Incorporated: 1993

After an earlier company of the same name was sold to CityAir Scandinavia, Malmö Aviation was formed in 1992 as Malmö Aviation Schedule by Wiklund Inter Trade. The airline was acquired by the Norwegian airline Braathens in 1998, and the following year Braathens Sweden, which had originated as Transwede, was merged into Malmö. A complete reversal came in 2001 when Malmö once again became independent following the acquisition of Braathens by Scandinavian Airlines System, SAS, which was prevented for legal reasons from increasing its share of the Swedish market. Ownership rests with BRZ Sverige.

Throughout the various changes of ownership, a small domestic and international scheduled network has been established, while the airline also undertakes passenger and cargo charters.

HQ airport & main base: Malmö Sturup, with a further hub at Stockholm Bromma
Radio callsign: MALMO
Designator: TF/SCW
Employees: 500
Route points: Brussels, Gothenburg, Malmö, Nice, Stockholm, Umea
Links with other airlines: Alliance with SN Brussels Airlines (qv)
Fleet: 9 BAe Avro RJ100ER; 1 BAe 146-200QT

NORDIC AIRWAYS/NORDIC LEISURE
Incorporated: 2003

Founded in 2003 as a subsidiary of Nordic NR Regional, Nordic provides cargo and passenger charters in addition to wet-lease aircraft for other airlines, and has developed a small, domestic scheduled network.

HQ airport & main base: Stockholm Arlanda
Designator: 6N/NRD
Route points: Lulea, Ostersund, Stockholm, Umea
Links with other airlines: Nordic NR Regional has a 100 per cent shareholding
Fleet: 1 McDonnell Douglas MD-87; 2 McDonnell Douglas MD-83; 1 McDonnell Douglas MD-82; 1 McDonnell Douglas MD-81; 1 Saab 340A

NOVAIR
Incorporated: 1997

Founded in 1997 as an inclusive tour charter airline, Novair initially operated mainly for Apollo Resor, but is now fully owned by the Kuoni Travel Group. Most operations are to the Mediterranean and the Canary Islands, but the airline also flies to resorts in Thailand.

HQ airport & main base: Stockholm Arlanda
Designator: 1I/NVR
Employees: 350
Fleet: 2 Airbus A330-200; 3 Airbus A321-200

SKYWAYS EXPRESS
Skyways AB
Incorporated: 1987

Skyways Express was originally founded in 1987 as Avia, operating internal commuter or feeder services with a fleet of Short 330s and 360s, but later adopted the title of Skyways. In 1991 it acquired another commuter operator, Salair, which also dated from 1987 and operated a fleet of 3 Saab 340s, following this with the acquisition of Highland Air in 1997. The airline entered into a partnership with SAS, which took a 25 per cent stake in the airline in 1998, and the airline also started to feed into the SAS system in addition to operating its own services, and later adopted the title Skyways Express.

Today, Skyways Express has a fleet of Fokker and Saab aircraft, and operates scheduled services within Sweden and to nearby countries. It has grown considerably over the past decade, with the Fokker 50 fleet trebling in size and displacing many of the smaller Saab aircraft.

HQ airport & main base: Linkoping, with a main base at Stockholm Arlanda

Radio callsign: SKY EXPRESS
Designator: JZ/SKX
Employees: 740
Route points: Arvidsjaur, Borlange, Copenhagen, Falun, Gothenburg, Halmstad, Hemavan, Jonkoing, Karlstad, Kramfors, Kristianstad, Linkoping, Lycksele, Norrkoping, Orebro, Skelleftea, Stockholm, Storuman, Sundsvall, Trollhattan, Vilhelmina, Visby
Links with other airlines: SAS (qv) has a 25 per cent stake
Fleet: 16 Fokker 50; 1 BAe Avro RJ100ER; 1 Saab 2000

VIKING AIRLINES
Incorporated: 2003

Formed in 2003, Viking is an inclusive tour charter airline specialising in flights between Sweden and Greece. The shares are privately held.

HQ airport & main base: Umea
Radio callsign: VIKING
Designator: VIC
Fleet: 4 McDonnell Douglas MD-83

WEST AIR SWEDEN
West Air Sweden AB
Incorporated: 1955

Originally founded in 1955 as LBF-Eda Varken, an air taxi operator, the name changed to Abal Air in 1963. A further name change followed in 1990, when it became Time Air Sweden, when cargo and passenger charter services started; then again to West Air Sweden in 1993, trading as Air Sweden, when the airline graduated to scheduled services. In 1997 the decision was taken to concentrate on cargo charter and scheduled services as West Air Sweden, with the main base moving from Karlstad to Gothenburg. West Air Luxembourg is a subsidiary.

HQ airport & main base: Gothenburg
Radio callsign: AIR SWEDEN
Designator: PT/SWN
Route points: Copenhagen, Gothenburg, Linkoping, Lulea, Malmö, Paris, Stockholm
Links with other airlines: West Air Luxembourg (qv) is a subsidiary
Fleet: 12 BAe ATP; 3 BAe 748 Srs 2A/B

SWITZERLAND – HB

Switzerland's reputation for reliability, most of all in business, suffered badly in 2002 with the collapse of the national airline, the Swiss Air Transport Company, more usually known by its branding, Swissair. Swissair was the most prominent airline victim of the events of 11 September 2001, when the terrorist atrocities that saw four US airliners seized and destroyed, two of them being flown into New York's World Trade Center and another into the Pentagon, had a serious effect on the volume of international air travel, and on security costs and insurance for airlines.

Despite the small size and population of Switzerland, at the time of its collapse Swissair was the world's eleventh, and Europe's fourth, largest airline by annual turnover. The airline's history dates from the merger of Balair of Basle and Ad Astra Aero of Zurich in 1931. Ad Astra was the older of these two airlines, dating from 1919, when it had appeared as the Ad Astra Swiss Air Transport Company, operating in competition with the Aero-Gesellschaft Comte Mittelhelzer & Co. and Avion Tourisme, and which it acquired in 1920. The acquisition led to the airline being named Ad Astra Aero Tourisme, or Ad Astra Aero, operating a fleet of sixteen aircraft. Balair dated from 1925.

At the outset in 1931, Swissair had a fleet of thirteen aircraft, mainly of Fokker manufacture. New aircraft were not long in arriving, with the single-engined, four-passenger Lockheed Orion being introduced in 1932 for the Zurich–Munich–Vienna service. In 1934 Curtiss Condor biplane airliners were introduced, and on these Swissair became the first European airline to employ female cabin attendants. A year later, all-year operations started on the Zurich–Basle–London service, using Douglas DC-2s.

Operations had to be suspended on the outbreak of the Second World War in Europe, despite Swiss neutrality, both for safety reasons and to conserve fuel. By this time, Swissair's fleet consisted of five Douglas DC-3s, three DC-2s, a de Havilland DH-89 Dragon Rapide, a Fokker F-VIIa and a Comte AC-4 – slightly smaller in terms of aircraft numbers than eight years earlier, but showing a massive advance in capacity. Operations were resumed in 1945 following the end of the war, when the fleet was enlarged by the addition of several more DC-3s. The following year, the airline introduced its first four-engined aircraft, Douglas DC-4s, and in 1949 these aircraft launched Swissair's first transatlantic service, linking Geneva and New York. By this time Swissair had become the national airline of Switzerland, although not the nationalised airline, since a 1947 agreement enabled the airline to become the official flag carrier in return for the state taking a 30 per cent shareholding.

Swissair became a loyal supporter of Douglas aircraft after the DC-4s, introducing first DC-6Bs and then DC-7Cs on its longer-haul routes, although the absence of Douglas from the short-haul market for many years following the DC-3, and the unsuccessful DC-5, meant that Convair 440 Metropolitans were the choice for the European routes. Swissair's first jet airliners, Douglas DC-8s, were introduced in 1960, and were later joined by Convair 990 Coronado airliners for the less-busy long-haul routes, and by Sud Aviation Caravelles for the European services, although these too were in due course replaced by Douglas DC-9s.

In 1958 Swissair entered into a collaborative agreement with SAS, Scandinavian Airlines System, covering the pooling of certain intercontinental services and technical collaboration, since the two airlines had almost identical fleets. This agreement was superseded in 1968 by a further agreement involving SAS, Swissair and KLM, covering collaboration on the DC-9, under which Swissair maintained all of the engines and the airframes of its own aircraft and those of KLM, and KLM maintained the airframes of the newly introduced Boeing 747s of all three fleets, while SAS maintained the engines. All three airlines became customers for the Douglas DC-10.

Swissair obtained a share of the fast-growing air charter market by taking a controlling interest in a charter airline, Balair, which, despite its name, had no link with the original airline of that name and had started charter operations as recently as 1957. In 1988, a 38 per cent shareholding was acquired in a new Swiss regional airline, Crossair, and that same year the airline took a 3 per cent interest in Austrian Airlines. In 1993, Balair merged with CTA, Compagnie de Transport Aerien, and in 1995 the merged Balair-CTA's operations were transferred to Crossair, in which Swissair had by then a 56.1 per cent interest.

A significant cross-border acquisition in the late 1990s was a 49.5 per cent stake in Sabena. Other alliances were marked by cross-shareholdings, with Swissair having 4.6 per cent of Delta Air Lines, which had a reciprocal 4.5 per cent stake in Swissair, as well as a token 0.6 per cent in Singapore Airlines in return for that airline's 2.7 per cent stake in Swissair.

In the late 1990s, the decision was taken to concentrate intercontinental services on Zurich, rather than dividing them with Geneva, although both airports still operate European services. This was a controversial decision, with French-speaking Geneva considering creating its own intercontinental airline in opposition to Swissair based in German-speaking Zurich. While language and cultural differences loomed far less prominently in Switzerland than in Belgium, the fact that the nation had four different languages – German, French, Italian and Romansch (in that order of the number of speakers) – had already meant that the airline's official title, the Swiss Air Transport Company, was spelled out in English.

In 2002, at the time of the collapse, Crossair operated a number of the less-busy routes on behalf of Swissair, sometimes with aircraft in Swissair livery. It was to be the continued existence of Crossair that enabled the Swiss to rebuild a substantial national airline so thoroughly and so quickly, using this smaller company as the basis for a new airline, Swiss International Airlines. Less fortunate was Sabena, Swissair's Belgian subsidiary, which failed following the collapse of Swissair.

In 2001 the Swissair fleet included five Boeing 747-300s, sixteen McDonnell Douglas MD-11s, nine Airbus A330-200s, eight Airbus A310-300s, of which at least one was in Balair/CTA livery for long-haul, low-cost holiday flights, as well as eight Airbus A321-100s, eighteen Airbus A320-200s and eight of the smaller Airbus A319-100s. More than 9,000 personnel were employed.

Unlike Sabena, the loss of Swissair sent shock waves through the airline industry. On the other hand, this was a high-cost airline from a high-cost country, already facing the challenge to its services from the low-cost carriers, and much leaner and fitter rivals elsewhere. Slimming down a large, well-established business would not have been easy, and perhaps collapse and the creation of what is, in effect, a new airline, was the only way to make it happen. Certainly, not only the Swiss International intercontinental route network, but that within Europe as well, is considerably different from that operated by Swissair.

Several other airlines have also emerged in recent years, although one of the older ones is perhaps the most interesting, Privatair, which operates VIP variants of airliners for KLM, Lufthansa and Swiss International on both up-market charters and long-haul scheduled flights.

BELAIR

Incorporated: 2001

Belair was established, following the collapse of Swissair, out of the airline's charter subsidiary Balair, by one of the latter's main customers,

Hotelplan, which remains the airline's sole shareholder. It provides inclusive tour passenger charter flights for Hotelplan and other operators, operating throughout Europe and to destinations in Africa, the Caribbean and the Far East.

HQ airport & main base: Zurich
Designator: 4T/BHP
Employees: 132
Fleet: 1 Boeing 767-300ER; 2 Boeing 757-200

DARWIN AIRLINE
Incorporated: 2003

Founded in 2003, Darwin commenced operations in 2004, operating scheduled passenger flights out of Lugano.

HQ airport & main base: Lugano
Designator: OD/DWT
Employees: 60
Route points: Berne, Geneva, London, Lugano, Rome
Links with other airlines: Alliances with Air One, Swiss (both qv)
Fleet: 3 Saab 2000

easyJet SWITZERLAND
Incorporated: 1988

The Swiss operations of easyJet originated as TEA Switzerland, one of the TEA group of airlines, an ambitious plan which saw charter airlines established using the TEA name in most of the main air-charter markets across Europe. The airline was rescued by its directors when TEA collapsed, and its main shareholder became Air Finance. In 1988 easyJet took a 49 per cent stake in the airline, the maximum permitted a non-Swiss investor, and the following year the airline commenced operations as an easyJet franchise, moving from its base at Basle/Mulhouse to Geneva. easyJet needed a Swiss-based, airline as otherwise the Swiss authorities would only permitt operations between the UK and Switzerland, and the airline's plans depended on being able to operate what would traditionally be described as 'seventh freedom' rights, that is, an airline flying traffic between two countries, neither of which is its country of origin.

HQ airport & main base: Geneva International
Radio callsign: EASY
Designator: DS/EZS
Employees: 400
Route points: Alicante, Amsterdam, Barcelona, Bournemouth, Budapest, Doncaster, Edinburgh, Hamburg, Lisbon, London, Madrid, Malaga, Naples, Nice, Palma de Mallorca, Paris, Prague, Rome
Links with other airlines: easyJet (qv) has a 49 per cent interest
Fleet: 10 Airbus A319-100

EDELWEISS AIR
Incorporated: 1996

A Swiss-based inclusive tour charter airline formed by the Kuoni Travel Group, Edelweiss Air operates to the main holiday resorts in the Canaries, Mediterranean and Red Sea, East Africa and the Caribbean.

HQ airport & main base: Zurich
Designator: 8R/EDW
Employees: 210
Fleet: 1 Airbus A330-200; 3 Airbus A320-200

FARNAIR SWITZERLAND
Incorporated: 1984

Originally founded in 1984 as an air taxi and express packet company, Farnair has developed into a passenger and cargo charter airline, but also provides regular express cargo services throughout Europe. Air transport support is also provided for humanitarian organisations and for the energy industry. In 1993, the Hungarian airline NAWA was acquired and renamed Farnair Hungary.

HQ airport & main base: Basle/Mulhouse Europort
Radio callsign: FARNAIR
Designator: FAT
Links with other airlines: Owns Farnair Hungary (qv) 100 per cent
Fleet: 1 ATR-72-300F; 3 ATR-72-200; 3 ATR-42-300/320

FLYBABOO
Incorporated: 2003

Operating from Geneva and Lugano, Flybaboo was founded in 2003 and has a network of scheduled internal services and also operates internationally.

HQ airport & main base: Geneva, with a further base at Lugano
Designator: F7/BBO
Employees: 54

Route points: Geneva, Ibiza, Lugano, Nice, Pisa, Prague, St Tropez, Valencia, Venice, Zurich
Fleet: 2 Bombardier Dash 8 Q400; 2 Bombardier Dash 8 Q300

HELLO
Incorporated: 2004

A new inclusive tour charter airline, operating from Switzerland to holiday destinations throughout the Mediterranean and North Africa. It also provides aircraft on wet-lease to other airlines.

HQ airport & main base: Basle/Mulhouse
Designator: HW/FHE
Employees: 84
Fleet: 2 McDonnell Douglas MD-90-30

HELVETIC AIRWAYS
Incorporated: 2002

Originally founded as Odette Airways and commenced charter and low-cost scheduled operations in 2003, changing its name to Helvetic Airways later that year. The name is based on the Latin name for Switzerland. In 2006 the airline was acquired by an investment firm, Patinex.

HQ airport & main base: Zurich
Designator: 2L/OAW
Route points: Alicante, Barcelona, Brindisi, Catania, Lamezia-Terme, London, Malaga, Naples, Palermo, Palma de Mallorca, Pristina, Skopje, Valencia
Fleet: 4 Fokker 100

PRIVATAIR
Incorporated: 1995

Privatair was formed to operate VIP versions of airliners such as the Boeing Business Jet, BBJ, and the Airbus equivalent on both corporate charters and as long-haul scheduled services, which it undertakes for Lufthansa, KLM and Swiss International, as well as providing a corporate shuttle for Airbus. The airline is owned by the Latsis Group through a subsidiary, the PrivatAir Group, and has expanded into acquiring executive jet and VIP handling facilities at a number of airports, including Paris Le Bourget. A major airline subsidiary is Privatair GmbH of Germany, which operates the A319-100LR on behalf of Lufthansa and Airbus.

HQ airport & main base: Geneva International
Radio callsign: PRIVATAIR
Designator: PTI
Employees: 500
Route points: In KLM, Lufthansa and Swiss International newtorks, as well as Toulouse–Hamburg for Airbus
Links with other airlines: Operates on behalf of KLM, Lufthansa and Swiss International (all qv)
Fleet: 1 Boeing 757-200; 1 Boeing 737-800; 2 Boeing BBJ; 1 Bombardier Global Express (On order: 1 Boeing 787-8)

SWISS EUROPEAN AIRLINES
Incorporated: 2005

Swiss European Airlines was founded in 2005 by its owner, Swiss International Air Lines, to operate wet-lease services throughout Europe for other airlines. Many of its aircraft do in fact operate the shorter and thinner routes for the parent company and have come from the fleet operated at one time by Crossair. As a wet-lease operator, it does not have its own designator.

HQ airport & main base: Basle/Mulhouse
Employees: 320 (almost all aircrew)
Links with other airlines: Owned 100 per cent by Swiss International Air Lines
Fleet: 19 BAe Avro RJ100ER; 4 BAe Avro RJ85ER; 9 Embraer ERJ-145LR

SWISS INTERNATIONAL AIR LINES
Incorporated: 1975

Swiss International Airlines was created in March 2002, following the collapse of Swissair, the national airline for Switzerland. The basis for the new airline was a small regional airline, Crossair, in which Swissair had been the majority shareholder, and which was restructured from being a regional airline, often flying the less-busy routes on behalf of its parent company, into being a worldwide airline. Crossair had in its later years also operated inclusive tour charter flights.

The changes also meant that Crossair employee numbers more than doubled, while the new airline soon became the thirty-third largest in the world by annual turnover, although fiftieth by passenger numbers.

Originally founded in 1975, Crossair had not commenced operations until 1979, initially operating domestic services. Swissair acquired a significant minority stake in 1988, and later increased this to a majority, 56.1 per cent shareholding, with a 59.8 per cent voting share, giving the national airline control.

Crossair was the first operator of the Saab 340 regional turboprop, and then developed into providing international and domestic feeder services for Swissair, as well as flying some of the parent airline's less-busy routes, or even in some cases sharing routes with the larger operator by operating them outside the peak periods.

In 1995 Balair/CTA's aircraft and services were transferred by its owner, Swissair, to Crossair, taking the airline into the inclusive tour charter market. In April 1996, a new McDonnell Douglas MD-83 for inclusive tour charter operations was delivered in the colours of McDonald's, the hamburger chain.

At the time Crossair was restructured into Swiss International Air Lines, its fleet included eight McDonnell Douglas MD series aircraft for inclusive tour charters, as well as sixteen BAe Avro RJ series aircraft, which were often used on Swissair flights and were known to Crossair as the 'Jumbolino', while its own route network mainly used twenty-four Saab 2000s, known as the 'Concordino', and fifteen of the smaller Saab 340B, known as the 'Cityliner'.

The 'new' airline operates most of the old Swissair and Crossair networks, but not all. The collapse of what was a high-cost airline has clearly shown that a substantial number of routes were not viable, and much of the network in Africa and Latin America has been abandoned, while flights to the Far East have been trimmed and some of the less important European destinations have also been dropped. The fleet has also changed, with the loss of the Boeing 747s and McDonnell Douglas MD-11s, and Crossair's BAe Avro RJ series, which are now part of Swiss European Air Lines, and the Saab turboprops, while Airbus and Embraer aircraft predominate. The airline has been taken over by the German airline Lufthansa, following the agreement by shareholders in March 2005, and although the separate identities will remain, there will be some rationalisation of the route networks and no doubt standardised procurement policies.

HQ airport & main base: Basle/Mulhouse, but long-haul operations are based on Zurich
Radio callsign: SWISS
Designator: LX/SWR
Employees: 5,970
Annual passengers: 9.2 million
Route points: Amsterdam, Athens, Bangkok, Barcelona, Basle/Mulhouse, Belgrade, Benghazi, Berlin, Berne, Birmingham, Boston, Brussels, Bucharest, Budapest, Cairo, Chicago, Copenhagen, Dallas, Dar-es-Salaam, Delhi, Doha, Douala, Dresden, Dubai, Düsseldorf, Frankfurt, Geneva, Graz, Hamburg, Hanover, Helsinki, Hong Kong, Istanbul, Jeddah, Johannesburg, Kiev, Krakow, Kuala Lumpur, Lisbon, Ljubljana, London, Los Angeles, Lugano, Luxembourg, Madrid, Malabo, Malaga, Manchester, Miami, Milan, Montreal, Moscow, Mumbai, Munich, Muscat, Nairobi, New York, Newark, Nice, Nuremberg, Oporto, Palma de Mallorca, Paris, Prague, Riyadh, Rome, Salzburg, Sao Paulo, Singapore, Skopje, Stockholm, Stuttgart, Tel Aviv, Thessaloniki, Tokyo, Tornoto, Tripoli, Venice, Vienna, Warsaw, Washington, Yaounde, Zurich
Links with other airlines: A subsidiary of Deutsche Lufthansa. Owns Swiss European Air Lines and Swiss Sun (both qv). Alliances with Adria Airways (qv), Air Alps Aviation (qv), Air Canada (qv), American Airlines (qv), British Airways (qv), Cirrus Airlines (qv), CSA Czech Airlines (qv), Darwin Airline (qv), Egyptair (qv), El Al (qv), Finnair (qv), Iberia Airlines (qv), Japan Airlines International (qv), Lufthansa (qv), Macedonian Airlines, Malaysia Airlines (qv), Malev (qv), Oman Air (qv), PrivatAir (qv), Qantas Airways (qv), Qatar Airways (qv), Scandinavian Airlines System (qv), SN Brussels Airlines (qv), Styrian Spirit, Thai Airways (qv), Ukraine International Airlines (qv), United Airlines (qv)
Annual turnover: US $2,836 million (£1,890 million)
Fleet: 9 Airbus A340-300; 11 Airbus A330-200; 4 Airbus A321-200; 14 Airbus A320-200; 7 Airbus A319-100; 1 BAe Avro RJ100ER; 15 Embraer 195; 15 Embraer 170

SWISS SUN

Incorporated: 2002

Effectively the charter airline subsidiary of Swiss International Air Lines, which owns it, in particular replacing the inclusive tour charters operations of the former Balair and Crossair. Formed in 2002, it does not have any aircraft of its own, but instead uses idle time on the Swiss International Air Lines fleet.

HQ airport & main base: Basle/Mulhouse
Links with other airlines: Owned 100 per cent by Swiss International Air Lines

SYRIA – YK

SYRIANAIR

Syrian Arab Airlines
Incorporated: 1961

The history of air transport in Syria predates the formation of Syrian Arab Airlines in 1961, to a private venture airline, Syrian Airways, which commenced operations in 1947 on domestic routes. The airline soon encountered difficulties, and in 1948 had to suspend operations, which did not begin again until 1951 with the support of Pan American World Airways. The first international routes, to neighbouring capitals, were not introduced until 1953.

The creation of the short-lived United Arab Republic of Egypt and Syria in 1960 led to the merger of Syrian Airways with the state-owned Egyptian airline, Misrair, to create United Arab Airways. On the division of the United Arab Republic in 1961, the Syrian government had to quickly re-establish an airline, creating Syrian Arab Airlines, which initially operated a mixture of elderly piston-engined aircraft on domestic routes, including Douglas DC-3s, DC-4s and DC-6s. Jet airliners were soon introduced, in the form of three Sud Aviation Caravelles, with which services to European capitals were steadily introduced during the 1960s. Later, the airline collaborated with Royal Jordanian Airlines to establish a joint service to New York in 1978, but this is no longer operated.

Syrian Arab Airlines adopted the fleet name Syrianair during the late 1990s and now has an extensive international network, and a limited domestic network, serving just four airports from its base in Damascus. The route network and the fleet have tended to reflect a close alliance with the former Eastern Bloc, although some Western types are in service. Even the arrival of the six Airbus A320s did not see the final retirement of the Tu-134 fleet, although the Caravelles were replaced. The airline remains in state ownership, with no plans for privatisation.

HQ airport & main base: Damascus
Radio callsign: SYRIANAIR
Designator: RB/SYR
Employees: 3,700
Route points: Abu Dhabi, Aleppo, Algiers, Amsterdam, Athens, Bahrain, Beirut, Berlin, Brussels, Bucharest, Cairo, Casablanca, Damascus, Damman, Deirezzor, Delhi, Doha, Dubai, Frankfurt, Istanbul, Jeddah, Kameshi, Karachi, Khartoum, Kuwait, Larnaca, Latakia, London, Madrid, Marseilles, Moscow, Mumbai, Munich, Muscat, Paris, Riyadh, Rome, Sana'a, Sharjah, Sofia, Stockholm, Tehran, Tripoli, Tunis, Vienna, Yerevan
Links with other airlines: Has a 25 per cent stake in Phoenician Express. Alliances with Austrian Airlines, Cyprus Airways, Hemus Air, Iberia Airlines, KLM, Royal Jordanian Airlines, Tarom (all qv)
Fleet: 2 Boeing 747SP; 4 Ilyushin Il-76; 6 Boeing 727-200; 6 Airbus A320-200; 1 Tupolev Tu-134B; 6 Yakovlev Yak-40; 6 Antonov An-26; 2 Antonov An-24

TAIWAN – B

CHINA AIRLINES

Incorporated: 1959

Although sometimes mistaken for the national airline of China (now Air China, but previously CAAC) China Airlines is the national airline of Taiwan, the only part of China not to have been swept into Communist rule after the Second World War. Formed by retired Nationalist Air Force officers in 1959, China Airlines operated charter flights initially and did not commence scheduled flights until 1962, when a domestic passenger service was started. Although state-owned at the time through the China Aviation Development Foundation, the airline was not officially recognised as the national flag carrier until 1965. The following year, the first international service was introduced, to Saigon (now Ho Chi Minh City), and transpacific flights commenced in 1970 with a service to San Francisco.

It is now the thirty-second largest airline in the world by annual turnover, and unplaced in passenger numbers, reflecting the importance of long-haul traffic and of cargo. A subsidiary is Mandarin Airlines, which operates flights to Sydney, Auckland and Vancouver with a fleet of three aircraft. In 1996, the airline acquired a 42 per cent stake in Formosa Airlines, the main Taiwanese domestic airline. At one time there was a 19 per cent stake in Far Eastern Air Transport, although this has now reduced to 7.6 per cent. Over the past decade, the China Aviation Development Foundation stake in China Airlines has been increased from 62 per cent to just over 70 per cent, although the airline has been listed on the Taiwan Stock Exchange since 1993.

HQ airport & main base: Taipei Chiang Kai Shek International
Designator: CI/CAL
Employees: 9,769
Route points: Amsterdam, Anchorage, Bangkok, Boston, Brisbane, Chiang Mai, Delhi, Denpasar Bali, Frankfurt, Fukuoka, Guam, Hanoi, Hiroshima,

Ho Chi Minh City, Hong Kong, Honolulu, Houston, Jakarta, Johannesburg, Kaohsiung, Kuala Lumpur, Los Angeles, Manila, Nagoya, New York, Okinawa, Penang, Phuket, Rome, San Francisco, Seattle, Seoul, Singapore, Sydney, Taipai, Tokyo, Vancouver, Vienna
Links with other airlines: Has 94 per cent of shares in Mandarin Airlines (qv), 25 per cent in Yangtze River Express (qv), and 7.6 per cent in Far Eastern Air Transport. Alliances with Alitalia, Delta Airlines, Garuda Airlines, Korean Air, Thai Airways and Vietnam Airlines (all qv)
Annual turnover: US $2,891 million (£1,920 million)
Fleet: 20 Boeing 747-400F; 15 Boeing 747-400; 7 Airbus A340-300; 16 Airbus A330-300; 1 Airbus A300-600R; 12 Boeing 737-800

EVA AIR
Eva Airways
Incorporated: 1989

Founded in 1989 by the Evergreen Corporation, a shipping conglomerate, Eva Airways began operations in 1991 as Taiwan's first private enterprise international airline, with the first services using two leased Boeing 767-300ERs. In the beginning, assistance was received from several airlines, including British Airways, Alitalia, All Nippon and Thai International. The initial destinations were in the Far East, but a route to the United States was opened in 1993, and the network has now extended to several points in Europe after tremendous growth which has seen the still relatively young airline projected into the world's top fifty airlines in terms of annual turnover.

A 25 per cent interest was held in Great China Airlines, but today its interests in other airlines consist of a 18 per cent stake in UNI Air, reduced from 51 per cent some ten years ago, and a nominal 5 per cent interest in Air Macau. The company is the thirty-ninth largest airline in the world by revenue, but is outside the 'Top 50' by passenger numbers, partly because of the predominance of long-distance passengers in its operations but also due to the importance of all-cargo traffic to the airline, reflected in the number of all-cargo aircraft in the fleet.

HQ airport & main base: Taipei Chiang Kai Shek International
Radio callsign: EVA AIR
Designator: BR/EVA
Employees: 4,934
Route points: Amsterdam, Auckland, Bangkok, Brisbane, Denpasar Bali, Fukuoka, Ho Chi Minh City, Hong Kong, Honolulu, Jakarta, Kuala Lumpur, London, Los Angeles, Macau, Manila, Newark, Osaka, Paris, Penang, Phnom Penh, San Francisco, Sapporo, Seattle, Sendai, Seoul, Singapore, Surabaya, Sydney, Taipei, Tokyo, Vancouver, Vienna
Links with other airlines: Owns 18 per cent of UNI Air and 5 per cent of Air Macau (qv). Alliances with Air Canada, Air New Zealand, Air Nippon, America West Airlines, American Airlines, Continental Airlines, Qantas Airways, UNI Air (all qv)
Annual turnover: US $2,485 million (£1,656 million)
Fleet: 5 Boeing 747-400; 10 Boeing 747-400 Combi; 3 Boeing 747-400F; 11 Airbus A330-200; 13 Boeing 777-300ER; 3 Boeing 777-200LR; 10 McDonnell Douglas MD-11F

FAR EASTERN AIR TRANSPORT
FAT Far Eastern Air Transport
Incorporated: 1957

Originally founded as a cargo charter airline, Far Eastern Air Transport moved into scheduled services in 1965, operating to the main Taiwanese cities. China Airlines acquired a 19 per cent shareholding at one time, but this has now reduced to 7.6 per cent, while the airline now also operates passenger services within Taiwan and to neighbouring countries.

HQ airport & main base: Taipei Sungshani
Designator:EF/FEA
Employees: 1,224
Route points: Hualien, Jeju, Kaohsiung, Kinmen, Koror, Makung, Seoul, Tainan, Taipei, Taitung
Links with other airlines: China Airlines (qv) has a 7.6 per cent stake
Fleet: 5 Boeing 757-200; 1 Boeing 757-200PF; 5 McDonnell Douglas MD-83; 6 McDonnell Douglas MD-82

MANDARIN AIRLINES
Incorporated: 1991

Founded as a joint venture by China Airlines, the majority shareholder with 66.6 per cent of the shares, and the Kuo Development Corporation in 1992, Mandarin initially operated charter flights and both domestic and international regional flights. In 1992, China Airlines took complete control of Mandarin, and in 1999 merged its subdiary, Formosa Airlines, into Mandarin.

Formosa Airlines itself dated from 1966, when it was started as a as a crop-spraying company, but then developed into a domestic carrier in Taiwan. In 1996 China Airlines acquired a 42 per cent interest, and the two airlines code-shared on certain domestic routes, before China Airlines acquired the remaining shares in the airline. In the reorganisation that followed, Mandarin acquired Formosa's aircraft, mainly Fokker and Saab regional turboprops, and domestic scheduled network, while Mandarin's own aircraft and most, but not all, of its international flights were transferred to China Airlines.

HQ airport & main base: Taipei Chiang Kai Shek International
Radio callsign: MANDARIN
Designator: AE/MDA
Employees: 630
Route points: Cebu, Chi Mei, Green Island, Hengchun, Hong Kong, Hualien, Kaohsiung, Kinmen, Makung, Orchid Island, Subic Bay, Taichung, Taipei, Taitung, Toyama, Wajima, Wonan, Yangon
Links with other airlines: Owned 100 per cent by Air China (qv)
Fleet: 2 Boeing 737-800; 5 Embraer 195LR/AR; 3 Embraer 190LR/AR; 6 Fokker 100; 5 Fokker 50

TRANS-ASIA
Trans-Asia Airways Corporation
Incorporated: 1951

Taiwan's first privately owned airline, originally founded in 1951 as Foshing Airlines. Douglas DC-3s were operated from Kaohsiung to Taipei and Makung, on the Pescadores Islands. The name Trans-Asia was taken in 1992 to reflect a major expansion into regional charter flights. The fleet expanded quickly from just four ATR-42s to include Airbus A320 and A321 aircraft, as well as ATR-72s for an expanded domestic network. Asmall, scheduled network covering domestic and international flights is now operated.

HQ airport & main base: Taipei Chiang Kai Shek International
Designator: GE/TNA
Employees: 1,142
Route points: Busan, Hengchun, Hualien, Jeju, Kaohsiung, Kinmen, Macau, Makung, Pingtung, Tainan, Taipei
Fleet: 5 Airbus A321-100; 3 Airbus A320-200; 7ATR-72-500; 3 ATR-72-200

UNI AIR
UNI Airways Corporation
Incorporated: 1988

Originally founded in 1988, UNI Air commenced operations the following year as Makung Airlines, operating from Makung in the Pescadores Islands to Taipei and Kaohsiung. The initial fleet included the last two BAe HS 748s to be built, and these were soon joined by two BAe 146-300s. The new Taiwanese international carrier, Eva Air, later acquired a 51 per cent interest in the airline, although this has since dropped to 17.9 per cent. The present title was adopted in 1996, partly reflecting the significance of other routes in the airline's growing network. The decision was further vindicated in 1998, when Taiwan Airlines and Great China Airlines were taken over.

Originally founded as an agricultural crop-spraying company, Great China Airlines started operating domestic scheduled services in 1990, initially using a single de Havilland Dash 8-100, although another five of these aircraft followed soon afterwards. At the time of the acquisition by UNI Air, Great China, in which Eva Air had a 25 per cent interest, operated an extensive domestic route network, taking a claimed 10 per cent of the Taiwanese domestic market. The airline's first jet equipment, a McDonnell Douglas MD-90, had been introduced in 1996. The airline was the launch customer for the Bombardier Dash 8-400.

In addition to scheduled services, UNI Air also operates charter flights.

HQ airport & main base: Kaohsiung International
Designator: B7/UIA
Employees: 1,420
Route points: Bangkok, Hanoi, Hiayi, Hengchun, Kaohsiung, Kinmen, Makung, Matsu, Nangan, Seoul, Taichung, Tainan, Taipei, Taitung
Links with other airlines: Eva (qv) owns 17.9 per cent of the shares. Evergreen (qv) owns 17 per cent of the shares
Fleet: 13 McDonnell Douglas MD-90-30; 10 Bombardier Dash 8 Q300; 1 Bombardier Dash 8 Q200

TAJIKISTAN – EY

TAJIKISTAN AIRLINES
Incorporated: 1992

A former Aeroflot division, Tajikistan Airlines was formed as Tajik Air in 1992 after Tajikistan became independent from the former Soviet Union. Scheduled and charter flights are operated for passengers and freight, while a small number of helicopters is also operated on charter. A subsidiary airline at one time was Khojand Air Enterprise. The number of employees has halved over the past decade. It remains completely government owned.

HQ airport & main base: Dushanbe
Radio callsign: TAJIKISTAN
Designator: 7J/TJK
Employees: 1,993
Route points: Almaty, Ashgabat, Bishkek, Delhi, Dushanbe, Istanbul, Karachi, Khudjand, Mashhad, Moscow, Novosibirsk, Piyndjikent, Samara, Sharjah, Tehran, Uralsk
Fleet: 9 Tupolev Tu-154B/M; 9 Tupolev Tu-134; 7 Yakovlev Yak-40; 4 Antonov An-28; 2 Antonov An-26; 6 Antonov An-24

TANZANIA – 5H

AIR TANZANIA
Incorporated: 1977

Air Tanzania was formed in 1977 to take over Tanzania's share of the routes that had hitherto been operated by East African Airways, after that airline collapsed. East African had been founded in 1946 with the financial and operational support of BOAC, British Overseas Airways Corporation, and the governments of Kenya, Uganda, Tanganyika and Zanzibar, with the last two merging after independence to form Tanzania.

Initially it had operated internal services in what were Britain's East African colonies, but it had moved into international services in 1957 with a Canadair DC-4M, a Canadian-built DC-4 with Rolls-Royce Merlin engines. This aircraft was superseded by first, a Bristol Britannia, later a de Havilland Comet 4, and eventually by four Vickers Super VC10s. An unusual feature of the airline, which it shared with SAS, was that aircraft were registered in different member states.

Initially, Air Tanzania concentrated on developing a network of domestic services and services to neighbouring states, but today the route network extends as far as Johannesburg. Until privatisation occurred in 2002, the airline was controlled by the Tanzanian government, which nevertheless now retains a controlling 51 per cent interest, while the remainder is held by South African Airways.

At one time Air Tanzania held a 10 per cent stake in Alliance Airlines–African Joint Service, a venture involving the airline and Ugandan Airlines, both governments and South African Airways, and to which it was intended that the equipment and routes of Air Tanzania and those of Air Uganda would have been transferred.

HQ airport & main base: Dar-es-Salaam
Radio callsign: TANZANIA
Designator: TC/ATC
Route points: Dar-es-Salaam, Entebbe, Johannesburg, Kilimanjaro, Moroni, Mtwara, Mwanza, Zanzibar
Links with other airlines: Marketing alliance with South African Airways (qv), which holds 49 per cent of the company's stock
Fleet: 3 Boeing 737-200; 1 Fokker F28 Mk4000 Fellowship

PRECISIONAIR
Incorporated: 1991

Originally formed in 1991, Precisionair commenced operations as an air taxi operator in 1994, mainly flying tourists. Scheduled operations started in 1999, initially in collaboration with Air Tanzania, and today a small domestic and international route network is operated, aimed at the tourist market. Kenya Airways has a 49 per cent shareholding.

HQ airport & main base: Arusha
Radio callsign: PRECISIONAIR
Designator: PW/PRF
Route points: Arusha, Bukoba, Dar-es-Salaam, Dubai, Kigoma, Kilimanjaro, Mombasa, Nairobi, Musoma, Mwanza, Shinyanga, Tabora, Zanzibar
Links with other airlines: Kenya Airways (qv) has a 49 per cent stake. Alliance with Air Malawi (qv)
Fleet: 4 ATR-72-200/500; 4 ATR-42-300/320; 3 ATR-42-500; 2 Let L-410UVP-E; 1 Cessna Caravan 675

THAILAND – HS

BANGKOK AIRWAYS
Bangkok Airways Co. Ltd
Incorporated: 1986

Originally founded in 1968 as Sahakol Air, Thailand's first privately owned airline, Bangkok Airways started as a charter airline with a single nine-seat aircraft, mainly supporting the oil, natural gas exploration and timber industries. The business was restructured and renamed Bangkok Air in 1986 and moved into scheduled domestic air services. One unusual feature of the airline's operations is that it has built and opened its own airports on the island of Samui and at Sukhothai, to tap the lucrative tourist potential of these destinations. It recently made a minor change to its name to become Bangkok Airways. The main shareholder is Dr Prasert Prasarttong-Osoth, with 91.6 per cent.

HQ airport & main base: Bangkok
Radio callsign: BANGKOK AIR
Designator: PG/BKP
Employees: 1,581
Route points: Bangkok, Chiang Mai, Guilin, Hangzhou, Hong Kong, Jinghng, Koh Samui, Krabi, Luang Prabang, Male, Phnom Penh, Phuket, Shenzhen, Siem Reap, Singapore, Sukhothai, Trat, Utapao, Xain, Yangon, Zhengzhou
Links with other airlines: Alliance with Thai Airways (qv)
Fleet: 3 Airbus A320-200; 4 Boeing 717-200; 9 ATR-72-500

NOK AIR
Incorporated: 2003

Founded in 2003, NOK Air began operations in mid-2004 as a low-cost subsidiary of Thai Airways, initially operating domestic scheduled services. The Thai Airways stake is now 39 per cent, with the rest held by financial institutions.

HQ airport & main base: Bangkok International
Radio callsign: NOK
Designator: DD/NOK
Employees: 130
Route points: Bangkok, Chiang Mai, Hat Yai, Nakhon Si Thammarat, Phuket, Udon Tahni
Links with other airlines: Thai Airways (qv) has a 39 per cent interest
Fleet: 6 Boeing 737-400; 1 ATR-72-200

ORIENT THAI AIRLINES
Incorporated: 1992

Almost an expatriate or offshore Kampuchean airline, Orient Thai was formerly Cambodian International Airlines, but ceased operating its own scheduled operations in 1998 and today operates charters, as well as flying under contract to Kampuchea Airlines, in which it has a 49 per cent stake. Orient Thai itself is owned 30 per cent by the government of Kampuchea, with Thai Trading owning the remaining shares.

HQ airport & main base: Bangkok International
Designator: OX/OEA
Employees: 644
Route points: On the Kampuchea Airlines network, but includes Bangkok, Hong Kong, Phnom Penh, Seoul
Links with other airlines: Owns 49 per cent of Kampuchea Airlines (qv)
Fleet: 1 Boeing 747-300 Combi; 1 Boeing 747-300; 3 Boeing 747-200B; 3 Boeing 747-100; 3 Boeing 757-200; 4 McDonnell Douglas MD-82

THAI AIRASIA
Incorporated: 2003

Thai AirAsia was founded in 2003 and commenced operations as a low-cost scheduled airline and passenger charter operator in 2004. A domestic and international route network has been established and, like many airlines of this kind, the fleet is standardised on one aircraft type, the Boeing 737-300. Ownership is divided between Asia Aviation and the AirAsia holding company.

HQ airport & main base: Bangkok International
Radio callsign: AIRASIA
Designator: FD/AIQ
Employees: 990
Route points: Bangkok, Chiang Mai, Chiang Rai, Hanoi, Hat Yai, Kota Kinabalu, Kuala Lumpur, Macau, Narathiwat, Penang, Phnom Penh, Phuket, Sinagpore, Ubon Ratchathani, Udon Thani, Xiamen
Fleet: 12 Boeing 737-300

THAI AIRWAYS
Thai Airways International Public Company Ltd
Incorporated: 1959

Thai Airways was founded in 1959 as a joint venture between Thailand's domestic carrier, Thai Airways Company, and SAS, Scandinavian Airlines System, with the latter taking a 30 per cent interest in the new airline. The new airline took over the external routes and equipment of TAC when it commenced operations in 1960. The initial equipment of Thai Airways consisted of Douglas DC-6Bs, but these were followed by leased Sud Aviation Caravelles and Convair 990 Coronados, which quickly replaced the DC-6Bs so that Thai could eventually claim to have the first all-jet fleet of any airline in Asia. A network of services was developed, initially serving destinations in South-East Asia, but gradually extending to Japan and Australia. By the early 1970s, the airline had standardised its equipment on several different variants of the Douglas

DC-8, ranging from the 140-seat DC-8-30 through to the 200-seat DC-8-63.

The SAS stake was steadily reduced over the years, and the airline became fully Thai owned in 1977, when the Thai government acquired SAS's remaining shares. The Thai Airways Company's domestic services were absorbed in 1988, adding eleven aircraft to what was, by then, Thai's own fleet of thirty wide-bodied aircraft. Privatisation began in 1991, with a stock-exchange listing and a share offer, which reserved 5 per cent of the new shares for the airline's employees. Although the airline was expected to become a completely privatised enterprise, this has been deferred and currently the state holds a 54 per cent stake in the airline, with most of the remainder held by financial institutions. The airline has a 39 per cent stake in Nok Air.

The airline is a founder-member of the Star Alliance, which brings together frequent-flyer programmes and other services for a number of airlines, including Air Canada, Lufthansa, SAS, United Airlines and, in late 1997, Varig, as well as Thai. It is the twenty-fourth largest airline in the world both by annual turnover and passenger numbers.

HQ airport & main base: Bangkok International
Radio callsign: THAI
Designator: TG/THA
Employees: 25,884
Route points: Amman, Antananarivo, Athens, Auckland, Bahrain, Bandar Seri Bagawan, Bangalore, Bangkok, Beijing, Brisbane, Busan, Cairo, Chengdu, Chennai, Chiang Mai, Chiang Rai, Chicago, Chittagong, Colombo, Copenhagen, Delhi, Denpasar Bali, Dhaka, Doha, Dubai, Frankfurt, Fukuoka, Guangzhou, Hanoi, Hat Yai, Ho Chi Minh City, Hong Kong, Honolulu, Islamabad, Jakarta, Kaohsiung, Karachi, Kathmandu, Khon Kaen, Kiev, Kolkata, Krabi, Kuala Lumpur, Kunming, Kuwait, Lahore, London, Los Angles, Madrid, Mae Hong Son, Manila, Melbourne, Milan, Moscow, Mumbai, Munich, Muscat, Nagoya, Nakhon Si Thammarat, New York, Osaka, Paris, Penang, Perth, Phitsanulok, Phnom Penh, Phuket, Rome, Sapporo, Seoul, Shanghai, Singapore, Stockholm, Surat Thani, Tel Aviv, Sydney, Taipei, Tokyo, Trang, Ubon Ratchathani, Udon Thani, Vienna, Vientiane, Yangon, Zurich
Passengers carried: 19.5 million
Links with other airlines: A member of the Star Alliance. Alliances with AeroSvit Airlines (qv), Air Madagascar (qv), Air India (qv), Bangkok Airways (qv), China Airlines (qv), China Eastern Airlines (qv), Egyptair (qv), El Al (qv), Emirates (qv), Gulf Air (qv), Japan Airlines International (qv), Malaysia Airlines (qv), Myanmar Airways International (qv), Nok Air (qv), PB Air, Phuket Air, Qatar Airways (qv), Royal Jordanian Airlines (qv), Swiss (qv)
Annual turnover: US $3,791 million (£2,128 million)
Fleet: 18 Boeing 747-400; 2 Boeing 747-300; 6 Airbus A340-600; 4 Airbus A340-500; 6 Boeing 777-300; 6 Boeing 777-200ER; 8 Boeing 777-200; 12 Airbus A330-300; 15 Airbus A300-600R; 6 Airbus A300-600; 6 Boeing 737-400; 1 ATR-72-200 (On order: 6 Airbus A380-800)

TRINIDAD AND TOBAGO – 9Y

CARIBBEAN AIRLINES

Incorporated: 2007

Successor to BWIA West Indies Airways as the national carrier of Trinidad and Tobago, Caribbean Airlines is developing a network of regional services on which it operates Boeing 737-800s, while also operating an Airbus A340-300 on a service to London with a code-share with British Airways.

HQ airport & main base: Port of Spain Piarco International
Designator: BW/BWA
Route points: Atlanta, Baltimore, Bonaire, Bridgetown, Chicago, Curaçao, Fort Lauderdale, Grand Cayman, Grenada, Kingston, London, Los Angeles, Miami, Montego Bay, Nassau, New York, Newark, Orlando, Philadelphia, Port of Spain, Toronto
Fleet: 7 Boeing 737-800
Links with other airlines: Code-share with British Airways

TUNISIA – TS

KARTHAGO AIRLINES

Incorporated: 2001

Formed as an inclusive tour charter airline by the Karthago Group, which is the largest shareholder with 58 per cent, and by financial institutions and investors, Karthago commenced operations in 2001. It has since introduced a scheduled service between Tunisia and Moscow.

HQ airport & main base: Djerba
Designator: 5R/KAJ
Route points: Djerba, Monastir, Moscow, Tunis
Fleet: 6 Boeing 737-300

NOUVELAIR TUNISIE
Incorporated: 1989
Tunisia's first charter airline, Nouvelair Tunisie was founded in 1989 and started operations the following year as Air Liberté Tunisie, an associate of a French airline, Air Liberté, which at that time was also confined to charters. The present title was adopted in 1994 after the airline was taken over by the Tunisian Travel Service. Control has now passed to the chairman, Aziz Milad, who has a 60 per cent stake in the airline. Nouvelair specialises in inclusive tour charter flights into Tunisia from major European centres, but more recently has added low-cost international flights to London and Düsseldorf. Over the past decade, the fleet has changed from McDonnell Douglas MD-83s to Airbus A320 and A321 aircraft.

HQ airport & main base: Monastir Habib Bourguiba
Radio callsign: NOUVELAIR
Designator: BJ/LBT
Employees: 614
Route points: Djerba, Düsseldorf, London, Monastir, Tunis
Fleet: 2 Airbus A321-200; 9 Airbus A320-200

TUNISAIR
Société Tunisienne de l'Air
Incorporated: 1948

Tunisair was founded in 1948, while Tunisia was still a French colony, with the support of Air France, and until Tunisian independence in 1957, the French airline was the major shareholder. The initial fleet consisted of Douglas DC-3s for domestic services. Post-independence, the connection with Air France remained, with the airline having a 49 per cent interest and the Tunisian government holding the majority 51 per cent. International services were developed, initially to France using Douglas DC-4s, which were later joined by Sud Aviation Caravelle jet airliners.

Today, the airline operates a mixed Boeing and Airbus fleet on scheduled and charter services, with the latter generally being for inclusive tour operators, reflecting Tunisia's popularity as a holiday destination. A domestic feeder airline, Tuninter, in which Tunisair has an 83.4 per cent stake, was established in 1991 and commenced operations the following year, with a small fleet of three ATR and Boeing aircraft.

The Tunisian government owns 74.4 per cent of Tunisair's shares, and is the largest single shareholder, while Air France has 5.6 per cent, with the remaining 20 per cent traded on the national stock exchange. The number of employees has dropped by a third over the past decade.

HQ airport & main base: Tunis Carthage
Radio callsign: TUNAIR
Designator: TU/TAR
Employees: 4,732
Route points: Abidjan, Algiers, Amman, Amsterdam, Athens, Bamako, Barcelona, Beirut, Belgrade, Benghazi, Berlin, Bordeaux, Brussels, Budapest, Cairo, Casablanca, Copenhagen, Dakar, Damascus, Djerba, Dubai, Düsseldorf, Frankfurt, Geneva, Hamburg, Istanbul, Jeddah, Lisbon, London, Luxembourg, Lyons, Madrid, Marseilles, Milan, Monastir, Munich, Nice, Nouakchott, Paris, Prague, Rome, Salzburg, Sfax, Strasbourg, Tabarka, Toulouse, Tozeur, Tripoli, Tunis, Vienna, Warsaw, Zurich
Links with other airlines: Air France (qv) has a 5.6 per cent stake. Owns 83.4 per cent of Tuninter. Alliances with Air Algérie, Air Europa, Air France (all qv)
Fleet: 3 Airbus A300-600R; 1 Boeing 727-200; 12 Airbus A320-200; 3 Airbus A319-100; 4 Boeing 737-500; 7 Boeing 737-600

TURKEY – TC

ATLASJET AIRLINES
Incorporated: 2001

Originally known as Atlasjet International Airlines when formed in 2001, Atlasjet was originally a charter airline mainly handling inclusive tour passenger flights for the German tour operator Oger, although work for other companies has been handled. Approval has also been obtained from the US authorities to operate between the USA and Turkey. In 2004, the ETS Group acquired a 45 per cent stake, and this has since been doubled by acquiring the Oger Tours 45 per cent in 2006, while the current name has also been adopted. The airline's current plans are to convert the current inclusive tour charter flights to low-cost scheduled services in the near future.

HQ airport & main base: Istanbul Ataturk International
Radio callsign: ATLASJET
Designator: KK/OGE
Employees: 730
Fleet: 2 Boeing 757-200; 3 Airbus A320-200; 3 Airbus A319-100; 2 Bombardier CRJ700-701ER

FREE BIRD AIRLINES
Incorporated: 2000

Formed as an inclusive tour charter airline in 2000, operations with a fleet of three McDonnell Douglas MD-83s began the following year. The original aircraft have since been replaced by three Airbus A320s. The airline is a sibsidiary of Gozen Air Services.

HQ airport & main base: Istanbul Ataturk International
Designator: FHY
Employees: 200
Fleet: 2 Airbus A321-200; 3 Airbus A320-200

KUZU AIRLINES
Incorporated: 2004

Named after the founders and owners, Kuzu operates charter cargo flights and is developing a scheduled cargo network based on Istanbul.

HQ airport & main base: Istanbul Ataturk International
Radio callsign: KUZU
Designator: GO/KZU
Employees: 170
Route points: Amsterdam, Istanbul, London
Fleet: 3 Airbus A300B4-200F

MNG AIRLINES
Incorporated: 1997

Originally founded as a cargo airline, since 2002 MNG Airlines has also been offering passenger services. Transatlantic operations started in 1998. Most of the work is charter, but there is also a scheduled network. Ownership is divided between MNG Holdings with 80 per cent and Yavuz Cizmeci.

HQ airport & main base: Istanbul Ataturk International, with further bases at Brussels National, Frankfurt Hahn
Designator: MB/MNB
Route points: Amsterdam, Antalya, Brussels, Frankfurt, London, New York, Paris
Fleet: 6 Airbus A300B4/F4; 4 Boeing 737-400; 4 McDonnell Douglas MD-82; 4 Fokker F27 Friendship Mk500; 1 Bombardier Challenger 601

ONUR AIR
Incorporated: 1992

Onur Air was founded in 1992 as a charter airline operating inclusive tour flights into Turkish holiday destinations for tourists from throughout western Europe, with two Airbus A320s. Deregulation of the Turkish market in 2003 encouraged the airline to introduce low-cost domestic air services in addition to its international charters, following which the airline has enjoyed rapid growth. It is owned by three individuals.

HQ airport & main base: Istanbul Ataturk International
Designator: 8Q/OHY
Route points: Adana, Ankara, Antalya, Bodrum, Dalaman, Diyarbakir, Erzurum, Gaziantep, Istanbul, Izmir, Kars, Kayseri, Malatya, Samsun, Trabzon
Fleet: 6 Airbus A300-600R; 4 Airbus A300B4-200; 6 Airbus A321-200; 2 Airbus A321-200; 4 Airbus A320-100; 5 McDonnell Douglas MD-88; 3 McDonnell Douglas MD-83

PEGASUS AIRLINES
Incorporated: 1990

An inclusive tour charter airline founded in 1990 by Aer Lingus and two Turkish companies, Net and Silkar, initially operating two Boeing 737-400s. In 1994 the Aer Lingus and Net holdings were sold, and in 2005 ESAS acquired the 85 per cent majority holding, with Silkar retaining 15 per cent.

HQ airport & main base: Istanbul Ataturk International
Radio callsign: PEGASUS
Designator: 1I/PGT
Employees: 720
Fleet: 17 Boeing 737-800; 2 Boeing 737-400; 2 Boeing 737-500

SAGA AIRLINES
Incorporated: 2004

Owned by the Kolot family, Saga is an inclusive tour charter airline flying passengers from western Europe into Turkish resorts.

HQ airport & main base: Istanbul Ataturk International
Radio callsign: SAGA
Designator: SGX
Fleet: 1 Airbus A300B2; 1 Airbus A310-300

SKY AIRLINES
Incorporated: 2001

Formed as an inclusive tour charter airline flying visitors to Turkey from western Europe, Sky is owned by the Kay Group. It operates Boeing 737s.

HQ airport & main base: Antalya
Designator: SHY
Employees: 255
Fleet: 1 Boeing 737-800; 5 Boeing 737-400

SUNEXPRESS
SunExpress Aviation
Incorporated: 1989

SunExpress was established in 1989 as a joint venture between Lufthansa and THY Turkish Airlines to cater for the inclusive tour charter market from elsewhere in Europe to resort destinations in Turkey. Operations began in 1990. Although initially shareholdings were divided 60 per cent to THY and 40 per cent to Lufthansa, the German airline transferred its shareholding to Condor, and this has now passed to Thomas Cook. Today the airline is owned equally by Thomas Cook and THY. In common with many inclusive tour charter airlines, SunExpress has moved into the low-cost scheduled market.

HQ airport & main base: Antalya International
Designator: XQ/SXS
Employees: 580
Route points: Antalya, Basle/Mulhouse, Berlin, Cologne, Düsseldorf, Frankfurt, Friedrichshafen, Hamburg, Hanover, Izmir, Leipzig/Halle, Munich, Nuremberg, Paderborn, Saarbrücken, Stuttgart, Zurich
Links with other airlines: A 50:50 joint venture between THY Turkish Airlines and Thomas Cook (both qv)
Fleet: 4 Boeing 757-200; 9 Boeing 737-800

TURKISH
THY Turk Hava Yollari/Turkish Airlines
Incorporated: 1933

THY's origins date from the formation in 1933 of Devlet Hava Yollari, or Turkish State Airlines, which was operated as a branch of the air force. This operation continued for more than twenty years, with the airline gathering a fleet of Douglas DC-3s for domestic services, mainly between Istanbul and Ankara, and to other destinations in the Middle East. THY itself was created in 1956 to take over DHY's services and equipment, and initially ownership was split between the Turkish government, with 94 per cent, and BOAC, British Overseas Airways Corporation, holding the remaining 6 per cent.

A fleet of five Vickers Viscount 700 turboprop airliners was introduced in 1957 for the international services, and these were joined in 1960 by ten Fokker F27 Friendships, although unusually the order was split equally between the F-27 and the US-built Fairchild FH-227 version. The DC-3s remained on a number of domestic services meanwhile, until, in 1968, after leasing a Douglas DC-9-10 from the manufacturer, THY introduced three Douglas DC-9-30s, allowing the DC-3s to be withdrawn. The airline later added Boeing 707s for the introduction of long-haul services, and Fokker F28 Fellowships. Meanwhile, the BOAC interest was gradually reduced so that for some years the airline was owned 98.2 per cent by the state Public Participation Administration, with the few remaining shares in private hands.

A regional airline was established in 1989, Turk Hava Tasimaciligi, or THT, and the following year THY took 64 per cent of the shares, intending to operate THT as a feeder. Initially, THT operated two Antonov An-24RVs, but these were soon joined by the first two of four BAe ATPs, or Jetstream 61s as they were later renamed. In 1993, THT's operations were absorbed into those of THY.

Over the years, THY acquired interests in other airlines, including including SunExpress, a joint venture in which Lufthansa had a 40 per cent stake until this was transferred first to Condor and then to Thomas Cook Airlines, and Kibris Turkish Airlines, a 50:50 joint venture with the Turkish Cypriot authorities. The most recent venture is a wholly owned subsidiary, Turkish Express, which operates low-cost scheduled services. THY is the forty-fourth largest airline in the world by revenue, down from thirty-ninth, but is forty-first in terms of passenger numbers.

THY's own ownership has also changed over the years, with first a joint stock company structure being introduced and then, in 1990, almost a quarter of the airline's shares being sold to the public. The remaining shares, just over 75 per cent, are held by the TC Privatisation Administration. Turkey's growing popularity as a holiday destination has seen the airline maintain strong growth in recent years, with the number of employees rising by almost a quarter.

HQ airport & main base: Istanbul Ataturk International
Radio callsign: TURKAIR
Designator: TK/THY

Employees: 10,956
Route points: Abu Dhabi, Adana, Adiyaman, Agri, Algiers, Almaty, Amman, Amsterdam, Ankara, Antalya, Ashgabat, Astrana, Athens, Bahrain, Baku, Bangkok, Barcelona, Batman, Basle/Mulhouse, Beijing, Beirut, Belgrade, Berlin, Bishkek, Bodrum, Brussels, Bucharest, Budapest, Cairo, Casablanca, Chicago, Chisinau, Cologne/Bonn, Copenhagen, Dalaman, Damascus, Delhi, Denizli, Diyabakir, Donetsk, Dubai, Dushanbe, Düsseldorf, Elazig, Ercan, Erzincan, Erzurum, Frankfurt, Gaziantep, Geneva, Hamburg, Hanover, Helsinki, Hong Kong, Istanbul, Izmir, Jeddah, Kahramanmaras, Karachi, Kars, Kayseri, Kazan, Kiev, Konya, Kuwait, Lisbon, Ljubljana, London, Lyons, Madrid, Malatya, Manchester, Mardin, Milan, Moscow, Munich, Mus, New York, Nice, Nuremberg, Odessa, Oslo, Paris, Prague, Pristina, Riyadh, Rome, St Petersburg, Samsun, Sana'a, Sanliurfa, Sarajevo, Seoul, Shanghai, Simerofol, Singapore, Sivas, Skopje, Sofia, Stockholm, Strasbourg, Stuttgart, Tabriz, Tashkent, Tblisi, Tehran, Tel Aviv, Tirana, Tokyo, Trabzon, Tripoli, Tunis, Van, Vienna, Warsaw, Zagreb, Zurich
Links with other airlines: Owns Turkish Express. Has a 50 per cent stake in SunExpress (qv)
Passengers carried: 12 million
Annual turnover: US $1,960 million (£1,307 million)
Fleet: 7 Airbus A340-300; 5 Airbus A330-200; 1 Airbus A310-300F; 5 Airbus A310-300; 1 Airbus A310-200; 17 Airbus A321-200; 2 Airbus A321-100; 31 Airbus A320-200*; 49 Boeing 737-800*; 14 Boeing 737-400; 2 Airbus A319-100 (*Includes options)

TURKMENISTAN – EZ

TURKMENISTAN AIRLINES
Incorporated: 1992

Based on the former Aeroflot divisions within Turkmenistan, Turkmenistan Airlines is the national airline and has also operated as a holding company for other airlines in the country, including Khazar Airline, Akhal and Lebap, although recently these have been integrated into its mainstream operations. Although Russian and Ukrainian equipment continues to predominate in the fleet, Western types are being introduced. At one time a BAe 125 was operated for VIP duties.

HQ airport & main base: Ashgabat
Radio callsign: TURKMENISTAN
Designator: T5/TUA
Route points: Abu Dhabi, Amritsar, Ashgabat, Bangkok, Beijing, Birmingham, Delhi, Dubai, Frankfurt, Istanbul, London, Moscow
Links with other airlines: Subsidiaries include Akhal, Khazar Airline and Lebap
Fleet: 2 Boeing 757-200; 5 Ilyushin Il-76TD; 2 Boeing 737-800; 3 Boeing 737-300; 7 Boeing 717-200; 5 Antonov An-26; 22 Antonov An-24B/RV; 10 Yakovlev Yak-40

UGANDA – 5X

The absence of the former East African Airways Corporation must have been keenly felt by both Uganda and Tanzania as, unlike Kenya, these have had difficulty in establishing their own national airlines, and a solution was found in the creation of Alliance Airlines, owned 40 per cent by South African Airways, 10 per cent each by Uganda Airlines and Air Tanzania, and 5 per cent each by the governments of Uganda and Tanzania.

The airline commenced operations in 1997, with backing from South African Airways, who provided the first aircraft, a wet-leased Boeing 747SP. In 1998, the airline was to absorb the operations of Uganda Airlines and Air Tanzania, but this failed to materialise and the airline has ceased operations.

Currently, Uganda's air transport effort is confined to a small cargo airline.

UKRAINE – UR

As with the Russian Federation, the Ukraine has a substantial number of airlines which have their origins in divisions either of the old Soviet Aeroflot, or of quasi-military operations similar to those once so prevalent in Latin America. True, there are many fewer Ukrainian airlines, but the country is that much smaller, and although it is far more prosperous than most of the rest of the former Soviet Union, the currency with which to obtain more reliable and economic Western types remains in short supply.

Since the national airline, Air Ukraine, was declared bankrupt by the government in 1992, the three main Ukrainian airlines can be taken as Ukraine International, Aerosvit and, of course, the Antonov Design Bureau, which has ensured the survival of its An-124 Ruslan project by well-considered marketing alliances outside the country.

Air Ukraine was formed as a direct result of the break-up of the former Soviet Union. Air Ukraine's operations were developed under Aeroflot after the Ukrainian Soviet Socialist Republic became part of the USSR in 1923. In terms of the number of aircraft and employees, this was one of the world's largest airlines, but not so in terms of annual turnover.

In addition to its role as a commercial airline, Air Ukraine was responsible for the operation of the country's main airports, and to some extent it bore a closer resemblance to the old Aeroflot and the Chinese CAAC than to Western ideas of a commercial airline. The airline had planned expansion, especially on the North Atlantic and to the Far East, using Western equipment, including Boeing 767s introduced in late 1997, but at bankruptcy, the bulk of its fleet consisted of Russian and Ukrainian types, with a marked absence of the latest types, such as the Ilyushin Il-96 and Tupolev Tu-204.

Following the demise of Air Ukraine and the resultant loss of confidence, the remaining airlines will have a much harder task in securing a stable, long-term future, and details of some of them are not completely reliable due to the sometimes poor availability of their equipment. Two airlines, Dniproavia and Lvov, were subsidiaries of Air Ukraine, but have been allowed to survive.

AEROSTAR
Aerostar Airlines
Incorporated: 1992

Formed relatively recently, Aerostar operates passenger charters mainly throughout the Ukraine and the CIS.

HQ airport & main base: Kiev Zulyany
Designator: UAR
Fleet: 6 Yakovlev Yak-40; 1 Raytheon Beech King Air 350; 1 Dassault Falcon 20

AEROSVIT
Aerosvit Airlines
Incorporated: 1994

One of the many airlines that emerged as the Soviet Union imploded, Aerosvit initially cooperated with Air Ukraine, operating flights from Kiev to Athens, Larnaca, Thessaloniki, Odessa and Tel Aviv. It initially used Antonov aircraft, but these were soon replaced by dry-leased Boeing 737-200s when Moscow was added to the network.

In addition to its international and domestic scheduled service, the airline also provides charter flights. Ownership is divided among tourist agencies, the state property fund, and a Dutch investment company.

HQ airport & main base: Kiev Borispol International
Radio callsign: AEROSVIT
Designator: VV/AEW
Employees: 1,450
Route points: Ashgabat, Athens, Baku, Bangkok, Beijing, Belgrade, Birmingham, Budapest, Cairo, Chernovtsy, Chisinau, Delhi, Dnepropetrovsk, Donetsk, Dubai, Hamburg, Istanbul, Ivano-Frankovsk, Kharkov, Kiev, Larnaca, Lvov, Moscow, New York, Odessa, Prague, Riga, St Petersburg, Simferopol, Sofia, Stockholm, Tallinn, Tel Aviv, Thessaloniki, Toronto, Uzhgorod, Warsaw
Links with other airlines: Air Baltic (qv), Azerbaijan Airlines (qv), CSA Czech Airlines (qv), Cyprus Airways (qv), Dniproavia, El Al (qv), Estonian Air (qv), Kras Air (qv), LOT Polish Airlines (qv), Malev (qv), Olympic Airlines (qv), Pulkovo Aviation Enterprise (qv), Tandem Aero, Thai Airways (qv)
Fleet: 2 Boeing 767-300ER; 5 Boeing 737-400; 2 Boeing 737-300; 1 Boeing 737-200; 1 Boeing 737-500

ANTONOV AIRLINES
Antonov Design Bureau
Incorporated: 1923

The Antonov Design Bureau first moved into aircraft operations in 1989, reaching an agreement with Air Foyle under which the British cargo airline marketed the capabilities of the Antonov An-124 Ruslan, still today the largest aircraft in commercial service.

The move into operating aircraft, as opposed to their design and construction, was vital for the company's survival, faced with the sudden collapse of its traditional markets in the former Soviet Union and the lack of funds for aircraft development. It has proven to be so successful that Antonov took an interest in Volga-Dnepr, the Russian heavy-lift specialist, and has since moved into the market on its own account, although only lately has the term 'airline' been added to the name.

Although the Antonov An-225, an even larger six-engined development of the An-124, is likely to join the fleet, development of this aircraft has stopped due to funding problems, and it is highly unlikely to be available commercially for some time yet.

HQ airport & main base: Kiev
Radio callsign: ANTONOV BUREAU
Designator: ADB
Employees: 600

Links with other airlines: Shareholding in Volga-Dnepr (qv)
Fleet: 7 Antonov An-124 Ruslan; 2 Antonov An-22 Antei; 2 Antonov An-12

ARP 410 AIRLINES
Incorporated: 1999

A passenger and cargo airline operating throughout the Ukraine, to Russia and to Europe and the Middle East.

HQ airport & main base: Kiev Borispol International
Designator: URP
Fleet: 2 Antonov An-30; 6 Antonov An-26; 11 Antonov An-24

BUSINESS AVIATION CENTER
Incorporated: 2003

A passenger and cargo charter airline which also offers VIP services and air taxi operations over much of Europe and the Middle East.

HQ airport & main base: Kiev Borispol International
Designator: BCV
Fleet: 4 Antonov An-26/B; 7 Antonov An-24B; 25 Let L-410UVP

DNIPROAVIA
Incorporated: 1933

Founded within Aeroflot in 1933 as the Dnipropetrovsk Integrated Air Squad, on the break-up of Aeroflot the airline became independent and in 1996 was re-established with the current name, with Dnipropetrovsk Airport as one of the shareholders. Later it became state owned through the national airline, Air Ukraine, but has been allowed to survive the bankruptcy of its parent. Cargo and passenger scheduled and charter flights are operated.

HQ airport & main base: Dnipropetrovsk International Airport
Designator: Z6/UDN
Route points: Berlin, Dnipropetrovsk, Frankfurt, Istanbul, Kiev, Moscow, Munich, Vienna, Volgograd, Yerevan
Links with other airlines: Alliance with AeroSvit Airlines (qv)
Fleet: 1 Boeing 737-400; 1 Boeing 737-300; 6 Yakovlev Yak-40/D/K

DONBASSAERO
Incorporated: 1933

Originally part of Aeroflot, Donbassaero has established itself as an operator of scheduled and charter flights from Donetsk and Kharpov.

HQ airport & main base: Donetsk
Radio callsign: DONBASS
Designator: 7D/UDC
Employees: 780
Route points: Aleppo, Athens, Baku, Beirut, Dnepropetrovsk, Donetsk, Dubai, Istanbul, Kharpov, Kiev, Moscow, Munich, Odessa, Riga, Tbilisi, Vilnius, Yerevan
Links with other airlines: Alliances with AirBaltic, Air Ukraine, FlyLal (all qv)
Fleet: 2 Airbus A320-200; 6 Antonov An-24B/RV; 10 Yakovlev Yak-42/D

KHORS AIR
Khors Air Company
Incorporated: 1990

Primarily an air cargo operator, although there are some passenger operations.

HQ airport & main base: Kiev
Designator: KHO
Fleet: 2 Ilyushin Il-76MD; 1 McDonnell Douglas MD-82; 4 McDonnell Douglas DC-9-50; 1 Antonov An-24B; 1 Antonov An-12

LVOV AIRLINES
Incorporated: 1992

A scheduled and charter airline for passengers and cargo, Lvov Airlines was formed from the former Lvov Division of Aeroflot's Ukrainian Directorate when the original Aeroflot was broken up in 1992. The move coincided with Ukrainian independence, and Lvov passed into the ownership of Air Ukraine until that airline was declared bankrupt in 1992.

HQ airport & main base: Lvov
Radio callsign: LVOV
Designator: 5V/UKW
Route points: Kiev, Lisbon, Lvov, Madrid, Moscow, Rome, Rovno, Uzhgorod
Fleet: 3 Ilyushin Il-76MD; 7 Antonov An-24B; 5 Yakovlev Yak-42/42D; 2 Antonov An-12

MOTOR SICH AIRLINES
Incorporated: 1984

Primarily a passenger and cargo charter airline, Motor Sich also operates a regular scheduled service between its base at Zaporozhye and Moscow.

HQ airport & main base: Zaporozhye
Designator: M9/MSI
Employees: 183
Route points: Kiev, Moscow, Zaporozhye
Fleet: 1 Antonov An-74; 2 Antonov An-24RV; 2 Antonov An-12; 2 Yakovlev Yak-40

RIVNE UNIVERSAL AVIA
Incorporated: 1992

In common with many airlines in the former Soviet Union, Rivne takes its name from it home airport. While a passenger and cargo airline – although mainly the latter as the fleet provides the UPS collection and distribution network in the Ukraine – Rivne, like many airlines in the former Soviet Union, has a number of unusual activities, including parachute dropping.

HQ airport & main base: Rivne
Radio callsign: RIVNE
Designator: UNR
Employees: 115
Route points: On the UPS network
Links with other airlines: Contract flying for UPS (qv)
Fleet: 10 Let L-410UVP/UVP-E

UKRAINE AIR ALLIANCE
Incorporated: 1992

Founded in 1992 on the dissolution of the old Aeroflot and the independence of the Ukraine, the airline was one of the first independent airlines in the country when operations started in 1993. Both passenger and cargo charters are operated throughout Asia, Europe and Africa, with the latter including operations for humanitarian relief agencies.

HQ airport & main base: Kiev Borispol International
Designator: UKL
Employees: 135
Fleet: 5 Ilyushin Il-76MD/TD; 1 Antonov An-32; 3 Antonov An-26

UKRAINE AIR ENTERPRISE
Incorporated: 1996

A wet-lease operator mainly used by other Ukrainian-based airlines and by the government.

HQ airport & main base: Kiev Borispol International
Designator: UKN
Fleet: 2 Ilyushin Il-62M; 3 Tupolev Tu-134A; 1 Yakovlev Yak-40

UKRAINE INTERNATIONAL AIRLINES
Ukraine International Airlines
Incorporated: 1992

Although not officially the national airline of the newly independent Ukraine, Ukraine International originally was a joint venture between the Ukrainian government, with a 68.4 per cent interest, the aircraft leasing specialists Guiness Peat Aviation, with 13.2 per cent, and a partnership of Austrian Airlines and Swissair holding the remaining 18.4 per cent. In the wake of the Swissair collapse, Austrian now has a 22.5 per cent stake, with a financial institution holding 6 per cent and the remainder held by the government. A relatively modest operation compared with Air Ukraine, nevertheless it has Western aircraft and expertise, as well as the prime destinations in western Europe, which suggests that this could become the leading Ukrainian airline in the longer term, while the number of employees has doubled in the past decade.

HQ airport & main base: Kiev Borispol International
Radio callsign: UKRAINE INTERNATIONAL
Designator: PS/AUI
Employees: 1,000
Route points: Amsterdam, Barcelona, Berlin, Brussels, Chemovtsy, Copenhagen, Dnepropetrovsk, Donetsk, Dubai, Düsseldorf, Frankfurt, Helsinki, Ivano Frankovsk, Kharkov, Kiev, Kuwait, Lisbon, London, Lvov, Madrid, Mariupol, Milan, Oslo, Paris, Odessa, Rome, Simeropol, Vienna, Zurich
Links with other airlines: Austrian Airlines holds 22.5 per cent of the airline's shares. Alliances with Air France, Austrian Airlines, Finnair, Iberia Airlines, KLM, SN Brussels Airlines, Swiss, TAP Portugal (all qv)
Fleet: 5 Boeing 737-400; 4 Boeing 737-300; 2 Boeing 737-500; 1 Antonov An-24RV

UKRAINIAN CARGO AIRWAYS
Incorporated: 1997

Founded in 1997 by the Ukrainian government, Ukrainian Cargo Airways operates charter services using former air force transport aircraft, as well as operating a major aircraft maintenance facility. A major element of the airline's operations has been humanitarian relief work for UN and other agencies, as well as transporting peacekeeping troops. This business has been so substantial that a base is maintained at Kinshasa in the Democratic Republic of the Congo.

HQ airport & main base: Kiev Borispol International
Designator: 6Z/UKS
Employees: 870
Fleet: 2 Ilyushin Il-78; 19 Ilyushin Il-76MD; 1 Tupolev Tu-154B; 1 Antonov AN-26B; 2 Antonov An-12

UM AIR
Ukrainian-Mediterranean Airlines
Incorporated: 1998

Founded in 1998, UM Air did not begin operations until 2000, and, contrary to its title, is mainly engaged in operating a small domestic and international network, with the latter serving CIS states and the Middle East. The airline is privately owned.

HQ airport & main base: Kiev Borispol International
Radio callsign: UMAIR
Designator: UF/UKM
Employees: 640
Route points: Almaty, Amman, Astana, Beirut, Chernovtsy, Damascus, Kiev, Kulaisi, Tashkent, Tehran, Uzhgorod
Fleet: 1 Airbus A320-200; 2 Tupolev Tu-134A; 1 McDonnell Douglas MD-83; 2 McDonnell MD-82; 4 McDonnell Douglas DC-9-30; 1 Antonov An-24RV; 1 Yakovlev Yak-42

VOLARE AIRLINES
Incorporated: 1994

Founded in 1994 as the Volare Aircompany, Volare Airlines started operations the following year, concentrating on cargo charters, including operations for the United Nations and other relief agencies.

HQ airport & main base: Nikolayev
Designator: 1L/VRE
Employees: 165
Fleet: 3 Ilyushin Il-76MD/TD; 5 Antonov An-12

YUZMASHAVIA
Incorporated: 1985

Formed from the aviation division of an aviation company, Yuzmashavia operates passenger and cargo charters and is developing a scheduled network.

HQ airport & main base: Dnepropetrovsk International
Designator: UMK
Fleet: 2 Ilyushin Il-76TD; 3 Yakovlev Yak-40

UNITED ARAB EMIRATES – A6

If only to drive home the fact that the Scandinavian example is so unusual, air transport in the United Arab Emirates is steadily moving away from joint operations to a more fragmented and individual approach. Nevertheless, the main carrier, Emirates, continues to grow and the deregulation of air transport in the area has encouraged many new services.

AEROVISTA
Incorporated: 1999

Aerovista is the main international charter airline in the UAE, operating cargo and passenger flights.

HQ airport & main base: Sharjah International
Radio callsign: AEROVISTA
Designator: AAP
Fleet: 2 Boeing 737-200; 1 Antonov An-26B; 1 Antonov An-24B; 2 Yakovlev Yak-40; 2 Let L-410UVP

AIR ARABIA
Incorporated: 2003

Founded by the Sharjah Civil Aviation Department and the Sharjah Airport Authority as a result of an Amiri decree, Air Arabia is a low-fares airline operating scheduled services within the Middle East and also to the Indian subcontinent, the source of many workers in the oil and related industries.

HQ airport & main base: Sharjah International
Designator: G9/ABY
Route points: Aleppo, Alexandria, Aqaba, Assiut, Bahrain, Beirut, Colombo, Damascus, Damman, Doha, Jeddah, Khartoum, Kuwait, Luxor, Mumbai, Muscat, Nagour, Riyadh, Sana'a, Sharm-el-Sheikh
Fleet: 8 Airbus A320-200

ARIA AIR
Incorporated: 1999

Established in 1999 as Aria Air Tour, Aria Air started scheduled and charter passenger and cargo operations between Iran and Dubai in 2000.

HQ airport & main base: Dubai
Radio callsign: ARIA
Designator: IRX
Route points: Bandar Abbas, Dubai
Fleet: 3 Tupolev Tu-154M; 2 Fokker 50

BRITISH GULF INTERNATIONAL AIRLINES
Incorporated: 1996

Originally formed in 1996 to operate air cargo services between the UK and Africa, in 2002 it was decided to concentrate on traffic to and from the Gulf States, and the following year it was allowed to relocate to the United Arab Emirates.

HQ airport & main base: Sharjah International
Designator: BGK
Fleet: 6 Antonov An-12

CARGO PLUS AVIATION
Incorporated: 2001

An air cargo charter operator specialising in ad hoc assignments, founded in 2001 by Nasir Khan in Dubai. A mixed Russian, Ukrainain and US fleet is operated.

HQ airport & main base: Sharjah International
Designator: 8L/CGP
Fleet: 1 McDonnell Douglas DC-8-63; 1 McDonnell Douglas DC-8-55F; 1 Ilyushin Il-76; 1 Ilyushin Il-62; 1 Boeing 707-320; 1 Antonov An-12; 1 Ilyushin Il-18

DOLPHIN AIR
Incorporated: 1996

A merger of Flying Dolphin and Santa Cruz Imperial Airlines, Dolphin Air is a charter airline handling passengers and cargo and based on Dubai.

HQ airport & main base: Dubai International
Radio callsign: DOLPHIN
Designator: ZD/FDN
Fleet: 2 Airbus A300-600R; 1 Boeing 707-300C; 2 Boeing 737-200C; 2 Dornier 228-212

EMIRATES
Emirates Airline Group
Incorporated: 1985

Although only dating from 1985, Emirates is the largest airline in the Arab world, ranking twentieth by turnover worldwide, but is thirty-seventh by passenger numbers, on which basis it lags behind the other large Arab airline, Saudi Arabian Airlines. Established in 1985 as an international airline for the United Arab Emirates by the government of Dubai, Emirates has developed an extensive internal and international route network with a modern fleet, reflecting the prosperity of the region. It remains in state ownership, and since 1998 has had a management contract for Air Lanka, later renamed Sri Lankan Airlines, in which Emirates also acquired a 43.63 per cent interest.

A wholly owned subsidiary is Emirates Sky Cargo, which not only sells cargo space on Emirates' own scheduled services, but also has a small air freighter fleet of its own.

HQ airport & main base: Dubai International
Radio callsign: EMIRATES
Designator: EK/UAE
Employees: 16,400
Route points: Abidjan, Abu Dhabi, Accra, Alexandria, Amman, Athens, Auckland, Bahrain, Bangkok, Beirut, Birmingham, Brisbane, Cairo, Casablanca, Chennai, Christchurch, Colombo, Damascus, Damman, Dar-es-Salaam, Delhi, Dhaka, Doha, Dubai, Düsseldorf, Entebbe, Frankfurt, Fukuoka, Glasgow, Hamburg, Hong Kong, Houston, Hyderabad, Islamabad, Istanbul, Jakarta, Jeddah, Johannesburg, Karachi, Khartoum, Kochi, Kuala Lumpur, Kuwait, Lagos, Lahore, Larnaca, London, Mahe, Male, Malta, Manchester, Manila, Mauritius, Melbourne, Milan, Moscow, Mumbai, Muscat, Nairobi, New York, Newark, Nice, Osaka, Paris, Perth, Peshawar, Riyadh, Rome, Sana'a, Sapporo, Seoul, Shanghai, Singapore, Sydney, Tehran, Tokyo, Tripoli, Vienna, Zurich
Passengers pa: 12.5 million
Links with other airlines: Owns Emirates Sky Cargo (qv). Has a 46.63 per cent stake in Sri Lankan Airlines, which it manages. Alliances with Air Mauritius, Air India, Continental Airlines, Japan Airlines, Korean Air, Oman Air, Philippine Airlines, Royal Air Maroc, South African Airways, Sri Lankan Airlines, Thai Airways (all qv)
Annual turnover: US $5,198 million (£3,436 million)
Fleet: 5 Boeing 747-400F; 18 Airbus A340-600; 10 Airbus A340-500; 8 Airbus A340-300; 54 Boeing 777-300ER; 8 Boeing 777-300F; 12 Boeing 777-300; 10 Boeing 777-200LR; 6 Boeing 777-200ER; 3 Boeing 777-200; 29 Airbus A330-200; 1 Airbus

A310-300F; 1 Airbus A310-300 (On order: 43 Airbus A380-800; 2 Airbus A380-800F; 10 Boeing 747-8F)

EMIRATES SKY CARGO
Emirates Airline Group
Incorporated: 1985

The air cargo division of Emirates, the airline uses the cargo holds of the parent airline's aircraft as well as operating an air cargo fleet of its own.

HQ airport & main base: Dubai International
Radio call sign: EMIRATES
Designator: EK/UAE
Route points: The Emirates network as above
Links with other airlines: A subsidiary of Emirates (qv). Alliances with Air Malawi, Finnair (qv)
Fleet: 5 Boeing 747-400F; 3 Airbus A310-300F

ETIHAD AIRWAYS
Incorporated: 2003

Formed as a national airline for Abu Dhabi, one of the Emirates, scheduled passenger and cargo flights are operated throughout the Middle East, and to much of Africa and Europe, as well as to the Indian subcontinent and to Thailand. It is owned outright by the government of Abu Dhabi. Despite only starting operations in 2003, the airline has grown rapidly.

A subsidiary is Etihad Crystal Cargo, which markets the airline's air cargo capacity and services.

HQ airport & main base: Abu Dhabi International
Radio callsign: ETIHAD
Designator: EY/ETD
Route points: Abu Dhabi, Amman, Bahrain, Bangkok, Beirut, Brussels, Cairo, Colombo, Damascus, Damman, Delhi, Frankfurt, Geneva, Johannesburg, Karachi, London, Manila, Mumbai, Munich, Riyadh, Toronto
Links with other airlines: An alliance with SN Brussels Airlines (qv)
Fleet: 4 Airbus A340-600; 4 Airbus A340-500; 1 Airbus A340-300; 5 Boeing 777-300ER; 15 Airbus A330-200; 2 Airbus A300-600F; 1 Airbus A310-300F; 1 Boeing 767-300ER (On order: 4 Airbus A380-800)

UNITED KINGDOM – G

Today, the United Kingdom gives the impression of having been the European leader in air transport deregulation and competition, but for many years the independent sector had to struggle to gain a foothold in the scheduled service network.

It is believed that the first air cargo flight occurred on 4 July 1911, when Horatio Barber flew a consignment of electric light bulbs from Shoreham to nearby Hove, both in Sussex, in a Valkyrie monoplane. Doubtless the light bulbs were an ideal cargo, being light and fragile, to prove the value of air transport. That the flight was something of a publicity stunt can be gauged by the fact that the manufacturer, Osram, paid £100 for the flight, which was US $500 at the then rate of exchange.

While the UK was one of the first to provide international services, with a flight from London to Paris on 25 August 1919, operated by Aircraft Transport and Travel using a converted Airco DH4a bomber, which could carry two passengers in addition to the pilot, the airline was soon competing against state-sponsored and subsidised rivals, so that within a very short time the company was bankrupt. Nevertheless, other airlines emerged as quickly as existing airlines passed from the scene, and in 1924 four of them, British Marine Air Navigation, Daimler Hire, Handley Page Air Transport (owned by the aircraft manufacturer) and the Instone Air Line, merged to form Imperial Airways. The airline was government sponsored in that it received preferential subsidies, and was an early example of a particular airline being the 'chosen instrument' for the development of air transport.

Imperial operated both landplanes and flying boats. The former used Croydon Airport, south of London and then known as Waddon, which opened in 1920 and replaced Hounslow Heath, west of London and now on the site of the present-day London Heathrow, from which the first international flights operated. Flying boats operated from Hythe, on Southampton Water.

Of the founding companies, Daimler Airways shared the distinction with the French airline, Grands Express Aeriens, of being involved in the first mid-air collision between airliners. On 7 April 1922 one of Daimler's de Havilland DH18s, flying from Croydon to Paris, and a Farman Goliath of Grands Express, operating in the opposite direction, collided over Thieuloy-St Antoine, some 18 miles north of Beauvais. Everyone aboard both aircraft – three aboard the DH18 and four aboard the Goliath – was killed.

Imperial became famous for its pioneering, long-haul, flying boat services to the far-flung British Empire, but it also developed a European network. Initially, aircraft were used simply to cover the stretches of water and desert along the route, with travel across France to the Mediterranean by train, but soon the flying boats were carrying passengers all the way, with twice-weekly departures from Hythe, near Southampton, to both Africa and Asia. The Empire Air Mail Scheme, providing a cheap, flat rate for airmail letters between any two points in the Empire, provided a significant boost to the industry.

The next major step was the appearance of a rival to Imperial Airways, British Airways, which was formed in 1935 from the merger of Hillman's Airways, Spartan Air Lines and United Air Lines (not to be confused with the American airline). This original BA always operated landplanes and its operations were confined to Europe.

Meanwhile, a number of small airlines had begun operating domestic air services to the many offshore islands and also between the mainland of Great Britain and Ireland. Prominent among these airlines was Railway Air Services, operated by the airline subsidiaries of the four mainline railway companies. The two railway companies that did most to promote internal air services were the Great Western Railway and the Southern Railway, which collaborated in Great Western and Southern Air Services. Flights were operated to the Isle of Wight and the Channel Islands, but there were also many cross-country legs on often long routes, with many stops. The appeal of air transport to the GWR was easy to see, with journeys such as Cardiff–Plymouth taking a lengthy 'V' route to avoid the Bristol Channel, while flights were direct. The Southern Railway at one time even offered to purchase the European operations of Imperial Airways, but was turned down.

In 1938, a report by the Cadman Committee recommended that Imperial Airways and British Airways be merged, but by the time the new merged airline, British Overseas Airways Corporation, appeared in 1940, the Second World War had started.

In wartime, most air services were curtailed, but a number of strategically important routes were operated. BOAC operated from Gibraltar to Malta and Alexandria, continued its African services and operated a horseshoe-shaped route from Cape Town to Australia via India. Once the Japanese captured Malaya, this involved flying 3,512 miles non-stop between Ceylon (now Sri Lanka) and Perth. A de Havilland Mosquito bomber was used to transport ball bearings from Sweden to Scotland, flying part of the way over enemy-occupied territory. A regular air service was maintained by flying boats between Poole and North America.

Air services continued over the Irish Sea. Other airlines had their aircraft and personnel absorbed into the British armed forces, with Jersey Airlines having its entire fleet transferred to become a transport squadron in the Royal Navy's Fleet Air Arm.

The return of peace saw a Labour government which was committed to a programme of nationalisation, and in this political climate it was decided that Britain's airlines would be in state ownership. In restarting operations within Europe, it was decided that the restarted European operations of BOAC and the operations of two RAF transport squadrons that had been providing regular services into Europe would form a new airline, British European Airways, BEA. Just as BOAC became the first airline to operate jet aircraft, BEA became the first to operate turboprop airliners, but BOAC's de Havilland Comet 1s failed and had to be withdrawn, while BEA's Vickers Viscounts were successful. Within a decade, BEA was Europe's largest airline.

Nevertheless, an independent sector began to emerge, often using ex-wartime Douglas C-47 transports, or Avro Yorks disposed of by the RAF. Nevertheless, there were tight restrictions on what the independent airlines could do. If they flew scheduled services, it could only be as associates of BEA or BOAC, usually the former. Many associates, such as BKS Air Transport and Cambrian, eventually became subsidiaries of BEA. Certain unusual operations were also allowed, such as car ferries, with Silver City and Channel Air Bridge providing links with the continent from the south-east of England. Charter flights were also permitted to the independent airlines, but as the inclusive tour holiday market had still to develop, many led a precaarious existence and were saved by the Berlin airlift and then by providing 'trooping by air' – transporting servicemen and their families on overseas postings.

Inclusive tour charters were a way around the restrictions on competition, with the flight being part of a package that included accommodation. On transatlantic services, with little inclusive tour traffic, charters were allowed for groups or associations.

The growth of the inclusive tour market created many new airlines, with Britannia, the former name for Thomsonfly, and Monarch being among those that survived and prospered. Many others fell by the wayside. At the same time, independent airlines finally started to operate scheduled services, although confined to the secondary routes not wanted by the two state corporations. Derby Aviation, a predecessor of today's bmi, operated scheduled flights and charters from the East

Midlands; Channel Airways did the same from the south and east of England; while British Eagle operated from the London area. A small airline called Autair operated to the north-west of England from what was then simply known as Luton Airport, before being acquired by the Court Line shipping group, and adopting its name and becoming an inclusive tour charter airline, initially with BAC One-Elevens, but later with Lockheed TriStars. Many of these airlines failed, including British Eagle, Channel Airways and Court Line.

Two small, independent airlines, Airwork and Hunting Clan, merged in 1960, forming British United Airways, which with British Eagle was to the fore in demanding the right to be able to compete with BEA on the domestic trunk routes – those from London to Belfast, Edinburgh and Glasgow. BUA soon acquired other airlines, including Silver City, Air Charter and its subsidiaries Transair and Channel Air Bridge, Morton Airways and the Jersey Airlines.

Both BEA and BUA were also among the European pioneers of helicopter operations.

BUA was acquired in 1970 by Caledonian Airways, a Scottish inclusive tour charter airline, and became British Caledonian Airways, known affectionately as BCal. By this time, Derby had become British Midland (now bmi), and was pushing to become a scheduled airline. After the formation of BCal, many of the BUA fringe activities were sold off, with services to the Channel Islands and Isle of Man passing to British Island Airways; the car ferry services were dropped, especially after the disappointing results of the deep penetration routes which used Carvairs, converted DC-4s and Argonauts, to fly to the south of France and Switzerland.

Other airlines continued to appear, including Monarch Airlines and Air Anglia. Monarch established itself as a leading inclusive tour charter operator. Air Anglia developed a network of scheduled services along the east coast of England and Scotland and to the Netherlands, using Norwich as its base and initially using Douglas DC-3s, before replacing them with Fokker F27 Friendships and then augmenting these with F28 Fellowship jets. In 1980, Air Anglia joined three smaller airlines, Air Wales, Air West and British Island Airways, to form Air UK. Air Wales and Air West were relative newcomers. In its turn, Air UK embarked on a programme of rationalisation and development, remaining a major operator to Amsterdam and along the east coast, and retaining the Channel Islands services which had been the core activity for BIA. The London Gatwick services to Edinburgh and Glasgow of British Caledonian were eventually taken over when that airline was acquired by British Airways, but were later dropped once British Airways had moved back onto these routes to support its growing Gatwick hub. The airline also developed its route network into Amsterdam, with KLM taking an increasingly large stake in the airline, and the two airlines enjoying code-sharing, through-booking and other arrangements, before KLM eventually acquired the remaining interest in Air UK of British Air Transport Holdings during 1997.

Air UK was to the forefront in developing London's fourth airport, the new London Stansted Airport, as a hub, which displaced Norwich as the airline's main base. Air UK was also first with domestic trunk operations into London City Airport, flying from Glasgow and Edinburgh.

During its existence, the Air UK fleet changed, with the original mixture, which included Handley Page Heralds and Fokker F.27 Friendships, being replaced by Fokker F 50s and 100s, while the airline was an early major purchaser of the BAe 146 series, at first the only jet airliner allowed to operate into London City. A number of Short 360s were operated for a period. Modernisation of the turboprop fleet was delayed by the collapse of Fokker. Eventually, Air UK was rebranded as KLMuk, before being integrated completely into KLM. Many of the internal routes were dropped, and some of these were absorbed by a new airline, Eastern Airways.

Eventually, the system began to fall into disrepute, with some of the inclusive tour charters offering accommodation in caves, which the client was not expected to use, so that passengers could enjoy cheap flights. There were so many violations of the clubs and groups rule on the North Atlantic that passengers were questioned at airports to see whether or not they were breaking the rules. Even so, a tentative step towards low-cost transatlantic travel came with Skytrain, a service operated by Freddie Laker, owner of Laker Airways, an inclusive tour charter airline. Skytrain offered no booking services, and passengers had to pay for all food and drink. Aggressive price cutting by the main transatlantic carriers, made worse by a railway industrial dispute that made it difficult for would-be passengers to travel to Skytrain's departure airport at Gatwick, contributed to the collapse of Laker and Skytrain in 1984.

Nevertheless, growing liberalisation of air services, first within the UK and then to Europe, also meant that many of the charter airlines began operating low-cost scheduled services. A small airline, Manx Airways, was established on the Isle of Man, abandoned by British Airways as unprofitable, while third-level services to the smaller Scottish islands were operated by Loganair. Eventually British Midland bought both Loganair and Manx, and also created a regional subsidiary, only for Loganair to be bought out by its management and the regional operation, including Manx, to be purchased by British Airways. Meanwhile, Lufthansa and SAS both took substantial minority stakes in British Midland.

If British Midland's sale of some of its operations to British Airways showed a degree of uncertainty, the national airline has also suffered from many changes of direction over the years. It was criticised, unfairly, for one of its many changes of corporate identity, seeing the word 'Airways' dropped off its aircraft, even though few other operators have the words 'airways' or 'airlines' on their aircraft (and Deutsche Lufthansa went one step further and dropped the Deutsche). The critics were on firmer ground with a later change of identity that saw the representation of the Union Flag dropped from aircraft tails in favour of a variety of ethnic designs, and this eventually was dropped. The airline began to invest in European airlines, starting with Deutsche BA, now DBA, in Germany, before moving into the French market, and also acquiring a substantial stake in USAir, now US Airways, but then reversed this policy. It started a low-cost airline, Go, but then sold it to easyJet. Franchised operations, with smaller airlines adopting the BA brand followed, but now this policy is under review. A number of regional airlines was acquired, including Brymon, operating from Plymouth, but later these services were dropped. Meanwhile, BA Connect is emerging as a low-cost regional operation.

The low-cost route has seen easyJet adopt the UK as its country of origin and main base, while Irish-based and -owned Ryanair has its main base at London Stansted. Nevertheless, while the most successful low-cost airlines have shown that air transport can be profitable, and not before time, it has not been a guarantee of success. Go! probably would have been a success had BA had the patience, with some in the airline industry joking that the then new chief executive knew that he had to sell an airline, but sold the wrong one! Debonair failed, probably because its BAe 146s were too costly to complete with Boeing 737s and Airbus A320s. Duo, formed out of what had been Maersk Air UK after a management buyout, suffered for much the same reason, with its Bombardier regional jets also being too expensive for the low-cost market, while it may also have been undercapitalised. Gill Air, while not strictly a low-cost airline, lost the support of its bankers within days of the 11 September 2001 atrocities, doubtless anticipating a downturn in air travel.

The UK market is both vibrant and fluid. That survival is possible can be seen with bmi, Monarch and Thomsonfly as proof. Even BA has to pay its way. Despite the demise of Laker, low-cost operations can also be successful. There is also scope for innovation, even on routes with relatively light traffic, as Aurigny showed. The questions for the future are many, but include whether or not the low-cost model can be adapted for longer-haul operations. Flyglobespan has started, and in the near future another airline, Zoom, with a Canadian sister company of the same name, plans to follow. The problem for low-cost operators on long haul, however, remains that of the established airlines dumping economy seats at marginal prices, simply because filling the first and business-class sections of the aircraft covers the costs and the economy passengers are needed as ballast to maintain trim. Not for nothing does one aviation magazine imply that airlines see economy passengers as 'self-loading cargo'.

There are seemingly intractable areas in which successful air transport seems to be difficult, however, such as the south-west of England and South Wales.

AIR ATLANTIQUE

Atlantic Air Transport Ltd
Incorporated: 1969

Air Atlantique was originally founded in 1969 as a Jersey-based aircraft sales and service company and air taxi operator, General Aviation Services. The first aircraft was a Cessna 336, which was soon joined by two other light aircraft, both Cessnas. The sales and service aspects of the business were hived off in 1974, leaving the company free to concentrate on air taxi work, standardising on the Cessna 310. The name Air Atlantique was adopted later that year. Two years later, operations started in the UK, using two Douglas Dakota aircraft on general freight and aerial survey work throughout Europe. In 1979, two Douglas DC-6s were used briefly for livestock flights to Europe and Africa.

Major expansion occurred in 1981, with the Dakota fleet expanding to eight aircraft, and a new base at Blackpool Airport. In mid-1984 the business was transferred from Jersey to London's Stansted Airport, but the development of Stansted as London's third airport forced a further move to a permanent home at Coventry Airport in the West Midlands.

A major part of the airline's business is the operation of two Dakotas and the much smaller Britten-Norman Islander aircraft on marine pollution control duties for the British Department of Transport. This work has been carried out since 1987, and the aircraft were involved with the aftermath of both the *Baer* and *Sea Empress* incidents off Shetland and South Wales respectively, with the aircraft flying at just 5m above the surface of the sea during spraying runs. Although the company operates freight and passenger charter flights within the UK and into Europe, its most high-profile activity is the operation of Atlantic Historic Flight, offering pleasure flights in a number of aircraft, including not only the Dakota but also such rare types as the Percival Prentice, de Havilland DH89A Rapide and the Scottish Aviation Twin Pioneer. The company is a subsidiary of Atlantic Holdings, while an offshoot is Atlantic Airlines, owned jointly by Atlantic Holdings and the airline's management.

HQ airport & main base: Coventry
Radio callsign: ATLANTIC
Designator: NL/AAG
Fleet: 2 Douglas DC-6; 1 ATR-72-300; 4 Douglas DC-3; 3 ATR-42-300; 1 Fairchild Metro III; 1 Britten-Norman BN-2T Islander; 1 Britten-Norman BN-2 Islander; 3 Cessna 404 Titan

AIR SOUTHWEST
Incorporated: 2003

Air Southwest was founded to take over the services from Plymouth and Newquay previously operated by British Airways, and which that airline had inherited when it acquired the small West Country airline, Brymon, including a service to London Gatwick. It is owned by Sutton Harbour Holdings, which also owns Plymouth Airport.

HQ airport & main base: Plymouth City
Radio callsign: SOUTHWEST
Designator: WOW
Employees: 95
Route points: Bristol, Dublin, Jersey, Leeds/Bradford, London, Manchester, Newquay, Plymouth
Fleet: 5 Bombardier Dash 8 Q300

ASTRAEUS
Incorporated: 2002

An inclusive tour charter airline operating from both London Gatwick and Manchester for around fifty tour operators.

HQ airport & main base: London Gatwick
Radio callsign: ASTRAEUS
Designator: 5W/AEU
Fleet: 4 Boeing 757-200; 2 Boeing 737-700; 1 Boeing 737–300

ATLANTIC AIRLINES
Incorporated: 1994

Atlantic Airlines was formed within Atlantic Holdings, owners of Air Atlantique, in 1994, but operations did not start until 1998. The management bought out control in 2004, although Atlantic Holdings still maintains an interest. Scheduled and charter cargo operations are provided by a fleet which includes Tupolev Tu-204C transports, while services are flown under contract to TNT Worldwide Express.

HQ airport & main base: Coventry Baginton
Designator: NPT
Links with other airlines: Alliance with Enimex
Fleet: 2 Airbus A300B4-200F; 2 Tupolev Tu-204C; 7 Lockheed L-188/L-188C Electra; 3 BAe ATP; 5 Fokker F27 Mk500

AURIGNY
Aurigny Air Services Ltd
Incorporated: 1968

Taking its name from the French name for the Channel Island of Alderney, Aurigny Air Services was founded in 1968 when the then British United Channel Islands Airways decided to withdraw the air service between Alderney and Guernsey. The first aircraft was the appropriately named Britten-Norman Islander. The airline then took over what has now become its busiest route, the inter-island service between Jersey and Guernsey, which at the time was served only by morning and evening British European Airways' flights – today the service is half-hourly at peak periods and hourly off peak throughout the day. The initial operations were intended to operate on a 'no-booking, turn-up and take-off' shuttle system, but passengers soon showed a preference for a reservation-based system.

The twin-engined Islanders were soon replaced by the stretched tri-motor Trislander; eventually a fleet of eight was assembled and routes operated between the three largest Channel Islands and to France and the British mainland. Experience with de Havilland

Canada Twin Otter aircraft proved that the Trislander was the ideal aircraft for inter-island flights, but since it was no longer in production, Aurigny's engineering subsidiary, Anglo-Normandy Engineering, located a kit of parts to produce a ninth Trislander in 1999. Meanwhile the fleet had also been strengthened with the addition of a Short 360 airliner. A relatively short-lived venture was the acquisition of Guernsey Airways.

The type of low-cost lifeline air service pioneered by Aurigny has been the model for many others worldwide, and the airline helps train personnel for other airlines operating in remote areas, such as the Falklands. Aurigny also claims to have been the first airline to have an aircraft sponsored, when G-OTSB was sponsored by a bank in 1984, while another aircraft, G-JOEY, featured in a series of books for young children.

The airline moved its main base from Alderney to Guernsey in the 1990s, and in 2000 ownership passed to a private equity company, before the States of Guernsey acquired Aurigny in 2003. The Trislander fleet is now slightly smaller, while the airline has obtained larger, pressurised, turboprop aircraft and also moved into providing night post services for the UK Post Office. Route expansion has also seen services introduced to London, Bristol and Manchester.

HQ airport & main base: Guernsey; with aircraft and crew also based at Jersey and Alderney
Radio callsign: AYLINE
Designator: GR/AUR
Employees: 290
Route points: Alderney, Bristol, Dinard, Guernsey, London, Manchester, Southampton. Mail flights operate between Jersey, London Gatwick and East Midlands
Fleet: 3 ATR-72-200; 1 ATR-42-301; 1 Saab 340A; 1 Short 360; 6 Britten-Norman Trislander

BA CITYFLYER
Incorporated: 2007

Following the sale of BA Connect to FlyBe, BA Cityflyer was formed to continue BA Connect's services to London City Airport, which were not included in the sale.

HQ airport & main base: Manchester International
Radio callsign: Bealine
Designator: BA
Route points: Birmingham, Bristol, East Midlands, Edinburgh, Glasgow, London, Manchester
Links with other airlines: A subsidiary of British Airways (qv)
Fleet: 10 BAe Avro RJ100

BA CONNECT
Incorporated: 2002

Originally formed as BA CitiExpress in 2002, combining the operations of British Regional Airlines, Brymon Airways and Manx Airlines, by this time all subsidiaries of British Airways, the airline was renamed BA Connect in February 2006, offering low-cost flights and feeder services into the BA network.

The largest of the merged companies, British Regional Airlines came into existence in 1990 as Manx Airlines (Europe), a subsidiary of Manx Airlines, set up to develop the parent company's growing network of operations based outside of the Isle of Man. A growing number of services was based on Cardiff, Manchester and Southampton, with services from the last two being boosted by the transfer of Loganair's operations outside of Scotland in 1994. The following year, Manx Airlines (Europe) became a British Airways Express franchise-holder, adopting British Airways colour schemes, uniforms and flight designators.

The current title was adopted in 1996, reflecting further growth in the network after British Airways decided to withdraw its operations within Scotland, handing these over to British Regional Airlines, and shortly afterwards Loganair's operations were incorporated into British Regional Airlines.

The fleet initially was largely based on BAe ATP, Jetstream 31 and 41 aircraft, and Shorts 360, but this soon included a BAe 146 and a Saab SF340, while the smaller Jetstream 31s were soon replaced by more of the larger 41s. In 1997, British Regional Airlines became the first British operator of the new Embraer 145 regional jet aircraft.

Manx Airlines had been for many years a subsidiary of Airlines of Britain Holdings, ABH, along with British Midland and Loganair while in 1996, ABH also took over Aberdeen-based Business Air, and in 1997 this airline became part of British Regional Airlines (Holdings), a new company set up as a parent for both British Regional Airlines as an operating company and Manx Airlines. Loganair, which had been operated as part of British Regional Airlines, was bought out by its management early in 1997, leaving the BRAL Group.

Brymon Airways took its name from those of the two founders, William Bryce, a New Zealander, and Chris Amon. Operations started in 1972, using a nine-passenger Britten-Norman Islander, flying to the Isles of Scilly and Jersey from the company's base at Newquay, and from Plymouth. The following year, Brymon moved its base to Plymouth and obtained a larger aircraft in the form of a de Havilland Canada Twin Otter, with twenty seats. A Plymouth–Guernsey service was also introduced that year.

In the years that followed, Cork and Exeter were added to the network, but a major step forward came in 1977, when the airline took over British Midland's Newquay to London Heathrow route, replacing the Vickers Viscounts used by BM with a smaller Handley Page Herald. Services from Plymouth to London Gatwick were introduced two years later, using Twin Otters. The restricted length of the runway at Plymouth had limited the development of services from that airport, but this changed in 1982, when Brymon introduced the short take-off and landing – STOL – de Havilland Canada Dash 7, initially for use on an oil industry charter because of the aircraft's ability to use another short runway at Unst in Shetland, the UK's most northerly airport. Brymon's Dash 7 was also used in experiments to prove the feasibility of an airport in London's docklands, encouraging the future development of what is now London City Airport.

A number of changes of ownership followed during the next few years. In 1983, de Havilland Canada bought a 75 per cent stake in Brymon from the founders, while three years later ownership passed to The Plimsoll Line, a company owned 40 per cent by British Airways, and in which Danish airline Maersk Air in 1988 acquired a 40 per cent stake before TPL acquired Birmingham European Airways.

Brymon launched flights from London City Airport to both Paris and Plymouth in 1987. Three years later, further expansion started with the introduction of the de Havilland Dash 8, and a new network of routes from Bristol to Glasgow, Edinburgh and Paris, with a feeder service between Plymouth and Bristol. The following year, services from Bristol were introduced to Aberdeen, Jersey and Newcastle. A short-lived merger of the two TPL subsidiaries followed in 1992, but this was reversed the following year, leaving Maersk with Birmingham European, and Brymon became a wholly owned subsidiary of British Airways, adopting the parent company's livery and flight designators.

Further expansion followed the acquisition by BA, although by this time the airline was no longer operating to London City Airport. Services were introduced from Newcastle and Southampton to Paris. In 1997, services from Newquay and Plymouth to London Heathrow were switched to London Gatwick, allowing a 25 per cent increase in flights. Despite the growth in the scheduled network, Brymon continues to operate oil industry-related charters out of Aberdeen.

The second largest regional airline in Europe, the merged airline provides one of the densest cross-country networks in Europe, flying within the UK and to the closer European destinations. Some rationalisation of the aircraft types in the fleet can be expected over the next few years.

In 2006 agreement was reached between British Airways and FlyBe for BA Connect to be sold to FlyBe, which took effect in March 2007, although during a transitional period both airlines will retain their separate identities before eventually adopting the FlyBe identity. The fleet will be rationalised on FlyBe Embraer 195s and Bombardier Dash 8 Q400s.

HQ airport & main base: Manchester International
Designator: TH/BRT
Route points: Within the BA network
Links with other airlines: A wholly owned subsidiary of FlyBe (qv)
Fleet: 13 BAe Avro RJ100ER; 1 BAe 146-300; 2 BAe 146-200; 1 BAe 146-100; 8 Bombardier Dash 8 Q300; 8 Embraer ERJ-145EP; 20 Embraer ERJ-145EU

BAC EXPRESS
BAC Express Airlines Ltd
Incorporated: 1992

BAC Express Airlines started life as BAC Aircraft in 1992, the name being changed in 1995. The early fleet included two Handley Page Heralds, an Embraer Bandeirante, a Shorts 330 and a Shorts 360. These aircraft were used on regular postal charters for the Royal Mail, while ad hoc passenger and freight charters were also operated. Although Fokker F27s were operated from some while, today the airline has standardised on Shorts 360. It continues to operate for the Royal Mail and express courier companies, as well as having aircraft available for ad hoc cargo charters, or for wet-lease on scheduled services. Originally based at London Stansted, its head office is now in Horley and its two main bases are Edinburgh and Exeter. It is a wholly owned subsidary of the 2morrow Group.

HQ airport & main base: Edinburgh, Exeter International
Radio callsign: RAPEX

Designator: ABR
Fleet: 1 Shorts 360-100; 3 Shorts 360-200; 1 Shorts 360-300

BIRMINGHAM EUROPEAN AIRWAYS
Incorporated: 2006

Not to be confused with another airline of the same name that later became part of Maersk Air, this new airline intends to commence operations shortly, initially using turboprop aircraft.

HQ airport & main base: Birmingham International
Designator: BHX

BLUE ISLANDS
Incorporated: 2001

Founded by the Channel Islands retailer Le Cocq's Stores as Le Cocq's Airlink, the company initially started to deliver perishable goods to Alderney from Bournemouth, and then moved into charters for tourists. In 2002 a scheduled service was inaugurated between Bournemouth and Alderney, and in August 2003 the airline's name was changed to Rockhopper, before being changed again to Blue Islands in 2006. It is owned by the Le Huret Group.

HQ airport & main base: Alderney
Radio callsign: ROCKHOPPER
Designator: XAX
Employees: 50
Route points: Alderney, Bournemouth International, Jersey
Fleet: 3 BAe Jetstream 32; 5 Britten-Norman BN2 Islander

BMED
Incorporated: 1994

Originally formed as British Mediterranean Airways in 1994, the airline initially served the Lebanon and later expanded into Jordan and Syria. At first the airline competed with British Airways, but it became a BA franchisee in 1997, and expanded later by taking over many routes abandoned earlier by BA, with a strong emphasis on the Middle East. The current title was adopted in late 2004. In February 2007 BMed was acquired by bmi, but will remain as a BA franchisee until October 2007 at least.

HQ airport & main base: London Heathrow
Designator: KJ/LAJ
Employees: 668
Route points: Addis Ababa, Alexandria, Amman, Aleppo, Almaty, Baku, Beirut, Bishkek, Damascus, Ekaterinburg, Khartoum, London, Tashkent, Tblisi, Tehran, Yerevan
Links with other airlines: BA (qv) franchisee
Fleet: 10 Airbus A321-200; 4 Airbus A320-200

bmi
British Midland Airways Ltd
Incorporated: 1938

Within a span of some seventy years, British Midland has grown from operating a small flying school at Burnaston, near Derby, to first a major British domestic and charter airline, and then, within the last twenty years, a significant major international airline.

The original company was known as Air Schools, providing pilot training, and became heavily involved in pilot training throughout the Second World War, with the schools at Derby and Wolverhampton training some 14,000 pilots. As the demand for pilot training reduced with the return of peace and the availability of ex-service pilots for airlines, the company diversified into ad hoc charters for both passengers and cargo, initially using eight-seat de Havilland Rapide biplanes.

The name was soon changed to Derby Aviation, but the first scheduled service did not come until 1953, when a Dragon Rapide operated from Wolverhampton to Jersey in the Channel Islands. Other routes soon followed, with services from Derby as well as Wolverhampton, and the small Rapides were soon replaced by larger Douglas DC-3 Dakotas and the four-engined Handley Page Marathon, albeit with just twenty seats. The Marathons were soon replaced by three Canadair DC-4M Argonauts for the rapidly growing inclusive tour charter market. A further name change came in 1959, when the airline became Derby Airways.

During the early postwar period, British commercial aviation had been dominated by the big nationalised British European Airways and British Overseas Airways Corporation, with private enterprise airlines being allowed charters and confined to a minor role on scheduled services, often as 'associates' of the state carriers. The establishment of an Air Transport Licensing Board in 1960 prepared the way for greater opportunities for the private sector.

In 1965, Derby moved to the new East Midlands Airport at Castle Donington, and changed its name to British Midland Airways, adopting a two-tone blue and white livery. More modern aircraft were soon acquired, starting in 1967 with Vickers Viscount turboprop airliners. Shortly afterwards, British Midland started its first service to a London airport, with a route from Teesside to Heathrow.

Boeing 707 aircraft were also operated for a period during the 1970s, and the airline provided an 'instant airline' start-up service for newly independent nations wishing to have their own national airline, helping to start twenty-five airlines over a seven year period. In 1978 the airline was purchased by the present chairman, Sir Michael Bishop, and two partners from the previous owners, Minster Assets, which had acquired British Midland ten years earlier. The new owners then set out to establish the airline as a major competitor on the domestic trunk routes from London's Heathrow Airport to Belfast, Glasgow and Edinburgh. Although the initial application for licences was made in 1979, because of strong objections from British Airways it was not until 1982 that the first services could be operated to Glasgow, with Edinburgh services following in 1983 and those to Belfast in 1984. A fleet of McDonnell Douglas DC-9s was acquired to operate the new routes.

In 1985, a new blue and white livery with red lettering was adopted, although this has since been modified and later changed to that used today. A new holding company, Airlines of Britain Holdings, was established in 1987 to take into account the company's ownership at the time of the main Scottish airline, Loganair and the rapidly expanding Manx Airways, while the following year Scandinavian Airlines System, SAS, took a 24.9 per cent stake in ABH. In 1986, British Midland inaugurated its first international service from Heathrow with a new route to Amsterdam. New Boeing 737 airliners started to augment, and then replace, the DC-9s throughout the late 1980s and early 1990s, with Fokker 100 airliners also being introduced. When SAS increased its holding to 40 per cent in 1994, British Midland took over that airline's Glasgow–Copenhagen service, increasing the flights to twice daily and then introducing a daily call at Edinburgh. Lufthansa now has 30 per cent of the airline's shares, with SAS having 20 per cent, while the remainder are in the hands of the BBW partnership, which includes Sir Michael Bishop, the chairman. The airline has reintroduced two-class air travel to British domestic flights as well as on its European network.

Today, British Midland is the second largest user of London's Heathrow Airport, and has code-share arrangements with a number of international airlines. The other ABH subsidiaries, which also came to include Business Air in 1986, transferred to a new company, British Regional Airlines, in 1997, and have since been sold to British Airways. Nevertheless, in 1987 BMI Regional was formed and this has since developed into a substantial carrier, providing regional scheduled services, while in 2002 a further development was the creation of a low-cost subsidiary, bmibaby.

In 1998 the first of an order for Airbus A320/321s entered service, which started to replace the Boeing 737 fleet, some of which were passed to bmibaby. The airline applied to operate transatlantic services in 1999, although these were delayed by the shortcomings of the UK–USA air services agreements. Code-sharing was introduced with a number of overseas airlines and the airline became a member of the Star Alliance in 2000. bmi adopted its current identity in 2001.

HQ airport & main base: London Heathrow is the main base, but the HQ airport is East Midlands
Radio callsign: MIDLAND
Designator: BD/BMA
Employees: 4,077
Route points: Aberdeen, Abu Dhabi, Alicante, Amsterdam, Antigua, Bahrain, Belfast, Birmingham, Bridgetown, Brussels, Calgary, Cape Town, Chicago, Cologne, Copenhagen, Cork, Dublin, Durham, Düsseldorf, East Midlands, Edinburgh, Esbjerg, Frankfurt, Glasgow, Gothenburg, Groningen, Halifax, Hamburg, Hanover, Inverness, Johannesburg, Las Vegas, Leeds/Bradford, London, Lyons, Madrid, Manchester, Milan, Montreal, Mumbai, Munich, Muscat, Newcastle, Nice, Norwich, Oslo, Ottawa, Palma de Mallorca, Paris, Pisa, Riyadh, St John's, Stavanger, Stockholm, Stornoway, Stuttgart, Toronto, Toulouse, Vancouver, Venice, Vienna, Warsaw
Links with other airlines: Lufthansa has a 30 per cent shareholding and SAS 20 per cent (both qv). Member of the Star Alliance. Alliances with: Air France, Gulf Air, Iberia, Malaysian Airlines, Qatar Airways, Royal Brunei Airlines, South African Airways, Sri Lankan Airlines, Virgin Atlantic Airways (all qv).
Fleet: 3 Airbus A330-200; 1 Boeing 767-300ER; 8 Airbus A321-200; 11 Airbus A320-200; 9 Airbus A319-100

bmi regional
Incorporated: 1987

Formed as a subsidiary of the then British Midland Airways, now bmi, to operate scheduled passenger services within the UK.

HQ airport & main base: Aberdeen Dyce
Designator: BD/BMR
Employees: 400
Route points: Within the BMI network, but with hubs at Edinburgh, East Midlands, Glasgow, Leeds/Bradford, Manchester
Links with other airlines: Subsidary of bmi (qv)
Fleet: 1 ATR-42-300; 11 Embraer ERJ-145EP/MP; 3 Embraer ERJ-135ER

bmibaby
Incorporated: 2002

bmi's foray into the low-fares market, bmibaby was founded in 2002 and is based at East Midlands Airport, operating mainly international scheduled services from a number of UK airports, using Boeing 737 aircraft.

HQ airport & main base: East Midlands
Designator: WW/BMI
Route points: Alicante, Amsterdam, Belfast, Birmingham, Bordeaux, Cardiff, Cork, Durham, Faro, Geneva, Glasgow, Jersey, Knock, London, Malaga, Palma de Mallorca, Manchester, Paris, Prague
Fleet: 13 Boeing 737-300; 6 Boeing 737-500

BRITISH AIRWAYS
British Airways PLC
Incorporated: 1972

Carrying more international passengers than any other airline, British Airways, BA, until recently was also one of just two airlines operating supersonic air services. It has been overtaken both by Lufthansa and by the merger of Air France and KLM, so that it is no longer Europe's largest airline, but it is eighth in the world by annual turnover, and twelfth by passenger numbers.

The airline's long history dates from 1924, when four small airlines, Handley Page Transport, Instone Air Line, Daimler Hire and British Marine Air Navigation, were merged to form Imperial Airways with a mixed fleet of just eighteen aircraft. Daimler Hire had been the successor to the world's first international scheduled airline, Aircraft Transport and Travel, AT&T, which had commenced a London–Paris service on 25 August 1919.

Initially the new airline developed services to Europe. It soon established a network of services to the countries of the British Empire using a combination of landplanes and flying boats. Services had reached Basra in the Persian Gulf by 1927, Karachi in 1929, Nairobi and Cape Town in 1932, Calcutta, Rangoon and Singapore in 1933, and Brisbane in 1935. The complete journey on the Australian service took 12 days and the route often had to be altered to avoid trouble spots. The Singapore–Brisbane section was operated by the then newly formed Qantas.

Meanwhile, other airlines had been established in the UK, and in 1935 three of these, Hillman's Airways, Spartan Air Lines and United Air Lines, merged to form British Airways, which operated landplanes mainly on routes between the UK and Europe.

The growth of Imperial Airways was given added impetus after 1937 when the British government introduced the Empire Air Mail Scheme, which enabled all letters between the countries of the British Empire to be sent by air, at a rate of 1*d* (0.625p) per half ounce, or 3 US cents at the exchange rate of the day. To handle this growing quantity of air mail, Imperial took the then unprecedented step of ordering twenty-eight of the new Shorts S.23 Empire flying boats off the drawing board, without a prototype aircraft. The first of these aircraft entered service on 31 October 1936, reducing the UK–Australia journey to 9 days. Later, the Empire flying boats were to take part in experiments in in-flight refuelling, and with Pan American World Airways conducted successful trials for transatlantic flying boat services.

Both Imperial Airways and British Airways were nationalised in 1939 as a result of the previous year's Cadman Report, which recommended a single British international airline. The new, merged airline, British Overseas Airways Corporation, BOAC, commenced operations in 1940. While air services were drastically reduced during the Second World War, BOAC maintained its African network, and a new service from Cape Town to Australia via Ceylon. Liberator bombers were used on the North Atlantic to return ferry pilots to Canada and the United States. Modified de Havilland Mosquito fighter-bombers were used to fly ball-bearings from Sweden to Scotland, flying over enemy-held territory, while obsolete Whitley bombers maintained an air line between Gibraltar, Malta and Alexandria in Egypt.

Postwar, the airline concentrated on intercontinental services, while domestic and European services passed to a new airline, British European Airways, BEA.

BOAC's fleet became increasingly landplane dominated and the last flying boats left the fleet in the early 1950s. The airline was the first to introduce jet airliners in 1952, but the de Havilland Comet 1 airliners had to be withdrawn in 1954 after several disasters. Nevertheless, the much-improved de Havilland Comet 4 enabled BOAC to launch the first transatlantic jet air services in 1958.

Meanwhile, BEA had been the first airline to introduce turboprop aircraft after successful trials with the prototype Vickers Viscount in 1951. The airline also experimented with the carriage of mail, and then passengers, by helicopter. A subsidiary, BEA Helicopters, was formed in 1964 to operate helicopter services to the Isles of Scilly, but the main boost to the helicopter operations came with the discovery of oil and natural gas in the North Sea.

While BOAC developed satellite airlines in Africa and the Caribbean, BEA became involved with regional airlines in England and Wales through involvement in BKS Air Services (which later changed its name to North East Airlines) and Cambrian Airways, which operated from Cardiff and Bristol, eventually establishing a subsidiary, British Air Services, to coordinate these two companies. In 1969 a charter subsidiary, BEA Airtours, was formed. Throughout its existence, BEA also operated a network of German domestic services radiating out of West Berlin, since East German airspace was closed to airlines other than those of the four occupying powers.

History repeated itself when another government-appointed committee, the Edwards Committee, recommended the merger of BEA and BOAC. A holding company for both airlines was established in 1972, while the merger itself was implemented in 1974, when the new British Airways appeared. The main subsidiaries included British Airtours and British Airways Helicopters.

Since the merger, British Airways has continued the tradition of 'firsts', by introducing transatlantic supersonic services with the Anglo-French Concorde airliner, while its 'no reservation' shuttle services on the UK domestic trunk routes were the first of their kind outside the United States. In 1987, BA became the first European nationalised flag carrier to be privatised. The following year, it bought its main British rival, British Caledonian, which was encountering financial difficulties, and merged that airline's charter activities with those of British Airtours under the Caledonian Airways name. Four years later, BA acquired another Gatwick-based airline, Dan Air.

British Caledonian had itself been created by the acquisition of British United Airways, a scheduled and charter airline, by the Scottish-based charter airline, Caledonian Airways. The airline had developed as a competitor to the state-owned airlines and was at one time selected as the 'second force' competitor to BA, competing on the North Atlantic and also flying to Africa and, at one time, South America. It had been the first British customer for the BAC One-Eleven jet airliner. Dan Air, by contrast, had been formed by aviation brokers Davies & Newman, and had operated a mix of inclusive tour charters, ad hoc charters and cross-country regional flights within the British Isles, later moving into the charter market for the offshore oil industry. It was unusual in that it operated charter flights out of West Berlin during the period of German partition. It usually operated secondhand aircraft. The one item that both these airlines had in common was the use of London's second airport, Gatwick, as their main base of operations, and this took BA into that airport for the first time.

BA sold off British Airways Helicopters in 1986, when the helicopter operation became British International Helicopters, and in 1995 sold the charter company, Caledonian Airways. After this, the priority following privatisation became one of acquisition to establish a global airline. In 1992, BA bought a 49 per cent holding in France's leading regional airline, TAT European Airlines, later increasing this to 100 per cent, and 49 per cent in Germany's Delta Air Regionalflug, which was renamed Deutsche BA. The following year, BA acquired a 25 per cent holding in USAir, leading to code-sharing on USAir flights to 38 cities in the United States. Later in 1993, BA acquired a 25 per cent interest in the Australian airline, Qantas. Smaller acquisitions during this period included the small West Country airline, Brymon Airways, and a 49 per cent interest in the Gibraltar Airline, GB Airways.

Further rationalisation has included selling BA's package holiday operations to Owners Abroad (now the First Leisure Group, who at the time had their own airline, Air 2000), in 1990, and its engine overhaul plant in Wales to General Electric of the United States in 1991.

This programme of expansion also included franchise operations with smaller regional airlines operating their aircraft in BA livery on flights with BA designators, while their staff wore BA uniforms. The franchise partners included not only the wholly owned Brymon, but also Loganair, British Regional Airways, as the successor to Manx Airlines Europe, CityFlyer Express, Maersk Air (UK), TAT, and Sun Air. British Mediterranean Airways took over BA's services from London to Amman, Beirut and Damscus in 1997, becoming a franchisee, using three Airbus A320s. BA also became involved in Airline Management, AML, a low-cost joint venture based at Gatwick. A 'low cost, no frills' operation started at London Stansted in April 1998, using four Boeing 737-300s for services to Amsterdam, Paris and Madrid, under the name Go!. This company was later sold to its Luton-based rival, easyJet. At the other end of the market, BA was one of just two airlines to operate international supersonic air services, using the Anglo-French Concorde supersonic airliner, starting in 1976 and operating a twice-daily schedule between London and New York until 2003, when the service was withdrawn.

BA later disposed of its interest in USAirways in favour of seeking a major global alliance with American Airlines, at the time the world's largest airline, during the late 1990s, but this alliance proved a step too far for the regulators on both sides of the North Atlantic. The airline became a member of the Oneworld alliance. Meanwhile, in 1997 a controversial new corporate identity was introduced, part of which entailed having no standardised identity on the tails of the company's aircraft, but after a few years this was abandoned.

At intervals, the airline has conducted substantial cost-cutting efforts, and has sold off many of its support functions, including catering. Employee numbers have fallen from around 54,000 to fewer than 48,000 over the past decade.

In recent years, BA has largely reversed its earlier plans. The 'no booking' shuttle services were converted to standard services and capacity on the UK trunk routes was reduced, with 757 flights often replaced by the smaller A320. Interests in other airlines have largely been sold, most significantly in the case of Qantas, while the airline has withdrawn from services in France and Germany. The one exception has been the creation of BA Connect, which now provides low-cost feeder services for the parent as well as operations on its own account. At the time of writing, the airline is reviewing the franchise strategy, which may be ended as current francise agreements expire.

HQ airport & main base: London Heathrow, but there are also extensive operations from London Gatwick, Manchester and Birmingham
Radio callsigns: BEALINE/SPEEDBIRD/SHUTTLE
Designator: BA/BAW
Employees: 47,472
Route points: (Many operated by franchisees or BA Connect): Aalborg, Aarhus, Aberdeen, Abu Dhabi, Abuja, Accra, Addis Ababa, Agadir, Aleppo, Alexandria, Algiers, Alicante, Almaty, Amman, Amsterdam, Antigua, Athens, Atlanta, Bahrain, Baku, Baltimore, Bangalore, Bangkok, Barcelona, Barra, Basle/Mulhouse, Beijing, Beirut, Belfast, Belgrade, Benbecula, Berlin, Bermuda, Bilbao, Billund, Birmingham, Bishkek, Bologna, Bordeaux, Boston, Bridgetown, Bristol, Brussels, Bucharest, Budapest, Buenos Aires, Cairo, Campbelltown, Cape Town, Casablanca, Catania, Chennai, Chicago, Cologne, Copenhagen, Cork, Dallas/Fort Worth, Damascus, Dar-es-Salaam, Delhi, Denver, Detroit, Dhaka, Doha, Dubai, Dublin, Dubrovnik, Durban, Düsseldorf, Edinburgh, Ekaterinburg, Entebbe, Faro, Fez, Frankfurt, Geneva, Gibraltar, Glasgow, Gothenburg, Grand Cayman, Grenada, Guernsey, Hamburg, Hanover, Harare, Hassi Messaoud, Helsinki, Hong Kong, Houston, Innsbruck, Inverness, Islamabad, Islay, Isle of Man, Istanbul, Jeddah, Jersey, Johannesburg, Khartoum, Kiev, Kingston, Kirkwall, Knock, Kolkata, Krakow, Kuwait, La Coruña, Lagos, Lanzarote, Larnaca, Las Palmas, Lisbon, Livingstone, Londonderry, Los Angeles, Luanda, Lusaka, Luxembourg, Lyons, Madrid, Malaga, Malta, Manchester, Marrakesh, Marseilles, Mauritius, Melbourne, Menorca, Mexico City, Miami, Milan, Montreal, Moscow, Mumbai, Munich, Muscat, Nairobi, Nantes, Naples, Nassau, Newark, Newcastle, New York, Nice, Orlando, Oslo, Paris, Paphos, Perth (Australia), Philadelphia, Phoenix, Pisa, Port Elizabeth, Prague, Pristina, Providenciales, Riga, Rio de Janeiro, Rome, St Lucia, St Petersburg, San Francisco, Sao Paulo, Seattle, Seville, Shanghai, Sharm-el-Sheikh, Shetland Islands, Singapore, Sofia, Southampton, Stockholm, Stornoway, Stuttgart, Sydney, Tampa, Tashkent, Tblisi, Tehran, Tel Aviv, Thessaloniki, Tiree, Tobago, Tokyo, Toronto, Toulouse, Tripoli, Tunis, Turin, Valencia, Vancouver, Venice, Veronna, Victoria Falls, Vienna, Vilnius, Warsaw, Washington, Wellington, Wick, Windhoek, Yerevan, Zurich
Links with other airlines: Owns BA Cityflyer (qv). Has an 18 per cent stake in Comair, 9 per cent in Iberia and 3.84 per cent in Air Mauritius (all qv). Alliances with BMED, Comair, GB Airways, Japan Airlines, Loganair, SN Brussels Airlines, Sun-Air of Scandinavia, Swiss (all qv)
Passengers carried: 35.5 million
Annual turnover: US $14,417 million (£9,500 million)
Fleet: 57 Boeing 747-400; 40 Boeing 777-200ER; 3 Boeing 777-200; 21 Boeing 767-300ER; 13 Boeing 757-200; 19 Boeing 737-400; 5 Boeing 737-300; 11 Airbus A321-200; 28 Airbus A320-200; 5 Airbus A320-100; 9 Boeing 737-500; 33 Airbus A319-100

BRITISH INTERNATIONAL
Brintel Helicopters Ltd
Incorporated: 1993

British International Helicopters can trace its origins to the formation by British European Airways of the BEA Helicopter Experimental Unit in 1947, which initially used an S-51 helicopter for experimental postal servies, and subsequently operated Westland WS-55 Whirlwinds on passenger feeder services to airports, although these were withdrawn in 1956 as an economy measure. During 1953, with heavy flooding in the Netherlands, two of the S-51s were used to rescue seventy-six people.

BEA Helicopters was formed in 1964, and within a few years was operating Sikorsky S-61 helicopters, mainly in support of the North Sea oil and gas industry, and also operated Britain's only scheduled helicopter service, between Penzance and the Isles of Scilly, off the south-western tip of Cornwall. Between 1971 and 1983, a Sikorsky S-61N was operated on behalf of the British Coastguard service out of Aberdeen, saving more than 260 people during this period. At one stage, large Boeing Chinook helicopters were also operated on behalf of the oil and gas industry. Although the helicopter operation survived the merger of BEA and BOAC to form British Airways, becoming British Airways Helicopters, the company was subsequently sold as BA endeavoured to concentrate on its core scheduled airline operations, becoming British International Helicopters in 1986. The present title was adopted in 1995.

In 1996 the company acquired Cardiff-based Veritair, operators of light helicopters in support of police forces, including South Wales Police.

Today, British International continues to operate helicopters in support of the oil and gas industries, and has developed a cost-effective aerial crane service for the construction industry.

HQ airport & main base: Aberdeen, with other bases at Sumburgh (Shetland), Penzance and Cardiff
Radio callsign: BRINTEL
Designator: UR/BIH
Employees: 372. Flight crew: 103; cabin staff: 7; engineering: 139; ground staff: 78; administration and sales: 45
Main destinations: Penzance–St Mary's; Penzance–Tresco
Parent company: CHC Helicopter Corporation (Canada)
Links with other airlines: Reciprocal training links with Helikopter Service of Norway
Annual hours flown: 22,000
Annual turnover: £47.663 million (US $78.644 million)
Fleet: 12 Sikorsky S-61N; 1 Sikorsky S-61NM; 1 Sikorsky S-76A; 8 Eurocopter AS.332L Super Puma; 2 Eurocopter AS.332C-L Super Puma; 1 Eurocopter AS.355; 1 Eurocopter BO.105

BRITISHJET.COM
Incorporated: 2004

A British inclusive tour charter airline formed in 2004 and which commenced operations between the UK and Malta the following year.

HQ airport & main base: HQ at Gatwick, main base Malta Luqa International
Designator: FHE
Fleet: 1 McDonnell Douglas DC-9-30

CITY STAR AIRLINES
Incorporated: 2004

A charter and scheduled service airline linking Scotland and Norway, City Star was founded in 2004 and began operations the following year. Much of its work is centred around the needs of the offshore oil industry. A controlling interest was acquired in Landsflug in 2005.

HQ airport & main base: Aberdeen Dyce
Designator: X9/ISL
Route points: Aberdeen, Bergen, Oslo
Fleet: 3 Dornier 328-110

DAS AIR CARGO
Incorporated: 1983

DAS Air Cargo was founded in 1983 as a cargo charter airline that also provided wet-lease operations for other airlines, before developing cargo services between the UK and Africa. It now serves much of Africa from London and Amsterdam, while also using Entebbe in Uganda as a hub for onward distribution. The network now extends to Bangkok and Dubai. After operating DC-8s, the airline now operates DC-10 freighters.

HQ airport & main base: London Gatwick
Designator: WD/DSR
Employees: 228
Route points: Include Amsterdam, Bangkok, Dubai, Entebbe, Lagos, London, Nairobi
Fleet: 3 McDonnell Douglas DC-10-30F

DHL AIR
Incorporated: 2001

Established in 2001 by Deutsche Post WorldNet, DHL, to operate its European network of scheduled cargo flights.

HQ airport & main base: East Midlands
Radio callsign: DHL
Designator: DO/DHK
Employees: 270
Links with other airlines: Owned 100 per cent by Deutsche Post WorldNet
Fleet: 22 Boeing 727-200SF

EASTERN AIRWAYS
Incorporated: 1997

Founded in 1997, Eastern Airways acquired the small regional operator Air Kilroe, based at Manchester Airport, in 1999. It has grown rapidly to establish a strong regional network, helped by the withdrawl of KLMuk from the British internal market, and in 2003 a number of routes and Jetstream 41 aircraft were transferred from British Airways Citiexpress. It is independent of other airlines, with ownership split between the chairman and managing director.

HQ airport & main base: Humberside International, with hubs at Aberdeen and Norwich
Designator: T3/EZE
Route points: Aberdeen, Birmingham, Bristol, Brussels, Durham, Edinburgh, Humberside, Inverness, Isle of Man, Leeds, London, Manchester, Newcastle, Norwich, Nottingham, Southampton, Stornoway, Wick
Fleet: 4 Saab 2000; 25 BAe Jetstream 41; 3 BAe Jetstream 31/32

easyJet
easyJet Airline Ltd
Incorporated: 1995

The first European low-cost 'no frills' airline to begin operations in Britain, easyJet started with operations out of London Luton Airport along the British domestic trunk routes to Edinburgh and Glasgow. International services followed. Initially the airline used the air operator's certificate of GB Airways, but later transferred to Air Foyle Charter Airlines, who also provided flight crew in the early days. Today, easyJet operates on its own account and has established further hubs and bases at Liverpool, Bristol and Stansted, the last two aided by its acquisition of its rival, Go!, from that airline's parent company in 2002. It has also developed services between other EU countries.

easyJet was floated on the London Stock Exchange in 2000, but its founder, Stelios Haji-Ionnou, still retains 27.6 per cent of its shares, with more than 30 per cent spread among other members of his family. Today, easyJet is the forty-seventh largest airline in the world by revenue, and eighteenth by passenger numbers, lagging behind its main low-cost competitor, Ryanair, which is sixteenth by passenger numbers. It has a 49 per cent stake in easyJet Switzerland, the maximum allowed a foreign airline.

The airline is steadily switching from an all-Boeing 737-300s and 737-700s fleet, to an all-Airbus A319-100 fleet.

HQ airport & main base: London Luton, with further hubs at London Stansted, Bristol and Liverpool
Radio callsign: EASY
Designator: U2/EZY
Employees: 200
Route points: Aberdeeen, Alicante, Almeria, Amsterdam, Asturias, Athens, Barcelona, Basle/Mulhouse, Belfast, Berlin, Bilbao, Bratislava, Bremen, Bristol, Budapest, Cagliari, Cologne, Copenhagen, Cork, Dortmund, East Midlands, Edinburgh, Faro, Geneva, Glasgow, Hamburg, Inverness, Knock, Krakow, Lisbon, Liverpool, Ljubljana, London, Lyons, Maastricht, Madrid, Malaga, Marseilles, Milan, Munich, Murcia, Naples, Newcastle, Nice, Olbia, Palma de Mallorca, Paris, Pisa, Prague, Riga, Rome, Shannon, Tallinn, Toulouse, Turin, Valencia, Venice, Warsaw
Links with other airlines: Has a 49 per cent stake in easyJet Switzerland (qv)
Fleet: 30 Boeing 737-700; 130 Airbus A319-100 (in course of delivery)

EMERALD AIRWAYS
Incorporated: 1987

Originally founded at Southend, Essex, in 1987 as Janes Aviation by Andy and Hilary Janes, the present title was adopted in 1992 as the airline had developed so that most of its business was on the Irish Sea air routes. The main base also moved from Southend to Liverpool. Exeter-based Streamline Aviation was acquired in 2002. Both scheduled and charter flights are operated for passengers and cargo, with a five-times-daily operation between Liverpool and the Isle of Man.

Operations were suspended in early May 2006, and the airline was put into administration. Its Liverpool–Isle of Man service is being operated by Euromanx meanwhile.

EUROMANX
Incorporated: 2002

Formed in 2002, Euromanx operates charter and scheduled services to and from the Isle of Man. In 2006, it took over the Emerald Airways service between the island and Liverpool.

HQ airport & main base: Isle of Man Ronaldsway
Designator: 3W/EMX
Route points: Belfast, Isle of Man, Liverpool, London, Manchester
Fleet: 1 BAe Avro RJ70ER; 1 Fokker 50; 1 ATR-42-300; 1 Bombardier Dash 8 Q300; 1 Bombardier Dash 8 Q200; 2 Dornier 328-110

EUROPEAN AVIATION
European Aviation Air Charter
Incorporated: 1993

Commencing operations in February 1994, some five months after it was formed, European Air Charter initially operated three BAe One-Eleven 500 aircraft. Ad hoc passenger and cargo charters, and wet-leasing operations to other airlines, are operated from airports throughout the UK and Europe, while the main base is at Bournemouth International Airport on the south coast of England. In 1997, a One-Eleven 500 was wet-leased to EuroScot Express for a short-lived low-cost service from Bournemouth to Glasgow and Edinburgh.

HQ airport & main base: Bournemouth International Airport
Radio callsign: EUROCHARTER
Designator: EAF
Fleet: 4 Boeing 737-200

FIRST CHOICE AIRWAYS
Incorporated: 1987

First Choice Airways was formed in 1987 as an inclusive tour charter airline, Air 2000, based in Manchester, initially operating two Boeing 757s. Three years later a second base was opened at Gatwick, at the time Britain's main departure point for holiday charter flights. Meanwhile, the fleet continued to expand, mainly through the addition of further Boeing 757s, although a Boeing 737 was operated for a short period. In 1996, taking advantage of the liberalisation of air transport within the European Union, a further base was opened at Dublin in the Irish Republic. Recently, the airline's first scheduled services have been introduced to Cyprus. By 2000, the airline was operating a fleet of thirteen Boeing 757s, augmented by four of the smaller Airbus A320s. A new corporate identity was unveiled in October 1996, with the entire fleet rebranded during the winter season which followed. In 1998 the parent company, First Choice, acquired a competitor, Unijet, and its airline subsidiary, Leisure International, was merged into Air 2000. The airline was renamed First Choice Airways in March 2004.

HQ airport & main base: Manchester, with extensive operations from London Gatwick and Dublin
Radio callsign: JETSET
Designator: DP/AMM
Employees: 2,000
Fleet: 6 Boeing 767-300ER; 10 Boeing 757-200; 4 Airbus A321-200; 5 Airbus A320-200 (On order: 8 Boeing 787-8)

FLIGHTLINE
Incorporated: 1989

Originally formed in 1989 as a dealer in executive aircraft, with its own maintenance base at Southend Airport, Flightline moved into air transport work in 1992, when it started flying inclusive tour charters from Bournemouth for the tour operator Palmair, an activity that lasted until 1999. Today the airline undertakes passenger and cargo charters and also flies contract charters and wet-leases aircraft and crews to other airlines. It owns British Airline Management.

HQ airport & main base: Southend
Radio callsign: FLIGHTLINE
Designator: B5/FLT
Fleet: 1 McDonnell Douglas MD-83; 2 BAe 146-300; 6 BAe 146-200

FlyBe
Incorporated: 1979

FlyBe traces its history back to a merger of Jersey-based Intra Airways, dating from 1967, and the passenger operations of Express Air Services of Bournemouth, to form a new airline, Jersey European, which started operations in 1979 using Douglas DC-3 Dakotas. These were soon replaced by more modern Embraer Bandeirantes and de Havilland Twin Otters, aircraft of a size well suited to traffic flows between the Channel Islands and many mainland destinations at the time. Meanwhile, another airline, Spacegrand Aviation, based in Blackpool in the north-west of England, was developing from an air taxi operation to a regional scheduled carrier, building up a network of services from Blackpool to Belfast, Dublin and the Isle of Man. Spacegrand's parent company, the Walker Steel Group, acquired Jersey European in 1983 and merged the two companies under the Jersey European name in 1985, headquartering the airline at Exeter Airport.

The combined airline started to introduce new routes, including services from Exeter to Belfast and Jersey, and the fleet also expanded with the addition of three Shorts 360 aircraft. Before the end of the decade, services between Belfast City and Birmingham had been introduced. Larger aircraft, in the form of six Fokker F27 Friendships, were introduced during the early 1990s, while route expansion continued and the airline enjoyed phenomenal growth, with passenger figures rising by 31 per cent during 1991, for example. It was at this time that a new livery was introduced.

Jersey European's first jet aircraft arrived in 1993, when three BAe 146s, renowned for their low noise levels, were introduced for use on services from London Gatwick to Belfast and to Jersey. Following this, additional aircraft of this type were introduced and the route network continued to expand, including taking over the London Stansted to Belfast service originally introduced by Air UK (which later became KLMuk, before being absorbed by its Dutch parent airline), and operating London Stansted to Marseilles on behalf of Air Inter, predecessor of Air France Europe, and code-sharing with Air UK on Belfast-Amsterdam.

A further development at this time was a franchise operation with Jersey European aircraft flying from London Heathrow to Toulouse and Lyons on behalf of Air France Express.

Nevertheless, by this time the Channel Islands accounted for a relatively small proportion of the airline's business, and in 2000 the name was changed to British European. This was followed by a further change in 2002, when the airline was repositioned as a low-cost airline, again with a change of brand and livery, to become FlyBe. A major policy decision in the face of rapidly rising oil prices was to use fast, modern turboprops on many routes, replacing the fleet of fourteen BAe 146s with Bombardier Dash 8s. More than 80 per cent of the airline's routes are UK domestic, with more than a hundred routes operated.

In 2006 agreement was reached between British Airways and FlyBe for BA Connect to be sold to FlyBe, with effect from March 2007, although during a transitional period both airlines will retain their separate identities before eventually adopting the FlyBe identity. FlyBe will standardise the varied FlyBe fleet and concentrate mainly on the Bombardier Dash 8 Q400 and Embraer E-195 series, eventually building a fleet of more than eighty aircraft of the two types.

HQ airport & main base: Exeter International, with hubs at Belfast City, Birmingham and Southampton
Radio callsign: FLYBE
Designator: BE/BEE
Employees: 1,638
Route points: Aberdeen, Alicante, Angers, Avignon, Belfast, Bergerac, Berne, Birmingham, Bordeaux, Brest, Bristol, Chambery, Dublin, Edinburgh, Exeter, Faro, Galway, Geneva, Glasgow, Guernsey, Isle of Man, Jersey, La Rochelle, Leeds/Bradford, Limoges, Liverpool, London, Malaga, Manchester, Murcia, Newcastle, Norwich, Palma de Mallorca, Paris, Perpignan, Rennes, Salzburg, Southampton, Toulouse
Links with other airlines: Alliances with Continental Airlines, Scot Airways (both qv)
Passengers carried: 5.5 million
Fleet: 45 Bombardier Dash 8 Q400; 7 Bombardier Dash 8 Q300; 14 Embraer 195; 28 Embraer ERJ-145EP/EV; 4 Boeing 737-300; 9 BAe 146-300; 3 BAe 146-200; 1 BAe 146-100

FLYGLOBESPAN
Globespan Group
Incorporated: 2002

Founded in November 2002, Flyglobespan started low-fare operations out of Scotland in April 2003, initially operating to Spain. The airline has since developed, with bases at Edinburgh andGlasgow and a further hub at London Stansted, and has started transatlantic flights, offering three-class travel.

HQ airport & main base: Glasgow International with a further base at Edinburgh
Radio callsign: GLOBESPAN
Designator: B4/GSM
Route points: Alicante, Barcelona, Calgary, Faro, Malaga, Nice, Orlando, Palma de Mallorca, Prague, Rome, Tenerife, Toronto, Vancouver, Venice

Fleet: 1 Boeing 767-300ER; 1 Boeing 757-200; 3 Boeing 737-800; 2 Boeing 737-300;1 Boeing 737-300QC; 4 Boeing 737-600; 1 Boeing 737-200 (On order: 2 Boeing 787-8)

FLYJET
Incorporated: 2002

An inclusive tour charter airline, founded in 2002 and operational since June 2003. It was acquired by Luton-based Silverjet in 2007.

HQ airport & main base: London Gatwick
Designator: Y7/FJE
Fleet: 1 Boeing 757-200

GB AIRWAYS
GB Airways Ltd
Incorporated: 1981

GB Airways was originally formed in 1931, as a subsidiary of the Gibraltar-based shipping and travel group, M.H. Bland, carrying the name Gibraltar Airways. The early operations were to Tangier, giving the airline the world's fastest intercontinental service, with a flight taking just fifteen minutes. Flights were also operated to London, using a wet-leased Britannia Airways Boeing 737. The name GB Airways was taken in 1981, as the airline prepared to broaden its area of operations and moved its base to London Gatwick Airport. The airline gradually developed a route network to destinations in the Mediterranean, and to Portugal and Madeira.

In 1995, the airline became a British Airways franchise operator, adopting the livery, uniforms and flight designators of the larger airline, and enabling BA to re-establish its presence on routes such as those to Malta which it had surrendered previously. The route structure is incorporated with that of British Airways, and is now predominantly focused on the eastern Mediterranean and Middle East. Over the past decade, the fleet has gone from one consisting entirely of Boeing 737s to Airbus A320s and A321s. Ownership still remains with the Bland Group.

HQ airport & main base: London Gatwick
Radio callsign: GEEBEE AIRWAYS
Designator: GT/GBL
Links with other airlines: British Airways franchise partner. Alliances with British Airways and Iberia Airlines (both qv)
Fleet: 10 Airbus A321-200; 11 Airbus A320-200

GLOBAL SUPPLY SYSTEMS
Incorporated: 2001

Formed by John Porter, with a 51 per cent stake, and Atlas Air in 2001, operations began in 2002 with a Boeing 747F on dry-lease from Atlas. The airline effectively provides wet-leased cargo aircraft for other airlines.

HQ airport & main base: London Stansted
Designator: XH/GSS
Employees: 111
Links with other airlines: Wet-lease aircraft to major airlines, including British Airways (qv)
Fleet: 3 Boeing 747-400F

HIGHLAND AIRWAYS
Incorporated: 1991

Highland Airways was originally formed as Air Alba, and for the first four years operated a flying school, before moving into air taxi and light transport work. It was renamed Highland Airways in 1997. It now operates scheduled and charter flights, including carrying mail and newspapers to the Western Isles.

HQ airport & main base: Inverness
Designator: HWY
Route points: Benbecula, Inverness, Sumburgh, Stornoway
Fleet: 3 BAe Jetstream 31

ISLES OF SCILLY SKYBUS
Incorporated: 1984

Owned by the Isles of Scilly Steamship company, Isle of Scilly Skybus has traditionally operated a high-frequency service between Lands End and St Mary's, but the route network has since been expanded to include services to the islands from other points in the south-west.

HQ airport & main base: Lands End St Just
Designator: 5Y/IOS
Employees: 50
Route points: Bristol, Exeter, Lands End, Newquay, St Mary's
Fleet: 2 de Havilland Canada DHC-6 Twin Otter Srs 300; 2 Britten-Norman BN2B-26 Islander; 1 Britten Norman BN2A Islander

JET2
Incorporated: 2002

Jet2 was founded as a low-cost scheduled passenger airline in 2002, by the Dart Group, parent company of Channel Express, and commenced operations from Leeds/Bradford in 2003 with a fleet of Boeing 737-300s.

Early in 2006, Channel Express was rebranded Jet2 to provide a higher profile for the Jet2 brand. Channel Express had been founded in 1978 as Express Air Services, commencing air freight operations using Handley Page Herald freighters on services between Bournemouth's Hurn Airport and the Channel Islands. During the early 1980s, a number of Royal Mail contracts was obtained, and the present name was adopted. Other traffic developed, with the airline introducing its own special cooling plant in Guernsey to prepare cut flowers for air transport to the British mainland. While the Herald fleet grew, so that eventually Channel Express had eight uprated and refurbished 'Super' Heralds, larger aircraft were seen to hold the key to the future, and the airline was the first to place Lockheed L-188C Electra freighters on the British register. The arrival of the Electras saw the airline begin to take an increasing share of the overnight parcels and freight market within the UK and Europe. Later, Fokker F27 Friendship freighters were added to the fleet, and in 1997 the airline introduced the Airbus A300B4-100F freighter, as launch customer for the BAe conversion of this type, able to carry loads of up to 45 tonnes. In addition to its own contracts, Channel Express also provided additional freight capacity for other airlines throughout Europe and the Middle East.

HQ airport & main base: Leeds/Bradford International
Designator: LS/EXS
Route points: Alicante, Amsterdam, Barcelona, Belfast, Blackpool, Budapest, Chambery, Cork, Edinburgh, Faro, Geneva, Leeds/Bradford, London, Malaga, Manchester, Murcia, Newcastle, Paris, Prague, Tenerife
Fleet: 8 Boeing 757-200; 5 Boeing 737-300QC; 15 Boeing 737-300

LOGANAIR
Loganair Ltd
Incorporated: 1962

Originally billed as 'Scotland's airline', Loganair has seen many changes of ownership, but throughout has managed to maintain the vital 'lifeline' services linking the Scottish islands to the mainland or to larger islands.

Loganair did not start life as an airline at all, but when operations commenced in 1962 it was as the aviation division of a civil engineering company, Duncan Logan (Contractors). Initially a single Piper Aztec was used to carry the company's own staff to construction sites and to meetings, but the demand for this type of service in Scotland, with mountains and a heavily indented coastline as well many island groups, was such that Loganair soon started to offer an air taxi service to other organisations. A regular service between Edinburgh and Dundee was operated for a while, and in 1964 the company won the contract to provide a regular newspaper service to Benbecula and Stornoway.

By the end of the 1960s, the company was operating two Piper Aztecs, two Britten-Norman BN-2 Islanders, a Beech 18 and a Piper Cherokee Six: The Beech 18 is now preserved in the Scottish Aviation Museum at East Fortune. Regular services had been introduced to Orkney in 1967, and Shetland the following year, in each case linking the outlying islands with the Orkney and Shetland 'mainlands'. Apart from the newspaper contracts, there was also a regular weekday operation flying computer cards from Glasgow to Blackpool for the then Post Office Savings Bank.

Out of the initial varied fleet, the aircraft which did most to transform travel in the more remote parts of the Scottish islands was the Islander. Using this aircraft to serve sparsely populated communities was more economic than using passenger-carrying ferries, leaving heavy items to less frequent cargo, sailings while passengers, mail, newspapers and light freight went by air. For a while, Loganair also operated the Islander's larger cousin, the stretched three-engined Trislander. The Islander also proved to be the ideal aircraft for the Scottish Air Ambulance Service, operated under contract by Loganair.

Financial difficulties led to Loganair being taken over by the National Commercial Bank in 1968, with ownership passing to the Royal Bank of Scotland following a banking merger. Control later passed to Airlines of Britain Holdings, the parent company at one time for British Midland Airways (now bmi), and later to British Regional Airlines, while for a period the airline was managed by Manx Airlines, before a management buyout early in 1997. The Manx Airlines involvement followed a period when Loganair had set up a hub operation at Manchester, followed by one at Southampton, attempting to expand beyond the confines of the Scottish market in what proved to be a costly experiment. Loganair lost its external routes in 1994, and by the end of 1995 its management had been largely taken over by Manx.

During this period the fleet changed. Islanders remained popular on the Orkney and Shetland internal services, and for the air ambulance flights, but the Trislanders were replaced by de Havilland Canada DHC-6 Twin Otters for flights to and between the Western Isles. BAe Jetstream 31 and 41 aircraft were introduced for some of the external services and also for flights from Glasgow and Edinburgh to the Northern Isles. Larger aircraft were also obtained for flights from Glasgow and Edinburgh to Manchester and Belfast, in the form of BAe ATPs, while two BAe 146 airliners were operated for a short period out of Manchester on routes to Brussels and the Channel Islands. Shorts 360 were introduced for some of the busier routes to the islands, and it was eventually hoped that these would replace the older Twin Otters, but the 360 proved too heavy for some routes, and especially those to Barra, where aircraft have to land on the beach at low tide. The Jetstreams and ATPs passed to Manx under the ABH-inspired reorganisation of 1994.

In 1996, British Airways announced that it was pulling out of the Scottish internal services, and operation of these passed to Loganair and British Regional Airlines, operating as British Airways Express franchise partners.

Loganair is now concentrating on the Scottish internal services which it knows so well. The management buyout did not affect the airline's status as a BA franchise partner. Apart from using the beach at Barra, other features of the airline's operations include the world's shortest air service, between Westray and Papa Westray, on the Orkney internal services, with a flight scheduled to take just two minutes – but timed by a television reporter at 100 seconds!

For the future, the airline's franchise agreement with British Airways will be due for renewal, and much will depend on whether the current management at BA intends to continue franchising its services.

HQ airport & main base: Glasgow International, but aircraft are also based at Kirkwall (Orkney) and Lerwick (Shetland)
Radio callsign: LOGAN
Designator: LC/LOG (or BA/BAW)
Route points: Aberdeen, Barra, Benbecula, Eday, Edinburgh, Fair Isle, Foula, Glasgow, Inverness, Islay, Kirkwall, Lerwick, North Ronaldsay, Outer Skerries, Papa Stour, Papa Westray, Sanday, Stornoway, Stromness, Stronsay, Tiree, Westray
Links with other airlines: British Airways Franchise Partner
Fleet: 13 Saab 340A/B; 2 de Havilland Canada DCH-6 Twin Otter Srs 300; 4 Britten-Norman BN-2B Islander

LYDDAIR
Incorporated: 1997

Airlines don't come any smaller than this. Lyddair was founded as Sky Trek Airlines by the owner of Lydd Airport, Jonathan Gordon, in 1997. The airfield had developed post-Second World War on the growth of car-carrying aircraft, but lost its business with the improvement in cross-Channel ferry traffic and the introduction of hovercraft. The new owner renamed Lydd as London Ashford, and in 2002 Sky Trek was renamed Lyddair. A single international scheduled service is operated to Le Touquet in France, but charters are also offered and a Piper Navajo Chieftain is operated for air taxi operations.

HQ airport & main base: London Ashford
Radio callsign: LYDDAIR
Designator: LYD
Employees: 6
Route points: Le Touquet Paris Plage, London Ashford
Fleet: 2 Britten-Norman BN2A Islander

MANX2
Incorporated: 2006

This regional passenger airline links the Isle of Man with destinations in Great Britain and Ireland, with flights timed to connect with those of budget airline Jet2. It largely replaces the services to the island operated by the defunct Emerald Airways.

HQ airport & main base: Isle of Man Ronaldsway
Radio callsign: Manx
Designator: BPS
Route points: Belfast, Blackpool, Leeds/Bradford, Isle of Man
Links with other airlines: Connects with Jet2 services
Fleet: 2 Let L-410UVP-E

MK AIRLINES
Incorporated: 1990

MK started operations in 1991 as MK Air Cargo with a McDonnell Douglas DC-8-54F and a DC-8-55F, operating from Gatwick to destinations in Africa, usually via Accra in Ghana. The airline and has five DC-8 freighter conversions, and there are subsidiary companies, MK Airlines Ghana and Flash Airlines in Nigeria. As a specialist in scheduled operations between the UK and Africa, MK has alliances with a number of major airlines. Aircraft are available for ad hoc charters. The airline was originally at London Stansted, but the main base of operations is now Ostend in Belgium.

HQ airport & main base: Ostend, with bases at Manston, Kent, and at Luxembourg and Accra
Designator: 7G/MKA
Route points: Accra, Harare, Kano, Lagos, Luxembourg, Manston, Nairobi, Ostend
Links with other airlines: Owns Flash Airlines, Nigeria
Fleet: 7 Boeing 747-200F; 1 McDonnell Douglas DC-8-62

MONARCH
Monarch Airlines Ltd
Incorporated: 1967

Monarch Airlines commenced operations from London Luton Airport in 1968, initially using two Bristol Britannia turboprop airliners, although these were later joined by BAC One-Elevens. The early aircraft were replaced by more modern aircraft during the 1970s, while the airline continued to concentrate on inclusive tour charters to Europe, and especially to destinations in the Mediterranean. Long-haul services started in 1988, using Boeing 757-200ERs on charter flights to Florida, and in 1990 charters to New York and Boston were introduced. A small scheduled network was also being developed by this time, with flights from Luton to Mahon, Malaga and Tenerife.

Today, Monarch operates out of a number of UK airports, and has further developed its scheduled network using the Monarch Scheduled Services name. A modern fleet is operated with aircraft of both Airbus and Boeing manufacture. It has an extensive engineering subsidiary, Monarch Aircraft Engineering, which undertakes work for the airline and for third-party customers.

HQ airport & main base: London Luton, although flights also operate from Birmingham International, London Gatwick or Manchester
Radio callsign: MONARCH
Designator: ZB/MON
Employees: 1,777
Route points: Alicante, Almeria, Barcelona, Birmingham, Faro, Gibraltar, Granada, Lanzarote, Las Palmas, Lisbon, London, Madrid, Malaga, Manchester, Menorca, Palma de Mallorca, Tenerife
Fleet: 2 Airbus A330-200; 4 Airbus A300-600R; 1 Boeing 767-300ER; 7 Boeing 757-200; 7 Airbus A321-200; 6 Airbus A320-200 (On order: 6 Boeing 787-8)

MYTRAVEL AIRWAYS
Incorporated: 1986

Originally founded in 1986 as Airtours, the name of the parent inclusive tour holiday operator, the airline commenced operations in 1991. Airtours' other activities included inclusive tour operations, including Airtours Holidays, Aspro Holidays, Suncruises and Tradewinds, and the Going Places travel agency chain. The fleet originally included McDonnell Douglas MD-83s, but is now composed of Airbus A330s, A321s and A320s, plus Boeing 757s and 767s.

Airtours absorbed Inter European Airways of Cardiff in 1993 and in 1996 the parent company acquired Spies, the Scandinavian leisure group, incidentally also giving it ownership of Premiair, the largest charter airline in Scandinavia.

In 2002 the parent company was rebranded as MyTravel, and both the Airtours and Premiair airlines were renamed as MyTravel. Later that same year, the airlines entered the low-cost scheduled airline field, with the establishment of MyTravelLite, but in 2005 this airline and its scheduled services were reabsorbed into the parent airline. At the time of writing the airline is merging with Thomas Cook Airlines (qv).

HQ airport & main base: Manchester, with a further major base at Newcastle, but flights are also operated out of many other major UK airports
Radio callsign: MYTRAVEL
Designator: VZ/MYT
Employees: 1,900
Route points: Arrecife, Agadir, Alicante, Almeria, Antalya, Banjul, Belfast, Bergamo, Birmingham, Bodrum, Bourgas, Bridgetown, Bristol, Calgary, Cancun, Cardiff, Catania, Chania, Corfu, Dalaman, East Midlands, Eilat, Faro, Fuerteventura, Gerona, Glasgow, Goa, Heraklion, Holquin, Ibiza, Innsbruck, Kefalonia, Kos, Larnaca, Las Palmas, London, Madeira, Malaga, Male, Malta, Manchester, Marrakesh, Menorca, Mombasa, Montego Bay, Newcastle, Palma de Mallorca, Phuket, Pula, Rhodes, Salvador, Salzburg, Sanya, Sharm-el-Sheikh, Sofia, Split, Tangiers, Thessaloniki, Trivandrum, Turin, Varna, Venice

Fleet: 2 Airbus A330-200; 2 Boeing 767-300ER; 1 Boeing 757-200; 3 Airbus A321-200; 6 Airbus A320-200

ROCKHOPPER
See Blue Islands

SCOTAIRWAYS
Incorporated: 1986

Originally formed at Ipswich in 1986 as Suckling Airways, named after the husband-and-wife proprietors, operating a single Dornier Do.228-200 between Ipswich and Amsterdam, and with a domestic route being introduced later between Ipswich and Manchester. During the early 1990s the main base was transferred from Ipswich to Cambridge, a more central point for passengers from East Anglia, and afterwards a secondary base was opened at London Luton. The airline then moved on to a number of routes discarded by larger airlines, including the then Air UK's Edinburgh–Norwich service, while the fleet grew to include the larger Dornier Do.328-100, as well as additional Do.228-200s.

In October 1999 Brian Souter, one of the founders of the Stagecoach bus and railway group, invested in the airline and became a majority shareholder. The airline restructured and renamed itself ScotAirways, and while retaining its base at Cambridge, its emphasis moved to operations between the east of Scotland and London City Airport. The number of Do328s increased, but the Do228s were sold off. The two founders remain shareholders, with Roy Suckling as managing director.

HQ airport & main base: Cambridge
Radio callsign: SCOTAIRWAYS
Designator: CB/SAY
Route points: Amsterdam, Dundee, Edinburgh, London, Southampton
Links with other airlines: Alliances with FlyBe, KLM Cityhopper (both qv)
Fleet: 7 Dornier Do.328-110

SILVERJET
Incorporated: 2007

A business-class scheduled airline initially operating between the UK and New York Newark and which also owns Flyjet (qv). Additional aircraft and other routes are planned.

HQ airport & main base: London Luton
Radio callsign: Silverjet
Designator: Y7/FJE
Route points: London, Newark
Links with other airlines: Owns Flyjet
Fleet: 1 Boeing 767-200ER

THOMAS COOK AIRLINES
Thomas Cook Airlines (UK) Ltd
Incorporated: 2000

Although Thomas Cook Airlines only dates from 2000, when it was created as JMC Airlines, named after the son of Thomas Cook, John Mason Cook, its origins go back much further. The airline was itself formed in 1998 when Thomas Cook acquired the Carlton Leisure Group and the airline operations of both companies, Caledonian Airways and Flying Colours Airlines respectively, were merged, but continued to operate under their own names until the creation of JMC in 2000. The title Thomas Cook Airlines was finally adopted in 2003.

The younger of the two airlines, founded in 1995, Flying Colours had commenced inclusive tour charter operations in 1997 with a single, leased Boeing 757-200. The airline was founded by Erroll Cossey, former head of Air 2000, and the Flying Colours Leisure Group, the parent company for a number of British tour operators, which itself belonged to the Carlton Leisure Group.

Much older, the name of Caledonian Airways can be traced back to the formation of the airline of that name in 1961. Caledonian's links with the original were tenuous. The original Caledonian Airways was founded to operate North Atlantic passenger charters, with the declared intention, never realised, that it should eventually become the Scottish international airline. In the event, the airline's business became increasingly London Gatwick-based, operating first a single Douglas DC-7C, then four Bristol Britannias, and then two Boeing 707-320s. A scheduled service between Glasgow and Barcelona was licensed, but never operated. Nevertheless, during the early 1970s the airline merged with British United Airways to form British Caledonian Airways, which at its peak operated a mixed fleet of BAC One-Elevens, Boeing 707s and Vickers VC10s airliners on a route network which included destinations in Africa and South America (abandoned by British Airways), as well as competing with BA on services to New York and Los Angeles. It also served many of the main European destinations as well as the UK domestic trunk routes from its London Gatwick base.

McDonnell Douglas DC-10 and Airbus A320 airliners were also introduced. The airline was officially recognised as being Britain's 'second force' airline, established to complement and on certain routes compete with British Airways. A route-swap with British Airways saw the South American routes exchanged for a number of destinations in the Middle East, before mounting economic difficulties saw British Caledonian, or 'BCal', taken over by British Airways in 1988. In the subsequent reorganisation the scheduled services and their aircraft were absorbed by BA, while the charter operations were combined with those of BA's then charter subsidiary, British Airtours, and the combined charter operation was renamed Caledonian Airways.

Caledonian was acquired from British Airways by Inspirations, a British inclusive tour operator, in 1994. Operations were mainly charter, and primarily for inclusive tour operators, although there was some wet-lease activity, with aircraft deployed for the London Heathrow to Manchester shuttle at one time. Later, control passed to the Thomas Cook tour operating and travel agency group. At the time of writing the airline is absorbing MyTravel Airways (qv).

The main bases are London Gatwick and Manchester, but in common with many inclusive tour airlines, flights are operated from a large number of UK airports.

HQ airport & main base: Manchester
Radio callsign: FLY
Designator: MT/TCX
Employees: 1,804
Links with other airlines: Owned by Thomas Cook with an associated company in Belgium
Fleet: 3 Airbus A330-200; 2 Boeing 757-300; 14 Boeing 757-200; 4 Airbus A320-200

THOMSONFLY
Incorporated: 1962

Thomsonfly is the name introduced in 2004 for Britannia Airways, one of the world's largest inclusive tour charter airlines, and which dates from 1962. Britannia originated as Euravia (London), operating from Luton Airport, now known as London Luton, using three former El Al Lockheed Constellations carrying holidaymakers for its parent, Universal Sky Tours. The airline was one of the first to be started by a tour operator, a practice which later became commonplace. The fleet of Constellations rapidly grew to eight aircraft. In 1964, Britannia started to re-equip with Bristol Britannia turboprop airliners, and the airline was renamed Britannia.

Thomson Industrial Holdings, which later became the International Thomson Organisation, acquired Universal Sky Tours in 1965, and Britannia as well. The business continued to develop, aided partly by the convenient location of its home airport, but before long charters were also being flown from Glasgow, Manchester and Newcastle. During the winter months, trooping flights for the British Ministry of Defence also provided additional work, and the airline also undertook charters carrying pilgrims to Mecca, so that by the late 1960s some 20 per cent of receipts were in foreign currency. The fleet of Britannias eventually totalled seven aircraft before these were supplemented and then replaced by Boeing 737-200s, the first of which were delivered in 1968, when they were the first 737-200s to be operated in Europe. Twenty years later, the Boeing 737-200 and 737-300 fleet amounted to almost thirty aircraft, and the airline was operating out of twenty UK airports.

In 1988, the former Universal Sky Tours, by this time renamed Thomson Holidays, bought Horizon Travel and its subsidiary, the East Midlands-based Orion Airways, whose operations were soon integrated into those of Britannia. By this time, Britannia was already re-equipping with larger aircraft, Boeing 767s, and these were followed by the smaller 757. The highly competitive nature of the package holiday market meant that the largest possible aircraft were necessary so that tour operators could enjoy the economies of scale. The larger aircraft also opened up longer-distance inclusive tour operations to Britannia, operating initially to Florida and then, as the market developed, destinations throughout the world. Nevertheless, by the start of the twenty-first century, the lower costs of ever-larger aircraft were perceived as being balanced by a lack of flexibility, and so the Boeing 737 returned to the fleet.

In 1997 the airline moved into the German market, initially with two Boeing 767-300ERs, with a wholly owned subsidiary, Britannia GmbH. The next stage was the acquisition by Thomson of the Swedish Fritidsresor tourism group, which also included an airline, Blue Scandinavia, which was promptly renamed Britannia AB, and then later Britannia Nordic.

In May 2000, Thomson's travel interests were acquired by Preussag, part of the German TUI Group. The next move was that the TUI group announced plans for a low-cost airline, Thomsonfly, which began services on 31 March 2004, and took the company into the UK domestic market for the first time. In 2005 the decision was taken to merge the Britannia inclusive tour charter and Thomsonfly low-cost scheduled operations using the Thomsonfly name for all operations.

HQ airport & main base: London Luton, with a further major base at London Gatwick
Radio callsign: THOMSON
Designator: BY/TOM
Route points: (In addition to inclusive tour charter operations) Alicante, Amsterdam, Barcelona, Bournemouth, Coventry, Doncaster, Faro, Jersey, Lyons, Malaga, Paris, Prague, Salzburg, Tenerife, Valencia
Fleet: 4 Boeing 767-300ER; 4 Boeing 767-200ER; 18 Boeing 757-200; 5 Boeing 737-800; 10 Boeing 737-300; 4 Boeing 737-500

TITAN
Titan Airways
Incorporated: 1988

Titan Airways began air charter operations in 1988, and within a couple of years was operating an Embraer Bandeirante, two Shorts 330s and a Shorts 360 from its main base at London Stansted. The fledgling airline was sold to its management in 1992, and since then it has continued steady growth, offering contract and ad hoc passenger and freight charters throughout Europe, and in North Africa and the Middle East. Titan often undertakes wet-lease charters for scheduled airlines, many of these at short notice.

HQ airport & main base: London Stansted
Radio callsign: ZAP
Designator: T4/AWC
Employees: 171
Fleet: 1 Boeing 757-200; 1 Boeing 737-300QC; 2 Boeing 737-300; 3 BAE 146-200QC; 1 BAE 146-200QT; 1 Raytheon Beech King Air 200

TNT
TNT International Aviation Services Ltd
See TNT Airways (Belgium)

TRANSAFRIK
Transafrik International, SARL
Incorporated: 1984

Formed by Erich Koch, Renato Hermino and Joao Rodrigues, who remain the shareholders, Transafrik is a cargo specialist operating ad hoc and contract charters mainly in Africa from its bases at Luanda and Sao Tome. Medical evacuation flights can be undertaken, while the company is able to handle difficult loads and relatively primitive airports with its Hercules fleet, which has more than doubled in size over the past ten years.

HQ airport & main base: HQ is at St Peter Port, Guernsey, but the main operating base is Nairobi Jomo Kenyatta International
Employees: 205
Fleet: 5 Lockheed L-100-20/30 Hercules; 1 Boeing 727-200; 2 Boeing 727-100F; 1 Boeing 727-100

VIRGIN ATLANTIC
Virgin Atlantic Airways
Incorporated: 1984

Britain's second-largest long-haul airline, Virgin Atlantic Airways is already the twenty-ninth largest airline in the world by turnover, up in one year from thirty-sixth, but is outside the top fifty in passenger numbers due to the long-haul nature of its business. The airline was founded in 1984 by Richard Branson, and was intended to be an offshoot of his popular music businesses. The first aircraft was a Boeing 747, used for a service from London Gatwick Airport to New York-Newark Airport. Two years later, a second route, to Miami, was introduced and a second aircraft acquired. The third and fourth aircraft arrived in 1988, and the following year a service from Gatwick to Tokyo was inaugurated. In 1991, the airline was allowed to operate its first flights from London Heathrow Airport, initially operating flights to Los Angeles, New York-JFK and Tokyo, while maintaining services from Gatwick.

Branson's sale of his original business, Virgin Music, in 1992 resulted in a pledge to invest the proceeds in the further development of the airline. That same year the airline started to franchise its name, with a service from Gatwick to Athens operated under the Virgin name by South East European Airways, although this service was transferred to Heathrow in 1993. A further franchise operation began in 1994 with a service from London City Airport to Dublin operated by CityJet. Meanwhile, Virgin Atlantic had introduced the first Airbus A300-300 aircraft to be operated by a British airline.

Further routes followed, and a change of corporate identity marked the airline's tenth anniversay. During 1995 Virgin Atlantic entered into a number of marketing alliances, first with Malaysian Airlines, then with Delta Air Lines, followed by a code-share with British Midland, and a partnership arrangement with Malaysia Airlines and Ansett Australia. The airline took advantage of growing liberalisation of the European air travel market to launch a Dublin–Brussels service, also in 1995, in conjunction with CityJet, but the franchise was terminated by mutual agreement the following year after Virgin acquired Euro Belgian Airlines, a low-cost Brussels-based operator, which it renamed Virgin Express. The first Virgin services to South Africa were launched that year, with a Heathrow–Johannesburg flight.

The arrangement with Delta Air Lines ended in 1997, and was replaced by a similar arrangement with Continental Airlines.

Although the airline considered a stock exchange listing, it has instead entered a partnership with Singapore Airlines, which owns 49 per cent of the shares while the Virgin Group holds the remainder. As an airline group, Virgin is the second largest British airline by turnover, and twenty-ninth in the world, up in one year from thirty-sixth. The number of employees has almost doubled in the past decade.

HQ airport & main base: London Heathrow
Radio callsign: VIRGIN
Designator: VS/VIR
Employees: 7,480
Route points: Antigua, Boston, Bridgetown, Cape Town, Delhi, Dubai, Grenada, Havana, Hong Kong, Johannesburg, Lagos, Las Vegas, London, Los Angeles, Miami, Mumbai, Nassau, New York, Newark, Orlando, St Lucia, San Francisco, Shanghai, Singapore, Sydney, Tobago, Tokyo, Washington
Links with other airlines: Singapore Airlines (qv) has a 49 per cent stake. Virgin Group has a 25.26 per cent stake in Virgin Blue, and a minority holding in Virgin America. Alliances with America West Airlines, bmi, Continental Airlines, Nationwide Airlines, Singapore Airlines, South African Airways, Virgin Blue (all qv)
Annual turnover: US$2,997 million (£2 million)
Fleet: 13 Boeing 747-400; 25 Airbus A340-600; 5 Airbus A340-300 (On order: 6 Airbus A380-800)

XL AIRWAYS UK
Incorporated: 1994

Originally founded in 1994 as an inclusive tour charter airline, Sabre Airways, the present title was adopted in 2000 following the acquisition of a 67 per cent interest in Excel by the Libra Group. Air Atlanta Iceland acquired a 40.5 per cent stake in Excel in March 2004, with the Icelandic holding company Avion Group acquiring the airline outright in 2005. This was followed by Air Atlanta Europe's wet-lease operations being merged into Excel Airways in May 2006. Air Atlanta Europe had been founded in 2002 by Air Atlanta Iceland and operational since 2003, providing wet-lease operations for Virgin Atlantic, among others. Meanwhile, the present title has been adopted to link with sister companies in France and Germany, and the airline has moved into low-cost scheduled passenger operations in addition to its charter and wet-lease business.

HQ airport & main base: London Gatwick
Radio callsign: EXCEL
Designator: JN/XLA
Employees: 600
Route points: Alghero, Alicante, Athens, Bodrum, Cagliari, Chania, Copenhagen, Dalaman, Faro, Fuerteventura, Grenada, Heraklion, Holguin, Hurghada, Ibiza, Katamata, Kefalonia, Kerkyra, Kos, Lanzarote, Larnaca, Las Palmas, London, Luxor, Madeira, Madrid, Malaga, Malta, Marsa Alam, Menorca, Naples, Orlando, Ovda, Palermo, Palma de Mallorca, Paphos, Paris, Puerto Plata, Pula, Punta Cana, Rhodes, St Kitts, Santa Clara, Sharm-el-Sheik, Skiathos, Split, Taba, Tel Aviv, Tenerife, Tobago, Tunis, Vancouver, Verona, Zakynthos
Links with other airlines: Owned by the Icelandic-based Avion Group
Fleet: 3 Boeing 767-300ER; 2 Boeing 767-300ER; 3 Boeing 757-200; 8 Boeing 737-800

ZOOM UK
Zoom Airlines Ltd
Incorporated: 2006

A new British airline based in Scotland and with a significant interest by the Canadian carrier of the same name, it is planned to commence transatlantic low-cost flights, initially linking Scotland and Canada. The Bank of Scotland is backing the project.

HQ airport & main base: Glasgow
Links with other airlines: Zoom Airlines of Canada (qv) is a major shareholder

UNITED STATES – N

As the country that made the first aeroplane flights, the United States also saw many of the early experiments in the practical application of aviation. The early development of the hydro-aeroplane, later to evolve into seaplanes and flying boats, was largely conducted in the United States. There was also an early experiment with airmail on 23 October 1911, when Earl Ovington flew from Garden City, New York to Mineola, Long Island, in a Bleriot monoplane. As with the British air cargo operation earlier that year, the distance was short, in this case just six miles.

As elsewhere, serious and sustained development of air transport had to await the period between the two world wars, although a regular airmail service was started in the United States before the First World War was over. The US Post Office inaugurated a regular airmail service between New York City and Washington, D.C., on 12 August 1918. The US Post Office was later to use the United States Air Corps, part of the US Army, for its mail flights, until a spate of accidents – doubtless due to the more ambitious flying of military pilots – cast doubt on safety levels and the task was put out to tender by commercial airlines. Before this decision, however, the Hubbard Air Service, one of the first American airlines, flew the first North American international airmail service, starting on 3 March 1919, when a Boeing Type C flew between Seattle, Washington, and Victoria, British Columbia. The US Post Office must have been pleased with the service as a contract was awarded to Hubbard on 14 October 1920.

At the opposite end of the United States, an international air service was inaugurated on 1 November 1920 by Aeromarine West Indies Airways, linking Key West in Florida with Havana in Cuba, a distance of ninety miles. The Caribbean, and especially links with Cuba, featured prominently in the history of US air transport.

The early aeroplane was unreliable, frail, slow and short on range. It was no mean achievement that the United States inaugurated a transcontinental airmail service as early as 1 July 1924. It should also be no surprise, however, that the service required no fewer than fourteen stops between New York and San Francisco.

Two of the airlines credited with making more than their fair share towards the development of air transport in the United States are no longer in existence: Pan Am and TWA.

Pan Am went into liquidation in 1991, after several years of declining fortunes. It had been founded in 1927 as Pan American Airways, when Juan Trippe put two Fokker F-VII/3M trimotors on a route between Key West in Florida, and Havana in Cuba. A year later, the new airline was flying across the Caribbean to South America, using the new Sikorsky S-38 amphibian, the first of many Sikorsky and Boeing aircraft to be designed to meet the airline's requirements. Further expansion into South America came in 1929, when an agreement with the W.R. Grace company led to the formation of a joint venture, Pan American-Grace Airways, or PANAGRA, to develop services to South America, and especially to the west coast. In 1966, PANAGRA was sold to the now defunct Braniff.

Meanwhile, Pan American had retained the famous aviation pioneer, Charles Lindbergh, who had made the first non-stop solo crossing of the Atlantic, to chart courses for transatlantic and transpacific services. The first flights were in 1935 across the Pacific with the Martin M-130 flying-boat *China Clipper*, and in 1939 across the Atlantic with the Boeing 314 flying boat *Dixie Clipper* operating jointly with Imperial Airways, predecessor of British Airways, and that airline's Short Empire flying boats. Postwar, Pan Am became a major force on the North Atlantic, and for many years did not have a domestic network. Instead, it acquired American Overseas Airlines in 1950, and acquired significant holdings in airlines in Latin America and the Philippines. A domestic network finally came with the takeover of Miami-based National Airlines.

Pan Am had not been exclusively a flying boat operator, and in 1933 had introduced the Boeing 247, often regarded as being the first modern airliner. The aircraft persuaded TWA to encourage Douglas to proceed with the DC-1 and its successors. Later, in 1940, with its main rival TWA, Pan Am was one of just two operators of the Boeing 307, the first pressurised airliner. Other 'firsts' attributed to the old Pan Am were the first 'Round-the-World' service in 1947, using a Lockheed Constellation, and, in 1955, the first order for an American jet airliner, the Boeing 707.

The 1980s were to see the airline disposing of assets and reducing its route network, even before the trauma of the destruction of a Boeing 747 over southern Scotland in December 1988 by a terrorist bomb. The name and trademark were obtained in 1993 by Martin Shugrue and Charles Cobb, and a new Pan Am airline was created with six Boeing 727-200s, operating low-fare services starting with routes from New York to Los Angeles and San Francisco in 1996, which were soon joined by services from New York to Chicago and Miami. The low-fare route being the way to success for many airlines, the new Pan Am suspended operations in late 2003, and was wound up early the following year.

Trans World Airlines, TWA, could trace its ancestry through one of its predecessor airlines, Western Air Express, which was formed in 1925 to take advantage of the opportunities offered when Congress passed the so-called Kelly Act, which allowed US mail contracts to be let to privately owned companies, having up to then been operated by the United States Post Office. Competition for the early contracts was intense, with more than 5,000 applicants, but Western was one of just five companies to be successful in winning a contract, being awarded the route between Los Angeles and Salt Lake City, a distance of 575 miles. A variety of equipment was operated on the route during the early years, including the Douglas Cruiser biplane and Fokker trimotors.

Among the other American airlines operating at the time were Maddux Airlines, flying Fokkers from Los Angeles to San Diego and San Francisco, and Transcontinental Air Transport, or TAT, an airline formed in 1929 and which retained Charles Lingbergh, who had made the first solo crossing of the Atlantic, as a consultant, and operated an early trans-USA rail and air service. Control of Maddux passed to Transcontinental in 1929, while Western Air Express acquired Standard Airlines, another Los Angeles operator. It was in 1930 that TAT-Maddux and part of Western Air Express merged to form Transcontinental and Western Air Express, which soon became known as 'TWA', even though it was to be another twenty years before the present title was adopted. The other part of Western Air Express became Western Airlines, for many years a major operator in North America.

Unlike its rival for many years, the old Pan American or Pan Am, TWA's development was for many years confined to domestic routes, and again in contrast to Pan Am, TWA's early days were of landplane operation rather than flying boats or amphibians. Spurred on by the challenge presented by Pan Am's purchase of Boeing 247 landplanes, TWA pressed Douglas to pursue an alternative, the DC-1 and DC-2. TWA operated both the Douglas DC-2, generally regarded as being one of the first modern airliners, and its more famous successor, the DC-3, before becoming, in 1940, the first to fly the world's first pressurised airliner, the Boeing 307 Stratoliner, of which just ten were built (five each for TWA and Pan Am) before the demands of wartime production and operation saw production stopped. This aircraft gave TWA its first experience of over-water operation, as the aircraft and their TWA crews were pressed into war service.

TWA had also cooperated with Lockheed before the outbreak of the Second World War on a new, long-distance airliner, the Constellation, and this aircraft saw the airline inaugurate its first intercontinental service in 1946, between New York and Paris with a refuelling stop at Shannon in Ireland. Reflecting the growing sphere of operation, the airline's name was changed to Trans World Airlines in 1950.

Throughout the 1950s, TWA continued to develop, introducing the Lockheed Super Constellation, and later embracing the jet age with the Boeing 707 and, in the 1960s, on domestic routes and European feeder services, the 727, so that at one time the airline was the world's largest operator of Boeing aircraft. Later, Lockheed L-1011 TriStars were introduced and, on short-haul routes, Douglas DC-9s, followed by McDonnell Douglas MD-80 series.

In 1979 the airline was acquired by the Trans World Corporation, only to be sold in 1984, when TWA once again became an autonomous company. Eighteen months later, in September, 1985, TWA was taken over by a New York investor, Carl Icahn, who acquired 52 per of the airline's shares.

In common with many of the older-established US airlines, TWA then passed through a difficult period. The difficulties partly reflected the economic cycle of the air transport industry, but also those in competing on international routes against airlines in Europe and elsewhere which were in state ownership and, at the time, often heavily subsidised by the taxpayers. TWA survived these problems, even though many of its contemporaries could not. Some of its services, including some into London, were sold. In addition, the airline sought Chapter 11 Bankruptcy Protection (equivalent to administration in Britain) twice in the four years before finally emerging from this in 1995, after a financial restructuring which saw TWA employees receive some 30 per cent of the airline's shares in return for wage and benefit concessions.

Despite these difficulties, the airline managed to make progress. In 1991, TWA acquired Pan Am Express from the liquidator of its old rival, renaming the operation Trans World Express, and boosting feeder services into the New York Kennedy and La Guardia hubs. The new subsidiary had started life as Ransom Airlines in 1967, and between 1970 and 1982 had operated as part of the Allegheny Commuter System, and between 1984 and 1986 became a franchisee of Delta under the 'Delta Connection' branding, before being bought by Pan Am and renamed Pan Am Express in 1986. At the time of its acquisition by TWA, the airline was operating eleven AI(R) ATR-42s, eight BAe Jetstream 31s, and eight de Havilland Canada Dash 7s. TWA, meanwhile, had already established a 'Trans World Express' operation, using the franchised services of seven smaller airlines, including Trans State Airlines, who took over the routes of TWA's new acquisition when it ceased operations in November 1995.

Nevertheless, a further filing for bankruptcy protection ended with TWA being acquired by American Airlines in 2001.

The development of air transport in the United States, nothwithstanding the similarities between the achievements of Pan American and Imperial Airways, differed widely from that of the United Kingdom, or indeed of the mainland European nations. Given the size of the country, internal air services had a far higher priority than in Europe. Because air transport was seen as something for the mass of the people in the United States, it soon lost the sophisticated image of air travel in Europe. Air fares became lower in the United States than in Europe, partly due to competition, but at first this was tightly controlled, and it was not until 1978 that deregulation occurred in the US. In fact, deregulation had the effect of encouraging growth. Small towns that had received a (sometimes subsidised) daily service with a Boeing 737 soon found themselves with a more frequent service using much smaller aircraft. The age of the feeder airline and of hub-and-spoke operations had dawned, but as traffic volumes increased, so too did the number of direct services. Given lower air fares, Americans did not have to resort to inclusive tour charters to obtain value in air transport, and so it was that in the US charter or, in American terminology, supplemental carriers accounted for just 10 per cent of the market, much of it under contract to the armed forces or to sports clubs, against more than 40 per cent in Europe.

The US did have a strong supplemental or charter airline industry. Some, such as Saturn Airways, did concentrate mainly on moving US service personnel and their families to overseas postings in Europe and the Far East, while others, such as World Airways, tended to look towards the consumer market and eventually became low-cost carriers.

Even so, it was the United States that invented the low-cost airline, with South-West Airlines being the first. As the 'new' Pan Am experience showed, low-cost has not always meant success, but there have been many airlines that have grown rapidly and profitably as a result, while, as in Europe, many of the established airlines have struggled.

ABX AIR
Founded: 2003

Originally formed as Airborne Express in 1979 and beginning operations in 1980 as a subsidiary of Seattle-based Airborne Freight. ABX was established in 2003, separating from Airborne Express when that airline was acquired by DHL. The company is active in cargo charter operations providing international and US domestic flights, as well as providing overnight small package and freight services within Canada, the US and Puerto Rico.

HQ airport & main base: Wilmington International
Designator: GB/ABX
Employees: 7,600
Fleet: 26 Boeing 767-200; 9 Boeing 767-200F; 8 McDonnell Douglas DC-8 Srs 61F/63F; 28 McDonnell Douglas DC-9-30; 29 McDonnell Douglas DC-9-40

AIR CARGO CARRIERS
Air Cargo Carriers, Inc.
Incorporated: 1986

Formed in 1986, Air Cargo Carriers originally used a small fleet of Shorts Skyvan, 330 and 360 aircraft to operate feeder cargo charters for major airlines, operating throughout North America and the Caribbean, but has now added Dassault Falcon jets to its fleet to provide passenger charters.

HQ airport & main base: Milwaukee General Mitchell Field
Radio callsign: NIGHT CARGO
Designator: 2Q/SNC
Fleet: 8 Shorts 360-100; 11 Shorts 330-200; 5 Shorts 360-300; 2 Dassault Falcon 20

AIR TAHOMA
Incorporated: 1995

Air Tahoma is a contract air cargo operator operating within the USA.

HQ airport & main base: Rickenbacker International, Colombus, Ohio
Designator: HMA
Fleet: 5 Convair 580

AIR TRANSPORT INTERNATIONAL
Air Transport International, Inc.
Incorporated: 1979

Originally founded as US Airways, the airline soon changed its name to Interstate Airlines. Originally an air cargo specialist supporting the express parcels sector, the airline included UPS among its early clients. The present title was adopted in 1988, a year after the airline had filed for Chapter 11 Bankruptcy Protection. In 1994, the airline absorbed the operations and assets of ICX International Cargo Express. The current fleet is entirely of McDonnell Douglas manufacture, including convertible passenger/cargo combis, while the original express parcels traffic has been augmented by contracts with manufacturing industry and the US Department of Defense.

ATI was owned by Active Aero/USA Jet, until it was taken over by the Brinks Company in 1998.

HQ airport & main base: Little Rock
Radio callsign: AIR TRANSPORT
Designator: 8C/ATN
Employees: 625
Fleet: 5 McDonnell Douglas DC-8-73AF; 2 McDonnell Douglas DC-8-72; 9 McDonnell Douglas DC-8-71; 3 McDonnell Douglas DC-8-62

AIR WISCONSIN
Air Wisconsin, Inc.
Incorporated: 1965

The present Air Wisconsin was purchased by three of its present executives, Geoffrey Crawley, William Jordan and Patrick Thomson, from United Airlines in 1993, after United had acquired the airline in early 1992. Originally, the airline was started in 1965, operating scheduled commuter services that summer. The first jet equipment, BAe 146-200s, appeared in 1983, and the airline became a United Express operator in 1986. In 1991, Air Wisconsin purchased another United Express operator, Denver-based Aspen Airways, which had originally been founded as an air taxi operator in 1953. At the time of the acquisition, Aspen had disposed of many of its routes to Mesa, and was operating four BAe 146-100 and ten Convair 580s on the remaining scheduled services and some charters. To some extent this fleet matched Air Wisconsin's ten 146s, five BAe ATPs, fourteen Fokker F27s and a single Shorts 360, but during the 1990s Air Wisconsin moved to an all-jet fleet, rationalised to consist of just BAe 146s, albeit of all three sizes on a route network reaching more than thirty airports in the midwest and eastern United States, operating mainly from Denver. Expansion resumed in 1998 with the acquisition of Mountain Air Express, enabling Air Wisconsin's network to extend further west, while in recent years the BAe146 fleet has been replaced by Bombardier CRJ200s.

HQ airport & main base: Headquarters is Appleton, Wisconsin, but the main base is Outagamie County Regional and hubs are Chicago O'Hare, Denver and Washington Dulles
Radio callsign: AIR WISCONSIN
Designator: ZW/AWI
Route points: All within the United Express network
Links with other airlines: Independently owned but part of United Express (qv)
Fleet: 4 Bombardier CRJ200ER; 66 Bombardier CRJ200LR

AIRBORNE EXPRESS
Airborne Express, Inc.

Purchased by DHL in 2003.

AIRTRAN
AirTran Airways, Inc.
Incorporated: 1994

Originally founded as Conquest Sun Airlines, the airline adopted its present title in 1994. AirTran, in which Northwest Airlines had a 30 per cent shareholding at one time, subsequently became the operating subsidiary of of its parent, Airways Corporation, and flew scheduled passenger services from its main base at Nashville. During 1997, agreement was reached over a merger with Valujet, a pioneer of 'low cost, no frills' scheduled operations, operating McDonnell Douglas DC-9 aircraft, with hubs at Atlanta, Boston, Orlando and Washington. Valujet had been grounded the previous year following a fatal accident caused by the inadvertent loading of dangerous cargo, and was only allowed to resume operations on a reduced scale. An outright merger took place in 1998, although before this the former Valujet McDonnell Douglas DC-9s carried the same livery as AirTran's Boeing 737-200s. Before the merger, Valujet had become the first airline to order the Boeing 717, the renamed McDonnell Douglas MD-95, and subsequently AirTran became the largest operator of this aircraft, operating them alongside the larger Boeing 737-700.

HQ airport & main base: Orlando International
Radio callsign: MANATEE
Designator: FL/MTE
Employees: 6,700

Route points: Akron, Atlanta, Baltimore, Bloomington, Boston, Buffalo, Charlotte, Chicago, Dallas, Dayton, Denver, Detroit, Flint, Fort Lauderdale, Fort Myers, Freeport, Gulfport, Hampton, Houston, Indianapolis, Jacksonville, Kansas City, Las Vegas, Los Angles, Memphis, Miami, Milwaukee, Minneapolis, Moline, New Orleans, New York, Newark, Orlando, Pensacola, Philadelphia, Pittsburgh, Raleigh/Durham, Richmond, Rochester, San Francisco, Sarasota, Savannah, Tampa, Washington, West Palm Beach, Wichita
Fleet: 100 Boeing 737-700; 87 Boeing 717-200

ALASKA
Alaska Airlines, Inc.
Incorporated: 1932

The main airline operating within and to Alaska, Alaska Airlines dates from 1932, when it was founded as McGhee Airways, before later taking the name Alaska Star Airlines and finally adopting the present title in 1944. Throughout the airline's history, it has followed a pattern of acquisition of smaller airlines, including Horizon Air in 1986, which retains its identity as sister company in the same Alaska Air Group. Most recently, in 1987, it absorbed Jet America. The end of the Cold War has resulted in services being introduced into Russia, to which Alaska belonged at one time.

In common with many interstate and international carriers, especially in the United States, a commuter airline network feeding traffic from sixty small communities into Alaska Airlines' hubs has been established, using aircraft operated by Bering Air, Era Aviation, LAB Flying Services and Peninsula Airways, as well as those of Alaska's subsidiary Horizon Air, operating under the name of Alaska Airlines Commuter Service. In turn, Alaska Airlines has a code-sharing agreement with Northwest Airlines.

Alaska is the thirty-fifth largest airline in the world by revenue, down from thirtieth, although twenty-seventh by passenger numbers, indicating a substantial proportion of short-haul travellers. The fleet is currently all Boeing 737, although in the past it has operated such interesting aircraft as the rare commercial variant of the Lockheed Hercules.

HQ airport & main base: Seattle, with further hubs at Anchorage, Los Angeles, Portland and Seattle
Radio callsign: ALASKA
Designator: AS/ASA
Employees: 9,960
Route points: Adak, Anchorage, Aniak, Arcate, Atka, Atlanta, Austin, Barrow, Bellingham, Billings, Bethel, Boise, Boston, Bozeman, Burbank, Butte, Calgary, Cancun, Chicago, Cincinnati, Cold Bay, Cordova, Dallas, Denver, Detroit, Dilllingham, Dutch Harbour, Edmonton, Eugene, Fairbanks, Fort Lauderdale, Fresno, Great Falls, Guadajara, Helena, Homer, Honolulu, Idaho Falls, Ixtapa, Juneau, Kahului, Kalispell, Kamloops, Kauai, Kelowna, Kenai, Ketchikan, King Salmon, Klamoth Falls, Kodiak, Kona, Kotzebue, Las Vegas, Lewiston, Long Beach, Loreto, Los Angeles, McGrath, Manzanillo, Mazatlan, Medford, Mexico City, Miami, Minneapolis, Missoula, Monterey, Moses Lake, New York, Newark, Nome, North Bend, Oakland, Ontario (Cal), Orlando, Palm Springs, Pasco, Petersburg, Phoenix, Pocatello, Portland, Prudhoe Bay, Puerto Vallarta, Pullman, Redding, Redmond, Reno, Sacramento, Saint George, Saint Louis, Saint Paul, Salt Lake City, San Diego, San Francisco, San Jose, San Jose Cabo, San Luis Obispo, Sand Point, Santa Ana, Santa Barbara, Seattle, Sitka, Spokane, Sun Valley, Toronto, Tucson, Unakakleet, Valdez, Vancouver, Victoria, Walla Walla, Washington, Wenatchee, Wrangell, Yakima, Yakutat
Links with other airlines: Alliances with American Airlines (qv), Big Sky Airlines, Continental Airlines (qv), Delta Air Lines (qv), Era Aviation (qv), Hawaiian Airlines (qv), Horizon Air (qv), LAN Airlines, Northwest Airlines (qv), Pen Air (qv), Qantas Airways (qv)
Annual turnover: US $2,724 million (£1,816 million) – includes turnover of other Alaska Air Group operators, including Horizon Air
Fleet: 12 Boeing 737-900; 37 Boeing 737-800; 39 Boeing 737-400; 22 Boeing 737-700; 5 Boeing 737-200C; 23 McDonnell Douglas MD-83

ALLEGIANT AIR
Incorporated: 1997

Commencing operations in 1998, a year after it was founded as WestJet Express, the airline adopted its present title in 1999. The airline concentrates on domestic scheduled and charter passenger flights.

HQ airport & main base: Las Vegas
Radio callsign: ALLEGIANT
Designator: G4/AAY
Employees: 432
Route points: Allentown, Belleville, Bellingham, Bismarck, Boston, Cedar Rapids, Chicago, Colorado Springs, Des Moines, Duluth, Fargo, Fort Collins,

Fresno, Green Bay, Idaho Falls, Lansing, Las Vegas, Missoula, Newburgh, Oklahoma City, Orlando, Palm Springs, Rapid City, Sioux Falls, South Bend, Springfield, Toledo, Wichita, Worcester
Fleet: 3 McDonnell Douglas MD-87; 21 McDonnell Douglas MD-83

ALOHA
Aloha Airlines, Inc.
Incorporated: 1946

The largest operator within the Hawaiian Islands, Aloha was founded in 1946 as Trans-Pacific Airlines, a charter carrier. The current title was not adopted until 1958. The airline proudly claims to be the only airline serving ten of the smaller airports within Hawaii, as well as offering high-frequency services between the major Hawaiian airports, and since 2000 has also operated to the west coast of mainland USA. An unusual aspect of Aloha's operations is a weekly charter from Honolulu to Christmas Island.

The airline has been privately owned since 1987, when it became a subsidiary of the locally based Aloha Airgroup, which has interests in aviation engineering and support services, and also owns a small airline, Aloha Island Air, trading as Island Air, which was originally founded as Princeville Airways. Aloha has marketing alliances and code-shares with United Airlines. The fleet is less highly standardised than in 2000, when it included seventeen Boeing 737-200s, but it continues to be a 737 operator exclusively.

HQ airport & main base: Honolulu International
Radio callsign: ALOHA
Designator: AQ/AAH
Employees: 3,668
Route points: Hilio, Honolulu, Hoolehua, Kahului, Kapalua, Kauai, Kona Lanai, Las Vegas, Oakland, Reno, Sacramento, San Diego, Santa Ana
Links with other airlines: Marketing alliance and code-share with United (qv). Marketing alliance with Canadian Airlines International and Island Air (qv)
Fleet: 8 Boeing 737-700; 17 Boeing 737-200

AMERICA WEST AIRLINES
America West Airlines Inc.
Incorporated: 1981

See US Airways. The two airlines merged in 2005, but with separate identities retained until 2007 or 2008.

AMERICA WEST EXPRESS
Desert Sun Airlines/Mountain West Airlines
Incorporated: 1992

America West Express was established in 1992 as a regional feeder network for America West through a code-sharing arrangement with Mesa Airlines, initially using the Phoenix services of Desert Sun Airlines. The service now reaches eighteen airports, including the hubs of Phoenix, Des Moines and Fresno, with aircraft belonging to the constituent airlines. At the time of writing the operation is merging with US Airways, although separate identities will remain for the time being.

HQ airport & main base: Phoenix, with additional hubs at Des Moines and Fresno
Designator: HP
Route points: Bullhead City/Laughlin, Columbus, Des Moines, Durango, Farmington, Flagstaff, Fresno, Gallup, Grand Junction, Gunnison, Kingman, Lake Havasu City, Montrose, Palm Springs, Phoenix, Prescott, Santa Barbara, Sierra Vista/Fort Huachuca, Yuma
Fleet: Aircraft belong to the operating companies

AMERICAN
American Airlines Inc.
Incorporated: 1934

Now the only major US airline never to have sought bankruptcy protection, American Airlines was the world's largest airline during the late 1990s, but is now fifth by annual turnover, although second in terms of passenger numbers. The company has a long history in which it has often been instrumental in drawing up the specifications of many successful airliner types, including the Douglas DC-3, DC-7 and DC-10, the Convair 340 and the Convair 990 development of the Convair 880, and the Lockheed Electra.

As with so many larger airlines, American's history is that of the amalgamation of many smaller airlines. The formation of the Aviation Corporation in 1929 involved the acquisition of several small, often single-route, airlines. The oldest of these airlines, the Robertson Aircraft Corporation, which operated a Chicago–St Louis–Omaha service, dated from 1921, and was acquired through its parent company, the Universal Aviation Corporation. Most of the other airlines had been founded between 1926 and 1929 and they included: Canadian Colonial Airways (operating New York–Montreal); Central Air Lines (Kansas City–Wichita–Tulsa); Continental

Airlines (Cleveland–Louisville); Colonial Air Transport (New York–Boston, Albany–Buffalo–Cleveland); Embry-Riddle Aviation Corporation (Chicago–Cincinnati); Gulf Air Lines (Atlanta–Houston–New Orleans); Interstate Airlines (Chicago–Atlanta, St Louis–Evansville); Northern Air Lines (Cleveland–Chicago–Kansas City); Texas Air Transport (Dallas–Galveston); and the Universal Aviation Corporation (Tulsa–Dallas). Some of these airlines had been subsidiaries of larger concerns.

The Aviation Corporation established American Airways in 1930 as its operating company, with the task of rationalising the wide assortment of equipment and integrating the widely scattered network of services. While this was being done, American continued to make further acquisitions, so that in 1930 Standard AirLines, with its Los Angeles–El Paso service, was acquired from its parent, Western Air Express; and from E.L. Cord in 1932, American bought Century Air Lines, with a network of routes in the midwest, and Century Pacific Lines. An Act of Congress in 1934 forced the Aviation Corporation to isolate its manufacturing and operating interests, and as a result American Airlines was formed as a separate operating entity that same year. The new airline started life with a network of services stretching across the United States, from the Pacific to the Atlantic coasts, and from Canada to close to the border with Mexico.

American spent the remaining years until the outbreak of the Second World War consolidating and expanding its domestic network. In 1942, licences were obtained for services from El Paso and Dallas to Mexico City, but these services could not be introduced until after the war ended, due to wartime equipment shortages and the number of flight crew conscripted into the armed forces. Looking further afield, the airline obtained a 51 per cent interest in American Export Airlines, a company formed in 1937 to operate services to Europe and countries around the Mediterranean, but which had only managed to obtained a temporaray permit for a service to Lisbon by 1940. Yet, in October, 1945, just two months after the end of the Second World War, AEA was able to introduce the first commercial New York–London landplane service, using Douglas DC-4s. AEA changed its name to American Overseas Airlines in 1948, the same year that American increased its stake to 62 per cent, although two years later the company was sold to Pan American World Airways, an old rival, almost certainly due to the difficulty in obtaining sufficient overseas bilateral rights.

The 1950s saw a further period of rationalisation for American Airlines, dropping many small communities from its network and handing these over to the feeder or local service airlines – companies that would be known as 'commuters' today. Some thirty years later, deregulation of air transport in the United States would see much of this repeated. The rationalisation was in effect a reshaping of the network, with airlines such as American becoming major transcontinental and, eventually, intercontinental carriers. Steps towards this end included the introduction of a Chicago–San Francisco service in 1955, which was followed later by a non-stop New York–San Francisco route, with the first transcontinental jet service introduced in 1959. A merger with what was then another major United States airline, Eastern Air Lines, was mooted during the early 1960s and approved by shareholders of both companies, but vetoed by the Civil Aeronautics Board in 1963. Sadly, Eastern then suffered an uncertain three decades before finally ceasing operations in 1991, after a dramatic slimming down and disposal of routes and assets, which included selling its Caribbean and South American operations to American Airlines.

American grew through other acquisitions, buying AirCal in 1986 to gain a network of services along the west coast of the United States. During the same decade, major advances were made in developing both a transatlantic network and a transpacific network. Its five main hubs at Dallas/Fort Worth (its main base), Chicago, Nashville, Raleigh/Durham and San Juan were joined by a sixth hub at San Jose. Realising that an airline geared for the busier and longer routes is almost invariably at a disadvantage, in 1987 the airline created the American Eagle system of feeder airlines and AMR Corporation, by this time the holding company for American Airlines, spent US $150 million (£90 million) acquiring five airlines, Air MidWest, AVAir, Command Airways, Simmons Airlines and Wings West. While expanding its fleet and operational area, the airline was responsible for another innovation, being the first to offer electronic ticketing in October 1998, providing this service in no less than forty-four countries, a major improvement in efficiency that may explain the company's ability to steer clear of bankruptcy protection. The following year, the company acquired Reno Air, and then in 2001 acquired the remaining assets of TWA, at one time one of the world's largest airlines.

TWA, Trans World Airlines, could trace its history back to 1925, although the airline itself was incorporated in 1930, when TAT-Maddux and part of

Western Air Express merged to form Transcontinental and Western Air Express, which soon became known as 'TWA', although it was not until 1950 that the Trans World Airways title was adopted. TWA's development was for many years confined to domestic routes. It was TWA that pressed Douglas to develop the DC-1 and DC-2, which the airline operated with its more famous successor, the DC-3, before becoming, in 1940, the first to fly the world's first pressurised airliner, the Boeing 307 Stratoliner, flying five of these before the demands of wartime production and operation saw production stopped. This aircraft gave TWA its first experience of overwater operation when the aircraft and their TWA crews were pressed into war service.

TWA had also cooperated with Lockheed before the outbreak of the Second World War on a new, long-distance airliner, the Constellation, and this aircraft saw the airline inaugurate its first intercontinental service in 1946, between New York and Paris with a refuelling stop at Shannon in Ireland.

Plans for a close transatlantic working relationship between American Airlines and British Airways were scrapped following objections from the regulators on both sides of the Atlantic. Nevertheless, American has a 1 per cent stake in the Spanish flag carrier, Iberia. American's parent holding company also owns American Eagle, the airline's feeder operation, and Executive Airlines. American was a founding member of the Oneworld alliance.

Today, American's distinctive silver aircraft with their blue and red cheat lines can be seen at more than 250 airports worldwide. Recent deliveries of Boeing 737-800s will have resulted in some reduction of the McDonnell Douglas MD-80 fleet from that shown below. In recent years, the airline has expanded its operations to China, Australia and New Zealand, and to the Caribbean. Code-share alliances have been in force since 1992, when an arrangement was made with South African Airways, and was followed by an arrangement with British Midland Airways.

HQ airport & main base: Dallas/Fort Worth International, with additional hubs at Chicago O'Hare; Miami; St Louis and San Juan
Radio callsign: AMERICAN
Designator: AA/AAL
Employees: 92,000
Route points: (Include destinations served by American Eagle) Abilene, Abu Dhabi, Acapulco, Adelaide, Aguascalientes, Albany, Albuquerque, Amarillo, Anchorage, Anguilla, Antigua, Aruba, Atlanta, Auckland, Austin, Baltimore, Bangor, Baton Rouge, Beef Island, Beijing, Belize City, Belo Horizonte, Bermuda, Birmingham (Alabama), Bloomington, Bogotá, Boise, Bonaire, Boston, Bridgetown, Brisbane, Brussels, Buenos Aires, Buffalo/Niagara Falls, Burbank, Burlington, Calgary, Cali, Cancun, Canouan, Cape Girardeau, Caracas, Cedar Rapids, Champaign, Charlotte, Chicago, Chihauhau, Christchurch, Cincinnati, Cleveland, College Station, Colorado Springs, Colombia, Columbus, Corpus Christi, Cozumel, Curaçao, Dallas/Fort Worth, Dayton, Decatur, Delhi, Denver, Des Moines, Detroit, Dominica, Dublin, Dubuque, El Paso, Eugene, Evansville, Fayetteville, Flint, Fort de France, Fort Lauderdale, Fort Leonard, Fort Myers, Fort Smith, Fort Wayne, Frankfurt, Freeport, Fresno, Geneva, George Town, Glasgow, Grand Cayman, Grand Rapids, Green Bay, Greensboro, Greenville, Grenada, Guadalajara, Guatemala City, Guayaquil, Gulfport, Gunnison, Harrisburg, Hartford/Springfield, Halifax, Hayden, Helsinki, Hong Kong, Honolulu, Houston, Huntsville, Indianapolis, Istanbul, Ixtapa, Jackson Hole, Jacksonville, Joplin, Kahului, Kalamazoo, Kansas City, Kingston, Kauai, Key West, Killeen, Kirksville, Knoxville, Kona, La Crosse, La Paz, La Romana, Laredo, Las Vegas, Lawton, Leon-Guanajuato, Liberia, Lexington, Lima, Little Rock, London, Long Beach, Longview, Los Angeles, Los Cabos, Louisville, Lubbock, Madison, Madrid, Managua, Manchester, Maracaibo, Marion, Marquette, Marsh Harbour, Mazallan, McAllen, Medellin, Medford, Melbourne, Memphis, Mexico City, Miami, Midland/Odessa, Milan, Milwaukee, Minneapolis/St Paul, Mobile, Moline, Montego Bay, Monterrey, Montevideo, Montreal, Montrose, Morelia, Muscat, Nadi, Nashville, Nassau, Nevis, New Orleans, New York, Newark, Newburgh/Stewart, Newburgh, Norfolk, Oakland, Oklahoma City, Omaha, Ontario (California), Orlando, Osaka, Ottawa, Owensburgh, Paducah, Palm Springs, Panama City, Paris, Pensacola, Peoria, Philadelphia, Phoenix, Pittsburgh, Pointe-à-Pitre, Port-au-Prince, Port of Spain, Portland, Providence/Newport, Providenciales, Puerto Plata, Puerto Vallarta, Punta Cana, Queenstown, Quincy, Quito, Raleigh/Durham, Reno, Richmond, Rio de Janeiro, Rochester (Minnesota), Rochester (New York), Sacramento, St Croix, St Kitts, St Louis, St Lucia, St Maarten, St Thomas, Salt Lake City, San Angelo, San Antonio, San Diego, San Francicso, San Jose, San Jose Cabo, San Juan, San Luis Obispo, San Pedro Sula, San Salvador, Santa Anna, Santa Barbara, Santa Cruz (Bolivia), Santiago (Chile), Santo Domingo, Sao Paulo, Sarasota, Savannah, Seattle/Tacoma, Seoul, Shanghai, Shannon, Shreveport, Spokane, Springfield, Steamboat

Springs, Stockholm, Sun Valley, Sydney, Syracuse, Taipei, Tampa/St Petersburg, Tegucigalpa, Texarkana, Tokyo, Toledo, Toronto, Torreon, Traverse City, Tucson, Tulsa, Tyler, Vail, Valparaiso (US), Vancouver, Waco, Washington, West Palm Beach, Westchester County, Wichita, Wichita Falls, Zacatecas, Zurich
Links with other airlines: A 1 per cent stake in Iberia (qv). Parent company AMR also owns American Eagle (qv) and Executive Airlines (qv). Alliances with: Aerosur, Air Pacific, Alaska Airlines, Chautauqua Airlines, China Eastern, Eva Air, Gulf Air, Hawaiian Airlines, Japan Airlines, Mexicana, RegionsAir, SN Brussels Airlines, Swiss, TACA, TAM Linhas Aereas, THY Turkish Airlines, Trans States Airlines (all qv)
Annual turnover: US $18,645 million (£12,430 million) (includes American Eagle)
Fleet: 34 Airbus A300B4-600R; 53 Boeing 777-200ER; 58 Boeing 767-300ER; 16 Boeing 767-200ER; 1 Boeing 767-200; 143 Boeing 757-200; 124 Boeing 737-800; 80 McDonnell Douglas MD-83; 211 McDonnell Douglas MD-82

AMERICAN EAGLE
AMR Eagle Inc.
Incorporated: 1986

American Eagle was established by American Airlines' parent, AMR, in 1986 to provide a network of feeder services linking smaller communities into major airports and, of course, the major hubs of the American Airlines network. Although the network was initially a franchise operation, four airlines – Executive Airlines, Flagship Airlines, Simmons Airlines and Wings West Airlines – were acquired and operate under the American Eagle name and with American Airlines designators. These airlines share the headquarters of American Airlines and were joined by Business Express in 1999, although this company's operations were not fully integrated with those of American Eagle until the end of 2000. The airline owns Executive Airlines and has a 20 per cent stake in Aeroperlas of Panama.

American Eagle was an early user of jet aircraft for feeder services, introducing a Chicago–Cleveland service using Embraer EMB ERJ-145s in May 1998. Today, American Eagle operates both Bombardier and Embraer regional jets.

HQ airport & main base: Dallas/Fort Worth, plus Chicago O'Hare, Los Angeles, Miami, Nashville, New York-JFK, Raleigh/Durham, San Juan
Radio callsign: EAGLE FLIGHT
Designator: EGF
Employees: 8,972
Route points: Integrated with those of American, above.
Links with other airlines: Owned by American Airlines' parent AMR and provides feeder services for American. Owns Executive Airlines and has a 20 per cent stake in Aeroperlas (both qv). Alliances with Continental Airlines, Delta Air Lines, Finnair, Hawaiian Airlines, Midwest Airlines, Northwest Airlines (all qv)
Fleet: 25 Bombardier CRJ700-701ER; 108 Embraer ERJ-145LR; 59 Embraer ERJ-140LR; 39 Embraer ERJ-135LR; 26 Saab 340B

AMERIFLIGHT
Incorporated: 1968

The largest Part US135, or light cargo carrier, operating both scheduled and domestic services throughout the Americas for light consignments, Ameriflight was founded in 1968 as California Air Charter and in 1971 was taken over by ATI Systems International and merged with its subsidiary, United Couriers. Fixed-wing operations of Wings Express were purchased in 1993, and the company acquired Sports Air Travel in 1997.

HQ airport & main base: Burbank
Designator: AMF
Employees: 618
Route points: Billings, Burbank, Cincinnati, Dallas/Fort Worth, Oakland, Ontario, Phoenix, Portland, Salt Lake City, San Juan, Seattle
Fleet: 20 Raytheon Beech 1900C; 7 Embraer EMB-120 Brasilia; 19 Fairchild Merlin 23; 24 Fairchild Metro III; 46 Raytheon Beech C99; 13 Raytheon Beech B99; 1 Raytheon Beech King Air 200; 5 Bombardier Learjet 35A

AMERIJET INTERNATIONAL
Amerijet International, Inc.
Incorporated: 1974

Founded by David Bassett, the current chairman, in 1974, originally the airline carried passengers and cargo, but the Fort Lauderdale-based airline now operates only cargo flights, both scheduled and charter, on domestic and international routes, although mainly in and around the Caribbean and Central American areas.

HQ airport & main base: Fort Lauderdale Hollywood International

Radio callsign: AMERIJET
Designator: JH/AJT
Employees: 577
Route points: Antigua, Aruba, Atlanta, Barbados, Belize, Cancun, Caracas, Chicago, Curaçao, Dominica, Fort de France, Fort Lauderdale, Georgetown, Grenada, Guadalajara, Houston, Los Angeles, Mérida, Mexico City, Miami, Montserrat, New York, Pointe-à-Pitre, Porlamar, Port-au-Prince, Port of Spain, Puerta Plata, St Kitts, St Lucia, St Maarten, St Vincent, San Juan, Santo Domingo, Toronto, Valencia (Venezuela)
Fleet: 7 Boeing 727-200F; 1 Boeing 727-200; 1 Bombardier Challenger 601

AMERISTAR AIR CARGO
Incorporated: 1999

Owned and founded by the president, Tom Wachendorfer. Since operations began in 2000, Ameristar Air Cargo has acted both as an air cargo broker and as an air cargo operator, operating charter and scheduled flights, with its fleet complemented by the business jets of its sister company, Ameristar Jet Charter. Both operators are based at Dallas/Fort Worth.

HQ airport & main base: Dallas/Fort Worth
Radio callsign: AMERISTAR
Designator: AJI
Route points: Dallas/Fort Worth, Detroit, El Paso, Nashville
Fleet: 4 Boeing 737-200; 3 McDonnell Douglas DC-9-10

ARROW CARGO
Arrow Air, Inc
Incorporated: 1947

Although originally founded in 1947 by George Batchelor as Arrow Air, Arrow has suspended operations on three occasions, resuming them in 1981, 1995 and again in 2004, even though it had been acquired by Fine Air in 1999. Fine Air renamed the airline Arrow Cargo. Originally operating passenger and cargo charters, passenger operations were ended in 1986 to leave the airline to concentrate on cargo charters and scheduled cargo services from Miami.

While McDonnell Douglas DC-8s formed the backbone of the fleet, the first TriStar was introduced in 1996, and was added to later, but the airline has since reverted to a mixed DC-8/DC-10 fleet.

HQ airport & main base: Miami International
Radio callsign: BIG A
Designator: JW/APW
Fleet: 1 McDonnell Douglas DC-10-40; 3 McDonnell Douglas DC-10-30F; 2 McDonnell Douglas DC-10-10F; 4 McDonnell Douglas DC-8-63F

ASA – ATLANTIC SOUTHEAST AIRLINES
Atlantic Southeast Airlines Inc.
Incorporated: 1979

Atlantic Southeast Airlines was established in 1979 with the primary aim of providing short-haul or regional services from its base at Atlanta. Given this operating philosophy, and the presence of Delta Air Lines, it was not surprising that the airline was one of the first to establish links with a major airline, creating the Delta Connection service in 1984. Aircraft have operated with the branding 'Delta Connection' along the fuselage, but with ASA on the tail. Operating in a niche market, ASA enjoyed rapid growth, with a second hub opening at Dallas/Fort Worth in 1986. A hub operation at Memphis developed with the introduction of services between 1983 and 1985, but this was discontinued in 1986, although further hubs have since been opened. The launch customer for Embraer's successful EMB-120 Brasilia, ASA has also operated the smaller Embraer EMB-110 Bandeirante, while larger aircraft have included the de Havilland Dash 7, before standardisation on Canadair regional jets.

ASA is a subsidiary of Skywest.

HQ airport & main base: Atlanta, with further hubs at Salt Lake City and Cincinnati. Maintenance bases are Macon and Texarkana
Radio callsign: ASEA
Designator: EV/CAA
Employees: 5,960
Route points: Within the Delta/Delta Connection network
Links with other airlines: Operates all services under the Delta Connection (qv) name
Fleet: 35 Bombardier CRJ700-701ER; 112 Bombardier CRJ200ER; 11 ATR-72-210

ASTAR AIR CARGO
Incorporated: 1969

Originally founded as DHL Worldwide Express, taking its name from the founders, Adrian Dalsye, Larry Hillblom and Robert Lynn, who established the company to expedite the movement of bills of lading between Hawaii and San Francisco. It became one of the leading carriers of express cargo and urgent documents worldwide, using the name DHL Worldwide Express, generally using its own aircraft and those of subsidiaries, such as European Air Transport in Belgium. It later adopted the name DHL Airways, leaving its original title for the wider, inter-nodal operations of what had become the parent company. Marketing arrangements existed with both Japan Airlines and Lufthansa, while a joint venture with Sinotrans saw the service extended to twenty-six Chinese centres, in addition to fourteen hubs worldwide, and another twelve hubs and seventy-six other airports in the United States.

In 2003, three partners, headed by the current chairman, John Dassburg, completed the acquisition of the company and changed its name to ASTAR Air Cargo, effectively a charter airline working under contract to DHL Worldwide Express, and moving its headquarters from Cincinnati to Miami. In recent years, there has been considerable rationalisation of the fleet, down to three aircraft types from seven.

HQ airport & main base: Wilmington Airpark
Radio callsign: DAHL
Designator: ER/DHL
Fleet: 6 Airbus A300B4-200F; 9 McDonnell Douglas DC-8 Srs 73AF; 5 Boeing 727-200; 29 Boeing 727-200F

ATA AIRLINES
Incorporated: 1973

ATA Airlines was formed as American Trans Air, and although founded in 1973 to manage the Ambassadair Travel Club, it was not until 1981 that the airline became a Common Air Carrier, able to develop charter and scheduled services. A holding company, Amtran, was established to take over the airline in 1984. During the Gulf War in 1991, the airline was contracted by the US military and took some 108,000 personnel to the Gulf on 494 flights. In 1996, the airline formed a feeder operation with Chicago Express, American Trans Air Connection, and later adopted its present title. The parent company, ATA Holdings, and a number of subsidiaries, including the airline, filed for Chapter 11 Bankruptcy Protection in October 2004, but after restructuring, the airline left bankruptcy protection in February 2006.

HQ airport & main base: Indianapolis, with bases/hubs also at Chicago Midway and New York-La Guardia
Radio callsign: AMTRAN
Designator: TZ/AMT
Employees: 7,900
Route points: Cancun, Chicago, Dallas, Fort Myers, Guadalajara, Honolulu, Indianapolis, Kahului, Las Vegas, Los Angeles, New York, Orlando, Phoenix, San Francisco, Washington
Fleet: 4 Lockheed L-1011-500 TriStar; 6 Boeing 757-300; 6 Boeing 757-200; 22 Boeing 737-800; 3 Boeing 737-300

ATLAS AIR
Atlas Air, Inc.
Incorporated: 1992

A scheduled and charter air cargo operator, Atlas Air operates a fleet of Boeing 747 freighters for long-haul international operations out of New York, although more recently the main base has switched to Miami. A subsidiary of Atlas Air Worldwide Holdings, the airline enables major airlines to outsource their trunk cargo operations, effectively operating these services for them while they concentrate on sales and marketing of cargo traffic. Clients have included major airlines such as China Airlines, Emirates, KLM, Lufthansa and Varig. Initially aircraft were bought secondhand, but in 1998 Atlas introduced its first aircraft bought new from the manufacturer, the first deliveries from an order for ten Boeing 747-400Fs. It is now planning a major fleet renewal and expansion programme with the new Boeing 747-8F.

HQ airport & main base: Miami International
Radio callsign: GIANT
Designator: 5Y/GTI
Route points: Anchorage, Hong Kong, Khaborovs, Miami, New York plus trunk services for major airlines
Fleet: 6 Boeing 747-400F; 15 Boeing 747-200F (On order: 12 Boeing 747-8F)

BARON AVIATION
Baron Aviation Services, Inc.

Baron Aviation Services uses a substantial fleet of Cessna 208 Caravan light freighters to provide feeder services into the Federal Express network. In addition, five Douglas DC-3 freighters are operated, mainly on cargo charters.

HQ airport & main base: Rolla National Airport, Vichy, Missouri
Radio callsign: SHOW-ME

Designator: BVN
Links with other airlines: Most operations are on behalf of Federal Express (qv)
Fleet: 34 Cessna Caravan 675; 1 Cessna 208 Caravan

CAPITAL CARGO INTERNATIONAL AIRLINES
Incorporated: 1995

An air cargo charter airline, Capital Cargo International Airlines was formed in 1995 and commenced operations the following year. Ad hoc, contract and wet-lease charters are provided.

HQ airport & main base: Orlando International
Designator: PT/CCI
Fleet: 12 Boeing 727-200F; 1 Boeing 727-200

CENTURION AIR CARGO
Incorporated: 1985

Centurion Air Cargo was originally founded in 1985, as a subsidiary of Challenge Air Transport, but remained dormant until 1999, when Challenge's assets were bought by United Parcels Service, UPS. Centurion took over the operating certificate of Challenge Air Transport. The company provides schedule and charter air cargo services, mainly between the United States and South America, usually handling perishable goods and horses.

HQ airport & main base: Miami International
Radio callsign: CENTURION
Designator: WE/CWC
Employees: 110
Fleet: 1 McDonnell Douglas DC-10-10F; 5 McDonnell Douglas DC-10-30F

CHAMPION AIR
Incorporated: 1987

An international and domestic passenger charter airline, Champion Air was formed in 1987. Its main business is providing charters for sports teams. The airline ran into financial difficulties in March 1997, but was rescued by Northwest Airlines and Carl Pohlad, and later that year five of the airline's executives staged a management buyout of the airline.

HQ airport & main base: Minneapolis-St Paul International
Radio callsign: CHAMPION
Designator: MG/CCP
Employees: 768
Fleet: 16 Boeing 727-200

CHAUTAUQUA AIRLINES
Chautauqua Airlines, Inc.
Incorporated: 1973

Founded in 1973, Chautauqua Airlines commenced operations the following year. In 1994 the airline was acquired by Wexford Management, and then by Republic Airways in 2004.

The airline mainly operates feeder services for the major US airlines, and is part of the American Connection, Delta Connection, United Express and US Airways Express networks, operating from its Indianapolis base.

HQ airport & main base: Indianapolis International
Radio callsign: CHAUTAUQUA
Designator: RP/CHQ
Employees: 2,304
Route points: Hubs at Dallas/Fort Worth, Indianapolis, New York, Newark, Orlando and Pittsburgh, serving destinations of the networks of the four US majors for which it provides feeder services
Links with other airlines: American Connection, Delta Connection (qv), United Express (qv) and US Airways Express (qv) carrier
Fleet: 3 Bombardier CRJ200ER; 63 Embraer ERJ-145 EU/MR; 15 Embraer ERJ-140LR; 17 Embraer ERJ-135LR

COLGAN AIR
Incorporated: 1991

Founded by father and son Charles and Michael Colgan as a regional scheduled passenger airline in 1997, the airline became a Continental Connection operator, followed by a similar arrangement with US Airways Express in 1999 and then in 2005 with United Express.

HQ airport & main base: Manassas Virginia, but main hubs are at Boston Logan International, New York La Guardia and Washington Dulles International
Designator: 9L/CJC
Route points: On the feeder networks of Continental, US Airways and United
Links with other airlines: Operates as Continental Connection, United Express (qv) and US Airways Express (qv)
Fleet: 35 Saab 340A/B; 9 Raytheon Beech 1900D

COMAIR
Incorporated: 1977

Today, Comair is one of the world's largest regional airlines, ranking thirty-sixth in the world by passenger numbers. It was founded in 1977 and began operations the following year using three Piper Navajo light aircraft. To fund its expansion, the airline went public in 1981, and in 1984 became a Delta Connection operator. Delta acquired a 20 per cent interest in 1986, buying Comair outright in 1999.

HQ airport & main base: Cincinnati Northern Kentucky International
Radio callsign: COMAIR
Designator: OH/COM
Employees: 7,000
Route points: In the Delta network
Links with other airlines: A wholly owned subsidiary of Delta Air Lines (qv). Owns Delta AirElite Business Jets (qv).
Passengers carried: 12.6 million
Fleet: 27 Bombardier CRJ700-701ER; 43 Bombardier CRJ200ER; 42 Bombardier CRJ100LR; 67 Bombardier CRJ100ER

CONTINENTAL
Continental Airlines, Inc.
Incorporated: 1934

Now the eleventh largest airline in the world, and sixth largest in the United States, by turnover, Continental is the tenth largest worldwide by passenger numbers.

The company's history started with the formation of Varney Speed Lines in 1934, although the present title was soon adopted, in 1937. The first services operated between El Paso in Texas and Pueblo, Colorado. A major step forward for Continental occurred in 1981, when Texas Air, the parent company of another airline, Texas International, acquired a controlling interest in Continental, and the following year the two airlines were merged using the Continental name. Texas International's history had dated from the airline's formation in 1940, but because of wartime restrictions and shortages of aircraft and aircrew, scheduled operations did not start until 1947, using the name of Trans-Texas Airways until the title Texas International was adopted in 1969.

The new and enlarged Continental acquired a number of other airlines, including Frontier Airlines in late 1986, and the following year both New York Air and People Express. Further regional acquisitions led to the formation of a wholly owned regional subsidiary, Continental Express, in 1987. By this time the airline had expanded into international operations, primarily on routes across the Pacific.

Nevertheless, this rapid expansion was not without its problems. In 1983, Continental filed for Chapter 11 Bankruptcy Protection, with a dramatic cut in the route network from seventy-eight airports to just twenty-five, while the number of employees was cut by almost two-thirds, from 12,000 to 4,200. These drastic measures worked quickly, and by 1985 Continental was able to put a plan of reorganisation before the Bankruptcy Court and emerged from Protection the following year. Continental again sought Chapter 11 Protection in 1990, emerging on this occasion in 1993, this time with fresh investments from Air Partners and Air Canada, although the latter's investment was substantially reduced over the following decade and no longer exists.

During its second spell of Protection, Continental sold its Seattle to Tokyo rights to American Airlines, but acquired rights from Newark (sometimes call New York-Newark) to Frankfurt, Madrid and Munich, and from Houston to Paris.

The fleet, which had become highly diversified, was rationalised during the second spell of Protection, with the airline reducing the number of types operated, losing its Airbus A300s and Boeing 747s. Eventually the fleet became entirely of Boeing and McDonnell Douglas manufacture, but over the past ten years it has become all Boeing. At the same time, Continental has accelerated the replacement of its older aircraft to reap the benefits of up-to-date aircraft which are quieter and more economical to operate.

The airline has expanded over the years and, in addition to its original hub at Houston, now has substantial hubs at Cleveland, Denver and Newark, with mini-hubs for its Pacific services at Honolulu and Guam. It owns Continental Micronesia outright, as well as having 49 per cent of Copa Airlines and 8.6 per cent of Express Jet.

HQ airport & main base: Houston Bush Intercontinental, with hubs also at Cleveland, Newark and Guam
Radio callsign: CONTINENTAL
Designator: CO/COA
Employees: 38,255
Route points: Abilene, Acapulco, Aguadilla, Aguascalientes, Albany, Albuquerque, Alexandria,

Allentown, Amarillo, Amsterdam, Anchorage, Andros Town, Antigua, Aruba, Ashville, Atlanta, Austin, Bakersfield, Baltimore, Bangor, Baton Rouge, Beaumont, Beijing, Belfast, Belize, Berlin, Bermuda, Bimini, Birmingham (UK), Bogotá, Boise, Bonaire, Boston, Bristol, Brownsville, Brussels, Buenos Aires, Buffalo, Burlington, Cairns, Calgary, Cancun, Caracas, Charleston, Charlotte, Chattanooga, Chicago, Chihauhau, Cincinnati, Ciudad del Carmen, Cleveland, College Station, Colorado Springs, Columbia, Columbus, Corpus Christi, Cozumel, Curaçao, Dallas/Fort Worth, Dayton, Daytona Beach, Del Rio, Delhi, Denpasar Bali, Denver, Des Moines, Detroit, Dublin, Durango, Edinburgh, El Paso, Elmira, Erie, Fayetteville, Flint, Flores, Fort Lauderdale, Fort Myers, Fort Wayne, Frankfurt, Frankfurt (Germany), Freeport, Fukuoka, Gainesville, Geneva, George Town, Glasgow, Governor's Harbour, Grand Cayman, Grand Rapids, Greensboro, Greenville, Guadalajara, Guam, Guatemala City, Guayaquil, Gulf Port, Halifax, Hamburg, Harlingen, Harrisburg, Hartford/ Springfield, Hayden, Hiroshima, Hong Kong, Honolulu, Houston, Huatulco, Huntsville, Indianapolis, Islip, Ixtapa, Jackson, Jacksonville, Kahului, Kansas City, Key West, Killeen, Knoxville, Koror, Kosrae, Kwajalein, Lafayette, Lake Charles, Laredo, Las Vegas, Leon, Lexington, Lima, Lisbon, Little Rock, London, Los Angeles, Los Cabos, Louisville, Lubbock, McAllen, Madison, Madrid, Majuro, Managua, Manchester, Manila, Manzanillo, March Harbour, Mazatlan, Memphis, Mérida, Mexico City, Miami, Midland/Odessa, Milan, Milwaukee, Minneapolis/St Paul, Mobile, Mondova, Monroe, Montego Bay, Monterrey, Montgomery, Montreal, Montrose, Morelia, Myrtle Beach, Nagoya, Nashville, Nassau, New Orleans, New York, Newark, Niigata, Norfolk, North Eleuthera, Oakland, Oaxaca, Okayama, Oklahoma City, Omaha, Ontario (California), Orlando, Osaka, Oslo, Ottawa, Palm Springs, Panama City, Paris, Pensacola, Philadelphia, Phoenix, Pittsburgh, Plattsburgh, Pohnei, Ponce, Port of Spain, Portland, Providence, Puebla, Puerto Plata, Puerto Vallarta, Punta Cana, Quebec, Queretaro, Quito, Raleigh/Durham, Reno, Richmond, Rio de Janeiro, Roatan, Rochester, Rome, Rota, Rutland, Sacramento, St Croix, St John's, St Louis, St Maarten, St Thomas, Saipan, Sal Salvador, Salt Lake City, Saltillo, San Angelo, San Antonio, San Diego, San Francisco, San Jose, San Jose (Costa Rica), San Jose Cabo, San Juan, San Luis Potosi, San Pedro Sula, San Salvador, Santa Ana, Santiago de Chile, Santo Domingo, Sao Paulo, Sapporo, Saranac Lake, Sarasota, Savannah, Seattle, Sendai, Shannon, Shreveport, South Bend, Stockhom, Syracuse, Taipei, Tallahassee, Tampa/St Petersburg, Tampico, Tegucigalpa, Tel Aviv, Texarkana, The Bight, Tokyo, Toledo, Toronto, Torreon, Treasure Cay, Truk, Tucson, Tulas, Tyler, Vancouver, Vail, Valparaiso, Veracruz, Victoria, Vieques, Villehermosa, Waco, Washington, West Palm Beach, Yap, Zurich

Links with other airlines: Code-share with Air Canada (qv). Marketing alliance with Air Micronesia

Annual turnover: US $9,744 million (£6,480 million)

Passengers carried:: 42.7 million

Fleet: 20 Boeing 777-200ER; 16 Boeing 767-400ER; 10 Boeing 767-200ER; 17 Boeing 757-300; 41 Boeing 757-200; 36 Boeing 737-900; 105 Boeing 737-800; 72 Boeing 737-700; 48 Boeing 737-300; 63 Boeing 737-500 (On order: 20 Boeing 787-8)

CONTRACT AIR CARGO

Incorporated: 1983

In addition to ad hoc cargo charters, Contract Air Cargo also undertakes longer-term contracts for both Ford and General Motors.

HQ airport & main base: Oakland Pontiac

Designator: TSU

Fleet: 5 Boeing 727-100F; 7 Convair 580; 3 Kelowna Flightcraft Convair 580

CORPORATE AIR

Corporate Air, Inc.

Corporate Air is a regional feeder specialising in charter and scheduled light freight and packages, with its scheduled operations feeding into the Federal Express network. For the airline's size, a very wide variety of aircraft is operated, although the number of types has been rationalised considerably over the past decade.

HQ airport & main base: Billings Logan International Airport, Montana

Radio callsign: AIR SPUR

Designator: DN/CPT

Links with other airlines: Federal Express (qv) feeder carrier

Fleet: 3 Shorts 330-100; 5 Raytheon Beech 1900C; 1 Dornier 228-212; 4 Embraer EMB-120 Brasilia; 2 de Havilland Canada Twin Otter Srs 300; 37 Cessna Caravan 675; 4 Cessna 208 Caravan; 1 Raytheon Beech King Air 200

CUSTOM AIR TRANSPORT
Incorporated: 1995

A charter airline which also flies contract services on behalf of CharterAmerica, including mail flights, and also operates flights for Eagle Global Logistics, the freight forwarder. Custom is owned by the chairman and chief executive, Anthony Romeo.

HQ airport & main base: Fort Lauderdale Hollywood International
Designator: SR/CTT
Fleet: 8 Boeing 727-200F

DELTA AIR LINES
Delta Air Lines, Inc.
Incorporated: 1924

Seventh among the world's largest airlines, but the world leader in terms of passengers carried, Delta was originally founded not as an airline, but as a crop-spraying company. The airline's history dates from the formation in 1924, at Macon in Georgia, of Huff Daland Crop Dusters by one C.E. Woolman; this was the world's first aerial crop-spraying company, brought into existence to combat the boll weevil, a persistent pest which frequently devastated the cotton crop in the southern United States.

Airline operations started in 1929, after the company had changed its name to Delta Air Service and moved to Monroe, Louisiana. Three Travelaire monoplanes entered service between Dallas, Texas and Jackson, Missouri, on a route which was later extended to Atlanta, which eventually became Delta's main base. During the years up to the outbreak of the Second World War, the route network grew steadily, and a succession of more advanced aircraft entered service, including Stinson As and Douglas DC-2s, the immediate predecessor of the famous DC-3.

Postwar, Delta made rapid progress, aided by three major acquisitions. First of these was Chicago & Southern Airlines, which dated from 1934 and which passed to Delta in 1953. Almost twenty years later, a more significant acquisition was that of Northeast Airlines in 1972. Northeast was founded in 1933 under the name of Boston-Maine Airways, using two Stinson trimotors, and by the time of its acquisition by Delta possessed a route network stretching from Montreal in the north to Miami in the south. The third major acquisition was that of Western Airlines in 1987, which finally propelled Delta into the position of the third largest US airline by passenger numbers. Western also helped expand Delta's network on the Pacific coast. Older than the other two airlines, Western had been founded in 1925 as Western Air Express, operating a Douglas M-2 biplane between Los Angeles and Salt Lake City.

During its early years, Delta remained primarily a North American operator, with routes throughout the United States and across the borders into Canada and Mexico. Expansion into the Caribbean area followed and, during the 1980s, transatlantic operations began to the main European hubs. A major leap forward occurred in 1991, when Delta took over no less than twenty-one routes from the by then defunct Pan American World Airways, and then added a further seventeen destinations later in the year, mainly in Europe. These moves meant that a seventh US hub was added to the six then in operation, with New York-JFK joining the main base at Atlanta and Cincinnati, Dallas/Fort Worth, Los Angeles, Orlando and Salt Lake City. Portland, Oregon and a European feeder hub at Frankfurt in Germany have since followed.

In common with other major carriers, Delta has franchised smaller regional airlines to provide feeder services into its major hubs, in this case operating under the Delta Connection name. One of these airlines is Comair, in which Delta had a small shareholding but then bought the airline outright in 1999. Comair's business included a business jet charter operation, Comair Jet Express, based in Cincinnati, which has now been rebranded as Delta Airelite Business Jets, operating almost twenty business aircraft of varying sizes. In common with many established airlines, Delta created a low-cost subsidiary, Song, in 2002, which began operations the following year operating Boeing 757-200s from Florida and also across the north-east of the United States. Nevertheless, in 2006 this operation was reintegrated into the parent airline and the aircraft converted to two-class accommodation. Delta is a member of the Sky Team alliance. At the time of writing, Delta has been in Chapter 11 Bankruptcy Protection since September 2005.

HQ airport & main base: Hartsfield-Jackson Atlanta International, with additional hubs at Cincinnati, Dallas/Fort Worth, Frankfurt, Los Angeles, New York-JFK, Orlando, Portland, Salt Lake City
Radio callsign: DELTA
Designator: DL/DAL
Employees: 69,150
Route points: Acapulco, Aguascalientes, Akron, Albany, Albuquerque, Alexandria, Allentown,

Amarillo, Amsterdam, Anchorage, Antigua, Appleton, Aruba, Asheville, Aspen, Athens, Atlanta, Atlantic City, Augusta, Austin, Bakersfield, Baltimore, Bangalore, Bangor, Barcelona, Barranquilla, Baton Rouge, Belize, Berlin, Bermuda, Billings, Binghampton, Birmingham (US), Bismarck, Bloomington, Bogotá, Boise, Boston, Bozeman, Bridgetown, Bristol (US), Brownsville, Brunswick, Brussels, Bucharest, Budapest, Buenos Aires, Buffalo, Burbank, Burlington, Butte, Calgary, Cali, Cancun, Caspar, Cedar City, Cedar Rapids, Champaign, Charleston, Charlotte, Charlottesville, Chattanooga, Chicago, Cincinnati, Cleveland, Cody, Colorado Springs, Columbia, Columbus, Copenhagen, Corpus Christi, Dakar, Dallas, Dayton, Daytona Beach, Delhi, Denver, Des Moines, Detroit, Dothan, Dublin, Duluth, Eau Claire, Edmonton, El Paso, Elko, Erie, Eugene, Evansville, Fargo, Fayetteville, Flint, Florence (US), Fort Lauderdale, Fort Myers, Fort Smith, Fort Wayne, Frankfurt, Fredericton, Freeport, Fresno, Gainesville, Grand Cayman, Grand Junction, Grand Rapids, Great Falls, Green Bay, Greensboro, Greenville, Grenada, Guadalajara, Guangzhou, Guatemala City, Gulf Port, Halifax, Hampton, Harlingen, Harrisburg, Hartford, Hayden, Helena, Helsinki, Hermosillo, Honolulu, Houston, Huntingdon, Huntsville, Idaho Falls, Indianapolis, Islip, Istanbul, Jackson, Jacksonville, Johannesburg, Kahului, Kalamazoo, Kalispell, Kansas City, Key West, Kingston, Kinston, Knoxville, Kona, La Crosse, Lafayette, Lansing, Laredo, Las Vegas, Leon/Guanajuato, Lewiston, Lexington, Liberia, Lima, Lincoln, Lisbon, Little Rock, London, Long Beach, Loreto, Los Angeles, Los Mochis, Louisville, Lubbock, Lynchburgh, Macon, Madison, Madrid, Managua, Manchester, Mazatlan, McAllen, Medellin, Medford, Melbourne (US), Memphis, Mérida, Meridian, Mexico City, Miami, Midland/Odessa, Milan, Milwaukee, Minneapolis, Minot, Missoula, Mobile, Moline, Monroe, Montego Bay, Monterey, Monterrey, Montgomery, Montreal, Moscow, Mumbai, Munich, Myrtle Beach, Naples (US), Nashville, Nassau, New Orleans, New York, Newark, Newburgh, Niamey, Nice, Norfolk, Oakland, Oklahoma City, Omaha, Ontario (US), Ottawa, Ouagadougou, Paducah, Palm Springs, Panama City, Papeete, Paris, Pasco, Pensacola, Peoria, Philadelphia, Phoenix, Pittsburgh, Pocatello, Portland, Prague, Providence, Providenciales, Puerto Vallarta, Punta Cana, Raleigh/Durham, Rapid City, Redmond, Reno, Richmond, Rio de Janeiro, Roanoke, Roatan, Rochester, Rome, Sacramento, Saginaw, St Croix, St George, St Louis, St Lucia, St Maarten, St Petersburg, St Thomas, Salt Lake City, San Antonio, San Diego, San Francisco, San Jose, San Jose Cabo, San Juan, San Pedro Sula, San Salvador, Santa Ana, Santa Barbara, Santiago de Chile, Santo Domingo, Sao Paulo, Sarasota, Savannah, Seattle, Seoul, Shannon, Shreveport, Sioux City, Sioux Falls, South Bend, Spokane, Springfield, State College, Stuttgart, Sun Valley, Syracuse, Taipei, Tallahassee, Tampa, Tel Aviv, Tokyo, Toledo, Toronto, Traverse City, Tucson, Tulsa, Tupelo, Twin Falls, Vail, Valparaiso (US), Vancouver, Venice, Vienna, Warsaw, Washington, Wausau, West Palm Beach, Westchester County, Wichita, Wilkes-Barre, Wilmington, Winnipeg, Zurich

Links with other airlines: Delta Connection is Delta's commuter system. Delta has a 100 per cent share in Comair and Delta Connection, and through Comair owns Delta Airelite Business Jets (all qv). Alliances with: Air Jamaica (qv), Alaskan Airlines (qv), American Eagle Airlines (qv), Atlantic Southeast Airlines, Avianca (qv), Chautauqua Airlines (qv), China Airlines (qv), China Southern Airlines (qv), Comair (qv), El Al (qv), Freedom Airlines (qv), Royal Air Maroc (qv), Shuttle America, SkyWest Airlines (qv), South African Airways (qv)

Passengers carried: 110.0 million

Annual turnover: US $15,002 million (£10,001 million)

Fleet: 5 Boeing 777-200LR; 13 Boeing 777-200ER; 21 Boeing 767-400ER; 59 Boeing 767-300ER; 24 Boeing 767-300; 8 Boeing 767-200; 121 Boeing 757-200; 107 Boeing 737-800; 10 Boeing 737-700; 7 Boeing 737-300; 30 Boeing 737-200*; 120 McDonnell Douglas MD-88*; 16 McDonnell Douglas MD-90-30* (* These fleets may be reduced as deliveries of 737-800s are completed)

DELTA AIRELITE BUSINESS JETS

Although a subsidiary of Delta Air Lines, albeit through Comair, Delta Airelite Business Jets is not strictly an airline, but provides executive jet and helicopter charter, which can be used to connect with Delta scheduled flights. It operates more than twenty fixed-wing aircraft and helicopters.

DELTA CONNECTION

Delta Connection is the feeder or commuter operation of Delta Air Lines, feeding into the airline's major hubs. The main carriers participating in the scheme include Atlantic Southeast, Business Express, Comair, and Skywest Airlines.

EMPIRE AIRWAYS
Incorporated: 1977

Originally founded in Orofino, Idaho, as a cargo charter airline, Empire now operates well over a hundred flights a day throughout the United States and Canada. A large fleet of Cessna Caravans provides a service for small packets.

HQ airport & main base: Coer d'Alene
Radio callsign: EMPIRE
Designator: EM/CFS
Fleet: 3 ATR-72-200F; 3 ATR-42-300F; 4 ATR-42-300/320; 4 Fokker F27 Mk600; 33 Cessna Caravan 675; 1 Cessna 208 Caravan

EOS
EOS Airlines, Inc.
Incorporated: 2003

Founded in 2003, EOS commenced operations in 2005, flying between New York and London Stansted using three Boeing 757s configured to be all-business class with just forty-eight seats apiece.

HQ airport & main base: New York Kennedy International
Designator: EO
Route points: London, New York
Fleet: 3 Boeing 757-200

ERA
Era Aviation, Inc.
Incorporated: 1983

A regional commuter airline that has grown out of a helicopter air work operation, Era participates in the Alaska Airlines Commuter Service, carrying passengers and cargo out of its main hub at Anchorage, while operations from Bethel form part of the Alaska Airlines Village Service, the latter using de Havilland DHC-6 Twin Otter aircraft. In January 2006, the airline filed for Chapter 11 Bankruptcy Protection – meanwhile, operations continue.

HQ airport & main base: Anchorage International, with a further hub at Bethel
Radio callsign: ERAH
Designator: 7H/ERA
Employees: 330
Route points: Anchorage, Bethel, Cordova, Homer, Iliamna, Kenai, Kodiak, Valdez, as well as Bethel to small Alaskan communities
Links with other airlines: Alaskan Airlines Commuter Service member
Fleet: 4 Bombardier Dash 8 Q100; 8 de Havilland DHC-6 Twin Otter Srs 100/200/300

EVERGREEN
Evergreen International Airlines, Inc.
Incorporated: 1960

Originally founded in 1924 as Johnson Flying Service, Evergreen adopted its existing title in 1975. Air cargo is carried under contract for other airlines, and ad hoc cargo charters are also available, operating worldwide. Major clients include both the US mail and United Parcels Service, UPS. In contrast to many air freight carriers, the fleet is centred around conversions of the Boeing 747.

HQ airport & main base: Columbus Metropolitan
Radio callsign: EVERGREEN
Designator: EZ/EIA
Route points: Operations are worldwide, and include a regular New York-JFK to Hong Kong service, but most services are ad hoc charter or contract charter for other airlines
Fleet: 5 Boeing 747-100F; 5 Boeing 747-200F; 2 Boeing 747-200C; 1 Gulfstream GIV

EXECUTIVE AIRLINES
Executive Airlines, Inc. (AMR American Eagle)
Incorporated: 1989

Originally known as Executive Air Charter, providing corporate aircraft services at San Juan in Puerto Rico, the company moved into regional scheduled services before becoming an American Eagle franchisee in 1986. In 1989, it became a subsidiary of AMR American Eagle. Since becoming part of AMR American Eagle, the fleet has changed, with the disposal of the fleet of CASA 212s used on regional services, and the Cessna 402 and two Riley Herons, conversions of de Havilland Herons, used for executive charters. A large fleet of Shorts 360s was built up, but these have now been replaced by AI(R) 42s and 72s. American Eagle acquired the airline in late 1989. All aircraft carry American Eagle branding.

HQ airport & main base: San Juan Luis Munoz Marin International
Designator: OW/EXW
Route points: *See* American Eagle
Links with other airlines: Subsidiary of AMR American Eagle (qv)
Fleet: 12 ATR-72-500; 27 ATR-72-210

EXPRESSJET
Incorporated: 1986

ExpressJet was founded in 1986 and commenced operations in 1987 as a regional airline based in Texas. In 1989, it became part of the Continental Express feeder network, adopting the name for its operations, and was later acquired by Continental. In 2002, it was renamed ExpressJet and a parent company ExpressJet Holdings was established and floated on the New York Stock Market, buying the airline from Continental. The commercial links with Continental remain and Continental Express services are provided from Houston, Cleveland and Newark.

A 49.9 per cent stake is held in ExpressJet Europe, based at Cork in Ireland, which is designed to offer feeder airline services to major European carriers, but this airline will only become operational once a customer has been contracted.

HQ airport & main base: Houston Bush Intercontinental, with further bases/hubs at Cleveland Hopkins International and Newark Liberty International
Designator: CO/BTA
Employees: 6,800
Route points: On the Continental Express network
Links with other airlines: A Continental Express carrier
Fleet: 104 Embraer ERJ-145XR; 117 Embraer ERJ-145LR; 23 Embraer ERJ-145ER; 18 Embraer ERJ-135LR; 12 Embraer ERJ135ER

EXPRESS ONE INTERNATIONAL
Express One International, Inc.
Incorporated: 1980

Originally founded in 1980 as Jet East International, Express One adopted the current title in 1983. The airline is primarily a charter cargo carrier, specialising in short-notice operations, but it also operates under contract to the US Parcels Service from Indianapolis, and to DHL to Brussels. Passenger charters are also available.

HQ airport & main base: Dallas/Fort Worth, with further bases at Indianapolis, Minneapolis/St Paul, Brussels (Belgium)
Radio callsign: LONGHORN
Designator: EO/LHN
Employees: 500
Links with other airlines: Operates under contract to DHL and EAT European Air Transport (both qv)
Fleet: 15 Boeing 727-200F; 1 Boeing 727-100F

EXPRESSNET
Incorporated: 1972

A cargo charter airline operating throughout the Americas and the Far East, Expressnet was originally founded in 1972 by Scott Kalitta but was sold to the present owners, David Clark and Michael Goldberg in 1999.

HQ airport & main base: Naples Municipal
Designator: XNA
Employees: 270
Fleet: 6 Airbus A300B4-200F; 3 Boeing 727-200F; 2 Boeing 727-200; 1 Boeing 727-100F

FedEx EXPRESS
Federal Express, Inc.
Incorporated: 1971

The world's largest air freight operator, and fourth largest airline by annual turnover, Federal Express was founded in 1971 by Frederick Smith, who is still Chairman, and President today. Operations started two years later, using a fleet of Dassault Falcon 20 business jets to carry documents overnight across the United States. Although a substantial fleet of aircraft and a strong route network were quickly established, the major catalyst in the development of Federal Express, or FedEx as it is often known, was deregulation of the American air cargo market in 1977. Deregulation allowed FedEx to operate larger aircraft and, building on its existing route network, a fleet of Boeing 727 and McDonnell Douglas DC-10 aircraft was created. In 1986, operations to Europe began with services to London and Brussels.

In 1989, FedEx bought the then largest air cargo operator, Flying Tiger, giving the company an extensive intercontinental operation into Europe, Asia and South America. The Flying Tiger Line had been founded immediately after the end of the Second World War by a group of former USAAF war veterans, who had fought as the 'Flying Tigers' in Burma and China. Initially 'Flying Tigers', as the airline was usually known, operated Budd Conestogas, but these were soon replaced by Douglas C-47 Dakotas and C-54 Skymasters retired from US military service. In 1949, Flying Tigers gained authority to operate scheduled cargo services across the United States from coast to coast, with its main base being at Los Angeles.

While using large, wide-bodied aircraft on the trunk routes, FedEx did not lose its link with small aircraft and the package market, building up a fleet of some 300 small Cessna Caravan aircraft on feeder services, most of which are operated under contract by the cargo equivalent of the commuter airlines. Operations within specific target markets have often been developed through the acquisition of locally based package or document carriers, such as Lex Wilkinson in the UK in 1986. Currently, the largest aircraft in the fleet are McDonnell Douglas MD-11s, following the run-down of the Boeing 747 freighter fleet with the transfer of the five remaining aircraft to Lufthansa in 1998, but a substantial Airbus A300 and A310 fleet is operated and the airline has ten Airbus A380-800F freighters on order for its busiest routes.

HQ airport & main base: Memphis International, with additional hubs at Anchorage International, Fort Worth Alliance, Indianapolis International, Newark Liberty International, Oakland International, Paris Charles de Gaulle, Subic Bay
Radio callsign: FEDEX
Designator: FX/FDX
Route points: Aguadilla, Almaty, Anchorage, Athens, Atlanta, Bangkok, Basle/Mulhouse, Beijing, Bogotá, Boston, Buffalo, Calgary, Casper, Cebu, Chicago, Cleveland, Cologne, Copenhagen, Dallas, Denver, Detroit, Dubai, Fort Lauderdale, Frankfurt, Grand Forks, Great Falls, Guadalajara, Hong Kong, Honolulu, Houston, Indianapolis, Jakarta, Kansas City, Kaohsiung, Kuala Lumpur, London, Los Angeles, Madrid, Memphis, Mexico City, Miami, Milan, Minneapolis, Monterrey, Montreal, Mumbai, Nagoya, New York, Newark, Oakland, Osaka, Ottawa, Panama City, Paris, Penang, Rochester, St Louis, San Francisco, San Juan, Sao Paulo, Seattle, Seoul, Shanghai, Shenzhen, Singapore, Spokane, Stockholm, Subic Bay, Sydney, Taipei, Tampa, Tel Aviv, Toronto, Valencia, Vancouver, Washington, Winnipeg
Links with other airlines: Feeder aircraft are operated on behalf of FedEx by a number of airlines, including Baron Aviation (qv), Corporate Air (qv), Mountain Air Cargo (qv), Union Flights and Wigins Airways
Fleet: 57 McDonnell Douglas MD-11F; 22 McDonnell Douglas DC-10-30F; 58 McDonnell Douglas DC-10-10F/CF; 57 Airbus A300-600F; 16 Airbus A310-300F; 49 Airbus A310-200F; 90 Boeing 727-200F; 10 Boeing 727-100F; 2 Boeing 727-100C; 3 ATR-72-200; 2 ATR-42-300/320; 3 Bombardier Challenger 601; 1 Bombardier Global Express; 6 Bombardier Learjet 45; 2 Cessna Caravan 675 (On order: 15 Boeing 777F)

FOUR STAR AIR CARGO

Four Star Aviation, Inc.
Incorporated: 1982

This regional air cargo specialist, owned by Four Star Aviation, operates both charters and scheduled cargo services from its base at St Thomas, in the US Virgin Islands. Interline agreements exist with several of the major US airlines, as well as British Airways and Lufthansa.

HQ airport & main base: Cyril E. King Airport, St Thomas, US Virgin Islands
Radio callsign: FOUR STAR
Designator: HK/FSC
Route points: Beef Island, Boringuen, St Croix, St Thomas, San Juan, Santo Domingo, Tortola
Fleet: 6 Douglas DC-3

FRONTIER

Frontier Airlines, Inc.
Incorporated: 1994

Frontier Airlines operates from the new Denver International Airport, and was formed to take advantage of a massive reduction in flights to and from that airport by Continental Airlines. During 1997, a merger was agreed with Western Pacific, but called off three months later.

The airline has adopted the low-cost model and is now the second largest user of Denver. The number of employees has grown almost sixfold over the past decade, while the number of aircraft is now almost seven times that of the late 1990s. The route network now includes international services, mainly to Mexico.

HQ airport & main base: Denver International
Radio callsign: FRONTIER FLIGHT
Designator: F9/FFT
Employees: 4,392
Route points: Acapulco, Akron, Albuquerque, Atlanta, Ustin, Baltimore, Billings, Boise, Cancun, Chicago, Cozumel, Dallas, Dayton, Denver, Detroit, El Paso, Fort Lauderdale, Fort Myers, Fresno, Houston, Indianapolis, Ixtapa, Kansas City, Las Vegas, Little Rock, Los Angeles, Mazatlan, Milwaukee, Minneapolis, Nashville, New York, Oklahoma City, Omaha, Orlando, Philadelphia, Phoenix, Portland, Puerto Vallarta, Reno, Sacramento, St Louis, Salt Lake City, San Antonio, San Diego, San Francisco, San Jose, San Jose Cabo, Santa Ana, Seattle, Spokane, Tampa, Tulsa, Washington
Links with other airlines: Alliance with Great Lakes Aviation, Horizon Air (both qv)
Fleet: 10 Airbus A320-200; 53 Airbus A319-100; 11 Airbus A318-100; 10 Bombardier Dash 8 Q400

GEMINI AIR CARGO
Incorporated: 1995

Originally a freight forwarder, Gemini was founded in 1995, and began cargo charter operations, wet-leasing aircraft from Sun Country Airlines until it obtained its own air operator's certificate in 1996. A controlling interest was acquired by the Carlyle Group in 1999. The airline now has a domestic and international scheduled air cargo network. The airline was in Chapter 11 Bankruptcy Protection for four months during 2006.

HQ airport & main base: Washington Dulles, but with bases at Miami International and New York Kennedy International
Designator: GR/GCO
Employees: 412
Route points: Amsterdam, Bogotá, Brussels, Cali, Cologne, Delhi, Frankfurt, Halifax, Medellin, Miami, New York, Panama City, Quito, Toronto, Vienna
Fleet: 4 McDonnell Douglas MD-11F; 7 McDonnell Douglas DC-10-30F

GO!
Incorporated: 2006

A new, low-cost subsidiary of the Mesa Airlines Group, Go! provides a high-frequency inter-island service within Hawaii using a fleet of Bombardier CRJ200s.

HQ airport & main base: Honolulu
Route points: Hilo, Honolulu, Kahului, Kono, Lihue
Links with other airlines: Subsidiary of Mesa Air Group (qv)
Fleet: 12 Bombardier CRJ200

GOJET
GoJet Airlines, Inc.
Incorporated: 2004

GoJet was established in 2004 and began operations the following year, operating a small network of US domestic services from St Louis. The airline is owned completely by Trans States Holdings.

HQ airport & main base: Lambert St Louis International
Designator: G7
Employees: 400
Route points: Chicago, Denver, St Louis, Washington
Links with other airlines: Alliance with United Airlines (qv)
Fleet: 15 Bombardier CRJ700-701LR

GRAND CANYON AIRLINES
Incorporated: 1927

Effectively not so much an airline as an aerial sightseeing operator and, as the name implies, its business is centred over the Grand Canyon.

HQ airport & main base: Grand Canyon National Park
Designator: CVU
Fleet: 5 de Havilland Canada DHC-6 Twin Otter Srs 300

GREAT LAKES
Great Lakes Aviation, Inc.
Incorporated: 1979

Although founded in 1979, Great Lakes Aviation did not commence operations until 1982. The airline soon joined the United Express network, and in 1995 entered into a marketing alliance with Midway Airlines under the name of Midway Connection, although this only lasted until 1997. Some services were also operated under the Arizona Airways Express banner. The airline has left the United Express network and now operates independently. In addition to the scheduled network, Great Lakes provides passenger and freight charter and fixed-base (i.e. general aviation support) services. The airline was floated on the New York Stock Exchange in 1994.

HQ airport & main base: Cheyenne, with hubs at Chicago O'Hare and Denver
Radio callsign: LAKES AIR
Designator: ZK /GLA
Route points: Alamosa, Albuquerque, Alliance, Amarillo, Chadron, Cheyenne, Chicago, Clovis, Cortez, Denver, Dickinson, Dodge City, Enid, Farmington, Fort Huachuca, Garden City, Gillette, Grand Island, Grand Junction, Hays, Kearney, Kingman, Laramie, Liberal, McCook, North Platte, Page, Phoenix, Pierre, Ponca City, Prescott, Pueblo, Riverton, Rock Springs, Sante Fe, Scottsbluff, Show Low, Silver City, Telluride, Williston, Worland
Links with other airlines: Alliances with Frontier Airlines, United Airlines (both qv)
Fleet: 25 Raytheon Beech 1900D; 1 Raytheon Beech 99A; 6 Embraer EMB-120 Brasilia.

GULFSTREAM
Gulfstream International Airlines, Inc.
Incorporated: 1988

Gulfstream International Airlines was founded in 1988, and operations began in 1990, initially using a Cessna 402 to provide an 'on demand' air taxi service between Miami and Cap Haitien, Haiti. The founder was a former Eastern Air Lines captain, Thomas Cooper, who remained the proprietor and Chief Operating Officer for many years.

The company has since expanded and provides a network of short, scheduled passenger services from points in Florida to the closer Caribbean resort destinations. The fleet includes a mixture of Beech 1900 and Shorts 360 aircraft. A code-share arrangement existed with United Airlines, but this has now been replaced by alliances with other airlines, including a code-share with Continental Airlines. The company was acquired by G-Air Holdings, which has a 72 per cent stake, and which acquired Paradise International Airlines in 1998.

HQ airport & main base: Fort Lauderdale Hollywood International
Radio callsign: GULF FLIGHT
Designator: 3M/GFT
Employees: 514
Route points: Freeport, Fort Lauderdale, Gainesville, Jacksonville, Key West, Marsh Harbour, Miami, Nassau, North Eleuthera, Tallahassee, Tampa, Treasure Cay, West Palm Beach
Links with other airlines: Code-share with Continental Airlines, and alliances with Copa and Northwest Airlines (all qv)
Fleet: 26 Raytheon Beech 1900D; 7 Embraer EMB-120 Brasilia

HAWAIIAN
Hawaiian Airlines, Inc.
Incorporated: 1929

Hawaiian Airlines dates from 1929, when it was formed by Inter-Island Steam Navigation shipping company as Inter-Island Airways, commencing operations on 11 November with flights from Honolulu's John Rodgers Airport on the island of Oahu, to Maui and to Hawaii. Given the absence of runways on most of the islands at the time, and a route network almost entirely over water, the choice of aircraft settled on two Sikorksy S-38 eight-passenger amphibians. Schedules were far less frequent than today, with three round trips per week on each of the inaugural routes. Frequencies and destinations increased steadily, nevertheless, and in 1935, with the support of a new, inter-island airmail contract, a fleet of sixteen-passenger Sikorsky S-43s flying boats was introduced.

The present title was adopted in 1941, a year during which, almost on the eve of America's involvement in the Second World War, Douglas DC-3s were introduced into the fleet. Although most of these aircraft had seating for twenty-four passengers, the airline became heavily involved with air cargo operations to the other islands following the outbreak of war. All inter-island traffic was placed under military control, and Hawaiian received the first air cargo certificate to be issued by the Civil Aeronautics Board.

Postwar, Hawaiian introduced its first pressurised aircraft, Convair 340s, to the inter-island routes, and in 1958 acquired a Douglas DC-6 for transpacific US military charters. Douglas DC-9 jet airliners were introduced in 1966, reducing many of the sector times on the inter-island routes to just twenty to thirty minutes. The charter market was not overlooked, and in 1984 Hawaiian moved into the long-haul charter market with three McDonnell Douglas DC-8 jet airliners, before later introducing the first scheduled routes outside of the islands, to American Samoa and Tonga. The following year, five Lockheed L-1011 TriStars were introduced for long-haul charter and scheduled services, with the first of these to the west coast of the US beginning that year, when a route was opened to Los Angeles, with San Francisco and Seattle being added to the network early in 1986.

In 1993, Hawaiian agreed to a programme of cooperation with American Airlines, including marketing and technical support, leading to the replacement of the TriStars by McDonnell Douglas DC-10s, maintained by American. These have since been replaced by Boeing 767s. In the late 1990s, Japan Airlines took a 8.5 per cent stake in Hawaiian, while Northwest Airlines took a 25 per cent interest, with a marketing agreement signed in 1996. The airline was forced to seek Chapter 11 Bankruptcy Protection in March 2003, but operations continued and the airline eventually emerged from protection in January 2006. It is now owned by Hawaiian Holdings and the airline is once again independent, although alliances exist with a number of other airlines.

A mixture of scheduled and inclusive tour charter flights are operated.

HQ airport & main base: Honolulu International
Radio callsign: HAWAIIAN

Designator: HA/HAL
Employees: 4,371
Route points: Hilo, Honolulu, Hoolehua, Kahului, Kapalua, Kauai, Kona, Lanai, Las Vegas, Los Angeles, Pago Pago, Papeete, Phoenix, Portland, Sacramento, San Diego, San Francisco, San Jose, Seattle, Spokane, Sydney
Links with other airlines: Alliances with Alaska Airlines, America West Airlines, American Eagle Airlines, Continental Airlines, Horizon Air, Northwest Airlines (all qv)
Fleet: 14 Boeing 767-300ER; 2 Boeing 767-300; 11 Boeing 717-200

HOOTERS AIR

Branding used on aircraft belonging to Pace Airlines.

HORIZON AIR
Horizon Air Industries, Inc.
Incorporated: 1981

Part of the Alaska Air Group since 1986, Horizon Air dates from 1981, when it was formed as a small regional carrier. Another airline, Air Oregon, was acquired in 1982, allowing the new airline to become one of the largest regional airlines on the north-west Pacific coast of the United States. Further expansion followed in 1984, when Transwestern was acquired, and Horizon introduced its first jet quipment, Fokker F28 Fellowships.

A marketing alliance exists with Alaska Airlines, the other major airline in the Alaska Air Group, and with Northwest Airlines. The network now extends north and south of the airline's Seattle base, and includes destinations as far south as California, and north to Canada.

HQ airport & main base: Seattle, with hubs at Portland and Spokane
Radio callsign: HORIZON AIR
Designator: QX/QXE
Employees: 3,800
Route points: Bellingham, Billigs, Bozeman, Butte, Calgary, Edmonton, Eugene, Eureka/Arcata, Great Falls, Helena, Idaho Falls, Kalispell, Klamath Falls, Lewiston, Medford, Missoula, Moses Lake, North Bend, Oakland, Pasco, Pendleton, Pocatello, Port Angeles, Pullman, Redding, Redmond, Sacramento, San Jose, Sun Valley, Twin Falls, Vancouver, Victoria, Walla Walla, Wenatche, Yakima
Links with other airlines: Owned by Alaska Air. Alliances with Alaska Air, Frontier Airlines, Hawaiian Airlines, KLM (all qv)
Fleet: 21 Bombardier CRJ700-701ER; 31 Bombardier Dash 8 Q400; 28 Bombardier Dash 8 Q200

ISLAND AIR
Hawaiian Island Air
Incorporated:1992

Originally founded as Princeville Airways, operating scheduled services between Princeville and Honolulu using two de Havilland Canada Twin Otters, the airline was purchased by Aloha in 1987 and became Aloha Island Air. It became Island Air in 1992, but it was not until 2004 that the airline was sold to a new owner and became legally Hawaiian Island Air, although continuing to fly as Island Air.

HQ airport & main base: Honolulu International
Designator: WO/PRI
Employees: 400
Route points: Hilo, Honolulu, Kahului, Kapalua, Kauai, Kona, Lanai
Fleet: 1 Bombardier Dash 8 Q200; 8 Bombardier Dash 8 Q100

JETBLUE AIRWAYS
Incorporated: 1999

Established as a low-fare airline in 1999, JetBlue began operations in early 2000, and has since grown rapidly from its original two routes out of New York Kennedy International. Future plans foresee the fleet more than doubling in size.

HQ airport & main base: New York Kennedy International
Radio callsign: JETBLUE
Designator: B6/JBU
Employees: 9,470
Route points: Aguadilla, Austin, Boston, Buffalo, Burbank, Burlington, Denver, Fort Lauderdale, Fort Myers, Las Vegas, Long Beach, Nassau, New Orleans, New York, Newark, Oakland, Ontario (US), Orlando, Phoenix, Ponce, Portland, Rochester, Sacramento, Salt Lake City, San Diego, San Jose, Santiago, Seattle, Syracuse, Tampa, Washington, West Palm Beach
Fleet: 97 Airbus A320-200 plus 81 on order; 23 Embraer 190 plus 77 on order

KALITTA AIR
Incorporated: 2000

Kalitta Air was established in 2000 by Conrad Kalitta, the owner of the defunct Kitty Hawk

International, using that airline's air operator's certificate and assets. Kitty Hawk International had operated domestic cargo and passenger charter flights within the United States since 1976, when it was formed as Kitty Hawk Airways. In 1997 it was taken over by the Kalitta Group, owners of American International Airlines, and the merged airline was renamed Kitty Hawk International, operating Boeing 727 passenger aircraft and Convair 580 cargo aircraft. Since its formation, Kalitta has introduced a small number of scheduled air cargo services.

A subsidiary of Kalitta is Kalitta Charters.

HQ airport & main base: Detroit Willow Run
Radio callsign: KALITTA
Designator: K4/CKS
Employees: 560
Route points: Christmas Island, Detroit, Nuku'Alofa, Pago Pago
Links with other airlines: Kalitta Charters (qv) is a subsidiary
Fleet: 8 Boeing 747-200F; 1 Boeing 747-200B; 5 Boeing 747-100F; 4 Boeing 727-200F; 1 Boeing 727-100

KALITTA CHARTERS
Incorporated: 2000

A charter subsidiary of Kalitta Air, operating cargo charters in the southern states of the USA, mainly with small business jet type aircraft, although there is a Boeing 747 and a McDonnell Douglas DC-9 in the fleet.

HQ airport & main base: Detroit Willow Run
Designator: K4/CKS
Links with other airlines: A subsidiary of Kalitta Air (qv)
Fleet: 1 Boeing 747-100F; 1 McDonnell Douglas DC-9-10; 3 Dassault Falcon 20; 8 Bombardier Learjet 35/35A/36A; 8 Bombardier Learjet 24/25

KITTYHAWK AIR CARGO
Incorporated: 1976

Originally founded as Kitty Hawk Airways in 1976, the airline adopted its present title as it became a dedicated scheduled and charter cargo specialist.

HQ airport & main base: Dallas/Fort Worth International
Designator: KR/KHC
Employees: 201
Route points: Atlanta, Baltimore, Boston, Charlotte, Dallas, Denver, El Paso, Fort Wayne, Houston, Kansas City, Los Angeles, Miami, Mineapolis, Nashville, Newark, Niagara Falls, Orlando, Philadelphia, Phoenix, Portland, San Diego, San Francisco, San Juan, Seattle
Fleet: 14 Boeing 727-200F; 2 Boeing 727-200; 7 Boeing 737-300SF

LYNDEN AIR CARGO
Incorporated: 1997

Lynden Air Cargo was founded in 1997 with a single Lockheed L-382 Hercules, and continues today operating scheduled and charter flights from Anchorage.

HQ airport & main base: Anchorage International
Radio callsign: LYNDEN
Designator: L2/LYC
Route points: Anchorage, Bethel, Dillingham, Kotzebue, Nome
Fleet: 6 Lockheed Hercules L-100-30

MARTINAIRE
Incorporated: 1978

Operating feeder services for overnight package carriers, Martinaire was founded in 1978, and in 1990 acquired the business of another company involved in the same type of operation, CCAir. The airline was acquired from its founder in 1993 by the current owners, the Acker Group.

HQ airport & main base: Dallas Addison
Designator: MRA
Links with other airlines: Operates feeder services for Airborne Express, DHL and UPS (all qv)
Fleet: 31 Cessna Caravan 675; 4 Fairchild Metro III

MAXJET
Maxjet Airways, Inc.
Incorporated: 2004

Founded in 2004 as SkyLink Airways, Maxjet began operations the following year, initially on passenger charters, but its objective is to develop all-business class services between the United States and Europe, initially with flights from Washington and New York to London Stansted, for which it has US Department of Transportation approval.

HQ airport & main base: Washington Dulles International

Radio callsign: MAXJET
Designator: MY
Route points: London, New York, Washington
Fleet: 2 Boeing 767-200ER; 1 Boeing 767-200

MESA AIRLINES
Mesa Air Group
Incorporated: 1980

Mesa Air Group is the holding company for a group of regional airlines, most of which are franchisees for major American airlines, with aircraft carrying the branding and using the flight designators of the larger airlines. One of the constituent airlines, Mountain West, was originally known as Mesa Airlines, but the name was changed to avoid confusion.

Inevitably there have been some changes at Mesa as alliances vary, with, for example, United Airlines terminating its arrangements with Mesa in 1998. Today the airline divisions are America West Express, Air Midwest and Frontier Jet Express. There are also technical support and pilot training divisions within the group.

Claiming to be the largest independent regional carrier based in New Mexico, in 1997 Mesa introduced sixteen Canadair Regional Jets, marking a major advance in the services offered, and today this fleet alone has grown to more than a hundred aircraft.

HQ airport & main base: Phoneix
Radio callsign: AIR SHUTTLE
Designator: YV/ASH, but individual airlines and franchise arrangements may have different designators
Main route points: (*See also* individual airlines, but 166 airports are served altogether) Boston, Dallas/Fort Worth, Kansas City, New Orleans, Orlando, Phoenix, Pittsburgh, Philadelphia, Tampa
Links with other airlines: Alliances with America West, US Airways (both qv)
Fleet: 19 Bombardier CRJ900; 15 Bombardier CRJ700-701ER; 34 Bombardier CRJ200LR; 16 Bombardier CRJ200ER; 3 Bombardier CRJ100LR; 3 Bombardier CRJ100ER; 8 Embraer ERJ-145LR; 14 Bombardier Dash 8 Q200; 16 Raytheon Beech 1900D

MESABA AIRLINES
Incorporated: 1944

Although founded in 1944, for most of the next thirty years Mesaba operated as a fixed-base operator, Mesaba Aviation, providing support for general aviation activities, and did not venture into scheduled airline operations until 1973, initially serving isolated communities in Minnesota. The airline was purchased by the Swenson family in 1977, and after US airline deregulation in 1978, Mesaba became an 'Essential Air Service' operator and started to provide commuter services not only in Minnesota, but also in the Dakotas and Iowa, operating from a base at Minneapolis/St Paul.

After briefly entering into an alliance with Republic Airlines in 1983, the following year Mesaba became the first regional feeder for Northwest Airlines and also entered into a code-sharing agreement – one of the first instances of this. The airline's route structure almost doubled in 1988 when Northwest got Mesaba to open a second hub at Detroit. In 1994, Mesaba acquired Conquest Airlines, and the following year Northwest acquired a 27.8 per cent interest in the airline's parent company, Mesaba Holdings.

Mesaba sought Chapter 11 Bankrutcy Protection in 2005, largely to protect itself from the possible loss of much of its fleet and route network once Northwest completes a major restructuring.

The airline is wholly owned by Mair Holdings, the renamed Mesaba Holdings, and in turn Mesaba owns Big Sky Airlines. In addition to the relationship with Northwest, Mesaba also has an alliance with Continental Airlines.

HQ airport & main base: Minneapolis/St Paul International
Radio callsign: MESABA
Designator: XJ/MES
Employees: 3, 625
Route points: On the US domestic networks of Continental and Northwest
Links with other airlines: Northwest Airlines (qv) has a 27.8 per cent stake in the parent company, Mair Holdings. Alliances and feeder services for both Continental and Northwest (both qv)
Fleet: 24 BAe Avro RJ85ER; 2 Bombardier CRJ200LR; 49 Saab 340A/B

MIAMI AIR
Miami Air International, Inc.
Incorporated: 1991

Miami Air International was founded in 1991 as a supplemental, or charter, passenger carrier, a type of airline operation which is still less common in the United States than in the United Kingdom and Europe. Operations extend throughout the United

States and to some thirty countries. The fleet is standardised on one aircraft type, the Boeing 737-800, replacing an earlier Boeing 727-200 fleet, which streamlines maintenance and marketing. The airline is privately owned.

HQ airport & main base: Miami International Airport
Radio callsign: BISCAYNE
Designator: BSK
Fleet: 8 Boeing 737-800; 2 Boeing 737-400

MIDWEST AIRLINES
Midwest Airlines, Inc.
Incorporated: 1984

Founded in 1984 as a subsidiary of Kimberley-Clark, through a holding company K-C Aviation, which dated from 1948, when the parent company started to provide corporate air transport for its senior personnel. Deregulation in 1978 saw K-C Aviation move from providing in-house air transport to becoming a regional carrier, laying the foundation for an airline, and in 1984 this emerged as Midwest Express. The new airline developed a network of services from its main hub at Milwaukee, while Kimberley-Clark sold the airline in two transactions in 1995 and 1996. In 2003, Midwest Express became simply Midwest, and its regional subsidiary, Skyway Airlines, also changed its name, becoming Midwest Connect.

The airline now has an additional hub at Kansas City. While the fleet had grown to include smaller aircraft, Beech 1900s, in addition to the McDonnell Douglas DC-9s which were the mainstay of the airline for most of its existence, the operation of smaller aircraft was passed to Midwest Connect, but the connection with McDonnell Douglas continued after the acquisition of the manufacturer by Boeing, with the inclusion of Boeing 717-200 (MD-90 series) airliners in the fleet. The name has recently changed to Midwest Airlines.

HQ airport & main base: Milwaukee General Mitchell Field, with an additional hub at Kansas City
Radio callsign: MIDEX
Designator: YX/MEP
Employees: 2,900
Route points: Appleton, Atlanta, Baltimore, Boston, Cleveland, Colombus, Dallas/Fort Worth, Dayton, Denver, Des Moines, Escabana, Flint, Fort Lauderdale, Fort Myers, Grand Rapids, Green Bay, Hartford, Indianapolis, Iron Mountain, Ironwood, Kansas City, Las Vegas, Los Angeles, Louisville, Madison, Manistree, Marquette, Milwaukee, Minneapolis, Muskegon, Nashville, New York, Newark, Omaha, Orlando, Philadelphia, Phoenix, Pittsburgh, Rhinelander, St Louis, San Antonio, San Diego, San Francisco, Tampa, Toronto, Washington, Wasau
Links with other airlines: Owns Midwest Connect. Alliances with Air Midwest, American Eagle Airlines (qv), Midwest Connect (qv)
Fleet: 25 Boeing 717-200; 2 Boeing MD-88; 3 Boeing MD-82; 7 Boeing MD-81

MIDWEST CONNECT
Incorporated: 1989

Originally founded as Skyway Airlines, the airline began operating as a feeder for Midwest Express and changed its name to Midwest Connect in 2003. It is wholly owned by Midwest.

HQ airport & main base: Milwaukee General Mitchell Field
Designator: AL/SYX
Employees: 637
Route points: Included in the Midwest route points
Links with other airlines: Owned by Midwest. Alliances with Midwest Airlines, SAS (both qv)
Fleet: 20 Embraer ERJ-140; 10 Dornier 328 Jet; 12 Raytheon Beech 1900D (being replaced by ERJ-140/Dornier 328)

MOUNTAIN AIR CARGO
Incorporated: 1974

Mountain Air Cargo dates from 1974 and is essentially a charter cargo operator, mainly operating under contract to FedEx and concentrating on the eastern seaboard of the United States and Canada, the Caribbean, and into Brazil and Argentina.

HQ airport & main base: Kingston
Radio callsign: MOUNTAIN
Designator: MTN
Employees: 289
Links with other airlines: Contract carrier for FedEx (qv)
Fleet: 10 ATR-42-300/300F; 18 Fokker F27 Friendship Mk500; 2 Shorts 330-200; 2 Cessna Caravan 208; 41 Cessna Caravan 675; 1 Raytheon Beech King Air C90B

MURRAY AIR
Incorporated: 1985

Founded in 1985, Murray Air commenced operations the following year using Mitsubishi Mu-2s for light cargo consignments, and has since developed into a cargo and passenger ad hoc charter airline.

HQ airport & main base: Detroit Willow Run
Designator: MUA
Employees: 90
Fleet: 1 McDonnell Douglas DC-8-70; 2 McDonnell Douglas DC-8-63CF; 1 Saab 340A; 2 CASA C212-200 Aviocar

NORTH AMERICAN AIRLINES
Incorporated: 1989

Originally formed in 1989 and starting operations the following year, North American Airlines was initially intended to provide feeder services throughout North America for El Al, the Israeli airline, as well as inclusive tour charters for Club Med. El Al had a 24.9 per cent of the shares at first, but sold these to the founder, Dan McKinnon, in 2003, while the airline was acquired outright by World Air Holdings in 2005. Inclusive tour charters continue to be operated, while the airline now has a small scheduled network linking New York with West Africa.

HQ airport & main base: New York Kennedy
Radio callsign: NORTH AMERICAN
Designator: NA/NAO
Employees: 650
Route points: Accra, Georgetown, New York
Links with other airlines: World Air Holdings owns 100 per cent
Fleet: 5 Boeing 767-300ER; 3 Boeing 757-200

NORTHERN AIR CARGO
Northern Air Cargo, Inc.
Incorporated: 1956

Claiming to be Alaska's first scheduled air cargo carrier, Northern Air Cargo was founded in 1956 by Robert Sholton and Maurice Carlson, and commenced operations a year later. The route network covers some thirty points throughout Alaska, which is sparsely populated and with a rugged terrain, which makes the state ideal for air transport. For many years, Douglas DC-6 freighters provided the backbone of the fleet, including rare swing-tailed examples, but a Boeing 727-100F was added during the late 1990s, and has since been joined by other Boeing jets.

HQ airport & main base: Anchorage International
Radio callsign: NORTHERN AIR CARGO
Designator: NC/NAC
Employees: 290
Route points: Anchorage, Dillingham, Fairbanks, Nome, Prudhoe Bay/Deadhorse
Fleet: 2 Boeing 727-100C/F; 3 Boeing 737-200

NORTHWEST
Northwest Airlines, Inc.
Incorporated: 1926

America's fifth largest airline by turnover, and tenth in the world, Northwest is seventh worldwide by passenger numbers. The airline's history dates from 1926, when it was formed as Northwest Airways, not taking the present title until 1934. The first services were for mail between Chicago and Minneapolis/St Paul, and the airline remained primarily a regional carrier until after the Second World War, when expansion saw the route network reach destinations in Canada and coast to coast across the United States. At this stage, the strategy was for international expansion to concentrate on services from the United States to the Far East, and although the airline's legal title remained unchanged, for many years aircraft, advertising and tickets carried the name 'Northwest Orient'. The first transpacific route operated in 1947, from Detroit and New York through Anchorage and Shemya, in Alaska, to Tokyo, Seoul, Shanghai and Manila, initially using Douglas DC-4s, although these were soon replaced by the larger and faster Boeing Stratocruisers.

The ambitious expansion across the Pacific soon ran into trouble. First, in 1949, the conflict between Communist and Nationalist forces in mainland China saw Shanghai dropped from the route. In 1950, the invasion of South Korea by North Korea resulted in services to Seoul being dropped. These problems were more than compensated for by Northwest being selected as the prime contractor for the Korean Airlift by the United States government. The following year, a service was introduced to Hong Kong, initially through a connection with a Hong Kong Airways flight.

In 1985, a reorganisation led to the formation of a holding company, NWA, which became the owner of Northwest and a number of other subsidiaries. The following year, Northwest took over Republic Airlines, expanding its domestic services within the United States still further. Although Republic itself only dated from 1979, it had been the result of a merger between North Central Airlines, originally founded in 1948 as Wisconsin Central Airlines, and Southern Airways, founded in 1949 and based in Atlanta. Republic had acquired Hughes Airwest in 1980, an airline which had been formed in 1968 as Airwest on the merger of several small airlines, and acquired by the Hughes Air Corporation in 1970.

Northwest expanded into the North Atlantic in 1979, with a cargo service from New York and Boston to Glasgow Prestwick in Scotland. A few weeks later, passenger services were introduced from New York and Detroit to Copenhagen and Stockholm. The following year, services to London, Oslo, Hamburg and Shannon were introduced.

Northwest was acquired by a group of private investors, known as Wings Holdings, headed by Alfred Checchi, Gary Wilson and Fred Malek, in 1989, but became a publicly quoted company once again in 1994, with the employees holding a 27 per cent interest and KLM Royal Dutch Airlines holding 19 per cent. Friction with KLM over ultimate control of the airline was resolved in 1997 by an agreement that KLM should sell all of its shares in Northwest in four tranches by 2000.

Today, Northwest operates a substantial route network within the United States and with both transpacific and transatlantic routes. Although the marketing alliance and code-sharing agreement with KLM was viewed as a model example of airline cooperation and enjoyed anti-trust immunity status from the United States government, this has now ended.

Marketing alliances exist with a number of regional airlines who operate feeder or commuter services under the Northwest Airlink banner, while Northwest has outright control of a subsidiary, Northwest Airlines Cargo and a 27.8 per cent interest in Mair Holdings, which in turn owns Mesaba Airlines. Northwest is a member of the Sky Team alliance.

Northwest sought Chapter 11 Bankruptcy Protection on 14 September 2005. Employee numbers have fallen by a quarter over the past decade.

HQ airport & main base: Minneapolis/St Paul International, with additional hubs at Detroit, Memphis and Tokyo Narita
Radio callsign: NORTHWEST
Designator: NW/NWA
Employees: 35,000
Route points: Acapulco, Akron, Albany, Albuquerque, Alexandria (US), Allentown, Alpena, Amsterdam, Anchorage, Appleton, Asheville, Aspen, Atlanta, Austin, Baltimore, Bangkok, Bangor, Baton Rouge, Beijing, Bemidji, Billings, Birmingham (US), Bismarck, Bloomington, Boise, Boston, Bozeman, Braiderd, Bristol (US), Buffalo, Burlington, Busan, Calgary, Cancun, Caspar, Cedar Rapids, Champaign, Charleston, Charlotte, Charlottesville, Chattanooga, Chicago, Cincinnati, Cleveland, Colorado Springs, Columbia, Columbus, Cozumel, Dallas/Fort Worth, Dayton, Denver, Des Moines, Detroit, Devils Lake, Duluth, Eau Claire, Edmonton, El Paso, Elmira, Erie, Evansville, Fargo, Fayetteville, Flint, Fort Dodge, Fort Lauderdale, Fort Myers, Fort Smith, Fort Wayne, Frankfurt, Gainesville, Grand Cayman, Grand Forks, Grand Rapids, Great Falls, Green Bay, Greensboro/High Point, Greenville, Guam, Guangzhou, Gulf Port, Hancock, Harrisburg, Hartford, Hayden, Helena, Hibbing, Hilo, Hong Kong, Honolulu, Houston, Huntsville, Idaho Falls, Indianapolis, International Falls, Ithaca, Ixtapa/Zihuatanejo, Jackson, Jacksonville, Jamestown, Kahului, Kalamazoo, Kalispell, Kansas City, Kauai Island, Kitchener, Knoxville, Kona, La Crosse, Lafayette, Lansing, Las Vegas, Latrobe, Laurel, Lexington, Liberia, Lincoln, Little Rock, London, Los Angeles, Louisville, Madison, Manchester, Manila, Manzanillo, Marquette, Mason City, Mazatlan, Memphis, Mexico City, Miami, Milwaukee, Minneapolis/St Paul, Minot, Missoula, Mobile, Moline, Monroe, Montego Bay, Montgomery, Montreal, Mumbai, Musle Shoals, Muskegon, Myrtle Beach, Nagoya, Nashville, Nassau, New Orleans, New York, Newark, Newburgh, Norfolk, Oklahoma City, Omaha, Orlando, Osaka, Ottawa, Paducah, Palm Springs, Panama City, Paris, Pellston, Pensacola, Peoria, Philadelphia, Phoenix, Pierre, Pittsburgh, Portland, Providence, Puerto Vallarta, Quebec, Raleigh/Durham, Rapid City, Regina, Rhinelander, Richmond, Roanoke, Rochester, Sacramento, Saginaw, St Cloud, St Louis, Salt Lake City, San Antonio, San Diego, San Francisco, San Jose, San Jose Cabo, San Juan, Santa Ana, Sarasota, Saskatoon, Sault Ste Marie, Savannah, Seattle, Seoul, Shanghai, Shreveport, Singapore, Sioux City, Sioux Falls, South Bend, Spokane, Springfield, State College, Syracuse, Taipei, Tallahassee, Tampa, Thief River Falls, Thunder Bay, Tokyo, Toledo, Toronto, Traverse City, Tucson, Tulsa, Tupelo, Vail, Valparaiso (US), Vancouver, Washington, Waterloo, Watertown, Wausau, West Palm Beach, Westchester County, Wichita, Wilkes-Barre, Winnipeg
Employees: 35,000
Links with other airlines: Owns 100 per cent of Northwest Cargo. Owns 27.8 per cent of Mair Holdings, parent company of Mesaba Air (qv).

Member of the Sky Team alliance. Alliances with Alaska Airlines, America West Airlines, American Eagle Airlines, Big Sky Airlines, Gulfstream International Airlines, Hawaiian Airlines, KLM Cityhopper, Malev, Mesaba Airlines, Pinnacle Airlines, PrivatAir (all qv)
Passengers carried: 55.4 million
Annual turnover: US $11,279 million (£7,600 million)
Fleet: 15 Boeing 747-400; 13 Boeing 747-200F; 4 Boeing 747-200B; 28 Airbus A330-300; 12 Airbus A330-200; 15 McDonnell Douglas DC-10-30; 16 Boeing 757-300; 50 Boeing 757-200; 76 Airbus A320-200; 71 Airbus A319-100; 29 McDonnell Douglas DC-9-50; 8 McDonnell Douglas DC-9-40; 67 McDonnell Douglas DC-9-30 (On order: 18 Boeing 787-8; 36 Bombardier CRJ900)

NORTHWEST AIRLINES CARGO

The marketing name for Northwest Airlines cargo services and for cargo capacity on the passenger fleet. It does not currently operate as an independent entity.

NORTHWEST AIRLINK

The branding carried by aircraft operating commuter or regional feeder services into the Northwest Airlines route network. Participating airlines include Express Airlines, Horizon Air, Mesaba Airlines and Business Express.

PACE AIRLINES
Incorporated: 1996

Pace Airlines was established in 1996 as a specialised passenger charter airline, serving sports teams and their supporters, and also undertaking executive charters. It was acquired in 2002 by the owner of the Hooters restaurant chain, and some aircraft are operated under the Hooters Air name.

HQ airport & main base: Winston-Salem Smith Reynolds, North Carolina
Radio callsign: PACE
Designator: PCE
Employees: 458
Fleet: 5 Boeing 757-200; 1 Boeing 727-200; 3 Boeing 737-400; 4 Boeing 737-300; 5 Boeing 737-200

PENAIR
Incorporated: 1955

Originally founded in 1955 as Peninsula Airways, it started charter operations in 1956, and did not begin scheduled services until 1973, serving offshore islands. The airline expanded its scheduled network with the acquisition of Air Transport Services of Kodiak in 1985, and later became a feeder operator for Alaska Airways. The name was shortened to PenAir more recently. Today, the airline is owned by the Seybert family, and in addition to scheduled and charter services, also operates ambulance flights.

HQ airport & main base: Anchorage International
Radio callsign: PENAIR
Designator: KS/PEN
Route points: Aleknagik, Anchorage, Aniak, Atka, Cape Newenham, Chignik, Clarks Point, Cold Bay, Dillingham, Dutch Harbour, Egegik, Ekwok, False Pass, Igiugig, King Cove, King Salmon, Levelock, Manokotak, McGrath, Nelson Lagoon, New Koliganek, New Stuyahok, Perryville, Pilot Point, Port Heidon, Port Moller, Portage Creek, St George Island, St Paul Island, Sand Point, South Naknek, Togiak, Twin Hills, Unalakleet
Links with other airlines: Alliance with Alaska Airlines (qv)
Fleet: 7 Saab 340A/B; 1 Fairchild Metro 23; 1 Cessna 208 Caravan; 1 Cessna Caravan 675; 1 Fairchild Metro III

PIEDMONT
Piedmont Airlines, Inc.
Incorporated: 1931

Originally founded in 1931 as Henson Aviation, Piedmont began scheduled services in 1962 as Hegerstown Commuter, which then became Henson Airlines. After an agreement was signed by Allegheny Airlines, the predecessor of USAir, the airline operated as Allegheny Commuter, before being bought by Piedmont Aviation and spending a short period as Henson – The Piedmont Regional Airline. The airline was absorbed by the then USAir, predecessor of US Airways, in 1989, and subsequently became a USAir Express (now US Airways Express) carrier. Aircraft carry US Airways Express colours and flights use the US Airways Express designators.

HQ airport & main base: Salisbury-Wicomico County Regional Airport, Maryland
Radio callsign: PIEDMONT
Designator: US/PDT
Employees: 3,328

Route points: Destinations on the US Airways Express network, from Toronto in Canada, to points in Florida, and offshore to the Bahamas, with hubs at Charlotte, Philadelphia, Pittsburgh, Washington
Links with other airlines: Subsidiary of US Airways (qv) and participant in US Airways Express (qv) network
Annual turnover: Included in figure for US Airways
Fleet: 12 Bombardier Dash 8 Q300; 2 Bombardier Dash 8 Q200; 35 Bombardier Dash 8 Q100

PINNACLE AIRLINES
Incorporated: 1985

Originally founded as Express Airlines, from the start the airline operated as a feeder airline with a code-share agreement with Republic Airlines. When Republic was taken over by Northwest Airlines, Express became part of Northwest Airlink, and in addition to its original base and hub at Memphis, also created a new operation at Minneapolis/St Paul. Northwest acquired Express in 1997 and was renamed Pinnacle Airlines in 2002. In 2003, the airline was floated on the New York Stock Exchange and is no longer part of Northwest Airlines, but continues to operate within Northwest Airlink, as well as having an alliance with Continental Airlines. Pinnacle reaches more than fifty airports spread across twenty-two states, and the number of employees has more than doubled over the last decade, with the fleet rising from 58 small turboprops to more than 120 regional jets.

HQ airport & main base: Memphis with a further hub/base at Minneapolis
Radio callsign: FLAGSHIP
Designator: 9E/FLG
Employees: 3,056
Route points: As part of the Northwest Airlink network, services reach more than fifty cities
Links with other airlines: Member of Northwest Airlink (qv) network. Alliances with Continental Airlines, KLM (both qv)
Fleet: 71 Bombardier CRJ440; 53 Bombardier CRJ200LR

PLANET AIRWAYS
Incorporated: 1997

Planet Airways began operations in 2000 as Airship Airways, and provides passenger and cargo flights within the United States and the Caribbean.

HQ airport & main base: Orlando International
Radio callsign: PLANET
Designator: PLZ
Fleet: 2 Boeing 727-200

POLAR AIR CARGO
Polar Air Cargo, Inc.
Incorporated: 1993

Polar Air Cargo provides international freight forwarders and their agents with an all-freight, contract scheduled service. The airline was founded in 1993 with just two Boeing 747 freighters, but by the late 1990s the fleet had grown to seventeen, although it has since dropped back slightly. Charter services are available worldwide, while scheduled services are operated within the United States, to Latin America and across the Atlantic and the Pacific. The airline was acquired by the current owners, Atlas Air Worldwide, in 2001, but in October 2006 DHL (qv) announced that it was taking a 49 per cent share in the airline. The base has moved from Long Beach to New York.

HQ airport & main base: New York Kennedy
Radio callsign: POLAR TIGER
Designator: PO/PAC
Route points: Almaty, Amsterdam, Anchorage, Atlanta, Chicago, Glasgow, Hong Kong, Honolulu, Los Angeles, Miami, New York, Port of Spain, Santiago de Chile, Sao Paulo, Seoul, Singapore, Shanghai, Tokyo
Fleet: 6 Boeing 747-400F; 1 Boeing 747-300SF; 3 Boeing 747-200F

PSA
PSA Airlines, Inc.
Incorporated: 1979

Originally known as Van Neal Airlines after the founder, the airline started life as a fixed-base operator supporting business and other general aviation activities, with its first scheduled air service following in 1980 using a Cessna 402 between Pittsburgh and Latrobe. In 1983 the name of Jetstream International Airlines was adopted when two BAe Jetstream turboprops were acquired, and in 1984 the main base was moved from Latrobe to Erie. The following year, Jetstream entered into an alliance with Piedmont Airlines and became a subsidiary in 1986. When the then USAir acquired Piedmont in 1987, Jetstream became part of the Allegheny Commuter network, but did not adopt its present title until 1995.

The airline's operations are fully integrated with those of the US Airways Express network, and it continues to be wholly owned by US Airways. Over the past decade, the number of employees has almost doubled and the fleet has increased and been modernised, with the retirement of turboprops and their replacement by regional jets.

HQ airport & main base: Dayton James M. Cox International
Designator: JIA
Employees: 1,737
Route points: Generally within the US Airways Express network, but including Akron/Canton, Burlington, Charleston (S. Carolina), Charleston (Wyoming), Charlotte, Cincinnati, Columbia, Evansville, Fairfax, Flint, Greenville/ Spartansburg, Hartford, Huntsville, Ithaca, Kalamazoo, Knoxville, Lansing, Manchester (US), New Haven, Philadelphia, Pittsburgh, Portland, Raleigh/ Durham, Reading, Richmond, Roanoke, South Bend, Toledo, Tri-City Airport, Washington Dulles, Washington National, White Plains, Williamsport
Links with other airlines: Member of US Airways Express (qv) network
Annual turnover: Included in figures for US Airways
Fleet: 14 Bombardier CRJ700-701ER; 36 Bombardier CRJ200LR

REGIONSAIR
Incorporated: 1996

Originally founded in 1996 as Corporate Express Airlines, and then becoming Corporate Airlines, the title of RegionsAir was adopted in 2005, but most flights are operated as American Connection, the feeder for American Airlines. The flight designator code remains that for the original title – CEA. Based at St Louis, RegionsAir also operates out of Nashville.

HQ airport & main base: St Louis
Designator: 3C/CEA
Employees: 184
Route points: On the American Airlines domestic destinations
Links with other airlines: Flies as American Connection for American Airlines (qv)
Fleet: 11 BAe Jetstream J32; 5 Saab 340A

REPUBLIC AIRLINES
Incorporated: 2003

Not to be confused with an earlier airline acquired by Northwest Airlines, Republic was founded in 2003, but did not begin operations until 2005. Although based in Indianapolis, operations are centred on Philadelphia and Washington and the airline is a US Airways Express operator.

HQ airport & main base: Indianapolis
Radio callsign: REPUBLIC
Designator: RW/RPA
Route points: On the US Airways Express network
Links with other airlines: US Airways Express (qv) feeder service operator
Fleet: 28 Embraer 170 (On order: 30 Embraer 175LR)

RHOADES AVIATION
Incorporated: 1968

Named after its founder and current president, Jack Rhoades, Rhoades Aviation dates from 1968. Business is entirely charter, mainly cargo, and includes support of humanitarian missions.

HQ airport & main base: Columbus Municipal
Radio callsign: RHOADES
Designator: RDS
Fleet: 3 Convair 640

RYAN INTERNATIONAL
Ryan International Airlines, Inc.
Incorporated: 1972

Founded in 1972 as Ryan Aviation by the eponymous Ronald Ryan, the airline soon established itself as a scheduled and charter operator carrying passengers and cargo, before being sold. Passenger charter flights were introduced in 1983, mainly for inclusive tour operators. The airline was bought again by Ronald Ryan in 1989, and that same year began operations for the US Postal Service from Indianapolis under contract to Emery Worldwide Airlines, using a fleet of Boeing 727s and McDonnell Douglas DC-9s, later joined by MD-87s.

The McDonnell Douglas fleet is now considerably reduced, and only two Boeing 727s are left as the Boeing 737 now predominates.

HQ airport & main base: Wichita Mid-Continent, with a further hub at Indianapolis
Radio callsign: RYAN INTERNATIONAL
Designator: HS/RYN
Employees: 721

Links with other airlines: Contractor to Emery Worldwide Airlines
Fleet: 5 Boeing 757-200; 1 Boeing 727-200; 1 Boeing 727-100F; 7 Boeing 737-800; 1 Boeing 737-400; 1 Boeing 737-300; 4 Boeing 737-200; 2 McDonnell Douglas MD-87

SCENIC AIRLINES
Incorporated: 1992

Founded in 1992 primarily to provide sight-seeing trips for tourists, but with a small scheduled network developing over the years. It was acquired by Eagle Canyon Airlines in 1998, although the Scenic name was retained, and the airline is now part of the Eagle Group.

HQ airport & main base: La Vegas North
Radio callsign: SCENIC
Designator: YR/YRR
Employees: 260
Route points: Elko, Ely, Grand Canyon, Las Vegas, Merced, Reno, Visalia
Fleet: 11 de Havilland Canada DHC-6 Twin Otter Srs300; 3 Raytheon Beech 1900C/D

SHUTTLE AMERICA
Incorporated: 1995

Founded in 1995, Shuttle America did not commence operations until 1998, initially as a scheduled pasenger operator on the east coast of the United States. It was acquired by the Wexford Management group in 2001 and shortly afterwards it became part of the US Airways Express network. A further change of ownership followed in 2005 when the airline was acquired by Republic Airways Holdings.

HQ airport & main base: Fort Wayne International
Designator: S5/TCF
Route points: In the US Airways domestic destinations list
Links with other airlines: Owned by Republic Airways Holdings. Alliances with Delta Airlines, US Airways Express (both qv)
Fleet: 47 Embraer 170

SIERRA PACIFIC
Sierra Pacific Airlines, Inc.
Incorporated: 1976

Sierra Pacific was founded as a charter carrier, and acquired by Mountainwest Aviation (not to be confused with Mountain West Airlines, part of Mesa Air Group) in 1978. Mountainwest adopted the Sierra name for the merged operations in 1981. The airline is owned by the Sierra Pacific Group, which in turn is owned by its President, G.M. Thorsrud. Much of the business consist of sub-charters for other airlines, but it also undertakes contracts for US government agencies.

HQ airport & main base: Tucson, Arizona
Radio callsign: SIERRA PACIFIC
Designator: SI/SPA
Fleet: 2 Boeing 737-200

SKY KING
Incorporated: 1990

Owned by the Lukenbill family, Sky King operates passenger charters, mainly for sports teams and their supporters, as well as corporate charters.

HQ airport & main base: Sacramento
Designator: F3/SGB
Employees: 70
Fleet: 6 Boeing 737-200; 1 Raytheon Beech King Air B200

SKYWAY ENTERPRISES
Incorporated: 1981

Originally formed as a Cessna light aircraft dealership in Michigan in 1981, Skyway entered the air cargo charter market in 1983. In 1989, the business moved south from Michigan to Florida, where it is now based, although Detroit is still used. Although ad hoc charters are available, most of the airline's operations are under contract to major parcels and package carriers such as DHL, FedEx and UPS.

HQ airport & main base: Kissimmee Municipal
Designator: SKZ
Links with other airlines: Operates under contract to DHL, FedEx and UPS (all qv)
Fleet: 1 McDonnell Douglas DC-9-10; 5 Shorts 360

SKYWEST
Skywest Airlines, Inc.
Incorporated: 1972

Skywest originally started as a small air charter and air taxi company, with a fleet which included four-seat single-engined Piper Cherokee Arrows. The move into scheduled services came in 1974, since when the airline has developed into a strong regional carrier. It acquired its first Embraer EMB-120 Bandeirante aircraft in 1987, and at one time this type comprised the backbone of the airline's fleet.

Acquisitions of other airlines have speeded Skywest's growth, including Western Airlines, followed by SunAire of Palm Springs in 1984, and Scenic Airlines of Las Vegas in 1993. The most significant acquisition was that of Atlantic South East Airlines, ASA.

In many ways, Scenic's history paralleled that of Skywest, although dating from 1967 when it had a single five-seat aircraft. In 1969, Scenic introduced the first automated air tour narration system, and in 1981 was the pioneer of aircraft simulators for regional aircraft. It became the largest sight-seeing aircraft operator in the world, carrying up to half a million passengers annually in a fleet of Cessnas and Twin Otters, the latter modified with larger windows than the standard aircraft.

While maintaining its financial independence, Skywest has followed the majority of airlines of its type in the United States by establishing operational and marketing alliances with major airlines, in this case with Delta, operating as the 'Delta Connection' at Salt Lake City, and with Continental at Los Angeles, as the 'Continental Connection', and in 1997 with United Airlines to operate as 'United Express'.

Starting in the late 1990s, the airline accelerated many of its services with the introduction of the new Bombardier (formerly Canadair) Regional Jet from its hubs, which also has provided opportunities for operating longer distance services.

HQ airport & main base: St George, with maintenance at Salt Lake City, and hubs at Los Angles, Portland, Salt Lake City and Seattle
Radio callsign: SKYWEST
Designator: 00/SKW
Employees: 7,625
Route points: On the Continental, Delta and United domestic networks
Links with other airlines: Owns Atlantic South East Airlines and Scenic Airlines. Alliances with Continental Airlines (qv) as 'Continental Connection', Delta Airlines (qv) as 'Delta Connection' and with United Airlines (qv) as 'United Express'
Fleet: 17 Bombardier CRJ900; 61 Bombardier CRJ-701ER; 100 Bombardier CRJ200LR; 6 Bombardier CRJ200ER; 12 Bombardier CRJ100ER; 67 Embraer EMB-120 Brasilia

SOUTHERN AIR
Incorporated: 1999

Although founded in 1999, Southern Air used the assets of an earlier airline, Southern Air Transport, which dated from 1947. Like its predecessor, Southern Air is an air cargo operator, wet-leasing aircraft to cargo airlines or to freight forwards and also operating ad hoc charters. It no longer handles the outsize items of freight or the low-level spraying of chemical dispersants and insecticides that were part of Southern Air Transport's business and which justified a fleet of fourteen Lockheed L-100 Hercules, commercial variants of an essentially military transport able to operate with the minimum of ground support. The current fleet consists entirely of Boeing 747s, while most of the company's business is between the United States, China and Korea.

HQ airport & main base: HQ at Norwalk, Connecticut, with operations at Dallas/Fort Worth
Radio callsign: SOUTHERN AIR
Designator: 9S/SOO
Employees: 175
Fleet: 4 Boeing 747-200F; 1 Boeing 747-200B

SOUTHWEST
Southwest Airlines Corporation
Incorporated: 1971

One of the first, and today by far the largest, low-fares airline – the fastest growing sector in air transport – in the world. Southwest Airlines is seventeenth largest in the world by annual turnover but third in passenger numbers, reflecting both the short-haul nature of much of its operation and, of course, the low fares. Dating from 1971, today Southwest is the eighth largest American airline.

Originally formed as Air Southwest, the present title was adopted before operations commenced. At first, a fleet of three Boeing 737-200s, surplus because of a recession in air transport, were obtained at a discount and operated the 'Texas triangle' routes, linking Dallas Love Field, Houston and San Antonio. Flights to Houston were eventually concentrated on the old Houston Hobby Airport, neglected by the larger airlines, while the airline fought a successful battle to continue using Dallas Love Field despite pressure from airport operators and the airline industry to move to the then new Dallas/Fort Worth.

The number of aircraft remained at three for the first two years, after a fourth aircraft had to be returned due to regulatory restrictions on the airline flying charters outside Texas, but a fourth aircraft finally joined the fleet in 1974. The route network also started to grow, with the Rio Grande Valley being added in 1975, and Corpus Christi, Lubbock, Midland/Odessa, El Paso and Austin in 1977, during which the fleet doubled from five to ten aircraft, still standardising on the Boeing 737-200. A Boeing 727-200 was leased from Braniff in 1978 for two years while the route network grew to include Dallas and Amarillo. The rate of growth continued to accelerate into the 1980s, requiring an order for ten new Boeing 737-300 aircraft, and more Boeing 727-200s were leased while deliveries were awaited. By the end of 1984, the airline was operating fifty-four aircraft.

Southwest acquired a competitor, Muse Air, in 1985, renaming it TranStar Airlines the following year, and operating a fleet of McDonnell Douglas MD-80 series aircraft. Unfortunately, TranStar passed into liquidation in 1987.

Despite its rapid growth, even as late as 1988 Southwest was still inaugurating services to airports abandoned by other airlines, and in that year it became the first airline in more than forty years to operate into Detroit City Airport. Sadly, five years later the airline had to move to the other Detroit airport because promised runway improvements were not made.

A further acquisition came in 1993, when Morris Air Corporation, another 737 operator, of Salt Lake City was acquired. By this time, Southwest was operating 178 aircraft.

Today, Southwest Airlines has survived well over a third of a century of low-cost air travel, and outlived well-established rivals such as Braniff, which in its early days had attempted to undercut the new airline. In addition to its main base at Dallas Love Field, Southwest has hubs at Phoenix, Chicago Midway, Oakland and Houston Intercontinental, from which it serves another forty-three cities. As with other successful, low-cost carriers, the fleet is highly standarised, in the case of Southwest on Boeing 737s. The airline was the launch customer for the new generation 737-700, which replaced the older 737-200s. Southwest Airlines claims to have been the pioneer of ticketless air travel.

Over the past decade, employee numbers have risen by more than 40 per cent, while the size of the fleet has grown from 263 aircraft to around 500, depending on whether any of the Boeing 737-300s or 737-500s are replaced by the continued influx of 737-700s.

HQ airport & main base: Dallas Love Field, with hubs at Chicago Midway, Houston Intercontinental, Oakland, Phoenix
Radio callsign: SOUTHWEST
Designator: WN/SWA
Employees: 31,729
Route points: Albany, Albuquerque, Amarillo, Austin, Baltimore, Birmingham (US), Boise, Buffalo, Burbank, Chicago, Cleveland, Columbus, Corpus Christi, Dallas, Denver, Detriot, El Paso, Fort Lauderdale, Fort Myers, Harlingen, Hartford, Honolulu, Houston, Indianapolis, Islip, Jackson, Jacksonville, Kahului, Kansas City, Las Vegas, Little Rock, Los Angeles, Louisville, Lubbock, Manchester (US), Midland/Odessa, Nashville, New Orleans, New York, Norfolk, Oakland, Oklahoma City, Omaha, Ontario (US), Orlando, Philadelphia, Phoenix, Pittsburgh, Portland, Providence, Raleigh/Durham, Reno, Sacramento, St Louis, Salt Lake City, San Antonio, San Diego, San Francisco, San Jose, Santa Ana, Seattle, Spokane, Tampa, Tucson, Tulsa, Washington, West Palm Beach
Passengers carried: 70.9 million
Annual turnover: US $6,530 million (£4,350 million)
Fleet: Up to 373 Boeing 737-700; 194 Boeing 737-300; 25 Boeing 737-500

SPIRIT
Spirit Airlines, Inc.
Incorporated: 1980

A domestic passenger operator, Spirit Airlines was formed in 1980 as Charter One, handling inclusive tour charters, mainly from its base which was then at Detroit. Scheduled services were introduced in 1990, and in 1992 the current name was adopted as being more relevant to the changed nature of the airline's operations. Oaktree Capital Management acquired a 51 per cent controlling stake in the airline in 2004. Over the past decade, the fleet has grown considerably, from ten aircraft to forty, with the McDonnell Douglas MD series fleet first augmented and then replaced by Airbus A319 and A320 aircraft.

HQ airport & main base: Detroit Willow Run and Fort Lauderdale Hollywood International
Radio callsign: SPIRIT WINGS
Designator: NK/NKS
Employees: 2,800
Route points: Atlanta, Atlantic City, Cancun, Chicago, Dallas, Detroit, Fort Lauderdale, Fort Myers, Grand Cayman, Grand Turk, Kingston, Las Vegas, Montego Bay, Myrtle Beach, Nassau, New

York, Orlando, Providence, Providenciales, Punta Cana, St Thomas, San Juan, San Salvador, Santo Domingo, Tampa, Washington, West Palm Beach
Fleet: 10 Airbus A321-200; 63 Airbus A319-100

SUN COUNTRY
Sun Country Airlines, Inc.
Incorporated: 1983

Originally formed by employees of the former Braniff Airways in 1983, at first Sun Country was a charter – or in US terminology a supplemental – passenger and cargo airline, operating within the US, Canada, Mexico and to the Caribbean, operating McDonnell Douglas DC-10s and Boeing 727s. It was acquired by the Minnesota Corporation in 1988, and in 1999 started its first scheduled services operating from Minneapolis/St Paul. Boeing 737-800s have replaced the original fleet.

HQ airport & main base: Minneapolis/St Paul International
Radio callsign: SUN COUNTRY
Designator: SY/SCX
Employees: 800
Route points: Acapulco, Bullhead City, Cancun, Cedar Rapids, Columbus, Dallas/Fort Worth, Denver, Fort Myers, Green Bay, Harlingen, Houston, Ixtapa/Zihuatanejo, Las Vegas, Los Angeles, Manzanillo, Mazatlan, Miami, Minneapolis, Montego Bay, New York, Orlando, Palm Springs, Phoenix, Puerto Rico, St Maarten, St Thomas, San Diego, San Francisco, San Jose Cabo, San Juan, Seattle, Sioux Falls, Tampa
Fleet: 12 Boeing 737-800

TED
Incorporated: 2003

Formed in 2003, TED commenced operations the following year and is the low-cost subsidiary of United Airlines, building up a route network that will initially serve tourist destinations in the western and southern states of the United States from its first base and hub at Denver.

HQ airport & main base: Denver
Radio callsign: TED
Designator: TED
Route points: Denver, Fort Lauderdale, Los Angeles, Miami, Orlando, San Francisco
Links with other airlines: A subsidiary of United Airlines (qv)
Fleet: 57 Airbus A320-200

TOLAIR
Tolair Services, Inc.
Incorporated: 1981

Tolair commenced operations in 1981, initially just one Cessna 182 for the movement of packages and other urgent light cargo. Today, the airline operates scheduled and charter cargo services from San Juan, in Puerto Rico, using a varied fleet of Douglas, Convair and Beech aircraft. The airline is owned by two directors, Jorge Toledo and Lisa Rosello.

HQ airport & main base: San Juan, Puerto Rico
Radio callsign: TOLAIR
Designator: TOL
Employees: 63
Fleet: 1 Convair 240; 6 Douglas DC-3; 4 Beech E18S

TRADEWINDS
Incorporated: 1969

Although founded as Wrangler Aviation in 1969, the airline did not commence operations until 1974, initially operating Lockheed Constellations on charter flights before developing a route network, initially within the United States but more recently to destinations in Asia as well. The fleet now includes Airbus and Boeing freighters. The current name was adopted in 1991.

HQ airport & main base: Greensboro/High Point
Designator: W1/TDX
Employees: 217
Route points: Anchorage, Aquadilla, Dallas, Fort Wayne, Greensboro/High Point, Hartford, Indianapolis, Los Angeles, Macau, Miami, Piedmont, San Francisco, San Juan, Seoul, Shanghai, Taipai, Tianjin, Xiamen
Fleet: 4 Boeing 747-200F; 5 Airbus A300B4-200F

TRANS STATES AIRLINES
Trans States Airlines, Inc.
Incorporated: 1982

Originally founded as Resort Air, Trans States Airlines became a franchised regional feeder for TWA in 1985, using TWA's designators. The Trans World Express operations of Air Midwest were acquired in 1991, and in 1995 the airline took over the operations of Trans World Express, the renamed Pan Am Express acquired by TWA four years earlier. In 1994, the airline completed an unusual arrangement to cooperate with Alaska Airlines,

Northwest Airlines and US Airways in the first triple code-sharing operation in the world, offering considerable economies for the airlines involved as compared with the usual type of feeder operation. This spared the airline the impact of the demise of TWA as employee numbers have doubled, and over the past decade the fleet has seen the large-scale introduction of Embraer regional jets, replacing the ATR fleet.

HQ airport & main base: St Louis Lambert, with a main base at Pittsburgh International
Radio callsign: WATERSKI
Designator: AX/LOF
Employees: *c.* 2,000
Route points: Include Baltimore, Birmingham, Bloomington, Boston, Burlington, Cape Girardeau, Cedar Rapids, Champaign, Chicago Meigs Field, Chicago Midway, Columbia, Decatur, Evansville, Fayetteville, Fort Smith, Fort Leonard Wood, Fresno, Hartford, Joplin, Knoxville, Lexington, Lincoln, Louisville, Memphis, Madison, Marion, Moline, Paduca, Peoria, Quincy, Sioux City, South Bend, Springfield City, Waterloo
Links with other airlines: Alliances with American Airlines, US Airways (both qv)
Fleet: 36 Embraer ERJ-145LR; 12 Embraer ERJ-145ER; 1 BAe Jetstream 41

UNITED AIRLINES
United Airlines, Inc.
Incorporated: 1934

At one time the largest airline in the free world, United is today the world's sixth largest airline by annual turnover, and fourth by passenger numbers.

In common with many of the oldest airlines, United can trace its history back to the merger of several of the early pioneering airlines, of which Varney Air Lines was the first, formed in 1926. Varney's initial operations were providing feeders to the transcontinental airmail service, at that time operated by the US mail. The small Swallow biplanes used by Varney were limited to the carriage of mail.

The other three airlines that were eventually to form United had also been created for the US mail's planned transfer of airmail to private contractors after a period in which the United States Army Air Corps had been flying the mail routes, and all three dated from 1927. Boeing Air Transport, owned by the eponymous aircraft manufacturer, had been awarded the contract for San Francisco–Chicago, National Air Transport received Chicago–New York and Pacific Air Transport operated the Seattle–Los Angeles feeder service. Boeing hastened its latest commercial design, the 40A, into service for the airmail contract, and using this aircraft could accommodate passengers as well as mail. The next step forward for these services was Boeing and Ford Trimotor aircraft capable of carrying up to fourteen passengers, and these arrived in 1929. The following year, Boeing introduced stewardesses and meal service on its flights.

The first steps towards consolidation had already occurred by this time, with Boeing taking over Pacific Air Transport as early as 1928 as a step towards single-carrier operation of the transcontinental service, and in 1930 Boeing also acquired both Varney and National. A new company, United Aircraft and Transport, was formed to manage the merged airlines in July 1931, and soon acquired a fifth airline, Stout Airlines, with services from Detroit to Chicago and Cleveland. In 1933, the year that Boeing introduced the 247, the first twin-engined, all-metal low-wing airliner, an Act of Congress forbade the grouping of manufacturing and operating interests. The following year saw United Airlines, at first known as United Air Lines, founded as an independent company, completely divorced from Boeing.

In its first year, the new airline suffered a major setback, with the loss of several of its US mail contracts as these were put out to fresh tender. Nevertheless, United managed to continue its expansion throughout the 1930s and into the early 1940s, until US entry into the Second World War slowed progress from late 1941 onwards. Nevertheless, United soon renewed its growth once hostilities ended, and in 1946 introduced its first route away from the continental United States, with a service to Hawaii. Six years earlier, the Civil Aeronautics Board had forbidden a proposed merger between United and Western Airlines, but in 1946 United took over Western's Los Angeles–Denver route.

Even before the outbreak of the Second World War, United had been responsible for what was an innovation for the time, introducing air stewardesses in May 1930.

As befits a major airline, United can claim a number of firsts in its history. In 1947, the airline was first with the Douglas DC-6 pressurised airliner, a development of the earlier unpressurised DC-4. The airline was also first to operate the first Douglas jet airliner, the DC-8 in 1959, and again with the Super DC-8, or DC-8-61 series, in 1967. In between, United was first with the Boeing 720 in 1960 and

727 in 1962, while being the first and only American airline to operate Sud Aviation's Caravelle jet airliner, which it introduced in 1961. Most recently, the airline was the launch customer for the Boeing 777, which it introduced in 1995.

Another major development in 1961 saw United acquire Capital Airlines, another major American carrier and which was in financial difficulties after very protracted negotiations, lasting some years, over the terms of a merger. The scale of the merger can be judged by the fact that Capital, despite its problems, immediately boosted United's annual sales figure by 25 per cent. Just as United had been the sole United States purchaser of the Caravelle, Capital had been the sole US purchaser of the Vickers Viscount, the world's first successful turboprop airliner (although Trans Canada, predecessor of Air Canada, also had a large fleet of this aircraft), and the merger brought almost fifty of these aircraft into the United fleet.

The difficulties facing other airlines at different periods contributed to United's further growth in the postwar period. In 1986, a major expansion by United came with the acquisition of Pan American's historic Pacific Division, the subject of much pioneering in long-distance, over-water flights during the late 1930s. That same year, United introduced United Express, using the services of a number of regional airlines to provide feeder services into United's hubs, of which the most important was Chicago. Other hubs also developed, aided in 1991 by the acquisition of Pan American's Latin American network, with United commencing operations to Latin America out of Los Angeles, Miami and New York in 1992. Operations to the Caribbean and then to South America had been behind the formation of Pan Am in 1927, reinforced by the absorption of the joint venture airline PANAGRA (Pan American-Grace Airways) in 1966, and much later by the Miami-based National Airlines in 1979, which had effectively given Pan Am a domestic route network for the first time.

One of the United Express operators was Air Wisconsin, which United bought in January 1992, but was sold again some eighteen months later to Air Wisconsin's present management team. The airline remains a United Express carrier.

Although United was spared many of the traumas experienced by the other 'first generation' major United States airlines, in 1994 a majority of the airline's employees took a 55 per cent shareholding in return for concessions on working practices. The airline took this opportunity to launch a low-cost operation, Shuttle by United, which it intended to build up to 130 aircraft, as a counter to the growing number of new, low-cost operators, but the operation has since been reabsorbed into the parent airline and instead United's ambitions to compete with the low-cost airlines is a Denver-based operation, known simply as TED. United has also kept a tight hold on its own costs, with employee numbers cut by almost a third over the past decade, but passenger numbers have also fallen and turnover has risen only modestly. The fact that such measures were necessary can be judged by United's parent company, UAL, filing for Chapter 11 Bankruptcy Protection in December 2002, and only leaving protection in February 2006.

Today, United is the world's largest employee-owned business, with the majority of the shares traded on the New York Stock Exchange being held by employees. The airline carries more passengers on a greater number of international flights than any other United States airline, although the international network has been thinned out in recent years, but it also serves more than a hundred domestic destinations in the United States, in addition to a large number of international destinations, although a number of these are reached through code-sharing arrangements with other airlines, such as Air Canada and Ansett Australia. The airline is a founder-member of the Star Alliance, which brings together frequent-flyer programmes and other services for Air Canada, Lufthansa, SAS, Thai International and, in 1997, Varig, as well as United.

HQ airport & main base: Chicago O'Hare, with additional hubs at Denver, San Francisco and Washington Dulles
Radio callsign: UNITED
Designator: UA/UAL
Employees: 61,000
Route points: Akron/Canton, Albany, Albuquerque, Allentown, Amsterdam, Anchorage, Apia, Appleton, Arcata, Aruba, Asheville, Aspen, Atlanta, Auckland, Augusta, Bakersfield, Baltimore, Bangkok, Beijing, Bermuda, Billings, Binghampton, Birmingham (US), Bismarck, Bloomington-Normal, Boise, Boston, Bozeman, Brisbane, Bristol (US), Brussels, Buenos Aires, Buffalo, Burbank, Burlington, Cairns, Calgary, Cancun, Casper, Cedar Rapids, Charleston, Charlotte, Charlottesville, Chicago, Chico, Christchurch, Cincinnati, Cleveland, Cody, Colorado Springs, Columbia, Columbus, Copenhagen, Cozumel, Crescent City, Dallas/Fort Worth, Dayton, Daytona Beach, Denver, Des Moines, Detroit, Durango, Düsseldorf, Edmonton, El Centro, El Paso,

Eugene, Fargo, Fayetteville, Fort Lauderdale, Fort Myers, Fort Wayne, Frankfurt, Freeport, Fresno, Gainesville, George Town, Grand Cayman, Grand Junction, Grand Rapids, Great Falls, Green Bay, Greensboro/High Point, Greenville, Guatemala City, Gunnison, Halifax, Hampton, Harrisburg, Hartford, Hayden, Hilton Head, Ho Chi Minh City, Hong Kong, Honolulu, Houston, Huntsville, Indianapolis, Inyokem, Islip, Ithaca, Ixtapa/Zihuatanejo, Jackson, Jacksonville, Johannesburg, Kahului, Kalamazoo, Kansas City, Kauai, Key West, Knoxville, Kona, Krakow, Lansing, Las Vegas, Lexington, Liberia, Lincoln, Lisbon, London, Los Angeles, Louisville, Madison, Manchester (UK), Marsh Harbor, Medford, Melbourne, Memphis, Mexico City, Miami, Milwaukee, Minneapolis, Missoula, Modesto, Moline, Montego Bay, Monterrey, Montevideo, Montreal, Montrose, Munich, Myrtle Beach, Nadi, Nagoya, Nashville, Nassau, New Bern, New Orleans, New York, Newark, Norfolk, North Eluethera, Oakland, Oklahoma City, Omaha, Ontario (US), Orlando, Osaka, Ottawa, Oxnard, Palm Springs, Papeete, Paris, Pasco, Peoria, Perth, Philadelphia, Phoenix, Pittsburgh, Portland, Providence, Puerto Vallarta, Punta Cana, Raleigh/Durham, Rapid City, Rarotonga, Redding, Redmond, Rio de Janeiro, Roanoke, Rochester, Rome, Sacramento, Saginaw, St George, St Louis, St Maarten, St Thomas, Salt Lake City, San Antonio, San Diego, San Francisco, San Jose, San Jose Cabo, San Juan, San Luis Obispo, San Salvador, Santa Ana, Santa Barbara, Sao Paulo, Sarasota, Savannah, Seattle, Seoul, Shanghai, Singapore, Sioux Falls, South Bend, Spokane, Springfield, State College, Stockholm, Sydney, Syracuse, Taipei, Tallahassee, Tampa/St Petersburg, Tokyo, Toronto, Traverse City, Treasure Cay, Tucson, Tulsa, Vail, Vancouver, Vienna, Warsaw, Washington, Wausau, Wellington, West Palm Beach, Westchester County, Wichita, Wilkes-Barre, Wilmington, Winnipeg, Yuma, Zurich
Links with other airlines: Owns TED (qv). Star Alliance member. Alliances with Aeromar (qv), Air China (qv), Air Japan (qv), Air Midwest, Air Wisconsin (qv), Aloha Airlines (qv), BWIA West Indies Airways (qv), Chautauqua Airlines (qv), GoJet (qv), Great Lakes Aviation (qv), Mesa Air Group (qv), Republic Airlines (qv), SkyWest Airlines (qv), South African Airways (qv), Swiss (qv), Virgin Blue (qv)
Passengers carried: 70.8 million
Annual turnover: US $16,391 million (£10,800 million)
Fleet: 30 Boeing 747-400; 33 Boeing 777-200ER; 19 Boeing 777-200; 35 Boeing 767-300ER; 96 Boeing 757-200; 59 Airbus A320-200; 78 Airbus A319-100; 64 Boeing 737-300; 30 Boeing 737-500

UNITED EXPRESS
Incorporated: 1986

United Express first appeared in 1986, and is the franchise for airlines operating regional and feeder services into United Airlines' main hubs. The five airlines involved are independent of United ownership, and include Air Wisconsin, Chautauque Airlines, Mesa Airlines, SkyWest Airlines and Trans States Airlines. Desitinations served are included in the United route points, but other details are included in the entries for these airlines.

Main hubs: Denver, Los Angeles, Portland, San Franciso, Seattle
Radio callsign: UNITED
Designator: UA/UAL

UPS
United Parcels Service, Inc.
Incorporated: 1988

One of the world's largest parcels and package delivery operations, with a scheduled network to some 200 countries, involving 385 US destinations and 446 outside the United States. UPS is the second largest all-cargo airline in the United States and in the world, and the twenty-sixth largest airline by annual turnover.

UPS first ventured into the air express parcels service in 1929, operating on the west coast of the United States until 1931. The company did not return to air transport until 1953, when it established a two-day 'UPS-Air' service between major American cities using aircraft belonging to other operators. In 1981, UPS entered the next-day overnight market, using its own aircraft but with crews provided by other operators, before finally establishing its own airline in 1988. The original two-day 'UPS-Air' service has now been rebranded as '2nd Day Air Delivery', as an economy option to the 'Next Day Air Delivery' service. Generally, UPS has grown through organic expansion, but in June 1999 it acquired the aircraft and routes of Challenge Air Cargo.

The current fleet includes Airbus, Boeing and McDonnell Douglas aircraft. In 1995 the airline was the first to operate the Boeing 767-300 freighter, and in 1997 the airline started to carry passengers to improve aircraft utilisation – using 'quick change' aircraft that would otherwise be left idle during the day.

HQ airport & main base: Louisville, with additional hubs at Cologne/Bonn, Dallas, Hamilton, Hong Kong, Miami, Montreal, Ontario (Cal), Philadelphia, Singapore
Radio callsign: UPS
Designator: 5X/UPS
Employees: 3,570
Route points: Major airports in some 200 countries, plus an extensive feeder network
Fleet: 8 Boeing 747-400F; 4 Boeing 747-200F; 7 Boeing 747-100F; 19 McDonnell Douglas MD-11F; 1 McDonnell Douglas MD-11; 52 Airbus A300-600F; 32 Boeing 767-300ER; 75 Boeing 757-200PF; 25 McDonnell Douglas DC-8-73AF; 17 McDonnell Douglas DC-8-70; 12 Boeing 727-100F; 2 Boeing 727-100C (On order: 27 Boeing 767-300; 10 Airbus A380-800F)

US AIRWAYS
US Airways, Inc.
Incorporated: 1939

Although it is the fifteenth largest airline by turnover and eleventh by passenger numbers, due to the predominance of short-haul routes, the merger with American West Airlines, the fortieth largest by turnover and twenty-third by passenger numbers, will push US Airways further up the league table to around eleventh or twelfth by turnover and perhaps sixth by passenger numbers, provided that no business is lost in any post-merger rationalisation.

The merger sees US Airways retain its identity, having earlier changed its name from USAir in 1997. The change was the latest of many since its formation in 1939 as All American Aviation. The name was changed first to Allegheny Airlines in 1953, and to USAir in 1979. The original airline was founded to operate airmail feeder and delivery services in Pennsylvania, Maryland and West Virginia, but after the Second World War the airline developed a strong network of passenger and cargo services, helped by a number of significant acquisitions, including Lake Central Airlines in 1968, Mohawk Airlines, who had introduced the BAe One-Eleven to North America, in 1972, Piedmont Airlines in 1988 and Pacific Southwest Airlines in 1989.

The parent company, the US Airways Group, also owns a number of smaller airlines, and these form the core of US Airways Express, the airline's regional feeder operation, which also includes a number of franchised airlines.

US Airways has had a difficult recent history, attempting to follow the other major airlines in cutting costs. British Airways acquired 24 per cent stake in 1993, but the relationship was uneasy and BA eventually disposed of its stake, preferring instead to press ahead with an alternative arrangement with American Airlines, although this was barred by the regulators on both sides of the Atlantic. During 1997, the airline cut a number of unprofitable routes and reduced its fleet by twenty-two aircraft.

A major element in the USAir Group portfolio of airlines is the US Airways Shuttle, which shares the branding of US Airways, although using different flight designators. At one time there was the possibility that the shuttle operation might be sold to American Airlines. The airline also attempted to launch a 'low fare, no frills' operation, provisionally known as US2, subject to the agreement of the unions. The largest merger in the history of US Airways has been the most recent, that with America West Airlines.

Famous for painting its aircraft in themed colour schemes, dedicating aircraft to individual states or to sports teams, and in one case to its ground staff, America West Airlines dated from 1981, founded in the mood of optimism which followed deregulation of air transport in the United States in 1978. The airline commenced operations in 1983, with three Boeing 737-200 aircraft flying from its main base at Phoenix to Colorado Springs, Los Angeles, Arizona and Wichita. A service was also operated to Kansas City, but this was discontinued after a year. Steady expansion followed, with the fleet growing to twenty-one aircraft in just two years, and to almost fifty aircraft in 1987, when the airline took delivery of its first Boeing 757. Ansett, the Australian airline, held a 20 per cent interest in America West from 1987 until 1994. America West itself bid for the Eastern Shuttle, operated along the Washington–New York–Boston corridor by Eastern Air Lines, in 1989, seeking the route and twenty-one Boeing 757 aircraft, but was unsuccessful. By this time, operations out of Las Vegas had grown to the extent that this had become a second hub, complementing the airline's main base at Phoenix.

The first Boeing 747s were introduced in 1990 although, at the other end of the scale, the airline had been developing a small fleet of de Havilland Canada DHC-8s, operated for some years on routes which were either less busy or had airfields with shorter runways. In 1991, Airbus A320 airliners were introduced to the fleet. While by this time America West's route network covered much of the United States, coast to coast, it was not until 1991 that the first international route was opened, to

Nagoya in Japan, although this was transferred to Northwest Airlines after just fifteen months. Nevertheless, the growing airline was kept busy at this period, helping to bring American military personnel home from Kuwait and Saudi Arabia after the Gulf War. A code-sharing agreement with Aeromexico in 1992 preceded America West's introduction of services to Mexico City.

In 1992 the airline introduced a commuter franchise operation, America West Express. The following year, America West celebrated the fact that it was the only survivor out of 150 airlines which had been founded following deregulation, but the celebrations were marred by the fact that, in common with many older airlines, the airline was by this time under Chapter 11 Bankruptcy Protection. America West finally emerged from Chapter 11 in August 1994. New investors in the airline at this stage included Continental Airlines and Mesa, owners of the regional airlines constituting America West Express. Later that year, America West and Continental introduced a code-sharing arrangement on a number of routes.

A service to Vancouver in Canada was launched in 1995, along with additional services to Mexico. Operations out of Columbus had by this time grown to the extent that the airport gained 'mini-hub' status.

At the time of the merger with US Airways, America West was the fortieth largest airline in the United States, having dropped in one year from thirty-fourth, operating as a 'low cost, low fare' airline, albeit with the availability of first-class accommodation on its flights. The network covered more than fifty airports in the United States, as well as a number in Canada and Mexico and another seventeen operated by America West Express, while another nineteen are reached through the code-sharing arrangement with Continental. The fleet is well standardised, with Boeing and Airbus products. The airline was owned by the America West Holdings Corporation and, a result of a reorganisation, America West Vacations has been moved from being a subsidiary of the airline to being a separate division of America West Holdings.

One advantage of the merger is that the two fleets are compatible, indicating considerable scope for rationalisation of engineering and support resources. Gone are the large numbers of McDonnell Douglas DC-9s and Fokker 100s of US Airways and the Bombardier Dash 8s of America West; instead the combined a fleet is one in which Airbus products predominate. It will take a couple of years for the merged airline fully to integrate and receive the necessary regulatory approvals, so in the mean time, both airlines will retain their identities, but once completed, the new airline will still have the name and identity of US Airways.

US Airways became a member of the Star Alliance in 2004. The airline has twice applied for Chapter 11 Bankruptcy Protection in recent years. The first time was in August 2002, lasting until March 2003, and the second was in September 2004. The airline has several wholly owned subsidiaries: in addition to US Airways Express and US Airways Shuttle, these include MidAtlantic Airways, Piedmont Airlines and PSA Airlines.

HQ airport & main base: Charlotte/Douglas International with an additional hub at Philadelphia International
Radio callsign: US AIR and, for America West, CACTUS
Designator: US/USA and HP/AWE
Employees: *c*. 37,000
Route points: Acapulco, Akron/Canton, Albany, Albuquerque, Allentown, Altoona, Amsterdam, Anchorage, Antigua, Appleton, Arcata, Aruba, Asheville, Aspen, Athens (US), Atlanta, Augusta, Austin, Bakersfield, Baltimore, Bangor, Bar Harbor, Beckley, Beef Island, Belize City, Bermuda, Billings, Binghampton, Birmingham (US), Bluefield, Boise, Boston, Bradford, Bridgetown, Bristol (US), Brussels, Buenos Aires, Buffalo, Burbank, Burlington, Cancun, Cedar Rapids, Charleston, Charlotte, Charlottesville, Chattanooga, Chicago, Cincinnati, Clarksburg, Cleveland, Colorado Springs, Columbia, Columbus, Cozumel, Dallas/Fort Worth, Dayton, Denver, Des Moines, Detroit, Dodge City, Dominica, Dubois, Durango, El Centro, El Paso, Elmira, Erie, Eugene, Farmington, Fayetteville, Florence (US), Fort Lauderdale, Fort Myers, Frankfurt, Franklin, Freeport, Fresno, Gainesville, Garden City, George Town, Grand Canyon, Grand Cayman, Grand Junction, Grand Rapids, Great Bend, Green Bay, Greensboro/High Point, Greenville, Guadalajara, Guatemala City, Guaymas, Gunnison, Hagerstown, Hampton, Harrisburg, Hartford, Hayden, Hays, Hermosillo, Hilton Head, Hong Kong, Honolulu, Houston, Huntington, Huntsville, Hyannis, Indianapolis, Islip, Ithaca, Ixtapa/Zihuatanejo, Jackson, Jacksonville, Jamestown, Johnson City/Kingsport, Johnstown, Kahului, Kansas City, Kauai, Key West, Kingston, Knoxville, Kona, Lake Havasu City, Lancaster, Las Vegas, Lebanon, Lewisburg, Lexington, Liberia, Lincoln, Lisbon, Little Rock, London, Long Beach, Los Angeles, Louisville, Lynchburg, Madison,

Madrid, Manchester (UK), Manhattan, Massena, Manzanillo, Mazatlan, Medford, Melbourne, Memphis, Mexico City, Miami, Milwaukee, Minneapolis, Mobile, Moline, Montego Bay, Monterey, Montgomery, Montreal, Montrose, Morgantown, Munich, Myrtle Beach, Nadi, Nagoya, Nantucket, Nashville, Nassau, New Bern, New Haven, New Orleans, New York, Newark, Newburgh, Norfolk, Oakland, Ogdensburg, Oklahoma City, Omaha, Ontario (US), Orlando, Osaka, Ottawa, Palm Springs, Paris, Parkersburg, Pasco, Pensacola, Philadelphia, Phoenix, Pittsburgh, Portland, Presque Island, Providence, Providenciales, Puerto Vallarta, Punta Cana, Raleigh/Durham, Redmond, Reno, Richmond, Rio de Janeiro, Roanoke, Rochester, Rockland, Rome, Sacramento, St Croix, St Kitts, St Louis, St Lucia, St Maarten, St Thomas, St Vincent, Salina, Salibsury/Ocean City, Salt Lake City, San Antonio, San Diego, San Francisco, San Jose, San Jose Cabo, San Juan, San Luis Obispo, Santa Ana, Santa Barbara, Santiago de Chile, Sao Paulo, Sarasota, Savannah, Seattle, Sioux Falls, South Bend, Spokane, Springfield, State College, Staunton, Sydney, Syracuse, Tallahassee, Tampa/St Petersburg, Telluride, Tokyo, Toronto, Tucson, Tulsa, Vail, Washington, Watertown, West Palm Beach, Westchester County, Wichita, Wilkes-Barre, Williamsport, Wilmington, Yuma
Passengers carried: US Airways: 41. 5 million America West: 21.1 million
Links with other airlines: US Airways owns 100 per cent MidAtlantic Airways, Piedmont Airlines (qv), US Airways Express (qv), US Airways Shuttle (qv), PSA Airlines (qv). Member of the Star Alliance. Alliances with Air Labrador (qv), Air MidWest, Air One (qv), Bahamasair (qv), Caribbean Sun Airlines, Chautauqau Airlines (qv), Colgan Air (qv), Mesa Airlines (qv), Trans States Airlines (qv)
Annual turnover: US Airways: US$7,117 million (£4,760 million); America West: US$2,339 million (£1,560 million)
Fleet: 9 Airbus A330-300; 10 Airbus A330-200; 10 Boeing 767-200ER; 43 Boeing 757-200; 41 Airbus A321-200; 83 Airbus A320-200; 106 Airbus A319-100; 15 Airbus A318-100; 40 Boeing 737-400; 71 Boeing 737-300; 57 Embraer 190 (On order: 20 Airbus A350-800)

US AIRWAYS EXPRESS

This is the commuter/feeder operation of US Airways, and it includes four airlines within the US Airways Group, Allegheny, Piedmont and PSA, as well as Air Midwest Airlines, Chautauqua, CommutAir, Mesa Airlines, Shuttle America and Trans States Airlines, as well as the America West Express airlines, effectively the Mesa Air Group.

US AIRWAYS SHUTTLE

Shuttle, Inc.
Incorporated: 1992

The pioneering 'no booking' shuttle service which has since been emulated by British Airways and Air France, the origins of the service lay with the now defunct Eastern Air Lines, which founded the service in 1964. After Eastern's demise, the service was sold in 1988 by Eastern's parent, the Texas Air Group, to millionaire Donald Trump, who renamed it the Trump Shuttle and recommenced operations in 1989. USAir Group bought the operation in 1992, and despite speculation in the industry at one time that the operation might be sold to American Airlines, it has remained with US Airways and continues to operate on an hourly 'turn up and go, no booking' basis. The original fleet of Boeing 727 aircraft dedicated to the service has been replaced by a fleet of Airbus narrowbodies.

HQ airport & main base: New York-La Guardia
Radio callsign: US SHUTTLE
Designator: TB/USS
Employees: 620
Routes: New York-La Guardia to Washington National; New York-La Guardia to Boston
Links with other airlines: Part of the USAir Group, parent of US Airways and US Airways Express (both qv)
Annual turnover: Included in US Airways figure
Fleet: 6 Airbus A320-200; 3 Airbus A319-100

USA 3000 AIRLINES

Incorporated: 2001

Originally founded in 2001 as an inclusive tour charter airline, USA 3000 introduced scheduled services the following year, operating low-cost services to tourist centres in Florida and Latin America, and also developing a domestic route network. It is owned by the Brendan Air group.

HQ airport & main base: Philadelphia International
Designator: U5/GWY
Employees: 860
Route points: Aruba, Baltimore, Bermuda, Buffalo, Cancun, Chicago, Cincinnati, Cleveland, Columbus,

Detroit, Fort Lauderdale, Fort Myers, Hartford, Ixtapa/Zihuatanejo, La Romana, Milwaukee, Montego Bay, Nassau, Newark, Orlando, Philadelphia, Pittsburgh, Puero Vallarta, Punta Cana, St Louis, San Jose Cabo, Tampa
Fleet: 13 Airbus A320-200

USA Jet
USA Jet Airlines, Inc.
Incorporated: 1979

Originally a subsidiary of the Active Aero Group but now owned by its directors, USA Jet Airlines operates an on-demand cargo charter service, as well as contract operations for major companies, including the Ford Motor Company.

HQ airport & main base: Willow Run Airport, Belleville, Michigan, with subsidiary hubs at El Paso, Little Rock and Memphis
Radio callsign: JET USA
Designator: U7/JUS
Fleet: 5 McDonnell Douglas DC-9-30; 6 McDonnell Douglas DC-9-10; 13 Dassault Falcon 20; 1 Bombardier Learjet 25

VALUJET
see AirTrans Airlines

VIRGIN AMERICA
Incorporated: 2005
Founded in 2005, Virgin America commenced operations in 2006 as a low-cost airline. The majority of the shares are held by US investors, but the UK-based Virgin Group has a minority stake, limited by US regulations on foreign ownership of airlines.

HQ airport & main base: San Francisco International
Designator:
Route points: TBA
Links with other airlines: The Virgin Group has a minority stake
Fleet: 13 Airbus A320-200; 8 Airbus A319-100

WORLD AIRWAYS
World Airways, Inc.
Incorporated: 1948

World Airways is a major US supplemental, or charter, airline. Originally formed in 1948, the airline was not immediately successful, amassing liabilities of US $250,000 by 1950, when it was bought by Edward Daly for just US $50,000 (£17,540 at the then rate of exchange). Starting with a fleet of two twin-engined Curtiss C-46 transports, the airline mainly concentrated on military charter work, expanding so that by 1962 the original fleet had grown to eight Douglas DC-6s and eleven Lockheed Constellations. With the advent of jet equipment during the early 1960s, the airline expanded into North Atlantic charter operations for the inclusive tour holiday market, and by 1969, the fleet comprised eight Boeing 707-373s and six Boeing 727QCs, the latter being rapid-conversion passenger/cargo aircraft.

In 1979 World Airways introduced scheduled, low-fare transcontinental air services, linking New York-Newark and Baltimore/Washington DC with Los Angeles and Oakland. Further scheduled expansion arose in 1981, with services from New York/Newark to London Gatwick and Frankfurt, and the US domestic network was extended to include Honolulu.

Three years later Edward Daly, who controlled 81 per cent of the airline's capital, died. In the years following his death the airline saw a period of retrenchment, closing down the scheduled services in September 1986, even though these comprised the bulk of the airline's business by that time, and concentrating on freight charter work. Neverthless, the airline has since returned to both passenger operations and scheduled services in recent years, while in 2005 it acquired North American Airlines, which dated from 1989 and had been operating passenger services since 1992.

Today, World Airways has moved its main base from New York-Newark to Atlanta and handles both passenger and freight charter and scheduled flights, including contract and ad hoc work, as well as wet-leasing activity. Employee numbers have risen by more than 50 per cent over the past decade. Customers for contract passenger services have included Philippine Airlines and VASP.

HQ airport & main base: Hartsfield Jackson Atlanta International
Radio callsign: WORLD
Designator: WO/WOA
Employees: 1,380
Route points: Atlanta, Kingston, New York
Fleet: 2 McDonnell Douglas MD-11ER; 3 McDonnell Douglas MD-11F; 7 McDonnell Douglas MD-11; 1 McDonnell Douglas DC-10-30

XTRA AIRWAYS
Incorporated: 1989

Originally founded in 1989 as Casino Express, after the purchase of 81 per cent of its stock by TEM Acquisition in 2005, the airline adopted the current title at the beginning of 2006. While currently primarily a charter airline, it is planning low-cost scheduled operations to the Caribbean and Mexico.

HQ airport & main base: Elko, Nevada
Designator: XP/CXP
Employees: 102
Fleet: 1 Boeing 737-800; 3 Boeing 737-400

URUGUAY – CX

PLUNA

Pluna Lineas Aereas Uruguayas
Incorporated: 1936

Founded in 1936, Pluna became established as the national airline of Uruguay, and operated internal scheduled servcies as well as operating into neighbouring states. The airline was nationalised in 1951, but in 1994 a 49 per cent stake in Pluna was sold to Varig of Brazil, which continues to be held although Varig's financial difficulties may mean that this will be sold in the future. The government retains a 49 per cent stake.

HQ airport & main base: Montevideo
Radio callsign: PLUNA
Designator: PU/PUA
Route points: Asuncion, Buenos Aires, Madrid, Montevideo, Porto Alegre, Punta del Este, Rio de Janeiro, Santiago de Chile, Sao Paulo
Links with other airlines: Varig has a 49 per cent stake. Alliances with Aeromar (qv), Rio-Sul Servicos Regionais (qv), Transportes Aereos de Mercosul, Varig (qv)
Fleet: 1 Boeing 737-800; 1 Boeing 737-300; 2 Boeing 737-200; 1 ATR-42-320

UZBEKISTAN – UK

UZBEKISTAN AIRWAYS

Uzbekistan Havo Yullari
Incorporated: 1992

Uzbekistan's national airline, Uzbekistan Airways, was founded in 1992 and based on the former Aeroflot divisions in Tashkent and Samarkand. Although still state owned, since its independence the airline has developed services to destinations outside the former Soviet Union and introduced Western aircraft types to its fleet, doubtless hoping to develop the area's tourist potential. The fleet still includes a majority of former Soviet types, although Airbus and Boeing products are represented, but most of these are relatively modern, although the An-24 and Yak-40 fleet were replaced by BAe Avro RJ85s.

HQ airport & main base: Tashkent Yuzhny, with a further base/hub at Samarkand
Radio callsign: UZBEK
Designator: 6Y/UZB
Employees: 16,500
Route points: Almaty, Amritsar, Andizhan, Ashgabat, Astana, Athens, Baku, Bangkok, Beijing, Birmingham, Bishkek, Bukhara, Chelyabinsk, Delhi, Ekaterinburg, Fergana, Frankfurt, Hanoi, Ho Chi Minh City, Istanbul, Karshi, Kazan, Kiev, Krasnodar, Krasnojarsk, Kuala Lumpur, Mineralnye Vody, Moscow, Namangan, Navoi, New York, Novosibirsk, Nukus, Omsk, Paris, Riga, Rome, Rostov, St Petersburg, Samara, Samarkand, Seoul, Shanghai, Sharjah, Simferopol, Tashkent, Termez, Tyumen, Ufa, Urgench, Zarafshan
Fleet: 2 Airbus A310-300; 4 Boeing 767-300ER; 6 Boeing 757-200; 2 Ilyushin Il-114; 10 Ilyushin Il-86; 19 Ilyushin Il-76TD; 3 Ilyushin Il-62; 13 Tupolev Tu-154M; 3 BAe Avro RJ85; 28 Yakovlev Yak-40; 11 Antonov An-24; 5 Antonov An-12

VENEZUELA – YV

The collapse of Viasa has left a major gap in Venezuelan air transport, although the growth in the number of international destinations served by Aeropostal has helped to fill the gap. Viasa itself only dated from 1961.

AEROPOSTAL

Alas de Venezuela
Incorporated: 1933

Originally dating from 1930, when the French Cie General Aeropostale commenced operations in Venezuela, which were taken over by the Venezuelan government in 1933 as Linea Aerea Venezolana. The airline suspended operations in 1994, but was sold to a private company, Alas de Venzuela, in 1997 and resumed operations. Originally a domestic airline, regional services were soon operated, while services to the United States commenced in 1998. Also in 1998 the first European route, to Madrid, was launched, although this has since been withdrawn. The company has a 45 per cent interest in Aero Honduras and 33 per cent in the Colombian airline Aero Republica.

HQ airport & main base: Caracas Simon Bolivar
Radio callsign: AEROPOSTAL
Designator: VH/LAV
Employees: 2,300
Route points: Aruba, Barcelona*, Barquisimeto, Bogotá, Caracas, Curaçao, Havana, Lima, Maracaibo, Maturin, Miami, Porlamar, Port of Spain, Puerto Ordaz, San Antonio, Santo Domingo, Valencia*
*Domestic destination, not to be confused with the Spanish city
Links with other airlines: 45 per cent stake in Aero Honduras and 33 per cent in Aero Republica (qv)
Fleet: 2 Boeing 727-200; 3 McDonnell Douglas MD-83; 5 McDonnell Douglas MD-82; 8 McDonnell Douglas DC-9-50; 3 McDonnell Douglas DC-9-30

ASERCA
Aeroservicios Carabobo
Incorporated: 1958

Aserca operates domestic and regional passenger charter flights and a small network of domestic scheduled services from its base at Valencia in Venezuela.

It is owned by Migdalia Garcia, although the executive president, Simeon Garcia, has a 5 per cent stake.

HQ airport & main base: Valencia (Zim Carabobo Venezuela)
Radio callsign: AROSCA
Designator: R7/OCA
Route points: Aruba, Barcelona (Venezuela), Caracas, Curaçao, Maracaibo, Maturun, Porlamar, Puerto Ordaz, Punta Cana, San Antonio, Santa Domingo
Fleet: 15 McDonnell Douglas DC-9-30

SANTA BARBARA AIRLINES
Incorporated: 1995

Formed in 1995, Santa Barbara Airlines started operations the following year, developing a domestic route network with international services in Latin America and to Madrid. Tenerife-based Islas Airways owns Santa Barbara completely.

HQ airport & main base: Caracas Simon Bolivar
Designator: S3/BBR
Route points: Aruba, Barquisimeto, Caracas, Cumana, El Vigia, Guayaquil, Las Piedras, Madrid, Maracaibo, Mérida, Miami, Quito, San Antonio, Valencia (Venezuela)
Links with other airlines: Owned 100 per cent by Islas Airways (qv)
Fleet: 1 Boeing 767-300ER; 1 Boeing 757-200; 2 Boeing 727-200; 4 ATR-42-320; 3 Cessna Caravan 675

VENSECAR INTERNACIONAL
Incorporated: 1996

Founded in 1996, Vensecar operates both scheduled and charter cargo operations, with DHL International having a substantial 49 per cent minority holding and Venezuelan interests the remainder.

HQ airport & main base: Caracas Simon Bolivar
Designator: V4/VEC
Route points: Aruba, Bogotá, Bridgetown, Caracas, Curaçao, Miami, Panama City, Port of Spain, Santo Domingo, Valencia (Venezuela)
Links with other airlines: DHL International Aviation has a 49 per cent stake
Fleet: 2 Boeing 727-200F; 1 Boeing 727-100F; 2 ATR-42-300

VIETNAM – VN

VIETNAM AIRLINES
Incorporated: *c.* 1955

Vietnam Airlines has its origins in the General Civil Aviation Administration of Vietnam, formed after the French withdrawal in 1954 and after the Viet Cong seized power in the north. Operations during the Vietnam War were severely restricted by American air power. Since the American withdrawal from Vietnam, an extensive network of domestic services has been established, and a growing number of international destinations, initially within South-East Asia and, more recently, as far afield as Australia and Japan. The title of Hang Khong Vietnam was adopted for a number of years, but more recently the current title has been taken.

Originally the fleet reflected assistance from the Soviet Union, with Antonov, Ilyushin, Tupolev and Yakovlev aircraft operated, but over the past few years there has been a strong preference for Western types, with Airbus, Boeing and ATR all represented in the fleet as well as some Fokker 70s. The airline is completely state owned.

HQ airport & main base: Hanoi Noi Bai International, with a further hub/base at Ho Chi Minh City
Designator: VN/HVN

Employees: 8,500
Route points: Bangkok, Banmethuet, Beijing, Busan, Da Nang, Dalat, Dien Bien Phu, Frankfurt, Fukuoka, Guangzhou, Haiphong, Hanoi, Ho Chi Minh City, Hong Kong, Hue, Kaohsiung, Kuala Lumpur, Kunming, Manila, Melbourne, Moscow, Nha Trang, Osaka, Paris, Phnom Penh, Phu Quoc, Pleiku, Qui Nhon, Rach Gia, Seoul, Singapore, Son-La, Sydney, Taipei, Tokyo, Tuy Hoa, Vientiane, Vinh City
Fleet: 10 Boeing 777-200ER; 1 Boeing 767-300ER; 1 Airbus A330-300; 16 Airbus A321-200; 10 Airbus A320-200; 6 Tupolev Tu-134A/B; 3 ATR-72-500; 6 ATR-72-200; 2 Fokker 70 (On order: 4 Boeing 787-8)

WESTERN SAMOA – 5W

POLYNESIAN BLUE

Incorporated: 2005

A joint-venture, low-cost airline owned by the government of Western Samoa with 49 per cent, through state-owned Polynesian Airlines, and Virgin Blue with 49 per cent, Polynesian Blue will take over the busier routes from Polynesian Airlines as well as introducing its own new routes.

HQ airport & main base: Apia
Designator: TBA
Route points: TBA
Links with other airlines: Virgin Blue (qv) and Polynesian Airlines each have a 49 per cent interest
Fleet: 1 Boeing 737-800

YEMEN – 4W

YEMENIA

Yemen Airways
Incorporated: 1963

Yemen Airways was founded in 1963 as the national airline of North Yemen, and in 1996 absorbed Alyemda-Democratic Yemen Airlines, which dated from 1961 and was the airline of the People's Republic of South Yemen, formerly Aden. The bringing together of the two airlines was long delayed by disagreements between the two territories, which were exacerbated by the Gulf War. Yemenia had originally been known as Yemen Airlines when it was first formed, and became Yemen Airways in 1972 on nationalisation.

The fleets of the two airlines were more broadly compatible, however, since both operated a mixture of Boeing and de Havilland aircraft, although Alyemda also had Tupolev and Antonov types in service. The merged airline is owned 51 per cent by the new united Republic of Yemen government, and 49 per cent by the Kingdom of Saudi Arabia.

HQ airport & main base: Sana'a, with a secondary hub at Aden
Radio callsign: YEMENI
Designator: IY/IYE
Route points: Abu Dhabi, Aden, Addis Ababa, Al Ghaydah, Amman, Asmara, Bahrain, Beirut, Cairo, Damascus, Dar-es-Salaam, Dhaka, Djibouti, Doha, Dubai, Frankfurt, Hodeidah, Jakarta, Jeddah, Johannesburg, Khartoum, Kuala Lumpur, Kuwait, London, Marseilles, Moroni, Mumbai, Paris, Riyadh, Riyan, Rome, Sana'a, Seiyun, Socotra, Taiz
Links with other airlines: Marketing alliances with Air India, Cathay Pacific, Gulf Air, Lufthansa, TWA (all qv)
Fleet: 2 Airbus A330-200; 4 Airbus A310-300; 4 Boeing 727-200; 3 Boeing 737-800; 1 de Havilland Canada Dash 7-100; 2 de Havilland DHC-6 Twin Otter

ZAMBIA – 9J

NATIONWIDE AIRLINES (ZAMBIA)

Incorporated: 2001
A franchisee of the South African Airline of the same name, Nationwide Airlines (Zambia) commenced operations in 2001, and uses aircraft from the parent company as required.

HQ airport & main base: Lusaka International
Designator: 4J/NWZ

ZIMBABWE – Z

AIR ZIMBABWE

Incorporated: 1961

Air Zimbabwe was originally founded in 1961 as Air Rhodesia, and from the outset was owned by the then Rhodesian government. The airline was formed initially to take over the services operated by the former Central African Airways Corporation, which had been founded after the Second World War with assistance and investment by BOAC, British Overseas Airways Corporation, and the then Federation of Rhodesia and Nyasaland. The breaking up of the federation into three separate countries on Northern Rhodesia and Nyasaland gaining independence also marked the end for CAAC.

The new airline found itself initially operating a fleet of Douglas DC-3s and Vickers Viscounts. The route network included domestic services and destinations in South Africa and the neighbouring Portuguese territories of Angola and Mozambique. Services to what had been Northern Rhodesia and Nyasaland, by this time Zambia and Malawi, were soon suspended following Rhodesia's unilateral declaration of independence and the application of sanctions against the country by most of the international community. Sanctions also inhibited traffic growth and acquisition of new equipment, so it was not until 1973 that the airline obtained its first jet airliners, three Boeing 720s.

Air Rhodesia became Air Zimbabwe Rhodesia in 1978 after sanctions ended, and in 1980 assumed its present title, reflecting the new name for the country. Post-independence, the airline undertook a modernisation programme, partly spurred on by a growing tourist trade, but this has now been offset by the country's acute economic and political difficulties, with a consequent reduction in the international route network in recent years.

HQ airport & main base: Harare International
Radio callsign: AIR ZIMBABWE
Designator: UM/AZW
Route points: Blantyre, Bulawayo, Harare, Johannesburg, Lilongwe, London, Lusaka, Mauritius, Nairobi, Victoria Falls
Links with other airlines: Marketing alliances with Air Botswana, Air Malawi (qv) and Aero Zambia
Fleet: 2 Boeing 767-200ER; 3 Boeing 737-200

ZIMBABWE AIRLINK
Incorporated: 2001

Largely taking over the routes of the former Zimbabwe Express, Zimbabwe Airlink established air services between Harare and Bulwayo as well as between these two cities and Johannesburg using Embraer ERJ-135 regional jets. The Harare to Johannesburg route was withdrawn in 2005, and the country's economic difficulties put operations in doubt.

Radio callsign: ZIM AIRLINK
Designator: FEM
Route points: Bulawayo, Johannesburg
Fleet: 2 Embraer ERJ-135

GLOSSARY

Every sector has its own technical words and phrases or 'jargon', and these even differ between different sectors of transport, or between civil and military aviation. While terms like 'short haul' and 'long haul' may be self explanatory, some others need definition.

ad hoc charter: a 'one off' charter that is not part of a regular programme.

air work: could be construed as another term for general aviation, but usually refers to aerial photography, aerial surveying, fire fighting, air cranes lifting items into position or extracting logs from forestry work, etc.

commuter flight/service: a short-haul, high-frequency service, usually of a duration of no more than 75–90 minutes.

contract charter: a charter that is part of a regular programme of flights, which could be operated on behalf of a freight company or companies engaged in activities that require large numbers of people to be moved around, as with the oil and natural gas industries, for example.

dry lease: the lease of an aircraft on its own.

general aviation: any aviation activity that is not air transport or military, and includes private flying, police and emergency services, crop spraying, etc.

inclusive tour charter/airline: the airline flight is part of a package, including accommodation at a holiday resort, and the package is sold by an inclusive tour operator either directly to the customer or through a travel agent.

scheduled flight: a flight that operates to a published timetable and on which passengers or freight forwarders/shippers can book a ticket or book cargo space.

seat only: a seat on an inclusive tour charter flight that is not accompanied by accommodation at the destination.

shuttle: a scheduled air service which does not require the passengers to make an advance booking or seat reservation, but guarantees a seat, as back-up aircraft are kept available.

supplemental carrier: US term for charter carrier.

wet lease: the lease of an aircraft with crew.

Index of Airlines